C000061134

Famous Occultists and Witches

and Witches

Their Biographies and Birth Charts

ANDREA J MILES

GREEN MAGIC

Famous Occultists and Witches
© 2022 by Andrea J Miles.

All rights reserved. No part of this book may be used
or reproduced in any form without written permission
of the Author, except in the case of quotations in
articles and reviews.

Green Magic
Seed Factory
Aller
Langport
Somerset
TA10 0QN
England

www.greenmagicpublishing.com

Designed & typeset by Carrigboy, Wells, UK
www.carrigboy.co.uk

ISBN 978 1 7399733 215

GREEN MAGIC

Dedication and Special Thanks

DEDICATION

This book is dedicated to, and in loving memory of, Alan J Miles.

SPECIAL THANK YOU'S

Love and thanks to my dear friend and teacher, professional astrologer and artist, Kathy Rowan. You are an inspiration not only to me, but also to many other astrologers and students of the occult.

Kevin Rowan-Drewitt, astrologer, rune-expert and author, who was there at the very beginning as the book was being formed. Thanks for his friendship, knowledge and extensive support throughout the process of writing this book; a true guardian to *Famous Occultists and Witches*.

Frank Clifford, author, professional astrologer, lecturer and teacher at the London School of Astrology, for sharing his experience, generosity of spirit and humour.

Mark Hetherington, artist and illustrator, for his time, infinite patience and technical expertise with various chapters.

Marilyn Stroud, for her assistance and understanding of genealogy, and her continued enthusiasm and passion for this book.

Andrew Jenkins for his invaluable friendship, interest and support.

Ian Radford for his spiritual light.

Astrodienst, for permitting the natal and transits charts generated on www.astro.com to be used in this publication.

Individuals and organisations (of which there are many) who have assisted along the way are thanked at the end of each chapter that they helped with.

And last, but not least, my family and friends, who have been there for me throughout the duration of the journey that became *Famous Occultists and Witches: Their Biographies and Birth Charts*.

"All the world's a stage,
And all the men and women merely players;
They have their exits and their entrances,
And one man in his time plays many parts,
His acts being seven ages."

– From Shakespeare's *As You Like It.*
Act II, Scene VII.

Table of Contents

CHAPTER ONE

George Pickingill 1816–1909

Farm Labourer, Alleged Cunning Man and Wizard of Canewdon

GEORGE PICKINGILL (known locally as 'Old Picky') was born in Hockley, Essex, England on 2nd April, 1816 and died on 10th April, 1909 (www.essex.gov.uk/ERO). He was the eldest of five children born to Charles and Hannah Pickingill. His father was an agricultural labourer and blacksmith. Pickingill married Sarah Ann Bateman when he was 40 and they remained married for 31 years until her death in 1897, when she died of dropsy of the liver. Together they had four children, two daughters; Martha Ann and Mary Ann, and two sons; Charles Frederick and George. Pickingill remained a widower living in Canewdon until his death in 1909.

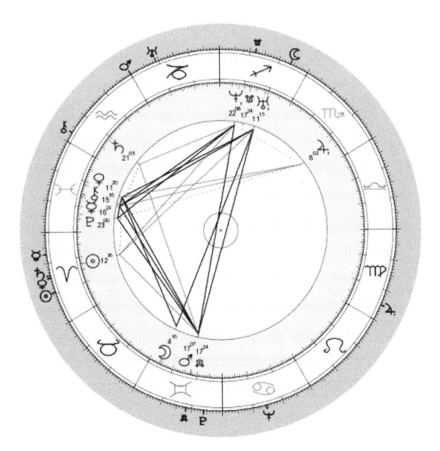

Natal and Transits Chart for George Pickingill on the day he died, 10th April, 1909.

Many claims have been made about George Pickingill, including the following which that state he:

- Was born and raised as Romany
- Was of dual heritage
- Frequently changed his age and the spelling of his surname in censuses. This may have been done in order to prevent people finding his baptism record at Hockley, as he needed to be in continuous employment and later claimed Parish Relief in his final years
- Was claimed to be one of the eldest men alive in England in 1908
- Could stop farm machinery working
- Could heal animals and was a horse-whisperer
- Got his imps (his familiar spirits) to do work for him
- Was a member of a hereditary witch-cult
- Wrote a *Book of Shadows*
- Lead a coven in Canewdon as well as others in southern England
- Was the last Master of Witches in Canewdon and created a form of witchcraft that would create the basis of Gardnerian Wicca in the 1950s
- Received visits from Aleister Crowley

WHAT HIS NATAL CHART SHOWS...

Pickingill was born on the 2nd April, 1816; when the Sun was in the assertive fire sign of Aries at 12 degrees, and the Moon was in the sociable air sign of Gemini at 4 degrees. Since Pickingill's exact time of birth is unknown, it is necessary to use a flat chart (*please see glossary*) to represent this unknown time of birth. As the Moon was at 28 degrees of Taurus at the start of the 2nd April 1816, it is more likely that Pickingill's Moon is in the sign of Gemini, since the Moon moves at a fast pace of approximately 13 degrees per day.

The general picture of the chart reveals conjunctions and several opposition and square aspects. This suggests that throughout Pickingill's life, he frequently had to adapt to many challenges and tensions. There is an absence of the earth element in Pickingill's chart; as there are no planets in the signs of Taurus, Virgo, or Capricorn.

When there is an absence of an element in a natal chart, often the subject compensates by 'searching' for the qualities of the missing element, sometimes in abundance. In this sense, Pickingill may have found balance and satisfaction from working on the land as a farm labourer being close with nature, as well as finding ways to apply practical skills such as organisation, productivity, and steadfastness. Duties that Pickingill was likely to have undertaken as a farm labourer include: preparing the ground, sowing seed and harrowing, hedge-maintenance and weeding; which all require planning, skill and practical application.

He also enjoyed spending time in his garden at 3 Canewdon High Street and in 1908, when he was in his nineties, he was described as still being able "to fill in odd moments by pottering about in the garden" (www.deadfamilies.com./EssexNewsman:1908). It was a sizable plot, described as, "a back boundary of 58 feet by a depth of 70 feet now used as a garden by George Pickingill" (www.deadfamilies.com/1899-advertisements), showing that he was still relatively mobile and strong for his age.

In his natal chart there are three planets in the water sign of intuitive and sensitive Pisces; Mercury, Venus and Pluto, whilst Jupiter is in the water sign of determined and powerful Scorpio. This reveals that Pickingill was perceptive and receptive as well as having the potential for healing and psychic and mediumistic ability. These areas will be discussed in detail later on.

There are three mutable T-Square (*see glossary*) configurations in his natal chart; this pattern is formed when planets in opposition also form a square with another planet. The squared planet is referred to as the focal point. T-Squares are made of up of each of the modes; cardinal, fixed and mutable and it is the latter mode that forms Pickingill's T-Squares. Adaptability, restlessness and agitation are also indicated in the natal chart, impacting on areas such as communication, health and independence, which would have been significant in his life. The three mutable T-Squares comprise of:

- Mars in Gemini is in opposition to Neptune in Sagittarius, with Mercury in Pisces square both planets, making Mercury the focus point. This makes Virgo at 16 degrees the release point of challenges for Pickingill
- Mars in Gemini is in opposition to Uranus in Sagittarius, with Venus in Pisces square both planets, making Venus the focus point. This makes Virgo at 11 degrees the release point of further tensions in Pickingill's natal chart. Venus and Uranus are both partile (*see glossary*) at 11 degrees
- Mars in Gemini is in opposition to Neptune in Sagittarius, with Pluto in Pisces square both planets. Therefore, Pluto becomes the focal point, making Virgo at 23 degrees the release point of further difficulties for him

We can see from the three mutable T-Squares that Virgo is the common release point in the configuration; Virgo is associated with nutrition, health and work and these areas will be discussed later in further detail, as will the aspects highlighted above in the mutable T-Squares. Overall, we can say that Pickingill's natal chart reveals a friendly, independent, restless and compassionate nature.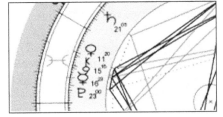

The Pluto in Pisces position (*see box on right*) suggests that Pickingill was intense and intuitive as well as compassionate and possibly mediumistic, as these are characteristics associated with Pluto and Pisces. He also had a talent for healing the sick, both human as well as domestic and wild animals.

Pickingill was apparently an effective and exceptional cunning man and healer, for in Glyn H. Morgan's, *Essex Witches*, it says of him that, "Injuries vanished at his touch and lost property was recovered with equal speed and facility" (Morgan, 1973, 48).

The other side of Pluto in Pisces suggests he may have yearned for privacy and seclusion, indeed he appeared elusive and secretive to some. When he lived in Canewdon, apparently "Nobody ever went inside the cottage. Visitors were strictly unwelcome" (ibid, 47). Eric Maple wrote *The Witches of Canewdon*, for the magazine *Folklore*. In it, Pickingill is described as "solitary and uncommunicative" (Maple, 1960, *Folklore/*Vol. 71, No. 1). Although this may describe him in his later years and not necessarily when he was a young man and had to work and live with other teams of labourers, and, where communication would have been necessary for work and socialising. Maple continued, "Pickingale practiced quite openly as a cunning man, restoring lost property, and curing warts and minor ailments by muttered charms and mysterious passes" (ibid).

INDEPENDENCE AND SOCIAL INTERACTION

Pickingill's Sun sign, Aries, is ruled by Mars, which associates with courage and vigour. It suggests that he was assertive and direct in his approach to life. The Moon was in the sign of Gemini which reveals Pickingill needed stimulation and thrived on socialising. His sense of humour which could be cheeky and mischievous, such is the nature of Mercury, the ruler of his Moon Gemini.

The nature of his Sun and Moon signs would have gone some way in helping Pickingill live to an old age. This is because Aries is courageous and Gemini is adaptable, which (when living in the harsh Victorian 1800s) probably helped Pickingill embrace the many changes that he saw in society.

In Pickingill's natal chart, the Sun was trine Uranus which reveals that Pickingill was free-spirited and enjoyed independence. Pickingill was 40 when he married, which was quite late for a bachelor in Victorian times. Perhaps he had other personal responsibilities or perhaps he enjoyed his freedom when he was a younger man?

The aspect Venus square Uranus also reveals a theme of valuing freedom, as Venus is associated with relationships and Uranus with independence and excitement. It also shows that friendships were important to him and in relationships strong companionship was integral.

Pickingill was also able to move on to pastures new. A New Zealand newspaper (Shepstone, correspondence with Author) obtained the story of Pickingill's long age from an English paper and in *The Star* newspaper in 1909 reported to its readers that he "... was able to look back on the past with pleasure.... He did not care to hear the old days run down ... there were privations, but there were happy memories of kind friendships" (www.deadfamilies.com/the Star1909).

The article continued that "... at the last, all the friendships of manhood had gone and he was left in what he called 'a new world'" (ibid). This shows that in his old age he still related to friends with feeling and fondness. He also recognised not only the changes of new generations, but also that he was living in a new and unfamiliar era.

LIBERTY AND EXPANSION

The position of Uranus in Sagittarius in his natal chart favours innovation and progress, as well as individualism and the freedom to pursue one's beliefs. The placement also indicates that he valued people's differences and the right of the individual to freedom on all levels. Pertinent to Pickingill is the symbolism associated with Sagittarius of being a 'gypsy-spirit' as well as the association of the horse through the image of the centaur.

Interestingly, there used to be an area in Eastwood, Essex, called the Bohemia Estate, which was occupied by Romanies. The name reflects the communities that (then) lived on the fringe of society, who were considered by some (both then and now) as outsiders. It is possible therefore that Pickingill was a neighbour to the Romany and Tinker communities as well as a co-worker in the fields where he worked.

In the past, *Gorjas* (non-Romanies) used to work together carrying out seasonal farm work, especially hop picking in September, and the Romany families were usually invited back each year as they were reliable workers (RTFHS, correspondence with Author). There was an area in Rochford, Essex, called the Anne Boleyn Estate, which was a popular rendezvous for Romanies who often met outside the Anne Boleyn Hotel, lining up their caravans ready for the road (Jerram-Burrows, 1983, plate 130

/photographs). Pickingill may well have valued people's differences and unconventionality and worked amicably alongside them, which is shown through the position of Uranus in Sagittarius.

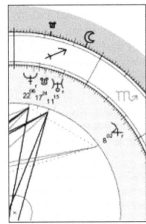

In 1861, Pickingill lived in Eastwood, in a farmhouse in Tinker's Lane. Farm wages were low and, up to the end of the nineteenth century, were no more than £1 a week, often there was a free cottage included as a perk. Farms for rent then cost approximately 20s–35s an acre, with the staffing ratio of one man and two horses to 40 acres of arable land considered sufficient (Cryer, 1978, 36). Apparently, Eastwood has for a long time had communities of Romanies (http://www.rootschat.com).

Uranus in Sagittarius is an ideal placement for being able to waive political change as well as seeing things in a new light in order to embrace a new era. We see this, for example, when Pickingill was visited by a London newspaper reporter who arrived in Canewdon in a car to interview him. Pickingill was excited at seeing the vehicle and elated when he was offered a ride; he said gleefully, "I'd like to go to London on it … I've never been to London." He very much enjoyed the experience too (www.deadfamilies.com/Essex Newsman:1908).

Apparently, the journalist's car was the first to be seen in Canewdon village and Pickingill was taken for a ride as far as the village pond (Webster, 1994, 14). Because of Canewdon's rather isolated location, Pickingill had never seen a train even though the railway system had been developed in Rochford almost twenty years before, in 1889.

It seems he enjoyed his work and proudly told the reporter that he was "… born in Hockley, and I have been in these parts working on farms all my life" (ibid).

A SAGE IN THE COMMUNITY

Saturn is in Aquarius in the natal chart (*see box below*) which indicates that Pickingill was respectful and tolerant of those with lifestyles alternative to his own. This repeats the theme about him valuing people's individuality and backgrounds which may have differed to his own.

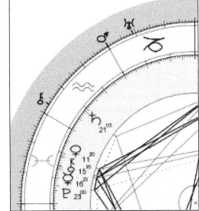

This may have manifested itself, for example, by way of him being respectful to landowners who employed him as a farm labourer and (as discussed above) the Romanies who also lived in Essex.

Apprehension and fear are also indicated through Saturn. It could be said that Saturn's position in Aquarius suggests that perhaps Pickingill had apprehensions about losing his identity amongst people; he had a need to be different. Saturn in the sign of Aquarius shows that Pickingill was original and independent and that he could be authoritative, commanding and respected in groups of people such as working teams of labourers, as an Aries he could direct and lead quite easily if he so wished. He may have cultivated an aura of fear too, with his blasting rod and the threat of paralysing others.

It seems that Pickingill's local community would have had a healthy respect for him (respect being associated with Saturn) and that, unlike his sons and wife; he did not fall foul of the law. Newspaper reports reveal that theft, cruelty to animals and fighting were some of the reasons his family had to attend court and, in some cases, were fined and/or went to prison, although George Pickingill senior does not appear to have been in the newspapers for breaking the law. Some of the crimes his family committed and were punished for included: stealing potatoes – Mary Ann his wife in 1862; cruelly beating four colts – son George Jnr. in 1885; being drunk and disorderly – sons George Jnr. & Frederick in 1891; trespassing looking for rabbits – George Jnr. in 1895. In 1891, Frederick paid his fine for being drunk and disorderly whilst his brother, George Jnr., served hard labour in Chelmsford prison (www.deadfamilies.com).

Saturn also depicts the wise old man or sage who has learnt hard lessons in life and learnt from his experience, whilst Aquarius represents generations and humanity. So, through the era of Saturn in Aquarius, Pickingill, in his long life, learnt a lot and had to break out of old established ways, giving way to innovation and progress. This can be seen through the examples of transport, particularly cars and railways. Therefore, whilst he could be inventive and original, he could also maintain the *status quo* when necessary (Saturn).

Mercury, the planet of communication, is square Uranus, indicating that Pickingill believed in free speech and may have had some radical thoughts as well as an inventive mind. As Mercury was in Pisces, it reveals that he was able to bring compassion and insight to his ideas as these are characteristics associated with Pisces (and its ruler, Neptune). Mercury is square Mars, indicating that Pickingill could put his thoughts into action and apply assertive communication; a less helpful side to this aspect is that Pickingill could get bored easily and so it would have been important to him to be stimulated by his environment which is in keeping with his lunar sign of Gemini.

WORKING ON THE LAND, CRAFTSMANSHIP AND LOVE OF NATURE

Mercury is conjunct Venus and reveals that Pickingill valued the language of beauty as well as understanding the language of nature. It is probable that he had a working knowledge of the seasons, and appreciated the beauty of Mother Nature and the gifts that she bestows. For example, harvest time was a very important period in the farmer's calendar and old customs dictated that the Corn Spirit was honoured. People made corn dollies in East Anglia as well as many other parts of Great Britain, this was an acknowledgement of the time of year as well as a magical, item, hoping for a prosperous year ahead for the production of corn and wheat. An example of the crops grown in the Parish of Rochford, in the fields surrounding Rochford Hall, shows that the fields were laid out as follows: fallow, oats or barley, clover, wheat and, where there was space, more oats or barley (Cryer, 1978, 33).

Interestingly, harvest time falls in the astrological sign of Virgo which is symbolised by the Corn Maiden as well as the Virgin. This sign is pertinent in Pickingill's natal chart as Virgo is the release point of challenges in his life and the areas associated with Virgo are health, nutrition and work (as discussed earlier).

Conversation, debate and exchange of ideas would have been a natural skill for Pickingill with the aforementioned aspect, since Mercury associates with ideas and debates, whilst Venus is affable and good natured. It also shows that Pickingill had an ease in communicating with loved ones, family and friends. The oral tradition of storytelling and sharing of knowledge is commonplace through most hereditary crafts. It is possible, therefore, that Pickingill's forbearers continued the line of sharing knowledge and storytelling through various generations of the family, perhaps, for example, in knowledge about farming and labouring as well as herbalism and traditional remedies and how to apply them effectively with precision and skill.

Another example of Pickingill's experience, knowledge and skill in craftsmanship can be demonstrated by him making his walking stick of blackthorn, assuming, of course, that it was he who made it!. He would have had to have first seasoned and then dried the material, straightened the shaft and shaped the handle, either by bending around a jig or smoothing and finishing the rounded knob-stick shape, and if the handle and shaft were made of two different woods then a collar had to be fashioned to firmly join the two together. The base of the stick also had to be finished to reduce the risk of slipping and often a ferrule, usually of metal at that time, was added to prevent the wood at the base from rotting. Possibly Pickingill blessed and created the walking stick in accordance with the Moon's cycle for energy purposes, as well as creating a unique mark on the stick for magical purposes, but of course this is just speculation and we do not know for sure.

EMBRACING LANGUAGE

Mercury (the ruler of Pickingill's Moon sign, Gemini) also indicates gravity towards languages. Many Dutchmen settled in the Canewdon area in the seventeenth century, and it is possible that some of the language and customs of the Dutch were absorbed by the community and were used in everyday speech, which members of the Pickingill family may have been familiar with and understood. Folklorist Eric Maple, when researching Pickingill, became aware of a character called 'Granny' who had lived in Canewdon village. He described her as being of "… old Dutch stock and her features bore something of the stamp of the seventeenth-century Hollanders who drained the Essex marshes and built sea-walls" (Maple, 1965, 185). She was a respected member of the Canewdon community and, whilst she believed in witchcraft, she did not fear it as "she was adept in white magic" (ibid).

The Pickingill family may also have been familiar with some of the Romany and tinker language, as they lived nearby and they may have worked together, particularly when the family lived in other parts of Rochford, such as Eastwood. As Canewdon was a very insular island, there may even have been remnants of the left-over Anglo-Saxon language which was still in use on the island. Recent observation reveals that dialect from areas such as Braintree, Halstead, Gosfield, Bardfield and Weathersfield in Essex contain many words from not only Saxon influences but also Belgic, Dutch and Friesian (http://www.essexlifemag.co.uk/people/essex-dialect-1-1779354).

Another example of Pickingill's development of language can be seen in an anecdote about him when he was administrating healing to a patient. Passing his hands over the injury, he started speaking in a seemingly gibberish language; "He used a little charming as well, passing his hands over an injury while mumbling some unintelligible litany" (Maple, 1965, 185). This was to help induce a magical energy and/or to create dramatic effect during his cunning work.

HORSE WHISPERING, MEDIATION AND HANDS ON HEALING

Returning to the aspect of Mercury conjunct Venus; both planets are in the sign of Pisces and this shows that Pickingill could have debated and negotiated with compassion and was able to appreciate both sides of an argument. We see this when folklorist Eric Maple (the subject of Chapter Eight) described how Pickingill was once called upon to help when "... the men of Dengie sought the advice of the Wise Man of Canewdon in a wages dispute" (Maple, 2008, 60). The area of Dengie was also in the Parish of Rochford, approximately 25 miles from Canewdon, so even travelling by horse or pony would have required real effort to travel to Canewdon to seek Pickingill's advice; this indicates he had high standing within the Rochford community.

Although Pickingill was considered illiterate, he seems to have developed his own, very effective language when looking after his horses and communicating with them through 'horse-whispering'. This he may have done through careful use of his vocal tone and volume, as well as hands-on healing (hands are also associated with Mercury). Horses trusted and understood him. In his natal chart, both Mercury and Venus in Pisces show that he had tremendous compassion and understanding for animals and for those that may be considered vulnerable.

A Canewdon villager, Jack Taylor, reminisced to historian Ronald Hutton a memory that he had of George Pickingill. He recalled how he and his sister as children were attempting to get to the Rochford Fair with their pony and trap, but their animal was being stubborn and not moving. Out of nowhere they saw Pickingill, "staring us with those terrible eyes of his."

Eventually Pickingill came over to them and requested they put the reins down and not interfere with the pony in any way. For a few minutes, Pickingill whispered in its ear, then stood back and hit it. Thereupon the pony started to move and, without any further interference from Jack and his sister, made its own way towards Rochford (Hutton, 1999, 297).

This tale shows that, despite Pickingill's rather menacing appearance, he had good intentions and would offer his help freely. The story further reveals his skill at communicating with animals and also that something about him must have allayed the children's initial fear. This shows not only his knowledge but also keen perception.

CREATING HIS OWN TRUTHS

The aspect of Mercury square Neptune indicates that Pickingill may have had a gift for distorting information; either by being highly creative or misleading by adjusting the truth. The latter can be seen, for example, when he gave different ages to different employers to gain employment (something we see through the various census records). This was not necessarily deliberate, of course, since he was born almost twenty years before the enforced registration of births, deaths and marriages in 1837. It was not unusual for people to be uncertain of their true age.

However, even when Pickingill was being interviewed by a London reporter about his longevity in age and he made headlines with: "A Canewdon Centenarian," he carried on the illusion that he was older than he was, telling the journalist "Yes I am one hundred and five. ... I only stopped working at ninety" (www.deadfamilies.com/EssexNewsman:1908). Claiming great age may have been a way of also claiming authority in his local area; he would have realised that some people would have read about him in the newspaper article.

This aspect (Mercury square Neptune) also suggests that Pickingill may have had a talent for working with images and symbols. This could have been helpful to him, for example in observing the Moon's cycle (which helps in agriculture) as well as weather-reading, such as reading the clouds. If he did indeed socialise with the Romanies, it is possible that he learnt some of the divination arts, such as palmistry. However, we cannot be sure of this and, besides, people other than Romanies also practised divination.

Since Mercury symbolises the mind and Neptune the infiltration, it could be said that Pickingill could easily permeate other people's psyches. This would have given him a capacity to tune-in to other people's feelings, frame of mind and disposition. Eric Maple's, *Dark World of the Witches,* describes Pickingill, as someone who "… always seemed to know what was in the mind of the person before they had spoken" (Maple, 1965, 185).

EDUCATION

It has been said that the historian's functional definition of 'literacy' is: "The ability of a person to sign his or her own name" (Reay, 1991, 24), as well as observing that the "attraction of using signatures or marks (usually crosses) as a gauge of literacy is that they permit measurement through time and across gender, class and occupational groups" (ibid).

It is notable that many of the agricultural classes were defined as illiterate in rural areas, while those who did go to school in the latter nineteenth century may have learned to read but were unable to write (as a technical skill), as they had to leave school and go to work to earn the family a much-needed extra income.

Charles Frederick *Pitengale* (Pickingill's eldest son) is recorded on the 1871 Census of Canewdon as aged nine and described as a scholar. However, on the death certificate of his father in 1909, the mark of an 'x' is entered next to the informant of 'Frederick Pettingale', suggesting he may have learnt to read but he could not write his name. We do not know if George Pickingill ever received any formal education, although the mark of the 'x' appears next to his name on his marriage certificate.

In the early nineteenth century there was no state education and no school-leaving age and although little is known about them, there were charitable and private schools. The existence at Canewdon of a "Day and Sunday School for teaching poor children" is confirmed by William White's *History, Gazetteer and Directory of the County of Essex.* The Schoolmasters of these schools had been instructed to "teach the children of poor parishioners in reading, writing, ciphering (mathematics) and religious knowledge, according to the doctrine of the established Church" (ERO, communication with Author).

We do not know for certain whether members of the Pickingill family attended the day school or the Sunday school (or both), although it seems unlikely that either Charles (born 1790) or his son George (born 1816) received a formal education. Charles Frederick Pickingill, however (one of George's sons), was born in 1861 and it is possible that he attended school although, regrettably, none of the local school records are known to survive from this period.

Although Charles Frederick was recorded as being a scholar on the 1871 Census of Canewdon, it is possible that he was a 'scholar' in that he was learning how to be an agricultural labourer. 'Scholar' could also mean, in those times, that he was learning the family business and labouring was the trade of the Pickingill family as well as most families in that area in the 1800s. Later on, he became a blacksmith, possibly learning that trade from Samuel Pickingill, his 'adopted' brother.

SURVIVAL AND VICTIMISATION

The aspect of Mars square Neptune also shows that Pickingill could fight for the underdog, as Mars is associated with fight and Neptune with the defenceless.

The aspect of Mars opposing Uranus also shows that Pickingill could at times be a 'freedom–fighter', since Mars associates with battle and Uranus with liberty. The Mars and Uranus contact also adds potential to be adventurous and original in action. Both of these aspects would have been helpful to Pickingill in any situation where his independence was at risk, and where he was in a position to help, for example, those who may have been without care and neglected.

The position of Mars square Neptune also indicates that Pickingill could have been a victim himself. For example, when Pickingill was working in a field at Canewdon Farm, his leather gloves and jacket (valued at four shillings) were stolen. The culprit, a homeless man named Jack Taylor, was charged on 17th August, 1887, and committed for trial (www.deadfamilies.com). In October, 1887, Taylor pleaded guilty to only stealing the jacket from Pickingill; he was imprisoned for six months with hard labour (ibid). When the theft occurred, Pickingill would have been 71 (Taylor was 63). It is worth mentioning here that in 1967, as part of his research, Professor Ronald Hutton interviewed a man named Jack Taylor who was then in a retirement home, but obviously this was not the same man who stole from Pickingill as he would clearly have been dead by that time.

A second example of how Pickingill sometimes found himself in the situation of victim can be seen in June, 1990, when his son George (Jnr.) was convicted at the Southend Petty Sessions and sent to jail for fourteen days, for failing to pay one shilling per week towards his father's upkeep (this was chargeable to the Rochford Workhouse Union) (ibid).

Mercury and Venus are conjunct in Pisces (as discussed earlier), the latter being ruled by Neptune; this shows a wealth of kindness and sensitivity. However, there is also a strong Martian side to Pickingill's nature which is shown by the various hard aspects created with other planets in his chart. This shows that, although Pickingill was very empathetic, he was definitely a force to be reckoned with and could both assert and defend himself when necessary; such is the nature of Mars.

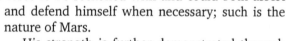

His strength is further demonstrated through the aspect of Mars square Pluto; Mars is associated with vigour and Pluto with determination and power. This indicates situations where Pickingill had to fight for survival and reveals that he possessed extraordinary courage and powers of endurance. This can be seen in his remarkable longevity through a period of economic depression when there was virtually no free medical help. Many poor people in those times had to rely on herbalism and old remedies as they could not afford to pay for doctors. It is possible that Pickingill had a thorough understanding of herbs and their medicinal purposes, which may have helped him to live to a great age, as well as being able to help his community and immediate neighbours with such treatments.

The characteristics of power and determination are revealed in the square aspect created between Mars and Pluto and can also be seen in the way that Pickingill was able to stop machinery using his extrasensory and telepathic skills. Even in his last days, he declared that his "... body was weak his power strong, and that he would demonstrate that he retained this power even after death" (Maple, 1965, 185).

There is also a competitiveness and sense of compulsive winning with this aspect, Mars being associated with the former and Pluto the compelling. Mars is in Gemini; the sign which connects with communities and neighbours. So it could be said that Pickingill had to assert himself in these areas to help gain work, for example, at the time in employment there were low wages in agriculture (his area of work) and much of the work was seasonal. Mars in Gemini also indicates that Pickingill could be grumpy and irritable at times, tetchy and crotchety (particularly in his older years).

Mars in Gemini also suggests he could enjoy debates, although at times friends, family and neighbours may have considered his anger and temper unnecessary. This is shown by the sometimes enraged nature of Mars as well as the light and superficial nature of Gemini and its ruler, Mercury; the planet of communication. It has been said that "... in his later years he was more interested in caging (sic) beer and getting a rise out of people" (*Haunted Palace Blog*); showing that he enjoyed seeing people rise to the occasion when he was teasing them.

ASSERTION AND ENDURANCE

Returning to the aspect of Mars square Pluto, it also indicates that he may have had to fight (Mars) to survive (Pluto), right until the end of his life. Although Pickingill was working, he was living on the breadline (like so many at that time) and when he was in his nineties, his son was meant to support him by way of maintenance, although, as we have seen; this did not always happen. It was not an easy life and he was a real survivor. The Pluto in Pisces placement shows that he survived an age of poverty and vulnerability, as Pluto is associated with survival and Pisces/Neptune the aforementioned areas of susceptibility and suffering.

Mercury is also associated with mechanical skill, which would have helped Pickingill to maintain, use and fix the tools and machinery that were used in agriculture in the nineteenth century. Tasks, such as sharpening (from bill hooks to knives and scythes), took time and skill.

Mars in Gemini suggests that Pickingill enjoyed debate and could be competitive (Mars) in communication (Gemini). Mercury square Mars also suggests that he could be assertive in his communications and that he was strong-willed, using his mind (associated with Mercury) as

Catherine Cox (née Pickingill) by very kind permission of Kimberli Shepstone.

a weapon (associated with Mars). This is borne out, for example, by the story that he used to wander the fields at harvest-time "threatening to bewitch the threshing machinery" (Maple, 1965, 184). He was apparently menacing, and farmers "bribed the wizard with beer to go away" (ibid). Harvest time is a crucial time in agriculture as it is the time of year for gathering ripened crops.

In Pickingill's life, there were many short journeys within the neighbourhood and a good deal of everyday comings and goings. This could certainly describe the daily effort of walking miles, since few ordinary people owned a horse for riding or a pony and trap. Mars indicates the application of energy and Mercury (the ruler of Gemini and Virgo) indicates the frequency and movement.

Another aspect involving Mars is its opposition to Neptune and this can indicate an illusion (associated with Neptune) of strength (associated with Mars). This adds to the sometimes 'menacing' nature of Pickingill as described above. Maple said that Pickingill was "feared with intensity," and people he interviewed described how "one word from Pickingill and you would be ill, and would remain so until he told you that you could be well again" (Maple, 1965, 184).

The following anecdote tells how, whenever Pickingill wanted water drawn from the local pump in Canewdon, the young local boys would be apparently reluctant to volunteer to fetch it for him because of the old man's rather sinister reputation (ibid). Eventually, the authorities had to employ a caretaker to supervise the people who needed water, thus ensuring they did not take more than their fair share (Smith, 1987, 42).

It was said of Pickingill's appearance, "In common with members of his family, he possessed eyes of peculiar intensity" (Maple, 2008, 59–60). This family presumably was his father, daughters and sons, and perhaps also his own siblings. A photograph of his sister Catherine definitely shows a strong family resemblance Pickingill was described as "tall and unkempt ... and had very long fingernails" (ibid). However, in the photograph of Pickingill as an old man, his fingernails do not seem particularly long, so perhaps he'd had them trimmed by then! It seemed that Pickingill kept up his masquerade of fear and intrigue until his final days and local villagers no doubt added strength to the illusion by their stories about him, recounted to researchers. In fairness to him, however, this illusion of menace may have been adopted as a protection, not only from local youths and children, but also from what he might have considered the prying eyes of officialdom, especially anyone connected with the local workhouse.

ILLUSION AND MYSTERY

Mercury is detriment (see glossary) in Pisces. This position can create confusion, distortion and misunderstandings as the nature of Pisces/Neptune at times is evasive and nebulous. However, there are other helpful energies to this position. For example, one of the positive aspects to this placement is that it can create an intuitive knowing and psychic ability in communicating; it also shows a gift for humour and mimicking which, like his Moon Gemini sign, enjoys frivolity and laughter.

Legendary stories connected with Pickingill include the following. It was claimed that local villagers saw "clocks and ornaments dancing on the mantelpiece" in his modest cottage, while "chairs and table waltzed elegantly together" (Maple, 1965, 165), until Pickingill, with one gesture, brought the "mad masque to an end" (ibid). Another (much disputed) Canewdon legend is that Pickingill was a 'Master of the

Witches' who could call up the nine secret witches of Canewdon merely by whistling. They then had to "… stand at their front doors exposed to the whole world as the ones responsible for all the evil of the village" (ibid, 184).

This ability to both intimidate and help his neighbours is echoed in Pickingill's chart; in particular the aspect of Mercury square Neptune, which suggests his ability to distort reality and shows the double-sided nature to his character. We know that local villagers both feared and respected him, presumably because they had witnessed or heard about his powers. Mercury corresponds with communication, conjuring and trickery and Neptune; being bewitching, magical and spellbinding. This is borne out by his varying ages and dates of birth shown on official census records (http://www.deadfamilies. com/Z3-Others/Pickingill/George-Pickingill.htm), as well as his effective healing work that he undertook as a cunning man and his success in finding lost property, which might have made people regard him as something of a wizard.

This aspect also indicates that Pickingill could be inspired, if taught in an imaginative way. He may have been gifted in working with art forms, images and symbols; this is because Mercury is associated with the mind and Neptune with the aforementioned media. This could have been helpful to him if he practiced the divination arts, such as astrology and palmistry as well as 'telling the bees' and weather-reading, for example.

Since Mercury symbolises the mind and Neptune the infiltrating, it could be argued that Pickingill could easily permeate other people's psyches, which would have given him a capacity to tune-in to other people's feelings and dispositions. Eric Maple said that, "In all the stories about Pickingill, there is a subtle undercurrent of horror which one finds hard to pinpoint" (Maple, 1965, 164); the delicacy and difficulty described here perfectly illustrates the Neptunian energy. The author continued that the local villagers who knew Pickingill and provided accounts about him may have experienced "a quiet terror when he passed them in the village street" (ibid). This suggestion also alludes to the possibility that Pickingill was held in awe within the village; the community may not have understood his cunning nature but knew that he was capable of extraordinary gifts.

An amusing tale which demonstrates Pickingill's gift of perception and telepathy is borne out by the following story told by Mr M. Burton, a villager of Dengie. Two labourers had decided to consult the 'Old Man Witch', George Pickingill of Canewdon, over a wages disagreement. Upon their journey to the village, one said to the other, "I wonder if the old b…… is at home?" Finally, they arrived at Pickingill's cottage, knocked on the door and "suddenly the window flew open and the wizard thrust his head out and hissed at them, 'Yes, the old b…… is at home!'" (Maple, 1962, 90).

If that story is true, it shows the remarkable powers of Pickingill's psychic gifts and must have given the labourers quite a shock. Of course, it might have been that Pickingill knew how the men were going to describe him, and was just waiting to surprise them with it. We do not know if Pickingill's consultation eventually helped smooth over the disagreement about their wages.

WISHING FOR A DIFFERENT LIFE

Neptune is also in Sagittarius which, (like most people of Pickingill's generation), indicates a yearning for a more meaningful life, as Neptune is associated with wishing and Sagittarius the adventurer and spirited. From Pickingill's perspective, it suggests that he may have yearned for a better life for his people where they could be free of poverty and suffering. Pickingill's sister, Catherine, and her husband George left Essex and emigrated to Powassan, Canada in approximately 1873. They remained in Canada, as did their future family generations (Shepstone, correspondence with Author).

Many people emigrated from England to Canada, especially when the British Government offered land there to the English and Irish. This was granted in exchange for the new immigrants helping to create the much-needed new infrastructure for the new settlements. However, the land was usually in the wilderness and families would be expected to build their own shelter as well as provide the basic necessities for their families. They were even required to clear the section of land on the edge of their property in order to build the concession roads for people to travel. Only once all conditions had been met were the families entitled to the property. It was a hard life and many perished during this time as it was too punishing an ordeal for them (ibid).

Although Catherine Pickingill survived, sadly her husband George died just six years after settling in Canada. Perhaps she had become accustomed to a harsh and stark way of life by living in the marshy and insular land of Essex. Like her brother George, who was hardy and lived to a ripe old age, Catherine lived to the age of 82 (copy of obituary from Shepstone to Author). The above example shows the Neptune in Sagittarius generation into which Pickingill was born; people yearned for a better life where optimism, faith and hope were key principles in their quest.

Beliefs, politics and religion may have been important to Pickingill since these are themes also associated with Sagittarius, whilst Neptune is associated with healing and vulnerability. It is also associated with the underprivileged, the unseen and unheard, in other words; those without a 'voice'. Saturn is sextile Neptune and suggests that Pickingill lived an uncluttered simple life, without excess and opulence; the realistic nature of Saturn shows that he could accept the limitations in his life by drawing upon his spiritual values to give him strength.

CUNNING ARTS, DEATH AND HEALING

Pickingill was 21 when Queen Victoria came to the throne and was still alive when she died in 1901, after a reign of 64 years. The Victorian era, although often portrayed as a period of great advances and tremendous wealth (for some people), was also a period of terrible grinding poverty for the majority. Poverty in towns and cities has been well documented; rural poverty was no less terrible, although it was not so well understood. This was the world that Pickingill knew. He was often on the breadline; forced to work well into extreme old age doing hard manual labour in all weathers. His wages were low and food often scarce. Poaching – even when prompted by the need for food – was punished harshly.

Neptune is square Pluto and reveals that anything 'hidden' and 'unspoken' would have appealed to Pickingill, since these areas are associated with both Neptune and Pluto. This would have been helpful to Pickingill in his work as cunning man, where healing and magic were applied. Compassion and understanding are qualities associated with Neptune, whilst Pluto, shows a breadth of understanding.

Pluto in Pisces suggests that Pickingill was perceptive and effective in his healing, as well as his magical pursuits, using his 'wit' and 'cunning' to help others in getting to the root of a problem. This placement would also help him to achieve his aims with determination and compassion – characteristics associated with Pluto and Pisces respectively.

Pickingill's strengths lay in the area of hidden powers as well as matters pertaining to life and death, and these are indicated by the placement of Jupiter in Scorpio. It shows a capacity for faith as well as willpower, since the former is associated with Jupiter and the latter with Scorpio. Death was a significant theme in Pickingill's life for he experienced grief and bereavement at an early age. There was a high infant mortality rate during the nineteenth century and, indeed, Pickingill's family experienced their fair share of loss in this way. Pickingill was one of the children who not only survived but went on to live to a great age in a harsh period of history.

Pickingill's mother died from consumption when he was 22 and his father Charles died of apoplexy when Pickingill was 51 (Walworth, 2016, 100). Pickingill's wife, Sarah-Ann, died from dropsy of the liver when she was approximately 59–60 years old (www.deadfamilies.com) and he was 71; he remained a widower until his death in 1909. His youngest son, George, died in 1902 when Pickingill was 86 (ibid).

Pickingill's parents had many children, most of whom died at a very young age, although this was common at the time. George was the first of his parents' children to survive, showing in keeping with the Aries nature; that he was truly a fighter (ibid). From this situation we can see that at an early age George was aware of death, and later he must have nurtured a philosophical and strong spirit which helped him to overcome grief as shown by the placement of Jupiter in Scorpio (*see box below*).

In his work as a farm labourer, he would also have seen a wealth of working animals born and die and it would have been easy for his sensitive nature to be overwhelmed by such events, yet his strong spirit enabled him to find a way to cope and remain optimistic. He saw birth and death as inevitable and so learnt philosophically to adapt to these forces and cycles of life. Jupiter's nature is optimistic and philosophical, whilst Pluto (the ruler of Scorpio) is associated with crisis, transformation as well as life-after-death issues.

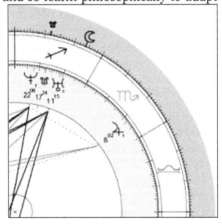

Venus is trine Jupiter and the aspect shows that he valued (Venus) religion (Jupiter), this is because Jupiter is associated with belief, faith and meaning. Venus trine Jupiter shows a love of life; Pickingill may have found pleasure in God or whatever he understood as a God – possibly a figure or spiritual force. This is because Venus represents the pleasure principle whilst Jupiter the organised religion and belief.

This planetary contact also indicates that, if he wished, Pickingill could be big-hearted and friendly, such are the qualities also associated with Venus and Jupiter.

TENDER LOVING CARE

Venus is exalted (*see glossary*) in Pisces and it is a position that is very co-operative as well as being accepting by nature. This creates the potential to heal others, as the subject is so easy to be around. They project a sense of calm, trust and peace; an ideal skill-set for any healer. Pickingill's own talents as a healer are quite well attested and may well have been, in part, due to this added aura of kindness and understanding. The position of Venus in Pisces can indicate empathy, kindness, care, sensitivity and understanding. In *Marsh Wizards-Witches of Canewdon* (Caduceus, 2008, 60), it reveals that, "One woman was said to have been cured by him of rheumatism ... he made no charge for his services." Considering his own penury, this generosity must have endeared him to friends and neighbours alike. He healed because he was a healer and felt compelled to do so, not in order to make money.

Another symbolism typical of Venus in Pisces is idealism, and perhaps Pickingill was idealistic in love. He may have wished to marry someone who needed help in some way, since Venus is associated with relationships whilst Pisces and its ruler Neptune also allude to themes of addiction and saving. Pickingill's wife died of dropsy of the liver, perhaps caused by alcohol addiction or even a virus, such as hepatitis which, if not properly treated, can be fatal.

Apart from addiction and dependency, other Neptunian themes include hospitals, prisons and workhouses, and these too featured in Pickingill's family life. His younger son, for example, not only served time in prison but eventually died from pneumonia in the Rochford Union Workhouse having died from pneumonia. Despite fighting desperately to stay out of the workhouse, Pickingill himself eventually died in the infirmary at the same workhouse; perhaps he'd had a premonition that if he were to be admitted, he too would meet the same fate as his son.

Venus in Pisces exalts in helping those less fortunate than themselves, and they can even sacrifice themselves for the good of others. It is also possible that many of his relationships thrived where there were themes of addiction, dependency, and escapism. In the Victorian world, with its oppressive levels of poverty, hunger and casual cruelty, such escapism may have been a way of coping with everyday life. Venus in Pisces is a passive placement and so there is an easiness and gentleness within, a compliant and giving nature. Relationships with the celestial, divine and heavenly are often found for a person with this placement. The numerous placements in Pickingill's chart repeat the message that he was indeed an independent and spiritual man.

EMPLOYMENT, WAGES AND FOOD

Venus square Mars indicates that Pickingill often had to fight for money, even though he does not seem to have charged patients and customers for his 'cunning work'. Yet, in terms of his employment as a farm labourer, this aspect suggests that it was not only difficult to find work (especially as he grew older) but that even when he did; it was poorly paid. This was largely due to a nationwide economic depression. Hours were long and, in winter when there was less daylight and poor weather; employees had shorter working hours, meaning they were paid less. Pickingill probably had to do 'piece work' as well as 'day work' during his working life as an agricultural and farm labourer.

To secure work, it appears he told potential employers that he was younger than he actually was. This in turn suggests that he looked young for his age, otherwise they would not have employed him. The charm and popularity of Venus coupled with the enterprising nature of Mars would also have helped him and, as far as we can tell from official records, Pickingill was always in employment.

Mars is trine Saturn in his natal chart, indicating that Pickingill faced tests (Saturn) of courage (Mars) and strength in his life. Any work he undertook which involved endurance and stamina would have been satisfying to him, the impulsive nature of Mars and disciplined nature of Saturn indicates that he could bring these qualities to his work. Mars and Saturn are both in air signs, Gemini and Aquarius respectively. The communicative qualities of the air signs indicate that Pickingill could be both innovative and sociable in his work, that he was enterprising (associated with Mars) and reliable (associated with Saturn).

The restricting nature of Saturn also suggests that Pickingill had to be economical and could live without excess; the vigorous nature of Mars would have helped him to be frugal and sparing. One area in which this can be seen is his diet, for Pickingill once said that he "... ate anything that came his way" (www.deadfamilies.com/The Star:1909). This statement shows how poor his diet must have been; mostly bread, vegetables, a little cheese and the occasional rabbit (one of his sons was convicted of poaching a rabbit on a Christmas Eve). He would probably have eaten oysters too, since these were easily and freely available to collect from the estuary and available for people who lived in that part of Essex.

At that time, oysters were a staple diet for the poor as the water (the sea and the river) was excellent for the production of oysters (www. rochford.gov.uk). Several oyster merchants lived in the area in the seventeen and eighteen hundreds and capitalised on the area for its

George Pickengale of Canewdon. Image Reproduced by the Kind Permission of Folklore Enterprises Ltd.

production of oysters. Pickingill also enjoyed his daily mug of beer (deadfamilies.com/EssexNewsman:1908). A newspaper article wrote that, "He still likes his pipe of tobacco and mug of ale," at the age of 92. According to folklorist Eric Maple's research, some of his interviewees told him that "Pickingill always ended the day drunk" (Maple, 1965, 184) and allegedly farmers would bribe him to go away with beer if they felt he had been intimidating their farm workers (ibid).

PHYSICAL TRANSFORMATION

Pickingill died on 10th April, 1909, and his death certificate reveals the cause of death was senile decay and cardiac failure (Death Cert. No. DYE 175655). Leading up to his death, he was experiencing some major astrological transits, and the symbolism of his source of death can be illustrated by two of his transits.

Firstly, transiting Neptune trine natal Mercury represents the senile decay. This is because Neptune denotes confusion, decay and loss, whilst Mercury denotes communication and intellect. The second transit, Saturn conjunct the natal Sun represents the cardiac failure, as Saturn represents obstructions and restriction, whilst the Sun represents life. In medical astrology the Sun also rules the heart through its rulership of Leo. He was described as being "... quite well and hearty until within a few days of his death" (www.deadfamilies.com/The Essex Newsman/April 1909/ Newspaper Obituaries).

The *Essex Newsman* newspaper on 17th April, 1909, in reporting the death of Pickingill wrote that Pickingill "to the last, retained all his faculties" and his memories of childhood were very distinct "He remembered the news of Waterloo coming to the village and the rejoicings over the victory. He worked hard all his life, and never had a holiday until he was 90" (ibid). Since the Battle of Waterloo took place in June 1815, a year *before* his birth, it seems unlikely he had such memories, although he may have claimed he did in order to support his claim to be older than he was.

Surprisingly, news of his death even reached a newspaper in New Zealand (as mentioned earlier); in *The Star* on 1st July, 1909, the article informed readers that, "He lived near the sea, and as a boy recalled the coming of the press gangs and the hiding of the seamen and fishermen in the inland villages" (www.deadfamilies.com/Pickingill/ newspaper reports). This memory is much more likely to be true, since impressments were a feature of coastal life up until the early 1830s.

When the journalist asked Pickingill if he had any advice as to how to live to be a centenarian he simply replied: "You just go on living that's all" (ibid), which reveals not only an uncomplicated but also fatalistic approach to life.

As previously noted, his sister Catherine died just four years after him in 1913, aged 82. She had emigrated to Canada with her Essex-born husband, George Cox (an agricultural labourer), in 1874 and in her obituary in the Canadian newspapers, the name Pickingill features (as her maiden name) as well as George Pickingill's beloved place of birth, Hockley in the County of Essex, where Catherine was also born. Although Pickingill never rode on a train or aeroplane, his name and reputation seemed do the travelling for him, since his death was mentioned as far afield as New Zealand and his surname and birthplace were mentioned in Canada.

Legend has it that, when Pickingill died, there was a sense of relief in Canewdon, since he was so feared. Apparently, at his funeral, his hearse approached the churchyard, only for the horse to bolt and take off into the open countryside. Supposedly, Pickingill had promised he would make his powerful presence known even after his death and villagers took the incident of the horse fleeing as proof. His cottage is said to have burnt down after his death, although it is thought this may have happened later, in the 1920s, when many wooden cottages in Canewdon were condemned (Webster, Canewdon Charities Trust, 1994).

George Pickingill was a hard-working farm labourer who lived through the difficult Victorian period when poverty was rife, both in the countryside and in the towns and cities. He came from a family where there had been high infant mortality and where he and family members regularly had to move around in the County of Essex to secure labouring work. During his lifetime, there was no free healthcare provided by the state. So, like so many millions of poor downtrodden rural folk in the nineteenth century, his – and their – medicines came from herbalism and handed-down remedies for medicinal purposes.

As far as we can tell, he was a law-abiding citizen (there is evidence of his family appearing before the magistrates, but not himself) who enjoyed life despite its hardships. Through astrology we can see by his nature that he was a born fighter, feisty though optimistic, who spent his life working amongst nature with other labourers as well as animals in his farm work, meeting different people across the County of Essex.

He was a natural healer and was able to help people through his 'cunning work', seemingly not charging them money or taking advantage of their situation; perhaps he asked for favours or payment in kind instead. He died in the Rochford Union Workhouse from natural causes, an ailing and aged man in dire poverty.

THE LEGEND OF A FARM LABOURER

We cannot leave this chapter without noting some of the controversy that has grown up around Pickingill.

He first gained public attention when newspapers claimed he was the oldest man alive in England. It was not quite true but, nevertheless, he went along with it. After his death, he became the subject of research about Canewdon and its folkore and witchcraft legends, investigated firstly by folklorist Eric Maple (subject of Chapter Eight) in 1959/1960, and later by historian Ronald Hutton in 1967.

Pickingill was again in the occult spotlight when *The Pickingill Papers: the Origins of the Gardnerian Craft*, written by W.E. Liddell and occultist Michael Howard, was published in 1994. Yet, whereas Maple had portrayed him as an old and wise cunning man who was feared by the villagers, Howard and Liddell's account stated he had hailed "... from an established line of hereditary witches who had been priests of the Horned God since Saxon times" (Howard, 2009, 51).

Michael Howard later admitted that many of Liddell's claims "... seem too fantastic to be true" (Hutton, 1999, 290). Indeed, historian Ronald Hutton's findings on Pickingill concurred with much of Maple's research about Pickingill being a traditional cunning man.

CANEWDON AND THE PARISH OF ROCHFORD

Canewdon lies approximately six miles off Southend, in the flat marshy country, close to the River Crouch, in the heart of Essex's 'witch country'. Legend claims that for as long as the St Nicholas' church tower stands, Canewdon will always have six witches. They must comprise of "three in silk and three in cotton." Legend says that when the last witch dies, the church tower inevitably will fall, but should the tower fall first then all six witches will die (Canning, 1974, 63). By the 1970s it was said that "some of the stories connected with the village have, over the centuries, become distorted beyond credulity" (ibid, 62).

The spinster Rose Pye was the first documented witch of Canewdon; in 1580 she was charged and tried for bewitching to death the one year-old daughter of Richard Snow, who also lived in Canewdon, but was acquitted (Maple, 2008, 51). The village has also inspired a book of poems called, *The Witch House of Canewdon* (Obby Robinson, 2014).

The sixteenth century Anchor Inn was very close to Pickingill's cottage in Canewdon (and likely to have been frequented by him). Dating from the sixteenth century, the inn is said to be haunted by a witch named Sarah who was put to death during the seventeenth century witch-hunts. The Anchor Inn is also said to be haunted by other restless spirits that have been seen by various landlords and members of the public (Sipple, 2001,17). It is even possible that the phenomena were also seen by Pickingill, as he lived nearby.

Author and folklorist, Eric Maple, in 1965 in his paper, *Witchcraft and Magic in the Rochford Hundred*, described the local population as "... narrow, bigoted and deeply superstitious and whose smuggling activities had created within them an inherent hostility to strangers" (Maple, 2008, 67). In his later years, Pickingill still possessed good recall about smuggling and other significant events which will be discussed later.

Many years after his death, George Pickingill joined the various legends of Canewdon as its very own cunning man. This was due to a combination of the aforementioned research as well as oral accounts by people who had known him (Hutton, 1999, 297).

Apparently, Pickingill's cottage eventually fell down as nobody wanted to live in it after his death (Canning and Smythe, 1974, 67). It has also been said that the villagers of Canewdon "... scoff or become irritated, or exploit the old tales according to their own interests" (ibid).

Interestingly, there seems to be no evidence of Pickingill's gifts as a cunning man or horse-whisperer in other villages in the Parish of Rochford in Essex where he lived (such as Hockley and Eastwood) before he moved to Canewdon. There also appears to be no tradition or account of him being a cunning man when he lived in Gravesend, Kent, with his wife Sarah Ann in the 1850s for a short while, before returning to Essex. It is possible that Pickingill was in Kent at that time, as his father, Charles, was also in Rochester, Kent, probably for employment purposes.

James Murrell was another famous cunning man who lived near Pickingill in a place called Hadleigh in the Parish of Rochford. He died in 1860 and it is possible that Pickingill attracted more clients after Murrell's death as, in the early 1860s, Pickingill was living in Eastwood, Essex, which was not far from Hadleigh.

Pickingill may have been practicing his cunning-arts there already, so that by the time he moved to Canewdon (sometime between 1864–68) he may have already built-up a reputation and client base. This would support Maple's comments about people travelling far to visit him in Canewdon, although the 'distance' that he speaks of was localised and mostly consisted of visitors from other parts of Essex, such as Dengie (now known as Billericay).

DATES, ERROR AND CONFUSION

No account of Pickingill's life would be complete without mentioning the problem of dates and the various spellings of his name, which have caused researchers considerable confusion. The Parish Registers of Hockley, Essex, show Pickingill's baptism on the 26th May, 1816 (www.essex.gov.uk/ERO) and that he was baptised as George Pickingill, son of Charles and Hannah *Pickingill*. During this period, some baptism registers also included the date of birth, although not in Pickingill's case. On occasions when the birth date *was* documented on the parish register, baptism usually occurred a few weeks or even months later.

Confusion arose regarding George Pickingill's age on the burial registrar when he was buried at the Church of St Nicholas, Canewdon. He was buried on the 14th April, 1909, but the registrar made an error by entering an incorrect age for Pickingill which made him 106 years old. At the bottom of the register page a note was subsequently added, which stated: "No. 484 born at Hockley in 1816, was only in his 93rd year," which corrected the original mistake (www.essex.gov.uk/ERO). Pickingill was also registered as 'Pettingale' in the register at St Nicholas' Church, Canewdon, which again shows a variation of his name (ibid).

Frederick was the middle name of Pickingill's eldest son (1861-1928) who was the last person in the family of his grandfather Charles, who bore the name 'Pickingill'. An Essex newspaper (*Essex Newsman*, 19/09/1908) reported on George's birthday in the article 'A Canewdon Centenarian' but referred to him as Frederick Pickingale and claimed he was 105 years old. Regarding the name, perhaps the reporter confused George with his son Frederick or it may have been that George deliberately gave them a different name and age for reasons known only to himself. Another possibility is that the error was due to his own senility. Certainly, the error created some confusion for later genealogists, historians and researchers in their investigations.

To add to the ambiguity of the Pickingill ancestry, it has been suggested that Charles Pickingill (George's father) was not really a Pickingill at all but was given the surname by Thomas Pickingill, the man who raised him, but who was not his biological father. Possibly Charles had been orphaned or his parent(s) were no longer able to look after him.

Another theory was that Charles was Thomas' illegitimate son, whilst one of George's descendants has suggested that Charles was an illegitimate son of Sarah (Thomas' daughter). Possibly, Thomas and his wife raised the child as their own in order to avoid any scandal. Official records indicate this as a possibility, and perhaps the reason there was no baptism record for Charles in that parish was because he had been born outside the Rochford area (Shepstone, correspondence with Author).

Between c.1786–1804, Thomas Pickingill was the gravedigger for St Nicholas Church in Canewdon, Essex (Walworth, 2016, 7). The first record of Thomas Pickingill being in Canewdon is found in his marriage record in 1773 to Martha Chilver. On the marriage bond, Thomas signed his name whilst Martha made the mark 'X'.

At the start of their married life, Thomas and Martha were poor and received assistance from the churchwardens (Walworth, 2016, 10). Surviving Church records reveal that later in their lives they did much work for the Church and there are also entries that provide information about their children. Interestingly, it is possible that the ancestors of both Thomas Pickingill and Martha Chilver originated from outside Essex. The name Pickingill has origins in Yorkshire, whilst Chilver originated from Warwickshire (Reaney & Wilson, 1997, 95).

From approximately the 1770s to 1804, the Pickingill's were paid by the Church to provide poor orphaned children with board and food and possibly these children were given the surname Pickingill after the family who fostered them. Some researchers believe that this may have been how Charles Pickingill became part of the family (Walworth, 2016, 12). Thomas' work included not only his grave-digging duties at St Nicholas Church in Canewdon; but he also became a church clerk and the church sexton around 1786. His job as sexton was to "take care of a church building and its graveyard, and sometimes … [ring] the church bells" (http://dictionary.cambridge.org). Interestingly, George Pickingill's nephew, George Charles Cox (who was the son of George's younger sister, Catherine), became a gravedigger when he emigrated to Canada (Shepstone, to Author).

Church life was clearly important to some members of George Pickingill's family; for example, his sister Catherine was a lifelong member of the Anglican Church and later descendants of Catherine's family were also churchgoing. It has been said that if Catherine had known that her brother George was a cunning man or witch, she would have kept it quiet to avoid any scandal (Shepstone, to Author).

Thomas was also hired to dig graves in Canewdon's churchyard and at times he and his wife would perform the 'Laying of The Dead' and 'Sitting Up with the Dead' rituals. Laying out the body involves cleaning and dressing it for the relatives and friends to see before the funeral in order to pay their respects. Sitting up with the Dead involves sitting with the body in the family home after it has been laid out, right up until the time of burial.

This was sometimes done by family members or friends and ensured that the deceased's body was always guarded by the 'sitter' who would be there to receive any mourners, come to pay their last respects before the funeral. Most traditions of laying out the dead involve local folklore, superstition and ritual and perhaps these were passed down the family line to Pickingill. Not only did sitting with the dead help deter flies and rodents, but it also acted as a kind of gatekeeper as the deceased's spirit entered its new spiritual home, passing through a veil from one world to another.

WHAT'S IN A NAME?

Throughout the years, the spelling of 'Pickingill' varied in official Essex records. For example, we have seen that he was baptised *Pickingill,* yet on his death certificate he is recorded as George *Pettingale.* He was married in Gravesend, Kent in 1856 and his surname documented as *Pickingill.* The official census revealed that in 1871 and 1881, Pickingill was recorded as living in his home at Canewdon under the name '*Pitengale*'.

It could of course be that, "… allowing for variations of accent, the difference between Pettingale and Pickingill is barely more than a change of spelling. In previous centuries it would hardly have attracted attention, although by the nineteenth century, spellings were generally becoming more rigid" (ERO: communication to Author April, 2015).

Official records show that George and his wife Sarah Ann, as well as their first son Charles (who identified as Frederick), were all illiterate. At their wedding, George and Sarah both signed their names with an 'X' indicating they could not sign their name, which was therefore written for them by the registrar. However, the witnesses at the marriage were two of Pickingill's sisters (Catherine Cox and Martha Smith), who were able to sign their names.

Sarah pre-deceased her husband and on George's death certificate, his eldest son Frederick was the informant of death, signing his name with an 'X'. A combination of inaccurate record keeping and less rigid laws about how surnames were written, together with widespread illiteracy, probably explain why George Pickingill, farm labourer and possible cunning man, was known by various surnames and ages.

It is likely that, because of the economic depression in Britain during Pickingill's lifetime, he lied about his age in order to help him gain employment, since he usually claimed to be younger than he was (at least until he was so old that nobody could expect him to work). The average farm labourer's wage steadily rose from about nine shillings and six pence per week in 1824 to approximately fourteen shillings and five pence in 1898. In addition, farm labourers were given various allowances such as 'potato ground and beer' (www.british-genealogy.com). This gives an insight as to how much Pickingill may have earned per week in his many years as a labourer. He was certainly never well-off and often in some considerable poverty, yet we repeatedly hear that he never charged for his services.

The empathic and selfless side of Pickingill's nature can be seen by the Neptunian energy in his natal chart through Mercury and Venus in Pisces, as well as the Pluto in Pisces era into which he was born. He – along with many others born during the Pluto in Pisces generation (particularly those living in poverty) – would have experienced suffering through themes such as death and survival, crisis and loss as previously discussed. His fighting Aries spirit shows how he could conquer such intense situations, whilst possessing an instinct for survival. If we knew Pickingill's exact time of birth, using the house system (*see glossary*) we would be able to see Pluto's exact position and thereby be enabled to gauge the area of life in which such themes were most prevalent to him.

Pickingill moved to Canewdon sometime between 1864 and 1868. In 1801, the village population had been just 569 and by 1831, it had risen to just 675 (Smith, 1987,

44–45), so it remained fairly small during his lifetime and most people living there would have known each other. Even today, the 2001 census gives a population of just 1477 (https://en.wikipedia.org/wiki/Canewdon).

It has been claimed that Pickingill was of Romany kin and was brought up in a caravan with his family in his formative years and that he was of dual heritage (Liddell and Howard, 1994, 90). However, since the census records of individual households did not start until 1841 (the earlier censuses were much vaguer and lacking in detail), it is impossible to check this information. He then lived with his father in a cottage, as well as lodging in his employer's home with seven other farm labourers for work purposes later in his life (www.deadfamilies.com).

In their book, *The Pickingill Papers,* Liddell and Howard claimed that as an adult, Pickingill "… travelled extensively as a horse dealer" (1994, 166). There were certainly fairs and markets he could have visited locally. Livestock and horse fairs were held in different areas of the Parish of Rochford, such as Canewdon, Hadleigh, Hockley, Pagelsham, Rayleigh and Little Wakering. However, visiting such fairs, and even selling or buying the occasional horse does not make him a horse dealer and his occupation is never given as such in the census returns.

Horse markets sold not only horses but also colts and ponies, whilst the livestock markets sold bulls, cows, calves, sheep, ewes, rams, lambs, pigs, hens, turkeys and ducks (Loveridge, 2003, various). In the late 1890s, there was also a horse racing course in Rochford (Jerram–Burrows, 1988, plate no. 122) which Pickingill may (or may not) have attended with his putative Romany friends and neighbours in the community, especially since horse dealing is associated with Romanies and their way of life.

As discussed earlier, he once claimed that only when he was 90 did he finally take a holiday (www.deadfamilies.com.:/Essex Newsman: 1908).

The 1901 Census reveals that 'George *Pickengal* (snr.)' was still living in Canewdon at 3, High Street in a four roomed home, which was also occupied by Pickingill and his sons Frederick and George, who had both returned to live with their father. By this time, Pickingill was reliant on parish relief as he was too old to work and had an 'infirmity'.

Parish relief was not without its problems however, and newspaper archives reveal that in 1900 his son George was "… committed for fourteen days, the order being suspended for a month, for failing to contribute one shilling weekly towards the support of his father, who is chargeable to the Union" (www.traditionalwitch.net/forums-/Essex Newsman, 08/06/1900). In 1902, the *Essex Newsman* reported in September of 1902 that George junior had been ordered to pay 13 shillings (65p in modern money) arrears to the support of his father and 12 shillings in costs (60p) or alternatively fourteen days imprisonment (www.traditionalwitch.net/forums).

In 1899 (www.deadfamilies.com/1899;advertisements section), Pickingill was living in a very precarious situation. His cottage was up for sale along with some other properties in Canewdon. The auction was held at the Old Ship Hotel in Rochford and the cottages up for sale were described as "A Timber Built and Tiled Range of Six Freehold Cottages. Abutting on the High Street, Canewdon, having back gardens" (ibid) and this then went on to describe the tenants, their type of tenancy and how much rent they paid for their properties.

Pickingill was described as a monthly tenant who was living on 'sufferance' whose rent per month was £3-5s-0. This is £3.25 in modern currency, yet still a sizable sum (just over 81p per week) when we consider his son could not manage a shilling (5p) per week towards his father's upkeep. A tenant on sufferance is defined as: "A tenant who stays in a building after the lease has ended and without the owner's permission," showing that Pickingill was not only liable to pay rent but also could be evicted by his landlord at any time (http://dictionary.cambridge.org).

George remained in his cottage until his death ten years later, so perhaps his cottage wasn't sold at auction, or if it was then the new owner was a compassionate landlord who did not pack the old man off to the workhouse.

MAGIC AND GEORGE PICKINGILL

As a wise old countryman, Pickingill (often referred to as 'Old Picky' by the villagers) may have gained experience and a magical understanding of the elements and nature that surrounded him. Possibly, this was a combination of hereditary knowledge passed from his parents, as well as obtaining knowledge from any Romanies he may have known (some of whom probably practiced the magical arts). Even if he did not know any Romanies (and it has not been conclusively proved that he did), he could have picked up other traditional lore from neighbours, relatives and fellow farming labourers. The sort of knowledge he may have acquired could have included:

• Animal and bird-lore
• 'Telling the bees'
• Weather reading, such as cloud–reading
• The Moon's cycle
• Knowledge about flowers, plants and herbs for medicinal remedies and cures
• Making corn dollies to honour the Corn Spirit at the crucial farming season of harvest time during late summer and early autumn

Apparently, Pickingill had a walking stick made of blackthorn which was used as a 'blasting rod'. It was claimed that if he ever touched a person with it they became totally immobilised and lost their senses until he touched them again with it to remove the paralysis (Howard, 2009, 49). Blackthorn traditionally has magical properties and if Pickingill knew that, it may be why he chose to use that material as a walking stick.

Blackthorn (*Prunus spinosa*) is a thorny plant and can be used as a natural protector against all kinds of harmful magic (Penry, 2009, 34), driving out "demons, vampires and ghosts" (ibid, 254). Apparently, Pickingill could stop farm horses and draw game from the hedgerows with his amazing stick; if he struck the hedge with it, all game would come rushing out, showing that his walking stick was a vehicle of his magical power (Maple, 2008, 60).

In astrology, thorns are associated with Mars, which is pertinent to Pickingill as Mars is the ruler of his Sun sign Aries, which is associated with energy and fight, so it is little wonder he would have felt at home with a blackthorn walking stick. There is a well-known but much disputed photograph of him standing outside his cottage and holding a walking stick, although it is not clear enough to be sure whether it was his famous 'blasting stick'. It may just have been a practical support in his old age. Pickingill must have had proficiency as a country craftsman in the raw materials around him to be able to make a walking stick from blackthorn. As for whether the photograph is truly of him, the similarities between the photograph and his sister (*see page 9*) are unmistakable.

Pickingill's back garden had elm trees in it (www.deadfamilies/1899-advertisements for sale of cottages) and there are magical properties also associated with elm. From a practical point of view, elm was popular as a coffin wood because it was durable in wet conditions (Penry, 2009, 179) and this would have been very necessary in areas such as Canewdon and Rochford as they were surrounded by water, including the River Crouch and marshes, for example. In the nineteenth century, there was a very high mortality rate, so coffins would have been in high demand. From Wych Elm (*Ulmus glabra*) one can obtain a yellow dye and traditionally this colour was associated with death (ibid).

Elm (*Ulmus sp.*) was also practical in the Parish of Rochford for it was durable enough to build boats and ships from (ibid, 371). There was a strong boat-building practice in Rochford as well as brick-making (because of the strong clay soil); bricks were made and sent on barges up to London. Pickingill had relatives who worked 'on the water' as brick-makers and his sisters Catherine and Martha both married brick-makers (www.deadfamilies.com/: point 10 + Part 1.–1st generation). Two of his granddaughters, Harriet and Sarah, respectively, married a waterman and lighterman for barges (www.deadfamilies.com/: 1881+1891).

On Pickingill's marriage certificate, his father Charles' occupation is recorded as a blacksmith and it is thought he learned the trade from his 'adopted' brother, Samuel Pickingill, who had been apprenticed with a family of two to three generations of blacksmiths in Rochford (www.pdf book: 23). It seems that George Pickingill did not continue his father's trade of blacksmithing, however, and always described himself as a labourer. It is quite possible though that he gained some knowledge about blacksmithing, farrowing and wheelwrighting, either from his father or even his co-workers, since the horse was such an integral part of farming back before new machinery was introduced.

In the 1800s, anyone with a garden grew what they could for the pot, along with herbs, flowers and even weeds. Pickingill had a garden when he lived at his cottage in Canewdon (from sources mentioned above), so he had the opportunity to cultivate herbs for any magical and medicinal purposes if he so wished, although we do not know for certain whether he had this sort of practice. However, if he did grow such plants, there would have been a ready – and profitable – market for them in towns and cities, where even the theft of thyme made a newspaper headline of the *Essex Standard* in 1842, reporting "... thyme roots which had been left for seed from a garden in Maidenburgh Street in Colchester"(Essex Society for Archaeology & History).

There may also have been a Freemason connection within the Pickingill family. In 1820, Charles' 'adopted' sister Mary (daughter of Thomas) and therefore an 'adopted' aunt of Pickingill, married Richard Bowton who was a master blacksmith in Ashingdon, Essex. He died in 1835 and before his death requested that he "... was carried to the grave by four blacksmiths with new white leather aprons" which suggests that he was a member of the Masons. White leather aprons in freemasonry symbolise purity and sacrifice, and at a mason's funeral, fellow masons are expected to wear their white aprons out of respect for the deceased (http://www.signology.org/masonic-symbols). Having four masons in white aprons may correspond to each of the cardinal points and elements; north and south, east and west and then fire, earth, air and water.

Richard Bowton's brother, John, was appointed executor of his estate and in 1809 had been listed in a membership document as a member of "The No. 375 Lodge of Hope and Trinity," a Masonic lodge in Romford, Essex. His profession was given as 'broker' (Wallworth, 2016, 76). Pickingill's granddaughter, Elizabeth Punt, married a master blacksmith called Walter Fellingham.

There is a loose connection to Pickingill in a magical sense through blacksmithing (and not just through his indirect family) as it holds such rich symbolism and magical associations. Blacksmithing is associated with Aries which (as we know) was Pickingill's

Sun sign. This is because Aires' ruling planet, Mars, is associated with fire, heat and iron. Horseshoes, for example, are forged from iron and associated with magical luck and protection, as are metals, sharp tools and weapons.

Interestingly, and as already discussed, there are several aspects made with Mars in Pickingill's natal chart, including Mars opposing Uranus. For some, this aspect can indicate skill with machinery and sharp instruments, such as cutting tools and such people have no fear in taking risks with machinery (Tompkins, 1989, 207). We see this in Pickingill's enthusiasm when he first saw a car and wanted to ride in it and go to London; he was not at all afraid of the vehicle even though it was new and strange to him. Also, during his labouring work he would have had to use a scythe, hoe, shears and other tools in his agricultural and farming work, which would have needed maintaining and being kept clean and sharp.

Little is known about George Pickingill's life, apart from the facts that are documented through official records. There is scarce information about his character and relationships, other than that which was shared by the Canewdon villager's memories when being interviewed by folklorists and researchers, along with various newspaper reports with statements from him when he was being interviewed for being the "oldest man alive in England."

Through the astrological interpretation of his natal birth chart, we can arrive at some greater understanding of Pickingill, his mind and his motivations, whilst also acknowledging the economic and social climate in which he lived.

If there is one thing that is true about George Pickingill, it is that he was and has remained a source of fascination and intrigue and will probably continue to do so for as long as people love a good story and mystery. This is hardly surprising, since he was a man capable of generating a captive audience with his intense nature, spell-binding appearance of later years and possible capabilities in the cunning arts, despite the wretched poverty-stricken environment and age in which he lived.

ACKNOWLEDGEMENTS, CREDITS AND REFERENCES

The Author and Publisher are very grateful to Kimberli Shepstone (third great-grandniece to George Pickingill) for permission to use her family photograph of Catherine, who was George Pickingill's sister, and also for her generous assistance and enthusiasm (George's sister, Catherine, married George Cox and is Kimberli's great-great-grandmother).

Thanks also to Doug Cox for his information on the Pickingill family from www.deadfamilies.com (Doug Cox is George Pickingill's third great-grandnephew. George's sister, Catherine, married George Cox and is Doug's great-great-grandmother).

Author and Publisher would like to thank The Folklore Society for permission to use image from *Folklore Journal*, 'The Witches of Canewdon' by Eric Maple, *Folklore*, Vol. 71, 1960, plate V, facing p248 *'George Pickengale of Canewdon.'* Reproduced by kind permission of Folklore Enterprises Ltd.

Moon's position www.astro.com/swisseph/ae/1800/ae_1816.pdf (04–04–2014)
Rodden Rating 'X' – Time of birth unknown

Essex Records Office, http://www.essex.gov.uk/ERO – Archive Search Service for Dates of:
Baptism/ – Source – Hockley St Peter & St Paul Baptism Register D/P 191/1/5
Birth/Death/ – Source – www.findagrave.com – B. 2 Apr 1816: Death: 10 April 1909 – Cemetery: Canewdon, St Nicholas Churchyard.

Corrected Note at Foot of Burial Register of Pickingill's Age
Source – Canewdon, St Nicholas Burial Register, D/P 219/1/11

Marriage Details of George Pickingill to Sarah Ann Bateman
Source – Registered: 1856 – Quarter: Apr/May/Jun – Registered District: Gravesend
Inferred County: Kent
Vol: 2a
Page: 389

Marriage Certificate
Certified Copy of an Entry of Marriage to George Pickingill and Sarah Ann Bateman: Number –
    MXD 710567, District of Gravesend & Milton.
Showing the Mark of 'X' for witnesses at George Pickingill's wedding, they being Catherine
    Cocks and Martha Smith. Source – Marriage Certificate for George Pickingill and Sarah Ann
    Bateman.

Death Certificate: Number DYE 175655 from the General Register Office, Southport, Merseyside,
    PR8 2JD, UK.

BOOKS

Caduceus Books *Marsh Wizards, Witches and Cunning Men* (2008). Published by Caduceus
    Books, featuring four papers of Eric Maple, referred to in this chapter:
'Witches of Canewdon.' *Folklore,* Vol. 71, No. 1, 960.
'Witchcraft & Magic in the Rochford Hundred.' *Folklore*, Vol. 76, No. 3 (1965).
Canning, J. (Editor): Clare Smythe; *Canewdon* from: *50 Strange Stories of the Supernatural.*
    Published by Souvenir Press/The Chaucer Press (1977).
Cryer, L.R. *A History of Rochford* (1978). Phillimore & Co. Ltd.
Douglas, John M. *Blackthorn Lore and the Art of Making Walking Sticks* (1984. Published by
    Alloway Publishing Ltd.
Howard, M. *Modern Wicca: A History from Gerald Gardner to the Present* (2009). Published by
    Llewellyn Publications.
Hutton, R. *The Triumph of the Moon: A History of Modern Pagan Witchcraft* (1999). Published by
    Oxford University Press.
Jerram-Burrows, L.E. *Bygone Rochford* (1988). Phillimore & Co. Ltd.
Liddell, W.E. & Howard, M. *The Pickingill Papers, the Origin of the Gardnerian Craft* (1994).
    Published by Capall Bann.
Loveridge, P. A *Calendar of Fairs and Markets Held in the Nineteenth Century* (2003). Published by
    the Romany & Traveller Family History Society.
Maple, E. *The Dark World of the Witches* (1965). Pan Books.
Morgan, Glyn H. *Essex Witches* (1973). Published by Spurbooks Ltd.
Penry, T. The *Magical Properties of Plants and How to Find Them* (2009). Published by Capall
    Bann.
Reaney & Wilson Oxford *Dictionary of English Surnames* (1997). Published by Oxford University
    Press.
Sipple, M. *Titbits and Tales of Essex Inns* (2001). Published by Brent Publications, Anchor Inn.
Smith, K. *A Record with Pictures - Old and New - Canewdon* (1979). Printed by H. W. Glanville Ltd.
Smith, K. *Canewdon: A Pattern of Life through the Ages* (1987). Published by Ian Henry
    Publications, Ltd.
Tompkins, S. *Aspects in Astrology* (1989). Published by Element Books Ltd.
Walworth, W. *Life and Death in an Essex Labourer Family* [pdf] (2016). W-003 – partial edition B,
    24th December, 2016. Published by The Exile's Publications.

Webster, S. *The Canewdon Witches: Mystery, Historical Facts, Folklore and Legend* (1994). Published by Canewdon Charities.

JOURNALS

Reay, B. Oxford Journals: *The Context and Meaning of Popular Literacy: Some Evidence from Nineteenth Century Rural England* (1991). Published by The Oxford University Press on behalf of The Past & Present Society: No. 131 May, 1991.

WEBSITES

www.ancestry.co.uk – Catherine Cox, obituary. – Accessed on 17/07/2017.
www.british-genealogy.com – Guy Etchells.
http://www.essexlifemag.co.uk/people/essex-dialect-1-1779354 – Adam Jacot de Boinod, Essex dialect article, published originally on 19/10/2012, updated August, 2013.
http://www.deadfamilies.com/Z3-Others/Pickingill/George-Pickingill.htm – Accessed on 11/07/2017.

* Theft of gloves and jacket/trial: Chelmsford Chronicle Aug and Oct, 1887: Petty Sessions at Southend – failure to pay one shilling per week to support George Pickingill Snr, 1900
* *Essex Newsman*, 1908: 'A Canewdon Centenarian'
* Page 6 re: occupation as brick makers and watermen on the barges

http://dictionary.cambridge.org/dictionary/english/sexton – Accessed on 17/06/2017.
http://dictionary.cambridge.org/dictionary/english/tenant-at-sufferance – Accessed on 13/07/2017.
http://www.historyhouse.co.uk/placeC/essexc01a.html – Accessed on 31/05/2017.
https://en.oxforddictionaries.com/definition/pikey
https://www.rochford.gov.uk – Oyster as staple diet for the poor.
http://www.rootschat.com/forum/index.php?topic=377171.9 – Accessed on 01/07/2017.
http://www.signology.org/masonic-symbols/freemason-apron.htm – White aprons symbolism.
http://www.traditionalwitch.net/forums/topic/8860-george-pickingill-revisited-information-about-him-and-the-family-and-history/ – Accessed on 07/06/2017.
https://hauntedpalaceblog.wordpress.com/2013/08/13/canewdon-the-village-where-witchfinders-feared-to-tread/ – Accessed on 21/07/2017.

PHOTOGRAPHS

Catherine Cox (née Pickingill), by kind permission of Kimberli Shepstone.
George Pickengale: *The Witches of Canewdon* by Eric Maple, *Folklore*, Vol. 71, 1960, Plate V, Facing p248: 'George Pickengale of Canewdon,' reproduced by kind permission of Folklore Enterprises Ltd.

CHAPTER TWO

Margaret Murray 1863–1963

Anthropologist, Author, Egyptologist Lecturer and Folklorist

MARGARET ALICE MURRAY was born on 13th July, 1863, in Calcutta, India, to a Christian English middle-class family; she was the daughter of James and Margaret Murray and younger sister to Mary. When she lived in India, her paternal grandmother and great-grandmother also lived with the family as well as family servants. Her father was a successful businessman and manager of the Seramore Paper Mills, whilst her mother was a missionary who also educated Indian women in various crafts and skills, continuing with this work even after the birth of her two daughters.

Encouraged by her elder sister, Murray eventually came to England to attend the Egyptian hieroglyph classes given by the celebrated archaeologist Sir Flinders Petrie at the University College of London (UCL), and in 1894 she became a full-time student of Egyptology. At college, she became a Fellow, specialising in Egyptology and was an assistant professor in Egyptology, until she retired at the age of 72. She carried out excavations, both in Britain and abroad.

Margaret Murray c. 1928 by unknown (Lafayette Ltd). Public Domain via Wikimedia Commons

Murray is probably best known nowadays for her theories about the origins and organisation of witchcraft as a religion. Her interest in witchcraft led her to field studies of the subject throughout Europe which included an examination of some written records of witchcraft trials.

Many academics and scholars both then and now refuted Murray's theories. However, she was a pioneer, both in the field of witchcraft and for her revelations on the continuity of antiquated Pagan practices through to the twentieth century. She continued lecturing independently after her retirement, and also continued writing. She died at the age of 100, shortly after her autobiography was published. She has been criticised by folklorists and historians for using selective sources to support her arguments and claims.

Murray was a woman of contrasts: she was the daughter of a middle-class Victorian family who became a professional scientist and educationalist. She forged her career in a patriarchal world, whilst standing up for the opportunities and rights of women from different classes and cultural backgrounds in society.

WHAT MARGARET MURRAY'S NATAL CHART SHOWS

Margaret Murray was born in India on 13th July, 1863, at 7.00am when the Sun was in the cardinal water sign of Cancer at 20 degrees and when the Moon was in the mutable air sign of Gemini at 18 degrees. The ascendant sign was in the fixed fire sign of Leo at 10 degrees. When Murray was born, her grandmother observed how "... the Moon-flowers were in their full glory and made a blaze of splendour" (Murray, 1963, 51). This is significant since the Moon is the ruling planet of Cancer and so perhaps the 'blaze of splendour' heralded the summer birth of a proud, pioneering trailblazer in the family.

In Murray's natal chart there is a configuration of a cardinal T-Square (*see glossary*), which involves one personal planet; Mercury, and two outer planets; Saturn and Neptune. Saturn is in Libra at the critical (*see glossary*) 0 degree and is opposing Neptune in Aries at 6 degrees. Mercury is in Cancer also at the critical 0 degree and is square both Saturn and Neptune; the focal (*see glossary*) point is 0 degree Capricorn in the fifth house and will be discussed further on.

The cardinal T-Square in Murray's chart reveals that she was ambitious, goal-orientated with plenty of drive and vigour, and at times met with confrontation from others. Again, these positions will be discussed later in more detail.

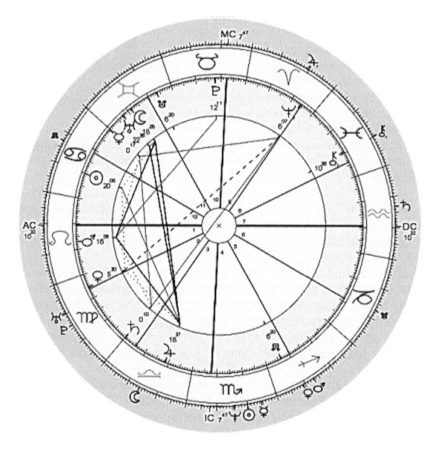

Natal and Transits Chart for Margaret Murray on the day she died, 13th November, 1963.

BEING FIRST

The first house (area of the self) is occupied in Murray's natal chart by both Mars and Venus; Mars will have given her a courageous and enterprising drive, whilst the gentle nature of Venus will have added a certain charm and pleasant disposition, as well as heightening her sense of self-worth and self-assertive nature. Mars is at home in the first house as it is the planet which naturally rules this area (along with Aries, the first sign of the zodiac). This can also give a sense of 'me first' in a natal chart, and this was true of Murray in various ways.

For example, she enrolled in the first class of Egyptology students trained by Flinders Petrie. She was the first female lecturer in archaeology in the United Kingdom when she was appointed a junior lecturer in 1899. Her entire working life was spent at the University College of London (UCL) and she was also the first assistant professor in the Egyptology department at UCL. At Manchester Museum she undertook public lectures and was the first woman to publicly unveil a mummy, something that attracted tabloid headlines (Sheppard, 2013, 156/Note 105).

CARE HUMOUR AND LANGUAGE

At the Calcutta General Hospital, she was the first lady-probationer in India, a post created to attract a "better-class of women into the profession" (Murray, 1963, 80). She also went on be in the first procession of the Suffragettes which went through Central London to West London; although she said she took no active part in any violent aspects of the campaign (Murray, 1963, 167).

The Sun in the sign of Cancer and is ruled by the Moon. This indicates that Murray was a caring, receptive and sensitive person who was inclined towards nurturing, protecting her family and loved ones, as well as having an interest in history and family heritage. In history and mythology, there were Moon goddesses in many civilisations, pertinent to Murray, both as an archaeologist and as a Cancerian.

The Moon in Murray's natal chart is in Gemini, which shows that Murray was interesting (and interested) as well as sociable. The Moon in Gemini also suggests she needed emotional stimulation and thrived on variety and change. She would have enjoyed fun, wit and light-heartedness since these are some of the areas associated with Gemini. She has been described as having a well-developed sense of humour and this is illustrated when, at the age of 96 she took part in a BBC broadcast and told the interviewer: "I have been an archaeologist most of my life and now I'm a piece of archaeology myself" (http://web.prm.ox.ac.uk). Even the title of her autobiography, *My First Hundred Years*, suggests a twinkling sense of humour.

Having an assortment of associations, contacts and connections would have enabled Murray to meet people from a variety of backgrounds. Language would have been no barrier as she had a talent for them; as a child she was fluent in French and German, while as an adult she translated Egyptian poetry (published in 1949 as *Egyptian Religious Poetry*). She also authored *Elementary Egyptian Grammar* (1905) and, six years later, *Elementary Coptic (Sahidic) Grammar.*

The lunar Gemini also suggests that she would have enjoyed younger people's company and that children were of interest to her (although she never had any of her own). She apparently made friends easily with children and young people (Cohen and Sharp Joukowsky, 2006, 132). The fifth house in natal charts is the area associated with children and recreation. In Murray's natal chart, the fifth house forms part of the cardinal T-Square configuration and its release point is at 0 degrees in Capricorn.

DISCIPLINE, OBEDIENCE AND TRAVEL

The focus point of 0 degrees in Capricorn suggests that, as a child, Murray may have been compliant and disciplined, perhaps putting duty before recreational pursuits. Indeed, she was described as being 'dutiful' (Sheppard, 2013, 19) particularly when, as a child, she lived with her uncle and aunt who were strict and religious (her Uncle being an Anglican vicar). Murray and her sister had to say their prayers in the morning and evening, were expected to say grace before a meal and also attend Sunday school. However, this was not uncommon in such households at that time.

MARGARET MURRAY AND ASTROLOGY

Murray was proficient in the science of astrology herself which is shown in her article, The Astrological Character of the Egyptian Magical Wands (1906). In it, she discusses astrological areas such as the ruling planet of a natal chart, the midheaven, as well as aspects, degrees, houses, planets and signs.

Murray's parents however seem to have been less religious, especially her mother. In fact, her brother (the vicar) once claimed she was almost an atheist (Murray, 1963, 65). Murray said that her mother rarely spoke about religion but one thing she did say which influenced her was, "The only way to live was to spend and be spent in the service of God" (Murray, 1963, 20). Although Murray dutifully obeyed her aunt and uncle while living under their roof, there were certain compensations and she later noted that her uncle inspired her mentally, since he was not only something of an antiquary but provided "a stimulating mental atmosphere" (Murray, 1963, 64). The compliant nature of Murray as a child can be seen here, which is in keeping with the Capricorn qualities (the release point) in the cardinal T-Square as discussed above.

Although the release point is at 0 degrees in Capricorn, the ruling sign of the fifth house cusp is Sagittarius (ruled by Jupiter). This indicates that Murray was not only inspired by children and younger people, but that she also enjoyed education as well as having adventures and travelling; something which continued into adulthood. Murray's entry for the 'Who's Who' regularly listed 'travel' under the heading for 'recreation'. She said that she loved travelling and would have liked to have had the opportunity to see more of the world; unfortunately, she lacked both the means and time to do so (Drower, 2006, 124).

LOYALTY AND AUTHORITY

The Sun is the ruler of Murray's natal chart since Leo is the ascendant and the Sun governs Leo; this shows that Murray had a confident and optimistic approach to life as these are qualities associated with Leo.

Murray could have commanded an audience and groups with dignity and nobility (qualities of Leo), as opposed to an imposing physical presence. This was because she was only 4' 10" tall. This would have been helpful to her, for example, when lecturing and directing a fieldwork team, but also when Petrie sent her out, as a test, to lead the local workmen across to the site at Abydos on a dig although none of the other academic male assistants had to do this.

Initially ignored, she strode back to the camp with them and ordered that their pay should be docked (Murray, 1963, 118–119). On one occasion, the University's vice-chancellor, the Duke of Athlone, came to visit with his wife, Princess Alice, Countess of Athlone. She took a genuine interest in the exhibits that Murray had shown her, returning informally to visit the University and a lifelong friendship began between the two women (Drower in Cohen and Joukowsky, 2006, 121).

This is a pleasing example of the Leo ascendant relating to royalty and nobility, also showing that Leo is loyal through the long-standing companionship between Murray and Princess Alice, as well as her ability to mix with people from different backgrounds.

Murray's diminutive stature may have made her feel she had to assert herself more than others, particularly as she was a woman in a male dominated world. For example, when she returned to England in 1866, her height prevented her from entering any English nursing schools as she did not meet their minimum requirements in this respect.

DETERMINATION AND COURAGE

Mars conjunct the Leo (*see box on right*) ascendant reveals her pride and courage and strength and also shows that she was prepared for action in her projects and undertakings. She has been described as having "… a combative and self-assertive nature" (Hutton, 1994), which describes all that Mars energy in her first house perfectly. Hutton further observed that her autobiography gave many examples of her "… physical toughness and belligerent courage" (ibid).

This is borne out, for example, when at the age of 68 she embarked on trip to Petra off the Red Sea, independently undertaking a small dig at a site that had not previously received much attention from archaeologists (Drower in Cohen and Joubowsky, 2006, 128). This reveals her zest for life as well as a courageous and enthusiastic nature, since the travel to Petra alone, besides the physical stamina in organising the digging and recording finds, is no easy feat by anyone's standards especially for a woman nearing her seventies. That she lived to the age of 100 shows just how much physical vitality and strength she possessed.

Mars is also associated with hostility, and in her natal chart suggests that conflict and confrontation were familiar themes to Murray in her life (as we will see later). She also had to assert herself in order to pursue her goals, and assertion is also a correspondence of Mars. The fiery nature of Mars and Leo shows an enthusiasm for life, and Murray certainly used her energy creatively, especially in taking opportunities to be centre-stage and taking the platform in order to surround herself with an audience, since these areas are all associated with Leo.

The Taurus MC (*see box on right*) (Medium Coeli, also known as midheaven) reveals that in her career Murray would have been both satisfied and successful wherever she was given the opportunity to work hard and achieve her goals. Patience and staying power are both qualities associated with Taurus and these areas would have helped her to attain her ambitions.

Pluto is conjunct the Taurus MC and indicates compulsion and obsession (as is the nature of Pluto) and shows that Murray had an intense drive to be successful in her career as well as in society. This is borne out by the fact she was still writing books when she was 100 years old, and she had seen and experienced many changes in the course of her long life. This is shown, for example, in Murray's extensive career, where many important transformations took place in the status of women in academia as well as society as a whole.

A RELIABLE STALWART

Mars square Pluto in the natal chart shows that Murray struggled for recognition in her career and experienced considerable discrimination in pursuing a career in an area that was mostly dominated by male contemporaries as previously discussed. The energy of Pluto in Taurus is enduring and steadfast; over a period of time it was to reveal just how powerful Murray was.

In 1927 she was appointed assistant professor and in 1928 was awarded an honorary doctorate. Although she reached retirement age in 1935, she continued to lecture independently and to publish her work. Her employers at UCL waived the retirement age for her and instead of being offered a five-year contract, she was reappointed on an annual basis which allowed her to continue working at the Institute of Archaeology.

Even after her retirement age, Petrie would ask Murray to assist him and she would do so since she was very loyal to him (although he barely mentioned her in his memoirs) and he surely benefited from her dependability and skills (Sheppard, 2013, 225). Murray's strong work ethic shows her qualities of endurance, longevity, perseverance and stamina which are in keeping with the nature of Saturn, the house cusp ruler of the sixth house in her chart, the area which governs work and health.

Many of her former colleagues and students attended her 100th birthday party in 1963 at the University College London. Murray was presented with "… an illuminated copy of the resolution passed by the Professional Board of the College at their last meeting" (Drower in Cohen and Joukowsky, 2006, 133). The resolution recorded, "… the high honour which, through her renowned scholarship, she has brought to the college where she taught for so many years" (ibid), showing Murray's importance not only to the college but also to society through her contribution to publishing, researching and writing.

At the end of the First World War in 1918, the Representation of The People's Act gave women over 30 the right to vote; by then Murray was 35 (it was only in 1928 that the Act was finally extended to allow all women over the age of 21 to vote). The work of the suffragettes and suffragists had successfully revealed much of the unfairness to which women were subjected, but this was less felt amongst middle and upper class women and Murray correctly observed that whilst the vote for women had given them confidence, "… it was among the working class that reform was necessary"(Murray, 1963, 173).

In her autobiography, Murray describes how she had "… lived through one of the most momentous periods of that miracle of world history, the advance of man" (Murray, 1963, 203), citing milestones such as the use of electricity in sound and vision, the X-Ray, germ theory about disease, as well as the motor car, air travel and the discovery of atomic power (ibid).

Murray's influence can be seen in the way she "… prepared two generations of Egyptologists for their careers in the field" (Drower in Cohen and Joukowsky, 2006,

109) in the 40 years between 1896 and 1936. Examples include Rex Englebach and Guy Brunton, who became directors in Cairo's Museum of Antiquities. Other students included Ernest MacKay, Randall MacIver and Gertrude Caton-Thompson who, after completing their apprenticeship with Professor Murray, went on to direct their own excavations or became inspectors of antiquities (ibid, 126). In particular, it was said that Caton-Thompson "… flourished under Murray's tutelage" (Sheppard, 2013, 98). These examples reveal what an effective lecturer Murray was, inspiring her students to carve a career for themselves in archaeology.

Given that Murray had received no formal education as a child, it was a tremendous accomplishment that she not only became one of the first Egyptology student of Sir Flinders Petrie but also became a lecturer at the Institute of Archaeology. At the end of her long life she said that, having lived through so many important changes, that her most important role in this 'great advance' was "… shown in my interpretation of the beliefs and ceremonies of certain ancient forms of religion" (Murray, 1963, 204).

The Taurus MC indicates that Murray needed to do something unequivocal in her career and in producing tangible work this may have brought her security. Pluto is conjunct the Taurus MC and shows her intense drive to be successful in her career. Pluto's nature (as mentioned previously) is sometimes compulsive and obsessed and these qualities would have helped Murray to achieve success. Pluto square the ascendant shows that she could have given the impression of being determined and indomitable in her career.

GEMS OF THE EARTH AND CREATIVITY

Venus is the ruler of Taurus, so art, music and nature would have been satisfying to Murray and may have been implemented in her work. For example, she took an interest in the jewellery and precious stones as well as pottery that she unearthed whist on excavations. She also observed how items such as pierced shells and animal teeth, for example, were strung on something made by human hands, and originally were worn as amulets; this was the start of ritual and amuletic magic (Murray, 1963, 194).

In 1937, Murray embarked on a small dig of her own at Petra in Jordan and became fascinated by the pottery she found lying about there; she described it as "… handsome painted pottery, a thin fine ware lavishly decorated with plant designs in red paint" (Drower in Cohen and Joukowsky, 2006, 128). This shows her aesthetic appreciation, as well as her keen observatory skills in her excavations.

Murray's student, Winifred Brunton, an artist and Egyptologist, painted a picture of the "gold and jewelled coffin of Tutankhamun Dynasty XVIII" which appears as a coloured-plate in Murray's book *The Splendour that was Egypt*. This reveals Murray's appreciation of Brunton's artistry by using it to support her writing (Murray, 1951, un-numbered) as well as showing how the two women became friends. Brunton painted portraits of both Murray and Petrie; they are still displayed in the Institute of Archaeology.

Some of Murray's Egyptology students recalled how in her class, *The Origin of Signs*, Murray did not lecture them as such but instead *talked* about art and architecture and "… used coloured facsimiles of painted hieroglyphics from tomb and temple inscriptions" (Drower in Cohen and Joukowsky, 2006, 125) to help generate discussion on areas such as the function of different tools used, as well as areas of clothing, house design, cooking and brewing in ancient Egypt. The aspect Mercury square Neptune indicates that Murray was an intuitive and creative thinker and that inspiration and insight fuelled her mental faculties.

The previous example shows Murray's versatile way of teaching and also that she could improvise in order to help her students. It was said that her classes were informal and pleasurable and she would even sometimes pass around a box of chocolates in lectures. Former student, Raymond Faulkner, noted that Murray's personality shone from the pages of her autobiography and "... that it is Dr Murray herself who is speaking, and not a pale simulacrum" (Sheppard, 2013, 231).

Returning to Pluto in Taurus, this sign is associated with tangibility as a practical earth sign, whilst Pluto is associated with evidence and investigation, and Murray "... was a true archaeologist who enjoyed concentrating on the material remains" (http://web.prm.ox.ac.uk). Together, these areas were helpful in Murray's chosen field of archaeology providing her with a dogged determination to achieve success and prosperity, whilst being seen by others as a powerful woman in her time.

Her courage can be seen, for example, when, in the early part of the twentieth century, she wrote about Pagan rites including an account of 'orgiastic rituals' in witches' covens, although anthropology was still considered inappropriate (ibid) for women at that time. Other associations of Pluto include: the buried, the hidden, mystery, research, uprooting and unearthing; all of which would have been invaluable to her in her work as an archaeologist, anthropologist and Egyptologist.

KINDLINESS AND SENSITIVITY

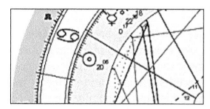

The Sun is in the cardinal (*see glossary*) water sign of Cancer and in the twelfth house of the natal chart (*see box left*). Cancer and the twelfth house are both governed by the element of water, which reveals that Murray was responsive and sympathetic, as well as nurturing (as previously discussed), since these are characteristics associated with the water element in astrology. Her sensitivity is revealed when, as an adult on the last day at UCL, she ran crying down the stairs, yet had the insight to realise that her tears were not caused by grief at "... leaving the place where I had spent so many happy years ... I was glad to escape from what was now a prison-house, full of bitterness and frustration" (Sheppard, 2013, 224). Possibly these feelings were because the department was quickly changing or perhaps because she resented the appointment of Stephen Glanville to the Edwards Chair (ibid).

Reflecting on her life as a young woman back in India, she once said, "I wanted something active and among people" (Murray, 1963, 79). These qualities, which she held so dear, would have helped her shine in particular areas of her work. For example, when she worked as a nurse in India and later as a social worker in Hertfordshire, England; these were jobs that required her to work with the sick and needy (careers associated with the twelfth house/Pisces).

She was a compassionate and hardworking nurse; for example, when she was a nurse in Calcutta, she worked twelve-hour shifts from 8am–8pm. Murray did not mind the long hours so much, it was the heat which was her greatest challenge; as a child and throughout her early adult years in India she suffered with 'prickly heat' (Sheppard, 2013, 24). Her mother had made her a uniform "of a simple white dress and a muslin cap" (ibid) which differentiated her in the role of lady probationer from the other nurses.

Murray's sister, Mary, however, seems to have disapproved of her sister being a nurse. Perhaps she did not like the idea of her sister serving the working or lower classes as they had been brought up in a middle-class environment where they were used to being served by working people. Or perhaps she felt she was capable of greater things.

As a child, Murray was fond of Teeloo, the Malay family cook who impressed her with his excellent skills in curry-making. She recalls in her autobiography that she always remembered his expression when he asked, "Did the Baba like today's curry?" (http://www.presentpasts.info). Apparently, as an adult, she shared her own recipes for her curries and dhal with a fellow Egyptologist, Gerald Lankaster Harding (ibid).

Murray's attitude towards service can also be seen in her description of the Egyptians who worked alongside her on an excavation in 1902. She stated that, "The Egyptian peasant is one of the best workers I have encountered, second only to an English one, but slower because he works longer hours" (Murray, 1963, 119). This shows that she had experience of workers from different backgrounds in manual working and service. It should be stressed here that the word 'peasant' belongs to her background and class of the time, although it would be frowned upon nowadays.

FACING GENDER BIAS

Murray often experienced male chauvinism in her life, for example in her excavations when some of the workmen were obstructive and adopted a 'know-it-all' stance, trying to teach Murray her own job. There were also those who would not listen to specific instructions (Drower in Cohen and Joukowsky, 2006, 129). She also encountered inequality from the male establishment when she wanted to publish her manuscripts on the subjects of social conditions and women in ancient Egypt, since at that time it was thought that only men should publish on these subjects (ibid, 13). However, the courageous and determined Murray did not let prejudice or chauvinism stand in her way, and was able to overcome many of the obstacles placed in her path.

The preponderance of the cardinal mode (*see glossary*) in Murray's chart reveals that she was not only a leader but also pioneering and self-motivated and was driven to get the job in hand done. Despite difficulties that others may have found insurmountable, she did achieve her ambitions.

Like her sister, Murrays' father was also opposed to her working as a nurse and felt it was not proper for a lady to be working outside the home earning her own income (even though Murray's mother did just that!). Undeterred, Murray clearly felt a calling for this work and in her early twenties, described it as being one of the most important things that she had ever done (ibid). She was not afraid of hard work and found satisfaction in caring and treating the sick, doing the work because she enjoyed it and liked to see patients heal and recover.

HERITAGE AND INSTITUTIONS

Murray's Sun sign, Cancer, is associated with history and memories as it is influenced by the past, heritage and legacy. This is illustrated in her autobiography when she wrote about her family's roots, "I always think that an autobiography should begin with some account of the immediate forbears and immediate family of the writer, so that one can understand some of the early influences which have affected the writer and have helped to make him what he is…. Though undistinguished, it is an ancestry to be proud of for its integrity, independence and family affection" (Murray, 1963, 11). The pride taken in her family genealogy is often seen in the family-orientated sign of Cancer.

Institutions are associated with the twelfth house, so perhaps it is unsurprising that Murray worked in places such as the Institute of Archaeology at UCL and the City Literary Institute, and also in hospitals, museums and libraries, which denote the 'behind-the-scenes' working of the twelfth house. As well as working at the British Museum, she worked with the Ashmolean Museum in Oxford (where she was responsible for the Egyptian section of the catalogue) and also the Dublin National Museum (where she made a catalogue of scarabs and other Egyptian antiquities and was asked to compile another in 1910). The sixth house cusp ruler is Capricorn, which is ruled by Saturn, while the sixth house also connects with cataloguing, by way of it being associated with Virgo/Mercury with its affinity for accuracy and organisation. Therefore, this placement shows that she was 'indexing the past' in her work since Saturn attributes to age and time.

In Scotland, Murray was invited to write a catalogue of the Egyptian objects belonging to the Museum of the Society of Antiquaries, which elected her a Fellow (FSA Scot). She repeated the same service for the National Museum of Antiquities in Edinburgh, producing a booklet which had photographs and Murray's own detailed drawings (Drower in Cohen and Joukowsky, 2013, 116). Murray also used the libraries at Girton College, Cambridge, the Ashmolean Museum, Oxford and of course the University College of London's Passmore Edwards Library where she researched and studied. In the Petrie Museum at UCL in London, there is an Egyptian vase which Murray had given to Petrie in 1915 (http://petriecat.museums.ucl.ac.uk).

In the Museum of Witchcraft and Magic in Boscastle, Cornwall, the library holds books written by Murray as well as articles relating to her. Murray also donated witchcraft artefacts to various museums, including "a witch in a bottle" and "a witches broom" (Sheppard, 2013, 173). She donated the bottle to the Pitt Rivers Museum in Oxford in 1925 (ibid) and the broom to the Cambridge Museum of Anthropology. It is thought that Murray uncovered it in the 1930s while working on an excavation near Cambridge.

As noted earlier, Murray worked at the Calcutta General Hospital and then, briefly, at a hospital in France. Inspired by the nuns who had worked at the hospital with her in India, Murray also considered joining the sisterhood, which is in keeping with the divine, sacrificial and devotional association of the twelfth house and its ruler Neptune. Murray once said that her "... special line of research has always been in religion .... groping towards something higher and better than the human being" (Murray, 1963, 201). This illustrates her spiritual yearning and demonstrates Neptune in the ninth house in the natal chart. Neptune alludes to the divine and spiritual, whilst the ninth house represents one's belief system (amongst other things).

FAMILY AND SACRIFICE

The twelfth house denotes an element of self-sacrifice and as the Sun is in Cancer here, it could be said that Murray sacrificed a family life for her work. Since Cancer symbolises the mother and family life, it is possible that she was extremely sensitive about this area of her life. In the twelfth house the Sun symbolises the hidden and secret self, so in not having been a mother in her life-time she may have concealed – or kept secret – her true feelings on this subject.

Self-sacrifice is something that Murray wrote about in the 'Suffragette Movement' chapter in her autobiography. She stated, "… there is latent in woman that passion of self-sacrifice which will make her give her life for a cause or for a person" (Murray, 1963, 169). Perhaps Murray was referring to her own experiences, as well as those of women generally, where her cause was her need to educate and research as well as combating the inequalities towards women in society. She also understood the inconsistency in that society regarded sacrificing one's life for motherhood as noble, but doing so for a cause made her "unbalanced" (ibid).

Although she never married or had children, Murray accrued her own family made up of friends and students to whom she remained very loyal. Education was her comfort blanket, somewhere she felt secure and satisfied. She even dedicated her book *Legends of Ancient Egypt,* "To my students, past and present." Written accounts of her forming long-lasting friendships with her students are also evidenced in essays and biographies written by them about Murray.

COMMUNICATION

Mercury, the planet of communication is in the sign of Cancer at the critical 0 degree (*see glossary*). This indicates that Murray was intuitive and sensitive to the feelings of others and had a well developed intuition that would have helped her communicate with her patients and colleagues as well as helping to reach conclusions when investigating archaeological matters. In her autobiography, she acknowledged that she had "a woman's intuition" (Murray, 1963, 201).

The placement of Mercury in Cancer also reveals that she gave great thought to the past and it held great memories; this would have been helpful to her when writing her autobiography, *My First Hundred Years*, as she reached her centenary. It must be said that it did not meet with universal approval and some claimed it "… included entertaining though wildly inaccurate memories of UCL in the late nineteenth century, including an account of her own part in the formation of a women's common room" (Harte and North, 2004, 144). This again suggests there was a persistent bias against her at UCL. For most people, writing an autobiography at the age of 100 would be both a challenge and achievement, because of the constraints that age places upon the mind and body. She was remembering a period many decades earlier, just one part of an extremely long and eventful life.

Mercury in Cancer shows that she enjoyed speaking, talking and writing about antiquities and history. This would have been invaluable to her in her field work as an archaeologist and lecturer, especially in Egyptology and in her work as an author.

RETREAT AND SANCTUARY

Returning to the Sun in Murray's natal chart; it is creating a square aspect (*see glossary: major aspects*) with Jupiter, which reveals her tremendous optimism. It also suggests she may have had great expectations about what she wanted to achieve in life, since the Sun represents the self and Jupiter greatness.

However, the Sun in the twelfth house further shows that, despite this ambition, she nevertheless needed retreat, solitude and withdrawal. She may have seen this as taking refuge from the stress and strain of the outer world, as she could have been vulnerable to the impact of her environment. For example, she undertook extensive long distance travel to places such as Egypt, Malta and Palestine, along with strenuous back-breaking activity in fieldwork. Earlier, she had worked in the hospital in India, which would have entailed being on her feet for long periods of time. No doubt Murray needed to take rest where and when she could in order to balance her very active life over so many years. Indeed, this approach may have helped her reach such a great age and be in relatively good health for a centenarian.

Such zest for life would have been invaluable to her when travelling abroad, especially at a time when transport was slow and arduous. Also, she had to deal with extreme heat and, even though she had lived in India as a child, she had suffered with prickly heat.

Murray probably needed to create a quiet, protective sanctuary in order to replenish her energies and rejuvenate her spirits. Disciplines such as meditation and prayer may have helped and, even though we do not know much about her spiritual life, she does seem to have been spiritually inclined, since she at one point considered becoming a nun. Meditative and prayerful practices are also associated with the twelfth house. This would have helped Murray in her writing, allowing her to focus on her inner creative self without interruption.

SPIRITUAL BELIEFS AND LONGEVITY

The twelfth house is associated with karma and the unconscious. Murray believed not only in an afterlife but also that human beings come into this world with a particular responsibility and task, and that it was up to them to accept or refuse this. If they accepted the challenge and did their best, they would move on to a higher sphere of activity and responsibility. If they refused, however, then they would be forced to keep returning until, eventually, the work was accomplished (Murray, 1963, 205).

The area of responsibility in work is very significant in her natal chart. The sixth house governs work (as well as health) in the natal chart and, in Murray's case; the planetary ruler of the sixth house is Saturn (as discussed earlier). This planet is associated with longevity and responsibility and is particularly pertinent to Murray as she continued working long past her retirement age, her strong constitution enabling her to reach her hundredth birthday.

There is also some interesting symbolism of Murray's long service at UCL (University College London) in her natal chart; this is seen not just by the sixth house data but also with the presence of Neptune in the ninth house. This is because associations of

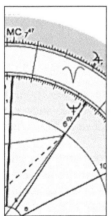

the ninth house include beliefs, higher education, long-distance travel, organised religion and publishing. The energy of Neptune can be addictive and absorbing at times and so it is unsurprising that she immersed herself in the realms of higher education, feeling very much at home in a place of learning and teaching (Moon in Gemini).

Neptune is also associated with magic and witchcraft and it is in the ninth house in Murray's natal chart. It indicates that Murray held beliefs in those areas, as belief is connected with the ninth house and Murray's published work on those subjects certainly generated controversy. Ensuring she obtained appropriate evidence from witchcraft trials to help support her theories about witchcraft would have been important to her logical and rational nature, which will be discussed later. It has been claimed that Murray once practiced casting spells, although in the part of her autobiography that deals with the occult, there is no indication of this (http://www.ai-journal.com/articles/10.5334/ai.1608/).

The Moon is in the eleventh house of her natal chart which governs clubs, friends, groups, humanity and societies. In this area it could be said that Murray had a somewhat maternal and an instinctual nurturing attitude in group activities, since the nature of the Moon is to cultivate and encourage. We can see these groups and societies at work through her excavation work as an archaeologist, which required team effort. In her forties, she even marched for the Women's Suffrage Movement, as previously discussed.

SOCIETIES

Murray was a passionate though not militant feminist who, as well as supporting the Women's Suffrage Movement, also defended women who faced discrimination in the field of education; demonstrating her humanitarian and reforming nature. She participated in large marches supporting the Suffragettes, for example, and the Mud March in 1907, which was organised by the non-militant National Union of Women's Suffrage Societies.

Murray was elected a member of The Folklore Society in 1927 and was president of the society between 1953–55. In 1954, during her presidency, her book *The Divine King of England* was published, showing her passionate commitment to writing, working and being involved in various projects simultaneously, which would have suited her stimuli–seeking Gemini Moon. Murray observed that in England, as a result of the First World War, several organisations of women replaced the men whilst they were fighting abroad, for example: The Women's Auxiliary Army Corps (WAAC), The Women's Royal Navy Service (WRNS) and The Women's Royal Air Force (WRAF).

Murray was 52 at the start of the First World War and decided she wanted to be of practical help, so once again returned to nursing. She became a major organiser of the Voluntary Aid Detachment (VAD) of the College Women's Union Society (Sheppard, 2013, 162). In 1915, she was called to a hospital in France (St Malo), where she was responsible for organising and cleaning the linens. After a short time in this role, she became ill and was ordered to return home for rest; it seems that her twenty years of continuous work had taken its toll on her health (ibid).

When she returned to England she decided to recuperate in Glastonbury; this is where her interest in the area's folklore developed. This reveals that Murray was responsive to instruction and pragmatic about what she needed to do. It also illustrates how sometimes she needed to recuperate and retreat, which is entirely in keeping with the Sun in the twelfth house as previously noted. Other groups and societies she was involved with included memberships of the Voluntary Aid Detachment, The Society of Biblical Archaeology and the Board of Studies in Anthropology.

UNORTHODOXY AND ATTENTION TO DETAIL

The Moon in the eleventh house also shows how Murray brought to the public attention the group called 'witches' through her research and writing. Whilst she alienated her colleagues and others (such as George Bernard Shaw and Montague Summers), generating controversy through her claims about Pagan and witchcraft rituals, she also inspired others such as T. C. Lethbridge (Keeper of Anglo-Saxon Antiquities at the

University Museum of Archaeology and Ethnology, Cambridge, from 1922–56). They became friends and Murray described his work as pioneering (Welbourn, 2011, 165, Note 156). Lethbridge himself was considered a radical by the academic establishment, largely because of his association with Murray as well as his investigations into occult phenomena.

Murray was criticised by Montague Summers regarding inaccurate and inconsistent information regarding the dates and geography. For example, when she wrote about the executions of two Northamptonshire women in *The Witch-Cult in Western Europe* (1921). Summers condemned Murray's lack of precision and accused her of maintaining her "… usual inaccurate slap-dash fashion" (Summers, 1927, 154). He *was* correct in that there was an inaccuracy: on one page a woman named Ann Foster was said to have been tried for witchcraft in Northampton in 1674, while on another page the date was given as 1673 and the place given as Northumberland.

However, Summers might have done well to pay attention to detail a little closer to home, for in his own book, *The Geography of Witchcraft*, Murray is not even listed in his index although he presumes that his reader knows who 'Miss Murray' is before launching into his attack about her lack of accuracy in logging information. He does not mention 'Miss Murray' before he makes criticism of her work and methods. This could be seen as yet another example of the prejudice, misogyny and double standards she regularly had to face.

Murray's book, *The Witch-Cult in Western Europe* met with furious opposition from Christian quarters, but nonetheless made substantial sales. Murray argued that witchcraft in the Middle Ages and Renaissance was not a phenomenon of Christian deviation, but a remnant of an organised Pagan fertility religion which dated back to Palaeolithic times. Murray used legal records of witch trials and pamphlets as supporting evidence, although some still criticised her for 'cherry-picking' her sources to help evidence her argument.

Another book, *The God of the Witches*, was published in 1933 and in it Murray portrayed the Horned God as a creative power force but not a malevolent one. It received positive reviews from three established publications such as *New Statesman* and *Nation*, while *Psychic News* described the book as "An important and fascinating book" and "A book of absorbing interest" (Murray, 1931, outside – back cover). In *The Divine King of England* (1954), Murray maintained that every English king from William the Conqueror through to James I, was a clandestine witch and that many of the country's statesmen were ritually killed.

Gerald Gardner (the subject of Chapter Four) enthusiastically embraced her work, which became popular with a new audience of Wiccans, Pagans and witches. Murray admired Gardner's work, and in her introduction to his book, *Witchcraft Today* (which used some of her research), she described his work as having an "easy pleasant style" (Gardner, expanded edition, 2004, 15).

Being on the fringe is associated with the qualities of the eleventh house and shows that Murray was controversial and unorthodox in her time, for example writing on the subject of witchcraft, something which was considered less important by her university colleagues and in society generally. It has been said that Murray's ideas were largely influenced by anthropologist Sir James Frazer, author of *The Golden Bough* (whose book inspired the original film, *The Wicker Man*), and he too was criticised for many of his ideas (http://www.witchcraftandwitches.com).

Other symbolism of the Moon in the eleventh house indicates that Murray had a diverse group of friends and worked in a variety of different groups. She seems to have felt very much at home in a group setting. For example, being connected with the NUWSS (National Union of Women's Suffrage Societies), which campaigned with the Suffragette Movement.

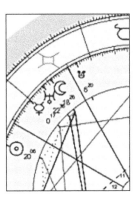

Her group activity work as well as the variety of the work involved would have suited her lunar Gemini energy. The Moon in Gemini in the eleventh house would have provided her with an ability to adapt, as well as the necessary versatility to work with a range of like-minded people. For example, she was close friends with the anthropologist Charles Gabriel Seligman, who taught at the London School of Politics and Economics, and they shared information with each other about the Egyptians in the early 1930s (https://archives.lse.ac.uk).

FURTHER RESEARCH METHODS

Murray's research and working methods included corresponding with other educated people who were often connected with local authorities and parishes. She would write asking them for detailed information and often they replied with very precise and helpful answers (Oates and Wood, 1998, 32). Her correspondents frequently obtained their information from people such as employees and servants, and through them she obtained first-hand accounts of people's experiences of fairies and witches, which helped her research. This also shows how she was able to work with a wide range of people and how, in this example, she was respected by them, since they agreed to carry out the requested enquiries.

However, Murray did not always experience a cordial response when she worked with other groups. For example, the first and only opportunity to dig in Egypt came in the winter of 1902 (Drower in Cohen and Joukowsky, 2006, 113). On the first day of work as previously discussed, Petrie had delegated Murray a task which would test her, instructing her to take the male workmen to the site herself. They refused all the directions of "this tiny woman … and began to disperse in confusion" (ibid). Promptly marching them back to camp, Murray let them know of her anger and told them they would lose a day's pay; after which, they co-operated (ibid).

DISCRIMINATION

Murray's Leo ascendant coupled with Mercury square Saturn shows that she could be confident and disciplined in speaking her mind about important issues, particularly where there was a sense of inequality and injustice (Saturn in Libra), and that she intuitively knew what to say (Mercury in Cancer) to achieve the desired result. Moon sextile Mars reveals that Murray enjoyed active involvement and needed to get on with the project in hand. The impulsive nature of Mars shows that she sought to take care of people and also had a quick and nurturing response to situations.

The direct nature of Mars also shows she expressed her feelings directly and could be fiercely protective of others. This would have been helpful whenever she saw others being ill-treated or subject to discrimination, such as female colleagues and students at the University experiencing unfair treatment from their male counterparts. In his unpublished autobiography, *The Ivory Tower,* T.C. Lethbridge described how Murray was badly treated whilst at Cambridge University during World War II (having been evacuated there with others from University College).

Lethbridge wrote that her books on witches struck Professor Ellis H. Minns of the Faculty of Archaeology and Anthropology as "obscene" and that he "did all he could to make the old lady's life difficult" (Welbourn, 2011, 156 and Note 144, 317). Such was Murray's passion for her specialist field that she offered to give a free course of lectures on the subject at Cambridge University. Minns deliberately shortened her proposal so that it would not qualify as a full university course, something that Lethbridge described as "… insulting as well as absurd." This clearly illustrates the sort of prejudice Murray experienced in the academic patriarchal hierarchy at that time.

STILL PLANNING AHEAD

The eleventh house is also associated with the energy of futuristic Aquarius/Uranus, so it is unsurprising that after completing her autobiography at the grand old age of 100, she considered writing another book! The autobiography was reviewed in the daily press and whilst being interviewed on radio she revealed that her next book would be about "early religion" and would be entitled, *The Genesis of Religion*. This was published in 1963 (Drower in Cohen and Joukowsky, 2006, 133) and reveals how Murray needed to be active in learning and research, retaining her ambitions and goals right to the end of her life, which is in keeping with the stimulating Moon in Gemini in the futuristic eleventh house.

In 1883, Murray began nursing in the Calcutta General Hospital, a time when malaria was rife. She remarked that this was not a true religious vocation or calling, but more of a response to the sheer boredom of her home life and "… an overwhelming desire for some active occupation" (Murray, 1963, 79). Boredom would not have sat well with Murray's nature which needed constant stimulation. In late Victorian India, genteel middle class English women were not expected to earn an income outside of the home. This shows her independent spirit and a break with the orthodoxy of the time, place and cultural context in which she grew up.

The Moon is conjunct Uranus in Gemini in the eleventh house, showing that Murray could break away (Uranus) from the past traditions of family life (Moon), and be emotionally independent. The Moon and Uranus in the sign of Gemini can cause great irritability and restlessness, which would have put a strain on her nervous system and made it hard for her to relax. The aforementioned aspect shows adaptability and an ability to make changes in her life.

LOGIC, SCIENCE AND THE OCCULT

The Moon is associated with instinct and Uranus corresponds with science, so the two together can symbolise a 'feeling for science,' given that Murray had these two planets positioned in the sign of Gemini, as well as logic and rationality. For example, in her autobiography, she subtitles the chapter entitled 'The Occult' with: 'Don't Believe all you Hear – Use your Common Sense'; here she talks scientifically about two aspects of the occult; ghosts and telepathy (Murray, 1963, 178–179), in a reasoned manner.

However, she also protests strongly about tales about some Egyptian objects being cursed (scarabs seem to have been particularly popular for this) and of course stories of the entire tomb of Tutankhamen being under a curse (ibid). She stresses a need for a scientific approach to the occult and concludes that, "... a ghost is the result of the striking of light-rays on some special combination of the elements of the atmosphere" (Murray, 1963, 183). This approach describes the Moon conjunct Uranus connection, in terms of Murray's need for experimentation with technology and science, i.e. the logical and rational side to her nature.

This position also suggests she could work with medicine and science, as she was able to think on her feet which would have been of tremendous help in her work as a nurse as well as when scientifically examining 'finds' from archaeological fieldwork. It is perhaps unsurprising that the reforming Murray is included in *The Biographical Dictionary of Women in Science – Pioneering Lives from Ancient Times to the mid-20th Century,* by Marilyn Ogilvie and Joy Harvey, published by Routledge in 2003.

Returning to the nature of Uranus, freedom and independence are integral for Uranus energy to work at optimum level. Positioned in the natural eleventh house (the area governed by Uranus), it reveals a strong affinity with the aforementioned areas of autonomy. Murray needed liberty and space, as domesticity and routine would not have appealed to her. She may well have been considered unconventional by her contemporaries and even by her own family. Her father died in 1891 and never lived to see her reach her full potential.

Symbolism associated with the aspect of the Moon conjunct Uranus and suggests an early experience of emotional independence and a distance from 'mother'. It suggests that Murray's mother was an independent and liberated woman who needed freedom and space away from domestic life. Murray once described her mother as being "rather silent and self-controlled," (Murray, 1963, 20) who rarely spoke about herself to the extent that she felt she knew almost nothing about her mother's earlier life. All of this is appropriate to the Moon/Uranus contact in Murray's natal chart.

Murray was raised by her nanny and other members of the family. Her mother went to Calcutta as a missionary and there taught local women practical crafts such as tapestry and knitting. Mrs Murray later helped set up an organisation called 'The Friend in Need' in Calcutta, where women worked and earned a small income for themselves. This was progressive and unusual in Calcutta at that time, showing the innovative and reforming nature of Uranus (ibid, 24).

EXPOLRATION, WEALTH OF COMMUNICATION AND WARM-HEARTEDNESS

The Moon trine Jupiter aspect indicates that Murray had a generous and warm nature that others may have seen as charitable, kind and big-hearted. This would have been helpful in relationships with her patients when she was a nurse and the women with whom she campaigned through the Suffrage Movement. The quincunx aspect created between Venus and Neptune also indicates Murray had a kind and sympathetic nature, since Venus and Neptune characteristics are associated with those planets respectively.

The Moon trine Jupiter aspect also indicates that she felt comfortable and secure exploring other countries and amongst other cultures. As an explorer, excavator and Egyptologist this would have been invaluable, and certainly Murray travelled to many countries.

Jupiter is in the third house, which is the area of communication and indicates that Murray could be direct and frank in her speaking, offering a wealth of information to

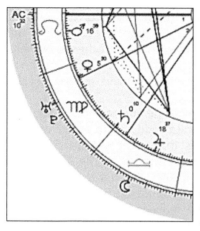

share with others which could be communicated in an enthusiastic and inspiring manner. It also shows her huge appetite for learning and a healthy respect for the value of education, intellectual fulfilment and enriching one's mind. Jupiter is in Libra, revealing that Murray was good at sharing and had good relationships with people; she infected others with her boundless enthusiasm. This is borne out, for example, in her lengthy working partnership with Flinders Petrie.

Venus is in the sign of Virgo and is unaspected (*see glossary*), which is a very rare occurrence; given that there are nine other planets it could be in aspect with. The unaspected Venus shows that it does not have to work with the energies of other planets and so has an abundance of its own energy.

Venus in the mutable earth sign of Virgo suggests Murray could be kind, helpful and practical in her partnerships. Venus symbolises both relationships and financial matters and indicates that Murray could be efficient and resourceful with money, as well as earning her money through being of service to others, since these are all areas associated with Virgo (*see box above*).

In loving relationships, the placement of Venus in Virgo seeks a sense of aloneness and seclusion as well as a sense of the completeness and impenetrable. Hence Virgo's image of the Virgin and in the tarot system, Virgo is associated with the Hermit in the major arcana. Virgo values self-sufficiency, yet at the same time seeks a relationship which can be depended on and where there is plenty of mental stimulation. Virgo seeks to analyse and perfect, therefore if Murray had been in a loving relationship, she may well have sought to improve the communication within the partnership, both on her own terms as well as that of her partner.

The Aquarius descendant in her natal chart suggests that in partnerships it was essential that she had mutual friendship and respect. Areas such as freedom and independence would have been crucial to Murray as these are areas associated with Aquarius and its ruler Uranus, and these qualities are echoed by the previously discussed Moon and Uranus in the eleventh house.

Saturn is in Libra (*see box below*) in the natal chart and reveals that she may have applied personal boundaries (Saturn) in her relationships (Libra), as well as fearing close relationships. In astrology, Saturn symbolises our fears, and in Murray's case this could have been fear of rejection, fear of losing personal freedom (echoed by the Aquarius descendant) and fear of losing a partner. Loss of independence is an area that Murray was aware of when she observed that, when her sister married, "... family

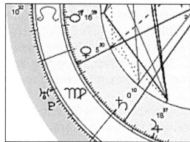

cares and responsibilities put an end to any hope of a career" (Murray, 1963, 30), something that would not have suited Murray's temperament at all.

Fairness and equality would have been areas that she looked for in any of her one-to-one relationships and she would have been able to bring consideration to her relationships (both business and personal), since kindness is associated with Libra. One example of how Murray lived with a limitation in a relationship is in her partnership with her mentor, Petrie. At the time, Murray lived in his shadow (Saturn) in the sense that, whilst she became established and recognised in her own right, she was always associated with Petrie, particularly in the field of Egyptology.

It has been said of Murray that she, "… devoted herself to Petrie as disciple and associate for the rest of her life" (Ogilvie, Harvey and Rossiter, 2000, 926). In her book, *The Splendour That Was Egypt*, published in 1951, she dedicated it, "To the memory of Flinders Petrie who, out of the hobby of antiquarianism, created the science of archaeology" (Murray, 1951, un-numbered dedication page). Petri died in Jerusalem in 1942; the last time Murray saw him was in Palestine in 1938.

ACADEMIC EFFORTS AND EARNING A LIVING

Interestingly, correspondences of Saturn include earth, confinement, form, structure, matter, rock, stone, frame, bones and the skeleton. These particular associations of Saturn are significant to Murray's archaeological area of work. For example, she joined Sir Flinders Petrie on his excavations in Abydos in Egypt, where the Osireion Temple was discovered. Later she investigated the Saqqara Cemetery. Her work in these areas made her an established and authoritative figure at this time, and both authority and established are associations of Saturn.

The aspect Mercury square Saturn shows that Murray had a disciplined mind, was thorough and conscientious, all of which would have helped her achieve her ambition, particularly where speaking and writing were concerned. Saturn in the second house reveals that she valued work and indicates that she could earn an income from a Saturnian career, which aptly includes archaeology.

Saturn is also the house cusp ruler of the sixth house in her natal chart and this is the area which governs health, service and work. Saturn also corresponds with authority, duty and responsibility, so in this sense it could be said that Murray became an authority and expert in her work, which is demonstrated by her formal qualifications, i.e. her doctorate and professorship.

The square aspect created between Mercury and Saturn also reveals that in her learning she experienced blocks, delays, frustrations and obstructions, since that is part of the less helpful nature of Saturn, it also suggests that she had hard lessons to learn. In comparing herself to her academic sister, Mary, Murray said that her sister passed with honours in the few exams that she took whereas she (Murray) "never got through any exam in my life till I took the full doctorate" (Murray, 1963, 30). She added that, whilst her mother's unorthodox style of teaching suited Murray, it did not "for anyone so versatile as Mary" (ibid).

Murray's position of Saturn in Libra shows the responsible and serious nature of Saturn, qualities that Petrie recognised in Murray, as he delegated much of his university teaching work to her whilst he was on excavations as well as promoting her to assistant professor in Egyptology at UCL. In Petrie's absences, Murray ran the department, planning seminar timetables, managing students and giving tours to important visitors such as Queen Mary in 1927 (Sheppard, 2013, 84). Murray had a heavy workload whilst Petrie was abroad and even when he was occasionally at University he was unable to offer a constant level of training for the students, due to his commitments abroad. Thus, training was left almost entirely to Murray, whose heavy workload included, "… teaching in all three terms of the semester, including evening classes twice a week" (ibid).

This reveals Murray's conscientious and diligent nature towards her work as well as her reliability; without her, Petrie would not have had the freedom to work abroad for lengthy periods of time. She was totally committed to promoting and developing UCL's Egyptology department. Sadly, in his autobiography, Petrie never acknowledged how much hard work Murray did at UCL for his department.

In his 269 page autobiography, he cites just *one* example of her working in Cairo with him in 1902, stating simply, "Miss Murray, my colleague, came to help with the Osireion" (Petrie, 1930, 185). His lack of acknowledgement and recognition speaks volumes about his attitude towards her and, perhaps, women in general, although his wife Hilda worked with him for many years. Murray, however, devoted an entire chapter to Petrie in her autobiography and clearly regarded him as a genius (Murray, 1963, 107). She also perceived Petrie as having a strong work ethic like herself and that at times, "he is ruthless in spending himself in his work and equally ruthless to his co-workers"(ibid, 108).

Returning now to the position of Venus in Virgo in relation to finances, the placement reveals she was thrifty with money, making it go a long way, while her organisation and planning skills and attention to detail would have helped her with budgeting and financial affairs. Murray continued to have a heavy workload whilst employed at UCL, yet she also secured extra income by teaching the evening classes at the college as well as Oxford extension courses which were held at the British Museum "… in order to supplement her annual UCL salary which started at £40 in 1898 and had grown to about £200 twenty years later" (Sheppard, 2013, 84).

In 1931, when Murray was awarded her honorary doctorate, she was unable to afford to buy the robes that she needed for the occasion. Her devoted students from the pre-war years pooled their finances to buy the robes for her, showing their appreciation and loyalty (http://www.ai-journal.com).

Murray's strong work ethic and concern for her own financial position is synonymous of Venus in Virgo. The National Probate shows that Murray's estate left the entire £13,012 to her niece (Sheppard, 2013, 231). This sum has been estimated to equal approximately £200,000 in 2013 (ibid).

When Murray died, she was experiencing some significant astrological transits which included:

- Transiting Saturn in the seventh house
- Transiting planets Pluto and Uranus in the second house
- Transiting Neptune in the fourth house
- Transiting Saturn was trine natal Moon and transiting Jupiter was trine natal Mars
- Transiting Uranus was trine natal MC
- Transiting Neptune was square natal Mars
- Transiting Pluto was trine the natal MC

FULL CIRCLE

Of the above transits, two are particularly significant, those which involve the natal Mars – which is concerned with the self – (the first house) as well as vitality; those two transits were:

- Transiting Neptune (in the fourth) square the natal Mars and
- Transiting Saturn (in the seventh) and was opposing natal Mars

Transiting Neptune – the planet of illusion and spirituality – was square natal Mars suggesting challenges in Murray's life. Part of Neptune's lesson is to try and connect us to the ethereal and intangible. As the energy and vitality of Mars was slowly dissolving at this time, Murray may have found herself questioning her goals and at times may have felt bewildered and confused since these are qualities associated with Neptune. It was said of her autobiography that it contained "wildly inaccurate memories of UCL in the late nineteenth century, including an account of her own part in the formation of a women's common room" (Harte and North, 2004, 144). In fairness however, not many autobiographies are written by centenarians!

Transiting Neptune was in the fourth house when Murray died. This suggests that she may have become confused about her past and family roots as well as becoming more idealistic than before. Neptune dissolves that which it touches, which in Murray's transit example here is Mars. The contact between the two planets reveals that Murray's energy levels and vitality had decreased and that she may have needed more sleep than usual (sleep is also associated with Neptune). She may have felt depleted and drained at times as the vigorous energy of Mars was softened.

> **THE SIGNIFICANCE OF THE HOUSES IN MURRAY'S TRANSITS CHART**
>
> The second house is associated with income, possessions and values.
>
> The fourth house is associated with home, parents and legacy.
>
> The seventh house is associated with relationships and partnerships – personal and professional.

Nonetheless, with sheer determination she harnessed her diminishing energy to help her complete her autobiography at the age of 100, preparing for her next spiritual life by naming her autobiography, *My First Hundred Years*. Murray passed away just months after her book was published and, as she believed in reincarnation (Neptune), she may have been looking forward to her next existence – hence the title of her memoirs.

Transiting Saturn opposing natal Mars also denotes a slowing down where one no longer has the previous levels of energy to accomplish projects. Murray had the necessary drive to accomplish completing her autobiography, but shortly afterwards she passed away in 1963. *The Genesis of Religion* was published after her autobiography in the same year, demonstrating her remarkable strength of mind and vitality to get complete those projects. Even in her hundredth year Murray was considered something of a progressive figure.

Her publishers, Routledge & Kegan Paul, described *The Genesis of Religion* as "… rather a feminist book because Dr Murray finds the origin of religion in the mother's power and discovery of creating life." It also describes the book as "… the focus of much thought and the research of a long life," which aptly describes the longevity and maturing nature of Saturn. The Grim-Reaper, Father Time (aka Saturn) was transiting the seventh house when Murray died.

This shows that professional partnerships were still relevant to her (as the seventh house is associated with partnerships), exemplified by her relationships with her publishers who clearly considered her to be dependable and reliable, someone who could honour her publishing contracts despite her advancing years and the restraints of ageing.

Another helpful transit (not listed above) that Murray experienced at the year of her death was transiting Jupiter in the ninth house trine the Leo ascendant. This transit could have added an optimistic self-belief to succeed in creative opportunities presented to her, with extra enthusiasm as this is a quality associated with Jupiter. It would have given Murray a tremendous self-belief that she could achieve her goals. Transiting Jupiter is in the ninth house and is in its natural home here; publishing is an area associated with Jupiter, which bestows fortune and opportunities.

It could be said therefore that Murray had the necessary drive and self-belief that she would publish two books in her centenarian year. She may have been philosophical about her 'first hundred years' coming to a close, accepting that part of the cycle of life was reaching a closure.

Chiron, the Wounded Healer was in the eighth house and in the sign of Pisces in the natal chart. This suggests that Murray may have experienced spiritual (Pisces) transformations (eighth house) in her life and felt intensely about 'life after death' issues. This we have already seen in the matter of the occult and ghosts. In her work as an Egyptologist, the themes of the afterlife and rebirth were significant in Egyptian culture and mythology.

The healing nature of Pisces and the transforming and rejuvenating nature of the eighth house indicate that Murray had the ability to be a natural healer, something she may have applied in her nursing work to aid her patients' recovery. Certainly, she took pride in seeing her patients' health improve under her care when she was a nurse and when she was abroad on excavations, her medical and nursing experience was often useful whenever health problems or injuries occurred amongst the excavating team and co-workers.

The eighth house 'transformation' also shows her ability to make new starts in her life and survive various crises, rather like a phoenix rising from the ashes. The phoenix is pertinent to Murray, as in Egyptian astrology it is the correspondence for the month of July (her birth month) covering the period from 25th June to 24th July (Richardson, 2007, 108). Also significant is that Murray's birthday, on 13th July, is the eve of one of the Egyptian extra days (in their calendar), that particular day being the day of Osiris, Lord of the Underworld, on the 14th July (ibid).

Chiron symbolises emotional wounds in childhood; perhaps Murray's family belittled any mystical insights and visions she may have experienced and her psychic and sensitive nature was ignored in favour of her family's own religious and scientific views. This could have been detrimental to Murray since she needed her emotions, intuition, sensitivity and psychic ability to help her find answers within.

Chiron is sextile the Taurus MC so, as she matured, she may have eventually found a way to channel her intuition and psychic ability by listening to her 'senses' in her work. Murray passed away when she was experiencing her second Chiron return, so one could say that her spiritual transformation was complete.

Margaret Alice Murray, a legend in the history of Wicca, was a pioneer and leader in various fields throughout her lifetime: anthropologist, archaeologist, author, Egyptologist, feminist, folklorist, nurse, scholar and a woman of her times. Having knowledge of the mystical association to the number thirteen, Murray surely would have been intrigued by the fact that she was born and died on the 13th and that she left over £13,000 in her estate.

ACKNOWLEDGEMENTS, CREDITS AND REFERENCES

The Author and Publisher would like to thank researcher and writer Elizabeth Crawford for her knowledge about the non-militant National Union of Women's Suffrage Societies (https://womanandhersphere.com/)

Natal chart generated by www.astro.com
Murray, Margaret: Monday, 13th July, 1863, 7.00am, Calcutta, India, LMT (Local Mean Time).
88e22, 22n32.
Rodden Rating 'B'

BOOKS

Cohen, G.M. and Sharp Joukowsky, M. (2006) *Breaking Ground: Pioneering Women Archaeologists*. Margaret Drower chapter on Margaret Alice Murray. Published by University of Michigan Press.

Gardner, G.B. (1954) *Witchcraft Today*. Rider & Company.

Harte, N. and North, J. (2004) *The World of UCL, 1828–2004*. University College London.

Hutton, R. (1999) *The Triumph of the Moon*. Oxford University Press.

Murray, M. (1905) *Elementary Egyptian Grammar*. London, Quaritch.

Murray, M. (1906) *The Astrological Character of the Egyptian Magical Wands*. Proceedings of the Society of Biblical Archaeology 28, Kindle version, Location 1062 of 7150.

Murray, M. (1911) *Elementary Coptic (Sahidic) Grammar*. London, Quaritch.

Murray, M. (1931) *The God of The Witches*. Oxford University Press.

Murray, M. (1921) *The Witch–Cult in Western Europe*. Oxford University Press.

Murray, M. (1949) *Egyptian Religious Poetry*. The Wisdom of the East.

Murray, M. (1951) *The Splendour That Was Egypt*. Readers Union, Sidgwick & Jackson.

Murray, M. (1954) *The Divine King in England: A Study In Anthropology*. Faber & Faber Ltd.

Murray, M. (1963) *My First Hundred Years*. William Kimber & Co.

Murray, M. (1963) *The Genesis of Religion*. Routledge & Kegan Paul Ltd.

Oates, C. and Wood, J. *A Coven of Scholars: Margaret Murray and her Working Methods*. (1998) Published by the Folklore Society.

Ogilvie, M.; Harvey, J. and Rossiter, M. (2000) *The Biographical Dictionary of Women in Science- Pioneering Lives from Ancient Times to the Mid-20th Century*. Routledge.

Petrie, Sir W.M. Flinders (1930) *Seventy Years in Archaeology*. Sampson Low, Marston & Co. Ltd, London.

Richardson, A. (2007) *The Magician's Tables – A Complete Book of Correspondences*. Godsfield Press, Division of Octopus Publishing Group.

Sheppard, K.L. (2013) *The Life of Margaret Alice Murray – A Woman's Work in Archaeology*. Lexington Books.

Welbourn, T. (2011) *T. C. Lethbridge – The Man Who Saw the Future*. O-Books.

WEBSITES

http://asketchofthepast.com/god-of-the-witches-the-cult-of-margaret-murray/
– Accessed on 13/06/2014.

https://archives.lse.ac.uk/Record.aspx?src=CalmView.Catalog&id=MALINOWSKI%2F36%2F1
– Accessed on 05/04/2017.

https://archives.lse.ac.uk/Record.aspx?src=CalmView.Catalog&id=SELIGMAN%2F15%2F2
–Accessed on 05/04/2017.

http://www.ai-journal.com/articles/10.5334/ai.1608/ – Author Ruth Whitehouse.

https://www.ucl.ac.uk/current-students/money/scholarships/sochistscl/margaret-murray
– Accessed on 10/04/2017.

http://www.presentpasts.info/articles/10.5334/pp.59/ – Accessed on 08/04/2017.

http://petriecat.museums.ucl.ac.uk/detail.aspx – Accessed on 08/04/2017.

http://web.prm.ox.ac.uk/england/englishness-Margaret-Murray.html – Author Alison Petch.
Accessed on 02/04/2017.

http://www.witchcraftandwitches.com/witches_murray.html – Accessed on 12/04/2017.

CHAPTER THREE

William Warner aka Cheiro 1866–1936

Astrologer, Numerologist, Society Palmist, Author and Entrepreneur

WILLIAM JOHN WARNER (Cheiro), was born on 1st November, 1866, in Bray County, Wicklow in Ireland, into a Protestant family. He was the youngest of three children born to William Warner and his wife Margaret. His sisters were Mary Jane Warner and Sarah Elizabeth Warner (who died in infancy). William Warner Snr had been an accountant, parish clerk and teacher. Warner Jnr. married Katie Florence Mena Hartland (née Bilsborough and known as Mena) in 1920 (daughter of a mahogany merchant); she outlived her husband.

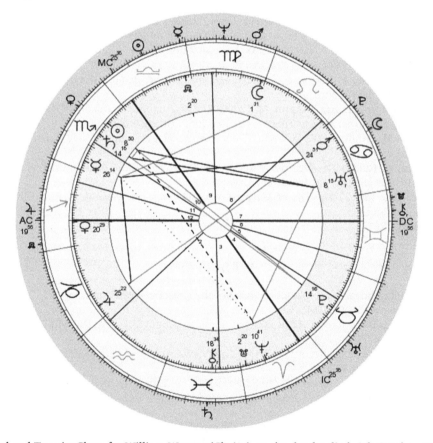

Natal and Transits Chart for William Warner (Cheiro) on the day he died, 8th October, 1936.

Warner Jnr. became celebrated worldwide under the pseudonym of Cheiro, travelling regularly amongst the affluent clientele of America, as well as working in London as a palmist whose fame became almost legendary. He later became a businessman although most of his enterprises were relatively short-lived, and he ultimately attained notoriety for criminal activities, including embezzlement.

Warner was a confident and self-promoting character, often described as courteous and charming. He spent his final years in Hollywood consulting as a palmist for clients (albeit on a more modest scale than previously), writing screenplays and completing his last book. The public were told his death was due to a heart attack but his death certificate reveals it was cirrhosis of the liver and organic heart disease, both of which had been diagnosed shortly before his death.

WHAT WARNER'S NATAL CHART SHOWS

Warner became globally famous as his alter-ego 'Cheiro' the palmist and seer. It is unsurprising that the ruling planet of his natal chart is Jupiter, which rules his ascendant sign Sagittarius. This sign is associated with celebrity, fame and fortune as well as adventure, education, long-distance travel, opportunities and philosophy. To avoid confusion, Cheiro will be referred to in this chapter as Warner, as he also had various other aliases including Count Louis Hamon, Count Leigh de Hamong and John Warner. The family surname Warner was "... an English name of dual old-French derivation in the county Cork since the mid-seventeenth century" (MacLysaght, 1985, 296) and his name change to Hamon will be discussed later.

In Warner's natal chart, there is a preponderance of planets in the water signs comprising: Sun, Mercury and Saturn in Scorpio; as well as Mars and Uranus in Cancer. This suggests that Warner had an artistic and sensitive nature and was very receptive to the feelings of others. The strength of this is shown by the dominance of female polarities (*see glossary*) in his chart made up of the five water signs in the aforementioned planets, as well as the three earth signs which comprise: Moon in Virgo, Jupiter in Capricorn and Pluto in Taurus.

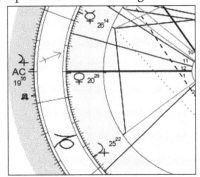

The emphasis of female polarities in the natal chart indicates Warner's exceptionally imaginative and intuitive nature. Warner was aware of his own sensitive nature and wrote that "... due to the influence of the more sensitive side of my nature, for many years I gave vent to my feelings by writing poetry, both sentimental and religious" (Cheiro, 1986, 145).

Sagittarius on the ascendant (*see glossary*) indicates that Warner was confident, restless and opportunistic. Long distance travel was important to his nomadic spirit, and he claimed to have visited China, Egypt and Russia which would have been a massive adventure in his time. Searching for meaning to life and living life to the full are typical of Sagittarius.

Warner's search for meaning in life can be seen by his exploration of occult subjects, spiritualism and other religious cultures, such as Hinduism. He once wrote "... in the study of the mysteries of life we are giving praise and glory to the Creator of Life, who in his infinite wisdom created all things to be used by man for the highest development of his kin" (Cheiro, 2013, Preface, 2). In his early book of poetry, *If Only We Knew*, his strong Christian religious background is very clear.

Venus in Sagittarius indicates that Warner needed freedom in relationships as he valued independence and saw love as an adventure, possibly he was reluctant to commit to a relationship as he prized his independence too much. He did not marry until he was 54, and the area of marriage and Warner's attitude towards it will be discussed later on. The Sun trine Uranus aspect suggests he was proud of being so original and distinctive, and of being part of Bohemian high society.

This aspect also suggests his need for freedom and independence in partnerships and relationships, while nevertheless appreciating any unique skills and talents that his partners (both personal and business) could offer him. The Sun represents self-expression whilst Uranus is associated with the aforementioned qualities of free expression and free will.

Warner's Gemini descendant (*see glossary*) shows that he needed a stimulating partner to prevent him becoming bored and frustrated. He was once described as "… a notorious womanizer (sic) and an Irishman who enjoyed his drink" (Carr, 2002, Introduction, 2). Warner was married for sixteen years, whether he remained faithful to his wife during their marriage is unknown.

NEVER JUDGE A BOOK BY ITS COVER

Venus in the first house shows Warner's concern with appearance; he liked to project charm and panache. One of his clients once described him as "… handsome with pale green eyes … with a quick bewitching smile and a gentle tenor voice" (Wiley, 2016, 61). Biographer, Anthony Carr, described him as "… tall, commanding and handsome, with deep-set, compelling eyes" (Carr, 2002, 9). A client who visited him for a palm reading, described him wearing "a long lavender silk robe" (Wiley, 2016, 293).

Venus is unaspected in Warner's chart which means that it does not have to work with the energies of other planets. It has full reign of its own pure energy rather like a wild horse and it becomes prevalent in the natal chart, because of its abundance of natural energy. This is borne out, for example, by Warner's extensive foreign travels, which shows the restless energy of Sagittarius that loves to adventure and explore.

VALUING EXCESS

The unaspected position of Venus in Sagittarius can also suggest an arrogance and self-belief with a gambler's approach to life, where the sky was the limit where money was concerned, and the end always justified the means. As a young man, he had inherited a substantial amount of money, and later earned a good income through his work as a palmist.

Yet nothing seems to have satisfied him and he embezzled huge amounts of money from some of his clients when he was a banker before going on the run.

Eventually, the authorities caught up with him after a Hungarian, Count Rudolph Festeric (one of his victims), insisted on Hamon's arrest and trial. However, Warner never appeared in court, having gone on the run, and returned to the UK in exile. He was found guilty in his absence, and sentenced to thirteen months in prison, fined 500 francs and ordered to repay the million francs he had swindled from the Count

(Wiley, 2016, 533), making newspaper headlines in the process. However, he fled justice, and left France, never to return (Wiley, 2016, 539). These examples show not only the irresponsible and unmanageable nature of the Venus in Sagittarius but also the criminal and underhand nature of Pluto, ruler of Warner's Sun sign Scorpio.

"Cheiro, Original Photo" by John Dyhouse (Licensed Under CC BY 2.0)

Apparently, Warner also had an adventurous and ardent love-life which included his famous and rich clientele, he even kept their passionate correspondence to him filed away. It has been suggested that Warner even turned some of these letters to financial advantage by using them for blackmail, with varying degrees of success (Wiley, 2012, 543).

A few years later, he left America for Paris with approximately $200,000 in his pocket (Wiley, 2016, 544). In 1909, the *Los Angeles Herald* carried a photograph of Warner (as Cheiro) and the headline read: "American Palmist Wanted in Paris" (ibid, 551). Jupiter is in the first house of his natal chart which is associated with one's *persona* and indicates Warner's charismatic and warm nature which so easily attracted people to him. However, since part of Jupiter's nature is to boast and exaggerate, this indicates that Warner was not only extravagant but also a master of exaggeration and self-promotion.

The aspect Mercury sextile Jupiter coupled with that of Venus in Sagittarius is less helpful for practical details in life, which may explain why he was less successful in his business ventures, particularly when he was not operating as 'Cheiro' (other interpretations of the aspect Mercury sextile Jupiter will be discussed later). Possibly, he over-extended himself, believing that he could achieve anything he wanted. This is seen in the aspect of Mars opposing Jupiter, a combination that indicates tremendous self-belief, as well as being overly enthusiastic. It also suggests that, although Warner was an inveterate risk-taker, he did not really think ahead to the consequences of his actions. He described people born on the 1st November (his birthday) as liking "large, bold enterprises" (Cheiro, 2009, 249).

The first house governs the image and the *persona* that we portray to the world and descriptions of Warner's physique show that he held a distinctive presence. He was, according to those who knew him, quite tall, athletic and muscular; facially he had a strong jaw and heavy dark eyebrows beneath which his pale green eyes appeared almost hypnotic (Wiley, 2016, 63 & 396).

These are fairly typical Scorpio attributes, since the eyes are associated with Scorpio and we can see his brooding presence in the photograph above. His naturalisation record from America more impassively describes him at the age of 66 as having a fair complexion with *brown* eyes and light brown hair, five foot 10 and ¾ inches and weighing 180 pounds (UN naturalisation card) and with no distinctive marks. Obviously, his eyes did not change colour and, from the photograph, certainly look darker than pale green.

The planets in Scorpio reveal Warner's determined and passionate nature. The Sun in Scorpio shows he was intense and passionate with tremendous inner strength, although his feelings were controlled and masked, such is the secretive nature of Scorpio. Warner wrote of Scorpios that, "The sex quality is an enormous factor in their lives ... in cases where the will and ambition are dominant, these people can keep the curb on their strong sex-natures" (Cheiro, 1980, 318), which clearly reveals the 'all or nothing' characteristic of Scorpio.

Mercury in Scorpio reveals that Warner was naturally gifted in understanding other people and perceptive in getting to the heart of what motivated them. Confidentiality and trust were qualities that mattered not only to him, but also to his alter-ego 'Cheiro', particularly in his work as a confidante in society palmistry where he read for the stars and celebrities of his day. However, as we shall see later, he was also capable of breaking trust and privacy. Warner also claimed to have read for royalty, including King Edward VII (Cheiro, 1912, 71). The controlled and disciplined nature of Saturn in Scorpio exacerbates the more ordered side of Warner's nature, particularly in business matters where he needed to be in complete control.

A STING IN THE TAIL

Warner had a penetrating mind that would have disliked superficiality; investigation and probing would have better appealed to his curiosity. Mercury in Scorpio also suggests that he was shrewd and had a talent for unearthing information which would have been invaluable when conducting palm readings. For example, it would have enabled him to understand and interpret areas such as body language. The placement also alludes to the idea of knowledge being power, since Mercury is associated with the former and Scorpio the latter.

Those who crossed Warner did so at their peril for the Mercury in Scorpio often possesses a biting and venomous tongue, transforming words into weapons. For example, when he appeared in court in Ireland regarding a compensation claim (which is discussed later), Mr Kupton KC (for the State) addressed Warner, asking about his *nom de plume*, Cheiro (Irish Independent, 1926, 8). Kupton accused Warner of not being truthful about "his precarious occupation as a palmist." Warner promptly replied, "There was nothing precarious about it, I earned more money than many of you barristers" (ibid). He wrote in his book, *Cheiro's Astrology*, that Scorpios "... are apt to reduce the most serious questions to ridicule by their love of the sarcastic which can sting like a scorpion's tail" (Cheiro, 2013, 222), clearly showing he was aware of his own sometimes venomous tongue, or perhaps he experienced a scorpion verbal sting himself!

Warner's Moon sign Virgo is ruled by Mercury and is a practical earth sign; being efficient and of service would have been important to him, since these are areas associated with Virgo. In his memoirs, he said he needed to dedicate two days of his working week "... at the service of those who cannot afford to pay my fees. I felt by so doing I was giving a part of what God had given me to His poor" (Cheiro, 1912, 52). This suggests he felt a debt owed to higher service that had provided him with his talents and was mindful of those who were less prosperous than his wealthy, high society clientele. However, it must be said that his lofty ideals did not match many of his actions; there is no evidence of charitable works, and considerable evidence of embezzlement.

Analysis, detail, minutiae and scrutiny would have been critical in his work, since Virgo's energy requires precision and meticulousness. It would seem that his writing skills were suited to occult subjects which is where he achieved greater success, and his book, *The Language of the Hand,* published in 1897 (first self-published in 1894), was his most successful; he wrote screenplays in his later life when he lived in America but none were ever produced.

Warner achieved better success in 1903 when he acquired an established newspaper called *The American Register*, and became both its editor and owner. The newspaper was the largest English language newspaper in Paris, with offices also in London; Warner also added a Brighton office (Wiley, 2016, 445). Monopolising on his freedom as editor, Warner started his own weekly column called *Occult Notes*, which he continued until the closure of the newspaper (by then, rather grandly renamed: *The American Register and Anglo-Colonial World News)* in 1908 (ibid).

The eighth house is associated with other people's resources, such as inheritance, loans and taxes; and in Warner's life he seems to have sought out situations where he could control other people's money. For example, he was director of Hamon & Co. Bank, and a director with the Threadneedle Syndicate which looked after various merchants; he was also a financier in Russia. In his memoirs, he described his "natural gift as given, claiming that he "endeavoured to return it as one would a loan – if possible, increased in value" (Cheiro, 1912, Forward, xiii). We see how he uses the imagery of finance to describe his gift of clairvoyance. However, he clearly betrayed his gifts by embezzling money from some clients and attempting to blackmail others. Crime and ruthlessness are characteristics associated with Pluto which rules the eighth house (and Scorpio, Warner's Sun sign) and demonstrates how Warner violated people by abusing his position of authority and trust.

INTRICACIES AND SKILL

As previously discussed Warner's Moon in Virgo is positioned in the eighth house the area, which is often in associated with the occult. The intricate and methodical nature of Virgo was applied in Warner's occult work, which can be seen by his analysis of the palms as well as calculations in astrology and numerology. This way of working would have appealed to his meticulous nature and added skill and techniques to his craft, all of which are characteristics of Virgo. Warner said of his occult work, "In my own work I use a system as regards time and dates which I have never found mentioned elsewhere. It is one which I consider exceptionally accurate. … It is the system of seven." (Cheiro, 1986, 125). Such precision is in keeping with Virgo's exacting nature.

The Moon in Virgo also indicates a good memory and bright and critical mind; this seems to be true of Warner in that he had the ability to learn and remember astrological calculations and systems in numerology. Apparently as a child he had "… a remarkable mathematical ability" (Carr, 2002, 10), and perhaps this talent was, in part, what drew him to numerology.

The perfectionist nature of the lunar Virgo can be seen in his writing about palmistry. Not only does he analyse the main lines on the palm (e.g. head, heart and life lines) as well as the shape of the hand, but provides other useful details, such as the fingernails in relation to health, the colour of the palm in comparison to the outside of the hand texture of the skin, joints on the fingers, as well as hair on the hands (Cheiro, 1986, 9). He is emphatic in his books in that he uses the ancient system of Chaldean numerology as well as zodiacal astrology, which rely on a method of numerology, which he clearly must have found reliable in his occult work. This shows how he strove to be accurate in his work and understood the importance of trustworthy sources.

In his book, *Language of the Hand,* in the chapter entitled 'Some Interesting Hands', Warner describes a distinctive lineage on his right palm called 'the double line of head.' This unique double head line has been described as "… a rare occurrence and indicates great versatility and awareness of what others want. It is found on those of us in command of our public persona" (Clifford, 2002, 197).

This accurately describes the various *personae* that Warner adopted in his life to help maintain privacy, as well as showing his ability to sense what his audience and public wanted. That Warner chose to use his own handprint as an illustration in his chapter about 'interesting hands' which suggests self-importance and resourcefulness in the information at hand (excuse the pun!), although one cannot help wondering whether, as a secretive Scorpio, this really was Warner's palm-print, or that of somebody else who did have a 'double line of head'.

The Moon creates a square aspect with Mercury in Warner's natal chart indicating that he worked hard at listening to others and became a skilled listener. It also indicates his ability to discuss domestic and mundane matters with others, irrespective of their background and class. Clearly, he could strike a rapport with others and encourage them to speak about their feelings, which made them more inclined to trust him. He claimed he had spent a considerable time visiting "… hospitals and even prisons, to collect impressions of hands of all sorts and conditions of humanity" (Cheiro, 1912, 15), showing his determination to obtain the material he needed from the unheard and unseen in society. The Moon square Mercury aspect would have helped him to communicate with these people and persuade them to allow their hand prints to appear in his book.

Emotionally, Moon in Virgo suggests that he was probably clinical and discerning in intimate relationships, since these are qualities associated with Moon Virgo in the eighth house (the area of intimacy and sex along with the occult). It is also possible that he was suspicious that any potential intimate partners were only seeking his money and/or power. This is borne out by the Moon being emotional and Virgo being analytical whilst the eighth house is also associated with deep intense feelings.

Given that Warner's Sun and Mercury are in the sign of Scorpio, which is associated with the eighth house (and Pluto), it is probable that this was a strong characteristic of Warner. It also suggests that, despite his outward show of self-assurance, he was in fact a deeply sensitive and insecure individual.

MONEY WORRIES

The Moon sign (*see box on right*) is an indication that Warner worried intensely, as anxiety is associated with Virgo, and this may have had a detrimental effect on his health. Towards the end of his life, he had tremendous money worries and, although during his bachelor years and without any family responsibility he had not worried about life insurance, when he married (in his fifties) he must have wanted some security for his much younger wife, but insurance companies declined him because of his health problems (Carr, 2002, 181).

At the end of his life, Warner lapsed into a coma (Carr, 2002, Photo section, 5, Newspaper article: Millen). After his death, however, Warner's secretive Scorpio nature was made even more apparent to his wife, for she discovered he had considerable debts and had not fully informed her of his true financial position (ibid). The Probate and Wills Register of 1948 shows:

'Probate London 28th January to Katie Florence Mena Hamon widow. Effects £1505 16s. 3d. In England'

(Probate & Wills Register, 1948, 69).

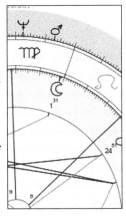

This would have been worth just under £40,000 nowadays (Moneysorter website – see bibliography), probably far less than their lavish lifestyle would have led her to expect. Moon square Mercury suggests that Warner not only wrote and spoke confidently about the future but also understood what his audience wanted to hear. This is shown by Mercury (planet of communication) in the eleventh house. This area is not only associated with groups of people but also with the future through the eleventh house's association with advanced Aquarius/Uranus. There is an example of this in Warner's book, *Cheiro's Language of the Hand*, where he provides the reader and students of palmistry with observations and his understanding of palmistry, learned over a considerable period of time. His work also benefitted from his highly developed gifts of intuition and clairvoyance.

Warner not only lectured on palmistry but had other interests such as psychic phenomenon, which he lectured on for the London Spiritualist Alliance in 1912. He wrote that Scorpios "… as speakers, appeal to the emotions and sentiments of their public … they sway their audiences as they choose" (Cheiro, 1980, 317) revealing his awareness of the effect he had upon his listeners and clientele.

Warner wished to see palmistry taken seriously and "acknowledged as it deserves to be" (Cheiro, 1986, 2), believing "… that the time is not far distant when, from considerations of health and demands from other fields of labour, I must perforce retire from the scene and leave others – I trust more competent – to take my place" (ibid). This reveals his concern for the future of palmistry and that he considered himself an authority and seasoned expert on palmistry. However, not everyone shared this belief. For example, he was often criticised for being unscientific and for not relying purely on the clinical hand analysis but also bringing his clairvoyance into play, since this was a skill that could never be taught as such.

It has been suggested that Katherine St Hill, founder of the Chirological Society of Great Britain in 1889, distrusted 'Cheiro', with whom she had corresponded briefly. She certainly disliked him using a pseudonym, feeling that this ran against her own principals of professionally practicing hand-analysis. Members of her society who were practicing chirologists were forbidden from using pseudonyms as it was seen to be unprofessional (http://www.johnnyfincham.com/history/ksthill.htm).

Although we cannot be certain whether these rules were specifically directed at Warner, he never became a member of the Chirological Society.

BROAD THINKING

Returning to the aspect of Mercury sextile Jupiter, this suggests that Warner had big ideas and often looked to the future. For example, as a young teenager, Warner was

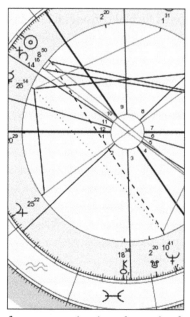

determined to travel overseas, as well as develop his knowledge and gift for palmistry. The aspect also suggests that Warner was a philosophical (Jupiter) thinker (Mercury), and an inspirational speaker and writer. Some of his poetry addresses philosophical and metaphysical themes in life. Examples include poems called *Dead, Fate, Life* and *Waiting* (Hamon, 1895), illustrating that Warner was inspired by such subjects and wished to share them with his readers through poetry.

To this day, his books remain popular even though hand-analysis and palmistry have progressed since Warner's times. No longer is the forecasting of death (as commonly used by *Cheiro*) considered appropriate in the practice, although it was once believed to help an individual better understand themselves and others.

The sextile aspect created between Mercury and Jupiter also suggests that Warner had a natural gift for communicating about the future, and one obvious indication of this is through the predictions he made for his palmistry clientele. Indeed, such was his confidence in his prophetic skills that he adopted the name 'Cheiro' which means 'The Seer'.

In medical astrology, Mercury governs the hands and the Greek word for hand is *Cheir*, and Chiromancy is the name given to palmistry. In *Cheiro's Memoirs: the Reminiscences of a Society Palmist*, Warner described how he was apparently inspired to use the name Cheiro. For a while he had been uncertain what to call himself as an alter-ego; he wrote "... my tired brain dreamt of names by the hundreds, til (sic) suddenly I seemed to see in Greek and English the name 'CHEIRO' standing out before me. The next morning I announced my discovery" (Cheiro, 1912, 31). However, Warner later used various other names once his career as a palmist was no longer his main source of income.

BANKRUPTCY, EMBEZZLEMENT AND GREED

Returning once again to the eighth house, this area is also associated with other people's money, inheritance, legacy and taxes. The Moon in this house suggests that, at one point in his life, Warner was made financially secure by means other than his own. This is borne out since, in his early life, Warner inherited a gift from a relative; a legacy of £20,000 (Carr, 2002, 28). At that time, this would have been an immense sum, enough to provide him with financial security for his future and enabling him to travel extensively. Yet, he seems to have spent most of this money quite quickly, and was later only able to make himself financially secure for a while when he "embezzled two American clients out of $500,000" (http://blog.museumoflondon.org.uk/the-champagne-years – *The New York Times*, January, 1909). Warner had no scruples about using his understanding of other people's vulnerabilities to his own advantage and defrauding his own clients. A year later, in London, he was declared bankrupt and his newfound situation made newspaper headlines.

Curiously, Warner would have done well to heed to his own advice, for in his book, *Cheiro's Astrology*, under the heading 'Finance', he advised readers that people born on

1st November (his birthday) can expect to make money in life and be successful, yet he stresses that the challenge would be to keep what they gain (Cheiro, 2013, 222). A combination of an extravagant lifestyle and sometimes poor decision making caused him to live out his final years in relative poverty. Warner also wrote that people born on the 1st November should guard against deferring and procrastination, citing it as "one of their besetting sins" (ibid, 219). One cannot help but wonder whether he ever reflected on this when he looked back on his own life in later years.

There is a quincunx aspect *(see glossary)* in Warner's chart created between the Sun and Neptune and has been observed by some astrologers that, amongst other possibilities, this aspect can be an indicator of "treachery concerning corporate money and joint finances" (Sakoian and Acker, 1972, 11). This is certainly borne out by the way he embezzled two of his clients when he was editor for the newspaper, *American Register*, in the early twentieth century. Warner was convicted of fraud for this offence and served a thirteen-month prison sentence in Paris (*The New York Times*, 9th October, 1936, Obituary for Cheiro). The quincunx relates to health issues too, and this area will be discussed later on in relation to Warner's health.

INFILTRATION, DELUSIONS OF GRANDEUR AND INSPIRATION

Neptune in the third house in his natal chart suggests an ability to communicate in a fanciful and imaginative way. This is borne out by how he enticed and persuaded his clients to do what he wanted. It has been said that what made Warner's palmistry so distinctive from other fortune-tellers was that he had "… an ability to deeply engage the imagination of his client to draw her close to share his apparent exotic world" (Wiley, 2012, 760).

The third house is connected with communications and, at times, Neptune has the capability to bewitch and create a mirage. The Sun (tenth house) quincunx Neptune (in the third house) shows that, in positions of authority, Warner could communicate poetically but also evasively, and thus was able to convince some customers to part with their extensive wealth which he then embezzled.

Passenger records for their sailing trips on the *President Garfield* in 1929 show that Warner's wife was recorded as being an author, while in 1933 (sailing on the *Heranger*) she was described as a housewife; on both trips however, she claimed the title of Countess. Their 1920 marriage certificate shows that his 'rank, trade, or profession' was recorded as Count but in the early days she does not seem to have called herself Countess.

The position of Neptune in the third house suggests deception, distortion as well as evasiveness in communication, and also reveals that, while Warner may have had a fertile imagination; learning bore more fruit when images and symbols were used. For example, he was inspired by the illustrated work of hand analyst Heron-Allen (1869–1943), as well as Casimir D'Arpentigny (b.1798) and Adrien Adolphe Desbarolles (1801–1886). There are distinct similarities in certain areas, between Edward Heron-Allen's life and the apparent 'memoirs' of Cheiro, so much so that one may be forgiven for thinking that Cheiro based his claims on events in Heron-Allen's life. For example, the latter wrote under a pseudonym (Christopher Blayre), he wrote books on palmistry and he also became famous in London society in the 1880s. He was friendly with Oscar Wilde and his wife Constance and towards the end of the eighteen-eighties embarked on a three year tour lecturing on the subject of palmistry, which was a great success (http://www.heronallensociety.co.uk).

Warner was certainly an inspiring speaker and writer hence his success in his writing, lecturing and also explaining his hand-readings to his palmistry clients. He also ran a correspondence course in palmistry when he was editor of *The American Register* newspaper (Wiley, 2016, 474). He used the newspaper to place advertisements for his 12–24 lesson courses stating that they would "… enable anyone of average intelligence to become successful in the art of reading hands for themselves" (ibid). This shows he was willing to share his knowledge of hand-reading and was enthusiastic about empowering his students through self-knowledge. It also shows how he used one business enterprise to support another.

Warner demonstrated his gift for poetry in his book of verse, *If Only we Knew and Other Poems,* which was one of his earliest publications. He claimed to have inherited his skill at writing poetry from his father (Kessinger and Cheiro, 1912, 3). He was versatile in speaking and writing on a variety of other genres too, including fiction, memoirs and the occult.

Neptune's appearance in the third house in Warner's natal chart adds sensitivity to his nature and its subtlety. The subtle nature of Neptune would have enabled him to read between the lines in any given situation. The energy of Neptune can be artistic and imaginative and when placed in the third house indicates that Warner had the ability to create illusion and communicate using his fertile imagination. This is shown, for example, by him adopting different personas in his life, e.g. 'Cheiro – palmist and seer' and Louis Hamon, etc. Some of his poems also reveal his religious and spiritual nature, as discussed earlier.

Another example of Warner's inspirational teaching can be seen when in 1926, when he still lived in England and he made a series of eight films entitled *Cheiro's Language of the Hand.* These taught the meaning of the lines in the palms (Carr, 2002, 149). He used black and white drawings, showing the distinctive lines of the hand with text to the side of the picture hand, which explained their meanings. He also used a pointer that moved from line to line as the text changed. This shows Warner's imaginative way of teaching, where viewers could learn for themselves through the media of film (Neptune) about palmistry. This would have been considered quite advanced and exciting for its time.

Warner also included images of imprints from the hands of famous people, taken from what he claimed was his own collection; some had been autographed and dated by the subject. Two examples included Lord Kitchener and Prime Minister William Gladstone. The films were shown at the Coliseum Theatre in London and proved very popular, as the number of viewers increased until the complete series of eight films had been shown. This shows how Warner was able to communicate and teach in an artistic and imaginative way, using the most up-to-date technology available to him.

UNCOVERED

The underhand nature of Pluto (ruler of the eighth house) indicates that Warner could, and did, misuse his position and use his understanding of people's weaknesses to his own advantage. Crime, police, investigation as well as the underworld are all associated with Scorpio and its ruler Pluto and reveal Warner's embezzling activities. Of course, not all Scorpios are criminals, although in Warner's case in the early twentieth century as a young man he was certainly known to Scotland Yard (Irish Examiner, 1926, 7). Another example of his misuse of power can be seen in the allegations that he blackmailed some of his famous and wealthy clients' husbands (Wiley, 2012, 543).

There is a compulsive and obsessive nature to Scorpio as these are qualities associated with this sign. Scorpio is ruled by Pluto, Lord of The Underworld, so it is perhaps unsurprising that Warner sometimes became involved with the criminal and darker nature of life as these are areas associated with the craft and mask of Pluto.

Warner became a director of the Threadneedle Syndicate, a financial organisation set up in 1914, and supporting different merchants, as well as supplying shells for the European war; Baron Max von Oppenheim was also connected with the organisation (Carr, 2002, 144). However, the company was short-lived, and was listed in *The Mining Manual Containing Full Particulars of Mining Companies* as resolved to 'windup voluntarily' (Skinner & Skinner, 1917, 643). According to *The London Gazette* (21st April, 1916), the company was no longer able to continue in business due to its 'liabilities', although it remained in voluntary liquidation as late as 1929 (*The London Gazette*, 27/09/1929, At that stage, the liquidator ordered "the disposal of the books, accounts and documents of the company" (ibid). The failure was most likely due to serious financial irregularities, since it was set up at the outbreak of World War I and should have been expected to make considerable profit supplying ammunition shells.

During the First World War, 1914–18, Warner spent some time living in London whilst director of the Threadneedle Syndicate (at least until 1916); he also spent time at his home in Henley-on-Thames in Oxfordshire. There, he spent time "on patrol duty over a section of the Thames River in his motor launch" (Carr, 2002, 120). It has been suggested that he may have been a civilian who aided with patrols along the River Thames as a local defence volunteer (correspondence between the Author and the River & Rowing Museum).

Warner also found himself the subject of an intriguing newspaper headline: 'Cheiro's Claim Against Irish Free State' (*The Times*, 26/04/1926, Page unknown). He had apparently brought a civil action claiming damages in the sum of £12,960 for the destruction of his peat works by the IRA. Several years earlier, in 1922, Warner (who also used the name Hamon) was director of The Artificial Coal Company which had a peat works site at Ballycumber, in County Offaly. He was visited at home by the members of the IRA who had allegedly burnt down most of the peat's work site. At the time, the IRA was fighting the War of Independence against British Forces and had been on a campaign to attack and destroy government buildings and British government related businesses. Warner was claiming a colossal amount of money for the time. During the court procedures it was revealed that the peat works plant was attached to James Nolan, a British M.P. who had approached Warner (Hamon) about running the business (*Irish Independent*, 26/04/1926, 8). The case was ultimately dismissed by the courts after an appeal by the Minister of Finance and, although initially there were some suggestions that Warner may have played a part in setting fire to the peats works, ultimately there was no evidence of foul play on his part. Perhaps Warner's criminal record made the court consider him less than honest.

INHERITED GIFTS AND BEREAVEMENT

Returning to the Moon in the eighth house, this placement suggests that Warner may have inherited some of his mother's characteristics and qualities (inheritance is associated with the eighth house). She may have been nervous and restless as well as being critical and discerning, as these are qualities associated with Virgo. The other possibility is that his mother was also psychic, as the Moon in the eighth house can indicate an intuitive and perceptive mother/care-giver. This idea is further strengthened by the position of Pluto in the fourth house, as Pluto is associated with insight and the occult, whilst the fourth house is associated with the care-taking figure, who is usually (although not always) the mother.

Warner claimed that his mother encouraged him to study the occult and that she was a gifted palmist herself (Carr, 2002, 10). It seems likely, therefore, that she passed this knowledge on to him, along with second sight, i.e. clairvoyance. In fact, Warner admitting this, saying that he inherited from her, "love of the occult in every form, combined with a curious religious devotionalism (sic) which has never ceased to exist," and that his mother's family were "bred on books" (Kessinger and Cheiro, 1912, 3). This supports the above interpretation of the Moon in the eighth house and Pluto in the fourth house being associated with his intuitive and psychic mother.

Pluto is a planet which, amongst other things, brings crisis and transformation in its wake, which often involves burying and concealing pain and trauma. Positioned in the fourth house in Warner's natal chart it reveals that when he was born, his parents were living with Plutonian themes, such as intense emotional angst. This is borne out by the fact that in 1865 their daughter, Sarah Elizabeth (born 3rd November, 1864), had died, aged just one year old. Her exact cause of death is unknown, but in Ireland at that time, in both affluent and poorer societies, measles and tuberculosis were common causes of infant mortality.

When their son William John was born on the 1st November, 1866, his parents would probably still have been processing the trauma of bereavement from the death of their daughter as well as rejoicing in the birth of their healthy son. The transformation in the family speaks for itself and reveals the Plutonian themes of survival, as well as life and rebirth. Warner, being of a sensitive disposition, may have been aware of the feelings of his parents when he was growing up as a child. Whether they spoke of the death of his sister to him, we do not know, but as a young boy he may well have become increasingly aware of the tensions brought about by his sister's death, particularly since they're birthdays were close together – Warner was born on 1st November and his sister had been born on 3rd November.

Possibly, his sister's death was never mentioned, and he may not have even known about her existence. It might have been a family secret. This would be in keeping with the hidden and secretive nature of Pluto in the fourth house, the area connected with family, heritage and legacy. If he *had* known about his sister's death, however, it may have helped shape his attitude towards life and death and account for why, in his work as a palmist, he seemed obsessed with the theme of death; often forecasting the death of his clients using his skills in numerology as well as his talent for clairvoyance.

RENEWAL AND TRANSFORMATION

In Warner's adult life, Pluto in fourth house suggests that he had to uproot and make dramatic changes in his domestic life, because the nature of Pluto uproots and generates transformations. One example is seen in the late 1920s, when he and his wife spent nine months organising selling property and leases and closing down a large house in London in order to emigrate to Hollywood, America. They finally set sail for America in July 1929, sailing on the *President Garfield* (Oak, sailing list) from Balboa, Spain. Such a transformation of domestic and home life must have been an emotionally intense time for the Warner's (as well as for their 22 servants who were about to become unemployed!).

Another Pluto in the fourth house example is illustrated when Warner became very ill in 1936 (he would later die at home that same year). Pluto is associated with death and the fourth house the area of the home, from this and the above examples we can see how Pluto, the ruling planet of his Sun sign Scorpio, was a powerful, persistent and transforming influence in the area of family and home in his life.

Heritage and legacy became important to Warner later in his life – he changed his surname from Warner to Hamon by deed poll in London, 1928 (*The London Gazette*, December, 1928), and then called himself Count Louis Hamon. He claimed that his father had carried out investigations into his own family history and concluded that he was of Norman heritage and descended from the Hamon family. Given that 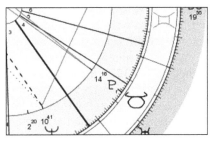 Warner senior was once a parish clerk, it would have been easy for him to access parish records and other necessary documents during his research, provided they had not been sent to the Public Record Office in Dublin, following the disestablishment of the Irish Church in 1869.

Clearly being a Hamon was important to Warner as was being called Count, which must have appealed to his imaginative nature.

At this point, it is also worth pointing out that Warner must have known that any claim to be a Count (or even a Hamon, for that matter) was going to be impossible to disprove, since just six years earlier, during the Irish Civil War, the Public Records Office in Ireland was bombarded for two days and many records were lost in the ensuing fire. It seems too much of a coincidence that he chose to legally change his name and give himself a title, once any means of disproving either was lost (it is true that not *all* records were destroyed, but it may have been enough for his purposes that many people *believed* that they were).

Pluto's energy is compulsive and intense – both words that describe Warner. His forceful and passionate nature probably made relations with his family somewhat painful and even vengeful (both qualities associated with Pluto). He seems to have had an uneasy relationship with his father, who had at first been a parish clerk and then trained to become a teacher, a profession shared by Warner's mother, Margaret (www.oakancestry.com). Apparently, Warner's father disliked the young man's interest in the occult so much that he sent him off to a theological school to study for the Anglican priesthood, in the hope that it would curb his obsession with palmistry (Carr, 2002, 10). Clearly it did not, and one of Warner's teachers even asked him to read his palm for him – which he did.

FATHER AND SON

Warner's parents are symbolised in the natal chart by the Sun in tenth house opposing Pluto in the fourth, since both of these houses are associated with parental figures. Some of his mother's intuitive qualities have been discussed previously and illustrated by Pluto in the fourth house. The Sun in the tenth house pertains to an authoritarian and disciplinarian figure, and Warner was indeed very much aware of his father's influence in the outside world as well as in the domestic environment. His father's occupations included accountant, parish clerk and teacher and he had passed an advanced exam in algebra for the Annual Examination of The Masters of Schools in 1860 for the Glandaulagh (sic) Church Education Society (*Wicklow Newsletter*, 02/06, 1860).

Warner's father was controlling and described as a "strict disciplinarian ... [who was] horrified and bitterly opposed to his son being connected to any superstitious nonsense" (Carr, 2002, 10). Such conflict would not just have affected father and son, but also both his parents, since allegedly his mother encouraged her young son's interest in palmistry. If true, this must have sorely aggravated her husband.

Warner's spiteful Scorpio nature is shown by the way he virtually reinvented his father on his 1920 marriage certificate. He told the registrar that William senior's full name was William Le Warner Hamon and that he was a man of 'independent means'. However, records show that his father died in 1898 (cause of death: paralysis) and his occupation was recorded as an 'Accountant and Clerk' (www.oakancestry.com).

This shows that Warner was cold, calculating and a compulsive liar when it suited him; he even gave his own age as a year younger than he really was. This example shows Warner's cunning and deceptive nature (Mercury in Scorpio) and how he could bend and distort the truth (Neptune in the third house).

Some of Warner's claims about his ancestry, e.g. that his father arrived as a Huguenot refugee, or that his grandparents were French nobility (Carr, 2002, 9) verge on the fantastical, especially since most French Protestants fled to Ireland before 1760, and their persecution ended with the Edict of Versailles in 1787. Warner's father simply could not have arrived in Ireland at such an early date.

Likewise, Carr's claim that Warner's lineage went back to a Pagan Scandinavian sea-king named Hamon is equally unlikely and unprovable (ibid). Whether that information originally came from Warner himself, we do not know but, like many 'family legends', it seems to have relied more on wishful thinking than the truth. It does reveal, however, that Warner desperately wanted to be regarded as somehow 'better' than he was, and better than everyone else.

Pluto positioned in the fourth house of his natal chart reveals that Warner could be very secretive about his true heritage and roots, as part of the nature of Pluto is to conceal and mask. Whatever his reasons, Warner fabricated a great deal about his life and family, as seen from the above example. Perhaps there was something more sinister and even taboo that he successfully hid, since hiding and repression are qualities associated with Pluto.

The Sun and Saturn in the tenth house (both opposing Pluto) shows that Warner could be calculating and manipulative as well as pompous. His self-importance and invented status in society can be seen by the aspect Sun quincunx Neptune, the latter planet positioned in the third house (the area of communication and mentality), which tends to falsify and bend the truth as previously discussed.

Returning to Warner's roots, The Primary Valuation Property Survey (1847–64) reveals that his surname was fairly uncommon in the nineteenth century and there were only 25 households headed by a Warner in County Cork, three in Dublin and just one in County Antrim (www.oakancestry.com). Warner was born in Castle Street, Bray, which is located in the old townland of Little Bray, part of County Dublin, in the civil parish of Rathdown. It seems likely, therefore, that Warner's family were amongst the three families in Dublin in the aforementioned survey (and possibly even related to the other two families there).

In his memoirs, Warner claimed he was of Norman descent on his father's side of the family (Kessinger and Cheiro, 1912, 2). However, one of the first rules in genealogical research is to begin with the present and work backwards, not to find a famous ancestor and try to work forwards from that. Again, we see how Warner's imaginative and romantic nature sometimes overcame his common sense.

ADDING IT UP

Calculated, logical thinking is certainly possible with Mercury in the eleventh house position and this would have been helpful in Warner's astrological and numerological calculations for long term predictions, which is significant with the eleventh house's association with the future. As a schoolboy, Warner had a natural talent for mathematics (Carr, 2002, 10) which he may have inherited from his father; such a talent would have been helpful when Warner needed to make calculations for astrology and numerology. Even embezzlement required a certain 'talent for numbers.'

No doubt his mathematical skills would have been helpful when, as an adult, he had to pay wages to domestic servants in his home, and also to the assistants who aided him when he toured as 'Cheiro'. For example, in 1910, *The Stage* newspaper published an advert that read:

> 'WANTED: Lady to Assist Gentleman Fortune-Teller (Astrology, Palmistry, Physiognomy) … Small premium – Write particulars, photo, CHEIRO, 397 High Street, Kirkcaldy, NB'
>
> (The Stage Archives, 1910, 23)

It has been said that the celebrated astrologer R.H. Naylor was one of Cheiro's assistants and, when Cheiro was invited to cast the horoscope for Princess Margaret's birth in 1930 but was unavailable, Naylor deputised and prepared the natal chart for the then editor of *The Sunday Express*, John Gordon, who had requested the chart in order to see what the future held for her (www.revolvy.com). This was to be a turning point in Naylor's career: he was given a regular Sun sign astrology column in *The Sunday Express* after his article about Princess Margaret's natal chart was published.

As assistant to Cheiro, Naylor had aided Cheiro in his work. In the Catalogue of Copyright Entries, New Series: 1929, Part 1, under the heading Hamon, Louis, we read: "Cheiro's year book for 1929 – By Cheiro (pseud) … Astronomical and astrological computations by R.H. Taylor – London, North Hollywood, California, The London Publishing company 1929."

As discussed earlier, the Moon is square Mercury in the natal chart and suggests that the communicative and reasoning skills of Mercury are softened by the caring qualities of the Moon. These can manifest in ways such as caring and sympathetic responses, which would have been helpful as a palmist in being able to communicate both kindness and logic to his clients. This aspect may have fuelled Warner's desire to write about his own life, for example, in his book, *Cheiro's Memoirs – The Reminiscences of a Society Palmist*. However, the book is mostly about his allegedly famous clients with pictures of their palms and reveals little about his private self (as is only to be expected with his secretive Scorpio nature).

KINDRED SPIRITS AND TEAMWORK

The eleventh house is also associated with groups of people such as clubs and societies and, in 1898, Warner had a lifelong Fellowship of The Royal Geographical Society. At this time, he was living at the affluent address of New Bond Street, Mayfair, London and it is possible he joined the society for the social opportunities that his membership afforded him. He never wrote any articles for any of the society's journals, though he may have attended some lectures as an interested lay person (Royal Geographical Society). Intriguingly, he joined the society under the name Count Louis de Hamon (before his official name change in the 1920s).

Another example of Warner being involved with a group can be seen through his involvement with the Wilson Barrett Theatre Company in 1866. At one point he had been described as a "... young Irishman and promising young actor" (*The Stage,* 1892, 9) and he had joined the popular theatre company on their tour in America, undertaking minor roles (Wiley, 2016, 63). However, it seems that Warner did not distinguish himself in the theatre company since he was not listed on the posters for even Barrett's most successful plays, such as *The Sign of the Cross* and *Claudian*, which were both triumphs in several American cities (Wiley, 2016, 72). When the theatre company returned to England in 1887, Warner remained in America; as far as we know, he did not pursue his acting career further, although, as we see from his subsequent career, he did become a remarkable showman.

Warner was also an active member of the London Spiritualist Alliance when he returned from America and in 1912 was writing for their membership journal, *Light*; he wrote several articles for the magazine as well as delivering lectures for the organisation. He was also a member of The Royal Thames Yacht Club, and his affiliations to such different groups show his diverse interests and desire to meet and mix with new people who might help him with his ambitions for power and wealth.

Warner claimed that, in his early twenties, he had been a member of a secret society based in Europe, whereby members undertook an oath not to marry. He did not name the society but claimed that, when he joined, there was a membership consisting of "... 500 hundred members bound under a common oath never to enter the bonds of wedlock" (Cheiro, 1931, 350). He described how "... each member paid dues of 100 pounds per year into a kind of pension fund, which money, with compound interest added, came to a considerable amount when one reached the supposed unmarriageable age of 60 years – called in our ritual, 'the age of wisdom'" (ibid). Clearly, he did not profit by this himself, since he married before he turned 60, and one wonders whether it was another dubious financial project.

In his first book of memoirs, Warner was photographed wearing a very ornate ring on his little finger (also known as the pinky finger). This is interesting, as in the Victorian era people often wore a ring on their little finger to signify that they were uninterested in marriage (Lamé, 2017, 25). He may also have been trying to suggest he was a member of the Freemasons, although he never claimed this himself (https://www.masonic-lodge-of-education.com/masonic-signet-ring.html).

If the above secret society scheme was genuine, however, this shows not just the eleventh house example of a society, but also demonstrates the value that Warner placed on freedom, shown by the astrological positions of unaspected (*see glossary*) Venus in Sagittarius, as well as Uranus in the seventh house, and Jupiter in the first house. The financial arrangements must have appealed to his Moon Virgo where he could see the practicality of accruing more money as years went by into his pension fund, it also indicates the thinking (Mercury) of the future (eleventh house). The position of Uranus in Cancer in the seventh house indicates his rebellion against marriage and family life, although this attitude changed when, finally, he married at the age of 54 and had a family; Mena his wife as well as Jack, his step-son.

Warner stressed that members of the secret society were not women haters but 'women lovers' and took an oath to help women, set up a fund for women in distress and helped the members' female relatives (ibid). The fact that he married just six years before he could have expected to receive a large payout from the society suggests that he either fell head over heels in love or that the society had ceased by that time. He seems to have been very ill when they married and, apparently, Mena had been determined ever since they first met that they would marry one day.

LEARNED FRIENDS

The eleventh house is also associated with friends, and with Mercury in this area it indicates that Warner not only had a variety of friends, but also that many were probably speakers, teachers and writers, as these are professions connected with Mercury. An example of this  can be seen through his friendships with the investigative journalist W. T. Stead and 'Thought Machine' inventor and scientist, Edouard Savary d'Odiardi. The latter was described by Warner as being a "... remarkable man who for years had been one of my best friends in London" (Cheiro, 1912, 155), from whom he "... learned a great deal of occult knowledge" (ibid). Not only was he a scientist but he was a musician and conducted experiments on hidden forces of the body, which would have greatly appealed to Warner's secretive nature, and they must have had many an interesting discussion about occult matters (*see box above right*).

It was not until 1929 that Warner (having changed his name by deed poll shortly beforehand to Count Louis Le Warner Hamon) and his wife, 'Countess' Mena, emigrated from England and became citizens of America in 1929 (US Neutralisation Record). It appears that both Warner and his wife Mena colluded in delusion and self-aggrandisement by calling themselves Count and Countess respectively, assuming titles to which they had absolutely no claim in order to raise their status in society.

The above examples show that Cheiro enjoyed meeting a variety of people, especially socialising with kindred spirits as well as speaking and writing about matters of mutual interest, thus demonstrating the communicating and networking energy of Mercury in the eleventh house, which governs clubs, friendships and societies. One problem for his claims of predicting the future, however, is that he usually claims success only after the event.

For example, in May, 1912, just one month after the sinking of the RMS Titanic, Warner delivered a lecture for the London Spiritualist Alliance and spoke about his twenty-year friendship with the newspaper editor, W. T. Stead, who had gone down with the great ocean-going liner. According to Warner, he had spoken to Stead in 1911, and warned that the biggest danger to his life was water and that travel would be dangerous for him in the month of April, 1912 (Eckley, 2007). This sort of claim is difficult to confirm or refute, but certainly Stead was a spiritualist in his later life and wrote books on the themes of life after death.

Mercury in Scorpio in the eleventh house indicates Warner certainly had a gift for psychic information and knowledge about the future, which would have helped when reading, writing and speaking about his predictions as well as aiding his clairvoyance. The eleventh house also corresponds with groups, teams and societies and, as discussed earlier, we know that Warner was a member of a variety of societies, including a spiritualist organisation.

There are harmonious aspects created with Mercury in Warner's chart, which are Mercury trine Mars and Mercury sextile Jupiter. The former aspect, Mercury trine Mars, denotes an agile, competitive and quick-thinking mind that may be prone to boredom. The latter aspect of Mercury sextile Jupiter, as discussed earlier, suggests that Warner was a philosophical thinker and was broadminded with many ambitious ideas and a wide range of interests. Writing and publishing books would have kept him occupied to some extent, avoiding boredom while giving him great pleasure in sharing his knowledge with other people.

SELF-APPOINTMENT

The Sun is opposing Pluto in the natal chart (as previously discussed), indicating Warner's powerful and magnetic energies. The silent screen actress, Lillian Gish, apparently stated that, "Cheiro was the sexiest man I ever met" (Carr, 2002, back cover), whilst another palmistry client, William Pirrie (owner and builder of the ill-fated ship, the Titanic), described Cheiro as, "... a beefy man with dark, wavy hair" (Matsen, 2008, 64).

The Sun is conjunct Saturn in the tenth house and shows Warner's determination to be special and to be acknowledged as important and successful. It reveals self-discipline as well as an iron will to succeed and above all desiring authority, glory and recognition. Warner, in his guise as 'Cheiro', certainly achieved that ambition as a palmist and seer.

However, it did not last and later in life he was involved in other business ventures, some of which brought him notoriety of a sort he might have anticipated but surely would not have desired. For example, when he was in his early forties, the *New York Times* reported in 1909 that he had been accused by two American women of stealing valuable stocks from them. The newspaper reported that Warner was not only charged with embezzlement but also that his sumptuous offices, where he owned and edited *The American Register* newspaper, and conducted a bank and other enterprises to which Americans loaned capital, were now bare and empty, as scores of creditors descended and seized everything (http://blog.museumoflondon.org.uk/the-champagne-years – *New York Times*, 07/01/1909).

The following year, in August 1910, Warner was subject of newspaper headlines yet again, when the *New York Times* reported 'Cheiro A Bankrupt: Palmist Who Became Broker Has Liabilities of $215,000, Assets $50 (http://blog.museumoflondon.org.uk/the-champagne-years – *New York Times*, 03/08/1910). This was certainly not the type of recognition he sought and craved.

AESTHETICS, PLEASURE AND STYLE

The MC in Libra suggests that Warner would have most enjoyed and succeeded in a career where art, beauty, design and partnerships were significant, since all these areas are associated with Libra and its ruling planet Venus. Being able to exhibit qualities of charm and grace as well as good taste and manners would have been important to him and part of his popularity was probably due to his courteousness to others. It was once said of his manners as a young man (aged about 21) that his "courtesy of manner would do credit to the Court of St James" (Wiley, 2016, 63), which is in keeping with the graceful nature of Venus. Certainly, he flourished in his role as Cheiro the palmist and seer, where the partnership situation was fulfilled by acting as confidant for his clientele when discussing their lives through hand-readings.

He nurtured the artistic side of his nature, for example, in designing the 'set' for his palmistry work; creating a dramatic setting through atmosphere and mood, where he would read the palms of his clients, many of whom were in artistic professions, such as the actresses Lillian Gish and Sarah Bernhardt. He revelled in creating an atmosphere whenever possible. For example, in 1893, a reporter visited his flat at Fifth Avenue where the reception room had sumptuous sage-green drapes along with gold and white furniture, a red Buddha and Persian carpets on the floor (Wiley, 2016, 291).

Libra is also associated with inequality and justice, in that it strives for balance, especially in business and personal partnerships. Certainly, justice featured in Warner's life when he found himself in court on two separate occasions; once where he was claiming compensation, and once when he was accused (and convicted) of embezzlement.

ASSERTION AND MOODINESS

Mars is square the MC, indicating that Warner was competitive and even wilful in his business relationships and career and could be assertive and enterprising. Sometimes he seems to have been too enterprising for his own wellbeing! Mars in Cancer reveals that he was sometimes emotional and had sensitive traits that may have been helpful to him when reading the palms of his clients. His wife once said of him, "The level of his sensitivity was so finely tuned that he could lock into the personal electro-magnetic force field of each individual and view the collected images of his past, present and future" (Carr, 2002, 10). Anyone with such a nature was likely to have also been unpredictable and moody, and this is shown astrologically in Warner's chart by not only the position of Mars in Cancer in the area of marriage, the (seventh house), but also by Uranus, which has its own erratic qualities.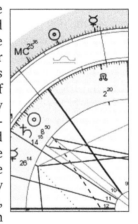

The Mars in Cancer position also suggests that Warner could be prickly and touchy at times, as the nature of Cancer can be moody whilst Mars is angry and headstrong. This may have influenced the events that caused him to be arrested and sentenced to prison (although, as we have seen, he fled before he could be arrested). He wrote that Scorpio's "… at some stage in their career, escape being attacked by calumny of scandal" (Cheiro, 1980, 318). There was plenty of scandal in Warner's life, but there may have been other scandals from which he escaped unscathed. He also wrote of the male Scorpio's domestic life that "… the men are inclined to be dogmatic, and expect to rule" (ibid); perhaps he was reflecting on his own domestic life and his assertive nature.

The position of Mars in Cancer also indicates that he could be enterprising within the home, since the nature of Mars is initiating and Cancer is associated with domestic life. This is borne out certainly in his final years when he lived in Hollywood and worked from home, writing screenplays (none of which were ever performed), as well as operating a consultation practice for palmistry, albeit it on a much smaller scale than previous years, when he was at the height of his success. Nonetheless, he still attracted clients, even after having been unmasked as an embezzler. His personal charm must have been considerable.

A LIFELONG PARTNER

The seventh house is the area which governs partnerships and marriage, and Warner married Katie Hartland (usually referred to as 'Mena') in St Helier, Jersey, in 1920, when he said he was 53, although he was actually 54 at the time (marriage certificate, St Helier, Jersey), having apparently gauged from his astrological and numerological knowledge that he would marry late in life. However, as a young man and member of an alleged anti-marriage society, he must have initially doubted that he would ever marry (Cheiro, 1931, 351). The couple lived for a while in Ireland in a beautiful and extravagant Georgian home called Prospect House, situated in Offaly.

Before they married, both had led very different lives until Mena apparently read in the *Daily Mail* that 'Cheiro' was seriously ill with double-pneumonia and was not expected to live. Any relatives reading the newspaper article were instructed to go to Devonshire Lodge, London, without delay (Cheiro, 1931, 352). Poignantly, no relatives came to visit Warner but Mena did, and when "she reached London and took charge of me like it was the most natural thing in the world ... I had a long hard fight for life; she nursed me day and night" (ibid). Her actions showed how much she loved him and that she could be caring, practical and reliable, such are the qualities of her Sun sign, Taurus.

At this point in his life, Warner was without control and freedom, which must have irked him since, up until then, he had always enjoyed both. He claimed in his memoirs that he originally met his wife when she was a sixteen-year-old client, and he had apparently predicted that she would marry twice and that her second husband would be somebody that she had met many times before (Cheiro, 1931, 351). Warner stated that he was taken with the teenager's beauty at their initial meeting and described her as "... a young girl whose small and beautifully formed hands attracted me even more than she did herself" (ibid).

Warner had also apparently predicted that Mena would lose her first husband in a mysterious way and would be prevented from marrying a second time for a long while, but eventually would overcome all challenges and would marry again (Cheiro, 1931, 351). Certainly, her first marriage was unusual. Mena married Henry Archibald Hartland in 1899, when she was seventeen and, in 1900, bore him a son called Jack. By 1902, they were all living in America, yet not together – Mena and Jack lived in Boston and Henry in New York, where he worked as a shipping clerk (https://horusastropalmist.wordpress.com).

Natal chart (time of birth unknown) for Katie Florence (Mena) Warner, née Bilsborough

In 1902, however, Mena was apparently informed that Henry had gone missing and later was told he had died (ibid). By some curious twist of fate, Henry was also told (before he went 'missing') that Mena had mysteriously disappeared (ibid). By the time of his registration for the US Draft for World War I, Henry gave his next of kin as Harriet Hartland, who was living with him at the same address.

By this time, Mena and Jack had returned to England where she had to wait for the statutory seven years before her husband, Henry, could be officially proclaimed dead, leaving her free to remarry (Cheiro, 1931, 352). Her marriage certificate to Warner reveals that she gave her status as 'widow' at the age of 37. Of course, these events were not written down until 1931, long after the events they described and therefore we have no way of knowing whether they are true or whether they were embellished to make them more interesting for Warner's readers.

Warner probably met his match in Mena, since her natal chart reveals that she had a stellium (see glossary and also box on previous page) of planets in Taurus, which indicates loyalty as well as strength of mind and will – just like Warner's own nature.

Apparently, Warner felt reassured by his wife's presence, feeling that "he could relax, undisturbed by major worries or trivial details" (Carr, 2002, 119), which demonstrates the stressful Moon Virgo position in his chart, as well as the free-spirited side to his nature that did not wish to shoulder responsibilities and avoided accountability, where and when he could.

Warner benefited from Mena's artistic and creative skills as she illustrated the front cover for his book, *True Ghost Stories*, and gives her name as 'Countess Hamon' on the front cover as the designer, showing that they worked together in a business partnership and presented themselves in the same way, both claiming titles for themselves, presumably in order to impress others.

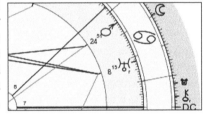

Returning to the area of the seventh house in Warner's chart, we can see that both Mars and Uranus are in the area of marriage and partnerships (see box above). Mars is in fall (see glossary) when positioned in the sign of Cancer. This suggests that in marriage Warner could be headstrong and passionate, perhaps even angry and volatile at times, such is the nature of Mars when in the sign of Cancer (as discussed earlier) and it also reveals a tendency towards moodiness.

The debilitated energy of Mars in Cancer also suggests an inconsistent sexual quality. Whilst Warner may have been amorous and even displayed bouts of promiscuous behaviour, there may at times also have been bouts of sexual problems.

Uranus in the seventh house suggests that friendship and truthfulness from his partners would have been important to him and he needed a partner who was also exciting and unique. A sense of freedom and openness in his relationships would also have been an important part of his marriage, as it provided him with a sense of mental and physical space. Deviation and experimentation are also associated with Uranus, so he probably enjoyed those relationships that offered detachment and impersonality. Given his alleged friendship with Oscar Wilde (*Chicago Examiner*, January 10th, 1909, Front page), he may have had homosexual relationships as a younger man. Uranus in Cancer also shows that, at times, Warner could have displayed unpredictable and temperamental moods, as the nature of Uranus can also be erratic and unexpected, although perhaps this was due to his ill health in later years, along with his growing dependency on alcohol.

Warner seems to have been immensely proud of his wife and respected her for her own achievements and talents. He said of her that she had an eventful and unusual career, and recognised her aptitude for chemistry (Cheiro, 1936, 354). A marriage partner who was independent and original is symbolised in Warner's natal chart with Uranus positioned in the seventh house (as previously discussed). This planet is associated with uniqueness, but also technology and science. This is especially pertinent to Mena as she was scientifically inclined. She and Warner had a laboratory when they lived in America, called Hamon Products Laboratories, where she developed a new process that helped to preserve bananas. These fruits do not travel well and were often damaged in transport, so any method that helped preserve them should have made a great deal of money for their inventors (http://blog.museumoflondon.org. uk/the-countess-chemistry-and-bananas/Behlan). This shows that Mena had her own interests. Something her husband would have appreciated, since he disliked partners being over-dependent in his own relationships. Nonetheless, it seems that Hamon Products Laboratories was unsuccessful as a banana preservation business; as there is no mention of their achievements anywhere, and it is another example of Warner's projects that do not flourish.

FIDELITY

Mena's loyalty may well have bordered on the excessive in some respects, for she played along with her husband's fantasies and may even have added to them. For example, she describes herself as 'Countess Mena', a completely fictional construct, and seems to have allowed her husband to write about her life with him in a way that was speculative, to say the least. Of course, it may have been that if they did indeed meet when she was a teenager and Warner was at the peak of his career as 'Cheiro' when they married later, he may have wanted to convince her that he was as financially secure as he was when she first met him.

Warner was extravagantly generous to Mena when they married and she possessed a large collection of designer clothes. Nonetheless, after her husband's death, she discovered that he was heavily in debt. Clearly, even in later life, Warner had not learned to accept his limitations and not only deceived himself but also his wife as to the reality of their financial situation. Warner had experienced a profound fall from grace; as a young man he had plenty of money that allowed him to court high society, as he had inherited a fortune from a relative. Yet he gambled, embezzled and deceived, losing himself in a mixture of recklessness and fantasy. For example, his decision to go to America with Mena was founded on the idea that producers there would fund his screenplays. This never happened, though, and he had to return to practicing palmistry again. It must have been deeply disappointing.

MAGNETISM, EMPOWERMENT AND MYSTERY

Returning to the powerful opposition aspect created between the Sun and Pluto, the energy between the two planets in Warner's chart suggests that he had intense relationships and was close to people in positions of power. He had the ability to maintain a confidence if he wanted to. Although, as we have seen through the example of blackmail, the dark and corrupt nature of Scorpio/Pluto came into its own, since Warner abused his position of confidentiality and trust with some of his clients, revealing how pathological and vindictive he could be.

Returning to people in positions of power, Warner claimed that he was an advisor to royalty, including King Edward VII, King Leopold of Belgium and Nicholas II, Czar of Russia. He also acted as seer to famous writers, such as Mark Twain and Oscar Wilde. Successful theatre actress, Sarah Bernhardt, visited Warner for palm readings, and an article about this appeared in *The Stage* magazine (14/07/1892, 9). Apparently, Cheiro explained to her that her palm held a distinctive mark, which indicated she was unique in some way. The same article goes on to inform readers that Cheiro was about to embark on a palmistry tour in Eastbourne, England. He had great skill in combining intuition, flattery and self-advertisement.

In his *persona* as 'Cheiro', Warner was not without his own sense of drama in appearance. Supposedly, at one point in his life as a younger man, when conducting consultations at his home, he'd adorn face powder and stage makeup and rouged his lips (Matsen, 2008, 64). This may have been simply to create a sense of the dramatic. Apparently, Warner also created a theatrical ambience by reading palms in "a dimly lit chamber" where his clientele had to sit "at a black-lacquered table lit by a single candle" (ibid). However, wearing rouge on the lips, and wearing makeup would also have given the impression – whether or not he self-identified as gay – that he was indeed homosexual (Hirschfeld, 2000, [1913], 823).

Warner was enamoured with playwright, Oscar Wilde, and claimed to have read his palm and predicted his eventual downfall, but there is another interesting connection between Warner and Wilde. The national press frequently observed that Wilde's followers wore striking makeup, including powder and rouge, to show they were affiliated with the author, and covertly indicate that they were gay, which at that time was still illegal. If Warner did identify as being gay at this time, it must have been very difficult for him and may account for why he was so secretive, weaving fantasies about his life so that his clientele and readership remained loyal to him.

Warner, at times, could execute tremendous self-control in not revealing private information (both his and that of others, for example; his wife, Mena) which is indicative of Pluto's determined energy. Hence, when he was alive, he was able, for the most part, to mask areas of his life that he did not want people to know about.

Other people in positions of power clearly respected and trusted the palmist in him as they recommended him to other acquaintances and possible clients. It also suggests that Warner took pride in his work and in being intimate with those in positions of authority and influence. However, when it suited him, he could cynically abuse this knowledge in the pursuit of money.

Pluto has the ability to illuminate the hidden, the secret and the taboo in society. It is unsurprising, therefore, that Warner was naturally able to use astrology, numerology and palmistry as occult practices to help reveal and permeate psychological profiles. His intuition and psychic ability would have enabled him to infuse his client's profiles. He had a great inner strength and had a capacity to transform his own life, as well as the lives of others; such is the powerful and strong energy of Pluto.

LORD OF KARMA

Saturn is opposing Pluto in the natal chart and indicates that Warner had an obsession with control – qualities associated with these planets – as well as being calculating and ruthless. It is possible that he was also controlling in his home as an adult; perhaps employing vast numbers of servants at his home in London was one way he could have many people doing his bidding unquestioningly.

As a child, he may have found his father disciplined and intense (as discussed earlier), as Saturn is associated with both authority and authoritarian figures. Saturn's nature is stern and creates barriers, particularly when in opposition to another planet. Saturn in the tenth house not only indicates responsibility, but also eventual success, as the nature of Saturn is deliberate and slow.

Other characteristics of Saturn include challenges, limitations and longevity and because Saturn is at home in the tenth house in Warner's natal chart, it indicates that his standing in society was successful; bringing with it status, hard work and responsibility. It is an ambitious and materialistic position and it can also indicate a 'fall from grace,' especially if this was caused by impulsiveness and irresponsibility.

This was borne out several times in Warner's life through the examples of embezzling money from two of his clients, as well as the liquidation of the Threadneedle Syndicate. Although he could reach authority and status (Saturn) as director of various companies, he did not hold on to such positions for very long and his tenure often ended in disgrace and debt.

Some of the significant transits that Warner was experiencing leading up to and at the time of his passing included:

• Transiting Pluto in the seventh house, trine natal Mercury
• Transiting Uranus in the fourth house, opposing natal Sun
• Transiting Jupiter in the first house, conjunct natal Venus on the ascendant

DEATH AND DECAY

Transiting Pluto in the seventh house of marriage and partnerships indicates that Warner's relationships probably became more intense as he grew older, and also that privacy and confidentiality were more important to him. Perhaps this was because he had indulged in so much deception that he did not wish it to be disclosed. At times, he may have felt that he was losing control and also any power he had in his marriage, due to his ill-health and being faced with his own mortality. Mena gave up some of her work and, with the assistance of a nurse, cared for him in his final days.

Mena was no stranger to nursing as, during the First World War (before she was married), she had been a nurse attached to a unit in northern France (Carr, 2002, 120). Apparently, Warner "... was a good patient, although, naturally, he chafed a little at the increasing restrictions imposed upon him" (Carr, 2002, 177).

Nonetheless, he was still mobile enough to leave the house occasionally, although his behaviour had become more unpredictable and erratic. Apparently, he had begun drinking heavily and at night would walk the streets of Hollywood, mumbling to himself (Wiley, 2016, 721). In his last hours, Warner was found by police; unconscious and sprawled out on a street corner (ibid), hardly the final ending he would have anticipated or desired.

Warner was under contract to finish some books he had been commissioned to write, one being an autobiographical book titled: *Fate in the Making; Revelations of a Lifetime,* which was published in 1931. Transiting Pluto was trine Mercury and indicates that, although he was weak and in poor health in his last few years with a combination of diabetes, cirrhosis of the liver and heart disease, he nonetheless demonstrated that he was still determined, and looking ahead to the future. He ensured that his final books were all completed; *Real Life Stories* was published in 1934, *Romances of the World's Greatest Occultists* in 1935 and in his last few months he finished *You and Your Star* (Carr, 2002, 177).

According to the death certificate, Warner's death was due to a heart attack and this is interesting, with regards to the aspect of transiting Uranus opposing the Sun, in medical astrology terms. This is because the Sun rules Leo in the natural (*see glossary*) zodiac and represents the heart. Uranus disrupts and changes the status quo. The aspect created between transiting Uranus opposing the Sun is an indication of Warner's fatal heart attack.

The transit of Uranus opposing the natal Sun not only suggests death from a heart attack but also that Warner is likely to have suffered diabetic and respiratory difficulties. As well as cirrhosis of the liver and heart disease, Warner had also experienced bouts of pneumonia and he had described this for people born on the 1st November, stating that those Scorpio's are likely to have ill-health connected with lungs and bronchial tubes (Cheiro, 2009, 249). His determined Scorpio nature shows his tremendous capacity for overcoming illnesses and crises in his life.

Transiting Uranus was in the fourth house (the area which corresponds with the family and home life) when Warner died. This is an indication that, in his last year, unexpected changes had to be made in the home and family. For example, Mena had to employ a nurse to help her care for him, whilst she had to visit her son Jack (from her first marriage), who was in a mental hospital. He had been a successful musician but unfortunately had an accident that occasioned severe head injuries which resulted in various long mental health issues.

The disruption and unexpected events at this time in the Warner household are indicative of the nature of Uranus. It created distance between the family, with Warner somewhat housebound through physical ill-health, his step-son temporarily living in a mental hospital due to his head injuries, and Mena having to divide her time between caring for her husband and visiting her son in hospital. This shows the detachment and unsettlement that Uranus characteristics can bring.

Transiting Jupiter was conjunct Venus on the ascendant, and this was particularly significant to Warner in terms of his health, as it suggests that, in the latter stage of his life, he had a tendency to undertake anything; even if it was likely to be too much for him. It warns – and Warner must surely have been aware of this – that immoderation and overindulgence would eventually play a significant part in his health. This is borne out by Jupiter (ruler of Sagittarius) which rules the liver and pancreas in medical astrology. Warner's heart was weakened by an overload, possibly by an excess of rich food (which would have damaged his pancreas and perhaps hastened the onset of diabetes), while his liver was weakened by an excess of alcohol.

The aforementioned aspect suggests that Warner was still confident he could push himself to the extreme (which we see in the above example of him writing his last book three months before he died) and that he always saw life with confidence and optimism – such is the nature of Jupiter – despite his terminal illnesses. It has been observed that the aspect in Warner's natal chart, Sun quincunx Neptune, can be an indicator of "overindulgence in alcohol ... can have an adverse effect on the health too" (Sakoian, 1972, 11). This is because the Sun represents our energy and vitality, whilst Neptune is associated with alcohol (as well as drugs and medications), and the quincunx aspect of 150 degrees creates a challenging energy, which generally impacts negatively on our health in some way.

Whatever his flaws, William John Warner lived his life with colour, gusto and zest. He was driven by a strong work ethic and a burning desire to be influential and successful in society. He befriended those of distinction and eminence in high society as a palmist, relishing the special relationships he had with them. Later generations thrived on his books and even today he remains a pioneer in the work of palmistry, although during his lifetime it was considered a precarious way to earn a living. Nonetheless, he made it acceptable in high society. He was not always honest in his various business dealings and paid the price by narrowly escaping his prison sentence and going on the run. After his disgrace, he could not rely on palmistry to the same extent as previously to earn an income and ventured into other businesses. He was determined, restless and secretive by nature as well as opportunistic and self-promoting. Yet his influence lingers on, and perhaps that was the real prize he sought so doggedly in life.

ACKNOWLEDGEMENTS, CREDITS AND REFERENCES

Rodden Rating 'A'
William John Warner natal chart: 10.53am, LMT, 01/11/1866, Bray, IRE.
6w06, 53n12.

Probate and Wills Register: (1948, 69)

Birth Certificate: for Katie Florence Bilsborough born on 26/04/1882 – Certificate number: BXCH 326765. General Register Office, Merseyside, UK, PR8 2JD.

Marriage Certificate: Extract from The Register of Marriages, of the Parish of St Helier in the Island of Jersey: Volume 23, 29, No. 87 – Documentation of Marriage between Louis Le Warner Hamon & Katie Florence Mena Hartland née Bilsborough on 15th April, 1920. Married at Office of the Superintendent Registrar by license.

THANKS TO

Beatrice Behlan: Senior Curator of Fashion and Decorative Arts at the Museum of London, for copy of Cheiro's obituary.
Johnny Fincham: Author, hand-analyser and lecturer, for information on Cheiro and palmistry.
Barry H. Wiley: Author, for sharing Count W. Le Warner Hamon's death certificate.
Oak Ancestry, for Baptist and Parish Records, for the Warner family as well as newspaper articles and additional support and general enthusiasm.
Assistant Curator at the Henley River and Rowing Museum.
Principal Librarian at the Royal Geographical Society.
Anna Baghiani: Library Assistant, Education Officer, Société Jersiaise, for research on 'Count and Countess Warner's' time spent in Jersey.

BOOKS

Carr, A. (2002) *Cheiro: Prophet of the End of the Times.* Carrino Publishing, Canada.
Cheiro. (2013) *Cheiro's Astrology.* Diamond Pocket Books (P) Ltd.
Cheiro. (1931) *Fate in the Making – Revelations of a Lifetime.* Harper & Brothers Publishers.
Cheiro. (1986) *Cheiro's Language of the Hand.* Arrow Books.
Cheiro. *Cheiro's Memoirs – The Reminiscences of a Society Palmist.* Kessinger Publishing's Rare Mystical Reprints. Originally published 1912, by William Rider and Son Ltd.
Cheiro. (1980) *The Cheiro Book of Fate and Fortune.* Hamlyn Paperbacks.
Cheiro. (2009) *You and Your Star.* Orient Paperbacks.
Clifford, F.C. (2002) *Palmistry 4 Today.* Rider Books.
Eckley, G.A. (2007) *Maiden Tribute: The Life of W. T. Stead.* Xlibris Corporation.
Hamon, L. (1895) *If Only we Knew and Other Poems.* Leopold Classic Library-On Demand. Originally published by Tennyson Neely, F. Chicago.

Hirschfeld, M. (2000) [1913] **Lombardi-Nash M.** (Trans) *The Homosexuality of Men and Women.* NY, Prometheus Books.

Lamé, A. (2017) *From Prejudice to Pride: A History of LGBTQ + Movement.* (Illustrated Edition) Wayland.

Lee Lawless, G. (2008) *The Hugenot Settlements in Ireland.* Heritage Books.

MacLysaght, E. (1985) *The Surnames of Ireland.* Published by Irish Academic Press Ltd.

Matsen, B. (2008) *Titanic's Last Secrets.* Twelve-Hachette Book Group USA, Inc.

Sakoian, A. and Acker, L. (1972) *That Inconjunct-Quincunx: The Not so Minor Aspect.* Copple House Books Inc., USA.

Wiley, B.H. (2016) *Master of the Telltale Hand: The Tumultuous Career of Cheiro, the Greatest Occultist of the Century.* Kindle edition.

NEWSPAPERS

Chicago Examiner Article headline: 'Oscar Wilde Gave 'Cheiro' his Start' by Vance Thompson. 10/01/1909, 1.

The Irish Examiner Article headline: 'Once a Palmist.' 26/04/1926, 7.

The Irish Independent Article headline: 'Tale of Crowded Career'. (Example of acidic humour quote) 26/04/ 1926, 8.

The Stage Archive Cheiro as promising actor. Thursday, 14th July, 1892, 9.

Untitled English Newspaper Article concerning Warner changing his name by deed poll to Hamon in 1928.

Untitled New York Newspaper Article about Cheiro being in New York and having been a member of the Wilson Barrett Theatre Company. 6th January (year unknown).

Wicklow Newsletter, **Vol. IV, No. 1** Article headline: 'Glandaulagh Church Education Society.' 02/06/1860.

WEBSITES

http://blog.museumoflondon.org.uk/the-countess-chemistry-and-bananas/
– Written on 30th December, 2010, by Beatrice Behlan. Accessed on 26/08/2017.

http://blog.museumoflondon.org.uk/countess-hamon-the-last-chapter/
– Written on 10th January, 2011, by Beatrice Behlan. Accessed on 26/08/2017.

http://blog.museumoflondon.org.uk/the-champagne-years/#comments
– Accessed on 26/8/ 2017.

https://books.google.co.uk – Mining Manual Containing Full Particulars of Mining Companies, by Walter Robert Skinner and Walter E. Skinner, published by *The Financial Times,* 1917.
– Accessed on 22/11/2017.

http://www.heronallensociety.co.uk/books-content.htm – Biographical areas of his life.
– Accessed on 27/04/2019.

https://horusastropalmist.wordpress.com/tag/countess-mena-hamon – Henry Archibald Hartland, Mena and Jack – marriage, family, move to America. – Accessed on 02/12/2017.

http://www.johnnyfincham.com/history/ksthill.htm/ – Katherine St Hill information. Accessed on 18/10/2017.

https://www.revolvy.com/topic/R.%20H.%20Naylor&item_type=topic
– Accessed on 01/10/2017.

http:// www.stagearchives.org.uk – Thursday May 12th, 1910, 23. –Accessed on 08/09/2017.

https://www.moneysorter.co.uk/calculator_inflation2.html#calculator
– Accessed on 21/04/2019.

https://www.masonic-lodge-of-education.com/masonic-signet-ring.html
– Accessed on 01/05/2019.

CHAPTER FOUR

Gerald Gardner 1884–1964

Author and Pioneer of the Tradition of Gardnerian Wicca

GERALD BROSSEAU GARDNER was born on Friday 13th June, 1884, in Great Crosby, a prosperous district in Liverpool, England. He died at sea on Wednesday 12th February, 1964, aged 79, whilst returning from Beirut. His upper middle class parents were William Robert Gardner, a magistrate, and Louise Burguelew and he was the third of their four sons. His parents profited from the hugely successful Gardner family timber business and when they died in the 1920s, he inherited a considerable private income.

Due to ill health, Gardner spent much of his childhood abroad in Madeira. He later moved to Ceylon and then to Malaya in 1911, where he gained employment as a civil servant until his retirement in 1936. He developed a fascination for anthropology and archaeology whilst abroad.

In the late 1930s, he returned to England and lived near the New Forest. He became interested and involved with the Rosicrucian Theatre and Players where he met Mrs Edith Woodford-Grimes (also known as 'Dafo') and other people who were members of the New Forest Coven into which Gardner was initiated, and Dafo became his magical partner. Some of Gardner's work included writing material for the eight festivals of the nature year and he also incorporated some of Aleister Crowley's poetry about the Great Goddess.

Gardner moved to London (in late 1944 or early 1945) intending to promote his Wiccan religion. This he did by courting media attention and writing about it, for example, in his fictional novel, *High Magic's Aid*. During his life, he initiated a series of very significant high priestesses including Eleanor Bone, Lois Bourne, Patricia Crowther and Doreen Valiente; all of whom achieved great success in their own right.

WHAT GERALD GARDNER'S NATAL CHART SHOWS

Gardner was born on Friday 13th June, 1884, when the Sun was in the mutable air sign of Gemini, and the Moon in the fixed air sign of Aquarius. Since Gardner's time of birth is unknown, it is necessary to use to use a 'flat' chart to represent an unknown time of birth (*see glossary for flat/noon chart*).

Gardner's Sun sign Gemini and Moon sign Aquarius are both ruled by the element of air, indicating he was a natural communicator, curious and sociable. High Priestess and close friend of Gardner's, Patricia Crowther said of him that, "... he was a true Gemini, though he had no interest in astrology" (Crowther to Author by telephone on 05/07/2016), and elsewhere described him as, "the Mercurial Herald of the Old Religion" (Crowther, 1981, 33). His biographer, Philip Heselton, stated that the general qualities associated with Gemini were accurate to Gardner, "His mind was very active. He read, thought and talked a lot" (Heselton, 2012, Vol. 2, 637).

The duality of Gardner's Geminian character was also described by historian Ronald Hutton, who said he had "... a taste for mischief and, at times, for duplicity" (Gardner,

2004, Expanded Edition, 164). Others remarked that Gardner "… was not above telling untruths" (Heselton, 2012, 641), yet he "… was a very colourful character, kindly with a great curiosity in people" (Crowther, 1981, 33). These descriptions all reveal the inquisitive and mischievous side to Gardner's nature.

Since the energy and nature of the air element which rules Gemini and Aquarius is cool and detached, these qualities of logic and reason were present in Gardner, who may have sometimes seemed to be abstract and distant, since these are also areas connected with the air element. The Moon was in Aquarius somewhere between 9 and 21 degrees on the day that Gerald Gardner was born, although we do not know the exact time. If he was born between 9am and 3pm then there were two aspects created during that time period which would have involved the Moon; these would have been Moon trine Saturn and Moon square Neptune, and it is worth considering both these aspects.

Moon trine Saturn suggests that, in his daily habits, Gardner was accomplished and disciplined, since these are areas associated with Saturn. We see these qualities in Gardner's management of his museum as well as his work as a civil servant. It also suggests that instinctively he was driven towards accomplishment and productivity, which is borne out in his work, not only as a tea and rubber planter, but also in his work as an author and pioneer of the Wiccan movement.

Saturn is in Gemini, indicating that he was serious about learning and possessed natural curiosity, along with an active intellect and a variety of interests. As a young

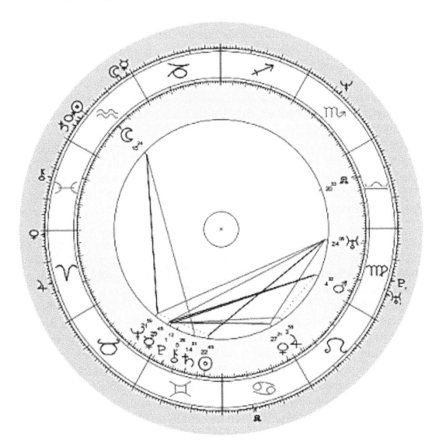

Natal and Transits Chart for Gerald Gardner on the day he died, 12th February, 1964.

child, on his travels Gardner, "… was to discover loneliness and unhappiness and from which there was no escape except into daydreams, and eventually books" (Bourne, 1998, 15).

HOME SWEET HOME

The potential hard aspect of the Moon square Neptune in Gardner's natal chart points to various possibilities. For example, Gardner may have dreamt of the ideal home, since the Moon represents the home and Neptune associates with dreaming and yearning. During his later years, Wicca was his consuming passion. In 1948, his friend Cecil Williamson (the subject of Chapter Seven) had bought the decaying 'Witches Mill' at Castletown on the Isle of Man. He first turned it into the 'Folklore Centre of Superstition and Witchcraft,' which was opened in 1949; with a restaurant adjoining it called 'The Witches Kitchen.'

Gardner acted as a guide in the museum, answering visitors' questions about the various artefacts and was also able to sell his book, *High Magic's Aid*, which at that time was not doing so well elsewhere. Williamson apparently thought that Gardner was a bit of a novelty and could entertain the visitors (Patterson, 2014, 169). Together with his wife, Gwen, Williamson helped Gardner find somewhere to stay and eventually Gardner purchased 77 Malew Street, Castletown, Isle of Man, which was very close to the museum. After the repeal of the Witchcraft Act in 1951, Williamson then renamed the enterprise 'The Museum of Magic and Witchcraft.'

Unfortunately, Gardner and Williamson's relationship deteriorated, and Williamson decided to return to mainland England. He sold the museum to Gardner in 1952, taking his artefacts with him. Gardner was able to use his own collection and continued to run the museum on the Isle of Man for the rest of his life. This may have been a dream home for Gardner in that it became a base, not only for the museum and its business, but also for magical initiation which could now take place at his covenstead, at his nearby home in Malew Street.

The Isle of Man, situated out in the Irish Sea, was at that time fairly isolated. Gardner was not only able to work at the Museum of Witchcraft there, but it may also have provided a sense of being in exile, on the edge or outside, which is in keeping with Aquarius/Uranus associations. In accordance with the duality of Gemini, it is perhaps unsurprising that Gardner had a home not just on the Isle of Man but also a flat in London.

However, this lifestyle was not without its problems, since the museum was only really busy during the tourist season and only of interest to a specific audience. Hence the challenge of the square aspect created by a possible Moon and Neptune aspect in the natal chart and Gardner feeling satisfied in a 'magical' home.

Another earlier example of his desire for a magical home can be seen when Gardner bought a cottage from a friend, the Reverend Ward, whom he had met in Burma. Ward and his wife had set up the Abbey Folk Museum in Hertfordshire (which closed in 1945). The museum was made up of several buildings, amongst which was a sixteenth century witch's cottage (Bourne, 1998, 22). Gardner bought the cottage, relocated and re-erected it in the grounds of the nearby Fiveacres Nudist Club where it was situated in woodland. Here Gardner was able to practice magic and ritual work sky-clad (i.e. naked) and initiate coven-members (known as neophytes).

The Moon also associates with the mother and care-taking figure, whilst Neptune associates with disillusion and loss (amongst other things). From an early age, Gardner had been a sickly child; his care-taking figures changed from his biological mother to a nursemaid and then, at four years of age, to yet another nursemaid, Com, with whom he travelled abroad for much of his childhood.

The energy of a square aspect creates challenges and so, with the Moon square Neptune aspect, it could be said that Gardner's home may have been a place of suffering in the sense that he may have often felt distressed, despite the care he received from his nursemaids and nannies, due to suffering from asthma since early childhood. Gardner was prevented from playing rough games with other children his age, causing him "… distress and discomfort and long hours of enforced inactivity" (Bourne, 1998, 15). Although the square aspect can create challenges, it can also produce success through effort and motivation. We can see this in Gardener's life where, despite the odds of having tremendous and lifelong problems with his health, he went on to accomplish much and achieve success.

The Moon and Neptune are associated with water through their rulership of water signs, which are associated with artistry, psychic receptivity and sensitivity, along with compassion and imagination. This would have influenced Gardner in his work as an author of fictional literature and also in his sensitivity to the indigenous people he met abroad, who inspired his love of anthropology. This placement reveals that Gardner was very much at home with magic and spirituality. He was also a talented artist who created interesting cartoons (Heselton, Vol. 2, 2012, 560–1). He was also interested in photography and used many of his own illustrations and photographs in his publication, *Keris and other Malay Weapons*, (Gardner, 1936, 3).

SECOND SIGHT

Returning to the intuitive and psychic sensibilities associated with the Moon and Neptune, we see Gardner's gift of clairvoyance in the following example. His friend puppeteer, ventriloquist and stage magician, Arnold Crowther, expressed an interest (early in their friendship) in the Craft. Gardner responded, "You will be initiated, but not yet. You must wait for a fair-haired young woman to do that for you – and she'll be damned pretty too!" (Crowther, 1998, 21). Gardner's prophecy came true. On the 6th June, 1960, Gardner initiated Patricia Dawson who then initiated Arnold Crowther that same night, with instruction from Gardner. The Crowther's were handfasted by Gardner later that year on the 8th November, and married the following day, 9th November, 1960 (P. Crowther, correspondence to Author).

Gardner also had the ability to see auras, although he does not seem to have always heeded his own psychic abilities and could sometimes be vulnerable, especially after his wife Donna died in 1960. They had been married almost 33 years. Bourne described Gardner at this time as being, "… like a ship drifting helplessly without a rudder" (Bourne, 1998, 66).

Neptune also associates with dreams and visions, which is particularly significant since Gardner had vivid and prophetic dreams which were sometimes experienced simultaneously by close friends (Crowther, 1998, 39; Bourne, 1998, 11 & 92). Moon square Neptune also reveals his need to escape the mundane through illusion, magic and spirituality.

Astrologer, Charles E.O. Carter, observed that in a man's natal chart, hard aspects created between the Moon and Neptune indicate not only "a kindly, rather easy-going character" but also "a scandal–engendering influence" (Carter, 1930, 77–8). The latter description is also emphasised by the position of the Moon in Aquarius which has the ability to astonish and shock, as well as possessing qualities of ingenuity and inventiveness.

DETACHMENT AND THE UNCONVENTIONAL

Gardner's lunar placement reveals his need to retain individuality and independence, since these are areas associated with Aquarius and its ruler Uranus. It reveals that emotionally Gardner could be cool, whilst intellectually he could be very stimulating, breaking with tradition and nurturing the extraordinary and unorthodox. The symbolism also shows that he felt comfortable around bohemian, independent and unusual women, since the Moon associates with women and Aquarius with the unconventional.

> **OPERATION CONE OF POWER**
> When Gardner lived in London, Eleanor Bone used to drive him down to Christchurch in Hampshire to see Dafo, who told her that the New Forest Coven was not a traditional coven but an hereditary one, and that when they worked the ritual to stop Hitler invading Britain, which was called "Operation Cone of Power" that she participated along with Gardner and Dorothy Fordham (who ran the New Forest Coven) in the ritual. (Crowther, 2010, 61)

Gardner's wife Donna was not especially unconventional however; she was the daughter of a clergyman, had trained as a nurse and later in life had dallied with the acting profession. Although she did not participate in Gardner's magical or ritual activities, she did give him the freedom and liberty to pursue his interests, which involved much travel. This meant he was often away from home which would have suited his independent nature and no doubt he appreciated the 'space' in their marriage that he needed.

There were some occasions, however, when Donna did accompany him abroad, for example, after they were married in 1927, they went to live in Malaya together before returning to England in 1936, when Gardner retired, settling in the New Forest area in Hampshire. She also accompanied him to America to visit his brother Francis who had become unwell.

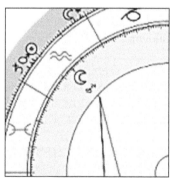

Gardner also enjoyed being around groups of people who enjoyed experimenting with matters that may have been considered unconventional and unusual at the time, e.g. naturist groups and covens, which is in keeping with the experimental nature of his Moon sign Aquarius and its ruler Uranus.

The Moon in Aquarius (*see box on left*) indicates that Gardner's mother was somewhat distant from him when he was a child, both physically and metaphorically speaking, since it is associated with Aquarius and its ruler Uranus which govern distance and space.

Gardner's mother, Louise Burguelew Gardner (née Ennis), "… was a literary minded woman who belonged to the Browning Society." She seems to have been quite liberated and progressive; Moon in Aquarius provides some indication (as previously mentioned) about her independent and reforming spirit. The house, "… would buzz with bazaars and meetings which Mrs Gardner would arrange to further her causes" (Bracelin, 1960, 13).

We also see the distance from his mother in her appointment of a succession of nurses and nursemaids, especially Georgina McCombie (affectionately known as Com), who not only became a mother figure in his life but also took him abroad to warmer climates, not only with his parents' blessing but also their full financial support and assistance to help improve his general ill-health and especially his asthma (Bracelin, 1999, 15).

McCombie was an exuberant and colourful Irish nurse, but whilst they were abroad she would apparently leave Gardner alone whilst she sought entertainment and good times elsewhere. This created further distance and space in the boy's life, thus demonstrating the detachment (Aquarius) from the care-taking figure (Moon) in his childhood. She could be abrupt and authorative with him and at times Gardner resented her manner although they remained friends when he grew up and he remembered her as "… a flamboyant, deep-bosomed, larneying Irish girl" (Heselton, Vol. 1, 2012, 30).

As previously discussed, it is possible that when Gardner was born, the Moon was trine with Saturn (depending on the exact time of his birth, which we do not know). This aspect would suggest he was emotionally stable and appreciated productive types of change, which would have been very helpful to him when moving from country to country and learning about other people's customs and folklore. The Moon in Aquarius suggests he could emotionally detach himself from people and places, perhaps because he felt like an outsider which is associated with Aquarius and its ruler Uranus.

LIVING WITH SUFFERING

It is well documented that throughout his life Gardner suffered terribly with asthma. In medical astrology, the lungs are one of the areas that correspond to Gardener's Sun sign Gemini, suggesting a predisposition to this illness, and it had been with him from a very young age, making him feel set apart from everyone else (Bracelin, 1998, 14). His health caused him pain, fatigue and distress, along with "long hours of immobility" (ibid).

Even in the twenty-first century, asthma is still difficult to control but back in Gardner's childhood, some of the remedies were not only harsh but worse than useless and included emetics made of mustard and even smoking cigars! (Victorian London website – see bibliography). Gardner was fortunate that his family were in a position to afford to try the 'change of air' remedy, which was usually a last resort, showing how serious his asthma attacks must have been.

In medical astrology, the hard aspect of Mercury square Mars reveals some of the other challenges that Gardner was to experience in his lifetime. Mercury represents health and mind, whilst Mars activates and energises. The square aspect indicates that Gardner could overcome many health difficulties, and his asthma was certainly a good example of this. Mercury in Taurus reveals his dogged determination to overcome the physical restrictions.

There are other interpretations of the Mercury square Mars that are worth considering, as they are pertinent to Gardner and other areas of his life. Mercury square Mars can also indicate defending one's thinking as well as writing about weaponry, since associations of Mercury include communicating, whilst Mars corresponds with defence and weaponry. We see this interest in weaponry in Gardner's writing, such as, *Keris and other Malay Weapons,* which he wrote while employed in the Johor Civil Service.

In that article, he wrote, for example, about blades, daggers and swords – all of which are associated with Mars. In the book's forward, Gardner wrote that he hoped it would be of "... interest and assistance to collectors of weaponry" (Gardner, 1936, 3), showing he intended it to have an educational function, something that would have been important to him as a Gemini.

In defending his thinking, Gardner certainly had to deal with opposition both from other witches and members of the public when publicising the Old Religion and Wicca and appearing on television broadcasts. Some members of the Craft did not appreciate him being so open about the subject and at the same time he also had to defend and educate the less enlightened members of the general public, who were too easily swayed by the many sensationalist articles in newspapers etc.

When he was in London, Gardner frequented the Atlantis Bookshop, an esoteric bookshop in London near the British Museum. The original owner, Michael Houghton, had published Gardner's first book on witchcraft, a novel called: *High Magic's Aid*. Gardner also went to the shop when he attended meetings of The Order of The Hidden Masters, a magical lodge group which met in the basement. The current premises is co-managed and owned by Geraldine Beskin who remembers as a young girl (when her father owned and managed the bookshop) seeing Gardner there and recalls, "There stood one asthmatic Gemini called Geraldine looking at another asthmatic Gemini named Gerald" (http://wildhunt.org). This is a wonderful example of Gemini's duality in action!

Astrologer, Wanda Sellar, observed that in medical astrology, Mercury affects the nerves and breathing as well as having potential for mental stress associated with a health condition. Contacts between Mercury and Mars indicate speeding up the nervous system, thus creating nervous irritation (Sellar, 2008, 119), which may explain why Gardner was so restless and constantly on the move. The nervous aspect can be seen in the way his asthma attacks were often stress-related; "... if Gerald was crossed, disagreed with or unable to have his way, an asthmatic attack would appear imminent or did indeed occur" (Bourne, 1998, 37).

Gardner was certainly aware of the effect and impact his nervous system exerted on his life. He once described the raising of energy in magical work as 'nerve power', and stated that this energy can be raised by chanting and dancing. By raising the nerve power in this way it can also act as a form of escape as it helps to induce a trance state (YouTube, 1960s, BBC Radio Broadcast: https://youtu.be/wcKfKdJrmUE).

In keeping with medical astrology, Saturn in Gemini also indicates Gardner's challenges with his breathing, since Saturn is a taskmaster, bringing barriers and obstructions, while Gemini/Mercury are connected with breathing and the lungs. Certainly, in the period that Gardner was born, medical treatment for asthma was nowhere near as advanced as it is today.

Licensed with Permission from PA Photos Ltd.

In medical astrology, Gemini is also associated with the hands, and Gardner often made 'metal jewellery' and 'magical tools' (Crowther, 1981, 28). His Gemini restlessness was often most noticeable in his hands, especially the way he "pushed his fingers through his hair, or tugged at his beard" (Crowther, 1982, 28), his hands "tugging at his goatee beard, or his thumb resting on his chin while his right index finger caressed the end of his nose" (Bourne, 1998, 18). These descriptions display his typical Geminian traits.

At the tender age of four, Gardner began travelling, crossing seas with his nurse to places such as the Canary Islands, Madeira, the Mediterranean and North Africa. If the Moon was square to Neptune when Gardner was born, this holds great symbolism. This is because Neptune governs the oceans and seas and also associates with areas of escape, loss and mysticism. Both the Moon and Neptune are associated with water through the sovereignty of the water signs (as mentioned previously) and it is surely no coincidence Gardner died whilst travelling overseas.

What is even more remarkable is that in world horoscopes (*see glossary*), Tunis – the place where Gardner is buried – is the same Sun sign as his (i.e. Gemini), and just two days away from Gardner's birthday (though not the year), 15th June, 1956, is the date when Tunisia achieved full independence (Campion, 1988, 275).

Neptune in Taurus (*see box above*) carries symbolism pertaining to a magical home and magical possessions. Lois Bourne described Gardner's cottage on the Isle of Man as being like "a miniature museum" containing almost a lifetime's collection of books on subjects such as archaeology, folklore, magic, weapons and witchcraft; while hanging on the walls were "swords, spears, daggers, pikes and medieval blades" (Bourne, 1998, 37). This placement is also pertinent to yet another 'dream home', i.e. the one that Gardner set up in Cyprus after he left Malaya.

Gardner had often experienced vivid dreams, whereby he dreamt of certain places from a bygone age; he came to recognise these were places in Cyprus, and he felt very much at home there and no stranger to the country (Bracelin, 1999, 141). He purchased the site of an ancient temple there which his friend, Cecil Williamson, described as "… a place for Aphrodite without her nightie, coming out of the sea" (Patterson, 2014, 171).

Neptune's energy is adaptable, impermanent and rootless; Gardner would have found adapting to different homes and even different countries quite undemanding. The changeable, flexible and versatile nature of his Sun sign Gemini would have enhanced these adjustments, enabling him to learn new subjects (especially languages) and meet new people, both of which are associated with Gemini.

CLAIMING AN EDUCATION

Saturn (as previously stated) is in Gardner's Sun sign Gemini and whilst it can be quick-witted, intelligent, and sociable, when Saturn is present in the sign of Gemini it produces cleverness tinged with a touch of sarcasm. Gardner's sense of humour could be sharp if provoked and friends remember he had "… a great sense of fun as well as a deep knowledge of occultism" (Burland, 1972, 120), and also "… loved a good joke and would laugh heartily, banging his fist, saying 'Damned good!'" (Crowther, 1981, 27).

Fear and insecurity also associate with Saturn whilst Gemini corresponds with education and knowledge. It is possible that Gardner feared appearing uneducated,

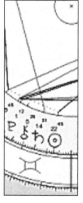

since he had little formal education, due partly to his ill-health but also because of the lack of attention and interest from his nursemaid, Com. He did have a hugely enquiring mind, however, and became enthralled with subjects as diverse as anthropology, archaeology, magic and the Old Religion.

Gardner worked hard to educate himself throughout his life, later collaborating with editors, publishers and those who wrote the forwards and introductions in some of his books; for example, author and Egyptologist, Dr Margaret Murray (the subject of Chapter Two), for *Witchcraft Today*, published in 1954. This would not only have helped his writing but also satisfied his Geminian nature which enjoys 'duality' and flexibility. Saturn would have provided the discipline and effort Gardner required in his studies, and perhaps he valued books and the printed word even more because of his earlier effort to self-educate.

His friend, Lois Bourne, thought that he may have been dyslexic; Gardner had written many letters to her during their friendship and she described his handwriting resembling "a drunken spider crawling across a page" (Bourne, 1998, 91). She even asked him to type his letters to her instead, which was when she began to consider that he might be dyslexic (ibid). Bourne may have been correct in her thinking, as it has been astrologically observed that Mercury and Neptune contact can indicate dyslexia. In Gardner's chart, there is a wide conjunction created between these two planets, so it is indeed possible that he was dyslexic. Gemini has also been observed as a sign that is connected with dyslexia (Stellar, 2008, 215).

Mercury with Neptune indicates a "... fantasy-rich imagination" (Ridder-Patrick, 1990, 57), which can be good for storytelling. This would have been helpful to Gardner in his fiction writing. It also suggests that any working with visual imagery, such as symbols, can be stimulating; something that would have been deeply satisfying to him in his magical work.

The position of Mercury in Taurus would have provided him with an indomitable attitude that enabled him to achieve his aims, since the nature of Taurus is determined and unwavering. He once remarked that "... the most successful people never had any schooling at all" (BBC Radio Broadcast: https://youtu.be/wcKfKdJrmUE), showing the mischievous and sardonic side of his nature. It could also show that he was defensive, and that this attitude was a way of perhaps downplaying his early lack of an education.

Some Saturnian barriers are seen in the difficulties Gardner faced in getting his manuscript for *High Magic's Aid* ready for publishing. Michael Houghton introduced Gardner to a journalist and writer, Dolores North (who was also known as the astrology and ceremonial magician, Madeline Montalban). At that stage, all Gardner had was "a mass of notes he had assembled and struggled with unsuccessfully to turn into something usable," and he had to pay her to help him revise and edit it for publication (Heselton, Vol. 2, 2012, 395).

In Doreen Valiente's (the subject of Chapter Eleven) book, *The Rebirth of Witchcraft* (Valiente, 2007, 41), she discusses her research around Gardner's claims regarding his academic qualifications, since he seems to have given the impression that he was made Doctor of Philosophy in Singapore, and a Doctor of Literature in Toulouse. On making enquiries, Valiente found such claims were bogus, although Gardner had written articles for *The Journal of the Asiatic Society*, and published *Keris and other Malay Weapons*, which suggested to Valiente that he could well have become an academic. Possibly, Gardner felt that the loss of educational opportunity was due to his poor health, and felt justified in claiming qualifications which he felt he deserved. Saturn also corresponds with authority and Gemini of learning so, astrologically speaking, one could say that he was a learned authority figure, even if not actually in possession of two doctorates.

However, it must also be said that, at the age of 53, Gardner *did* receive a doctorate in philosophy for his book, *Keris and other Malay Weapons*, which was a remarkable achievement for a person who had received no formal schooling. The documentation for this doctorate, along with a certificate, is held by the New Wiccan Church International of Canada in Toronto (Crowther, 2009, 74). The entry in Gardener's library reads that his doctorate came from the Meta Collegiate Extension of the National Electronic Institute "… graduating G.B. Gardner with the degree of Doctor of Philosophy, signed Sept 21st, 1937," and museums in different parts of the world used his academic award-winning publication (ibid, and also correspondence from P. Crowther with the Author).

The Sun is creating a square aspect with Uranus in Gardner's natal chart. This suggests he had an urge to be distinct and unique from others, possessing an independent and liberated spirit. Individuality would have been important to him. In his later life, his shock of white hair and pointed beard may have appeared unconventional and unusual at the time; both traits associated with Uranus, along with the ability to surprise and shock. The square aspect would have helped motivate Gardner to achieve individuality by using his determination and willpower. It is possible he may have sometimes felt alienated from the world, since the Sun represents the self and Uranus corresponds with the odd, peculiar and the eccentric, as well as brilliance and genius.

FITNESS AND WELL-BEING

Uranus is in the earth sign of Virgo (*see box on right*), suggesting that Gardner had an original and inventive attitude towards his health and diet. For example, he may have valued absent healing, yoga, and incantations for improvement of health. While living abroad, Gardner would have had to be open to trying different foodstuffs  and, as he had an interest in Buddhism and spiritualism, he probably practiced meditation and yoga to help with his health problems, since these are associated with these two religions.

In 1936, when Gardner returned to his London flat after some months spent abroad, he caught a cold which would not go away. He took the usual conventional remedies of the time, which were unsuccessful. His doctor advised that he could suggest something that would cure Gardner but felt he would refuse it; the proposal was that Gardner should visit a nudist club. Gardner, taken aback, replied, "I'll die there." However, he did attend, and not only was his cold cured but he also made many new friends (Bracelin, 1999, 139). This shows that Gardner's doctor was also unorthodox in his approach to healing and treatment.

When Gardner was in hospital in Singapore in the 1920s, he was apparently diagnosed with synovitis of the knee (a medical term for synovial membrane inflammation in the joints). At that time, the recommended treatment comprised of contrast baths, limited exercise and massage (Atkins, 1922, 948). Patients also had to keep the affected leg perfectly straight, which would have entailed extensive rest, perhaps outside, as he lived in a warm climate. Possibly, this treatment, along with the fresh air that helped his asthma, helped stimulate Gardner's interest in naturism. There is no evidence of Gardner being interested in naturism until his doctor advised him to visit a nudist club in 1936. This reveals that Gardner was open-minded about seeking alternative (connected with Uranus) approaches to health (associated with Virgo) and could be progressive in his thinking.

Gardner's individuality was further emphasised in the way he communicated and thought. In his natal chart, there is a trine aspect created between Mercury and Uranus. This suggests he possessed original and independent ideas and opinions along with radical thoughts. His distinct viewpoint and way of thinking is further echoed through the hard aspect created between Mercury and Mars, indicating his ability to look at things in an original and enlightened way; he could both communicate and promote liberal thinking and also teach progressively.

ACCURACY AND PRECISION

Mars in Virgo suggests that Gardner was industrious and conscientious, probably seeking perfection in everything he did, since the nature of Virgo is to be analytical, precise and specific. Efficiency and productivity are synonymous with Virgo, and in Gardner's natal chart there are two planets in the sign of Virgo: Mars and Uranus (as previously discussed). Craft, technique, method and ritual are all associated with Virgo. This would have helped Gardner, for example, when making his jewellery that was specifically for magical purposes; he made items in silver because it is the metal of the Moon Goddess.

Gardner was very precise about the timing of rituals, feeling that the best results could be achieved "... when nature had reached her greatest potential" (Crowther, 1998, 21). The same Virgoan qualities would have helped him perfect his written words and allowed him to be open to advice from editors; it would also have helped him as a museum curator, when he needed to precisely classify exhibits. In his work as a civil servant, being of help and use is another correspondent of Virgo, while his work as a tea and rubber planter would have required efficiency and productivity. Part of the skill in the horticulture part of this work would have been in assessing the health of the plants, and health (as previously stated) is another correspondent of Virgo.

All in all, Mars in Virgo is a very industrious and hardworking placement. The diligent side to Gardner is again shown by his voluntary work during the Second World War when he was an air-raid warden, filling sandbags in Parliament Square in London (Howard, 2009, 64). He was unafraid of physical work, despite his age and shaky health. This can be illustrated, for example, by the 'back-breaking' digging that he undertook in 1936 in Palestine in his archaeological work. Gardner "... tackled a mysterious pit" and worked on uncovering gate fortifications. Eventually, important finds were discovered (Bracelin, 1999, 136).

WOMEN AND CHILDREN

Venus is in the emotional and intuitive sign of Cancer, which is ruled by the Moon and governs family, feelings, maternal matters (including nurturing), heritage, women and the past; whilst Venus governs relationships, beauty, money and security. The placement of Venus in Cancer suggests that Gardner was sentimental and expressed affection with care and sensitivity, whilst having strong attachments to his family and friends, as well as old familiar places, memories and the past. There is also a sense of the 'Earth Mother' with this placement, as Venus rules earthy Taurus (as well as Libra), whilst Cancer rules the mother. Venus in Cancer also suggests that Gardner was naturally good at coaxing and nurturing, since the nature of Venus is gentle, and Cancer is associated with encouragement and support. He initiated Doreen Valiente into the Craft in 1953, and then promoted her to High Priestess of Bricket Wood Coven. Later he initiated Patricia Crowther in 1960, and raised her to the position of High Priestess in October, 1961 (Crowther, 1998, 40).

Permission of Manx Heritage Centre.

Lois Bourne, Gardner's friend and High Priestess, whom he initiated, described him as having "... two great weaknesses; one was for Machiavellian intrigue, the other for genteel, well-bred ladies" (Bourne, 1998, 27). This shows the wily nature of Mercury (the ruler of Gemini) and the penetrating intelligence through the Mercury conjunct Pluto aspect in his natal chart. The sextile aspect created between Mercury and Venus reveals that Gardner was a skilled communicator who could be very charming and diplomatic.

Gardner remained childless; perhaps his friendships with various women provided him with opportunities to create the family he never had, for example, with daughters and sisters. He once said he regretted never having had a sister (Bourne, 1998, 14). Youthfulness and younger people are associated with Gemini, so it is perhaps unsurprising that Gardner related well to children and did not patronise them. Perhaps this was because he never really grew up; even when he was an elderly gentleman on the outside, he remained a small boy at heart. Gardner's love of heritage, history and the past provided much inspiration when managing The Museum of Magic and Witchcraft. Gardner bought the premises (as previously discussed) from the founder Cecil Williamson (subject of Chapter Ten), and it was known originally as the 'Folklore Centre of Superstition of Magic and Witchcraft.' In his role as curator of the museum, Gardner would have assumed the role of custodian and guardian, which is in keeping with his Cancerian caring, home-making and protective nature.

Museums also educate and help younger generations to learn about past generations and lifestyles, which in turn can inspire them to keep certain customs and traditions alive. The educational aspect to museum life would have been satisfying to his Gemini-Mercury nature.

As the ruling planet of Cancer, the Moon suggests changes, flux, cycles and phases; while Venus symbolises (amongst other things) both money and relationships; it is likely that Gardner's finances fluctuated. However, his relationship with his wife, Dorothea (affectionately called Donna), remained steadfast and devoted. Such dedication is in keeping with Venus in Cancer, indicating that Gardner cherished his wife and was caring and protective towards her.

Dorothea Gardner was born on 24th August, 1893, which made her a Sun sign Virgo and Moon sign Capricorn, revealing that she was practical, reliable and resourceful.

Like her husband, she had the planetary placement of Mars in Virgo, which lends itself to a hard-working nature.

The earth element that rules her Sun Virgo and Moon Capricorn shows that her realistic and sensible nature would have balanced Gardner's more extrovert and generous personality, especially since he could sometimes be a little over trusting, allowing the unscrupulous to take advantage of his kindness.

Virgo symbolises the Corn Maiden and its enjoyment of independence would have suited Dorothea when Gardner was away from home. Their marriage was described as "... a contented relationship," where "... her own interests did not interfere with his" (Bourne, 1998, 32). Her Virgoan nature would have helped her sort the proverbial wheat from the chaff when it came to alerting her husband to those who may have wanted to take advantage of his kind nature. In a way, it is a kind of quality control.

Dorothea's training as a nurse coupled with a Virgoan interest in health must have played an important part in their relationship, especially since Gardner's life was constantly hampered with asthma and he was also ageing, which would have brought with it certain inconveniences and limitations.

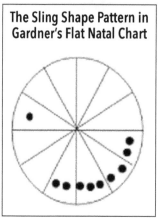

The Sling Shape Pattern in Gardner's Flat Natal Chart

The astrological planetary shaping in Gardener's flat natal chart is called the 'sling shape' (*see box on left and glossary*). This shape shows there is one solitary planet (in this case, the Moon) and the other planets act as a 'bundle-shape' (*see glossary*). It is through the other planets all 'bundled' together within a 150 degree area that the Moon channels its energy.

This configuration is very similar to the 'bucket', but the 'handle' planet(s) holds much more significance. Not only might this person be somewhat obsessed, as in the bundle, but the energy from the bundle of planets is directed towards the 'handle'. This often indicates someone who has a vocational calling or who feels they have a mission in life. Special attention should be given to the placement by house (if time of birth is known) and sign of the handle planet(s).

It is therefore not surprising that the Moon was such an important feature in Gardner's life, both through his work as a Wiccan and in resurrecting the Old Religion which worshipped the Moon. His interest in anthropology corresponds with past ages and people, both of which are correspondences of the Moon.

FIRE, EARTH, AIR AND WATER

In this flat natal chart (*see glossary*) there is a preponderance of the earth and air elements, as well as the mutable mode (*see glossary*). The planets in the air signs are:

Sun in Gemini
Moon in Aquarius
Saturn in Gemini
Pluto in Gemini

The planets in the earth signs in his natal chart are:

Mercury and Neptune in Taurus
Mars and Uranus in Virgo

The strong mutable presence in Gardner's chart indicates a profile that is distinctly adaptable, flexible and versatile. However, he may also have often been agitated, anxious and restless, since these qualities are attributed to the mutable mode (*see glossary*).

The strong prevalence of the earth and air elements suggests that Gardner could build upon and achieve his ideas. His thoughts could be put into action since the air element represents ideas and thoughts, and the earth element is practical and productive.

The weaker presence of the fire and water elements in his natal chart (present only in Venus in Cancer, and Jupiter in Leo), shows that Gardner probably overcompensated in the areas associated with them. For example, the under-represented fire element suggests it may have manifested in Gardner's life by way of an abundance of enthusiasm, recreation and spontaneity. The weaker presence of the water element suggests that, occasionally, he may have found it difficult to empathise and at times perhaps he seemed unfeeling.

Had Gardner's exact time of birth been known then the chart could have revealed whether any of the planets were in those houses that are ruled by the elements of fire and water. Fire rules the first, fifth and ninth houses, while water rules the fourth, eighth and twelfth houses. If any of the planets were in any of these houses, it would indicate the areas of Gardner's life where these qualities would have played out along with the planetary aspects.

In addition to the Sun, Saturn and Pluto in the sign of Gemini, there is the asteroid Chiron, which represents the Wounded Healer. Chiron's placement in a natal chart represents the area in one's life which requires healing and where individuals can assist others to heal within themselves. Astrologer, Judy Hall, in her book, *Past Life Astrology*, observes that Chiron in the sign of Gemini indicates that "… the wound is in making one's self heard. It can affect breathing. Healing comes through speaking one's truth" (Hall, 2006, 149).

The planet Saturn symbolises the Lord Karma and, with the placement of Saturn in Gemini, the lesson is about communication. This placement often signifies an old block on communicating clearly. Fear and insecurity may create physical impediments and the soul must learn to express itself clearly (ibid, 86). Although Hall's book was published long after Gardner's death, he did believe in reincarnation, and may well have agreed that his asthma and other health problems could have been a residue or tremor from a previous incarnation. It has been said that Gardner's memories of his own past lives was impressive; he was able to recall a succession of dreams and strange experiences that extended over a period of years (Bourne, 1998, 40).

There are four aspects in Gardner's natal chart involving the asteroid Chiron: Mercury conjunct Chiron, Mars square Chiron, Jupiter sextile Chiron, and Pluto conjunct Chiron. The aspect of Mercury conjunct Chiron is especially significant, since Mercury is the ruling planet of his Sun sign Gemini which, as we know, corresponds to the area of communication. Perhaps in a past life there was some problem that resulted in trauma concerning communication. For example, in a past life he may have been unable to read or communicate with his siblings or pass on knowledge, since these are all areas associated with Mercury (although of course these possibilities are only conjecture).

ROOM TO BREATHE

In the area of relationships, Gardner would have valued his freedom, liberty and space, together with open and unconventional relationships. This is demonstrated astrologically by the soft aspect created between the planets Venus sextile Uranus. The loving nature of Venus coupled with the independent spirit of Uranus denotes a love of freedom, and a relationship with the unusual. Gardner and Dorothea Rosedale married in London in 1927 and remained married until her death in 1960. His wife was not a witch and never wanted to be initiated into her husband's coven, but she *was* supportive and did not interfere with his pursuits. She was courteous and polite to his network of friends, regardless of their background and interests (Valiente, 2007, 44). Gardner, appreciating individualism, would have valued his wife's different views and the space and liberty she gave him to pursue his own activities and interests, as discussed earlier on.

Uranus pertains to the unusual, something seen in Gardner's personal style. His distinctive shock of white hair and beard was head-turning in his time. Astrologically, in medical terms (as discussed previously), Mercury rules the hands, fingers and the wrist, which corresponds with Gardner's Sun sign of Gemini, so it is significant that he chose to adorn these parts of his body with jewellery.

In 1953, Doreen Valiente was initiated into Gerald's coven, and she recalled him as being, "... tall, stark naked with wild white hair, a suntanned body, and arms which bore tattoos and a heavy bronze bracelet" (Valiente, 2007, 47). The bracelet was decorated with symbols denoting the 3 degrees of the Craft and was certainly a conspicuous personal statement in the rather drab, post-war period of the early 1950's. Gardner also often wore a large silver ring with his witch name, *Scire,* written in the Theban alphabet; again it must have looked very eye-catching, especially since at that time most men did not even wear a wedding ring.

Venus creates a sextile aspect with Pluto, which can suggest money and power, beauty and control, as well as love and loyalty; all areas in Gardner's life that are covered in this chapter. Pluto creates a sextile aspect with Jupiter in the natal chart, which exudes various potentials. For example, it suggests exploration of the 'Underworld' which Gardner did through his learning and application of the occult; it also suggests tremendous control, mastery and power in this area.

Pluto corresponds with healing, regeneration and transformation, while Jupiter corresponds with exploration and seeking; taken together, it shows how Gardner made a conscious decision in his quest to revive witchcraft. It also suggests a fascination with global travel, researching and investigating other cultures; all topics which frequently recur in his life.

In his archaeological pursuits, Gardner would have not only researched but also made discoveries, both activities being Plutonian in nature. For example, he once unearthed some ancient lamps in the Johor Lama defences. He began his international travels at a very young age and saw many different lands during his lifetime, which would have suited his curious, enquiring and infinitely restless solar Geminian spirit.

Secondly, the Pluto sextile Jupiter aspect denotes an abundance of power, secrets, lust and passion, coupled with intensity, ruthlessness and even vengeance. It can also indicate belief and teaching of the occult and the afterlife, with a philosophical attitude towards death. Gardner wrote about his memories of a previous incarnation in his book, *A Goddess Arrives,* and this shows his beliefs about the afterlife and meant that physical death would have taken on a metaphorical meaning; he viewed the spirit as being able to be reborn, even though the physical body had died.

EXUBERANCE AND GENEROSITY

Jupiter is in the sign of Leo and this placement suggests that Gardner enjoyed hosting situations where he had an adoring audience, where he could entertain and share his joy and knowledge with others. He showed generosity of spirit and was "generous to a fault, both materially and by temperament" (Valiente, 2007, 42).

The presence of the Sun in Gemini coupled with Jupiter in Leo indicates that Gardner was fun to be around; and with his Moon in Aquarius, he would instinctively have enjoyed the eccentricity, independence and quirkiness he found amongst his friends and partners.

Gemini collects acquaintances and contacts, while Aquarius collects loyal friends so, with his solar Gemini and lunar Aquarius, Gardner would rarely be without company to stimulate his enquiring and sociable mind and widen his network. His friend, Cottie Burland, (who worked at the British Museum and later wrote about magic and mysticism) described Gardner as, "… a man with a sense of fun as well as a deep knowledge of occultism" (Burland,

Permission of Manx Heritage Centre

120, 1972). Gardner frequented the museum for research and once remarked that witchcraft gave him, "… peace, contentment and joy … a sense of wonder (and) … a sense of companionship" (YouTube 1960s BBC Radio Broadcast: https://youtu.be/wcKfKdJrmUE).

As previously discussed, the aspect created between Mercury (the sign of communication and communicating), is trine Uranus. It is possible that Gardner deliberately adopted a mischievous attitude in order to shock for its own sake. For example, he once invited an elderly gentleman whom he knew vaguely into his home. The guest began bragging about his ancestors, and claimed to be related to an Earl, as well as a Knight of The Garter. He then asked Gardner if he had any significant ancestry.

Choosing his timing of delivery well, Gardner replied, "Well you know, *Adam* was a gardener!" (Crowther, 1998, 44).

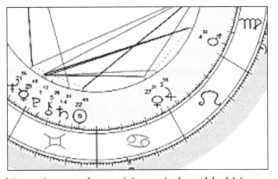

Mercury, the ruling planet of Gemini (and Virgo) creates three other aspects in Gardner's natal chart (*see box on right*); these involve contact with Mars, Pluto and Venus. Mercury is square Mars, suggesting that Gardner enjoyed every opportunity to learn. For example, when he was a child (as we know), he had no formal education, but his curious and enquiring mind enabled him to formulate his own opinions and to think for himself.

As a young boy staying in Madeira with Com (his nanny), he became bored and restless because she partied so much, neglecting her young charge for most of the time. Gardner was inspired by a kindly nearby elderly resident, who would debate religion with him, and this in turn stimulated him into believing that he might be able to "… find his own answers to perennial metaphysical questions. Or he would teach himself to read" (Bracelin, 1999, 19).

Using his initiative and practical nature, Gardner used an old copy of *The Strand* magazine and asked various people to explain each of the letters to him. When he had the letters securely memorised, he "... would practice on the fairy tale published in the back of each issue" (ibid). Before long, he was reading by himself.

Mercury square Mars also denotes a competitive mind and quick-thinking with an ability to put his ideas into action. It also shows he was mentally sharp and quick to communicate directly and frankly.

The hard aspect of the square here suggests that Gardner had a low boredom threshold, so it was important for him to be mentally engaged and stimulated. Mars is creating a square aspect with Pluto, suggesting that Gardner had a compulsion to be 'first', and was very competitive (Mars); it also suggests an affirmation of command (Pluto), which can be seen through his magical work, where sexual power was generated as a creative force.

More significantly, perhaps, for Gardner with this aspect, is the potential to fight for survival, since Mars corresponds with struggle and fight and Pluto with death. This is appropriate as he had suffered relentless ill-health since infancy. The planetary contact between Mars and Pluto heightened in its intensity later in Gardner's life. On 30th January, 1960, Gardner was widowed at the age of 75. At this period in his life, transiting Pluto was conjunct natal Mars; Pluto symbolises death and rebirth and Mars energy and vitality.

After his wife's death, Gardner's asthma attacks increased. In his natal chart, Mars is in Virgo, the sign which denotes health, so it could be said that his will to live was devastated, and he passed away four years later with heart failure (it is thought that asthma raises the risk of a heart attack). The nerves are a correspondence of Virgo in medical astrology and as Mars was in the sign of Virgo (which is also ruled by Mercury); it is possible that Gardner's asthma attacks were triggered by stress and nerves, since part of Mars' nature creates conflict. Thus, when Mars is in Virgo it can aggravate and create tension, triggering an asthma attack in the case of Gardner.

FIXATION WITH KNOWLEDGE

Pluto in Gemini indicates Gardner's determination to learn, and also that he was knowledgeable about the occult. His enquiring nature shows a curiosity about society and the world around him. Mercury is conjunct with Pluto and echoes the theme of an obsession to know. This could include holding secret knowledge, understanding the power of language, the ability to identify others' secrets, a compulsion to communicate and good researching skills. As previously discussed, Gardner's Craft name 'Scire' means 'to know', and in this sense there is definitely an indication that 'knowledge is power'.

Mercury is also creating a sextile aspect with Venus, giving an ease and natural ability. It denotes Gardner's appreciation of art, beauty and language; showing that he gained pleasure from learning and reading. He wrote creatively, stylishly and with an eye for the aesthetic. He also painted several pictures one of which is called '*The Magician*' and is in the ownership of his loyal friend, Patricia Crowther (it can be seen in her book, *Covensense*, 2009, Page 3 of photos section), along with another unfinished and unnamed painting.

Gardner authored several books and created his own elaborate and beautiful book containing the 3 degrees of the Craft (P. Crowther, correspondence to Author). These two examples of his creativity reveal his love for the aesthetic and language which is in keeping with Mercury sextile Venus. Having travelled extensively to many different countries, it is possible that, with his curious and enquiring mind, he would have wanted to understand and learn other languages, this would have educated him further.

One example of this is illustrated when Gardner was in Malaya. He discovered that the local people had a method of protecting themselves from great disasters. Gardner observed, though, that unless the chanted word was chanted with accuracy, it "... either killed the invocant" or made the misfortune "... worse than it would otherwise have been" (Bracelin, 1999, 94). He therefore recognised that, if words were chanted incorrectly, it would have a negative effect on their magical outcome formula, enforcing his belief that detail and intention were powerful in the ritual of magic, as well as the language used.

Gardner also realised that, although the words were carefully enunciated, their actual meaning was unknown to the Malays. He even recognised that some of the chanted words were the same as those used by Arabs and Persians. This shows again Gardner's appreciation of precision, as well as his knowledge of other languages.

Gardner's older brother Robert was also very artistic and drew pictures, "... a skill Gardner had always respected" (Bracelin, 1999, 14). Again, this is in keeping with the skill of art through the aspect of Mercury sextile Venus. Other symbolism connected with this aspect denotes Gardner's ability to communicate tactfully, something that may have been helpful to him both as a teacher and also as a civil servant. Any work in the area of public relations would have suited his temperament, where a combination of co-operation, mediation and even peace-keeping was needed.

INCARNATION AND KARMA

The lunar nodes in a natal chart are an indicator of the karmic purpose of the incarnated soul which, in this lifetime, helps to progress spiritual advancement and development. The North Node denotes which area needs to be developed and the South Node denotes the area that needs to be suppressed. In Gardner's chart, the North Node is in the sign of Libra and the South Node in the sign of Aries (*see box below right*). The North Node in Libra suggests, however, that Gardner could have benefitted from being more co-operative with others in relationships and rather less selfish.

Adaptation could have helped enhance his soul's needs, although this needed to be balanced, since being overly adaptive would potentially make him forget his own needs (Aries), especially in the area of personal relationships (Libra).

The South Node in Aries suggests that in a past incarnation he may have been too bombastic and egotistical. The challenge for him in his nineteenth-twentieth century lifetime was therefore to release the highly developed 'Me, Myself and I'. In doing so, Gardner's karmic purpose was to relate to himself and other people cordially and fairly. Partnerships, relationships and significant one-to-one relationships would have brought the karmic issues to the fore.

Gardner believed in the concept of reincarnation and held that "... if one was a witch in this life, one had been a witch in a past life and would be a witch in a future life" (Bourne, 1998, 40). He illustrated the point by quoting a Buddhist saying,

"What you are, what you have been, what you will be is what you do now" (ibid). Astrologically speaking, the symbolism of the Moon's Nodes, houses and signs reveal what qualities and character-building lessons were achieved in a past incarnation and what needed to be developed in this incarnation as discussed above.

Gardner died on 12th February, 1964, aged 79, having collapsed and died of heart failure whilst at sea on the ship, *SS Scottish Prince*, returning home from Beirut. His body was transported to the next port, which was Tunis and he was buried in the Belvedere Cemetery in Carthage (Crowther, 2009, 72). In 1968, Eleanor Bone learnt from the Tunisian authorities that the cemetery was to be turned into parkland and, upon suggestion from the authorities; Bone was able to have his remains placed in a different cemetery in Tunis (ibid).

It is significant that Gardner returned to a 'spiritual home' on the *SS Scottish Prince*, as Gardner's heritage in part was Scottish. It is also pertinent that Gardner was sailing in the Mediterranean when he died, as he believed he had, "... been very attached in previous lives to the area of the Mediterranean" (Bourne, 1998, 45). As previously discussed, the Moon is symbolic of home and legacy, and Gardner's remains were finally laid to rest in the ancient city of Carthage, a city that was home to the Moon Goddess, Tanith. He believed that between the time of physical death and rebirth people rested in what he called "the Land of Faery" (Valiente, 2007, 44). This seems to have been a concept similar to the Summerland of the spiritualists, theosophists, Wiccans and some Druids.

BEGINNINGS AND ENDINGS

One of the major transits that Gardner was experiencing when he died was that of transiting Neptune square the natal Moon and this gives further significance to the channelling of energy provided by the Moon in the planetary shaping of his natal chart. The Moon can indicate being 'at home' while Neptune indicates being 'at sea'. Each year, Gardner travelled abroad for health reasons, and so will have felt at home travelling abroad.

Because the nature of a square aspect is challenging, it could also symbolise potential tensions in his personal life. Since Gardner became a widower in 1960, it may have been that he was still trying to come to terms with the loss of his wife, as loss is also connected with Neptune. He may have been experiencing feelings and moods which left him feeling confused and vulnerable, and he may have been dreaming about and reflecting on the years he was married to Donna. The sea may have enabled Gardner to connect spiritually with the Divine. A less helpful side of this aspect is that it could have caused Gardner to ignore his intuition, perhaps causing him to make poor decisions, especially in relation to his health.

It is interesting that Gardner was born on Friday 13th. Many people believe that the superstition of this date being 'unlucky for some' arose from the time when all the Knights Templar were arrested on that date in 1307.

Amongst his wide network of associates and friends, Gardner would not have been short of conversation or different topics to talk about. In true Geminian style, he not only acquired much information but also had the generosity of spirit to share this with others. The wider Pagan community are deeply indebted to this knowledgeable man for reviving witchcraft, whilst at times putting his own life in jeopardy by damaging his health. He certainly worked more than his doctors advised, and probably he risked ridicule and threats for being one of the first in modern times to 'come out' as a witch.

In reviving Witchcraft as Wicca, Gardner gave the world the only religion ever created in Britain. Although various forms of Witchcraft are practiced all over the world, Gerald Gardner is responsible for the renaissance of the Craft of the Wise and the rebirth of Witchcraft today.

ACKNOWLEDGEMENTS, CREDITS AND REFERENCES

The Author and Publisher would like to thank Patricia Crowther for her generosity of spirit and time in assisting with this chapter, as well as her graciousness in sharing memories about her friend Gerald Gardner, as well as information and knowledge about the Craft of The Wise.

Thanks to John Parrott for confirmation of Dorothea Frances Rosedale's date of birth, taken from the Texas Passenger Lists 1893–1963 (and the Ennis Family information).

Flat natal & transits charts for Gerald Gardner generated by www.astro.com

Birth Certificate Data: Gerald Gardner's Birth Certificate – BXCG 881099: Copy issued by General Register Office, Stockport, Cheshire, UK, SK1 3XE.

Rodden Rating 'X' – Time of birth unknown.

Gardner, Gerald: Fri 13th June, 1884, GMT, Lancashire, England.
2w30, 53n45

BOOKS AND JOUNALS

Atkins, G.G. (1922) 'Treatment of Chronic Synovitis of the Knee-Joint.' *The British Medical Journal*. June 17th (p948).
Bourne, L. (1979) *Witch Among Us: The Autobiography of a Witch*. Robert Hale Ltd.
Bourne, L. (1998) *Dancing with Wolves*. London, Robert Hale.
Bracelin, J.L. (1999) *Gerald Gardner: Witch*. I-H-0 Books.
Burland, C.A. *(1972) Secrets of the Occult*. Ebury Press.
Carter, C.E.O. (1930) *Astrological Aspects*. L.N. Fowler & Co. Ltd.
Campion, N. (1988) *The Book of World Horoscopes*. The Aquarian Press.
Crowther, P. (2010) *Covensense*. Robert Hale.
Crowther, P. (2002) *From Stagecraft to Witchcraft: The Early Years of a High Priestess*. Capall Bann Publishing.
Crowther, P. (1998) *High Priestess: The Life and Times of Patricia Crowther*. Phoenix Publishing Inc.
Crowther, P. (1981) *Lid off the Cauldron*. Frederick Muller Ltd.
Gardner, G. (1936) *Kerisa and Other Malay Weapons*. The Progressive Publishing Compagny (sic).
Gardner, G. (2004) *Witchcraft Today* (Expanded edition). Citadel Press, Kensington Publishing Corp.
Hall, J. (2006) *Past Life Astrology*. Godsfield Press.
Howard, M. (2009) *Modern Wicca: A History from Gerald Gardner to the Present*. Llewellyn Publications.
Heselton, P. (2012) *Witchfather: A Life of Gerald Gardner, Vol. 1 – Into the Witch Cult*. Thoth Publications.
Heselton, P. (2012) *Witchfather: A Life of Gerald Gardner, Vol. 2 – From Witch Cult to Wicca*. Thoth Publications.

Patrick-Ridder, J. (1990) *A Handbook of Medical Astrology* Arkana Penguin Publications.
Patterson, S. (2014) *Cecil Williamson's Book of Witchcraft: A Grimoire of the Museum of Witchcraft.* Troy Books.
Sellar, W. (2008) *An Introduction to Medical Astrology.* The Wessex Astrologer.
Valiente, D. (2007) *The Rebirth of Witchcraft.* Robert Hale Ltd.

WEBSITES

http://www.astro.com – August 1893 Ephemeris to obtain astro data for Rosendale's date of birth (time unknown). Accessed on 11/08/2016.

https://www.youtube.com/watch?v=wcKfKdJrmUE – Accessed on 28/09/2016. BBC Radio broadcast from the early 1960s, interview with Gerald Gardner.

http://www.astro.com/tmpd/ctmofilePzRk1t-u1206289177/astro_d5eph_93_gardner_gerald_ hp.39158.1762.pdf – Gerald Gardner's astro data for flat chart. Accessed on 11/08/2016.

http://wildhunt.org/2014/03/legends-stories-in-british-witchcraft-history-with-geraldine-beskin.html – Accessed on 01/08/2016.

Asthma treatments: *Etiquette and Household Advice Manuals, Cassell's Household Guide*, New and Revised Edition (4 Volume). Victorian London Publications, c. 1880s.

Domestic medicine can be read online here:

http://www.victorianlondon.org/cassells/cassells-17.htm – Accessed on 16/08/2016.

CHAPTER FIVE

Dion Fortune 1890–1946

Author, Ceremonial Magician, Occultist and Teacher

D ION FORTUNE was born Violet Mary Firth on 6th December, 1890, in Llandudno, North Wales, to Arthur and Sarah Firth. Her father's family had manufactured steel in Sheffield, Yorkshire, from the mid 1800s, although he was not involved in the industry but instead became a solicitor. Her mother's parents were John Smith and his wife Agnes, who was also from Yorkshire.

Dion Fortune was the significant pen name of Ms Firth; others included Violet M. Firth and Violet M. Steele. She was also known as Mrs Violet Evans after she married Dr Thomas Penry Evans in 1927. Fortune became an outstanding British occultist, author, lay psychologist, mystic, teacher and trance-medium. For the purposes of continuity in this chapter, the name Dion Fortune shall be used to avoid confusion, apart from when her other names are used in references and quotations.

Little is known of her childhood education whilst she was living in Llandudno. However, the 1901 Census shows that her family were then living in Mortlake, Surrey, in England. The household included a governess, one Mabel French (Conwy archive services to Author). It was not unusual for a person of her class and background to be home-schooled at that time. At around the age of 21, she enrolled at Studley Horticultural College, then in 1914 she enrolled at the pioneering Medico-Psychological Clinic in London and studied psychoanalysis, just as the subject was becoming established; her training included undertaking a personal analysis of herself (http://www.dionfortune.co.uk). The clinic was formed by Suffragette, Dr Jessie Murray and her companion, Julia Turner. Sadly, there appears to be no archives in existence which evidence Fortune's time at the Medico-Psychological Clinic (either as a patient or lay analyst). This is unsurprising, as record-keeping at the clinic was informal and sparse (Crick to Author in conversation).

The clinic (also known as the Brunswick Square Clinic) was opened between 1913 and 1922; it developed the first psychoanalytical training programme in Britain and offered other forms of therapy to an extensive range of patients including shell-shocked soldiers (Raitt, 2004, 4). The personnel comprised a "wide range of personalities and backgrounds," and a variety of "psychotherapeutic treatments [were] accessible there" (ibid). During this period, the National Health Service did not yet exist. Apparently, Violet Evans enrolled in the newly formed clinic as a lay analyst in June of 1914 (Kuhn, 2017, 342).

In 1916, Fortune left the clinic and enrolled in the Women's Land Army. Later, in 1919 when the war was over, she was initiated into the Alpha et Omega Temple (originally the Hermetic Order of The Golden Dawn). This education in Western Esotericism helped her find her niche, and she became influential in the modern renaissance of the magical arts, running Occult groups and schools, as well as writing a vast amount of literature in different genres on diverse subjects. She died in 1946 from Leukaemia aged 55 and was buried in Glastonbury, Somerset.

Dion Fortune was born on 6th December, 1890, and the time believed to be have been around 02.11am (Rodden classification – www.astro.com), when the Sun was in the mutable fire sign of Sagittarius at 13 degrees and the Moon had just entered the cardinal air sign Libra at the critical (*see glossary*) 0 degrees. Her natal chart shows tremendous self-belief and confidence and the data shows a preponderance of masculine polarities (*see glossary*) comprising of:

Sun, Mercury and Venus in Sagittarius
Moon and Uranus in Libra
Mars and Jupiter in Aquarius
Neptune and Pluto in Gemini

The masculine air and fire signs reveal qualities of assertiveness and confidence; whilst the weaker presence of the earth and water signs in Fortune's natal chart suggest that the qualities of responsiveness and sensitivity were less apparent (although, as we shall see later, she *did* have such qualities). This is because the aforementioned characteristics are associated with the feminine earth and water signs. Her chart shows that Saturn is the only planet in a feminine sign, i.e. Virgo. There are no planets in any of the water signs (Cancer, Pisces and Scorpio); when an element is lacking in a chart, it can manifest itself in different ways. For example, in the case of Fortune, she may have had less control over areas such as sympathy and understanding (qualities associated with the water element) or she may have been slower in demonstrating and responding to both her own and others' feelings.

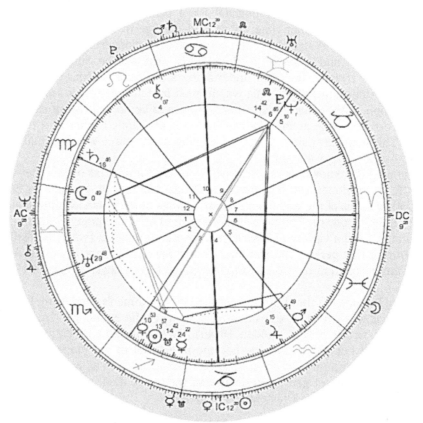

Natal and Transits Chart for Dion Fortune on the day she died, 6th December, 1946.

WHAT DION FORTUNE'S NATAL CHART SHOWS

Astrology is a multi-faceted subject and if we look at the house system (*see glossary*) in Fortune's natal chart, we can see that there are planets present in all of the houses governed by the water element in the natural zodiac: fourth house corresponding with Cancer/Moon, eighth house Scorpio/Pluto and twelfth house Pisces/Neptune. The more emotional and gentle nature of Fortune may be found in these areas, and the position of the planets in those water-ruled houses will be discussed later.

Earth signs are also less prominent in her natal chart, the only planet in an earth sign is Saturn, which is positioned in Virgo (as noted earlier and will be discussed later), and there are no planets resident in any of the earth-ruled houses, i.e. the second, sixth and tenth house. The earth element relates to body and matter, as well as practicality, resourcefulness and security; suggesting that Fortune may have needed routine and ritual to help balance the material and mundane aspects of her life.

The prevalent blend of fire and air elements in Fortune's chart is productive in the world of ideas and imagination but can be less favourable in everyday life. The combination also indicates bursts of volatile energy followed by mental exhaustion; this will be discussed further on, as Fortune did experience several 'burn-outs' which had a significant impact on her life.

Other astrological data in her natal chart indicates that she would need to be careful not to overstretch herself, and this can be seen by the position of the Moon's Nodes. These symbolic karmic points are able to provide guidance on how to live one's life, in order to advance on one's spiritual path.

To illustrate this, in Fortune's natal chart, the North Node is in Gemini in the ninth house, and the South Node is opposite in the third house in Sagittarius. The North Node indicates areas and qualities that should be developed whilst the South Node reveals areas that need to be inhibited.

The Nodal positions in her natal chart suggest that Fortune needed to find a way to fully express herself and had to be careful not to take on too much work. The Sun is in opposition to the North Node and conjunct the South Node. Given that, in astrology, the Sun is the heart of one's personality and the key to self-expression, it suggests that Fortune was very aware of a past life. It also suggests that in her present incarnation she was working through unfinished learning from a previous lifetime, and wanted the opportunity to expand, teach and understand what she had learnt from previous incarnations.

Some of this speculation is borne out when, at a very early age (approximately four years old), she had very vivid dreams, later wondering "...if they were memories of a previous life in some ancient civilisation" (Knight, 2000, 14). It has been suggested that the memories may have been of Atlantis, and certainly this seems to have been her belief since, as an adult, she reported that that the memories may have been of Atlantis (https://www.golden-dawn.com). In fact, it has been suggested that Fortune's description of Atlantis is almost an exact description of the area where she was born – in Llandudno! (Personal correspondence to the Author from the David Conway).

Addressing the modes (*see glossary*) in the natal chart, the dominant mode is the mutable one, associated with the signs of Gemini, Virgo, Sagittarius and Pisces. The planets positioned in the mutable signs in Fortune's chart, are:

Sun, Mercury and Venus in Sagittarius
Saturn in Virgo
Neptune and Pluto in Gemini

Qualities of the mutable mode include adaptation, restlessness and versatility, showing that significant energies were channelled in ways where she could be flexible, be of service to others, and where she could learn and gain experience. It has been said of her that she "was a changeable person as well as possessing a chameleon-like tendency at times" (Chapman, 1993, 19–20). This observation is in keeping with the mutable energy of her chart which shows her ability to not get fixated or stuck in any area of her life, although she could also be unsettled sometimes.

Looking at the angles of the chart, i.e. the AC, IC, DC, MC we can see that the cardinal signs are (*see glossary*) dominant shown by:

AC – Libra
IC – Capricorn
DC – Aries
MC – Cancer

The cardinal signs on both sets of axes suggest that Fortune was ambitious, driven, self-motivated and able to use her initiative, as the cardinal mode strives to assert itself and is not afraid to challenge in certain situations.

Venus is the ruling planet of the chart, as it governs the ascendant sign Libra, suggesting that Fortune sought balance in her life and had a strong sense of equality and justice. Libra is symbolised by the scales and Fortune may have gone to great lengths to find an inner sense of balance by creating a sense of beauty and peace that would help her find her own, unique intellectual expression.

Many people found Fortune appealing and charming, which are certainly qualities associated with Libra. It was said that she could even place people who disagreed with her "… under the spell of her persuasive charm" (Knight, 2000, 27), showing just how charismatic yet assertive she could be when she chose.

The ascendant sign (also known as the 'rising sign') represents the impression we initially give to others, the mask that we immediately present to the world. Fortune's ascendant sign Libra governs areas such as co-ordination, design and style. We get a sense of her flamboyance from author and occultist, Bernard Bromage, "She had the posture of some elected oracle proclaiming the Unescapable (sic) Law. … She was a striking figure. … Her rather plump figure was swathed in a crimson gown of hieratic cut; on her head she wore a black, flapping hat" (Chapman, 1993, 182).

This illustrates that she was aware of the impact her style and choice of colour, design and fabric would make. For example, the colours red and black are very powerful and striking. The curviness described above as 'plumpness' is also a characteristic of Venus.

In 1945, a year before her death, she met with Aleister Crowley. His secretary, Kenneth Grant, described her as "… very old and sick-looking, thin and emaciated. She wore a beige cape and a large, brass sun medallion. She was also wearing a lot of rings …" while under her cape she wore "… a tan shirt and a jacket with panels of suede or leather" (Chapman, 1993, 144–145). This reveals how appearance was still important to her; even when she was very ill, she remained co-ordinated and stylish.

Interestingly, in medical astrology, Jupiter is associated with fat in the body which can accumulate over time. It has been observed that those with Jupiter in the fourth house are likely to acquire "the middle-age paunch" (Jansky, 1977, 145). It was perhaps inevitable that because of the strong Jupiter energy in Fortune's natal chart, she became bigger as she matured (although in fairness, many women do, especially during and after menopause).

Jupiter is trine (*see glossary*) the ascendant, suggesting she was confident, generous and hospitable and destined for fame and success in the world. This is because the aforementioned areas and qualities are all associated with Jupiter, and Jupiter is the ruling planet of her Sun sign Sagittarius.

MR AND MRS PENRY EVANS

Photo Licensed by
Press Association
Photos Limited

Returning to the ascendant sign Libra, it is an air sign and this element needs to communicate and socialise with others for intellectual stimulation. It is interesting to note that she wrote about Libran themes of partnerships, in the sense of love and marriage, polarities and magical relationships, in some of her books and articles.

One of the better-known photographs of Fortune shows her with her husband, Thomas Penry Evans (*see photograph on right*), who has been described as "the very embodiment of manly virility" (Fielding and Collins, 1998, 83) with "a dark, rather Welsh complexion" (ibid). He certainly must have cut a striking and athletic figure; he had excelled on the sports-field and was a rugby captain (*Cambria Daily Leader,* 1919, 5). When he was 23, he was described as five feet, eleven and a half inches tall, of fair complexion with grey eyes and grey hair (National Archives, Army Form B.268A, 1916).

From an astrological point of view, Fortune and Evans were a mirror image of each other, in that she was a Sun sign Sagittarius and Moon sign Libra, whilst he was a Sun sign Libra and Moon sign Sagittarius (www.astro.com – Evans' birth certificate and ephemeris). She was more open and philosophically minded (Mercury in Sagittarius), while he was more analytical and clinically minded (Mercury in Virgo). The mutual attraction and pairing shows that, for both of them, freedom and partnerships were important, and that both had strong ideals and principles. They were both born in Wales, yet may have held dissimilar values and political views, especially as they were from different social classes; she from an upper middle class background, and he originally from the working classes.

Penry Evans' father, Kercy Evans, was a tin shearer and member of the South West Wales Tin Plate Workers Union, who, when his son was young (in 1899), supported a young and radical Liberal M.P. – David Randell (*South Wales Daily Post,* 1895, 3). Later, in 1938 (and after qualifying as a doctor), Penry Evans was invited to Spain by the Republican government to help and advise on the nutritional problems of Spanish children. Evans accepted the invitation (*Bucks Examiner*, 1959, 6). It was the time of the Spanish Civil War and the Nationalist General Franco was about to capture Barcelona. Children there were living with malnutrition, starvation and lacking essential dietary elements. By supporting the Republican government, it suggests that Evans perhaps felt he had a moral duty as a doctor to help save the children, and politically he believed in a system of government that permitted a country to function democratically.

If this *is* correct, it is possible that his viewpoint was largely formed from his experiences on the front line during the First World War. He entered military service as a private in the Second Artists Regiment, and later rose to the rank of temporary second lieutenant in the Machine Gun Corps Infantry (*London Gazette*, 1916, 8598), where he probably saw many traumatic situations, particularly serving in the Battle of Cambrai, an offensive on the Western Front, which marked the first and significant use of tanks in warfare.

Penry Evans moved socially to the middle classes when he became a schoolmaster and then a doctor. In the latter role, he specialised in treating smallpox and tuberculosis, securing various positions of employment in Buckinghamshire, East Ham and Southwark (*Bucks Examiner*, 1959, 6).

Aside from the astrological similarity between Evans and Fortune, there was another similarity between them. They both had lived with conditions which had affected their nerves, she with nervous breakdowns and he with shell-shock. He held a Diploma in Psychiatric Medicine (Fielding and Collins, 1998, 82) and was a member of the Royal College of Physicians. He was a licentiate of the Royal College of Physicians (LRCP) as well as member of the Royal College of Surgeons (MRCS) and wrote about medical issues. For example, in the *British Medical Journal*, he wrote an article about smallpox (bmj.com/ archive 1947, 807). Fortune had been a lay psychologist (as well as undergoing treatment for herself), showing they were both interested in curing the mind, body and spirit, and wrote in varying degrees about their specialist subjects.

Fortune was treated for her mental and nervous conditions, while Evans experienced pain (both mental and physical) during his service in the First World War. For example, proceedings from a medical board in 1917, which reported on Evan's injuries and wounds received in action, documented that he had blurred vision and sore eyes, regularly knocked against people, had attacks of giddiness and was unable to walk straight, as well as having slurred speech and short bouts of unconsciousness (Army Form A. 45A, Proceedings of a Medical Board, 1917). Other reports show that he was suffering with debilities and shell-shock (Army Form A. 45, Confidential: Medical Board Report on a Disabled Officer, 1918), yet he was instructed to still serve with his unit. Penry Evans was hospitalised at least twice during his active service, and was treated at military hospitals in Grantham and London.

People who knew Mr and Mrs Evans described their marriage as going through "a number of phases;" Penry Evans could be "difficult" and "not an easy personality" (Chapman, 1993, 84) – perhaps he was still living with PTSD (post-traumatic stress disorder) from his wartime experiences. However, this still did not prevent him from training, qualifying and working in the medical profession. Others remarked on his "most remarkable speaking voice and a very kind personality" (ibid).

Apparently, the couple had first met at one of Fortune's lectures. Both were mutually impressed with each other's work, and she was adamant that he was a priest companion she had known in a former incarnation (Fielding and Collins, 1998, 82).

In 1919, Penry Evans was living back in Wales and working for the Ministry of Pensions, they had appointed him as an 'officers' friend'. His duties included watching over all matters affecting the interests of disabled officers regarding awards of temporary retired pay, their treatment, and training; to advise and give assistance to the widows, dependents and relatives of deceased officers in matters relating to their pensions and the various allowances (*Cambria Daily Leader*, 1919, 6). Clearly, his responsibilities as lieutenant in the army put him in good stead for this position, and experience of disability himself would have enabled him to bring empathy and understanding to his role. After Evans died, a health department officer said that he could "think nothing but good to say about him ... he was really well liked by the whole staff" (*Bucks Examiner*, 1959, 4). In spite of some problems with occult studies (which are discussed later in this chapter), the Pagan work that he was given by his wife to deliver at the society (which was called the Green Ray) was apparently 'very suited' to him (Chapman, 1993, 84). The Green Ray was part of three major strands taught at the Society of Inner Light (the other two being The Orange Ray and The Purple Ray). The Green Ray embodied nature contacts and encapsulated forms relating to the earth such as elemental and faery traditions (http://garethknight.blogspot.com). It seems that Penry Evans maintained his belief and interest in Paganism, as his death certificate in 1959 documents the name of his house as 'Pan' (Fielding and Collins, 1998, 89). He also worked with his wife on the Isis Formula, an Egyptian ritual work which increased the goddess's strength (Fielding and Collins, 1998, 91). It has been claimed that several excerpts from the Rite of Isis, which appear in the fiction of *The Sea Priestess* and *Moon Magic* derived from Fortune's work with her husband (ibid).

Interestingly, later – after the two novels were published – the author and witch, Doreen Valiente (subject of Chapter Eleven), who was greatly inspired by Dion Fortune, said that Fortune's "fictional books are much more meaningful because there is a lot that is conveyed in fiction that can't be conveyed in non-fiction" (Jordan, 1998, 168). This was certainly true of the Isis formula, which was applied practically in magic by Fortune who also found a place for it in her fictional literature.

Penry Evans and Fortune married in 1927, and separated approximately ten years later, although did not divorce until 1945 – just six months before her death (Fielding and Collins, 1998, 91). She likened the breakdown of their marriage to being "like a leaf withering and falling off" (Chapman, 1993, 84). Some suggested that Evans "suffered himself to be henpecked by this big, powerful woman" (Chapman, 1993, 45), whilst others believed that "the separation between the two of them was amicable" (Fielding and Collins, 1998, 91).

Fortune had strong views on marriage and in 1924 had published a book called, *The Esoteric Philosophy of Love and Marriage*. The book addresses various areas, including 'The Ideal Marriage,' 'The Modern Conditions of Marriage' and 'The Esoteric Teaching Concerning Twin Souls.' One wonders whether, had she written the book after or during her marriage, she might have written differently, having by then had practical experience of it, rather than simply an ideal.

Eight years into her marriage, she wrote in *The Mystical Qabalah* that "A man's soul is like a lagoon connected with the sea by a submerged channel; although to all outward seeming it is land-locked, nevertheless its water-level rises and falls with the tides of the sea because of the hidden connection." (Fortune, 1987, 17). Her observation seems to suggest that a man's spirituality and libido waxes and wanes along with the cycle of the Moon, which in turn has an impact on the sea, which is symbolic of the soul.

The descendant (*see glossary*) is positioned at the seventh house, the area that represents marriage and other significant partnerships. It reflects 'our other half,' that is, the qualities that we project onto other people as well as qualities we seek in partnerships. Aries is the descendant sign (*see glossary)* in Fortune's chart and indicates that she was assertive and could project such qualities in her relationships. She could be forthright in her partnerships and equally would have sought relationships where a person could be courageous, defend themselves and assert action rather than procrastinating.

The aforementioned qualities are all associated with Mars, the ruling planet of her descendant, which is enterprising, headstrong and passionate by nature. Fortune's zealous nature is also shown by Mars being positioned in the fifth house, the area governing affairs of the heart (as well as children, entertainment and creativity).

Fortune's husband, Penry Evans, was, as previously stated, a Pagan and psychic, who also lectured on esoteric subjects. From 1933 onwards, he undertook a great deal of lecturing at the Fraternity of Light, along with his wife and Colonel Seymour. His lectures were advertised under his formal name and title Dr T.P. Evans, MRCS, LRCP and included subjects such as 'Where Mind and Matter Meet,' 'The Healing Gods' and 'Pan Within' (Knight, 2000, 207).

AN INSPIRATION

Another significant partnership in Fortune's life was her magical mentor, Dr Theodore Moriarty, an Irish Freemason and author who was very knowledgeable in esoteric subjects. She met him when she was approximately twenty-four and still studying at the Medico Psychological Clinic in London. Moriarty had been called in to help her deal with a difficult patient whom she was unable to help. Moriarty, however, was successful; apparently, he was dealing with subjects known today as "modern vampirism, allied to psychic phenomena and necrophilia," and Fortune was greatly inspired by him (http://garethknight.blogspot.com).

Moriarty has been described as "a Mason of considerable erudition, remarkable occult abilities, and wide-ranging freedom of thought" (ibid). He published two books on the subject of Masonry: *The Freemason's Vecum* and *Notes on Masonic Etiquette and Jurisprudence,* the latter being co-authored with Thomas N. Cranstoun Day who was another noted Freemason (ibid).

Such was Moriarty's influence on her that Fortune gave up working at the clinic and decided to dedicate her time to researching psychic subjects. She even created a fictional version of Moriarty, named Dr Taverner, and wrote and published a book of short stories about this character entitled, *The Secrets of Dr Taverner*. In it, Dr Taverner ran an unusual nursing home where patients with psycho-physical problems were treated unconventionally.

This was an exhilarating time in Fortune's life, as this was her first book to be penned under the pseudonym 'Dion Fortune'. Clearly, Moriarty's treatments were pioneering and he used his occult knowledge to help treat those patients for whom orthodox methods had been unsuccessful. This shows how Fortune was instinctively drawn to courageous and pioneering people, as shown by the Aries descendant in her natal chart. Apparently, Fortune once remarked, "If there had been no Dr Taverner, there would have been no Dion Fortune" (ibid).

DEPLETION AND SENSITIVITY

During World War I, Fortune was again depleted of energy and suffering from "recurring spells of mental exhaustion" (Fielding and Collins, 1998, 42); a condition similar to that which she had experienced at college (ibid). Possibly, she was working too many hours as a lay analyst and did not receive sufficient support and supervision from her employers.

Another possibility is that she was susceptible to her patients' negative energy. If so, this may have inspired her literature about possession and vampirism. Being a natural healer and psychic as well as having mediumistic qualities can make one especially sensitive to the external environment. Through her natural drive and hardworking nature, Fortune may have unwittingly ignored her own emotional and spiritual health, and this could have accounted for some of her feelings of exhaustion and oppression.

Certainly, in her natal chart there are aspects indicating that she was sensitive to others' auras and energy levels such as Moon trine Neptune and Pluto, which potentially could have depleted her own exuberance and vitality. In her book, *Psychic Self-Defence*, she wrote, "We need to realize that the human consciousness is not a closed vessel but, like the body, has a continual intake and output. The cosmic forces are circulating through it all the time, like sea-water through a living sponge" (Fortune, 1930, 127). This shows her awareness and knowledge of the everyday energies we encounter and produce, and how they can be both beneficial and detrimental to us. It shows that we are not static human beings and that we live in a world of polarities that can impact on one's aura and vitality. The aspect of Moon square Mercury also suggests possible tensions within with her emotions and mentality. The above three aspects of the Moon will be discussed in detail further on.

DAUGHTER OF JUPITER

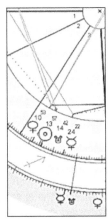

Sun, Mercury and Venus in Sagittarius in Fortune's natal chart (*see box on right*) show that themes of belief, freedom, higher education and learning, as well as philosophy and travel, were important to her. It has been claimed that "when she was a child, she was given more freedom than most girls of that period" (Fielding and Collins, 1998, 19). She has also been described as "a rather difficult child and this could have easily been a result of too much freedom before she was capable of accepting it properly" (ibid). This may suggest her parents felt she was sensible enough not to warrant close guidance and nurture or, alternatively, that they were not all that interested in what she did. Although, when she became an adult, her father at least seems to have been interested and involved in her co-lodge work.

In Fortune's natal chart, Mars is in the fifth house as mentioned before (*see box below right*), indicating that perhaps, as a child, she wanted to be 'first'; the one and only. As far as is known, she *was* the only child of Mr and Mrs Firth, and was born four years into their marriage. Possibly, her parents had other children who were stillborn or otherwise did not survive; and if so, perhaps this was why Fortune was treated as 'special'. We do not know who first described her as a difficult child but maybe some found her psychic and sensitive nature challenging; particularly if they were not of the same disposition. This may have been true of her parents and/or other members of her family, and even her teachers.

It is possible that her maternal grandfather, John Smith, understood Fortune's clairvoyant and sensitive nature more than her parents. He apparently adored his granddaughter (Richardson, 1987, 24) and may even have been clairvoyant or psychic himself. Certainly, Fortune was very attentive to the effects of direct inheritance, and not just those of a past life. "She was remarkably alive to the importance of heredity: 'work on their grandmother' was a favourite maxim of hers!" (Bromage, 2016, 172).

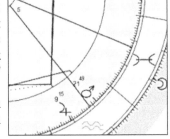

In astrology, the eighth house is associated with inheritance and, in Fortune's chart, Neptune is resident in that area. Therefore, it could be argued that she inherited psychic ability, compassion and spirituality (all associated with Neptune) from one of her ancestors, although this is speculation and cannot be proved. More interpretations of Neptune in the eighth house will be discussed further on.

After her death, Fortune communicated through a medium, Hope Todd, in 1974, revealing that she had been sent to Studley by her family, "after trying to cope with a number of psychic experiences which were disturbing because I did not understand them completely" (Chapman, 1993, 98). The communication continued, "My family became alarmed and then frightened for my sanity" (ibid). It was observed that, when Fortune went to Studley Horticultural College in 1911, she "was not in perfect mental health" (ibid, 178).

These early psychic experiences may have been just one of the driving forces that led Fortune to later want to understand and study psychology. She once said that she "... had attained the greater part of her knowledge of magical techniques solely by a study of psychological principles" (Chapman, 1993, 160) – clearly Fortune regarded magic and psychology as closely intertwined and part of the same thing.

Many children are born with psychic sensibilities but unless those gifts are harnessed and understood, they can be lost as they grow into adulthood, and perhaps even veer out of control. Fortune's early psychic experiences may have included trying to control psychic phenomena, developing mediumistic abilities and cultivating other spiritual gifts. She may have learned from her own experiences how important it is for intuitive and sensitive individuals to recognise their psychic and mediumistic potential, and this was why she made it a crucial part of her teaching when she taught at her magical societies.

Healing was very important to Fortune, who was motivated to help others, "especially those involved in unusual psychological obsessions and pathologies" (ibid). Indeed, it was said that Fortune would have been unafraid to "confront Satan himself in order to save someone's soul" (ibid); showing the lengths to which she would have gone to help somebody.

Teaching is also associated with Sagittarius and Jupiter, and it played an important role in Fortune's life, along with freedom, philosophy and travel (both mentally and physically).

Jupiter is the ruling planet of Sagittarius, and this sign is symbolised by the Centaur and its arrow. By nature, Jupiter is confident, expansive and exuberant, optimistic; thriving on exploration and enjoying growth both mentally and physically. Indeed, Fortune was once described as having an "unconquerable zest for life" (Knight, 2000, 27).

The symbol of the Centaur aiming its arrow high into the air symbolises the quest that drives Sagittarius. There is a duality to the sign symbolised by the centaur being half-man and half-horse, as it indicates a fusion of instinct and intellect. Sagittarius is ruled by the fire element, which gives an instinctive and warm nature to the sign, although at times it can also be tactless, opportunistic and irresponsible.

Horses featured in Fortune's earlier life, perhaps unsurprisingly, as Sagittarius is symbolised by the half-horse centaur. As a child, her only interest outside the home was in horses, and she often attended horse and pony shows, which gave her some freedom away from home (Fielding and Collins, 1998, 22).

Mercury, the sign of communication and mentality, is detriment (*see glossary*) in Sagittarius, and likes to explore the world of ideas, learning and teaching and enjoys discussing beliefs and ideas with others. The position indicates that Fortune could be broad-minded in some areas, as Mercury governs the mind and Sagittarius is expansive.

It also indicates that she was philosophically minded and enjoyed intellectual challenges, seeking the answers to life's big questions, such as the meaning of life. She was once described in a spiritualist journal as having "… an active, intellectually curious mind that speculated constantly on many subjects" (Chapman, 1993, 11).

Details and minutia are less significant to the Sagittarian, as this sign is concerned with the broader vision of life and the higher principles which inform it. Mercury in Sagittarius is less helpful when it comes to addressing the more mundane and practical areas of life. However, Mercury in Sagittarius *is* a good planetary position for management roles where areas such as development and forward thinking are needed, which would have been helpful in her position as warden (see below); helping her communities remain progressive and not complacent. Saturn in Virgo in her natal chart is a very practical and resourceful placement that will be discussed later, when we shall see how this position helped to balance the visionary nature of Fortune with pragmatism and stamina.

UPSTAIRS, DOWNSTAIRS

Apparently, when living at 21b Queensborough Terrace, West London (the community house for students interested in the occult), Fortune delegated tasks to the women who lived there. She was nicknamed 'Fluff' as, apparently, she used to check the rooms; running her finger over surfaces looking for any speck of dust or fluff that hadn't been removed by the person responsible for that task (Fielding and Collins, 1998, 49). This demonstrates her expectation of high standards, even with regards to relatively mundane tasks; clearly she was something of a perfectionist (Virgo) with high standards (associated with Saturn). It also shows her rather Edwardian attitude towards servants, expecting exemplary standards from them. She once claimed that one of the reasons why standards in domestic servants had declined was due to "… the practice of orphanages and workhouses of training most of their girls for that occupation," which was regarded as an unskilled calling (Maloney, 2011, 103). However, when she was in service as a gardener, she developed strong views about how employers should treat their staff fairly, as discussed further on.

THE WINGED MESSENGER

Positioned in the third house, Mercury shows a strong energy for communication and mentality. This is because, in the natural zodiac (*see glossary*), Mercury is the ruler of the third house. It indicates that Fortune had an agile and restless mind and probably found it difficult to switch off; it also suggests she was observant and witty as these are all areas are associated with Mercury. Messages, correspondence and short courses are also connected with Mercury, which is particularly pertinent to Fortune in terms of the Correspondence Courses that she offered to students.

The *Occult Review*, in December 1932, advertised the Fraternity of Inner Light's Correspondence Courses, emphasising that:

- They are for those serious about studying the occult but are unable to attend the lectures in London
- They provide a thorough grounding in esoteric science
- The genuine courses are only available from the address of 3 Queensborough Terrace, London, W2

(Chapman, 1993, 12)

Students undertook a comprehensive syllabus of programmes and lectures. For example, the spring programmes of lectures in 1938 covered subjects by Dion Fortune, Charles Seymour and Dr T. Penry Evans; the latter spoke on 'Spiritual Healing: Its Power and Limitations' and 'The Mental Factor in Health' (Knight, 2000, 237). Fortune's lectures that spring included 'The Esoteric Tradition, Ceremonial Magic, The Esoteric Doctrine of Sex and Polarity, A Reconstruction of Isis Worship' and 'A Reconstruction of the Worship of Man'. Fortune collaborated with Seymour on other lectures that spring while her husband opened and closed the season's programme of lectures.

In medical astrology, the nervous system is governed by Mercury and, if there is a strong planetary presence in the third house, this can generate agitation, restlessness and anxiety. It is perhaps unsurprising that in her earlier life, Fortune experienced what would have been described at the time as nervous breakdowns. Neptune is also in Gemini and this planet and sign are mutable by nature, which is strewn in energy, especially when the mutable mode is strongly developed in a natal chart, as it is in Fortune's. However, in her natal chart, Mars and Jupiter are in Aquarius, which will have helped to stabilise the energy (since Aquarius is a fixed sign), as would the planets, which are resident in the fifth, eighth and eleventh house. These three areas are associated with the fixed mode, which gives a determination and strength, which would help to balance the restless energy and enable Fortune to complete tasks and anything requiring tenacity.

Both Neptune and Pluto represent generations of people and these planets are conjunct in Gemini in Fortune's natal chart. This indicates that she lived amongst a generation of people who were intuitive and sensitive, and who also enjoyed exploration of life mysteries, as well as having to apply flexibility in an increasingly collapsing world. This is reflected by many people's experiences of death and survival, grief and loss during two World Wars.

Spiritualism flourished and grew during the First World War, and its aftermath in England was quickly followed by the Spanish Influenza epidemic which killed millions around the world. Violet Firth and Thomas Penry Evans were typical of two of the people from the Neptune and Pluto in Gemini generation, people who survived the two World Wars and the developments of the early and mid-twentieth century.

BELIEF AND POLITICS, CRISIS AND LEARNING

Looking at Pluto on a personal level, it is retrograde (see glossary) in the sign of Gemini and is in the ninth house in Fortune's chart. This planet belongs to the fixed mode and is more rigid in energy than the mutable mode (as discussed previously). This indicates Fortune had faith (the ninth house has spiritual and religious associations) and a strong will, coupled with a determination to survive and ability to learn from any crises she experienced. Pluto in Gemini also reveals her curious and restless nature.

Fortune may have applied coping mechanisms and tools for herself in some situations, an obvious example being psychic-self-defence. This includes practices such as cleansing the aura, banishing negative energies and visualisation. Healing, purging and transformation are all associated with the dark and intense nature of Pluto.

Qualities of compulsion and obsession are also associated with Pluto. She may have applied these to areas that govern the ninth house, for example; beliefs, morals, philosophy, religion and teaching, along with politics, publishing and travel. The Moon trine Pluto aspect certainly reveals that she had an instinctive feel for these areas.

Some people who have Pluto in the ninth house in their natal chart "may project unacceptable parts of their psyche onto another race, religion or culture, persecuting and blaming something outside themselves for what is dark or evil in the world" (Sasportas, 1998, 330). This is borne out by some of Fortune's political and social attitudes. It has been said that she was essentially right-wing and a passionate supporter of the British Empire and its divine right to rule (D. Conway, correspondence to Author).

In some of her earlier writings, Fortune made critical and derogatory remarks about the Germans and their allies during the First World War (ibid). In fairness however, such 'jingoism' was rife at the time and positively encouraged by the government and popular culture. It is also believed that she was homophobic (during her lifetime, same sex relationships were still illegal in Britain). Perhaps, she altered her beliefs as she matured, for this did not seem relevant too her when it came to her connection and meetings with Aleister Crowley, who was known for having gay relationships. Even if she did still object to homosexuality at the time she met him, she seems to have been discreet about her views.

Fortune believed that different races and cultural groups had their own particular esoteric traditions. For example, she rejected the eastern and orientalism elements favoured by Madame Blavatsky in theosophy (ibid) (D. Conway, correspondence to Author). Instead, Fortune ran a 'Christian' tradition of her own rather than conform to the established Theosophical Society in England. Again, she was driven to set herself apart (just as she did with the Golden Dawn organisation) and run a different faction of the Theosophical Society.

Astrologically, 'foreigners' are associated with the ninth house (and Jupiter/Sagittarius) so perhaps this fixated nature of Pluto in Fortune's ninth house (see box on right) may have made it difficult for her to change her mind about other cultures and races. It has even been claimed that, as an adult, she never made long journeys and had little experience of life (Fielding and Collins, 1998, 25), thus remaining stuck in her opinions about people outside of the British Empire and her own social class.

However, we know that, as a teenager, she travelled overseas at least twice with her family in 1907 and 1909, from Liverpool to Quebec, Canada, before crossing the border into New York, US (Conwy Archives, family database). It is unclear whether they travelled for business purposes; whatever the reason for the journey, it must have been quite an adventure for the young Fortune to cross the sea on a steamship and would have appealed to her Sagittarian nature.

The ninth house is also associated with higher education and it is interesting that Fortune's parents sent her to (as previously discussed) the Studley Agricultural College, where she stayed for approximately two years (1911–13). Although she started as a student there, she was apparently so proficient that she was eventually employed as a supervisor (Knight, 2000, 24).

Evelyn Heathfield, a fellow classmate and friend of Fortune's (whom she affectionately called Vi) at the college, was once asked by Fortune early in their friendship, "Oh, are you mad? Or don't you get on at home? Or have you been crossed in love?" (Chapman, 1993, 165). This suggests that Fortune understood that the college did not just train women in light horticultural skills, but also offered recuperation and perhaps even refuge for students. Heathfield replied that she wasn't at the college for any of the aforementioned reasons and was there simply because she wanted to become a gardener (ibid).

Interestingly in 1922, Fortune's parents suddenly moved from Westminster Bridge Road in London, they also resigned from their church membership and moved to the up and coming area of Letchworth, Hertfordshire, which was the world's first garden city (Knight, 2000, 18). Fortune's classmate, Heathfield, recalled that Fortune had been sent to Studley Agricultural College because she had already had a breakdown (Chapman, 1993, 64) *before* she enrolled into the college. Indeed, the establishment had advertised itself as "ideal for girls with psychological problems" (https://en.wikipedia.org). The breakdown at Studley Agricultural College was therefore Fortune's second, and it largely inspired her to write *Psychic Self-Defence* decades later, since she was apparently bullied by the then warden, Dr Lillias Hamilton, who had taken control of the college in 1908 and turned it "into a semi-nursing home for neurotic young girls" (Chapman, 1993, 193).

The problem, of course, was that Dr Hamilton may have caused some of the girls to become neurotic in the first place. She tormented Fortune by chanting to her for hours on end, repeating, "You have no self-confidence. You are incompetent,' over and over in her (the warden's) office. Fortune became dazed and exhausted for days afterwards and had to recuperate in bed. Apparently, the warden had a violent temper and was also controlling and manipulative to other employees and students at the college (Richardson, 1987, 44).

Some years later (as previously noted), this profound experience led Fortune to write *Psychic Self Defence,* first published in 1931; and parts of it were obviously autobiographical. She wrote in the preface, "I cite my own experience, painful as it is to me to do so, because an ounce of experience is worth a pound of theory" (Fortune, 2001, xxv).

Fortune also believed that she had been the subject of psychic attack by Moina MacGregor Mathers, after articles had been published (written by Fortune) that apparently contained 'secrets' of The Golden Dawn. Fortune described the event in some detail in her book, *Psychic Self-Defence,* but although she wanted her readers to infer that Mathers was the perpetrator, some feel these claims were untrue (Greer, 1995, 410).

Traumatised and having returned to the family home, the Firth's family doctor diagnosed that she had been hypnotised by her employer (Hamilton) when she had her breakdown. Unable to return to work for a long time as she needed recuperation, she was left in a depleted condition subject to extreme prostration when put under any stress whatsoever." Eventually however, she recovered and was healthy enough to re-undertake employment (Fielding and Collins, 1998, 25).

In her book, *Psychic Self-Defence,* she revealed that she was subjected to hypnotism and she believed hypnotism to be largely used in black magic as well as in telepathic suggestion – both being a large part of the power of hypnotism (Fortune, 2001, xxv). She believed her traumatic experience of being hypnotised "… was not an hallucination, but an actual fact that one could rise up and cope with" (Richardson, 1987, 50).

STILL WATERS RUN DEEP

As discussed earlier, the Moon is trine Pluto and shows an intense emotional life wherein Fortune could delve deep into her feelings. At times she may have needed solitude to help digest and absorb her experiences; this is further emphasised by the Moon

being positioned in the twelfth house. This area
governs respite, hospitals and retreat. Sometimes,
however, she could be undecided even about her
own feelings, probably due to the presence of her
Moon sign Libra in the twelfth house (*see box on
previous page*) Libra is associated with (amongst
other things) indecision and imbalance; hence the

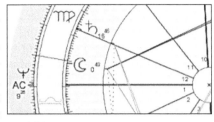

Libran nature strives to find balance and equilibrium within.

It has been observed that a person with the Moon trine Pluto aspect can be alert
and attuned to a misuse of power, especially where psychic invasion has occurred,
leaving the subject feeling invaded and exposed (Tompkins, 1989, 155). Consequently,
cleansing and purging the emotions may be necessary through counselling, healing
or therapy. Certainly, at Studley College, Fortune was aware of the warden's alleged
misuse of power towards some of her students and staff.

Both the Moon and Pluto are sextile Chiron (the Wounded Healer), the latter being
positioned in Leo in the tenth house. The Moon aspect created with Chiron suggests she
was highly sensitive to both her own and others' feelings. The Wounded Healer shows
us where there has been unresolved emotional hurt in her childhood, which has carried
on into adulthood; while the Moon sextile Chiron suggests that she was very much
aware of and in tune with her feelings.

FATHER'S INFLUENCE AND LEADERSHIP

The tenth house and Leo are both associated with authority figures and the father
figure. This suggests that she may have been aware of her father's wishes, especially in
terms of how he would have liked her to pursue a career. Perhaps her father projected
onto her during her early life that he wanted her to be powerful and successful, perhaps
even become an authority figure. This can be seen to some extent when her family
funded the publication of two editions of her poetry, which went on sale to the public
when she was a young teenager.

Her family were also interested in her research work on the soya bean and became
involved in the distribution of vegetarian products; the company was called Firth, Weir
& Co. Ltd. Her father was also involved with her esoteric work, along with Fortune
(and one of her cousins) and Penry Evans. Firth Snr was a member of his daughter's
Co-Lodge, which was formed in her London headquarters in 1925 (Knight, 2000, 113).

Chiron in the tenth house (*see box on right*) also indicates her
natural authority, and when young she may have found this resulted
in confrontations with other authority figures, such as teachers. It
has been said that when she was a student at Studley Agricultural
College, "Violet obeyed rules, but she was not in awe of authority"
(Chapman, 1993, 168), showing her strong independence. Accepting
her own natural leadership qualities would have helped her, although
it wasn't really until she delved into the world of magic and the occult
that she eventually became an author, ceremonial magician and
teacher and found her niche, which enabled her to lead and teach.

W.E. Butler, a long-term friend and member of Fortune's closed
magical group, provides some insight into Fortune's leadership when
she was Warden of the Fraternity of Inner Light. He stated that the

initiates accepted her as the decision-maker and obeyed her because it was obvious to them that *she* was the leader and had the necessary authority and power. This was not only because she held the authority of the Lodge but also because, like Mme Blavatsky, she could produce phenomena at will (Chapman, 1993, 120–121).

It has been observed that people with Chiron positioned in Leo "... feel something special about themselves which attaches itself to the ego in the early stages ... the way to break the ego hold is to minimize oneself, to identify with a purpose larger than the self" (Hand Clow, 2007, 90). Perhaps her indulgent family were partly responsible for making her feel she was special and this, along with her own psychic experiences from an early age, helped her to realise there was something greater than herself in the Universe. She may have fantasised a little, since the Atlantean scenery which she describes in her Akashic memories uncannily resembles the grounds of the Craigside Hydro Hotel which was owned and managed by her family (email correspondence to Author by David Conway). This shows that she may have enhanced her earlier memories of her earlier life, making them seem more special. Indeed, her memories of what she called 'Atlantis' have been described by biographer and occultist, Alan Richardson, as 'phantasies of childhood' (Richardson, 1987, 31).

It has also been said of Fortune's work that "there is a curious contradiction between her many flights of fancy and the sober approach to magic she ceaselessly advocates" (Conway, 1988, 271). Jupiter is opposite Chiron in the natal chart, suggesting that she may have been aware of her extended family's success and heritage, but may at times have exaggerated (Jupiter) about her childhood (Chiron in Leo).

Jupiter opposite Chiron may "stimulate occult perception to the maximum" (Hand Clow, 2007, 150) and, as a child, the opposition can create challenges: "the perceptions into the very core of existence are so amazing that this native seesaws between being completely ordinary to being a wizard" (ibid). One cannot help wonder if some of the challenges were the real reason why Fortune was described as "a difficult child" (Fielding and Collins, 1998, 22).

PAIN AND SORROW

Returning to the Pluto sextile Chiron aspect, this position suggests that Fortune was able to transform herself through healing and overcoming emotional pain. Pluto represents the underworld as in psychology and the subconscious, whilst Chiron is able to heal wounds that have been buried and hidden.

An obvious example of this is in Fortune's life when she experienced her nervous breakdowns: one occurred in her early twenties, the other was earlier. Another possibility is that she may have been affected by the death of her grandparents, who died when she was about sixteen (Knight, 2000, 17). When Fortune was fourteen, her parents had converted to the Christian Science religion, whose followers did not believe in medicine (even for the terminally ill). It is possible, therefore, that Fortune watched a grandparent die in agony, which would have had great impact on her. Perhaps, during her time working at the clinic and attending lectures at UCL, she discovered that such illness was preventable or treatable, irrespective of her parents' beliefs. She later went on to study and practice as a lay healer in psychology and psychoanalysis at London University between 1914 and 1916 (as previously noted). The buried wounds could have included mourning her grandparents who died (Pluto is also associated with bereavement and grief), especially if she felt their deaths were preventable.

Fortune received a certificate of proficiency for her studies, and although she did not complete her degree, she went on to practice as a Freudian lay analyst supporting qualified staff, at the Medico-Psychological Clinic in Brunswick Square, London, between 1914 and 1916 (as noted previously).

Barbara Low reviewed Fortune's, *The Machinery of the Mind,* for *The International Journal of Psychoanalysis,* in 1924, somewhat contemptuously, "It is a little difficult to see the *raison d'être* of this volume, since so many small books are already in existence at the time of its publication." This suggests that Fortune did not have an extensive knowledge of books on the market at that time when dealing with the subject, although she (Fortune) was modest enough to say that as far as she knew there was, "no book that dealt with psychopathology, not from the point of view of the student, but from that of the patient who needs an elementary knowledge of the laws of the mind in order to enable him to think hygienically" (Fortune, 2018, 4)

However, four years later, another reviewer, Dr T.R. Forsythe, was more enthusiastic, listing the book with other titles as 'recommended reading', for the British College of Nurses in the *British Journal of Nursing* in 1928 (*British Journal of Nursing*, May 1928, 116).

EXPERIENCE AND THE MEANING OF LIFE

Jupiter is trine Pluto in Fortune's natal chart, indicating that she would have enjoyed exploring the Underworld. In this case the 'underworld' would mean investigating the unconscious, as well as the occult, psychology and religion; a theme which recurs in her natal chart and discussed above. There is also a sense of buried (Pluto) wealth (Jupiter), the wealth being buried in the unconscious; something she tapped into through her study of magic and psychology.

As Jupiter is associated with philosophy and Pluto with death, Fortune had an understanding of an afterlife. She was mediumistic and able to work in trance as a channel for a higher force. She is thought to have demonstrated her mediumship in spiritualist churches as early as 1927, for example, at the Spiritualist Mission in Bayswater, West London and the Groatian Hall in Wigmore Street (Richardson, 1987, 165). Her work was inspired by hidden realms and her guides from a higher plane, whom she called 'The Masters'.

In August 1942, the spiritualist newspaper, *Psychic News*, announced that she was giving lectures on the *Deeper Esoteric Teachings* (not demonstrations of mediumship) at Marylebone House in Russell Square for the Marylebone Spiritualist Association Limited. The lecture was repeated in October that year at the same venue. She appeared to be the only person lecturing at the venue, whilst other mediums (such as the popular trance medium, Joseph Benjamin) participated in group séances. Despite the Blitz, Fortune seemed to confine her lecturing activities at that time to Central London, whilst other mediums travelled across different parts of London.

The contact between Jupiter and Pluto also indicates that she was philosophical about life and that it held a deep meaning; this can be seen for example in the Qabalah Tree of Life philosophy about which she taught and wrote extensively.

Another trine aspect in Fortune's chart is created with Jupiter and Neptune; this indicates mystical (Neptune) experiences (Jupiter) as well as religious yearnings. It also shows her need to escape rigours of everyday life through meditation, ritual, magic and writing. In these areas she could lose herself in mind or body and could find spirituality in the material world.

The aspect shows a great (Jupiter) understanding of the intangible (Neptune) and unseen forces in life, showing her need to work towards a higher order of reality. We can see this in her Western Mystery School, which she founded in 1924. It was later renamed the Society of Inner Light and still runs today in London. Fortune's potential initiates had to successfully complete correspondence courses before being then initiated into the Lesser Mysteries. Only later could they progress to the Greater Mysteries.

STUDENT AND TEACHER

Fortune seems to have been well regarded as a teacher. William E. Butler, an initiate and close friend said, "If you made a mistake, she gave you a polite ticking off. She never attempted to dominate you," adding, "she always was of the opinion that things could be done" (Chapman, 1993, 119 & 120). However, others, including occultist and writer, Kenneth Grant, claimed that Fortune tried to dominate initiates and interfere with their personal lives (ibid). He described her as "... a very dominating woman who did not scruple to tell her followers how they should arrange their private lives – sometimes with disastrous effects" (Chapman, 1993, 41).

If Grant's claim is true, it shows the assertive, blunt and often forthright nature of her Sun and Mercury sign of Sagittarius. It must be said, however, that Butler who knew her for six years, did not agree, although he did admit that people can and do change over time. He remembered her as a teacher saying, "Experience is a very good teacher....You've got to find out for yourself" (Chapman, 1993, 120).

Helah Fox knew Fortune from the 1930s right through until her death in 1946. She had been a member of the Inner Light Fraternity and lived in both London and Glastonbury with Fortune. She said that Fortune taught her students to concentrate and meditate and that, "The training that she gave me and several others was really of the utmost value to us. It made the difficult period of adjusting to life after the war much more possible" (Chapman, 1993, 79). This shows that Fortune was proficient in teaching and effectively provided life-learning skills to her initiates.

CHRISTIANITY

Returning again to the aspect of Jupiter trine Neptune, this suggests that Fortune was naturally drawn to divinity, religion and spirituality. Brought up in a strongly Christian household (her parents were Christian Scientists), she carried her Christian beliefs into many of her teaching groups. For example, The Christian Qabalah and The Christian Theosophical Guild of Jesus Christ. She passionately believed that 'The Master Jesus Christ' was her spiritual guide. Some of her earlier work also included themes of Christianity; for example, in her novel, *The Demon Lover* (1927), the Christian heroine was pitted against dark forces. She also discussed Jesus Christ when she wrote about obsession and overshadowing in an article about 'therapeutic methods' in *Principles of Esoteric Healing* (2006, 94). Advising the reader on how to protect themself against the influence of an obsessing entity, she advised, "taking care to protect yourself in the Name and the Sign of the Master of Masters whom we all serve –Jesus the Christ" (ibid).

SACRIFICE, SEX AND POLARITIES

Neptune is positioned in the eighth house, indicating that Fortune had to make sacrifices in the most intimate areas of life (since Neptune is associated with sacrifice and the eighth house governs intimacy and sex — as well as death, investigation, shared resources and transformation). It has been suggested that sex was infrequent during her married life (Chapman, 1993, 147) although only Fortune and her husband would have known that for certain! Magic is also associated with Neptune and so unsurprisingly, Fortune had a great interest in tantric and Sex Magic, writing extensively about 'polarities' between men and women.

Interestingly, in her early book, *The Machinery of the Mind*, she wrote, "Excessive sexual activity may lead to jaded powers of response to normal sexual stimuli, and the individual may then deliberately turn to abnormal forms of gratification in the hope of obtaining satisfaction" (Fortune [Violet M. Firth], 2018, 24). However, what is excessive and abnormal for one may not be so for another. Perhaps she was unwittingly drawing upon her own inhibited attitude towards sex and pleasure. For example, in *The Laws of Mating upon Each Plane* and *Abstinence and Asceticism* she claimed that people abstain from sexual intercourse as they "believe that asceticism is the path to spirituality" or because it either disgusted them or they "are not in a position to meet the obligations so incurred" (Fortune, 1974, 93).

THE AFTERLIFE AND MEDIUMSHIP

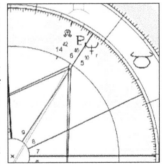

Neptune in the eighth house (*see box on right*) also reveals that Fortune was psychic and sensitive, possibly with precognitive dreams, astral experiences, an interest in spiritualism and a natural attunement with metaphysical and mystical subjects. Indeed, Aleister Crowley accurately observed that people with Neptune in the eighth house of their natal chart "... may be on the borderland between life and death ... liable to fall into trances, lethargies, catalepsies, and the like" (Crowley, 1987, 119).

Fortune undertook much trance-work, especially when she was with the Fraternity of Inner Light, and some mediums claimed to have received messages from her after she departed from her physical life. This shows her skill at communicating, both by channelling spirit when she was alive and also as a spirit communicator for other mediums after she had died.

INEXPERIENCE AND PROCESSING INFORMATION

Returning to Mercury, the planet of communication and mentality, and some of its aspects, the Moon is square Mercury in Fortune's natal chart, suggests she could rationalise her feelings and perhaps could be cool and detached when necessary, for these are the logical and reasoning qualities of Mercury. The Moon provides caring and sympathetic responses, thus the Moon in Libra would have added a softened quality to this aspect. This would have helped when Fortune was employed as a lay Freudian analyst at the Medico-Psychological Clinic, where she would have had to spend time listening to her clients and rationalise her initial feelings about their problems.

She was in her early twenties when she was in this post and, although she had some life-experience, there would have been areas in her patients' lives with which she was unfamiliar, one obvious example being that of war trauma and shell-shock, which must have been harrowing to observe.

Several years later, Fortune's work, *The Problems of Purity,* was published, giving an indication of the type of counselling she practiced. This included advising many of her clients on areas such as contraception, which was very forward-thinking, especially at a time when the repressive society of her time regarded sexual urges and sexual gratification as causing deep guilt (Knight, 2000, 31). Apparently, she tried to "...instil a sense of the sacredness of sex....to analyse its true physiological causes, and come to terms with it by means of controlling the imagination" (Knight, 2000, 31). The themes of celibacy and purity may also be in keeping with her Christian upbringing and attitude towards sex as noted previously.

JUSTICE AND CAREER

The Moon in Libra would have helped Fortune to redress any imbalances she encountered, as the Venusian energy of Libra includes approachability and co-operation, and any one-to-one situations such as that of client and therapist would have required calm, tact and diplomacy, all of which are associated with Libra. Other attributes of Libra include equality, fair-play and justice (suggesting that Fortune had little difficulty resolving taxing situations) or taking the initiative to redress any imbalance and take action. This is in keeping with the cardinal modes (*see glossary*) that are found on the axis of her natal chart.

For example, when she worked for the Women's Land Army, and wages were paid late to her and her co-workers, she threatened to drop the keys of the establishment into the sewage tank unless the wages were paid (ibid, 37). This shows her determination and fearlessness when confronting those in authority.

The Moon is the ruling planet of the Cancer MC (*see glossary*) in Fortune's chart, indicating she was caring and intuitive in her career, possessing great ambition and drive. Cancer belongs to the cardinal mode and, as discussed earlier, indicates she could assert herself and initiate projects.

The Cancer MC position also indicates that she could be a 'professional parent', which is seen in the way she coached and nurtured those she worked with. She was interested in the lives of others, and found helping them very rewarding. Sometimes she tailored courses and study for the individual on her courses.

As a teacher, Fortune transferred some of her knowledge and skills gained from the Agricultural College to nurturing her occult students, depending on their characteristics and knowledge. For example, she applied the (then) newly-grasped concept from genetics of "adapting the fruit to the soil" (Chapman, 1993, 179). Recognising how to get the best out of her trainees and help them achieve their goals shows that she was flexible and open minded in her thinking (Mercury in Sagittarius). Those qualities are in keeping with the Cancer MC and the vast mutable energy of Sagittarius in her natal chart.

The Moon has great significance within Fortune's magical and written work, as well as her experience of working with many women in various fields, for example, the Women's Land Army, members of her Western Traditional School, and her work as an employee and student at the Studley College of Agriculture, which was for female students only. The latter is particularly significant, since the Moon is symbolic of the female principle.

As previously discussed, history is also an association of Cancer and manifests in Fortune's life as her interest in the past. For example, ancient philosophies such as the Tree of Life, the Jewish Qabalah as well as the Arthurian Legends, Egyptology and Pagan deities (such as Pan). These subjects were very pertinent to her profession and are in keeping with the Cancerian connections with heritage and the past.

STRAIGHT TALKING

Copy of Ticket with Permission of Conwy Archive Service

Mercury is sextile Mars in Fortune's natal chart, indicating her assertive communication and straight talking, which may have been sometimes construed as insensitive or opinionated by others. For example, it was sometimes said that she henpecked her husband and (as previously mentioned) in her obituary in *The Times* it said that "… she made great demands on others" (Knight, 2000, 27).

A more favourable side to the Mercury and Mars aspect was that she could be incisive and quick-thinking, and could learn quickly, although easily became bored, especially if in the company of others who were slower in their thinking and understanding. The obituary in *The Times* remarked that "… she could not suffer self-conscious fools gladly" (ibid).

The Mercury sextile Mars aspect also bodes well for effective debating, speaking and writing as it keeps to the point and does not wander. Astrologer, Charles E.O. Carter, observed that the favourable Mercury and Mars contact "tends to literary work and is often childless in a physical sense, its books being its offspring" (Carter, 1930, 82). This was certainly an accurate description for Fortune.

Mars is positioned in the fifth house (the area of recreation) and suggests she could be irrepressible, able to play hard and work hard if she wanted to, although other areas of her chart indicate that recreation was less important to her than her work.

In 1937, when she was almost 47, she returned to her birth town of Llandudno and delivered a lecture called '*Occultism – Past and Present*' that was described as 'popular', suggesting both she and her subject were admired. The Sun Sagittarius is in the third house which governs communication, indicating Fortune's thirst for knowledge, and that she was curious, clever and could speak from the heart (*copy of original lecture ticket, above right*).

LOVE AND MARRIAGE

Venus is square Saturn in Fortune's natal chart, indicating her reluctance to commit herself in affairs of the heart. In fact, she did not marry until she was 36, which was quite late for a woman of her class and background at that time. Her husband later filed for divorce, as he wished to marry someone else. Since he was the petitioner, yet was also the one to leave the marriage, it may have been that Fortune's beliefs would not accept the concept of divorce. The Divorce Registry in January, 1945, documents that Penry Evans petitioned for divorce and in that in July of that year, the decree was made final and absolute (Fielding and Collins, 1993, 88). The Matrimonial Causes Act of 1923 gave either party the right to divorce their spouse, based on the grounds of their adultery. Then in 1937, a new act was introduced which gave other means to petition for divorce on the grounds of cruelty, desertion and incurable insanity (https://www.parliament.uk).

In Penry Evans' petition, no grounds for divorce were ever stated and it is interesting that Mr and Mrs Penry Evans divorced just six months before her death. One can only speculate what really led to the divorce. It has been claimed that "Evans was believed, not least by his wife, to have had an eye for the ladies, left her in 1939 and later remarried" (Conway, 2017, 339). It was also rumoured that as far as their sex life was concerned it "... was somewhat of a disappointment to Dion Fortune" (Fielding and Collins, 1998, 83). Perhaps Fortune did not want him to remarry, or held out for financial reasons. The new divorce act introduced in 1937, just two years before Penry Evans left his wife, may have finally given them the means to initiate divorce proceedings.

The Venus and Saturn aspect also suggests that Fortune was controlling in relationships and even found giving and receiving affection difficult, perhaps feeling awkward or embarrassed about physical displays of affection. This is because Saturn is associated with fear and restrictions, whilst Venus is associated with relationships.

An opposition aspect is created between Venus and Neptune in the natal chart, again indicating that Fortune was perhaps reluctant to maintain commitment in her relationships. Possibly she found living with somebody in a domestic setting too stifling. As Venus is associated with relationships, and Neptune with the celestial, divine and spirituality, it may have been that she needed a mystical and spiritual axis in her personal relationships.

To a large extent this was resolved by her husband's involvement in her magical work whilst they were still married, and he was given the magical name Merlin. Fortune always called him Merl rather than Thomas, although, apparently, he disliked this and found it patronising (email correspondence to Author from David Conway). Their joint magical work may have satisfied her need for a spiritual pivot in their relationship. As Neptune is associated with sacrifice, perhaps Fortune sacrificed personal and romantic love in order to pursue her calling. She may even have preferred a relationship that was a meeting of souls, rather than one that was more physically active.

The principle of independence in Fortune's natal chart is further emphasised by Uranus being positioned in the sign of Libra, which is associated with partnerships. It indicates that she needed space and interchange in her close partnerships, possibly feeling torn between her need to be loved and a desire for freedom. Her commitment to any relationship needed to be based on friendship and mutual understanding, as these are themes associated with Uranus.

Uranus in Libra also shows that she was forward thinking about partnerships and significant relationships, since Uranus is associated with futurism and goals. The planetary position shows her determination to achieve her ideals fairly.

The failure of her marriage must have been a disappointment to her, but she continued with her work to support the cause of humanity, as shown by Jupiter in the sign of Aquarius (ruled by independent Uranus). For example, she worked at developing the Western Esoteric Tradition, and also in the development of the soya bean used in vegetarian food products, which will be discussed further on.

Uranus positioned in the first house indicates that she actively sought freedom to be herself and needed constant stimulus to avoid boredom. Uranus in this area shows that she could make her mark in the world in an original and unique way, for such are the correspondences of Uranus.

Interestingly, author and magician, Aleister Crowley, a man certainly famed for his distinct and original approach to life, also had Uranus in the first house. Both he and Fortune wrote about sex magic, which was considered controversial at that time.

We see her progressive nature when she broke away from the Alpha et Omega Lodge (a branch of the Hermetic Order of The Golden Dawn organisation; she had been a member since 1919). Later, in 1927, she formed an outer branch of the Golden Dawn called the Fraternity of the Inner Light. Eventually, this organisation evolved into the Society of the Inner Light and was no longer affiliated with the Golden Dawn. This organisation became a landmark for the work of Dion Fortune and her disciples and initiates and remains active today.

Crowley and Fortune met and corresponded, and it seems they mutually respected each other although, unlike him, she preferred to stay out of the limelight, remain mainly behind the scenes and avoid the media. This illustrates the Moon in the twelfth house of her natal chart, and shows she avoided the public spotlight, unless it was for educational purposes, e.g. giving public lectures.

After Fortune's death, Crowley confided to a close friend that they had "a very secret understanding" and also that he wanted to take over her organisation, the Fraternity of Inner Light (Chapman, 1993, xi). Both Crowley and Fortune were members of the Hermetic Order of The Golden Dawn organisation, although Crowley had joined in 1898 when Fortune was just eight years old and had left the organisation before she joined.

Other aspects with Venus in Fortune's natal chart include an opposition created between Venus and Pluto. This suggests that Fortune's relationships were controlling and intense, both qualities associated with Pluto. At times, she may have felt overwhelmed by the force, strength and passion of others, such as the warden who had allegedly mistreated her at Studley Horticultural College. She may also have been attracted to wealth and power, as they are areas connected with Venus and Pluto (another example of this will be discussed later.)

Venus in the third house suggests that Fortune had an intellectual appreciation of literature and the arts. As Venus is gentle and graceful, it indicates her talent for verse and poetry, something borne out by her magical rituals and also her book of poetry, *Violets*, published when she was just thirteen years old. The *Evening Express* (1904, 2) newspaper described her as "… a poetess, a bright little lady of thirteen summers" (ibid) and the verses "… are of considerable interest and merit" (ibid). The article continues (somewhat prophetically) that "… if Miss Firth continues to cultivate the muse, she will be heard of again." The following year, another collection of her poetry was published entitled, *More Violets*.

Whilst at Studley Agricultural College, Fortune co-wrote and produced two satirical plays about the college, showing her ability to co-operate and collaborate (in keeping with her Libra ascendant) as well as a talent for communication through observation, writing and production, coupled with a keen sense of humour. However, if she was not inspired or stimulated by individuals or a project, she would walk away showing she could adapt and open new doors for herself which is in keeping with the strong, yet adaptable energy in her chart.

The Libra ascendant and the aspect Sun conjunct Venus show that Fortune could be tolerant and reasonable, but if she witnessed injustice then she would try to redress the situation. Sun conjunct Venus indicates that she valued the Divine feminine, since the Sun is associated with the ego and Venus with the feminine. We can see this for example, in her writing about the goddess and priestess. Meditation and prayer would have helped assist her on her spiritual path, helping her to find inner comfort and peace (which are associated with Venus).

MONEY AND SECURITY

Other associations of Venus include security and, because it is positioned in Sagittarius in her natal chart, this suggests she had an optimistic and philosophical attitude towards money. She certainly was lucky in some financial areas. For example, her working partner, Charles Thomas Loveday, whom she met in Glastonbury in 1922, was financially secure and owned property there (Benham, 1993, 256). It was he who bought the Chalice Orchard and the building on it, and was also responsible for securing the property in London for the Community of the Inner Light, selling some of his other properties to finance the venture (illustrating the earlier example of how Venus opposing Pluto results in being attracted to people in positions of power with money) (Chapman, 1993, 109). This shows Loveday's belief and devotion to Fortune and her work, and also illustrates Fortune's need to be financed by others to help fulfil her dreams and vocation.

Loveday was the co-founder of the Community of the Inner Light at 3 Queensborough Terrace, London with Fortune, and helped her to form The Guild of the Master Jesus within the Community of Inner Light. He not only assisted her financially in setting up the home of the society, but also provided moral support. As previously said, he was also responsible for securing the 40-foot-long wooden army building in Glastonbury which became her base from 1924 onwards (Benham, 1993, 259).

However, Fortune's independent nature did not wholly rely on others and she even wrote detective romantic novels in order to contribute towards the society's funds (Fielding and Collins, 1998, 140).

The Venus sextile Jupiter aspect suggests that a love of God and philosophy, together with religious conversions and experiences, were immensely important to her. This can be seen, for example, in her magical work during the Second World War, when members of her inner circle met on a Sunday and claimed to have sent out energy through prayer and visualisation to defeat the Germans.

AT HOME WITH PHILOSOPHY, RELIGION, PUBLISHING, AND TEACHING

Jupiter is positioned in the fourth house, the area governing domestic life, family, home, heritage and legacy and is positioned in Aquarius. Correspondences associated with Jupiter include, faith, law, publishing, philosophy, religion and teaching. Jupiter in this area suggests that Fortune was at home with these subjects, which is borne out by the abundance of work that she had published; a wealth of genres that included poetry, novels and non-fiction.

Fortune was deeply religious with beliefs and interests in many different spiritual areas, such as the Mystical Qabalah, spiritualism and Christian theosophy. An advertisement in 1928 for the Community (later Fraternity) of Inner Light described its purpose was "... to pursue the study of mysticism and esoteric science. Its ideals are Christian and its methods Western" (Knight, 2000, Opp. p284, Plate 4). A previous advertisement in 1926 for the Christian Mystic Lodge of the Theosophical Society, advertises the society's monthly journal and describes it as "a monthly magazine dealing with ESOTERIC CHRISTIANITY, Editor: DION FORTUNE" (ibid).

In 1935, the *Church Times* reviewed *The Mystical Qabalah* (*Church Times*, 1935, 400) while her book, *The Goat Foot God*, was also featured by *Readers' Digest* in the *Daily Express* in 1936. *Psychic News* spiritualist newspaper also carried regular advertisements and reviews of her books. For example, in December 1938, an article headlined 'Author Writes a Psychic Thriller' and describes how Fortune had to self-publish *The Sea Priestess*, as no publishers viewed the fiction as a commercial proposition. The article praised her enterprise, stating that she "has made it happen in a very enjoyable novel that deserves success in spite of publishers' blindness" (*Psychic News*, Dec 1938, 7).

Not all reviews were complimentary. In 1957 (after Fortune's death), Stephen Lang reviewed both *The Sea Priestess* and *Moon Magic* for Psychic News. He felt the former was "repetitive and often dull ... its meaning not only evades the reader but raises the suspicion that it has slipped from the grasp of the author" (*Psychic News*, March, 1957, 7). However, his review of *Moon Magic* said it was "material ripe for publication" (ibid).

During the Second World War, the Fraternity was bombed out of its headquarters in Bayswater, London but Fortune wrote letters to the members, directing the future of the group and their work during the world crisis. A religious and spiritual home is also associated with the Jupiter in the fourth house, and one example of this can be seen by her spiritual home in Glastonbury, which included a small temple with an altar.

In Glastonbury, Fortune had a cottage set in extensive grounds; it was called Chalice Orchard, and was home to "... apple, walnut, plum, quince and peach trees" (Chapman, 1993, 139). Although she adored the landscape in Glastonbury, she was in no hurry to become a contributor to the local community (Benham, 1993, 259), instead using her home there solely for the purposes of her magical and spiritual work. Possibly she felt her magical work took precedence over everything else.

The Chalice Orchard was situated near the foot of Glastonbury Tor, which would have been inspirational to her work on the Arthurian tradition and here she also wrote, *Glastonbury, Avalon of the Heart*. Her love for Glastonbury and adoption of it as her spiritual home remains relevant, in that she is buried in Glastonbury Cemetery, close to the grave of Charles Loveday, who also was a member of her inner spiritual circle, and not only her secretary but, in later years, her protector.

It was at Glastonbury that she was inspired by the elements and nature. For example, she and her inner circle friends performed a ritual invoking the element of air whilst walking upon the Tor (Knight, 2000, 116). As a child, she was equally inspired by nature to write poetry and in her book, *Violets*, she composed verses with titles such as 'Music in Nature' and 'The Song of the Sea' (Richardson, 1987, 36).

The dynamic of the group changed when Thomas Penry Evans joined the community at Glastonbury, becoming less Christian and more Celtic and Pagan. He has been described as a "... bright-minded fiery Celt, a Christian to a degree but with a strong leaning towards Pagan magic" (Benham, 1993, 257). Although, when he was 23, he identified as Anglican (National Archives, Army Form B. 121, 1915).

In 1927, Fortune had written that, "Christianity has for its work the manifesting of spiritual force to mankind, and nature worship has for its task the manifesting of elemental force, and both these types of force are necessary for the full functioning of the soul" (Benham, 1993, 261).

The circle performed group rituals using archetypes such as Arthur, Morgan le Fay and The Holy Grail. Other spiritual homes which Fortune had occupied included the Belfry in West London and, of course, the Fraternity of Inner Light (later the Society of Inner Light), also located in London. These residences acted as a base and home for officiated groups to educate and practice magical and spiritual endeavours. Here,

Fortune was able to teach, and therefore her homes were temples, not just places of comfort, domesticity and shelter.

LARGE PROPERTIES

Photo by Kind Permission of Conwy
Archive Services

Jupiter is also associated with abundance and when positioned in the fourth house suggests that Fortune lived in homes with plenty of space, where she wouldn't feel trapped. This was essential for her Sagittarian nature which needed openness (both mentally and physically) to avoid feeling trapped or imprisoned. For example, she was born in a house named Bryn-y-Bia, which comprised, "… Four Entertaining Rooms and Nine Bedrooms with Two Staircases and every convenience" (Conwy County Borough Council/archives) (*see photograph on left*).

Even more significant is that when Fortune was a child, the colossal Craigside Hydro hotel (which was managed and owned by the family) sat alongside the family home, practically dwarfing the Firth's residence.

When she was about five, Fortune's family moved to Somerset where they ran, 'a superior rooming house which catered to the more elite gentlemen and ladies of the middle class (Fielding and Collins, 1998, 19), again suggesting a large property, a boarding-house or lodging house, which is an example of a large property.

According to the 1901 Census, by the time Fortune was eleven years-old, her family had moved to East Sheen in Surrey, England, and were living in a home that was described as a club for playing chess (https://mannchess.org.uk). It was documented that Arthur, wife, daughters, parents-in-law John and Jane E. Smith, as well as four domestic staff and five employees of the club were all living there (ibid), suggesting a very large property. The next Census (1911) reveals that the Firth family had moved to South Kensington, West London, yet again with live-in servants, showing they were wealthy enough to afford a home in affluent areas as well as employing several servants.

Heritage is one of the correspondences of the fourth house. Jupiter is positioned here and governs areas such as law, publishing, religion, fame and wealth. Certainly, Fortune's paternal side of the family were both relatively famous and wealthy. Two of her ancestors, Mark and Thomas Firth Jnr, founded the Firth Sheffield Steel Company in the mid-nineteenth century. Indeed, Thomas Firth Jnr went on to supply industrialist and inventor Samuel Colt with much of the iron and steel used at his firearm factories. Mark Firth was a successful entrepreneur and philanthropist, who was elected Master Cutler in 1867 and became Mayor of Sheffield in 1874.

The Firth's adopted the Latin motto *Deo Non Fortuna,* which appeared on their family crest, meaning 'of God, not luck.' This is a clear manifestation of Jupiter's association with good fortune and spiritual riches and Violet Firth adapted it in her pen-name of Dion Fortune.

Fortune's father was a solicitor and in 1886 formed a partnership with Frank Bowman, to start his own law firm of Bowman & Firth, Ltd, Sheffield (Richardson, 1987, 19). However, his practice seems to have been short-lived as in 1893 his registration as a solicitor expired and was never renewed, although at his death in 1943 his profession was still given as a solicitor. After retirement, he self-published quarterly journals called

Chess-Nuts, which were small journals for beginners and social chess players (https://mannchess.org.uk/). His brother, Edward Harding Firth studied theology at Bristol University and became a Rector, Rural Dean and Honorary Canon (Richardson, 1987, 18). These examples again show Jupiter in action in the fourth house of Fortune's natal chart, since it governs law, publishing and religion.

THE MOTHER CHURCH

The fourth house is also associated with the mother and qualities associated with one's mother/care-giver, as previously discussed, suggesting that Fortune's mother, Sarah, was enthusiastic, philosophical and religious; as Jupiter governs these areas. She became a "keen Christian Scientist" (Richardson, 1987, End notes, 249) and a registered healer.

Fortune was fourteen when both her parents converted to this religion, a time when Christian Science was still relatively new – the first church was founded in London, barely six years earlier (Richardson, 1987, 34). This swift conversion shows how unorthodox Sarah Firth must have been, something quite in keeping with the unconventional and freedom-loving symbolism associated with Jupiter in Aquarius in the fourth house.

Dion Fortune was obviously affected by her parents' religious conversion. A family friend once described Sarah Firth as, "a most cultivated and religious woman who had imprinted in her daughter the principle of the Christian Science creed" (Chapman, 1993, 22).

Jupiter's presence in the fourth house suggests Fortune was comfortable with religion, along with the legacy of daily prayer and Bible study, handed down to her by her mother. Jupiter in the fourth house also suggests that Fortune's home life was happy and comfortable; and that she had tremendous belief in herself.

Her parents must have been very proud when, as a young teenager, two books of her poetry were published (possibly financed by her maternal grandfather) to relatively good acclaim (Richardson, 1987, 35). The first book received a review in *The Girls Realm* (Richardson, 1987, 37). She also had a poem published in the *Christian Science Journal* when she was seventeen, called *Angels* (Richardson, 1987, 42).

Jupiter's presence in Aquarius in the fourth house also suggests that Fortune enjoyed living among groups of people, especially kindred spirits. Her home had been busy since childhood and possibly she carried this on into adulthood.

Aquarius is associated with individuality and progress, and Fortune had many original ideas to offer humanity. She was also independent and unorthodox. When Jupiter is in Aquarius, it indicates enthusiasm for reform, humanitarian causes, and is open to innovation, metaphysics, theories and scientific advancement. For example, she became more interested in spiritualism in the Second World War and was reassured by the presence of "psychic researchers" as she insisted "on tangible validity and proof" (Chapman, 1993, 160). Being a trance-medium, she would have also appreciated any rational explanations that explained her gift.

Fortune's eager, experimental and open nature is seen also by Mars in Aquarius in her natal chart, showing she could be assertive and courageous. Experimentation, invention and science are all correspondences associated with Aquarius and its ruler Uranus. Apparently, Fortune had a particular interest in biology, chemistry, mathematics and physics (Chapman, 1993, 182). She was once employed in a laboratory where she worked alone, watching over bacterial cultures while pursuing research into the soya bean (Knight, 2000, 38).

ADVERTISING AND FOODSTUFFS

It has been claimed that she discovered a method for making milk from soya beans – quite groundbreaking at the time, although she does not appear to have patented her discovery (Chapman, 1993, 7). She is not, however, credited as the first to discover this method; *The Vegetarian Messenger* journal in September 1919, carried a small article showing a patent for soya milk by W.J. Melhuish of Dorset. It seems that Fortune did not patent her own *discovery* of the product.

In 1925, Fortune's book, *The Soya Bean – An Appeal to Humanitarians,* was published, promoting the work of The Garden City Pure Food Co., Ltd, Letchworth, which manufactured vegetarian food made from the soya bean (Fortune's parents had moved to the town of Letchworth in Hertfordshire). An advert appeared in *The Occult Review* in 1924, advertising that the sole distributing agents of pure vegetarian foods from the soya bean were Firth, Weir & Co., Ltd (ibid), founded with the help of Fortune's father.

Jupiter is in Aquarius in the fourth house (as stated previously) in Fortune's natal chart and suggests that Fortune's family heritage was independent and progressive by nature. In 1876, her maternal grandfather, John Smith, came to the West of England and with his partner, George Crawford, ran the Hydropathic Establishment in Limpley Stoke, which was first opened in 1860, for twelve years (Richardson, 1987, 22). Alternative healing methods are very much in keeping with the unconventional nature of Aquarius, whilst Jupiter is associated with expansion and growth.

DEVOUTNESS, SPIRITUALITY AND WRITING

Regarding the Moon in Fortune's natal chart and particularly the aspects of the Moon trine Neptune and Pluto both positioned in Gemini, the Moon trine Neptune is a soft aspect and provides an ease and gentleness, a natural and relaxing energy, that would have helped balance Fortune's more assertive and forceful energies. It also suggests that she needed something or someone to whom she could devote herself and escape from the daily drudgery of material life. She found solace through magic, poetry and meditation. The twelfth house is associated with the imagination, sub-conscious and 'behind-the-scenes' work.

The Moon's position in her twelfth house suggests she sometimes needed to retreat and withdraw, in order to replenish her energies. For example, when she was an adult, she visited Glastonbury in Somerset; a place steeped in myth and legend, and it has been said that, "Glastonbury was everything to Dion Fortune" (Benham, 1993, 259). Perhaps retreating from city life was a way she could relax and replenish her batteries in a rural setting.

The aspect created between the Moon and Neptune shows that Fortune found spiritual sustenance in healing, magic, mysticism and spirituality. Her devotion to healing, occult magic and the mysteries can be seen by Neptune's (the ruler of the twelfth house in the natural zodiac) position in the eighth house. When she died in 1955, she left the bulk of her estate (£9,781) to the Society of Inner Light, so they could continue their work.

A STRONG WORK ETHIC

Saturn is in Virgo in the eleventh house (*see box below left*) in Fortune's natal chart, indicating that she was able to forward plan and worked hard to achieve her goals; it also shows she was serious, hardworking and wise; all characteristics associated with Saturn. The position also suggests she was a workaholic, since Virgo is associated with service and work, while Saturn is associated with discipline, organisation and stamina.

These practical qualities must have helped Fortune in the role as editor for her group's magazines, *The Occult Review* and *Transactions of the Lodge,* and it was said of her that, "To her, work spelled salvation" (Knight, 2000, 27). During the Second World War, she described her fraternity as unique, holding, "… no part of the age in which they live, but of an age that is yet to come" (Fortune, Knight, 2012, 9). This reveals how Fortune saw both herself and her group as people of the future.

The eleventh house is associated with communities, groups, kindred spirits, friends and societies, and also hopes for the future. The 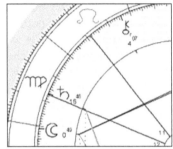 authoritarian nature of Saturn in the eleventh house is evident in Fortune's position as warden at the Fraternity of Inner Light (later the Society of Inner Light) and also when she was president of the Christian Mystic Theological Society. She was also the junior warden for a short time in Dr Theodore Moriarty's Co-Masonic Lodge in Hammersmith, West London, between 1919 and 1920 (http://garethknight.blogspot.com).

We see her authoritative and practical leadership qualities (associated with Saturn) when she wrote to her members during the war; "Life maybe difficult … but it is not bewildering. We have to endure" (Fortune, Knight, 2012, 12). No doubt her faith would have inspired and helped her through such difficult times, as it had done previously during the First World War.

There was one occasion, however, when she did not act wisely; this was when her husband had been initiated into her society. She forced him through various grades of the system so quickly that, when he was initiated into the Greater Mysteries, he had no understanding of them. Perhaps Fortune had let her heart rule her head in this situation and pushed through her husband's learning, without any regard for his own abilities (https://www.golden-dawn.com). It is possible that Penry Evans' war injuries caused him to be slower in learning some subjects.

Other associations of Saturn include defence and obstruction and Fortune sometimes met some difficulties, especially within groups. For example, towards the end of World War I, she joined the Brodie-Innes Lodge of the Hermetic Order of the Golden Dawn called the Alpha et Omega and was quickly initiated into the group. She had been described as being "… a model neophyte within the Golden Dawn" (Fielding and Collins, 1998, 43), but soon became dissatisfied and described the group as "… a set of bearded old men, more interested in the antiquities than in the living force of the tradition" (ibid). She asked many questions but received few answers that satisfied her and eventually left the established group.

In 1927, the leader of the Alpha et Omega Temple, Moina MacGregor Mathers, expelled Fortune for apparently "… not having the right inner sigils in her aura" (http://www.dionfortune.co.uk). This could suggest that Fortune found it difficult to apply herself as a student, although when she was teaching students in her later life, she applied herself in a disciplined and thorough way.

She later wrote about that time in her life, *The Psychology of the Servant Problem: A Study in Social Relationships,* was published in 1925 under her given name of V. M. Firth. It was a scathing insistence in a class-conscious society for downtrodden servants to be treated as human beings. She disapproved of servants being treated as inferior and "ignoring one's existence" (Horn, 2010, 147, Taken from *The Psychology of the Servant*). She also wrote of her time as a lady-gardener, "I found that my interests were identical with those of the servants, I made common cause with the kitchen, and because I was also a servant, and had to come in at the back door, I got to know the minds and feelings of the girls I met during those three years in a way that I could never have done had I descended upon them from an above-stairs" (Knight, 2000, 36). It is also possible she was influenced, one way or another, by how her family treated servants in her own childhood home.

Unsurprisingly, *The Church Times* reviewed this title dismissively, stating, "... we think that Miss Firth allows her sympathies to run away with her" (ibid). This shows not only the Church's indifference and desire to maintain the status quo, but also how she was regarded as both humanitarian and radical. The aspect Sun square Saturn suggests she wanted to be well-regarded and that she allowed herself little recreational time. This theme is also echoed in her chart by the position of Mars in the fifth house, which suggests she would work hard even when there was room for 'playtime', showing the hardworking and 'driven' side of her nature.

As discussed earlier, the eleventh house is associated with friends and kindred spirits. Astrology has a wealth of symbolism and interpretations, and one explanation of Saturn positioned in this area is that she had difficulties forming friendships. Certainly, as a child, her lack of friendships with her peers has been remarked upon by other writers. For example, Alan Richardson observed that little is known about her childhood, suggesting that, "Like all great magicians, she probably went through great and intense periods of loneliness" (Richardson, 1987, 34).

Richardson's comment is pertinent as Saturn is also associated with loneliness and isolation. The Sun square Saturn shows that Fortune learnt to develop tremendous self-discipline and self-sufficiency, which was self-imposed. This is borne out when *The Girl's Realm,* in May 1905, reviewed her book of poetry, *Violets,* and wrote, "... wise little Violet Firth works hard at her school in Weston-super-Mare all the term, and reserves verse-making for her holidays" (Richardson, 1987, 37). Her choice of title, where violets could mean not only flowers but also 'Violet's own work,' must have been deliberate!

It has also been said that, "She was terribly snobbish, a trait her parents had developed in her by not letting her play with other girls of lower class" (Fielding and Collins, 1998, 25). Certainly, she may have been forced to work with women from other classes when she volunteered in the Women's Land Army. This surely must have opened her eyes as to how 'the other half' lived. As an adult, there is little information about any friends outside of her magical and spiritual circles.

SUSCEPTIBILITY AND PSYCHIC SELF-DEFENCE

Returning again to the aspect of Moon trine Neptune – as Neptune is also associated with elusiveness – Fortune may have been reluctant to commit herself to romantic and intimate relationships, a theme previously recognised in her natal chart and discussed earlier in this chapter. This aspect also suggests she had a need to escape through imagination and fantasy. This is an ideal position for authors, particularly of fiction or poetry, and of course Fortune wrote novels such as, *Hunters of Humans* (under the name of Violet M. Steele), as well as *The Goat Foot God* and *The Sea Priestess*, and – as already mentioned – poetry and verse as a child. As previously discussed, Neptune is associated with meditation, prayer and ritual – all areas connected with mysticism and spirituality, as well as ephemeral and magical matters.

There is also something of the 'psychic sponge' when the Moon is trine Neptune, because the Moon is emotional and feeling, whilst Neptune is susceptible to those atmospheres and people around them and so can absorb both positive and negative energies. This was an area Fortune discussed in her *Psychic Self-Defence*, in which she draws upon her own experience of being psychically assaulted as a young adult. It also shows her awareness of the importance of vitality and magnetic energies, as well as how to protect oneself against them.

As Neptune's energy is compassionate and sensitive by nature, when it is trine the Moon it shows that Fortune may have been empathic to any suffering and vulnerability. We see this in her empathy with her fellow co-workers who were treated in an inhuman way by their employer. Another example was when Fortune was employed at Studley College and its warden was allegedly "tapping the assets of some of the wealthier students" and abusing her position of power. When Fortune discovered the warden's deceitful behaviour, she came to the assistance of the victims (Knight, 2000, 25). She once reflected on her work as a lay analyst that, "I had very little success in alleviating human misery, and this was a thing for which I was sincerely concerned" (Richardson, 1987, 66). She was deeply affected by seeing patients spend all they had in the hope of an impossible cure and this shows her frustration at her inability to heal all her patients.

Fortune died of Leukaemia in 1946 in a London hospital and her body was eventually taken to her spiritual home in Glastonbury, where she was buried in Glastonbury Cemetery. At the time of her death, she was experiencing some major transits including:

- Transiting Uranus (ninth house) opposing natal Sun
- Transiting Saturn (tenth house) quincunx natal Mars

A NEW CHALLENGE AHEAD

Seven months before Fortune died, transiting Uranus was in the ninth house and opposing the natal Sun. This suggests that there may have been a sudden and unexpected event in her life that challenged her to adjust her thinking in order to help with flexibility. Her divorce may have been one example of the unanticipated experiences in her life. This should have been relatively easy for her, since her natal chart shows great potential for adjustment and flexibility. Any major changes in her life were likely to bring a sense of freedom and self-expression, and those areas of her life where she felt imprisoned would have embraced the change as it gave way to progression; such is the advancing energy of Uranus. Possibly, Fortune may have felt a sense of freedom and liberty as a divorcée – a new situation for her.

Health-wise, the aspect between transiting Uranus and the natal Sun can indicate suppressed vital energies, so she may not have had the same energy levels as before. This aspect can also point to accidents, broken hearts and even a coronary. The Sun represents the heart and the pulse of Uranus can break, deviate and bring unexpected events; perhaps the decree absolute in her divorce proceedings, which arrived just six months before her death, may have had some impact on 'breaking her heart.'

Transiting Saturn was quincunx natal Mars when Fortune died, and this is an interesting aspect when considering areas of health. Transiting Saturn was positioned in the tenth house and shows that by this time of her life, Fortune had become well-established and respected as a stalwart in her magic and occult society.

Saturn is associated with bones, knees, skeleton, skin and teeth, whilst Mars is associated with blood, and muscle. Fortune had leukaemia which is a malignant production of white cells in the blood and is also known as blood cancer. It is believed that Fortune once contracted blood poisoning from a badly extracted tooth. Here we can see the associations of Mars and Saturn as well as the transiting Uranus unexpected event (as discussed earlier) of contracting a life-changing illness. Those who knew her in her final years saw the evident symptoms of her disease, which included persistent fatigue, weakness and undesired weight loss.

Mars and Saturn are sometimes considered to be malignant planets due to their association with blood and gore (Mars) as well as karma, Father Time and the Grim Reaper (Saturn). The quincunx aspect denotes challenges and strains with health and stress issues.

Saturn's ageing and decaying associations may have brought other health problems to Fortune in her last few years. Problems that are connected with the body's hardening processes include arthritis and, since Mars governs blood, it may have been possible that she had high-blood pressure too, which would have further weakened her heart and blood vessels. The quincunx could also symbolise the 'decay' and 'death' of blood, which would eventually kill a human being, since the nature of Saturn is to restrict, while the function of blood is to maintain life.

In her 55 years, Fortune taught and inspired many people to develop their own spiritual and mystical pathways. She was devoted to the arenas of the magic, the occult, religion and spirituality and in doing so developed Western esotericism. She endlessly explored and sought inspiration from the intangible areas of life. She also shared her knowledge of magic and mysticism through her teachings and through her published books, both fiction and non-fiction.

Fortune produced work in a variety of genres and also participated in magical groups and set up the Fraternity of Inner Light (later renamed the Society of Inner Light), which still exists and practices today. She was a prominent author, free-thinker and occultist of her generation. Little did she know just how important her influence would become in the occult world, in terms of developing Western esotericism and writing. An extraordinary woman who lived by her beliefs and devoted herself to God, magic, teaching and writing – set against a backdrop of a patriarchal society – what a huge achievement for her.

ACKNOWLEDGEMENTS, CREDITS AND REFRENCES

Natal chart generated by www.astro.com
Rodden Classification 'C'
Fortune, D: Saturday, 6th December, 1890, 0.55am, Llandudno, North Wales, UK. 53n19, 3w49.
Data Collector Starkman /Source rectified from approximate time.
Birth Certificate for Thomas Penry Evans /WBXZ 549838 – from General Register Office, Southport, Merseyside, PR8 2JD, UK.

SPECIAL THANKS TO:

Amersham Museum, Bucks. The curator, for information about Evelyn Ann Evans and her family, as well as the newspaper image of Thomas Penry Evans' obituary.

David Conway, who was kind enough to give his attention and time to this chapter; and for providing personal family memories of Thomas Penry Evans and also the area where the Frith family lived.

Conwy County Borough Council Archives Service, for images and information of Dion Fortune lecture ticket and also the home where she was born.

Penelope Crick, former director of Institute of Psychoanalysis – for sharing historical information about the context and early times of the Medico-Psychological Centre, as well as papers on the subject.

Hertfordshire Archives and Local Studies, for their search of Firth's presence in Hertfordshire whilst in Women's Land Army.

Andrew Jenkins, for knowledge of http://www.pep-web.org

Llandudno Historical Society, for copy of newspaper article from *The Evening Express* on Violet Firth's book of verses.

Leslie Price, for information about the Friendship Centre.

National Museum of Wales, for information about the article in *Cambria Daily Leader* newspaper, in 1919, about the appointment and duties of Thomas Penry Evans as officers' friend, working for the Ministry of Pensions.

Kathy Rowan, for her experience and knowledge of S.I.L. and understanding of Dion Fortune.

Royal College of Physicians. Enquiries Officer, for details of Penry Evan's membership details of the R.C.P.

Soy Info Center, for content details from Violet Firth's, *The Soya Bean: An Appeal to Humanitarians* (October, 1925). Published C.W. Daniel Co., London.

The Vegetarian Society. Enquiries and Advocacy Officer, for access to the adverts of Firth & Weir, and also the Garden City Pure Food Co., Ltd, from archived society journals.

Cherish Watton. Women's Land Army Historian, for assistance with collecting Women's Land Army First World War information (www.womenslandarmy.co.uk).

JOURNALS

British Journal of Nursing. 'Elementary Psychology and its Application to Nursing: A Course of Lectures to the British College of Nurses' by Dr T. R. Forsythe (May, 1928, 116) – 'Books recommended' supporting Lecture Ten of April 17th, 1928.

Oxford University Press JSTOR. 'Early British Psychoanalysis and the Medico-Psychological Clinic' by Suzanne Raitt (Autumn, 2004) (www. jstor.org./stable/25472754).

Psypioneer Electronic Journal. Vol. 7, No. 6, June 2011, 178 – 'Dion Fortune Magical Medium' by Price, L.

BOOKS

Benham, P. (1993) *The Avalonians*. Published by Gothic Images Publications.

Brashear, J.A. (1924) *A Man who Loved the Stars*. Published by University of Pittsburgh Press.

Bromage, B. and Gaunt, P. J. [Ed] (2016) *Psypioneer Journal*. Vol. 12, No. 5 (First published in *Light*, Spring, 1960. Vol. LXXX. No. 3442. 5–12).

Carter, C.E.O. (1930) *Astrological Aspects*. Published by L. N. Fowler & Co., Ltd.

Chapman, J. (1993) *The Quest for Dion Fortune*. Published by Samuel Weiser, Inc.

Clow Hand, B. (2007) *Chiron, Rainbow Bridge Between the Inner and Outer Planets*. Published by Llewellyn Publications.

Conway, D. (1988) *Magic – An Occult Primer*. Published by The Aquarian Press.

Conway, D. (2017) *Magic – An Occult Primer* [New ed.]. Published by The Witches' Almanac, Rhode Island.

Crowley, A. *Aleister Crowley – The Complete Astrological Writings* (1987). Published by A Star Books, Paperback Division of W. H. Allen & Co. Plc.

Fielding, C. and Collins, C. (1998) *The Story of Dion Fortune.* Published by Thoth Publications.

Firth, V.M. (2018) *The Machinery of the Mind.* Published by Aziloth Books (edited from first edition of 1922).

Firth, V.M. (1925) *The Soya Bean: An Appeal to Humanitarians.* Published by London, C.W. Daniel & Co.

Fortune, D. (1987) *The Mystical Qabalah.* [1935] Wellingborough: Aquarian Press.

Fortune, D. (2006) *Principles of Esoteric Healing.* Edited with an introduction by Gareth Knight Published by Thoth Publications.

Fortune, D. (1998) *Psychic Self-Defence: A Study in Occult Pathology and Criminality* [1930] (Repr. Wellingborough: Aquarian Press).

Fortune, D. *The Magical Battle of Britain: The War Letters of Dion Fortune* (Edited by Gareth Knight, 2012). Published by Skylight Press.

Greer, M.K. (1995) *Women of the Golden Dawn – Rebels and Priestesses.* Published by Park Street Press.

Horn, P. (2010) *Life Below Stairs in the Twentieth Century.* Published by Amberley Publishing Plc.

Jansky, R.C. (1977) *Astrology, Nutrition & Health.* Published by Whitford Press.

Kuhn, P. (2017) *Psychoanalysis in Britain 1893–1913, Histories & Historiography.* Published by Lexington Books.

Knight, G. (2000) *Dion Fortune & the Inner Light.* Published by Thoth Publications.

Knight, G. (2000) *Esoteric Orders and their Work.* Published by Samuel Weiser, Inc.

Maloney, A. (2011) *Life Below Stairs: True Lives of Edwardian Servants.* Published by Michael O'Mara Books Limited.

Richardson, A. (1987) *Priestess.* Published by The Aquarian Press.

Sasportas, H. (1998) *The Twelve Houses.* Published by Thorsons (An Imprint of Harper Collins Publishers).

Tompkins, S. (1989) *Aspects in Astrology.* Published by Element Books Limited.

NATIONAL ARCHIVE DOCUMENTS

For Thomas Penry Evans, accessed on 08/11/2019.

Record of Military Service, Reference WO339/124011 (original department 132986).

Army Form B. 268A, no.5248 – Private Thomas Penry Evans – Physical description in 1916, trade information as schoolmaster, regiment Artists Rifles, 2nd Batallion, discharged 4th August 1916, in Ayshire at 23 years old.

Army Form B. 121, no.5248 – Evan's documented religion as being Church of England, whilst serving with 2nd Artists Rifles regiment in 1915.

Army Form A. 45A, Proceedings of a Medical Board assembled by Order of G.O.C. London District, for the purpose of examining and reporting on the present state of a wound or injury sustained by Lt. T.P. Evans 15 M.G.C. at (place of injury) France on the (date of injury) Dec 16th and Jan 17th. Proceedings took place at Caxton Hall in 1917.

Army Form A. 45, Confidential: Medical Board Report on a Disabled Officer: Disability a) Debility b) Shell-Shock, dated 22nd Feb 1918, stationed at Grantham. Date of origin of disability March 13th 1917. Place of origin of disability Cambrai, France. Form stamped 28th Feb, 1918.

NEWSPAPER ARTICLES

Bucks. Examiner "Doc' Evans Dies Aged 66.' Obituary 4th September, 1959, 6.

Cambria Daily Leader 'Mr T. P. Evans Officers' Friend for Wales.' 20th October, 1919, 6.

London Gazette 'Cadets to be Temporary Second Lieutenants on Probation.' 1st September, 1916, Issue No. 29730, listings from War Office of Machine Gun Corps (Infantry).

Psychic News 'Dion Fortune Appearing on Wed. 12th August at 6.30pm at Marylebone House, Russell Square.' 22nd August, 1942, 8. Announcement of Church Listings.

Psychic News 'Dion Fortune Appearing on Wed. 4th November at 3pm at Marylebone House, Russell Square.' 31st October, 1942, 8. Announcement of Church Listings,

Psychic News 'Author Writes a Thriller.' 3rd December, 1938, 7. Article about Fortune changing publisher in order to get *The Sea Priestess* published.

Psychic News Book Review: *Psychic Self Defence.* 22nd October, 1955, 2.

Psychic News Book Review: Stephen Lang review on *Moon Magic* and *The Sea Priestess.* 9th March, 1957, 3.

South Wales Daily Post 'Gower Division-Nominations.' 20th July, 1895, 3. Article about Kercy Evans supporting David Randell as their local M.P.

The Church Times Book Review: *The Mystical Qabalah.* 11th October, 1935.

The Daily Express New Books, Readers Digest Feature: *The Goat Foot God.* 31st December, 1936, 4.

The Evening Express (Weston-super-Mare) Book Review: *Freemasonry* (no author) and a review of Violet Firth's book of verses, '*Violets*'. 19th November, 1904, 2.

WEBSITES

www.astro.com/ – 1892 Ephemeris for T. P. Evans' birth date.

www.bl.uk/ – Correspondence between Firth/Evans/Fortune and The Society of Authors, between 1923–1946/MS 63239 ff.1–80.

https://www.bmj.com/archive – 'Treatment of the Maladjusted Child' – Medical Memoranda – Smallpox: A Case with Minimal Lesions. Accessed 29/10/2019.

http://www.dionfortune.co.uk/resources/biographical-history – Fortune's clinic training included undertaking a personal analysis. Accessed 28/07/2019.

http://garethknight.blogspot.com/2006/11/talk-given-at-canonbury-masonic.html – Accessed 06/10/2018.

https://www.heraldry-wiki.com/heraldrywiki/index.php?title=Deo_non_fortuna – Definition of Latin motto. Accessed 14/05/2020.

https://www.parliament.uk – Grounds for divorce from the 1900s, accessed 21/09/2019.

http://www.pep-web.org – Review article on book: The Machinery of the Mind, written by Barbara Low in 1924. Accessed 14th August, 2018.

https://www.societyofauthors.org/About-Us/History – Accessed 30/09/2018

http://www.victorianturkishbath.org/3topics/atozarts/aapix/limpleystoke_w.htm – Accessed 21/10/2018.

https://en.wikipedia.org/wiki/Lillias_Hamilton – Accessed 12/09/2018.

CHAPTER SIX

Helen Duncan 1897–1956

*Materialisation Medium and the Last Person in Britain to be
Charged and Imprisoned Under the Witchcraft Act of 1735*

HELEN DUNCAN, the last person in Britain to be imprisoned and charged under the Witchcraft Act of 1735, was born Victoria Helen McCrae MacFarlane, on 25th November, 1897, in Callender, Scotland. Callender is situated near the River Teith, Perthshire, near Stirling, which is often described as the gateway to the Highlands in Scotland. She was the fourth child of Archibald and Isabella MacFarlane, a hard-working and religious couple, and she was baptised into the Scottish Presbyterian Church. Helen's father was stern and deeply religious, taking great pride in his faith. Naturally he became concerned when his quiet daughter began to develop psychic talents, especially since Helen probably did not even realise she was psychic; what she did came very naturally to her (Armour, 2000, 14). He was described as "God-fearing and loyal to the Crown" (Gaskill, 2002, 31).

Trance Mediumship:
Deep trance is usually used in physical mediumship and is a sharing of mental and physical energies between the medium and spirit communicator.

At the age of 20, Duncan became wife to Henry Duncan who was supportive of her gifts as a trance medium, and together they raised a family of six children (others died in infancy). She worked hard in various positions of employment and due to her husband's ill health as a result of injuries sustained in World War I, as well as his cabinet-making business going bankrupt; she was the breadwinner in the family, although Henry did receive a small army pension from being in the war.

In 1944, Helen Duncan was charged under the Witchcraft Act of 1735 and accused of fraud in pretending to conjure spirits. Her trial significantly contributed to the repeal of the Witchcraft Act. After she was released from prison, she vowed never to participate in mediumship again. However, two months later, she was called back to work by spirit, and was conducting a séance. She was in trance when the police raided the premises, under the pretence of looking for beards, shrouds and masks, taking flashlight photographs. In doing so, they not only abruptly touched her whilst she was still in trance, which is dangerous for any medium, but they also strip-searched her and subjected her to treatment which was brutal and violating, including a thorough gynaecological examination. The police found nothing. A doctor was called and found two second degree burns on her stomach. She returned to her Scottish home, and then was rushed to hospital. On 6th December, 1956, five weeks after the police raid, Duncan passed to spirit.

WHAT HELEN DUNCAN'S NATAL CHART SHOWS

Duncan was born on 25th November, 1897, when the Sun was in the fire and mutable sign of Sagittarius at 3 degrees and when the Moon was also in the sign of Sagittarius at 13 degrees. In Duncan's chart there is a stellium created by Uranus in Scorpio and Sun, Mars and Saturn in Sagittarius (*see box on right*). The latter three are an indication of a great visionary who is able to far-see in a clairvoyant way; someone who is precognitive, with an ability to see the wider picture far into the future. A collection of conjunct planets in the formation of a stellium denotes a significant focus

> **Stellium:** Multiple conjunctions of planets, a close cluster of three or more planets in one sign and/or house.

in a chart. The Sun in Sagittarius indicates that Duncan needed new adventures and exploration in her life, with an area of religion or spirituality to 'believe in'. Those who knew her said she had natural warmth, buoyancy, inspiration, generosity of spirit and a philosophical and optimistic outlook on life. Fiery Mars in the sign of Sagittarius suggests that Duncan enjoyed challenges, had an exuberance of energy and was a capable fighter, both physically and spiritually.

Mars in Sagittarius can indicate great physical energy and also manifest in terms of having a temper and being brutally outspoken. In the biography, *The Two Worlds of Helen Duncan,* by Duncan's daughter, Gena Brealey, she writes of her mother, "All her life Helen was quick to anger, yet like a true Sagittarian, within minutes she would be sorry for her lack of control, but also true to her birth sign – she had an innate sense of what was just" (Brealey and Hunter 2008, 23). The 'justice' here perhaps pertains to the Libra ascendant symbolised by the scales and fairness, which was especially pertinent later in Duncan's life, in significantly representing the 'Scales of Justice' when she appeared at the Central Criminal Court at The Old Bailey.

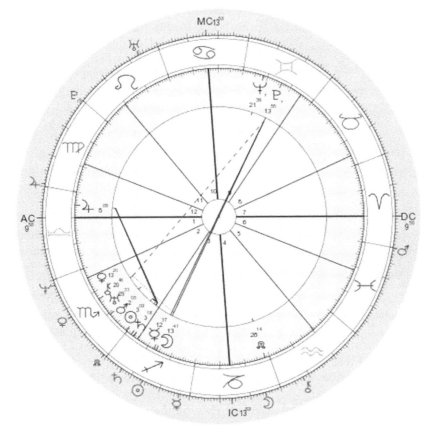

Natal and Transits Chart for Helen Duncan on the day she died, 6th December, 1956.

The physical strength in Duncan's nature would have helped in her work as a materialisation medium, since the nature of the work requires a physical strength and zest of both mental and spiritual health (materialisation mediums are able to allow the spirits with whom they are communicating to make themselves visible to the sitter, either completely or partially). Mars in Sagittarius is a positive placement for sport too, and as a young girl Duncan's sporting activities included ice-skating on the quarries, swimming, country walks and dancing (Brealey and Hunter, 2008, 25). The Sun conjunct Mars suggests that bravery and courage were important to her, and she could have accomplished much through her ability to be daring and enterprising. Certainly, her impulsive and spontaneous nature would have left little room for calm and poise.

It has been said of her that her character traits included "sudden outbursts of hysterical rage" (Gaskill, 2002, 37). Apparently, at school she brazenly gave predictions to the other children and this led her to be treated "with a mixture of respect, fear and contempt" by them (ibid).

The Sun is in the second house, the area representing earnings, possessions and values. This denotes Duncan's focus and need for material possessions or money. Uranus is also present in the second house, it indicates that she earned money in an unusual way and held unorthodox and independent principles in the world of employment. In 1944 when she was scheduled to appear at the Master Temple Psychic Centre, the price of admission for the special occasion of seeing Helen Duncan was twelve shillings and sixpence. This was a considerable sum then, since in today's value it equates to

Commons. Wikimedia.org.uk
Public Domain

approximately between £20–25 (Gaskill, 2002, 6). Before she was this popular, at one time, in order to sustain her large family and her disabled husband, by day she worked in the local bleach factory, while by night she carried out her domestic chores and spiritual work.

The strong Sagittarian energy in her natal chart also indicates that she did everything in excess and, at times, this was to her detriment. For example, the abundance of materialisation trance-sittings that she undertook. She was advised by other spiritualists and her family that she should reduce her work schedule, or it could be to the detriment of her health. It has been observed that, unless mediums look after their health, they may discover that the production of phenomena (especially for the materialisation mediums) can be an exceedingly weakening process (Carrington, 2000, 62).

Unless they have adequately cared for their health, they may become run down and nervously exhausted. This can potentially subject them to conditions such as insomnia and depressing mental emotions – should the latter get worse; it could lead to obsession and even greater challenges (ibid). In Duncan's natal chart, there is some indication that she had a compulsive drive where her faith and religion was concerned.

This is shown by intense and obsessive Pluto in the ninth house, the area which is associated with faith and religion. Pluto is opposing the Moon in the third house (the area of communication and mentality) and reveals how compelled she felt about her faith. These areas will be discussed in greater detail further on.

Duncan chose to ignore advice and recommendations about reducing her workload, determined to bring as much comfort as possible to her sitters, who had lost many loved ones during the wars.

Returning to Mars in the second house, this denotes that Duncan was assertive and resourceful. This placement also indicates that self-employment was possible and, coupled with her abundant energy, she could have put it to good use in this way. Duncan's husband, Henry, had been in the army but was released due to injury and ill health, receiving just eight shillings a week army pension, so Helen became the main earner in the family (as previously stated). Therefore, her competitive and enterprising nature would have helped in earning an income and seeking financial security for herself and her family. During one of the many times when the Duncan's were experiencing financial difficulties, Helen had to move to a smaller house, taking in washing and shirt repairing, even patching sheets; charging a penny for each repair (Brealey and Hunter, 2008, 45). This demonstrates that Duncan would do whatever was necessary in order to earn a basic income and that she was not greedy in what she charged for her work. Before she was married, Duncan had worked in the jute mills and as a nursing aid in Dundee Royal Infirmary. Venus is in the second house and this is particularly interesting, since this planet governs the second house in the natural zodiac (*see glossary*).

Did Helen Duncan Achieve her Potential?

Looking at Duncan's life, she not only came from a poor working-class background, but constantly had to struggle with finances and also with her own and her husband's many health problems. The presence of so many planets in Sagittarius shows that she would not have done anything by halves and also that she needed something to believe in. This she achieved with her belief in life after life, together with her drive to believe that it was her mission in life to help others. The Sun in Sagittarius indicates the 'want' and the Moon the 'need', so she did accomplish and reach her potential.

Venus is detriment (*see glossary*) in Scorpio and suggests that Duncan could attract people with her intensity and willingness to commit. Two obvious examples of this are through her relationship with her husband and her dedication to Spiritualism.

Venus' presence in the second house also indicates characteristics of determination and willpower. This can be seen, for example, when as a young child her mother warned her daughter not to speak about her premonitions to anyone outside of the family, as she may be taken away to the local mental asylum. However, Duncan refused to curb her ways, stubbornly believing that her behaviour and visions were natural (Gaskill, 2002, 35).

Venus in the second house not only denotes a value of earning money but also an appreciation of owning beautiful and valuable items. For example, Duncan was a very skilled at sewing and embroidering. In her home there was a large piano above which hung a picture she had embroidered of a man and woman dancing a minuet together. Her hall dresser was covered in items given to her over the years in appreciation of her work and she always worried that the "presents may be broken" if anyone dusted them. Her niece Mary remembered how she always carried two large handkerchiefs, one used exclusively for flicking away any dust she spotted around her home (Armour, 2000, 22).

Saturn in the second house values bricks and mortar and investments. It is a position that indicates having to work hard for one's money, and it adds a level-headed and realistic approach to earning money. The Sun conjunct Saturn indicates self-responsibility and positions of authority. We see this when Duncan had to become the sole breadwinner for her family after her husband had a heart attack.

Saturn is in the sign of Sagittarius and denotes a fear of intellectual studies, along with a fear of restriction in education and religion. This was true in Duncan's life in as much as she was not particularly driven whilst in formal education as a young girl. In one biography, she was described as having a "lack of academic aptitude" (Gaskill, 2002, 37). She has also been summed-up by another as being "Unintellectual, domestic, anthropomorphic and materialistic, Duncan personified stigmatised working-class and female culture (Hazelgrove, 2000, 279). Coming from an impoverished background, it is perhaps understandable that Duncan's focus was often on financial security and providing for her family.

Later on in her life, as a mature student, however, she fostered an honourable and hard-working application and attitude towards her education. For example, when she was studying for her diploma certificate for the Psychic Union, she patiently underwent diverse examinations and extensive tests until she was finally granted her diploma.

Mercury is detriment (*see glossary*) in Sagittarius at 12 degrees. This placement shows that she would have, at this stage of her life, enjoyed learning and discussing her ideas with other people and gained enormous pleasure from exploring the world of ideas. However, she would have found the arena of detail and minutiae far less interesting and attractive, since her great Sagittarian nature was largely interested in the broader vision of life, aiming high for a more materialistically secure base and wanting to nurture her communication skills.

The lack of earth signs in her natal chart suggests that she may have been unsystematic and disorganised, and probably would have benefited from method and routine. She may have found some balance in marrying her husband (who was born on the 8th May, 1886, i.e. in the earth sign of Taurus), who would have been more earthy and practical in his approach to life (http://www.helenduncan.net/ –No longer extant). The Moon's Nodes in the natal chart indicate one's karmic purpose and is able to offer spiritual advice helping to understand one's present relationships in terms of one's past life. Duncan's North Node is in the sign of Capricorn, which advises that Duncan would have benefitted from being more cautious, practical and realistic. The South Node advises that release of emotional possessiveness of the past would help Duncan to progress along her path in life.

Duncan's diploma as a qualified medium enabled her to serve many churches throughout the country. Before she became an accredited medium, she used to 'communicate in the home' which is symbolic of the Moon conjunct Mercury. She used to give freely her time and services to people in distress and need, by providing them with evidence of their loved-ones who had passed over, or by talking to people in a coaxing, sensitive and nurturing way. Mercury is in the third house, which is naturally ruled in the zodiac by Mercury and by the element of air. This placement suggests that Duncan had a restless and agile mind, was a natural communicator, always quick with an opinion and naturally witty.

For example, once, having collapsed into a diabetic coma at her home, her doctors were concerned about permanent kidney damage and strongly advised her to give up work. Her response, "I've got to die of something ... don't worry, doctor," is typical of the natural philosopher in her Sagittarian nature. On another occasion, her friend and fellow medium, Jack MacKay, were talking together and Jack described an incident when he was suffering from dizziness due to his own diabetes and began staggering, having to cling onto the railings for support. Passers-by unkindly jeered at him for drunkenness, although he was in fact teetotal. Duncan's response was, "Never mind, Jack, names won't kill you. It's only shortness of breath that does that" (Brealey, 2008, 144 & 148).

The third house also corresponds with siblings and neighbours, and with the Moon resident in that house it suggests that Duncan may have adopted a motherly role with her siblings and amongst her neighbours. For example, although Duncan rarely had much money, according to her niece, Mary, she always gave readily to those who had less. If she could not give money then she gave bread or milk, or even – to the poorer children – jam sandwiches. Mary remembered her aunt giving money so that a neighbour could get the doctor for her sick child (Armour, 2002, 22). The Moon is opposing Pluto, which gives a suggestion of being controlling and over-protective, perhaps even being obsessed with being a mother, with a need for emotional and intense interaction. Duncan had eleven or twelve pregnancies, but only six of her children survived. Of these, only one (Gina Brealey) became a spiritualist (Armour, 2000, 17). The Moon in the third house and opposing Pluto in the ninth house denotes communicating spiritually with the afterlife, and that Duncan was guided and nurtured by spirit. Since the Moon symbolises the domestic and home life and Pluto crisis, it could be said that Duncan experienced a very intense home life.

Returning to Duncan's communication skills, there are indicators in the chart that Duncan would have made an effective public speaker for congregations and other audiences. For example, the Moon sextile the ascendant Libra and Venus trine the MC in Cancer. The good natured and co-operative side of Libra will have helped Duncan in one-to-one sittings, while Venus trine the MC would have helped in relating with the general public.

Working for the Psychic Union certainly entailed a great deal of travelling for her work, and this is supported by the fusion of planets in Sagittarius in her natal chart, since this can indicate a great deal of travel in the subject's life. Duncan felt more confident when accompanied by her husband, who frequently joined her as she travelled throughout Britain, demonstrating her mediumship. The Duncan's decided to put two of their children into a council-run boarding school and employed a young girl to manage their home in order to care for their eldest working daughter whilst they were working away from home; clearly their financial situation had improved by this time. The Moon is conjunct and Mercury denotes that Helen Duncan needed to talk about domestic and home life and it also denotes movement from the home and being away from home.

The signs at the angles of the chart all belong to the cardinal mode, which suggests a leading and pioneering individual (which she certainly was!), together with a focus on the self (Aries), home (Cancer), partner (Libra) and career (Capricorn).

The Moon is the ruling planet of the MC and indicates the potential to work with the general public where using her intuition, sensitivity and fluctuating responses were important to the recipient of her work. It also shows the potential to work in the home and for the public, and Duncan undoubtedly did both during her career. She also worked as a nursing aid in Dundee Royal Infirmary, where she was able to offer care, coaxing and support to patients.

The sense of freedom in being released from the full-time domestic responsibilities would have been nurturing and satisfying to Duncan's Moon in Sagittarius, enabling her to pursue her adventures; to travel, explore and indulge in her love of spiritualism.

This is somewhat illustrated by the aspect created by the Sun sextile Jupiter, showing her adventurous, exploring, confident, optimistic and sometimes naive nature. It also denotes a self-expression through God and religion, which brings joy to others, and can be seen through her service as a medium in spiritualist churches. Jupiter in Libra shows a confidence in partnership with her husband and that she enjoyed sharing with other significant people in her life. The sign is also associated with co-operation and diplomacy. This we can see, for example, by her co-operation with Harry Price, in that she agreed to be subject to his psychic experimentations at the National Laboratory of Psychical Research in 1931. She may well have agreed to assist Price as she knew she had nothing to hide and was a genuine medium. One of his experiments included subjecting her to stomach X-Rays; he believed she had a second stomach where she regurgitated cheese-cloth, pretending it to be ectoplasm! Price wrote a chapter dedicated to his work with Duncan called 'The Cheese-Cloth Worshipers' in his book, *Leaves from a Psychist's Casebook*, published in 1933 (http://www.harrypricewebsite. co.uk).

Journalist, film critic and spiritualist, Hannen Swaffer, told the court (when Duncan appeared at the Old Bailey, Central Criminal Court in 1944) that he had been present at other tests that Duncan undertook by Price. He described how she was tied up with 40 yards of sash cord and handcuffed with police regulation handcuffs. Not only that, but her two thumbs were tightly tied together with thick thread which bit into her flesh. This was carried out by a magician, and yet, despite this brutal act, Duncan was still able to produce phenomena, which must have left them nonplussed to say the least! (Crossley, 1999, 84).

Another illustration of her diplomacy can be seen whereby, during her one-to-one private consultation sittings with her clients, she did not always tell them what she could see clairvoyantly, (especially if an unpleasant situation was impinging, such as death). She said "I exercise discretion in these matters ... It would be criminal folly to make such a disclosure to a client" (Gaskill, 2002, Photos on plate 11).

As previously discussed, Libra is the sign on the ascendant and depicts one's impression, image and physical appearance. Libra ascendants often have large eyes and like to be well colour co-ordinated. Jupiter is conjunct the ascendant and, since Jupiter grows, expands, can generate an abundance and indulgence; this can be a signification of a sizeable person. In the biography, Duncan's physical appearance as a young girl is described as being always rather plump, but "... her beauty lay in her large deep brown eyes, unusual blue-black hair and wonderful personality"(Brealey, 2008, 17).

The ruler of the ascendant and of the chart is Venus, which symbolises beauty, appeal and style as well as idealism. Libra is symbolised by the scales, and it is significant that these Libran scales of justice were to be metaphorically tilted in Duncan's life, where she strove for fairness and justice, having been hounded by the authorities, police and popular press on more than one occasion. The Aries descendant shows that in her life she faced battles and challenges, and that she had to remain assertive, brave and headstrong in dealing with those that opposed her.

Pluto is trine the ascendant and makes for a charismatic though intense and magnetic impression. Pluto symbolises rebirth, transformation and regeneration, which is significant, in that Duncan had the gift to empower others by providing evidence of survival by way of materialising those that had passed over to the spiritual realms. Evidence and survival are both correspondences of Pluto.

In 1914, when the First World War was declared, Duncan was just seventeen and offered her services in a munitions factory. She was sent for the mandatory medical examination but was declared unfit for service due to her weight. Yet that medical examination turned out to be something of a blessing, since it revealed that she had tuberculosis of the left lung. She had to spend time at a sanatorium, where she did make a remarkably recovery.

The presence of Jupiter in the twelfth house (which governs isolation, secrets, institutions, prisons and hospitals) indicates Duncan's spiritualist faith. It also symbolises a tremendous impressionability and optimism, revealing a belief by the individual that one is blessed and lucky in life and indeed Duncan is recorded as always saying that God and spirit were with her (Brealey, 2008, 45). Her time as a patient in hospital made a great impression on her, and must have influenced her decision to nurse others. The twelfth house also corresponds with sacrifice, the sick and the suffering, martyrdom and victimisation. Experience of time spent in seclusion is symbolised here, for example in hospital and in prison, both of which Duncan endured.

> **Uranus:** There is a rebellious side to Uranus where ideals and truths are of paramount importance, which often meets with opposition and resistance. In the sign of Scorpio, the Uranus energy may have exposed concerns around death and life-after-death issues, since uncompromising Scorpio associates with crisis, investigation, research and transformation.

Correspondences of Jupiter also include law and politics and Duncan undoubtedly experienced both during the course of her trial in 1956. The abundance of optimism and confidence in this area indicates that Duncan could draw upon her rich inner resources with confidence and faith to carry her through difficult times. The twelfth house (and its ruling planet, Neptune) also symbolises spirituality and the mediumistic, psychic and healer, and is also able to respond to the Divine and higher service with delicacy and sensitivity.

Duncan became known in various ways amongst different audiences. Amongst spiritualists, she was known for her mediumistic gifts of healing, materialisation and trance mediumship. In the spiritualist movement, she was considered to be one of the most tested and hounded mediums, becoming known as a martyr for spiritualism. To the audience of the popular press and general public, she was known as the woman accused of fraud, which was the centre of a World War II legal battle. The sextile aspect created between Jupiter and Saturn suggests a test of faith, and that faith would have given Duncan a foundation in testing times. It also denotes an abundance of patience and persistence, as well as an optimistic and philosophical principle about materialism and work.

In 1944, Duncan was convicted of 'conspiracy to pretend to conjure up the dead,' under the ancient Witchcraft Act of 1735. At the Old Bailey, in Central London, she had offered to do a test séance in order to prove her authenticity, but the offer was declined by the court. When she left the dock weeping, she exclaimed in her broad Scottish accent, "I never hee'd so many lies in a'my life!" (Brealey, 2008, 228).

Duncan was imprisoned at Holloway Women's Prison, North London, for nine months and served her full sentence. She was the last person to ever be convicted under The Witchcraft Act. Generationally, Uranus in the sign of Scorpio denotes that she could have helped influence deep seated and humanitarian changes in society. This is because Uranus is an outer planet, meaning it takes a long time to move into another sign (seven years in Uranus' case) and therefore affects generations of people. During her trial, there was cross-border co-operation and developments when the Law Societies of both England and Scotland jointly and simultaneously came together in saying that the case was a travesty of justice. This demonstrated the Uranus humanity and Scorpio taboos in society (whatever was culturally perceived as a taboo in those times). On a more personal level, Uranus in Scorpio suggests Duncan may have experienced a wealth of upheavals and unpredictability in her life; such is the surprising and shocking nature of Uranus.

Duncan's case had generated anger, concern, interest and sympathy from significant governmental and political figures, such as Sir Winston Churchill and Lord Hugh Dowding. Sir Winston Churchill was Prime Minister at the time and he himself was psychic and had many sixth sense experiences, which he describes in his autobiography. He had also been ordained into the Grand Ancient Order of Druids. Lord Dowding, who had led the Air Force in the Battle of Britain, was also a spiritualist who had authored the spiritualist book, *Many Mansions* (amongst others). Saturn conjunct Uranus shows opposing principles of authority and anti-establishment and suggests a breaking with tradition and guarded reform. It is also a helpful aspect in providing form and foundation to new ideas and principles in society.

Mars sextile Jupiter indicates that Duncan had to fight for her beliefs, and the aspect created between Mars conjunct Saturn, is an indication that she also had to fight for and against authority. While it reveals tests of strengths, courage and hard labour, it can also indicate aggressive manifestations, i.e. outbursts of temper. Mars conjunct Uranus denotes sudden aggression and violence as well as highly strung nervous system. As a child Duncan had been described as being timid and passive but also had "sudden outbursts of hysterical rage" (Gaskill, 2002, 37). The preponderance of the mutable Node in Duncan's chart would have added to her fidgety and restless nature, while Mars conjunct Uranus is also indicative of a freedom fighter and a revolutionary.

The Sun is also conjunct Uranus, suggesting that Duncan liked to do things in an individual way and needed freedom and space. She had a determination, drive and impulse to be different from others, satisfying her independent spirit and detaching herself from others. In doing so, this could have brought her attention and recognition, yet in her uniqueness she may have felt alienated in some ways. When she was seven-years-old, she first began to show signs of her gift as a medium and psychic and prophetically, her mother had warned "… if she continued to say things like that, people would say she was a witch and put her in prison" (Brealey and Hunter, 2008, 18). Forty years later, that warning would come to fruition.

Neptune is in the ninth house, which governs higher education, law, philosophy and travel; it is unaspected in the chart. This indicates that Duncan was looking for spiritual enlightenment and was naturally drawn to meditation, mysticism and philosophy and trance mediumship. Being able to travel would have enabled her to escape physically from the domestic and mundane. By venturing into higher education in studying for her diploma, this would have enabled her to escape the limitations of the mind. Neptune and Pluto are in the sign of Gemini and this indicates a curious, restless and imaginative person who could be talkative and liked to get to the heart of a matter in communicating. Serving spiritualist churches is in keeping with the Neptunian divine, as is being absorbed in the realms of spirit.

Healing was also a gift of Duncan's and she could heal by her compassionate spoken word and by hands-on healing. During the First World War, she brought comfort to many families who experienced bereavement, channelling messages from those that had passed-over, and often she did so whilst not charging payment for this, giving her services selflessly with compassion and a warm heart. Pluto is also in the ninth house and suggests that Duncan had a deeper understanding about the meaning of life than many other people. Crisis and devastation may have helped formulate her life philosophy, and as Pluto corresponds with the afterlife, it suggests meaning and philosophy from life and death themes.

Venus is creating a quincunx to Pluto in the natal chart, suggesting that Duncan may have suffered emotionally because of ill health or the death of a loved-one, which in turn may have impacted on her health in an intense way. The poor health and death of loved-ones may have created an obsessive intensity in her relationships with partners and in her work. Apart from her husband's and her own ill health, several of Duncan's children returned to the spirit world very quickly through their ill health, which inevitably would have brought grief pain and sorrow to her as a mother.

As far as her health is concerned, it is known that she lived with angina, diabetes, kidney problems and excess weight. Shortly after she married, she was admitted into hospital with pneumonia and was strong enough to survive the episode after rest and treatment (Hartley, 2007, 29).

Returning to Duncan's Neptunian compassion, empathy and understanding, this can be illustrated by the way distressed neighbours would visit her, seeking 'answers' and 'evidence' about what had happened to their loved-ones who were lost in active war service. At Duncan's home development circle, she used prayer and hymn to cleanse, elevate and protect the 'circle' from any confused or lost souls – confused and lost being in keeping with Neptune.

UNASPECTED NEPTUNE

Neptune is significant in Duncan's chart in that it does not have to confront hard and challenging aspects, allowing greater freedom for her to develop her imagination and inspiration. It symbolises here that she had the potential for strength in mediumship and clairvoyance, and an abundance of intuition and sensitivity.

> **Unaspected Planets**
> Peregrine is another word used to describe an unaspected planet. It originally came from a Latin word meaning 'foreign'.

Neptune can also signify escapism and depravity, as well as confusion and indefinable upsetting disturbances. Duncan often experienced poverty in her life, along with confusion when, as a child, she was unable to understand why others around her could not see or hear 'spirit' in the same way that she could. She also had the ability to produce ectoplasm (a physical substance that can manifest as a result of psychic phenomenon and/or spiritual energy) whilst deep in trance, and she could produce phenomena whereby items could move independently of any human aid, as well as manifesting spirits which could be seen to the naked eye. This is a controversial aspect of her work, and controversy can be seen in her chart. The natal Uranus is in the second house the area, which governs money and self-value. Here Uranus calls for Duncan to be an individual; different, original and unorthodox. The adventure and freedom-loving planets in Sagittarius, coupled with Uranus in the second house, commands a tremendous sincerity coupled with independence, as well as frankness and truth. Saturn conjunct Uranus suggests that Duncan may have experienced limitations and restrictions in her originality, since the nature of Saturn is to barricade and obstruct. One obvious example of this is the appalling experience of her being charged by the authorities of conspiracy, fraud and witchcraft, using an antiquated act from 1735 (as discussed above). By the government not understanding her gifts and

By Kind Permission of Psychic News.

that she was a genuine medium, they assumed that she was a threat to the security services. When she appeared at the Old Bailey in 1944, the country was preparing the forces for what is/was referred to as D-Day. Interestingly, the operation was codenamed 'Operation Neptune' (presumably because Neptune is the god of the sea).

Neptune can and indicate martyrdom and vulnerability. Victimisation can take many forms. As a child, Helen's nickname was 'Hellish Nell' (also the title of one of her biographies), simply because the locals in her superstitious village of Callender misunderstood her. Once she was even unjustly accused of being responsible for the death of one of the younger villagers (Armour, 2000, 16). Her notorious reputation continued to also have an effect on the rest of the MacFarlane family. For example, her daughter, Gina Brealey (neé Duncan), said that Duncan knew how resentful she felt about what had happened to her mother, even though they never discussed it later in life (Crossley, 1999, 4). Duncan's last words to her daughter were, "God knows how I love you lass, but you must forgive them as I have done" (ibid). This remark shows the forgiving and philosophical nature of Helen Duncan, as well as her unwavering belief and faith in God, all of which is indicative of her strong Sagittarian characteristics. Even one of Helen Duncan's granddaughters felt the wrath of being the granddaughter of Britain's last convicted witch (https://www.theguardian.com). She recalled how she would regularly come home from school having been subjected to physical and verbal abuse by fellow students (ibid).

It has been said of Helen Duncan that she "was very much victimised by her times and that she suffered too" (ibid).

Helen also had to cope with becoming estranged from her family as her reputation and popularity increased. Her father and siblings all distrusted anything different from the teachings of their Presbyterian faith. Matters may have come to a head when she predicted the death of her mother-in-law, and after that she and Henry lost the support of her entire family, apart from her loyal brother, Archie Macfarlane. Right to the end of his life, he continued to defend his sister. For example, when their father died, Helen was warned by the rest of the family to stay away from his funeral, but Archie insisted on taking her with him (Armour, 2000, 20). From this, it is easy to see just how many sacrifices Helen Duncan had to make for her work and calling.

Quite apart from family difficulties, Duncan was on the receiving end of several unpleasant attempts to 'prove' she was a charlatan. The most notable – and unjustifiable – of these attempts was by Harry Price (as discussed previously), the self-styled ghost-catcher of Borley Rectory and founder of the National Laboratory of Psychical Research (as discussed above), he was also a long-time member of The Magicians Club (Hartley, 2007, 31). His vilification of Duncan was in fact a projection of his own trickery, since it was eventually proved that *he* was a charlatan, but not, alas before he had permanently damaged Duncan's reputation. Despite his conviction that Duncan was a fraud, he did not appear as a prosecution witness when she appeared at the Central Criminal Court at the Old Bailey in 1944, although some claimed that they had seen him in the vicinity (Crossley, 1999, 79).

Duncan's ability to produce ectoplasm was just one of the reasons that brought about Duncan being tested by other psychic investigators, to see if she was genuine in her manifestations, or to identify if she was committing fraud. Such was her accuracy in her mediumship that she became a threat to the establishment and national security during the Second World War.

Duncan was arrested in 1944 at one of her séances in the naval town of Portsmouth. However, before that event and on another occasion, a sailor whose hatband bore the name HMS Barham, materialised at one of her séances and addressed his mother who was in the séance congregation (Guiley, 1999, 107). He informed her that his ship HMS Barham had exploded and sunk off Malta and many sailors had been drowned and there was a huge loss of lives. Neptune's influence and correspondence is recognised here as it symbolises the sea, drowning, loss and sorrow.

The recipient of the sailor's message protested when the information about the sunken ship was given. She said that it could not possibly be true as she had not been notified formally by the Admiralty. The mother was however notified formally three months later that her son had been drowned, thus demonstrating the accuracy of the message and the authenticity of the materialised spirit, channelled by the mediumistic and clairvoyant Duncan. However, the authorities did not see it that way, and unwittingly, she had betrayed some wartime secrets. The Admiralty had not declared the information instantly as they believed it would affect morale.

As soon as Duncan was released from prison, the Spiritualist National Union campaigned to get The Witchcraft Act reformed, and issuing a statement: "Helen Duncan was charged under an Act which is antiquated and obsolete. In the course of the case, rules relating to rules and procedure were laid down, which in our view, render inevitable the conviction of any innocent person similarly placed" (Valiente, 2007, 10).

After World War II had ended, supportive Members of Parliament concluded that the position for spiritualists, psychics and students of the occult was intolerable in a free society. It was in June 1951 that The Fraudulent Mediums Act became law, and the antiquated Witchcraft Act was finally repealed. Under this new act the only circumstances under which a prosecution could be brought forward was where deliberate fraud was committed for gain. Fraud is in keeping with Neptune since it corresponds with deception, distortion, illusion and scandal and the new act of that time illustrates just how significant unaspected Neptune was in Duncan's chart and made a significant contribution in her life. The repeal of the Witchcraft Act and the introduction of The Fraudulent Mediums Act is indicative somewhat of the Uranus in Scorpio placement which has the capacity to shock into reform, and also an intense pursuit of freedom and liberty.

DOORS, KEYS AND LOCKS

Duncan's granddaughter, Margaret Hahn says on 'The Official Website of Helen Duncan', that 'For the entire nine months of her unjust incarceration, Helen Duncan's prison cell door was never once locked! What's more, she continued to apply her psychic gifts as a constant stream of warders and inmates alike found their way to her cell for spiritual guidance.' (http://helenduncan.org.uk/imprisonment.html). It seems inevitable that

Duncan with the stellium of planets in Sagittarius in her natal chart should become involved with law and politics during her life, and that the theme of freedom would be of significance in her life (*see chart on right*).

When Duncan passed away, her luminaries in Sagittarius had progressed into the unconventional air sign of Aquarius, and the remaining inner planets of Mercury, Venus and Mars had progressed into the earthy and responsible sign of Capricorn. This suggests that she had become somewhat experimental, progressive, radical and a social reformer, although themes of freedom, humanity, liberty and truth would have been of great significance to Duncan throughout her life. Application, hard-work, responsibility, trials and tribulations would have all been second nature to Duncan. When Duncan was released from prison, she announced that she was no longer prepared to offer her services again as a medium, whether for religious, scientific, or any other purpose (Brealey and Hunter, 2008, 108). However, after a while, she changed her mind as the spirit again called her to serve and help others.

	Natal	Prog	Transit
☉ Sun	3 Sag 9' 9"	3♒12'
☽ Moon	13 Sag 40'59"	14♒38'
☿ Mercury	12 Sag 36'41"	9♑21'
♀ Venus	13 Sco 19'41"	27♑28'
♂ Mars	2 Sag 4'59"	15♑49'

Progression Date: 23rd January, 1898, 3:41:44, UT

LONGEVITY AND PERSEVERANCE

Areas connected with time would have been key to Duncan. For example, time spent in prison and being ahead of her time through clairvoyance and mediumship, which may have caused her much stress and hardship. The lesson around time is further indicated through Duncan's transit of her second Saturn return, the planet which rules Capricorn and which represents endings and beginnings. Transiting Saturn in the third house was conjunct her natal Saturn, which brings a maturity to her life and a realisation that pragmatism, realism, duty and responsibility were crucial to the next phase of her life. Areas of life which were futile and no longer necessary or crucial in Duncan's life will have inevitably crumbled away from the fundamental and essential Capricorn/Saturnian nature.

The progressed luminaries in the sign of Aquarius coupled with natal Uranus in Scorpio gives a distinct Uranus influence to Duncan's chart. Some of the Aquarian/Uranus influences which had an effect on Duncan's life are illustrated as follows:

- She was futuristic progressive and visionary
- She was unconventional and original, emancipating and open-minded
- She was honest and truthful in her co-operation and willingness to be subject to scientific experimentation to prove and understand the authenticity of her mediumship
- She was seen as anti-establishment by the authorities and establishment
- She was independent and liberated and liked to feel free from limitations in society
- She experienced many shocks in her life including the loss of some of her children, and being shocked by external influences whilst working in trance-state as a medium, i.e. when detectives raided a séance whilst she was still in trance

In Duncan's natal chart, Uranus has learnt its lesson in Scorpio, almost completing its cycle at 29 degrees and is almost ready to commence a new cycle in Sagittarius. When Duncan passed away, her ascendant Libra had progressed into the sign of Scorpio, the sign which corresponds with death and rebirth, healing and transformation.

Returning to the transits in Duncan's chart for 6th December, 1956, there were a number of aspects that transiting Jupiter in the twelfth house was creating on the day that Duncan passed away. Transiting Jupiter in the twelfth house suggests that she was at the end of a cycle in her life, concerned about spiritual truths and wisdom and finding that spirituality gave her comfort and support. At this time of her life, she would have found meaning in her being and learnt a tremendous amount about spiritual dimensions and existence. However, she may have needed an abundance of healing and rest and may have wanted to withdraw from life needing retreat and solitude.

Transiting Jupiter creates a wide conjunction with her natal Jupiter at this time, so she may have wanted more freedom and space in her life (*please see box on the right*). Another possibility is that Duncan may have wanted to share with others what  she had learned. One example of this is that she encouraged her daughter to sit in a 'Development Circle' in order to help advance her psychic gifts. Transiting Jupiter sextile natal Saturn with an orb of 3 degrees suggests that she fostered an optimistic approach to duties and obligations, making plans with caution and realism. She also had the ability to set down foundations to ensure success in order to turn her ideas into reality. Also with an orb of 3 degrees transiting Jupiter is sextile the natal Sun and Mars, we can see her enormous willpower and strength coupled with courage and exuberance.

Throughout her life, Duncan had suffered with poor health, including diabetes and heart problems. Sagittarius and Jupiter rule the liver and pancreas (where insulin is made) in medical astrology. With so many aspects created with transiting Jupiter at the time of her death, it is possible that Duncan could have died of diabetic-related illnesses. As Jupiter expands and creates abundance and plenty, the excess weight that she carried may have contributed to her heart problems. Natal Jupiter being conjunct the ascendant, the ruler of her Libran ascendant suggests a person with a big heart and a love of socialising, travelling and spiritual exploration.

The two transits comprising of transiting Mars trine Uranus and transiting Pluto square Mars are both significant to this period in Duncan's life. Both transits correspond to the area of accidents, burns and health. Transiting Mars was in the sixth house – the area which governs work, exercise and health. It is also the house of service which, in this case, could denote 'service to spirit' – and it was trine Uranus. This indicates that work was challenging and that there may have been health difficulties too. It denotes taking risks, as well as accidents, burns, fevers and infections. This is illustrated when Duncan was grabbed by the police whilst she was in trance during a séance that she was participating in, just weeks after she was released from prison. In lacking spiritual knowledge, the police would have been unaware that it was dangerous to touch a medium in trance, and may have unintentionally caused some damage to her health. Second degree burns were also found on Duncan's stomach after the raid.

Transiting Pluto is in the eleventh house – the area which governs long range goals, associations, groups, societies or a movement – and here it is making a square aspect with Mars. This suggests a regeneration of goals, and involvement with a movement that wants to reform society. Since Pluto has dark and dangerous energies, it could be said that there were crafty, dangerous and vengeful persons among her associations, and there were some determined attempts to discredit her and her work throughout her life, and even after her death. Other correspondences of Pluto are criminals, enemies, detectives, spies and researchers, all who could work 'undercover', which is

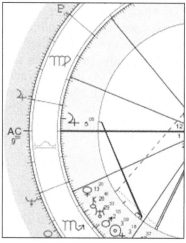

Plutonian by nature. This transit (transiting Mars square natal Pluto) also denotes tremendous physical energy which, if not managed carefully, could lead to a physical breakdown as well as accidents through sheer exhaustion from the subject working too hard.

The distinct Sagittarian and Jupiter influence in Duncan's natal chart shows a tendency to excess, immoderation and overload (as previously discussed). Her Centaur's arrow never failed to look to the higher realms for guidance, with a belief and faith in spirit which was immovable. Law, politics, and publishing, are all well-known correspondences of Sagittarius, and were apparent both during and after Duncan's passing. Indeed, much has been written and published about Helen Duncan's life and trial. In April 2008, the European Union passed a piece of legislation called The Consumer Protection from Unfair Trading Regulations. It replaced a number of Acts of Parliament including The Fraudulent Mediums Act of 1951.

At a very early age, Duncan had been aware of the spiritual and psychic areas of life and knew she possessed a unique ability to see and hear 'spirit'. Her niece, Flossie, daughter of the ever-loyal Archie, described her as "... a kind, generous, ordinary woman, but with an exceptional mediumistic gift" (Armour, 2000, 22). Duncan developed these gifts into trance mediumship where she was able to materialise spirit while in trance, an exceptionally unique and rare gift. She never forgot her beginnings however, and her ashes were scattered in her home village of Callender, in a secret location between two trees where she had played as a child (Armour, 2000, 119). In a newspaper feature in 1933 she claimed that her gift of second-sight was the "power to peer into the past and forward into the future to see things that have been and yet to be in the lives of others" (Gaskill, 2002, Photos, Plate 11).

Helen Duncan brought tremendous comfort to many people and courageously travelled up and down the country during and before the Second World War, but, in the end, it was a gift which greatly impacted on her earthly life. To this day she remains famous as the last person to be imprisoned under the Witchcraft Act. In 2007, a campaign was launched to pardon and clear Duncan's name, however the Criminal Cases Review Commissions rejected the petition claiming that, it was not in the public's interest (www.dailymail.co.uk).

Had Helen Duncan not been found guilty under the ancient Witchcraft Act of 1735 (which was repealed in 1951) and imprisoned for nine months, it may have been that mediums of today may never have been free to practice their philosophy and religion, which includes demonstrating life after physical life through clairvoyance and/or materialisation trance sittings, without fear of being accused of witchcraft (which was totally irrelevant) and sent to prison.

In this sense Duncan was a martyr to her cause and the theme of freedom and independence is so pertinent in her birth chart. Jupiter the ruling planet of Sagittarius her Sun sign, is associated with fame and royalty. It is somewhat ironic therefore that Victoria Helen Duncan was named after Queen Victoria who was also a spiritualist, and who enjoyed a close friendship with John Brown who was mediumistic. Little could Duncan's parents know just how infamous their little Victoria was going to become. She possessed a rare gift which she always described as God-given, and she used it to bring comfort and hope to others, reassuring them that life is eternal.

ACKNOWLEDGEMENTS, CREDITS AND REFERENCES

Natal, progressions & transits chart generated by http://www.astro.com
Rodden Classification – Rating 'AA'
Duncan, Helen: Thu 25th November 1897, 3.00am, GMT, Callender, Stirling, Scotland, UK. 4w14, 56n15.
Collector Gerard. Source of data Birth Certificate/Birth Record.
Also Malcolm Gaskill's biography on Helen Duncan, *Hellish Nell*.

BOOKS

Brealey, G. and Hunter, K. (Republished in 2008) *The Two Worlds of Helen Duncan*. Saturday Night Press Publications, England.

Carrington, H. (1975) *Your Psychic Powers And How To Develop Them*. Published by Newcastle Publishing Inc.

Crossley, A.E. (1999) *The Story of Helen Duncan Materialisation Medium*. Published by Psychic World Classic Publications (Imprint of Con-Psy Publications).

Gaskill, M. (2002) *Hellish Nell*. Published by Fourth Estate.

Guiley, R.E. (Ed.) (1999) *The Encyclopaedia of Witches & Witchcraft*. Published by Checkmark Books.

Hartley, R. (2007) *Helen Duncan: The Mystery Show Trial*. Published by H Pr Publishing.

Hazelgrove, J. (2000) *Spiritualism and British Society between the Wars*. Published by Manchester University Press.

Valiente, D. (2007) *The Rebirth of Witchcraft*. Published by Robert Hale, London.

WEBSITES

https://www.theguardian.com/uk/2007/jan/13/secondworldwar.world/ – Mary Martin grand-daughter and campaign to pardon Helen Duncan. Accessed on 24/08/2019.

http://www.harrypricewebsite.co.uk/Seance/Duncan/duncan-intro.htm – Price's book including chapter about 'Helen Duncan – The Cheese-Cloth Worshippers.' Accessed on 26/08/2019.

http://www.helenduncan.net/ – Accessed 22/06/2014 but appears to be no longer in existence.

http://www.helenduncan.org.uk/trial.html – Number of children died and survived, Helen Duncan trial, police last raid on Helen, burns. Accessed 23/06/2014

http://helenduncan.org.uk/imprisonment.html – Accessed April, 2015.

CHAPTER SEVEN

Cecil Williamson 1909–1999

Founder of Museum of Witchcraft, Soldier, Director, Editor, Photographer and Film Screenwriter

CECIL HUGH WILLIAMSON was born on 18th September, 1909, in Paignton, Devon; the eldest of three children. He had two younger sisters; Charmain Gay (b.1914) and Maureen Elay (b.1916). His father was Hugh Alexander Williamson, born on 29th May, 1885, in Edinburgh, Scotland, who died on 15th November, 1979, in Torquay, Devon. His mother was Ermyntrude Alberta Alexandra (née Walsh), born on 15th November, 1885 in Cork, Ireland; and died on 16th November, 1975, in Exeter, Devon, UK.

Williamson's parents spent much of their time abroad, largely because of his father's eminent Royal Naval career and his various postings overseas. He became a lieutenant and was awarded the distinguished Royal Naval Medal of the CMG (Order of Saint Michael and Saint George). In 1913, he undertook a course at the Central Flying School at Salisbury Plain and, by summer of 1917, he was appointed as flying officer. By 1919, he was granted a permanent commission as a wing commander in the RAF (http://www.dreadnoughtproject.org/tfs/index.php/). As a very young child, Williamson spent time with his nanny; later, he was sent to boarding schools, spending the school holidays with various relatives (Patterson, 2014, 123).

When he was 27, Williamson married film make-up artist, Gwendolyn (Gwen) Vera Wilcox, on 21st February, 1933. They had two daughters; Marlena Corina born 29th August, 1938, and Anita Christina on 28th August, 1947 (http://www.thepeerage.com). Like their father, both daughters were born Sun sign Virgo. Williamson went on to become a film director, influential witch and founder of the Witchcraft Research Centre and The Museum of Witchcraft. He also managed other museums, such as the Polperro Museum in Cornwall. It is sometimes claimed he worked for MI6 and the 'Secret Service', but most of this evidence is anecdotal; the Author's enquiries of the various authorities have thrown up no proof to support this assertion and will be discussed in more detail further on.

WHAT WILLIAMSON'S NATAL CHART SHOWS

Cecil Hugh Williamson was born on Saturday 18th September, 1909, at 9.00am, when the Sun was in the mutable earth sign of Virgo at 24 degrees, and when the Moon was in the fixed water sign of Scorpio at 5 degrees.

The Sun in Virgo suggests he was kind and industrious, sought perfection and enjoyed being of service to others in a practical way, since all these areas are associated with Virgo. Administration and archiving collections, data compilation and organising exhibits are also areas associated with the analytical and methodical Virgoan nature and, indeed, Williamson once described himself as a "born collector" (The Museum of Witchcraft, 2011, 13).

Friends connected with some of the large museums in London encouraged him to exhibit his own private collection, assuring him that it was too good to be hidden away (ibid). At first, Williamson thought they were teasing him but soon realised they were sincere.

The Moon in determined and passionate Scorpio reveals that he had very deep emotions and needed privacy. The nature of Scorpio is to bury, conceal and veil and shows that confidentiality and trust were important to him. This can be seen, for example, in his silence about his family, although not in the way he claimed to have worked for MI6 and the Secret Service since, even if he had, he would have been required to sign the Official Secrets Act. Perhaps he enjoyed fostering a sense that he was a man of mystery.

This can be seen in an interview with the *New York Times* journalist, Peter Bloxham, at the Witchcraft Museum in 1970. When asked about his own claim of magical powers, Williamson said that he was a "strictly academic researcher" (wwwnytimes.com, 1970). He continued that "sorcerers are men of a learned and serious disposition ... sorcerers concern themselves in isolation with celestial magic" (ibid). This reveals his experience and understanding as a solitary practitioner and how seclusion was important to him in his magical work.

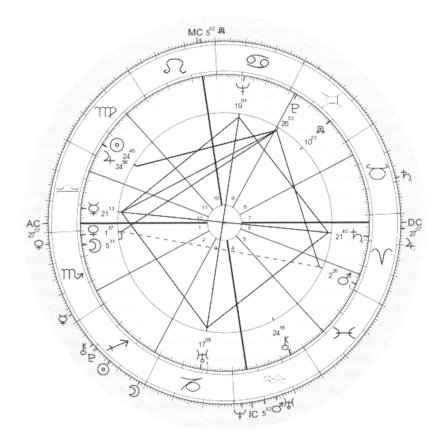

Natal and Transits Chart for Cecil Williamson on the day he died, 9th December, 1999.

Williamson was nevertheless something of a showman and involved in the film world and exhibitions of magic; this is in keeping with his Leo MC (*see glossary*) in the natal chart. This indicates that a career which offered creativity and public recognition would have been satisfying to him. At heart, however, he needed sanctuary and seclusion. He once remarked, when he had to leave England for the Isle of Man because the authorities resisted his idea of a witchcraft museum, "As in war, the road to victory is often found in retreat" (The Museum of Witchcraft, 2011, 13).

His natal chart contains a Grand Cross configuration (*see glossary)* which is an aspect pattern consisting of four squares and two oppositions, making a cross in a square box shape. The configuration is generated by Mercury, Neptune, Saturn and Uranus. The two oppositions are between Mercury and Saturn; and Uranus and Neptune, and they are all in the cardinal signs (*see glossary*) comprising: Mercury in Libra, Saturn in Aries, Uranus in Capricorn and Neptune in Cancer. As this is quite complex, they will now be examined in turn.

The Grand Cross configuration is an unusual pattern and has been described as being a "heavy cross to bear," and, "a constant fight with opposition from all quarters" (Clifford, 2012, 84). The first of the two oppositions in the Grand Cross configuration, Mercury opposing Saturn, shows that Williamson was conscientious, serious-minded, and hard-working. The restricting nature of Saturn suggests he would also have been cautious; for example, in knowing there was opposition to his witchcraft museum, he would have understood the need for a certain amount of circumspection.

Williamson's reservation in speaking about himself and his practices can again be seen in his interview with Peter Bloxham in 1970, from *The New York Times* (as mentioned above). Bloxham commented, "Adroitly, Williamson sidestepped the imminent question about the phenomena that he himself claims to produce." This shows he preferred to deflect any discussion of his own magical and psychic abilities.

The Moon conjunct Venus in Scorpio indicates that Williamson was capable of being cryptic and secretive. Positioned in the first house, the Moon and Venus reveal that adopting a mysterious *persona* helped him veil his private life. Pluto, the ruler of Scorpio, at times can be obsessive, manic and even paranoid; so perhaps Williamson felt compelled to keep his private life more confidential, even if there was no practical reason to do so. Alternatively, perhaps he really did have something to hide, or wished to seem as though he did.

Another example of how he manipulated questions about himself that he did not wish to answer is seen in a comment by his biographer, Steve Patterson, who described him as, "a great weaver of yarns and tales," and that at times it was "difficult to stop him talking" (YouTube video, *see bibliography*). Patterson also said that Williamson would speak about anything but that which had been asked about him personally (ibid). This was another way of Williamson maintaining control of his private self and any information that he wished to conceal.

Returning to the natal chart, Libra is the ascendant sign, which means that the whole chart is ruled by Venus – the governing planet of Libra (and Taurus). Associations of Venus include art and design, beauty, aesthetics and style, as well as relationships – especially those of an intellectual and sociable nature. This is because the Libra Venus gravitates towards others who can stimulate the mind. Williamson would therefore have been eager to find intellectual equals to stimulate his own mental abilities.

Venus is in the first house (as mentioned before) and reveals that, for Williamson, appearance (his own and that of others), finesse and style would have been important to him. For example, in his early sixties, when he was owner of the museum in Cornwall, he was once described as, "… not the half-expected sombre Faustian figure in flowing robes, nor did he materialize at the quayside in a puff of green smoke. Instead, he arrived by station wagon, was wearing a tweed jacket and looked every inch a seaside businessman and absurdly unlike a wizard" (Bloxham, *New York Times*, 1970).

Style and appearance are not just concerned with clothing, however; for Williamson chose to situate his museum at Bourton-in-the-Water, in a late seventeenth century building; Boxbush House. Now a Grade II listed building, it is built of Cotswold stone with mullioned windows. Its appearance did not seem to please Williamson however, who proceeded to remove some of the mullions and make other alterations, much to the annoyance of the parish council (Bourton-on-the-Water parish records, 1956). In fact, Gloucester County Planning Department wrote to Williamson on 18th May, 1956, complaining that he had erected two unauthorised signs and instructed him to either remove both signs or submit a formal application for them to be erected. One of the signs was attached to a tree and advertised the Museum of Witchcraft, while the other was positioned at a car park (Museum of Witchcraft and Magic website, *see bibliography*).

Williamson's design skills can be seen through his film directing work as well as setting up his various museums, particularly the House of Shells in Buckfast, Devon; which housed beautiful, crafted exhibits, including flower displays; all made of shells. An example that shows Williamson's sense of art and aesthetics was an item entitled, 'White Summer Roses'; part of its description reads: "This study in mother-of-pearl is an excellent example of colour matching and graduation using the medium of the shell as nature created it" (Williamson, Date unknown, *House of Shells*, 7).

Venus is on the ascendant at 1 degree of Scorpio in the natal chart, indicating that relationships were important to Williamson (both personal and professional) and that he could be diplomatic and tactful when necessary. Mercury in Libra also shows he could be fair-minded, charismatic and charming.

His ability to communicate and 'get things done' was recognised by his senior officers when he was a member of The Royal Corps of Signals and became involved in the building of the transmitter hall for the covert 'Aspidistra' radio transmitter, c.1942. This was a powerful British radio transmitter used for broadcasting propaganda against Nazi Germany during World War II.

Williamson had to approach some of the wealthy landowners living nearby to request that they rent out their homes "… to a small party of very respectable civil servants" (Howe, 1982, 79). No doubt this project allowed Williamson to be at his charming and diplomatic best, pointing out that it was better to choose one's tenant than to have the house requisitioned (as many were) and used, for example, for gunnery practice. This often resulted in houses being completely uninhabitable after the war. Williamson was successful in securing them a place to rent at nearby Wavendon Tower.

Venus is detriment (*see glossary*) in Scorpio and shows that Williamson had deep and intense feelings, could be passionate in love, and expected a high degree of loyalty from others. Mars in the fifth house also indicates that he lived life to the full in matters of the heart. His chart indicates there may even have been a possibility of extra-marital affairs, as Mars is associated with sex, and the fifth house with love affairs. There is also symbolism in his chart that suggests private and clandestine interaction. This is seen by the presence of Mercury, the planet of communication in the twelfth house, which is the area of privacy and secrets, and also shows the potential for introspective thoughts and hidden communications. This is evidenced by his wife writing to him during their marriage and clearly she was very unhappy about his extra-marital affairs (presumably

Kind permission of Museum of
Witchcraft & Magic

they were separated, as she wrote to him). The letter is in the archives of The Museum of Witchcraft and Magic (Document 619), although unavailable to the public to read.

Other symbolism of Mars in the fifth house suggests there may have been conflict with his children, since this house also rules the area of children, and Mars is associated with discord (amongst other things). It is possible that Williamson's relationship with his two daughters broke down later in life, although it is not certain. His daughters lived in Australia and Canada and came to England to sort out his affairs in order to pay for his care in a nursing home following a massive stroke towards the end of his life. However, there were no family members at his funeral (Graham King to Author in email correspondence). Although, in fairness, this could have been due to the distances involved and the cost of travel.

Along with Venus in the first house, there is also the Moon in Scorpio; which echoes Williamson's strong and powerful feelings. At times, these may have been brooding and obsessive, for such is the nature of Scorpio. The Moon conjunct Venus indicates that he needed reassurance and security and was ultra-sensitive in his feelings.

Pluto is the ruler of Scorpio and, at times, can be dark and toxic, since its energy can be compulsive and manic, controlling and possessive (as discussed earlier). The first house governs the self, so perhaps Williamson was attracted to the occult, mysteries and taboo subjects in order to better help understand himself.

COLLECTIONS AND EXHIBITIONS

Williamson's exacting and precise mind meant he would have found planning and organising his thoughts and information a welcome challenge, and most challenging it was as we shall find out. Certainly, acquiring a collection that was suitable for display as a public exhibit would have required money, energy and time to establish. He told Peter Bloxham, in 1970, that he had been building his collection for 25 years (www. nytimes.com) which shows his commitment and abiding interest in folklore, magic and witchcraft.

Williamson once stated that he had made a hobby from collecting memorabilia connected with folklore from a very early age and any small amount of money he had to spare seems to have been used to fund this (*The Museum of Witchcraft*, 2011, 13). This not only illustrates his passion for folklore but also suggests that innately he *knew* that in the passage of time (an association of Saturn) he would be sharing them for educational purposes (Mercury). Williamson's own scrying mirror that he used as an adult is nowadays exhibited in The Museum of Witchcraft and Magic, showing how he is still 'educating' people about his 'magical' self even today.

Form and structure may have played an important part in his thinking too, as Saturn corresponds with definition and structure. This can be seen, for example, when he converted the rather derelict outbuildings into a Museum of Witchcraft, restaurant and domestic quarters on the Isle of Man. Various documents held at The Museum of Witchcraft and Magic show the numerous invoices, letters and receipts between Williamson and building and glass contractors and other parties involved in helping him construct his various sites to the way he desired. This required commitment and organisation, along with the ability to plan ahead.

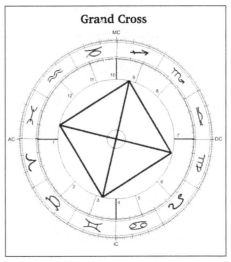

Grand Cross

Some of Williamson's photography can also be seen at The Imperial War Museum of England in collection 8108–23 of Mr Harold Robin, a colleague in the Second World War (www.iwm.org.uk).

The subject of the photography included the construction and equipment of the 'Aspidistra' secret wireless transmitter at Crowborough, Sussex, from 1941–45. It has been suggested (though it is not certain) that the photographs of these secret operations could have been taken for reference purposes. Perhaps it was felt that they would be useful if they were going to build similar transmitters in the future, as well as for repair purposes (Imperial War Museum website). The collection of photographs was not acquired from The Royal Corps of Signals but probably from a donor connected with Harold Robin.

It has been claimed that Williamson was also responsible for some of the large Odeon cinemas built in the 1930s (Broadcasting –'The Biggest Aspidistra'). However, extensive searches with the Royal Institute of British Architects have revealed no record of Williamson ever training and qualifying as an architect. It is extremely unlikely therefore that he played a significant role in designing cinemas, especially since the term 'architect' is a protected title. In architecture, the head architect is always named as architect although, in practice, it would often be a more junior architect who takes control of the project. Sometimes – where known – credit *would* be given to the architect whose firm designed the building and also an individual in the firm (Theatre Cinema Association correspondence).

The aspect Mercury opposing Saturn also relates to the business and communications involved in setting up the enterprise, such as having to deal with planning permission, use of business names, etc. Williamson could be quite cavalier about this, as the parish records for Bourton-on-the-Water show, although the experienced and wise nature of Saturn indicates that, at times, he could also be circumspect. For example, when planning to buy the museum on the Isle of Man, he decided not to use the word 'witchcraft' (previous experience had taught him that the word could attract unwanted controversy) and opted instead to focus on the folklore aspect. Thus, it became 'The Folklore Centre of Superstition and Witchcraft' (ibid, 13).

Returning to the Grand Cross the second opposition in the configuration is, as discussed earlier, created between Uranus and Neptune. This suggests that Williamson dreamt of freedom, innovation and independence, yet his ideals and visions may have met with resistance, which would have disappointed him. It may also have required him to make sacrifices in his family and domestic life, which in turn may have caused detachment, since the aforementioned areas are all associated Neptune and Uranus.

Mercury is square Neptune and Uranus, while Saturn is square Neptune and Uranus. Interpretations for these aspects will be discussed later.

Williamson's dream of owning a witchcraft museum was not without its problems, and it took many years before his vision became a reality. He had to uproot and move home several times before finally finding a secure site for it in Boscastle, Cornwall. He claimed that his previous museums had met with opposition from local authorities and various members of the neighbourhood, including members of the local Christian community. However, the Author's own research suggests that much of the opposition was created and embellished by Williamson himself, rather than by local people.

The Grand Cross in his natal chart also suggests that despite Williamson's tremendous capability and talent, many of his achievements had to overcome challenges and opposition, and some of these will be discussed later. The Grand Cross (*see glossary*) is in the cardinal signs in Williamson's natal chart, suggesting that he had a high degree of ambition, drive, initiative and collaborative ability. The cardinal (*see glossary*) mode indicates initiation and drive, and this significant energy in his natal chart suggests that Williamson was assertive, dynamic and perhaps even forceful when he felt it was necessary. It seems likely he may sometimes have over-reacted.

CONTROL, DETERMINATION AND WILLPOWER

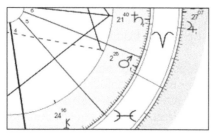

Enterprising Mars is in its natural sign of Aries (*see box below left*), which reinforces the cardinal energy in the natal chart. It indicates that Williamson was courageous and pioneering, as well as enthusiastic. He could also be quite impetuous. Mars is square Pluto in the chart, indicating he had the necessary courage and endurance to help achieve his ambitions. It also reveals that he could be ruthless with himself. His determination to have a museum of witchcraft from which the public could benefit required all the grit and wilfulness of Mars and Pluto in order to achieve his goals.

This aspect may also have affected his health, as Mars symbolises anger, and Pluto the buried and hidden. It is therefore possible he suppressed his anger rather than expressing it. Medical astrologer, Jane Ridder-Patrick, observes that people with hard aspects between Mars and Pluto in their natal chart, "… have a tendency to push themselves to the limits of endurance" (Ridder-Patrick, 1990, 62).

Yet if Williamson *did* hide his rage as a relatively young man, he also had the magical knowledge that enabled him to cast spells at his discretion. This would be in keeping with the vindictive nature of Pluto, the ruler of his Moon and Venus sign. Pluto, in the sign of Gemini also indicates his knowledge of the occult, since Pluto and Gemini are both associated with those areas. It also suggests he was determined and obsessive in his learning, as well as in reading and speaking about magic and the occult, since the aforementioned qualities are associated with Pluto and knowledge with Gemini.

In December, 1952, Williamson wrote to the BBC, offering to deliver a talk on witchcraft for a television programme, presumably with the intention of better educating and informing their viewers about the subject. This was a bold move on Williamson's part given that the Repeal of the Witchcraft Act had only happened, in 1951, and became The Fraudulent Mediums Act (this in turn was repealed in 2008 and replaced by EU Consumer Protection Regulations). The Northern Region Talks Department politely declined his offer of delivering a talk on the subject for the near future, although they advised that they acknowledged he was a specialist and would contact him should a future opportunity arise for a talk on witchcraft (www. museumofwitchcraftandmagic.co.uk/).

Mars square Pluto also reveals that sometimes Williamson needed to fight for his own survival, including facing quite violent abuse on several occasions (*see example further on*). Winning was the only option for him since Mars symbolises courage and competition and Pluto has fixed determination and is associated with survival. Some of the violence had repercussions that affected him for the rest of his life.

For example, he was regularly bullied and beaten at Norfolk House, his second boarding school. On one occasion, he was given a black-eye by a student called Bulstrode (The Museum of Witchcraft, 2011, 41). A school cook, hearing about the incident, took pity on Williamson and introduced him to a very capable wise woman who taught him some spell craft. She advised him how to make a witches swing and to make a wish through a tantra. Williamson followed her instruction, made and sat on the swing and then, as the swing went backwards and forwards, chanted his tantra (ibid).

The magical remedy seems to have proved effective, for shortly afterwards the culprit Bulstrode had a skiing accident in the school holidays, was confined to a wheelchair as a result and never returned to school. This shows a way of Williamson 'owning' his personal power and fighting back, taking some control of his life through cursing and seeking revenge. It is also interesting that he obviously shared this story with others, and seems not to have felt any regret about his actions. This example also alludes to the Uranus opposition Neptune aspect in his natal chart, where innovative Uranus is able to challenge Neptune's vulnerability.

Williamson's magical education continued when he left school and worked in Rhodesia on a tobacco plant. There he befriended African witchdoctors, observing they had similar beliefs to the English cunning women and witches. This reveals that Williamson could relate to many different people and thrived on intellectual stimulation and knowledge. He also had the ability to change society's point of view, for example, in promoting a gradual and slow shift in attitude towards witchcraft.

This is again borne out when, as an adult, he created a 'curse-puppet' in order to counteract a curse he had received in the form of a letter (Patterson, 2014, Caption to first set of photographs from *Illustrated News*, 27th September, 1952). What is particularly interesting is that he allowed himself to be photographed in a sequence of photographs, from the start to the finish of creation, suggesting these were intended to be educational or perhaps for publicity purposes. It contrasts starkly with his secrecy on other occasions.

This was not the only curse item that Williamson claimed to have received; he once found a dog's heart with nine pins stuck in it on the path leading to his home, when he first moved to Cornwall. Although this is usually cited as evidence that local Christians did not welcome him, it seems more likely that the culprit was as well versed in the magical arts as himself. While the local minister of Bourton delivered a sermon to his congregation about "the evil that had moved to the village" (document in Museum of Witchcraft and Magic archive), it seems unlikely that any clergyman would have approved of sending curse items to anybody and the incident will be more fully discussed later in this chapter. Williamson's response to such intimidation was to fight fire with fire and use magical mirrors to reflect back the evil. This shows he could successfully resist (Uranus) any opposition regarding his magic and susceptibility (Neptune).

Returning to the Mars square Pluto aspect, there is another example of a childhood life-changing event for Williamson when he survived a brutal attack whilst staying at the home of his uncle, a Devonshire vicar. Williamson had heard a commotion outside his uncle's garden, beyond a huge stone wall. Describing himself as "… an inquisitive little so-and-so" (ibid, 122), he went to see what was happening and was appalled to see four labourers had stripped a little old lady stark naked. They apparently thought she was witch, and intended to prove this, "… by finding a third nipple on her" (ibid).

Without stopping to think that the odds were against him, Williamson charged in and threw his arms around the woman. The four men kicked and beat him, and he was only saved when his uncle, who had heard the disturbance, came to their rescue.

These examples reveal how Williamson's formative years shaped his understanding of what it was like to be the persecuted and for others to be victimised. He looked to magic for help in claiming back his 'hidden power' and 'ownership' of his life, yet he was also capable of taking physical risks when necessary. This shows his courage (Mars) and determination (Pluto) not to see 'power' abused and people subjected to cruelty.

Pluto also symbolises what is taboo in society, something that can vary depending on the time and place. The previous example shows how witchcraft was very much the 'taboo' at that time and place. Pluto is also associated with the afterlife and death, and Williamson was aware of his own spirit guide, whom he referred to as 'Shadow'. His philosophy about death is borne out, for example, when in the Witchcraft Research Centre pamphlet he wrote, "Death is another fact facing all of us. No need to be gloomy about that" (Patterson, 2014, 261).

Pluto is in the eighth house and is at home there, as it is associated with Scorpio which is ruled by Pluto in the natural zodiac *(see glossary)*. It adds an exceptional inner strength as well as a capacity for survival and an ability to survive any crisis. A good example might be surviving the Second World War as well as fulfilling his dream to create his Witchcraft Museums despite several setbacks.

Death, investigation and research, and all subjects associated with matters hidden and secretive (such as the occult and underworld) are associated with Pluto, Scorpio and the eighth house so this placement would have been helpful to Williamson in any covert or investigative work which he may have undertaken.

PERSISTENCE AND OPPERTUNITY

The Sun is square Pluto, again suggesting that Williamson could be very wilful and yet also exercise self-control. It indicates his awareness of personal power and how to use it to advance himself. Hidden power was important to him, borne out by Pluto's association of the occult and personal power. Sun conjunct Jupiter also reveals his tremendous faith in life and in himself. He was a great visionary, ever seeking opportunities for personal expansion and growth, all areas associated with Jupiter.

During 1947, Williamson met Gerald Gardner (the subject of Chapter Four) at the esoteric Atlantis Bookshop in London, which was a significant turning point in both their lives. It quickly became apparent they shared an interest in folklore and witchcraft. Gardner later arrived at the Witchcraft Centre on the Isle of Man; his introductory words to Williamson were, "I had to come, my dear fellow, to see how things are going" (*The Museum of Witchcraft*, 2011, 15).

Williamson later offered employment to Gardner, inviting him to work at the Witchcraft Centre when it was completed, and to take up position there as 'resident witch'. Presumably the strategically minded Williamson hoped Gardner's presence would generate further interest in the museum. Initially the two men were great friends and Williamson observed how Gardner loved to gossip and mingle with the customers of the museum (which is in keeping with the latter's sociable Geminian nature).

Williamson was clearly industrious, practical and resourceful; all attributes in keeping with his Sun sign Virgo. Sun square Pluto reveals determination, passion and tenacity and this, coupled with the entrepreneurial energy of Mars in Aries, indicates that Williamson probably felt driven to accomplish his ambition to own a witchcraft museum. Even though he was disappointed with its inability to generate a better income, he did not abandon his dreams. Instead, in 1955, he sold the museum building to Gardner, and relocated once again.

FAMILIARITY BREEDS CONTEMPT

By the time Williamson moved back to England with his various artefacts and collections, the relationship between himself and Gardner had become tense and difficult. Although Williamson was fair-minded (Mercury in Libra), he did not appreciate being put in difficult positions especially by those he had previously helped. For example, he (and the group membership) was unhappy that often Gardner was unable to complete various research tasks that had been delegated to him at the Museum.

When he heard of Williamson's plans to sell the museum, Gardner asked to be allowed to buy it – a process that was not "without a lot of rather underhand wrangling, the details of which are best left unmentioned" (*The Museum of Witchcraft*, 2011, 15). This shows that Williamson could keep confidences (characterised by Pluto), although his efficient Virgoan nature must surely have been frustrated by the flaws of the business relationship between him and Gardner, which he once described as 'vexed' (the vex here being another association of Pluto). However, it is worth noting that he only kept secret the *details* of the wrangling, not the fact that there had been underhandedness!

The close, but by no means always smooth, relationship between Williamson and Gardner can be seen in the position of Pluto in the sign of Gemini, since the nature of Pluto is intense and probing, whilst the mutable nature of Gemini is changeable and mercurial. The differences that appeared between Gardner and Williamson in their relationship were perhaps partly due to the fact that they had very different approaches to magic and witchcraft. Gardner's interest was in coven and group-working, creating Wicca as a modern form of witchcraft; whilst Williamson's priority was the solitary practitioner, the village wise-woman and charmer, and he was not averse to casting the odd curse or hex (as we saw earlier).

CHRISTIANS, ROYALTY AND PREMISES

In 1955, Williamson relocated to the Royal Borough of Windsor and Maidenhead, in Berkshire, England, and later claimed to have opened a witchcraft exhibition in Windsor High Street (opposite the Guildhall). Posters proudly announced it was open every day including Sunday. This residency was short-lived and he was again forced to relocate because of alleged opposition from the 'Royal Household' who lived in Windsor. According to Williamson, it was felt that a witchcraft museum in such close proximity to the head of the Church of England was inappropriate. The Sunday opening might also have raised a few eyebrows at that time.

However, the Author's research even casts doubt on the exhibition's existence. The posters may have been printed, but perhaps the exhibition did not in fact take place. The Kelly's Street Directory for Windsor shows that Williamson was living at a residential place which he called 'The Studio', in Goswell Hill in 1956, behind the railway arches there. In the directory, there was no mention of an exhibition or a museum at that site, and neither was Williamson's occupation listed (Royal Borough of Windsor and Maidenhead, Librarian Museum, Arts & Local Studies). What is particularly interesting is that the drill hall, where his exhibition/museum was said to have been situated, was actually pulled down in the 1940s, i.e. long before Williamson moved there (https://windsorhistoricalsociety.org).

Furthermore, the indices of the Royal Borough of New Windsor council minutes show no entry for Williamson (ibid). He may well have had his collection with him when he was living at Goswell Hill, but it seems the exhibition did not take place. Besides it seems an odd place to want to host an exhibition – at a site, which was located in a dark and inaccessible alleyway, behind railway arches – although perhaps it was not so odd for Williamson, from what we already know about him.

We see this pattern again and again in his life: exaggerated claims of opposition and victimisation. The Sun conjunct Jupiter in Virgo suggests boasting and embellishment, particularly in the area of his work, since work is an association of Virgo, whilst the Mercury square Neptune aspect suggests distorted and fabricated communications.

Still determined to pursue his dream, Williamson next opened a museum in Bourton-on-the-Water, Gloucestershire. There he claimed to have met with even greater opposition than before, and claimed that the local Christian community actively tried to intimidate him. However, the parish council records of the 9th April, 1956, reveal a different story; most of their complaints initially were in regard to planning matters, such as removing mullions from the windows, removing plant pots, erecting unapproved signs and fencing-off land near the property. Clearly this was going to be contentious and indeed, just a few years later in 1960, Boxbush House – which was the name of the premises – became a Grade II listed building (as previously noted). Yet Williamson accepted none of this; he apparently approached one of the parish councillors and not only accused him of, "… stirring up trouble against him," but also, "… threatened legal proceedings" (Parish Council Records, 1956).

A few weeks later, on 14th May, the minutes for the meeting recorded councillors' anger that someone had contacted the national press and, "attempted to make a big issue of the matter." It seems more than likely that the 'someone' was in fact Williamson, who used the publicity generated in this way to attract visitors to his exhibition. The chairman of the parish council also stated there was little or no opposition to the witchcraft museum and of all the complaints they received, only two were local. Despite some misgivings (mainly because Williamson had said he was opening a folklore museum and then devoted it to witchcraft instead), members of the parish council went to inspect the museum and decided not to oppose it. They were hardly unfair to him.

Claims that attempts were allegedly made to burn his premises down and a dead cat left hanging outside the door (Patterson, 2014, 135) seem all the more unlikely in the light of the above. The parish council at that time was very concerned with anti-social behaviour and littering and it would certainly have been raised had the allegations been true.

Whilst living in Gloucestershire, Williamson purchased two properties in Cornwall and eventually decided to relocate again, this time to East Cornwall where he opened a smuggling museum (which is *not* the present day Polperro Heritage Museum of Smuggling and Fishing). Williamson's museum focused solely on the smuggling aspect, unlike the Heritage Museum, founded in June 1994 by Bill Cowan, which covered the community's marine traditions and history. Today a letter from the local authorities held in the archives (No. 6084) at The Museum of Witchcraft and Magic shows that Williamson did not pay his rent for the smuggling museum and did not open the museum on the terms agreed. They asked him to vacate the premises and restore it to the condition that it previously was, and he did finally leave.

The Heritage Museum was just starting up and looking to purchase exhibits when Williamson closed his museum. However, despite repeated requests, Williamson refused to sell to them, and instead sold them elsewhere so that most items left Polperro. However, some years ago, an old sign, complete with bells, that Williamson used to wheel around the town, advertising his museum, was found and refurbished. This is now on display in the Heritage Museum.

According to some who were connected with the Heritage Museum, Williamson was not well liked in Polperro and described as 'a queer object.' Ever confident and enthusiastic, he tried to open the 'House of Spells' in another town in Cornwall. This enterprise however, was not so well tolerated and was unsuccessful; again, Williamson claimed that the local Christians ran him out of town (Patterson, 2014, 136).

In Buckfast, Devon, Williamson opened and ran the 'House of Shells', probably between the mid 1960s – early 1970s, which was managed by his wife. They described this 'Museum of Shell Craft' as "… devoted solely to the study of the art of the shell craft workers of the world" (Williamson, un-dated pamphlet, inside front cover).

Williamson was then drawn to North Cornwall with its magical and mystical town of Tintagel; here he tried to open another tourism enterprise, which he named 'The Museum of Sorcery.' Unfortunately, it generated little income so he once again relocated, this time to Boscastle a few miles away, where legend has it that sea-witches used to sell the wind to sailors in the harbour (*The Museum of Witchcraft: A Brief History & Guide to the Displays,* 2007, 24).

In 1960, he opened the 'Witches House', now known as 'The Museum of Witchcraft and Magic.' Previously, it had been a warehouse on the harbour of Boscastle. Here he seems to have finally found security and achieved his ambition, remaining there until, in 1996, when aged 87, he sold the museum to the then director, Graham King. As mentioned above, the Grand Cardinal Cross in his chart shows Williamson had strong leadership skills with a tendency to seek out challenges; with this aspect pattern, there is no path of least resistance.

Mercury in Libra (*see box on right*) suggests diplomacy, equality and fairness may have been important to Williamson, as would having intellectual affinity in one-to-one situations, for example, in partnerships and collaborations 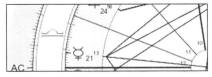 (Libra) as discussed previously. This can be seen too in his marriage, since his wife was also his business partner and ran some of the museums he had set up. There is also the partnership between himself and Gerald Gardner, where Williamson (while he owned it) employed Gardner as 'resident witch' of the Isle of Man museum to help generate interest there, whilst at the same time trying to help Gardner sell his book, *High Magic's Aid*. However, he could also be stubborn when he wished, such as when he flatly refused to sell any artefacts to the Polperro Heritage Museum of Smuggling and Fishing.

LESSONS TO BE LEARNED

Saturn is challenging in the sign of Aries since this position is in fall (*see glossary*) and there is conflict between the authoritative and restricting nature of Saturn, which prohibits the impulsive nature of Aries. Although he worked in business partnerships, this astrological position also suggests that Williamson feared dependency and reliance and so working alone on areas where he could be independent would have been his ideal. We can see this characteristic through his pioneering work as director of a witchcraft museum, and also in his film work, editing scripts.

After World War II, Williamson set up his own production company, Do–U–Know (D-U-K) Pictures, from 1946–50 (http://www.bfi.org.uk). This shows that he could use his initiative and had the focus and vision to set up his own businesses. Even when some of them failed, he was not deterred.

Since Saturn forms boundaries, it could be said that Williamson defended himself to safeguard and protect his self-interests. The accommodating nature of this position reveals that as a leader he will have used Aries' combative nature and self-sufficiency to spur him on to greater achievements, irrespective of how much time it would take. In the passage of time, the almost childlike nature of Aries learns wisdom through experience, just as Williamson would have learned from his mistakes (which again echoes the theme of Mercury opposite Saturn as mentioned above).

In fact, in *The Museum of Witchcraft – A Magical History*, Williamson admitted, "One learns from experience ... [that] ... these unexpected rebuffs and setbacks only served to strengthen my determination to open a museum of witchcraft." This shows his single-minded resolve to achieve his aims.

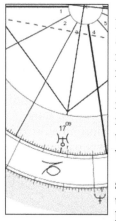

Uranus is in Capricorn in Williamson's natal chart. This suggests he could have created progressive change within authoritative and traditional structures, whilst at the same time wanting to rebel against authority. This is because Uranus is associated with rebellion as well as progress, and Capricorn is associated with authority and tradition. We see this, for example, in his choice to follow a more unorthodox path into the world of witchcraft and the film industry. Typically, he also claimed to have caused uproar by unsettling various local authorities when he set up his exhibitions of witchcraft. For example, in Windsor and at Bourton-on-the-Water.

However, as we have seen, the parish records show that he seems to have exaggerated somewhat in the case of Bourton-on-the-Water, and the Author's research with the authorities at Windsor has revealed no information or records pertaining to Williamson's alleged exhibition there.

The magician and occultist, Aleister Crowley, observed that the position of Uranus in Capricorn in a natal chart shows that, "The magical will of the man, his mission in the world, are everything to him" (Crowley, 1987, 170). This is evident, for example, in Williamson's determination to have a museum of witchcraft, despite several setbacks.

Eventually Williamson found a safe haven in Boscastle, where his museum of witchcraft (now called the Museum of Witchcraft and Magic, and owned by Simon

Costin) to this day educates generations who are interested in witchcraft. The position of Uranus in the third house indicates that Williamson was unique, forward-thinking, ahead of his time and controversial. Some also viewed him as eccentric and strange (hence the comment from Polperro locals about him being 'a queer object'), since these characteristics are also associated with Uranus.

Commons. Wikimedia. org Public Domain

The symbol of Uranus resembles that of an old-fashioned television aerial, and this is also relevant to Williamson, as the planet is associated with computers, radio and television and technology. During the Second World War, the Political Warfare Executive (P.W.E.), which was a branch of the British Secret Intelligent Services (S.I.S.), commissioned a purpose-built radio station at Crowborough, East Sussex, near the Ashdown Forest, to house a special transmitter which was codenamed 'Aspidistra'. Williamson, then a member of the Royal Corps of Signals was involved in the construction as well as some of the design of the transmitting hall (as previously discussed).

The RCA transmitter was powerful and able to change airwave quickly. In a sense, it could be described as 'mercurial'. As a result, the P.W.E. saw its potential for propaganda as it could "... intrude on enemy wavelengths and transmit misleading information". Interestingly the badge of the Royal Corps of Signals (Williamson's regiment) is the symbol of Mercury (*see image above right*), the winged-messenger, and this planet is also the ruler of the third house in natural astrology (*see glossary*) as well as governing Virgo (and Gemini), Williamson's Sun sign.

MAKE-BELIEVE AND MAGIC

Neptune is in Cancer in the natal chart, suggesting that Williamson was imaginative, enjoyed fantasy and illusion and was receptive to art, film, magic, poetry, romance and spirituality. His life behind the lens in his film work, for example, would have benefitted from a sense of enchantment and imagination as would his magical work.

Neptune is in the ninth house and reveals that he was willing to sacrifice himself for his beliefs; it also indicates that Williamson could find spiritual enlightenment through mystical channels. He certainly found escapism through meditation, magic and witchcraft, which allowed him to free his mind from the constraints of everyday life. His beliefs may have helped form his philosophy about life, as the ninth house is associated with belief and spirituality, and Neptune the divine and ephemeral.

Williamson wrote about chants, divination and spells in his private Witchcraft Manuscript, and the exacting nature of Virgo can be seen in the detail of his magical work. For example, his instruction and tantra for *Washing Hands in Moon Rays Charm* (Patterson, 2014, 31) provides a meticulous guide as to how to cleanse one's hands for a moon ritual, together with a three-lined chant for the spell.

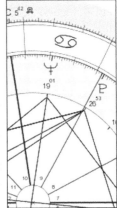

When Williamson returned to Britain, after a spell of working on a tobacco plant in Rhodesia, he became involved in the film industry (as previously noted), employed by companies such as Paramount and Ealing Studios. He undertook a variety of positions there, such as director, editor, producer and photographic director, right up until his final work on *Action Stations*, in 1959. During this period, he was still pursuing his interest in the occult and witchcraft.

Film, lenses and vision are all correspondences of Neptune and its ability to create illusion and glamorise, whilst Uranus is original and innovative. The opposition between Uranus and Neptune can also allude to the technological and scientific nature of Uranus, meeting with the illusionary nature of Neptune. This would have been helpful in Williamson's film and production work as he was also willing to work on different types of film genre, including comedies, costume drama, documentaries, educational films/school programmes, musicals and war programmes (ibid).

It has been suggested that Williamson was fascinated by Shakespeare, especially his play, *Macbeth*, in which the three witches make an appearance (Patterson, 2014, 132). Williamson made a documentary called *The Upstart Crow* (1948), which was a tour of Shakespeare's country (ibid). The previous year, he claimed he had attempted to open a witchcraft research centre in the Bard's birthplace, Stratford-Upon-Avon, but met with so much opposition that he was forced to abandon it and change his plans. However, the Author's research with the authorities at Stratford-Upon-Avon concludes that no such attempt ever took place.

Neptune is in the sign of Cancer (which is associated with the family and home). It could be said that Williamson had a magical home, since Neptune corresponds with bewitching, enchanting and spells – thus his museums were a type of home for him. Cancer can be patriotic, enjoying its country's ancestry, heritage, and history, which would have been nurturing to Williamson in his collection of artefacts, with his sensitivity to the persecution of witches in bygone days.

The placement also alludes to magic and spirituality (Neptune) in the family (Cancer) and this was true for Williamson, in that his grandmother apparently had a great interest in the occult arts and mediumship and mingled with people who practiced them. Whether any other members of his family were also involved with such subjects is unknown.

FEELINGS, PARENTS AND SUSCEPTIBILITY

Other associations of Neptune include guilt, sacrifice, vulnerability and victimisation. This is borne out not only in the bullying Williamson experienced at school but also at home. His father would describe him as 'The Idiot', while his beauty-obsessed mother wished to pass him off as "... a younger brother visiting from Ireland" (Patterson, 2014, 122). His parents' cold and detached attitude may have left him feeling rejected and unloved, perhaps even unwanted.

Moon was conjunct Venus (*see box above*) when Williamson was born and, as previously discussed, this aspect suggests he had intense and profound feelings. He may have managed to hide these, preferring not to express his anger or pain, and perhaps even fearing to reveal his vulnerability.

As discussed previously, the Moon in Scorpio is conjunct Venus in Scorpio in his natal chart and provides some interesting insight about his mother. Significantly, his mother was a Sun sign Scorpio, showing that she could be as uncompromising as her son. This could have created an intense and even unhealthy energy in their relationship.

The contact created between the Moon and Venus supports the claim that his mother was vain; since this trait is associated with Venus and certainly the example above reveals she could be conceited and narcissistic. As discussed earlier, Venus is detriment (*see glossary*) in Scorpio. This suggests that if Williamson ever felt betrayed, then his vengeful Scorpio nature could seek reprisals, for Scorpio is capable of channelling feelings quite ruthlessly. He was unlikely to forgive or forget any slight – real or imagined. This *might* explain his refusal to sell anything to the new museum in Polperro; perhaps he felt the community had slighted him in some way. Scorpio in this part of a natal chart shows the subject can hide their feelings very well and can take a while before they use the sting in their tail as an act of revenge.

EMPLOYMENT, HEALTH AND SERVICE

The sea corresponds with Neptune. It is interesting, therefore, that Williamson took and passed his entry examination to become a naval officer, although it seems he was not offered any employment with the Navy, and this may have been disappointing to his father, who had flourished in the Royal Navy. He then considered entering the Church, another area of work that is a correspondent of the divine and spiritual Neptune.

His father, however, fiercely opposed such a move and sent him to Rhodesia (Patterson, 2014, 126). There Williamson worked on a tobacco plantation and got to know and work with a retired witchdoctor called Zandona, who became a friend as well as a source of inspiration. The earth element rules Virgo and so he probably enjoyed working with plants. The earth element in astrology is associated with practicality and tangibility, shown where he would have tended to the vegetation and ensured the health of the plants was adequate.

Williamson was eventually dismissed from his post when his employer discovered he had been providing basic first aid to his co-workers on the plantation, because he was so appalled at the conditions in which they were expected to work. Later, he briefly worked for the Imperial Tobacco Company as a driver and general assistant to a German scientist. Being of 'general assistance' suggests that he could be helpful, resourceful and useful – all qualities associated with Virgo. We do see a pattern emerging here though, in that he was restless, particularly in his early life; Sun and Jupiter in Virgo as well as Pluto in Gemini shows the adapting and nervous energy of the aforementioned signs. He did not return to England until the early 1930s.

Williamson did not maintain any ties that did not suit him and could be ruthless when cutting himself adrift. For example, when as a student boarding at the school house at the prestigious Malvern College, from 1923–26 (Malvernian Society in correspondence to Author), he visited the poverty-stricken dockland area of London's East End. There, as part of his Christian Aid voluntary work, Williamson helped out by feeding the poor at the soup kitchen scheme (Patterson, 2014, 124). Malvern College had a long association with the 'Mission' at London Docklands at that time (ibid).

Through Williamson's voluntary work, we can see the Virgo motivation at play, by way of being helpful in a kind and practical way. However, once he left the college, he cut all ties with the college and fellow students.

Saturn is in the sixth house in his natal chart and is the area associated with work, and this illustrates that Williamson took his work responsibilities seriously and that detail, organisation and planning would feature in his work, as these are themes associated with the thorough nature of Saturn. In mundane astrology (*see glossary*), the sixth house associates with the army. His military work saw Williamson (army number 142144) promoted to rank of second lieutenant in the Royal Corps of Signals in July,

1940. (https://www.thegazette.co.uk/London/issue/34926/supplement/5081). This was the first rank obtained on commissioning and was usually held for up to two years, although Williamson does not seem to have been promoted again. His commission was not a 'normal' one, but part of the Royal Corps of Signals Regular Army Emergency Commissions (RAEC). Normal commissions were cancelled early in the war, and RAEC ones were granted only for the duration of the war.

He was, however, awarded two medals for his service (www.ancestry.co.uk); the British War Medal and the Star (www.ministryarchives.com). Neither medal was awarded for bravery, but instead for service; the British War Medal was awarded for serving at least 28 days, between September 1939 and September 1945. The 1939–45 Star marked six months' service in certain operational commands overseas, between 3rd September, 1939, and 2nd September, 1945.

Part of the Grand Cross's configuration includes Mercury opposing Saturn and Saturn square Neptune (as mentioned earlier). These two aspects indicate possible health problems in Williamson's life and it would have been significant to him, as health is one of Virgo's main associations. Saturn (as previously noted) is in the sixth house, which is also associated with health/ill health (as well as work). Some of Saturn's health conditions included arthritis and depression, and areas of the body ruled by Saturn are the bones, skin and teeth. Mercury opposing Saturn can indicate (amongst other areas) serious thinking and depression and, given that Saturn brings challenges and restrictions in itself, it exacerbates the theme of ill health in Williamson's chart. The aspect of Saturn square Neptune indicates a long-term health problem that won't go away. For example; some sort of chronic illness.

Although we do not know for certain, it is possible that Williamson may have been living with depression, perhaps stemming from the bullying he endured as a child, and/or his parents' neglect of his emotional well-being. He may even have had a form of PTSD (post-traumatic stress disorder) following his time in the army. The area of health/ill health in his natal chart indicates long-term issues, and yet his drive and grit helped him accomplish much in his life and he lived to an old age.

OVERLOAD AND PRECISION

Jupiter in Virgo is detail-orientated and enjoys a wealth of analysing, critique, dissemination, perfection and research. This placement would have helped Williamson in his work as editor and screenwriter, although some large projects may have been held up by him over-focussing on detail. When taken to extremes, this placement has the potential to be overly analytical and critical. Indeed, Williamson's chart does suggest he may have had workaholic tendencies and found it difficult to rest and relax.

We see examples of this in how he persisted in seeking an ideal site for his Museum. In 1992, for example, he even contemplated moving the museum site from Cornwall to "somewhere between Birmingham and Manchester" (Museum of Witchcraft and Magic archive, letter to Michael Howard). His gradual progress in the film industry, starting out as an editor and then progressing to screenwriter and director, also shows his focus and diligence.

The quincunx aspect between Venus and Mars indicates that professional responsibilities may have interfered with Williamson's marriage and social life. In his business partnership with his wife, it was she who had the idea of opening 'The Witches' Kitchen' and she also ran 'The Shell Museum'. Possibly she felt that Williamson was taking on too much work and she wanted to help.

No doubt, when he was in the Royal Corps of Signals, he would have appreciated the formal and routine duties and tasks that serving officers had to go through as part of their military service. For example, cleaning their uniforms and rifles, as well as marching and participating in daily inspections. In particular, The Royal Corps of Signals requires officers to enable "reliable communications and the swift accurate passage," as well as providing "military commanders with their information requirement and ability to command and control their forces" (http://www.army.mod.uk/signals).

Working in a company of men would have been agreeable to Williamson, as his Sun and Jupiter are in Virgo and in the eleventh house – the area of groups and teams. In the past, some men from the Signals were often involved with intelligence duties, although not all of them (Blank, 2017, correspondence to the Author).

Jupiter in the eleventh house also suggests a sense of reward in a group setting as well as pomp and ceremony. This can manifest in various ways. For example, Williamson's desire to appear more mysterious or influential than was the case can be seen in the way he often told people in Polperro (and probably elsewhere) that he was in the 'Secret Service' (Heritage Museum, Polperro, 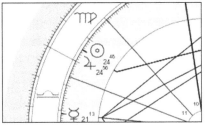 conversation with Publisher). Likewise, by claiming people were against him (perhaps in order to draw attention to his museum in Bourton-on-the-Water) and going to the national press with this story, even though the parish records reveal quite a different account, again suggests his determination to be centre-stage.

Sun conjunct Jupiter suggests that Williamson enjoyed organising, detail, working in a capacity where he could apply classification, ordering, routine, method; striving for perfection and precision. One example of this is shown through his use of the card indexing system (Steve Patterson: Youtube). Although, nowadays regarded as old fashioned, nevertheless it would have helped him with analysis and data collection in his work.

His quest for excellence and perfection, are areas connected with Virgo. The aspect of Sun conjunct Jupiter in Virgo is capable of creating nervous energy, due to the restless nature of Virgo, so Williamson may at times have experienced nervous exhaustion in his drive and search for accomplishment. As previously discussed, the element of earth rules Virgo and in doing so it produces an efficient and industrious nature; Williamson was once described as a "resourceful colleague" (Howe, 1982, 160), showing how practical and skilful he could be.

Williamson's educating and methodical nature can be seen, for example, in his visitor's guide book for The House of Shells Museum. He provides the reader with guidelines for the potential shell crafter; "A few helpful thoughts for the would-be shell crafter." He enters into great detail under four headings about the cleansing and preparation, selection and application of shells in the artwork of shell craft (Williamson, *The House of Shells*, Buckfast, un-dated).

In magical work, preparation and precision are of tremendous importance if the desired outcome is to be successful. Williamson's accuracy and skill were significant to him, particularly in the areas of cursing and spell craft. Apparently, he would use the term "*Malificea* finely ground," meaning that in magical matters it was critical to 'fine-tune' what he did in order to achieve precision (Bad Witch blog, *see bibliography*).

The contact between Sun and Jupiter also shows generosity of heart and spirit, combined with a willingness to share knowledge – traits that are ideal for a museum curator and librarian. Williamson had kept a manuscript, which was a small personal notebook that he had named: 'Witchcraft'. Inside was a wealth of information about folklore and magic, charms and spells, as well as some wry observations.

Williamson was an enthusiastic letter-writer (Steve Patterson: YouTube). Anyone who wrote to Williamson for witchcraft information would usually receive a reply, thus revealing his enthusiasm for helping others and sharing his knowledge. For example, an eager Doreen Valiente (subject of Chapter Fourteen) wrote to Williamson in 1952, after reading an article about him and witchcraft in the *Illustrated News* magazine. In her letter, she asked if she could be put in touch with the witch cult (Heselton, 2012, 491). Williamson passed her letter on to Gerald Gardner (subject of Chapter Four) who contacted Doreen Valiente directly. This was the beginning of a mutually beneficial relationship between Gardner and her. Williamson kept many of the letters written to him, and these are now preserved in the archives the Museum of Witchcraft and Magic.

Sun and Jupiter are in the eleventh house (as previously discussed) – the area which rules friendships and kindred spirits (along with goals, objectives and social reforms and causes). It was important for Williamson to have like-minded people around him who could understand him and he formed friendships with the likes of Sir Wallis Budge, Gerald Gardner, Dr Margaret Murray (the subject of Chapter Two) and Montague Summers.

Jupiter is creating a square aspect with Pluto, indicating Williamson's interest in exploring the secretive and taboo, along with magic. Venus trine Pluto indicates his natural love of research and investigation, both of which he put to good use in his career. The tight conjunction created between the Sun and Jupiter is almost exact at 1 degree and so is creating a partile (*see glossary*) aspect. It reveals that Williamson was always optimistic about the future, full of confidence and enthusiastic about in finding opportunities to find locations for his museum, despite the many setbacks he encountered.

PUSHING AND PULLING

Saturn is creating a square aspect with Uranus, which creates a tension, as the two planets represent conflicting impulses. Saturn needs boundaries and restraint, whilst freedom-loving Uranus needs independence and unconventional ways of living. One example of Saturn square Uranus is shown where Williamson broke with family tradition by not embarking on a naval career. He felt he had a calling to be a clergyman but instead his father ordered him to go to Rhodesia and work on a tobacco plantation (as discussed previously). Even less conventional in the 1950s was his career as a curator for a museum of folklore and witchcraft. Here we can see that the Old Order of Saturn has been drastically superseded by progressive Uranus, although interestingly Saturn is associated with museums in mundane astrology (*see glossary*).

Saturn is established and traditional while Uranus is anti-establishment and progressive. Williamson was committed to conserving and preserving old customs and traditions, e.g. by his innovative and humanitarian approach to safeguarding the Old Religion. For example, in 1960, he negotiated with Essex council and purchased the skeleton of the famous Essex Cunning Woman and Midwife, Ursula Kemp, who was tried for witchcraft and hanged in Chelmsford, Essex, in 1582. However, when Graham King brought the museum from Williamson in 1996, the skeleton was not included.

It seems that shortly before his death in 1999, Williamson sold Kemp's remains to the artist Robert Lenkiewicz for £5,000. Eventually, and some years after Lenkiewicz's death in 2002, the bones were reburied back at St Osyth, in the parish cemetery. There is an interesting footnote to this: the remains that were believed to be that of Ursula Kemp were examined by mitochondrial DNA testing, and was found to be a young male, possibly in his twenties (St Osyth Parish Council).

Saturn is also square Neptune in the natal chart and suggests Williamson's determination to make his dreams a reality, even in the face of opposition. It is also seen in the way he rebuilt the various buildings, setting up museums at different locations, as well as the rebuilding work, he undertook at the Isle of Man to create a museum, restaurant and domestic quarters. Saturn's discipline and persistence would have helped him achieve his vision.

Hugh Williamson, Father of Cecil Williamson. Kind permission of The Royal Aero Club Trust.

Williamson was (as we already know) passionately interested in the solitary practitioner – for example, the village wise-woman and charmer – as well as folklorists and scholars. He did not belong to a coven but quietly practiced his own form of witchcraft. Although he sometimes described himself as a showman, he nonetheless guarded his private life and never even wrote an autobiography (Patterson, 2014, 119–120). This is indicated by the Moon square Leo MC aspect in his natal chart.

As a young man, Williamson was introduced to astrology through a friend of his grandmother's; Miss Mona Mackenzie, who in turn had a friend who was a medium, palm and tarot reader (ibid, 272). This shows that from very early on, Williamson was aware of the unorthodox side of life. He gathered much of his knowledge of witchcraft from traditional West Country witches, and this helped him form his own magical practice. In doing so, he kept with the traditional, whilst reforming ways of working for himself.

Uranus is in opposition to Neptune in the natal chart, as previously discussed. Neptune corresponds with dreams and visions, while Uranus corresponds with foresight and the future; it is therefore possible that Williamson experienced prophetic dreams and flashes of insight – something that is indicative of the energy of Neptune and Uranus, respectively. Dreams interested Williamson who wrote about 'oneiromancy' (divination through dreams) in his manuscript called, *Witchcraft*, where he described dreams as giving insight into one's inner soul as well as being "an invaluable tool to the wayside witch" (ibid, 64).

As already discussed other qualities associated with Neptune and Uranus include emotion and sensitivity, as well as eccentricity and originality, respectively. Williamson's sense of uniqueness was demonstrated in his being the first to open a museum about magic and witchcraft in England (in 1951, on the Isle of Man). No amount of opposition seems to have deterred him. Given that Uranus' nature is experimental, it could be said that Williamson was 'experimenting' with his 'vision' of a museum of witchcraft.

Although he eventually had at least five museums, it seems that Uranus' erratic and unpredictable nature created a delay in achieving his dream, and instead brought inconsistency and upheaval in its wake.

THINKING OUTSIDE THE BOX

Mercury, the planet of communication, is square Uranus; indicating a progressive thinker with original ideas, slightly sceptical towards authority and bureaucracy. Williamson certainly was a liberal thinker ahead of his time – mentally alert, bright and perhaps seen by others as controversial and eccentric – qualities that are echoed by Uranus in the third house in his natal chart. Mercury is also creating hard aspects with Saturn and Neptune, opposing the former and square the latter in his natal chart.

Mercury opposing Saturn suggests Williamson was serious-minded and wanted to be respected and taken seriously for his opinions and views. Mercury corresponds with learning and Saturn with obstacles so, as discussed previously, it could be said that Williamson had to 'learn the hard way' in his life, as noted earlier. The theme of 'learning the hard way' is also symbolised in the aspect pattern of the Grand Cross in the chart.

There is also a sense that he had the voice of authority, since Mercury also corresponds with speaking and Saturn with authority. Williamson in his later years reflected upon the experience of owning five museums over the period of fifteen years, and wrote about the six "lessons learnt" from the experience (*The Museum of Witchcraft*, 2011, 18), part of which included: "A museum, like a magnet, draws to itself all manner of information on its subject," as well as: "Never lose sight of the fact that witchcraft gets a bad press. Too many modern witches do not seem to realise that in the public eye they are regarded as figures of fun or just slightly loopy" (ibid).

Mercury square Neptune suggests that Williamson could express himself imaginatively and in a poetic way, especially through the written word. Imaginative learning would have appealed to him, and he could teach others in the same way, for example, through visual and symbolic means. This aspect would also have been helpful to him in his role as 'story-teller' in his film work.

Williamson was able to use his artistic and visual skills by creating dramatic and sensational exhibitions at the witchcraft museums. For example, he painted protective 'evil eyes' on the outside of the museums; he also painted signs that declared: 'This Museum is Devoted to the Study of Black Magic and Witchcraft.'

The use of the term 'black magic' alludes to the darker side of magic which involves cursing, hexing and revenge. This can be associated with Williamson's lunar sign of Scorpio and its ruler Pluto, since the aforementioned areas are associated with them. It is well documented that Williamson used curses against those who had done wrong to him or others. The infiltrating Neptune suggests he may have had insights into others' motives, suggesting sensitivity towards the realms of intuition – something that would have been helpful to him in his magical work and perhaps also his film work.

Mercury square Neptune also suggests that Williamson could be the subject of gossip and scandal, as Mercury connects with communication and Neptune with distortion and fantasy. This was certainly the case when he opened his museum in the Easter of 1955 in Bourton-on-the-Water, which led to immediate confrontations with the parish council; and in the way he treated the fabric of the Boxbush (the name of the building that housed the exhibition). He removed mullioned windows and erected signs without planning permission, while still portraying himself as the hapless victim.

Press headlines included 'Black Magic Fear Grips Village' and 'Witchcraft Exhibition not likely to Stay' (The Museum of Witchcraft, 2011, 17), and apparently a local minister gave a sermon about "... the evil that had moved to the village" (Museum of Witchcraft and Magic archive). Indeed, he only stayed a few years and soon after moved his exhibition again. Williamson was also the subject of scandal amongst the Bourton Baptist church congregation on the August Bank Holiday of 1957. Mr and Mrs Williamson were discussed by the then Reverend J.K. Nettleford, as Gwen Williamson had claimed that her husband had, a year previously, successfully cursed several members of the Bourton village (Museum of Witchcraft and Magic archives, Williamson's draft letter & Nettleford's letter to Williamson). The couple's behaviour was intimidating and sent ripples of fear amongst the congregation where the Reverend had to reassure his flock and told them to "ignore Mrs Williamson's claims" (ibid).

In Polperro, he often told people he had worked for the 'Secret Service' and locals remember hearing him state this during a radio broadcast (conversation with Polperro Harbour Heritage Museum, August 2017). However, given that anyone working for the Government must sign the Official Secrets Act, it seems highly unlikely he would have openly bragged about this, had he really been any sort of spy. One only has to recall the furore surrounding Peter Wright and his book, *Spycatcher*, in the 1980s to realise the dangers of divulging state secrets. It was as though Williamson, the editor, screenwriter and director, was inserting himself into a fiction of his own creation, a potential revealed also by the Mercury square Neptune aspect.

LIFE AFTER LIFE

The aforementioned aspect of Mercury square Neptune also reveals Williamson's ability to communicate with the spirit world, showing he was mediumistic and able to channel. His spirit guide was known as his 'Shadow', and he consulted with it for direction and guidance when making critical decisions (Patterson, 2014, 210). This shows he found comfort and trust in the spirit world – a place where he sought inspiration. It also indicates the qualities of Mercury's communication and Neptune's spirituality and transcendence.

In the 1940s, Williamson was a member of The Ghost Club which was originally founded back in 1862 and, as its name suggests, was associated with psychical research (Patterson, 2014, 86). Eric Maple, author and folklorist (the subject of Chapter Eight), was also a member of this long-established organisation, as was psychic researcher Harry Price (discussed in Chapter Six – Helen Duncan).

Williamson married film make-up artist, Gwen (Gwendolyn) Wilcox in 1936, the niece of celebrated film director, Herbert Wilcox. Born on 21st November, 1912, in Sydney, Australia, Gwen was born when the Sun was in Scorpio and the Moon in Aries. In her career as one of the foremost make-up artists for the Max-Factor organisation, she would have been able to put her Scorpio/Pluto energy to good use by being able to transform a person's appearance – transformation being a correspondence of this sign and its ruling planet Pluto – she also had plenty of drive and loyalty to offer Williamson in their marriage.

Gwen's artistic abilities were not confined to being a make-up artist, for she was a talented 'shell-crafter' with a real gift for shell-work. Over a long period of time, she and her husband had collected shells from many different places. These they repaired and restored, then put on public display. Gwen had developed a natural 'feel' for and understanding of shells and could use them as a channel of artistic expression. Much of her work, along with that of other shell-crafters, was exhibited at the House of Shells (Williamson, un-dated, inside front cover).

Gwen's Sun sign Scorpio instinctively would have understood Williamson's Moon Scorpio nature which was quietly intense and perceptive. It was her idea to set up their restaurant, 'The Witches' Kitchen', in order to help finance the centre on the Isle of Man.

The initiating and entrepreneurial side of this situation is in keeping with her Moon in Aries, since Aries is an assertive, driven and pioneering sign. Apparently, she had remarked, "At least we shall be able to eat on the firm" (*The Museum of Witchcraft*, 2011, 13), showing her understanding of the business-side of running the museum. Williamson remarked that, "... the revenue from it enabled him to stay in business with the museum, in its first infant and unprofitable two years" (ibid).

From Left to Right: Gerald Gardner, Cecil & Gwen Williamson and Mr W. A. Clang. Permission of Manx National Heritage.

The Venus trine Pluto aspect in Williamson's natal chart reveals that he was a passionate partner with a capacity for affection, involved in deep and profound relationships. He could be charming and intense, since these are qualities associated with Venus and Pluto, respectively. He coped well with crises in relationships, as he had a strong survival instinct. In their domestic life, Mr and Mrs Williamson had two children and remained married until Gwen's death in 1989. Williamson survived her by ten years.

The Moon's Nodes (*see glossary*) show that, in Williamson's natal chart, the North Node of the Moon was in the sign of Gemini and the South Node of the Moon was in the sign of Sagittarius. The Nodes are karmic points and the spiritual advice with this position counsels that, in the current lifetime, Williamson needed to find a way to fully express himself in his life, yet needed to be cautious not to take on too much. This would help him advance on his spiritual path.

However, it is hard to see what 'too much' actually meant for Williamson. During a lifetime immersed in folklore, magic and witchcraft, during which he acquired five museums (some more successful than others), he worked tirelessly in the film industry and had family responsibilities. Although never published as an author on the subject of witchcraft, at the age of 82 Williamson is known to have been writing, perhaps setting down information for future generations. Possibly he wanted his legacy to be known on a wider scale, and being a Virgo he would have wanted accuracy, facts and precision about his life.

He outlined his autobiography in an appendix (which is held at the Museum of Witchcraft and Magic) and ends the piece by saying to readers that he hopes the enclosed information illustrates that he has "a working knowledge of witchcraft and the occult arts." He adds cryptically, "... you will know of this dormant and virgin source of information" (Patterson, 2014, 277).

HEALING, HUMANITY AND VALUING INDIVIDUALITY

Chiron the Wounded Healer is in the sign of Aquarius and in the fourth house in the natal chart (*see box on right*). This suggests that Williamson may have felt a sense of alienation and detachment from his parents, feeling that he was different and unusual in some way, perhaps even disconnected or isolated.

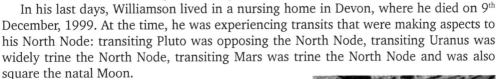

It also suggests that, as he matured, he may have preferred to stick rigidly with old ideas, and if he did embrace new ideas, then he surrounded himself only with those that shared the same interests as him. However, as we have seen, other data in his natal chart reveals that he was capable of both. He not only collected things on the subject of witchcraft but also contacted people who had a wide range of witchcraft interests.

The 'healing' of Chiron in Aquarius suggests that Williamson needed to learn to embrace the unique and unconventional side to his nature, which he certainly did through both film and magic.

In his last days, Williamson lived in a nursing home in Devon, where he died on 9th December, 1999. At the time, he was experiencing transits that were making aspects to his North Node: transiting Pluto was opposing the North Node, transiting Uranus was widely trine the North Node, transiting Mars was trine the North Node and was also square the natal Moon.

The transiting planets creating an aspect with the North Node suggest that there would be plenty more for Williamson to do in his next incarnation. Transiting Mars trine the North Node suggests that, as his life came to an end, he may have become more of a loner, acting on his own decisions and perhaps feeling frustrated.

There is much to thank Cecil Williamson for, including his relentless search for a permanent museum for witchcraft, which he eventually achieved. Also, we are indebted to him for his generosity of spirit in wanting to share with others what he knew, thus educating and allowing others to study and research for their own purposes at the Museum of Witchcraft and Magic. At the museum, in Boscastle,

Cecil Williamson, by kind permission of the Museum of Witchcraft and Magic

one can see many of the items and artefacts he acquired and conserved, and explore the collections for inspiration, learning and enjoyment.

Born with the challenging astrological Grand Cross in his natal chart, Williamson rose above the predictable difficulties in his life, revealing his tremendous inner strength. His determination and motivation show that he was intense, worked hard and overcame challenges in his life.

ACKNOWLEDGEMENTS, CREDITS AND REFERENCES

The Author and Publisher would like to thank the following:
Peter Hewitt at the Museum of Witchcraft and Magic Archives, for providing Cecil Williamson's time of birth and granting permission to use some photos from the archives of Williamson.

Geoffrey Spender at The Imperial War Museum, for archives/photography and curator services. The Polperro Heritage Museum of Smuggling and Fishing.

Author, Nigel West.

Author and former owner of The Witchcraft Museum, Graham King.

Dr Stuart C. Blank, Military Archive Research: http://www.militaryarchiveresearch.com

The secretary at The Malvernian Society; and Alumni Association of Malvern College, for dates that Williamson was a boarder at Malvern College 'Mission' at London Docklands.

The Cinema Theatre Association Archive Service.

Bourton-on-the-Water Parish Council, for providing extracts of the Parish Council Minutes for 1956.

Clerk of the Council, St Osyth Parish Council; Stratford-upon-Avon Library;

Librarian Officers at; Royal Borough of Windsor and Maidenhead Library Museum; and Local Studies Officer.

Windsor Historical Society.

Rodden Rating 'A'
Source – Museum of Witchcraft and Magic, audio cassette, Cecil Williamson speaking.
Williamson, Cecil: Sat. 18th Sep, 1909, GMT, Paignton, England.
3w34, 50n26

E. Williamson (nee Walsh): England & Wales, Civil Registration Death Index, 1916–2007, Date of Birth: 15th November, 1885. Date of Registration: December 1975. Age at Death: 90. Registration District: Exeter. Inferred County: Devon. Vol. 21, p1021.

H. Williamson: England & Wales, Civil Registration Death Index, 1916–2007, Date of Birth: 29th May, 1885, Date of Registration: December 1979. Age at Death: 94. Registration District: Torbay. Inferred County: Devon. Vol. 21, p225.

BOOKS

Clifford, F.C. (2012) *Getting to the Heart of your Chart: Playing Astrological Detective*. Flare Publications in conjunction with the London School of Astrology.

Crowley, A.; Symonds, J. (ed.) and Grant, K. (ed.) (1987) *The Complete Astrological Writings*. Star Books.

Heselton, P. (2012) *Witchfather – A Life of Gerald Gardner –Volume 2 – From Witch Cult to Wicca*. Thoth Publications.

Howe, E. (1982) *The Black Game*. Queen Ann Press/Futura.

Patrick-Ridder, J. (1990) *A Handbook of Medical Astrology*. Arkana Penguin Group.

Patterson, S. (2014) *Cecil Williamson's Book of Witchcraft – A Grimoire of the Museum of Witchcraft*. Troy Books.

Williamson, C.H. & G.V. (undated) *The House of Shells, Buckfast*. Produced in Great Britain by Photo Precision Ltd, St Ives (Huntingdon).

A Brief History & Guide to the Displays. Published by The Museum of Witchcraft (2007).

A Magical History – A Collection of Memories Celebrating 60 Years. The Museum of Witchcraft (2011), The Occult Art Company in conjunction with The Friends of The Boscastle Museum of Witchcraft.

JOURNALS

Hawker, J.P. (1992) 'Broadcasting – The Biggest Aspidistra in the World.' *Radio Bygones*. August–September, pp22–26.

Porter, D. and Matheson, A. 'Tricks of The Trade' article from *Signal* magazine. Issue 12, p17.

WEBSITES

www.ancestry.co.uk – Gwen Wilcox birth data and children, year of marriage. Accessed on 31/10/2014.

www.ancestry.co.uk – Military information about Williamson's war medals. Accessed on 28/05/2017.

http://www.army.mod.uk/signals/24935.aspx – Accessed on 02/08/2017.

www.astro.com – Generated natal chart.

http://www.bfi.org.uk/films-tv-people/4ce2b9f60fb15 – Film info. Accessed on 04/09/2016.

http://www.bfi.org.uk/films-tv-people/4ce2b94905c84 – Information about DUK Company. Accessed on 26/07/2017.

http://www.birminghammail.co.uk/news/nostalgia/spy-who-hoodwinked-nazis-sorcery-13098320 – Article entitled 'The Spy Who Hoodwinked the Nazis with Sorcery' by Mike Lockley (28th May, 2017). Accessed on 30/07/2017.

http://www.dreadnoughtproject.org/tfs/index.php/Hugh_Alexander_Williamson – Hugh Alexander Williamson: life & career. Accessed on 23/03/2021.

http://en.wikipedia.org/wiki/Cecil_Williamson_Gardner_and_the_Museum – Accessed 04/09/2016.

https://www.gov.uk/guidance/medals-campaigns-descriptions-and-eligibility – Accessed 01/08/2017.

https://historicengland.org.uk/listing/the-list/list-entry/1392333 – Accessed on 26/07/2017.

http://www.iwm.org.uk/collections/item/object/205005122/photography collection 8108-23) – Accessed 01/08/2017.

https://museumofwitchcraftandmagic.co.uk/document/document-2719/ – Letter from Gloucestershire County Planning Dept. to Cecil Williamson re: unauthorised signs advertising the Museum of Witchcraft, File 24. Accessed on 23/03/2021.

https://museumofwitchcraftandmagic.co.uk/document/document-2712/ – Letter from the BBC to Cecil Williamson, File 24. Accessed on 23/03/2021.

http://www.nytimes.com/1970/04/19/archives/the-devil-and-cecil-williamson.html – 'Evil and Cecil Williamson' by Peter Bloxham (19th April, 1970). Accessed on 23/07/2017.

https://windsorhistoricalsociety.org/ – Information about Drill Hall and Railway Arms/Arches. Accessed on 16/09/2017.

http://www.royal-windsor.com – General communications with editor to Author on 17/18th September, 2017.

http://www.thepeerage.com/p45038.htm – Detail of daughters. Accessed on 07/09/2016.

https://www.thegazette.co.uk/London/issue/34926/supplement/5081

https://youtu.be/nb5g4XAX-OY – 'The Magic of Cecil Williamson', an interview with Steve Patterson. Accessed on 27/07/2017.

http://www.badwitch.co.uk/2017/06/spells-cecil-williamson-spiders-web.html – Accessed on 25/07/2017.

http://www.iwm.org.uk – Geoffrey Spender, photography curator at Imperial War Museum. Accessed on 01/08/2017.

CHAPTER EIGHT

Eric Maple 1915–1994

Author, Folklorist and Speaker

Eric William Maple was born on 22nd January, 1915 (time of birth unknown), in Forest Gate, which at that time was part of the County of Essex in England, and is now in the borough of Newham in Greater London. He was born to William Alfred Maple and Edith Ann (née) Baker (birth certificate). As a bachelor, William Maple had served in the Royal Navy as Acting Chief Stoker and when Eric was born, his father was then employed as an "electrical wireman" (ibid). Eric also had a younger brother, Sydney J. Maple. Eric Maple married twice, firstly in 1938 to Patricia V. Carter by whom he had a son, Alan John. Sadly, Patricia Carter died just ten years into their marriage. Maple later married Dora Savage in 1951 (ibid), and they remained together until his death.

It is unclear exactly what Maple did in the Second World War. He may have remained in employment in a reserved occupation or perhaps he was a conscientious objector. In the mid-1940s, Maple was working for the Gas Board (https://libcom.org/history/north-east-london-anarchist-group), some jobs in utility industries such as gas, electricity, etc, were reserved occupations; when he commenced employment with the company is unknown. There was certainly a political aspect to Maple, who attended local meetings of The Anarchist Society, and wrote articles for anarchist publications such as *Freedom* and *The Word*.

Later, while he was still working for North Thames Gas as a senior clerical officer, Maple became an avid collector and researcher in the field of folklore in his spare time. In the early 1960s, he wrote four folklore papers for The Folklore Society: *Cunning Murrel, The Witches of Canewdon, The Witches of Dengie* and *Witchcraft and Magic in The Rochford Hundred*. Much of the material from these papers later helped him to form his books including: *The Dark World of the Witches, Magic, Medicine, Quackery & Old Wives Tales, The Secret Lore of Plants and Flowers, Supernatural England* and *The Ancient Art of Occult Healing*. These all contributed to knowledge of English witchcraft.

Maple also helped with collaborations and contributed to popular journalism. In the mid-1960s, he became a full-time author, lecturer and broadcaster at the BBC where he became affectionately known as 'The Witch Man' ('Local Man's Book on Witchcraft.' Undated, unnamed newspaper article). The popular press consulted him on a variety of psychic matters and this relationship continued for approximately 25 years, until failing eyesight and fragile health made it difficult for him to continue.

WHAT ERIC MAPLE'S NATAL CHART SHOWS

In Maple's natal chart, the Sun is in Aquarius at 1 degree. When the Sun is in Aquarius, it is known as being 'detriment' (*see glossary*) because the Sun is in the sign opposite the one it naturally rules, which in this case is Leo. The elemental combination of the luminaries in his natal chart comprises of the air sign Aquarius and the fire sign of Aries. There is a preponderance of the air signs in Maple's natal chart, mainly in the sign of Aquarius which comprises of Sun, Mercury, Jupiter, Uranus and the North Node as well as Saturn in Gemini, all of which will be discussed later.

There is a weaker presence of the earth element in Maple's chart, suggesting he was perhaps less talented in practical and financial matters. However, the one earth placement he does have is that of the exalted (*see glossary*) Mars in Capricorn, which helps to balance out the lack of earth element. The preponderance of male polarities (*see glossary*) in the chart also shows that Maple was assertive, confident and direct. This can be seen in his talks and broadcasts, where his style is certainly very confident and clear.

The air element governing Aquarius indicates sociability and reveals curiosity, a need for debate and discussion, exchange of ideas and a thirst for knowledge. All these characteristics are clearly apparent in Maple's achievements throughout his long life. The fixed mode air sign of Aquarius so prevalent in the chart indicates that the energies of Aquarius would have been intensified, showing that Maple was independent, reliable and even sometimes wilful, while at the same time he sought freedom and liberty. Other qualities bestowed by Aquarius are that of logic, tolerance, originality and truthfulness. The unwavering fixed nature of Aquarius also suggests that Maple could be inflexible and obstinate because of the detriment position of the Sun in Aquarius.

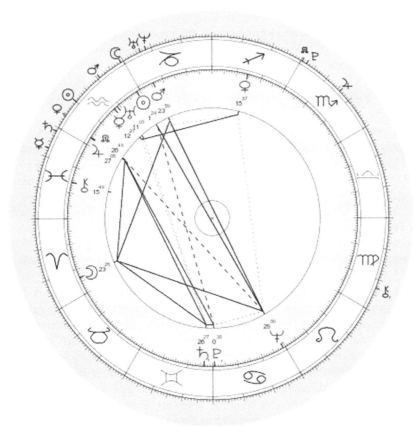

Natal and Transits Chart for Eric Maple on the day he died, 9th February, 1994.

Humanity, innovation and progress will have been important to Maple, since the nature of Uranus, the ruling planet of Aquarius, is to challenge reform and liberate. This can be seen by the image of Aquarius the Water Bearer, who pours fresh water from an urn onto old and tried values; symbolising reform and innovation – cutting through hierarchies, red-tape and traditions. This provides a unique perspective on social issues, bringing enlightenment to support anything that helps further society's progress and recognise that everyone is unique and equal. The sign is also known as 'The Brotherhood of Man,' which again is in keeping with the Aquarian humanitarian spirit.

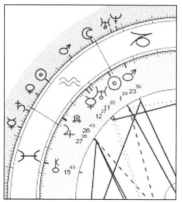

Maple is a strongly developed Aquarian, in that he has several planets in Aquarius, as well as his North Node (*see box on left*), as previously mentioned. Also in Maple's chart, Uranus is in Aquarius, which is the ruler of the sign in the natural zodiac. Such Uranus strength in the natal chart suggests that Maple may have been viewed by less progressive thinkers in society as anarchic, eccentric, rebellious, trailblazing and unconventional.

Mercury is in Aquarius in the natal chart and Uranus is in its ruling sign of Aquarius. Mercury governs professions that deal with speaking, writing, education and books. This placement would have helped Maple as a lecturer, broadcaster and writer, dealing with topics considered unconventional and unusual at the time. Mercury conjunct Uranus reveals that Maple was a progressive speaker who believed in free speech and radical thought, since these attributes are all associated with Uranus.

FREEDOM, POLITICS AND SOCIAL JUSTICE

Maple was once described as a "level-headed rationalist" (Smith, 1995, 87), which demonstrates the cool and detached nature of Mercury in Aquarius position. The Aquarius/Uranus energy also bestows enlightenment, indicating that Maple experienced flashes of ideas and insights, and was able to shed light on a situation by looking at it in a novel and unique way.

For example, in his early thirties, Maple wrote an article for the anarchist publication, *Freedom Press,* published on 6th September, 1947 (Maple, 1947, 8). At that time, he was a member of a then newly formed North East London Anarchy Group (NELAG). In the article, he argued that people should refuse to allow themselves or their groups to be isolated. He believed that small groups had the advantage that they could meet in private houses, thus avoiding having to pay rent and other overheads. Also, he believed that small groups were more intimate and prevented acrimony. He reasoned that such an arrangement would be better placed to create a socially conscious and active anarchist with the will to promote ideas, in order to create yet more groups. This, he suggested, was the movement's best chance of growth, rather than just forming larger groups. He felt that small groups could better introduce the movement into areas where hitherto it had been unknown, as well as providing the best opportunity for scattered readers of the *Freedom* newspaper to come together. In this article, he suggested that the newspaper should set up a register to put people in touch with each other.

From this example, we can see how the innovative and reforming nature of Aquarius comes into play within the non-conforming anarchist movement, and how Maple regards that 'small groups' are the way to advance and progress. NELAG meetings included debates, discussions and lectures; one of Maple's contributions was called 'Trends of Modern Capitalism' (https://libcom.org/history/north-east-london-anarchist-group).

From 1947, NELAG published a journal called, *The Libertarian*. Its purpose was described by Maple's fellow NELAG member and close friend, Alan W. Smith, as "... primarily for the purpose of bringing the ideas of the group to wider audience" (https://libcom.org/history).

Maple wrote other articles, for example, for the publication, *The Word*, which was edited by the Scottish anarchist and communist, Guy Aldred. Here Maple described how NELAG "... pursues an independent path, relying upon its own strengths" (ibid). He also wrote on occasion for *The Freethinker* journal which was a publication for the free-thought radical movement (Foote, 1975). In 1967, Maple was also listed in the publication written by David Tribe (one-time editor for *The Freethinker*) called *100 Years of Free-Thought* (Tribe, 1967, 195). This placed Maple in an influential exhaustive grouping of free-thinkers, who were described as 'aridly intellectual', as well as writers included for their political and social activities.

Interestingly, the area where Maple was born, Forest Gate, had a long tradition of political protest and social struggle for over 60 years. In the early 1890s, local anarchists had been arrested for trying to give speeches on Wanstead Flats (close to Forest Gate, Essex) – all tales that Maple must have heard while growing up. Indeed, he may even have met some of the participants.

The highly inventive, tolerant and humanitarian qualities of Aquarius can also be seen in Maple's research on customs, folklore and witchcraft. He was then in his late thirties and still in full–time employment with the Gas Board. In 1966, he became a full-time author, folklorist and speaker; and his work on folklore and witchcraft was to provide an important resource for future generations.

> **Maple Surname**
>
> It is also interesting – and Maple must surely have discovered this in his research – that his family name derived from the sycamore maple tree. Variants include Marple and Maypole – the latter is particularly significant considering Maple's interest in folklore!
>
> In fact, pegs made of sycamore wood were often hammered into doors and crossbeams to prevent witches from entering stables, and when going out at night people often carried a sycamore twig with them. The belief in the power of sycamore leaves is widespread across Britain (De Cleene and Le Jeune Vol. 1, 686).

EXCITEMENT AND THE UNUSUAL

Maple once described himself as a 'ghost-broker', referring to the vast number of ghost stories that he had collected over a long period of time (*Guardian Gazette & Independent*, 1972, 18). This description indicates a quirky sense of humour and it alludes to the qualities of Mercury conjunct Uranus present in Maple's natal chart, where Mercury symbolises humour, whilst Uranus symbolises the original and unusual.

In fact, when asked by a newspaper reporter what he would do if he was a ghost, Marple replied that "I would probably find myself a stately home and haunt a few American tourists" (*Essex and East London Newspaper*, 1973, 11), which again shows his quirky sense of humour. In that same interview he states that he has never been afraid of a ghost but has been more alarmed by the strange people that he had encountered in his work and goes on to provide examples of such people and their odd behaviour towards him.

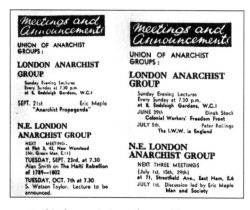

By kind permission of www.libcom.org

His humour was often remarked upon. In an interview with *The Washington Post*, for example, it was noted, "For one thing, he has a light touch. For another, he refuses to exploit the fear of death or the unknown. He keeps his equanimity" (Kernan, 1979). In that same interview, he was also described as "invincibly chipper and cheerful," and someone who "refuses to be infected by fear." Maple was also very aware of his audiences, aiming for example to "… tell the story of witchcraft in a way that will be easily understood by the non-specialist reader" (Maple, 1965, vii). Even though the topic was serious, he knew the importance of humour in bringing a "dark page of history to life" (ibid).

Author and High Priestess, Lois Bourne, met Maple when they both recorded a television programme for the BBC, which was a discussion on witchcraft. Bourne had read his book, *The Dark World of the Witches,* and described it as "… an erudite exposition of the subject" (Bourne, 1985, 37), and when she met Maple at the BBC, she reported finding him to be "… a pleasant unassuming man" (ibid). Bourne was also amused when Maple admitted to her that he had phoned his wife Dora to say he was dreading meeting Bourne, as she sounded "regal and matriarchal" (ibid). Actually, the two of them got on very well and Maple found her "very humorous". However, Maple's comment about Bourne being matriarchal reveals that he was somewhat wary of the possibility of being dominated by Bourne, since this would have clashed with his own independent and freedom-loving nature. He probably understood this side of his nature, once confiding, "I like women – in a sort of supernatural way" (Kernan, 1979).

FRIENDS, INDEPENDENCE AND KINDRED SPIRITS

Maple was also involved with and included in The Ghost Club, which was formed in 1862. Being a member meant he was able to do public speaking on the subject and explore other people's experiences of ghostly matters, this probably influenced his later book, *The Realm of Ghosts*. The prestigious club met regularly for dinners and other past members of the club had included the psychic investigator Harry Price, actor Peter Cushing, author Charles Dickens, poet Siegfried Sassoon and the author Peter Underwood, who eventually became the president of The Ghost Club Society as well as president of The Society for Physical Studies.

He and Maple were to become friends, and in Underwood's book, *Haunted Gardens,* he describes how Maple interviewed a family about their ghostly experiences, whilst living in a former fifteenth century farmhouse.

Maple was also a member of The Savage Club, which was founded in 1857 and is described today as one of the leading bohemian Gentleman's clubs in London. Maple became a member in 1969, being classified under the membership category of literature. He was friends with the actor and comedian 'Wee Georgie Wood' OBE, who was a stalwart of the club. The Aquarius/Uranus qualities of the unusual, needing kindred spirits in friendships, clubs, groups and societies are demonstrated in the above examples.

Jupiter is in Aquarius and repeats the theme that Maple was altruistic, open-minded and innovative. Jupiter, the ruling planet of freedom-loving and visionary Sagittarius, provides enthusiasm in being able to see the bigger picture. Placed in individualistic Aquarius, this indicates again that Maple was progressive in thought and reforming in spirit. It also suggests that Maple had a wide social circle and held strong beliefs about freedom and humanitarianism. It was said of Maple that he could mix with people from different circles, for example "… soldiers, psychologists, the pensioners at his club meetings and infant school children who loved his stories" (Smith, 1995, 87). Maple illustrates the belief that people with this placement in their natal chart "… can believe in the power of ordinary people to do good" (Tompkins, 2006, 164).

Jupiter in Aquarius also reveals faith in mankind, since these are areas that are associated with Jupiter and Aquarius, respectively. Maple reveals his optimism for a progressive society where he writes, for example, in the introduction for *The Ancient Art of Occult Healing*: "Little wonder then that so many intelligent men and women are turning away from the false promises of science to the hidden mysteries and miraculous cures of the lost ages of faith. For faith is the key to physical and mental health, the only complete antidote to the toxic influence of despair for both the individual and the society in which he lives" (Maple, 1974, 7). His words also show how he values a bygone era when faith was paramount in people's thinking.

The theme of freedom and independence is also echoed by the placement of Venus in Sagittarius at 15 degrees (*see box on right*). This reveals that Maple valued liberty and seeing the bigger picture of life and the higher principles which create it. Venus in Sagittarius also suggests that Maple would have been attracted to the adventurous and explorative opportunities in life that are associated with Venus. Sagittarius is associated with overseas travel and unknown places, as well as philosophy, religion, politics, teaching and publishing. With Venus in this sign, it is very likely Maple was attracted to such areas and pursued them with confidence and enthusiasm. Certainly, he worked abroad at a time when overseas travel was only just becoming more popular in the UK. He was a frequent broadcaster on both the American networks and German radio. He also toured the USA 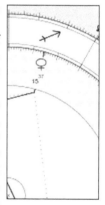 giving lectures on 'haunted Britain' for The British Tourist Authority, and was a regular contributor to a Finnish magazine called *Atlantis* (Maple, 1977, inside back-cover). This shows his confidence in his work, and his aptitude for educating and sharing his knowledge abroad. Money and earnings are also associated with Venus and it can be seen that Maple earned an income through some of the areas mentioned here.

However, it was not until 1966, when Maple was in his fifties, that he became a full-time author. Just around the time he had published *The Dark World of Witches* in 1962, a local newspaper ran an article entitled, 'Local Man's Book about Witchcraft.' Asked whether he would consider leaving his day job at the Gas Board to focus on broadcasting and writing as a living, Maple dryly replied; "I doubt it … writers usually starve" ('Local Man's Book about Witchcraft,' newspaper cutting, *c*.1963).

Even before publication, Maple was making programmes about folklore and witchcraft for the BBC. His reticence about becoming a full-time author is puzzling. Possibly he did not wish his employers to know his plans. However, something clearly happened around that time to make him change his mind, perhaps it was his burgeoning popularity, as he began publishing with a wider range of publishers, including Hale, Octopus Books, Pan, Readers Digest and The Aquarian Press. He also

Kind permission of London Newsquest
Newspapers

travelled extensively in Britain as well as abroad not only to give talks but also to research further information about folklore, ghosts, psychic matters and witchcraft. Combining this with a full-time job was clearly not a viable option, so at some point, he must have made the decision to pursue a full-time researching and writing career. His first book, *The Dark World of the Witches* was published by Robert Hale Ltd in 1962, as a hardback. It soon became available in paperback formats too.

Maple made it clear that although he investigated, researched and wrote about ghosts, magic and witches, it was the folklore of the supernatural that really interested him. Since he had already written on the subject of politics back in the late 1940s, it is possible that, with the unique thinking associated with Mercury in Aquarius, he realised he could focus on a gap in the literary market – for books on folklore and the supernatural. He revealed in 1973, that he had experienced seeing a ghost and that was the only ghost that he believed in (*Essex and East London Newspaper*, 1973), although his friend Peter Underwood subsequently claimed there were other, later sightings (Underwood, 2009, 157).

Similarly, Maple does not really seem to have believed in magic, claiming it was "non-existent" ('Local Man's Book about Witchcraft,' newspaper cutting), although he may have been trying at this time (*c.*1963) to avoid being associated with the more sensationalist aspects of press reporting. Certainly, in an interview in the *Guardian Gazette and Independent* (June 30th, 1972) he claimed that modern attitudes to witchcraft were "still feudal" and that people believed atrocious things took place. It seems likely that he was protecting himself and his family and was also determined to be taken seriously as an author and researcher.

He was friends with Alex Sanders (the subject of Chapter Thirteen) and interviewed both him and his wife Maxine for an article that *The Sun* newspaper published in the period leading up to Samhain in 1970 (*The Sun* newspaper, 'What it's Like to Live With a Witch.' 29th October, 1970). Yet, although advocating freedom of religion, he was also well aware that some people were exploiting witchcraft, remarking that, "These fantastic witches with their suburban orgies and comic covens belong to the horror comic rather than to history" (Kernan, 1979).

The presence of Venus in Sagittarius would have provided Maple with a less materialistic attitude towards money. For example, in *The Secret Lore of Plants and Flowers* (1980), he describes the world as "... overwhelmed by materialism." Perhaps this is what enabled him to retire from his clerical job at the gas board and become a full-time writer, which even then would have been a more precarious existence. It is likely that the attraction of adventure and exploration, educating and learning and the love of the philosophical and religious combined to give him an optimistic belief that he could be successful in his new full-time work.

ADVICE, COMPANIONSHIP AND CAUTION

Another manifestation of Venus in Sagittarius is that, in relationships and significant one-to-one partnerships, there may remain some longing for freedom and space to explore. There may also be tremendous friendship, idealism in love and an enjoyment of relating to a variety of people. Maple married his second wife Dora in 1951, and they remained married until his death in 1994. In Dora's natal chart, there is some indication of her astrological compatibility with Maple, which is worth exploring a little further.

Dora Maple's Sun sign Scorpio is a fixed sign, as is Maple's Sun sign Aquarius; both belong to the fixed mode (*see glossary*). The nature of the fixed sign shows that they both possessed determination, loyalty and tenacity. Their Sun signs respectively show potential interest in the supernatural and the unusual. Dora was also receptive to spirit, and once saw a ghost while she was with Maple when they visited The Royal Botanical Garden in Spain (Underwood, 2009, 157).

Venus in Sagittarius and Uranus in Aquarius associate with valuing friends and their individualism. We see this loyalty in their friendship with the author, broadcaster and parapsychologist Peter Underwood and his wife, who were friends with the Maples for many years. Underwood was president of The Ghost Club from 1960–1993, and Maple had been a member of The Ghost Club in the 1960s as previously discussed. Underwood wrote that the Maples were "old friends" of him and his wife (Underwood, 2009, 157).

In his autobiography, *No Common Task*, published in 1983, Underwood describes talking to Maple about his concerns when both he and his wife were thinking about becoming full-time writers. By then Maple had been writing full-time for a number of years. *The Dark World of the Witches,* his first book, was published in 1962 and Dora his wife knew about the practicalities of being married to a full-time writer. Underwood noted, "Our friends Eric and Dora Maple said we ought to think very carefully before we came to such a decision" (ibid). Maple's caution is reflected in his Mars in Capricorn placement, governing planning, strategy and timing. He may even have been 'projecting' his own caution in becoming a full-time writer, since it took him many years to finally make the break and leave the Gas Board.

APPEAL, CHARISMA AND THE VALUE OF KNOWLEDGE

Mercury is sextile Venus indicating that Maple was a naturally skilled communicator who obtained great pleasure in reading, speaking and writing. It was not 'just a job' to him. It also denotes a love of language and certainly Maple could be amiable, charming and diplomatic. This can be seen in his public speaking – he participated in numerous radio phone-ins and television programmes discussing subjects such as Christmas customs, ghosts and witches, during which he comes across as invariably patient and humorous. He also worked in public relations for the British Tourist Board promoting his spiritual homeland, East Anglia, and wrote articles for the popular press and was interviewed in the local and specialised press.

Maple wrote many books and some journals on the afore-mentioned areas and subjects, showing he was able to communicate with different audiences through different media. It has been said of Maple that he was comfortable with "all sorts and conditions of men," reflecting how Mercury associates with humour and wit, and Venus with charm and kind-heartedness; it is perhaps unsurprising that he was said to have "a kindly wit" (Smith, 1995, 87).

Little, if anything is known about Maple's educational background but his close friend Alan W. Smith once said that "he had little formal education" (ibid). It seems likely therefore that, like most boys of his day, he left school at the age of fourteen. Clearly, he did not allow this to hold him back, and he must have either educated himself or sought further study after leaving full-time education. Saturn is in Gemini (*see box on previous page*) at 26 degrees in Maple's chart and as authority and knowledge are associated with Saturn and Gemini, respectively, it probably influenced Maple's decision to become an authority and specialise in folklore, ghosts and witches. The author, Peter Underwood (2009, 157), has described him as "a knowledgeable and erudite expert on witchcraft" (ibid).

Saturn also represents fear and perhaps Maple secretly feared appearing uneducated, particularly as he did not (as far as we know) pursue any further formal education after he left school. Interestingly, Gerald Gardner also had this placement in his own natal chart (see Chapter Four). However, the aspect of Jupiter trine Saturn reveals that Maple was realistic enough to know his own limitations and could compensate for these with his strengths.

For example, his lack of education (though not of knowledge) meant he could sympathise with and reach out to people who liked his work and subjects, without appearing to talk down to them. The placement also reveals he was a philosophical thinker who was honest and straightforward, since these are areas associated with Jupiter and Saturn, respectively. Certainly, his lack of a formal education did not stop him from pursuing a learned and successful career. Michael Howard (2010, 47) once referred to Maple rather dismissively as an "amateur folklorist" but it is important to remember that Maple was writing and researching at a time when interest in these subjects was only just re-emerging and he was reaching out (successfully) to an audience that had never previously been interested in these topics.

Saturn is conjunct Pluto, indicating that Maple may have been something of a workaholic, since these are areas which bestow qualities of Pluto and Saturn; Pluto seeks to transform, whilst cautious Saturn restricts Pluto's action. This can be seen in the way Maple remained in his full-time work with the Gas Board whilst at the same time collecting the anecdotes and research for the papers that he wrote for The Folklore Society. This work must have occupied a lot of his time. It has been said that Maple

at this time "... encountered folklore as a field for systematic research" (Smith, 1995, 87), and he applied himself to this with great diligence, planning his visits to Essex country villages to help with his investigations, before writing up the information he obtained and indexing it so he could later access it more easily ('Local Man's Book about Witchcraft.' Newspaper article, *c*.1963).

Investigation and research are both associations of Pluto, whilst the systematic (as we see with the indexing) is associated with practical Saturn – his work required intense self-discipline. Jupiter is trine Pluto and would have influenced Maple's enthusiasm for magic and the occult. This made the transforming nature of Pluto apparent, and, in Maple's case, his

Kind permission of London Newsquest Newspapers

passion for magic, the occult and witchcraft transformed his life. He literally "… spent a lifetime investigating witchcraft and ghostology" (Underwood, 2009, 26).

As already mentioned, the Moon was in the cardinal (*see glossary*) fire sign of Aries, and was a crescent moon when Maple was born. The cardinal energy of the Moon and of Aries will have helped him to not only assert himself, but also to initiate and lead in his pioneering field. Astrologer, Dane Rudhyar, observed that people born under a crescent moon "… may be characterised in some cases by a deep subconscious sense of being overwhelmed by the momentum of the past and the power of 'ghosts' or karma" (Rudhyar, 1971, 50–51).

PUTTING THE PAST TO RIGHTS

Maple's passion appears to have been radically retrieving old traditions, superstitions and customs of days gone by. The outer (*see glossary*) planets Neptune and Pluto are both in the sign of Cancer in Maple's natal chart. These two placements indicate that the generations of people who were born at this time may have romanticised about the past and fiercely held onto family and security at this time, since these are areas connected with Neptune and Pluto. This is significant, as society was living through the First World War, where many families were destroyed through the tragic effects of war and mass bereavement.

Up until he researched George Pickingill of Essex (the subject of Chapter One), few people knew about the man who later was to become known as the Last Wizard of Canewdon. Maple also undertook exhaustive investigation and research on James Murrell, known as 'Cunning Murrell' of Hadleigh, Essex. During his investigations, Maple obtained Murrell's last surviving book (although it did not turn up until shortly after his own death). Maple also owned Murrell's 'treasure chest'. His work on these two significant Essex men was an exceptional contribution to the literature of English cunning men and witchcraft for future generations and when Maple died; his widow gave Murrell's book to The Folklore Society (Smith, 1995, 87).

The Moon in Aries indicates willingness to defend others if necessary and often achieves its best when going solo or leading projects. Maple may have secretly wished to use his strengths and talents to redress some of the wrongs of previous times, i.e. when the disabled, impoverished and 'wise men and women' of villages, were victimised and targeted by those in positions of authority and power. His Aquarian/Uranus energies could have helped champion their cause to help try and achieve social justice for them, albeit long after the event. He once remarked that ghosts were "… souls on our conscience, a debt that humanity owes the dead" (Kernan, 1979).

This position of Moon in Aries (*see box on right*) also reveals Maple's need for action and excitement in his life. He responded instinctively to people and his enthusiasm could be easily aroused by the right subjects, as shown in his many interviews and broadcasts, some of which are still available on YouTube. He enjoyed a challenge and could be bold and courageous when required – as we see in giving up his steady job in order to pursue writing full-time.

On the 22nd January, 1915, at noon, both the Moon and Mars were at 23 degrees; in allowing an orb of 6 degrees either side, it is more than likely that the Moon and Mars were square (*see glossary*) all day on his birthday. This aspect can indicate "a radical politician" (Tompkins, 1989, 139), since the

Moon and Mars contact needs to be able to channel its anger and express its outrage. This is seen in Maple's younger years, where he expressed his anger about capitalism and society when writing for the *Freedom Press*, as well as writing for the periodical, *The Word*, which was edited by the Scottish anarchist and communist, Guy Aldred (www. libcom.org), as previously discussed.

The Moon square Mars also suggests that Maple may have been sensitive to conflict because of the hard square aspect. He may have found it challenging to express his feelings, perhaps preferring to concentrate on the facts and traditions he found in folklore rather than the conflicts of the present. If so, then folklore would have offered him a form of escape.

Certainly, anarchists were very resistant to war and conscription, many of them preferring to be conscientious objectors, although it is not known whether this was the case with Maple, who may have been in a reserved occupation (as he worked for the Gas Board, as discussed earlier) or he may have been called up. Astrologer, Robert Pelletier, observed that for people with Moon/Mars hard contacts, their "... professional distress tends to cross over into your domestic life and cause painful situations to develop between you and your partner" (Pelletier, 1974, 136).

This is relevant as in Maple's, *The Ancient Art of Occult Healing*, where he advises: "... try to create a home environment free of discordance into which you can retire at the end of the day's labours to renew the strength required for facing the difficulties of daily life" (Maple, 1974, 64). Perhaps he realised that 'bringing his work home with him' might cause tension in his own domestic life or he may have witnessed this happening in the homes of friends or other family members. Certainly, it cannot have been easy for his family with him working full-time for the Gas Board while pursuing his folklore research and writing. By the late 1970s, he was lecturing "... four or five times a week" (Kernan, 1979). The Moon square Mars suggests that he felt protective about his home and work yet was driven in each of these areas. There is an element of ambition and courage too in his work, since these areas are associated with Mars. Writing about ghosts was often regarded as sensationalist, and it took courage to carve a path for himself, without descending into the style of tabloid journalism.

HARD WORK AND STRATEGY

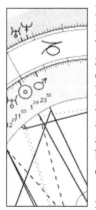

Mars in Capricorn (*see box on left*) emphasises the theme of difficulty in expressing anger, in the sense that Capricorn obstructs and restricts, whilst the energy of Mars is assertive, heated and passionate – so it gives a sense of keeping a stiff upper lip in order to retain a reserved external shell and helps to avoid appearing vulnerable. This is a less helpful side of this position, but of course Mars is exalted in Capricorn and shows that Maple was totally focused on his ambitions. Once he achieved recognition, energy was even more reliable and persistent, although it demanded great self-discipline. However, this would have been a great help to him in his work, particularly when he became self-employed as a full-time writer.

The assertive and energising planet Mars and ruler of the sign Aries, is in exaltation in the sign of earthy and hardworking Capricorn. This gives a patient, pragmatic, and steady edge for working in business and indicates that Maple was a grafter. Certainly, with over 20 years of service from him, North Thames Gas Board had had a loyal and reliable member of staff on their payroll.

Maple's pioneering self can be seen whereby, after he had spent considerable time collecting tales about witches, he approached the BBC and they invited him for a voice test which led to several recordings on programmes such as *Roundabout, Tonight* and *Town and Country* ('Local Man's Book about Witchcraft' undated, unnamed newspaper article, c.1963).

Maple was a clever strategist and only when the time was right did he make the move to retire from the Gas Board in order to work full-time as a folklore collector, ghost-hunter, author, broadcaster and lecturer. He was anything but amateur. Saturn in the sign of Gemini in the natal chart suggests sincerity in issues concerning communication and learning, which may have enabled Maple to become an authority in his chosen field.

Mars in Capricorn can also symbolise struggle against authority since Mars and Capricorn are associated with these areas, respectively. This probably influenced Maple's earlier life as a proactive anarchist where the anger (associated with Mars) is channelled against conservative attitudes and status quo (associated with Capricorn).

However, Mars in opposition to Neptune suggests that Neptune's energy could have helped to diffuse Maple's potential anger. It also symbolises that Maple may have 'fought' for the underdog. This can be seen in his politics, where he was fighting (associated with Mars) for an ideal (associated with Neptune), yet as far as we know, he did this by employing his greatest skills, compassion and writing. This can also be seen in his investigative and research work, where he was sensitive and compassionate towards the people he interviewed. This would have encouraged them to open up to him, especially when discussing topics that others might have ridiculed. People were happy to confide in him.

Returning to the area of the Moon sign Aries, this placement also symbolises the mother and care-taking figure and provides some insight into their qualities. The Moon in Aries reveals that Maple's mother, Edith Ann (née Baker), 1888–1963, was probably pioneering for the time in which she lived. Like her parents, she worked in the post office (Census, 1911) and in her younger days was a spiritualist medium (Smith, 1995, 87). She may not have been a certified and registered medium, as the Greater World, Spiritualists National Union and the Spiritualists Association of Great Britain hold no records of such a person (email communications to Author, April 2016). It is possible that Edith Maple served local spiritualist churches even though she did not hold a diploma but, more likely, that she worked at home with sitters and home circles were popular then.

Maple was influenced by his mother's qualities. Edith Maple lived through both world wars, it is possible that, perhaps she worked from home as a medium offering comfort and information to people seeking news of their loved-ones who were missing in the war. Perhaps her work as a medium helped shape Maple's fascination with the occult and witches.

THE COMMON TOUCH

The Sun is in opposition to Neptune in Maple's chart, indicating that Maple was receptive and sensitive and had an active imagination. He may have tended to float off in daydreams, for example, since the Neptunian nature is without boundaries and finds it easy to transcend into other realms and escapism. It has been said of Maple and his work that he "... had effectively taken his own favourite nook of England, the scene of his own research, and given it a spurious national status" (Hutton, 1999, 296). This suggests an element of glamorisation and perhaps romanticising on Maple's part, which is also an association of the Sun in opposition to Neptune.

This aspect also suggests that Maple could have sympathised with those he interviewed; his kindly manner made it easy for them to trust him and not be intimidated by his questions. This would have been especially useful when meeting people who were 'suffering' or 'victimised', perhaps because they had been disturbed by paranormal activity in their homes. Maple was "… a great teller of tales himself, he also had the gift of getting others to tell their tales to him" (Smith, 1995, 87). Maple was also interested in healing, magic, spirits and witches, sacrificing much of his time in order to, in effect, escape back into earlier times.

The sea is the symbol for planet Neptune, which rules Pisces. This sign is symbolised by two fish swimming in opposite directions and belongs to the element of water, which is associated with being emotional, sympathetic, imaginative, healing and impressionable. When Maple was born, Neptune was in exaltation (*see glossary*) in the sign of Cancer at 29 degrees. This sign is symbolised by the crab and its ruler is the Moon, water is also the ruling element of Cancer.

This placement therefore holds a strong affiliation to cycles, rhythms and tides and so it is interesting that his publisher wrote the following: "Eric Maple spent his early life in that strange Essex marshland district near Southend, still known as the Witch Country, where even today the terror of witches, ghosts and demons is not entirely dead. Here he fell under the spell of the arcane and was never to escape from its influence. In his youth he was a sea-front orator and an investigator of the curious byways of political history" (Maple, 1962, back cover).

Neptune in Cancer suggests Maple had well-developed intuition and this, coupled with the placement of Pluto in Cancer brings intensity and insight to his nature. A less helpful side to this placement is that his very strong imagination could have potentially caused him unnecessary worry. The adoring, dreamy, and starry-eyed Neptunian energy is nurtured here by the emotional, leading and sensitive crab. Neptune and Pluto in Cancer can suggest an obsession and passion; addiction and escape to the past, which can be seen in Maple's drive and determination in collecting archives, memoires and records from times past. He could, absorb and retell old chronicles, history, memories, etc, that had long been lost or hidden. His story-telling may have been delivered creatively and imaginatively but is no worse for this, since it enabled him to reach a wide audience of readers and listeners. Maple brought the important qualities of; perception, tolerance and understanding to those that had once lived in an intolerant and until then, mostly hidden, bygone age.

Pluto is at 0 degrees in Cancer. This degree is described as a 'critical degree' (*see glossary*) since it is at the beginning of a sign, which in Maple's case is Pluto at 0 degrees and 36 minutes into the sign of Cancer. It has been observed that, when at the position of 0 degrees, the planet "embraces the very pure, undiluted nature of the sign" (Clifford, 2014, 191). This is especially pertinent to Maple and his passion for ancestry, customs, ghosts, history and witches.

Neptune and Pluto are both outer planets (*see glossary*) and whilst the above offers interpretations on a personal level about Maple's natal chart, it is important to remember that Neptune and Pluto in Cancer socially represented generations of people (*see box overleaf*). Maple was born during the First World War, a turbulent time when one's country, family and home could no longer be taken for granted, in that those areas had to be fought for – often they were devastated in the process. War was followed by a worldwide economic depression as well as a great flu epidemic which killed millions of people worldwide. Towards the end of Pluto's passage in patriotic Cancer, the world saw the rise of Fascism and the start of World War Two.

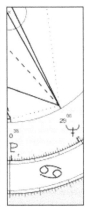

Maple had clearly been much affected by these changes and wrote in his introduction to *The Ancient Art of Occult Healing* (1974), "We live in an age of anxiety, beset by wars and rumours of wars and bombarded by bad news from dawn to dusk. Newspaper, television and radio bulletins constantly remind us that even if the end of civilization is not exactly at hand, it cannot long be deferred. Our society is sick, strained by intolerable pressures and poisoned by fears" (Maple, 1974, 7). This shows his concern for society and this description of society as 'sick' and 'poisoned by fears' well illustrates the qualities of Neptune and Pluto.

He goes on to say, "In recounting the remarkable story of the ancient art of occult healing, it is hoped to widen your understanding of the secret processes which determine the health, wealth and happiness of mankind." Here we see the Aquarian area of the happiness of mankind, as well as Neptune's healing and Pluto's secret processes (ibid).

ENERGIES AND PARENTAL INFLUENCE

As previously stated, the Sun can symbolise the father in the natal chart and this is pertinent to Maple and his father, William Alfred Maple, who was born in 1879, in Kent, and died in 1948. During World War I, he worked in the Royal Navy as an Acting Chief Stoker. He returned from the war apparently unscathed and with service medals which included: British War Medals for services between 5th August–11th November, 1918 and The Victory Star (also called The Allied Victory Medal) 1914–15, for having served at sea in many of the operations (www.ancestry.co.uk/1911census). The father is symbolised by the Sun and the seas, and service by Neptune.

The Sun in opposition to Neptune reveals that Maple may have glamorised or idolised his father. When Maple Senior moved from his birth county of Kent to Essex, he brought with him the lore of that county, and would regale others with tales of highwaymen and smugglers and Canterbury's 'Mad Messiah' of the 1830s (Smith, 1995, 87). This almost certainly influenced Maple's future as a collector of tales and researcher of the occult.

Maple's birth certificate describes his father's occupation as an 'electrical wireman' and again this is indicative of the Sun in Aquarius, since electricity and technology are associated with Aquarius and its ruler Uranus. It is significant therefore that his father worked both as a stoker in the boiler rooms at the heart of the Royal Navy ships and also as an electrician.

Electricity and technology also appear in Maple's understanding of magic and ghosts; he once said of magic that it is "… non-existent. Nothing can influence events other than remote control" ('Local Man's Book about Witchcraft.' Undated, unnamed newspaper article, *c*.1963). About ghosts he remarked that, "the greatest enemy of the ghost is the electric light" (*Guardian-Gazette and Independent*. June 30th, 1972, 18). Presumably he came to such conclusions after his ghost-hunting experiences and interviews with those who had seen a ghost.

Maple's awareness of psychic energy and magnetism is also illustrated by an experience recounted to him by Lois Bourne. One evening, after a visit by Maple,

Bourne saw "… an animal-type face with thick black bristling hair, red glowing eyes and bared teeth" pressed against her window so forcefully that it left an imprint on the glass (Bourne, 1979, 38).

Some days later, she telephoned Maple to tell him of her experience, and surprisingly he took some responsibility for it, explaining, "I think it's my fault; this sort of thing is always happening whenever I have visited someone" (ibid). He then explained how, before he visited Bourne, he had paid a visit to a haunted barn in Essex. A farm labourer had seen an apparition of a monkey-like creature so malevolent it had almost persuaded him to hang himself.

Both Bourne and Maple came to the conclusion that Maple "carried with him a trail of undisciplined psychic energy which had that day shaped itself into a thought-form," which then materialised and made itself visible to Bourne (ibid, 39). This shows that Maple realised he was a magnet for psychic and spiritual energy and understood how energies could generate in different ways.

There are two conjunctions (*see glossary*) in Maple's natal chart; Sun/Pluto and Jupiter/Neptune. Sun conjunct Pluto reveals that Maple had a strong will and great determination in work. It has been observed that "… investigators of life and death, reincarnation and other occult forces are apt to have this aspect" (Sakoian and Acker, 1972, 12), and it describes Maple and his work perfectly.

The conjunction aspect in a chart indicates a tension or an area of one's life which creates stress, as it involves a relationship with someone who generates a sense of friction and pressure, which nonetheless has to be tolerated. It has also been observed that the Sun and Pluto in conjunction may indicate that, "… someone may be constantly putting him under pressure to improve his work" (ibid). Possibly this could refer to his work in the Gas Board, which may have seemed constrictive and mundane to him, although there seem to have been some tensions in his fieldwork as a collector and investigator, since "… his colleagues in the Folklore Society rued his abandonment of scholarly standards" (Hutton, 1999, 296). Yet a review of Maple's *Realm of Ghosts* by Geoffrey Palmer, which was published in *Folklore Society Magazine* (1964, 212) describes him writing "… with scholarly precision," suggesting it is a "… book for historians, theologians and archaeologists, as well as for laymen."

If it is true that Maple did not follow the discipline and regulations of The Folklore Society, this would be very much in keeping with his independent Uranus nature, where he made progress in his work in a unique way. However, it was precisely by this method that Maple was eventually able to retire from his day work and support himself by researching and write full-time.

Jupiter in conjunct Neptune in the chart suggests that Maple's artistic and creative nature would have been best expressed in behind-the-scenes work, especially since he would have needed privacy and solitude to write his books. The aspect again suggests

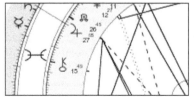

Maple's understanding and sensitivity when dealing with the general public, since excess is associated with Jupiter, and the other areas mentioned are associated with Neptune. These influences would have enabled him to spend so many years talking with the public via books, articles, radio, television and public appearances.

EMPATHY AND HEALING

The theme of compassion, intuition and sensitivity is shown in Maple's natal chart with the placement of Chiron (*see glossary*), The Wounded Healer, in Pisces) suggesting that Maple needed to 'heal himself' by developing his inner knowing and in doing so cultivate his intuition so that he could be of the best service possible to those around him. This healing may have taken him a long time since the 'wound' manifests itself in one's early years and can take a lifetime before it can be cured. Chiron in Pisces also suggests that Maple possessed past-life esoteric knowledge and that in this lifetime he needed to 'heal' and find an outlet for his familiarity with this area.

Pisces and its ruler Neptune bestow qualities that include empathy, kindness and sensitivity. It is possible, therefore, that Maple was able to feel a sense of oneness with the many people that he met in his lifetime, who were willing to share their experience and knowledge with him. He could also feel a strong connection to bygone ages, where cunning folk, healers and witches were essential to the community.

Maple may have also felt a sense of duty to those who were victimised and tortured years ago. He was particularly passionate about Essex, which is where his family name originates (https://www.houseofnames.com/Maple-family-crest); an area famed for its self-styled 'Witch-finder', the puritan General Matthew Hopkins, who had many men and women tortured, tried for witchcraft and hanged. As Pisces has an affinity with past-life and reincarnation, perhaps Maple felt he owed it to those previous generations to ensure they were remembered and to highlight the torture and victimisation they experienced.

Venus is square Chiron in the natal chart, suggesting that Maple may have lacked self-esteem in love and other significant relationships. Perhaps he felt that he gave more than he ever received, as the square aspect reveals challenges and tensions. Chiron represents the area in our lives where we lack self-esteem and feel insecure, and the Chiron/Venus contact symbolises that "the soul has been hurt in love many times" (Hall, Godsfield Press, 2006). Maple was widowed relatively early in life, after just ten years of marriage. He may therefore have felt reluctant to get involved with another partner after his wife had died, and it may have taken him a long time (perhaps even continuing after his second marriage to Dora) to heal from his experience of bereavement, and complete his grieving process.

The North Node in Aquarius and South Node in Leo (*see glossary for Moon's Nodes*) in Maple's chart symbolise the karmic lessons which have been brought into this life and show both the areas needing to be developed, and those needing to be inhibited if one is to advance and grow spiritually. The position of these nodes suggests that Maple needed to let get go of fears in relationships by offering freedom to his partners, instead of expecting them to act as he wanted them to. Learning to let go and moving instead towards more logical objectives in his life would have helped achieve balance, as would learning to cultivate true friendships. In growing into this throughout his life, Maple will have helped his relationship with himself and his outer world.

The position of Venus in Sagittarius would have helped Maple to value freedom in relationships as it is an association of Sagittarius and its ruler Jupiter. There is a conjunct aspect created between Jupiter and the North Node is partile (*see glossary*), suggesting he may have found emotional security through his beliefs and spirituality (all areas associated with Jupiter). He may have gained enormous satisfaction from taking up his opportunities to explore and travel, since these areas are also associated with Sagittarius and Jupiter. Trusting in parts of life which are infinitive, such as faith, would have been helpful to him; for example, healing, nature and spirituality.

It is interesting that Maple wrote about these things, and presumably he enjoyed being able to share his knowledge and educate others through his spoken and written words. He was not just noticed by ordinary readers; other distinguished authors have referred to Maple in their work, such as historian and author Ronald Hutton, Essex folklorist Sylvia Kent and High Priestess and author Doreen Valiente (see Chapter Eleven).

After a long and active life, Maple died on the 9th February, 1994, aged 72. His death certificate cited the cause of death as 'Degenerative and Ischemic Heart Disease'. At the time of death, there were several planets transiting in the sign of Aquarius including the Sun, Moon, Venus, and Mars. These planets would have been activating all the natal planets in Aquarius; Sun, Mercury, Jupiter and Uranus.

There were astrological transits (transiting Pluto sextile the natal Sun, and transiting Saturn semi-sextile the natal Sun) taking place at the same time, indicating death, rebirth and transformation. Pluto and Saturn indicate the end of Maple's cycle and transformation, and since both the sextile and semi-sextile are easy/harmonious/soft aspects, this can indicate that his passing was peaceful. Since the condition of his heart was degenerative, it would have caused a heart attack and seems likely to have been a quick and peaceful passing, rather than a prolonged and lingering death.

Eric William Maple was the most unique investigator and storyteller. His personal identity may have been carefully hidden, but in his work as a truly self-made man and scholar, he was a colourful character with kindliness and interest towards others and he continues to inspire.

ACKNOWLEDGEMENTS, CREDITS AND REFERENCES

Flat/noon natal chart generated by www.astro.com

Maple, Eric: Fri, 22nd January, 1915. Time of birth: Unknown, GMT, Forest Gate, London, England.

0w10, 51n30.

Rodden Rating 'X'

Eric Maple's Birth Certificate – Copy issued by General Register Office, Stockport, Merseyside – BXCG 822691.

Dora Maple (nee Savage) Birth Certificate Copy issued by General Register Office, Stockport, Merseyside – BXCG 862907.

Eric Maple's Death Certificate (Copy Issued by London Borough of Redbridge) – BBB 620201.

William Alfred Maple birth/death data: Reg. year 1879, Reg qtr April/May/June, reg District: Canterbury. Inferred County: Kent. Vol. 2a, p749.
Edith Ann Baker birth/death data: Date of birth 1888, Date of death Reg, March 1963, reg district: Hendon. Inferred County: Middlesex. Vol. 5a, p686.
Sydney John Maple birth/death data: Born 11th Dec 1916, Date of death registration, Nov 1985, reg district: Chelmsford. Inferred County: Essex. Vol. 9, p1821.

BOOKS

Bourne, L. (1985) *Witch Amongst Us.* Robert Hale, London.

Clifford, F.C. (2014) *Horoscope Snapshots: Essays in Modern Astrology.* Flare Publications and The London School of Astrology.

De Cleene, M. and Lejeune, M-C. (2003) *Compendium of Symbolic and Ritual Plants in Europe.* Vol. 1. Man and Culture Publishers, Ghent, Belgium.

Hall, J. (2006) *Past Life Astrology.* Godsfield Press.

Howard, M. (2010) *Modern Wicca: A History from Gerald Gardner to the Present.* Llewelyn Worldwide.

Hutton, R. (1999) *The Triumph of the Moon: A History of Modern Pagan Witchcraft.* Oxford University Press.

Maple, E. (1962) *The Dark World of the Witches.* Robert Hale Ltd.

Maple, E. (1974) *The Ancient Art of Occult Healing.* The Aquarian Press.

Maple, E. (1977) *Supernatural England.* Robert Hale Ltd.

Maple, E. (1980) *The Secret Lore of Plants and Flowers.* Robert Hale Ltd.

Palmer G. (1964) *Folklore.* Review of: *Realm of Ghosts,* by Eric Maple. Vol. 75, No. 3 (Autumn), pp211–212.

Pelletier, R. (1974) *Planets in Aspect: Understanding Your Inner Dynamics.* Whitford Press.

Rudhyar, D. *The Lunation Cycle.* Shambhala, Boulder and London.

Sakoian, F. and Acker, L. (1972) *That Inconjunct-Quincunx: The Not So Minor Aspect.* Copple House Books, Inc.

Smith, A.W. (1995) 'Eric Maple, 1916–1994.' *Folklore.* Vol. 106, p87.

Tompkins, S. (2006) *The Contemporary Astrologer's Handbook.* Flare Publications: The London School of Astrology.

Tribe, D. (1967) *100 Years of Free Thought.* Elek Books Limited.

Underwood, P. (2009) *Haunted Gardens.* Amberley Publishing Plc.

Underwood, P. (1983) *No Common Task.* Harrap, London.

Various contributors. *(1975) The Freethinker.* Vols. 95 & 96. G. Foote and Company.

NEWSPAPER ARTICLES

Essex and East London Newspapers. 'Interview with Dick Tidiman.' Wednesday, January 17th, 1973, 11.

Express and Independent. 'Dark World of the Witches.' Friday, 26th October, 1962.

Guardian-Gazette and Independent. 'That Old Black Magic.' 30th June, 1972, 18.

Copy of article provided by Redbridge Library Information and Heritage Services-Article headed 'Local Man's Book about Witchcraft' with photo of Maple by local man Arthur Hands. No record of publication or date but it is c.1962/3.

The Sun. 'What it's Like to Live with a Witch.' 29th October, 1970.

The Washington Post. 'The Fearless Phantom Hunter.' By Kernan, M. October 25th, 1979. https://www.washingtonpost.com/archive/lifestyle/1979/10/25/the-fearless-phantom-hunter/7a386303-b367-4ae2-9704-db3a9f5d18de/

CREDITS

International Institute of Social History (Amsterdam) *Freedom Journal,* 6th September 1947, article by Eric Maple. Accessed 21/04/2016.

SPECIAL THANKS TO

Alan W. Smith's widow, for her time.
Alan Murdie, Chairman of The Ghost Club, for his time and information (May, 2016).
Essex Records Office.
Michael Gray, Assistant Archivist of The Savage Club, for his time and information about Maple's membership of the club.
The International Institute of Social History (Amsterdam), for copy of *Freedom* (06/09/1947).
Norman Burton and the Romany & Traveller Family History Society (R&TFHS).
Redbridge Library Information and Heritage Services.
Sittingbourne Heritage Museum.

WEBSITES

https://www.libcom.org/history/north-east-london-anarchist-group – Maple's article in The Word (25/09/1947). Accessed on 17/04/2016.

http://www.historyextra.com/feature/school-leaving-age-what-can-we-learn-history – Accessed on 18/04/2016).

www.ancestry.co.uk – Accessed on 18/03/2016.

http://www.ancestry.co.uk/1911Census – Eric and Dora's marriage details – Dora Savage, Spouse. Maple, Date of Registration: Oct/Nov/Dec, 1951. Registration District: Essex South Western. Inferred County: Essex. p444.

https://familysearch.org/ark:/61903/1:1:QV8N-JQ45 – Eric Maple's first marriage: England and Wales Marriage Registration Index, 1837-2005, database, family search. Accessed on 09/06/2016.

https://familysearch.org/ark:/61903/1:1:QVDD-HQ6N – Eric Maple's second marriage: England and Wales Marriage Registration Index, 1837-2005, database, family search. Accessed on 09/06/2016.

CHAPTER NINE

Stewart Farrar 1916–2000

Author, Journalist, Screenwriter and Wiccan Priest

FRANK STEWART FARRAR (known to many as Stewart Farrar) was born on the 28th June, 1916, in the area of Highams Park which at that time was part of the county of Essex in England, and is now in the borough of Waltham Forest in Greater London. His parents were Francis Joseph Farrar who, like millions of others, was serving in the war at that time, but would later return to his position as head of current accounts at the London office of the Hong Kong and Shanghai Bank; and his mother Agnes Farrar (née Picken), who would eventually become manager and teacher in a private school.

Having studied journalism at university, Farrar volunteered at the outbreak of World War II, entering the army as an officer cadet at the age of 23. His military career was impressive; by the time he was discharged in 1946, he had reached the rank of major, a remarkable achievement. Whilst serving in the forces, he had travelled to different parts of the country, undertaking various duties and training. Although Farrar had volunteered to serve his country abroad, this was denied, since his superiors considered he was more valuable if he remained in the UK, teaching new army recruits in diverse combat techniques at various barracks. In Kent, in 1940, he was an instructor in anti-aircraft gunnery during World War II, using his communication and supervisory skills to teach his less experienced colleagues. In August 1940, *The London Gazette* listed him as being in the Middlesex Regiment as Frank Stewart Farrar – army service number: 140013 (*London Gazette*, 1940).

Farrar was very politically minded and joined the Communist Party. Much of his political stance was borne out of his gruesome and painful experiences and observations of the war and its effects, both at the time and in the ensuing years. This may have helped shape his peaceful, humanitarian, philosophical and political outlook. He put his writing talents to good use, becoming a journalist, novelist, poet and scriptwriter. He is perhaps best known however, for being a well-known Wiccan priest and he authored his first Wiccan book, *What Witches Do,* in 1971. He was married six times and had four children, moving to Ireland with his last wife, Janet, and living there with her until his death in 2000.

WHAT STEWART FARRAR'S NATAL CHART SHOWS

Stewart Farrar was born on Wednesday, 28th June, 1916, at 11.59am, when the Sun was in the cardinal water sign of Cancer at 6 degrees and the Moon was in the mutable air sign of Gemini at 14 degrees. The chart shape is that of a locomotive driven by the 'engine' planet Uranus, which is in its natural sign of Aquarius at 19 degrees. In a locomotive (*see glossary*) shape the planets span an arc of approximately 240 degrees, leaving the other area of the chart void of any planets.

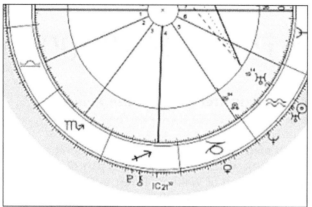

In Farrar's chart, this shape signifies that he was driven to succeed in a very individual way and that on his life's journey he may have felt a detachment from the more inner and personal areas of his life as symbolised in his chart by the empty first four houses, which span the signs Libra, Scorpio, Sagittarius and Capricorn (*see chart on left*). These four houses represent the areas of the self, earnings and possessions, communications and siblings, and domestic and family life. The ruling planets of the house cusps of the aforementioned signs are: Mercury, Venus, Pluto and Jupiter, the aspects of these planets will be discussed later on.

The engine planet Uranus dominates the chart, giving us critical clues about Farrar's nature – since qualities such as being humanitarian and progressive, while also possessing so much in the way of originality and creative thinking, together with the ability to shock and to be unpredictable – are notable Uranus traits.

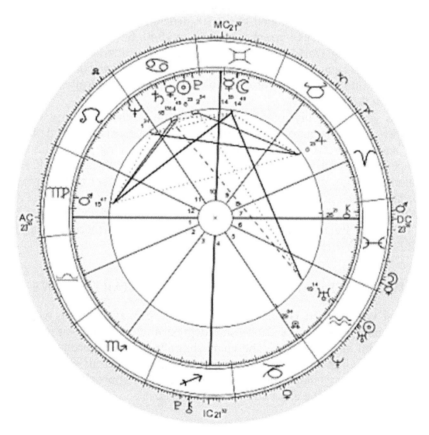

Natal and Transit Chart for Stewart Farrar on the day he died, 7th February, 2000.

Despite the emptiness of the first four houses, Farrar's personal life was unusually intense, even by the standards of wartime. By the time he left the army in 1946, he was already married for the second time, having divorced his first wife who had left him in 1943, taking their son with her. Farrar was on leave, waiting to be demobbed in May 1946, when his second wife, Shindy, gave birth to their son. Shortly afterwards however, Farrar went to work in the Allied Control Commission in Germany, serving as a civilian officer, while Shindy remained in England with their child. The ACC was based in Berlin and governed the military occupation of Germany by the US, UK and Soviet Union after the war.

Farrar was a public relations officer and press officer for North German Coal Control and Krupp Control at Villa Hugel (the Krupp family palace), outside Essen. There he met the "love of his life" and "the woman who was to haunt his memories for years to come," Hilke Carstens (Guerra and Farrar, 2013, 53). She was his personal assistant, beautiful, intelligent and tri-lingual. They became lovers while he was still married to Shindy, and Hilke became pregnant.

Against Farrar's wishes, Hilke had an abortion which was performed by a Catholic doctor for 200 cigarettes. Farrar delivered the dead foetus himself and buried it in the grounds of Villa Hugel, a traumatic experience for both of them. The affair with Hilke continued even in 1947, when Shindy and their son moved out to Germany. Farrar even persuaded his wife to let Hilke move in with them as she was very ill. Shindy heard rumours about her husband, of course, but did not find out the truth until after Hilke had moved out.

Over the years, Farrar never forgot Hilke or their dead son, and his sixth wife, Janet, claims that she always knew Hilke was his true love even though Farrar protested that Janet was the love of his life. When Farrar was dying, he called out Hilke's name and claimed to see an apparition of her standing before him (ibid, 53).

Farrar lived at a time when divorce was slightly more acceptable than it had been, but even so, marrying six times was uncommon, and may reflect the unusual layout of the first four houses in his chart. He certainly *had* a domestic life, including wives, mistresses and children, yet his chart clearly shows that his real interests lay elsewhere, in pursuing his career and status in society. The determination, focus and success in his career is symbolised by the cluster of planets present in the tenth house, the area of career and status in society.

The Virgo ascendant is part of the mutable angles in Farrar's chart, the rest of the angles comprise of Gemini MC, Pisces DSC and Sagittarius IC. The preponderance of mutable signs on the angles indicates that Farrar had the ability to adapt, experience, learn and to be of service. In other words, to flow with life's impermanence. Being involved in processes and dissemination are indicative of this mutable presence. This we see through the ease with which Farrar flowed from one position of employment to another, having the ability to achieve in different types of jobs; and also through his tremendous talent in writing for various audiences, the way he was able to uproot home for both personal and professional reasons, and his need for multiplicity in partnerships and significant relationships.

The ascending sign (*see box on right*) is in 23 degrees of Virgo, which makes the ruling planet of the natal chart Mercury, since that is the planet which rules Virgo. The ascendant Virgo suggests he viewed the world through a lens of scrutiny and had strong critical and observation skills. It also indicates

Stewart Farrar. Photo by kind
permission of Janet Farrar.

that his liked being organised and productive, and also being of service to others. This was certainly borne out by his employment in the army, as well as being a reporter for various publications, and also as a teacher. Virgo is also associated with diet and health, so it may well have been that Farrar was quite aware of any ill health and other matters related to his body, such as allergies, diet, nervous energy and stress – all of which are associated with Mercury the ruler of Virgo (and Gemini).

The emphasis on Mercury is given further significance in Farrar's chart, as Mercury is also in its other natural sign of Gemini, which is at 14 degrees; the Moon is also in the sign of Gemini at 14 degrees. Interestingly, as mentioned above, Farrar was born on a Wednesday, the day of the week that is ruled by Mercury.

The correspondences of Mercury (when associated with Gemini) include learning, languages, speaking, teaching and writing – since this is the planet which governs the mind and communication. It is unsurprising that Mercury significantly manifested itself in Farrar's life in his career as a journalist, radio-playwright, screenwriter and author of fictional and non-fictional books; the latter he penned with his last wife, Janet Farrar. He also wrote books with both Janet Farrar and his friend Gavin Bone, and all three became prominent and significant figures in contemporary Wicca and Neo-paganism. He wrote numerous books with Janet Farrar and Gavin Bone including, *The Pagan Path: The Wiccan Way of Life* and *The Complete Dictionary of European Gods and Goddesses*; works written by him and Janet Farrar include, *A Witches' Bible: The Complete Witches' Handbook*, *The Witches' Way*, and *The Witches' God: Lord of the Dance*.

After joining the Craft, Farrar developed a strong belief in reincarnation and experienced several regressions. He recollected clear memories of having been a scribe in Egypt at the time of Ramesses II. Perhaps it is no coincidence that Ramesses the Great (as Ramesses II was better known) was famous for his military successes, just as Farrar had experienced a successful military career. The Pharaoh was famous for obliterating evidence of the earlier Amarna Period of Akhenaton, which has some similarities with the way Farrar sought to establish Wicca as 'new/old' religion, which may not have replaced Christianity but perhaps challenged it.

Farrar's twelfth house cusp is ruled by the Sun/Leo and the Sun's energy could have enabled him to 'shine his light' in order to gain attention. By doing this, Farrar could have been placed (or, indeed, placed himself) in positions where he was able to share the spotlight with others. It would have been satisfying for him to share his 'light' with others, since the twelfth house calls for service and selflessness. Leo, and its ruler the Sun, have a creative, generous, sharing and warm disposition. In Farrar's life, we see this application of self-expression through his work as a writer and teacher. Although writing is a solitary and subliminal practice, it ultimately benefitted others, i.e. allowing his readers to follow their own spiritual paths and, before that, the trainee army recruits.

Since the Sun rules the noble and regal sign of Leo, there is a real sense of 'the power behind the throne' with this position. This is because the twelfth house energy is unseen and its power is hidden and secretive. Other areas associated with the twelfth house include, 'behind-the-scenes' activities, the subconscious and sacrifice.

Since the Sun represents the self and the twelfth house represents sacrifice, it could be said there was an element of self-sacrifice throughout Farrar's life. Possibly this explains the empty first four houses in the natal chart, which relate to personal areas of his life, showing how these were forfeited in the service of the absorbing and dissolute energy of the twelfth house. Mars (associated with impulse, lust and sexuality) is positioned in the twelfth house, which is of a private and secret nature – a combination that could be interpreted as an indication of the secret affairs in his life.

The energising Mars in the twelfth house suggests that Farrar may have lived in frequent states of internal excitement and impatience, but was endowed with the determination and self-motivation to channel his restlessness into solitary activities such as diary-keeping, reading and writing, along with channelling his impulsiveness into his love affairs.

Since Mercury is so prominent in Farrar's chart, it is worth examining his oeuvre in more detail here as it shows where his energies were focussed and goes some way to explaining the emptiness of the first four houses of his chart. Amongst his prodigious output, Farrar wrote radio serials, and co-wrote a screenplay with Sir John Betjeman. In 1968, he won the Writers' Guild Award for another radio series, *Watch the Wall my Darling*. He also wrote episodes of various TV series including, *Armchair Theatre, Dr Finlay's Casebook, Special Branch* and the long-running soap-opera, *Crossroads*.

His work as a journalist on the magazine, *Reveille,* proved to be a significant move for him at this time in his life, and will be discussed later. Whist employed there, he explored and reported on a variety of subjects, which led him to be photographed for the publication in diverse settings. For example, climbing a ladder to a skycrane, modelling tartan clothing, as well as participating in the annual Brighton Veteran car run (http://www.callaighe.com/photo_archive/On_the_job.htm).

For three years, Farrar worked for Associated British Pathé as a commentary writer and documentary scriptwriter and sometimes he appeared in the films. Topics covered included a documentary on phone tapping, *Is Your Phone Tapped* (1957); smoking, *Coffin Nails* (1957); and the Lord Mayor, *My Lord Mayor* (1960). Before that, he had worked for a PR company, F. H. Radford; its readership was chiefly Trade Union Members. Earlier, in 1939, he had worked for the Communist newspaper, *The Daily Worker;* his very first job was as an editor working for Odhams Press Book Department, a position he held after graduating from college.

In 1949, after the Second World War, Farrar worked for the media company, *Reuters,* for several months, leaving in 1950 to then work for the *Soviet Weekly* newspaper. The newspaper was first published by the Soviet Information Bureau in the UK and later by the Novosti Press Agency (email communication from SCRSS to Author). Articles written during the 1950s were rarely by-lined and the names of *Soviet Weekly* staff were probably not openly recorded, given the nature of the Cold War conditions under which they worked. For example, people suspected of being a member of the Communist Party in the UK may have been subjected to blacklisting, phone tapping and vetting of their mail.

Other tactics could have included MI5 surveillance and other tricks to try and undermine the Communist Party and its membership. The colophon (which normally gives information about the publisher) was absent from the publication, listing only an address and telephone number for subscriptions (International History of Social History).

The above examples show the challenging conditions in which Farrar worked during the Cold War, and his stamina to work covertly which was essential. For example, he attended many Communist Party meetings and even held gatherings at his family home (the latter was not appreciated by his then wife, Shindy, who was not a Communist and felt the gatherings an intrusion (Guerra and Farrar, 2013, 56).

As a member of the Communist Party's editorial team (*Daily Worker*, Sat, June 3rd, 1953) he reported on a large variety of issues in 1953 including, *inter alia,* railway workers' pension schemes, an engineers' rally in Trafalgar Square to support demands of a pay increase, landlords raising rents, and increasing the State Pension rate for old-age pensioners. However, Farrar became increasingly disillusioned with Communism and eventually left both his position of employment and the Communist Party simultaneously.

Farrar's drive and interest in politics can be seen in his natal chart, by Mercury and the Moon positioned in the ninth house. This is because Mercury is associated with communication and the Moon with instinct and nurture; whilst freedom, law and politics are associated with the ninth house. Further interpretations about these planets in the ninth house will be discussed further on.

Later, aged 53, whilst working on the magazine, *Reveille,* Farrar met and interviewed Alex (the subject of Chapter Thirteen) & Maxine Sanders, who would later initiate him into their coven. In Farrar's book, *What Witches Do,* he describes this meeting which took place at the press review of the film, *Legend of the Witches.* He wrote, "After the screening, free scotch in hand, I manoeuvred my way through the crowd around Sanders. Alex was a slim, balding man in his early forties, wearing dark glasses, answering questions in a soft northern voice and giving a quick, genuinely humorous smile every now and then" (Farrar, 1995, 3).

This shows Farrar's ability to capture a fleeting mood and present an arresting image of Alex Sanders. His description of Maxine is equally vivid, "... Maxine, taller than Alex and twenty years younger, a striking figure with long blonde hair and a diaphanous white gown, looked a very believable witch" (ibid, 3). Again, we see Farrar's ability to evoke the moment in which he met the woman who was to initiate him into the Craft and become a considerable influence in his life.

These, along with many other examples, show Farrar's gift of communication and his driving desire to communicate. Mercury, the winged messenger, was dominant in Farrar's natal chart and lends itself to a restlessness as well as flexibility and diversity. We can see this in the variety of positions he held when he was in the army, the number and variety of writing jobs which he held, and in moving home frequently with his ever-changing families).

LANGUAGE, LESSONS AND ACTION

Farrar had been educated at the privately run City of London School and, whilst there, joined the Officer Training Corps where he learnt about military intervention. During his training however, he began to loathe the military and embrace left-wing politics; first socialism and then communism – while at the same time rejecting Christianity. He then went on to University College London, where he studied journalism, becoming editor of *The London Union Magazine,* and president of the London University Journalism Union. After gaining his degree, he went on an exchange trip to Germany where he became fluent in German, and grew to despise the Nazis. During World War II, Farrar was stationed in Britain where his work included training new recruits in various combat techniques and also working as an instructor in anti-aircraft gunnery as previously discussed.

Farrar's Virgo ascendant also suggests that he liked to be kept busy and was naturally industrious. Mars is in the sign of Virgo indicating that he constantly strove for perfection, showing great attention to detail and facts. An example of this can be seen in his military work where he wrote gun drills and training pamphlets. He also spoke fluent German, and translated and edited the drill book for the German anti-aircraft gun, the *Flakvierling*. This enabled British troops to use such weapons when they captured them. The Mars in Virgo position can indicate 'military servitude', since the military is governed by Mars and servitude is governed by Virgo. Languages are governed by Mercury which is the ruling planet in Farrar's natal chart, and is the ruling planet of both Gemini and Virgo (as previously discussed).

The twelfth house also governs the solitary, and we can see that this placement was helpful to Farrar in his 'behind-the-scenes' work. Mars in Virgo can also indicate activities requiring detail, precision, technique and practicality – all useful attributes when translating the German *Flakvierling* handbook. Mars in the twelfth house can also symbolise a secret desire to be successful, revealing that working behind the scenes probably suited Farrar. He not only kept private diaries and journals but also his solitary work as a novelist, poet and screenwriter would be helped by this placement. The twelfth house is also at ease with compassion, escapism, imagination, healing, mysticism, poetry, romance, spirituality and sympathy – all of which were significant in Farrar's life.

The courageous, vigorous and fiery Mars in the twelfth house shows his drive, and enthusiasm for these areas of his life. Mars sextile Saturn in the chart suggests he may have experienced tests of bravery and courage in his life, since Saturn is 'testing' and Mars is 'brave'. One example of this can be seen in his wartime service, which began as a volunteer and saw him rise eventually to the rank of major. Mars governs the military while Saturn provides authority, commitment and endurance – all attributes that would have aided Farrar's rapid rise through the ranks. Achieving a position of authority is yet another Saturnian attribute. The blending energies of Mars and Saturn would also have helped Farrar with editing, reaching deadlines and achieving targets, collating data, and those areas of work where ambition, discipline, rules and strategy were required.

The Moon in Gemini at 14 degrees and in the ninth house suggests that Farrar needed emotional stimulation, thrived on change and variety, and loved to have fun. Author, Francesca Ciancimino Howell, once recalled him as "... a delightful gentleman and an engaging scholar, with a marvellous wit (and frequently a naughty one) ... he was also always ready to share a laugh" (Guerra and Farrar, 2013, 187). Farrar enjoyed communications of all kinds and networked well, creating wide circles of acquaintances, contacts and friends.

Stewart Farrar. Photo by kind permission of Janet Farrar

Mercury and Gemini also indicate his youthful mind, and he would have enjoyed having like-minded people around him. Humour was important to him, and he would have appreciated joking about the absurdity of life. The three personal planets; the Moon, Mercury and Venus are at 14 degrees in his natal chart, meaning that every time a transiting planet hits that degree, all the Lunar, Mercurial and Venusian areas in the chart will be activated.

The Gemini MC (*see glossary*) indicates that Farrar could have enjoyed (and excelled in) a career as librarian, linguist, messenger, teacher and writer, all of which are correspondences of Mercury, the ruler of the Gemini MC (*see box below left*). This placement also suggests that Farrar needed diversity in his work and was a gifted and able communicator.

The Sagittarius IC (*see glossary*) suggests he moved home frequently and in fact his family had moved eight times by the time Farrar reached college age. The Sagittarius IC also reveals that his domestic and family life was shaped by strong religious principles. His parents were both Christian Scientists, and his mother taught at a Christian Science girl's school in Surrey which his younger sister also attended. Farrar's conversion and initiation into Wicca later in his life shows the repeat of strong religious principles, albeit on a different path, which is also in keeping with the explorative and independent nature of Sagittarius (positioned at the IC).

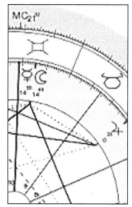

Jupiter, the ruling sign of Sagittarius also corresponds with publishing and it is interesting Farrar's aunt, Kathleen, had three novels published. This illustrates again Sagittarius/Jupiter on the IC. Perhaps his aunt's writing helped inspire Farrar, and certainly he *did* write fiction, including seven novels about witchcraft (official obituary on Witchvox – *see bibliography*). From these examples, we can see how publishing was not only prevalent in the Farrar family (Sagittarius IC), but also in his own life, which is indicated by the planets resident in the ninth house (associated with publishing) in his natal chart and is discussed further in detail below.

James Farrar, one of Stewart's cousins, was also a writer but his bright future was cut short when he was killed in the Second World War when he was only 21. A book of James' poetry, short stories and sketches was published posthumously in 1950 entitled, *The Unreturning Spring*, by the English author, Henry Williamson, who also edited it. The third house is associated with cousins and siblings (as well as communication) and in Farrar's natal chart, the third house cusp is ruled by Pluto, which governs deaths and transformations.

The Moon in the ninth house (*see box above*) indicates travel and even restlessness. Farrar needed to be on the move, experiencing life. He travelled for recreational purposes and also to lecture and teach others about Wicca and Paganism. Some of the places he visited included America, Canada, Egypt, Greece and Spain, and he always embraced and was receptive to the different cultures he experienced on his travels. The Moon in the ninth house suggests that Farrar saw not only goddess but also feminine energies more generally as a guiding force in his life. For example, he and his sister both admired their mother's profession. It was very unusual in those days for a married woman, especially one with children, to work, yet Agnes Farrar was very successful in both teaching and running a school, and loved her work (Guerra and Farrar, 2013, 28).

Agnes Farrar's profession allowed her to be home with her children in the school holidays, although, at some point, she also home-schooled her son for a year; he must have learned a great deal as he even helped her with her students' homework. Whilst Farrar's mother was pregnant with him, she used to read every day, believing that what a pregnant woman thought about during her pregnancy would be communicated to the child whilst still in the womb. As she wanted her first child to be a writer, she tried to nurture this by reading good quality literature every day. Unsurprisingly as a young child, Farrar's reading skills were outstanding and he was moved up a level in his English classes. In this area, we can see how his mother was indeed a guiding force in his life, teaching him the value of learning, reading and writing, so that later he was able to share knowledge with others.

Janet Farrar and Maxine Sanders were also important nurturing forces in his life. The former in matrimony, spirituality and writing; and the latter by introducing him into the Craft and initiating him into her and her husband's coven – this bears out the influence and power of the Moon in his ninth house.

The ninth house (as previously discussed) governs politics, publishing, law, principles, and religion and spirituality and with the Moon in this house suggests that he cared very much about these areas. The Moon conjunct Mercury shows that Farrar accommodated different viewpoints and ideas. The Moon symbolises everyday life and Mercury symbolises speaking and writing. This would have helped Farrar in keeping a diary and provided a narrative to his everyday life; it may even have helped him in writing for soap-operas and women's magazines!

Mercury in the ninth house suggests Farrar may have been involved in the law, for example, through copyright, since the ninth house is an association of publishing. Mercury in the ninth house also indicates a curiosity and enquiring mind, especially in relation to other cultures, philosophy and religion and spirituality, since these are also associations of the ninth house.

For example, he married a woman called Rachael in 1950. She was Jewish but did not practice her faith, apart from a few traditions she enjoyed (Guerra and Farrar, 2013, 57). She could, however, speak fluent Yiddish and taught Farrar, who was an enthusiastic student. However, his in-laws were observant Jews and he learned a great deal about the Jewish customs and faith from them (Guerra and Farrar, 2013, 58). This reveals his eagerness to learn about other cultures and religions.

Mercury in the ninth house shows a mind that can see the wider picture of life, although as it enjoys a broader overview – this suggests Farrar was perhaps not so adept in mundane, domestic matters, although the resourceful Virgo ascendant would have helped bring some balance to this. It also denotes a lively intelligence, and Farrar was enthusiastic when sharing his knowledge with others. This placement also helped in his coven working as a teacher. This is supported by Geraldine Beskin, co-proprietor of the esoteric Atlantis Bookshop in London, who fondly remembered that Farrar, "… was a gentleman, well-motivated with a fine intelligence. He had a beautiful voice and was a chuckle, forever with a cigarette and a pen in his hands …" (Guerra and Farrar, 2013, 195). She also remembered serial philandering and political interests. Above all though, she recognised his generosity in sharing what he learned with others, when he could have kept it to himself instead.

The contact between Mercury square Mars indicates Farrar's ability to translate thought into action and to communicate assertively. His active and agile mind needed opportunities to keep it alert and sharp. Mercury trine Uranus shows not only that he communicated in a unique and unusual way, but also that he had original and radical ideas and thoughts. This can be seen when he and Janet had left the coven of Alex and Maxine Sanders, and went on to create their own.

Farrar's first non-fiction book was the influential, *What Witches Do,* which helped make Wicca accessible in the wider Wiccan community, giving it a voice and helping to educate and inspire not only those practitioners already on the path, but also those just setting out. Farrar's independent and original thinking can also be seen in the progression of his religious practice; having been raised as a Christian Scientist in a middle-class family, he became an agnostic by the time he was twenty, and later a

Wiccan. These progressions show the independent, unconventional and even rebellious side to his nature.

At the core of the natal chart, Farrar's self is illustrated by the Sun in the sign of Cancer, ruled by the Moon and governed by the element of water. The other planets in the sign of Cancer are Venus, Saturn and Pluto. There are two conjunctions created by the Sun and Pluto, and Venus and Saturn. The Sun in the sign of Cancer suggests that Farrar was a caring, compassionate and sensitive person, who may have tried to hide his feelings under a crab-like shell, since the sign of Cancer is symbolised by the crab. The Sun is in the tenth house, where it denotes an ambitious, high-profile position in society, with a need to be regarded as important and powerful.

The Sun conjunct Pluto shows a magnetic and powerful presence. There is also a sense of the 'hidden-self', since the nature of Pluto can be to conceal and cover. We see the theme of 'life and death' in the tenth house of career in Farrar's chart. This is because the Sun symbolises life and vitality, while Pluto symbolises death and transformation, therefore the Sun and Pluto are creating a conjunction – in this case, a hard aspect in the natal chart.

For example, during WWII, when Farrar was working in the anti-aircraft unit, an RAF Lancaster Bomber that had flown off-course while returning home from a mission over Germany had been damaged during its return, and it was dark, making it difficult to identify. Farrar was on duty commanding an AA gun unit and gave the order to shoot the plane down. The crew were all killed. This event haunted him for the rest of his life, even though he knew it had been a terrible accident and was not his fault. It also strengthened his belief in the futility of war (Guerra and Farrar, 2013, 46). The Cancerian crab often hides and protects its feelings, indicating the sense of a hidden self, and it is likely that Farrar could veil himself from things he did not wish to remember. Cancer's other correspondences include history, memories and the past.

Pluto is in the tenth house of authority, career, profession and status (as discussed previously) – showing that Farrar was ambitious and determined; wielding control and power which could be used for the good of society. Pluto is an outer planet and so represents a generation of people that were born during the age of Pluto in Cancer. During the era that Farrar was born, many people worldwide experienced destitution, unemployment and starvation. The First World War brought thousands of deaths and devastation to families and nations on a massive scale. Cancer represents families, history and roots, as well as being a correspondence of the arena of domesticity and security. Pluto is akin to destruction and transformation.

On a more personal level, the position of Pluto in Cancer suggests Farrar was intuitive, perceptive and sensitive. The interpretation of this placement is echoed by a remembrance in his biography, when Cate and Frank Dalton described him as "... very tall, very perceptive and insightful" (Guerra and Farrar, 2013, 183).

Saturn is in its natural tenth house which corresponds with authority and tradition. Old Father Time corresponds with Saturn, and represents age, maturity and wisdom. In this sense, it could be said that in Farrar's career, he was treated with high regard and respect. This was certainly true, as he was well respected not only in the hierarchy of Wicca, but also accomplished much whilst in the army, and as a professional writer. The archetypal image of Saturn as Old Father Time was pertinent to Farrar, especially in his later years, in terms of his physical appearance, since he had a tall frame (the frame is connected to Saturn), white hair and a distinctive white goatee beard.

Given that the Sun, represents the self, and is also in the tenth house, it could be said that Farrar was seen in the public eye as an authority figure and, coupled with

Venus in the tenth house, that he courted the Establishment successfully. This can be seen during his army career where he received several promotions, and also when he worked for the BBC producing scripts for television dramas. Both the army and the BBC are often regarded as part of the Establishment.

There is frequently a marked sense of ancestry, family, heritage and 'roots' with Cancerians. Saturn is detriment (*see glossary*) in the sign of Cancer, and it is detrimental because the fearful and obstructing nature of Saturn indicates that Farrar had some anxieties about domestic life and also of being unloved, which may seem surprising in the light of his private life and numerous marriages. Yet Venus in Cancer suggests that the loves in his life were almost like a family to him and he may also have clung to past loves, finding it challenging to let them go. The affectionate and loving nature of Venus indicates that he 'loved to love' and could be caring and protective, enjoying being able to indulge his loved-ones.

However, the breakdowns of Farrar's earlier marriages should not be overlooked. Up until he met and married Janet Owen, there had been a consistent pattern in the breakdown of his marriages and relationships. These are indicated somewhat by the dissolving and elusive energy of Pisces, the sign on the descendant at the seventh house, the area which governs marriage and significant partnerships (*see chart below*). Some associations of Neptune (the ruler of Pisces) include deceit and pretence – perhaps suggestive of Farrar's extramarital affairs.

It is interesting that Janet Farrar's natal chart shares the same position of Mercury in Gemini with Farrar. This would have been nurturing and stimulating to him since his Moon sign and Mercury are both in the sign of Gemini. Between the two of them, there would have been plenty of conversation, dialogue, exchange of ideas, interest and stimulation and therefore, with her, he finally found the most intellectually, physically and spiritually satisfying relationship of his life, one that satisfied his mind, body and spirit. Both easily bored, they would have complemented each other by being open to new ideas with an agile mind and a need to experiment with as many ideas as possible.

Farrar's Moon in Gemini could nurture others by being adaptable and flexible and by lightening the mood with wit and humour. His placement of Venus in Cancer indicates a love of the goddess, history and of women, which is reflected in his spiritual practices. Geraldine Beskin once remarked that he had found a religion, "... that suited him ... a serial philanderer and politically-minded man" (Guerra and Farrar, 2013, 195).

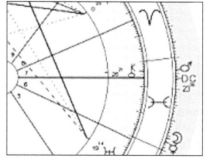

Venus in the tenth house suggests that Farrar was regarded as attractive and stylish, and was naturally attracted to people with good connections, who could help him. For example, Alex and Maxine Sanders initiated him into their coven, after they had initially met him through his work as a journalist when he went to interview them. Diplomacy and tact are qualities associated with Venus and these qualities would have been helpful to Farrar in his work as a journalist, where interviewing, listening and obtaining information were required.

Saturn is in the tenth house, which is its natural house (as previously noted), since it is akin to Capricorn, which is ruled by Saturn. This position suggests that Farrar sought recognition for his qualities, and wished to be shown respect and public recognition.

Farrar was a pioneer of Wicca, and is always honoured as such, along with his wife, Janet, Gerald Gardner and Alex Sanders. Having had a relatively prominent media career, he was prepared to be quite open about his beliefs and practices, at a time when Wicca and witchcraft were usually misunderstood and misrepresented, and people tried to conceal their involvement.

Farrar's determination and drive to ensure projects were completed, and his enterprise in doing so is illustrated by the sign of Cancer, which belongs to the cardinal mode. This is an energy that can activate, initiate and pioneer, yet often in a coaxing rather than a dominant way. The cardinal energy of the Moon and Mars comes together in the square aspect created between the two planets. Farrar was fiercely protective of his work, reflected in Cancer's need to protect and Mars' desire to activate and work. This would have helped him 'protect' his solitary work when it was in process, keeping it private and secret – attributes that aptly symbolise Mars in the twelfth house.

Venus conjunct Saturn suggests that it may have taken a long time for Farrar to be convinced that he was safe in a relationship, and secure in his partner's affections. This position also suggests that once the initial attraction had worn off, he *could* maintain a relationship, even over a long period of time, since he was in touch with Saturn's pragmatism and reality, which gave him the ability to maintain a relationship over nearly 25 years. Despite having been already married five times, his final marriage to Janet Owen (who was also a Sun sign Cancer) was enduring and steadfast and was maintained over a long period of time, up until his death. As a couple, they had a high-profile relationship which fits with the conjunction of Venus and Saturn in Farrar's tenth house, as well as the Sun, which is creative, individual and proud.

Venus is sextile Mars, suggesting that Farrar was a romantic adventurer, who related easily to the opposite sex. There is also symbolism of charm and personal magnetism with Venus sextile Mars. This aspect can make one affectionate and tolerant, and so Farrar may have found it easy to embrace the 'romantic triangle', which is evident in his later years, when he and Janet entered into a relationship with Gavin Bone, a Seax Wiccan friend and business partner. All three accepted that they would remain faithful to each other and that sexual relations would stay amongst the three of them, so maintaining fidelity amongst them.

This relationship could not always have been easy. By the time they married, Farrar was 59, while Janet was just 25, and it may be no coincidence that their wedding on the 19th July, 1975, took place in the season of Cancer, which of course was the Sun sign for them both. It was accepted by all three that Gavin and Janet should also enjoy a sexual relationship together. Farrar once said of Gavin that he was the "… gifted manipulator of technicalities, and I am the gifted user of words" (Guerra and Farrar, 2013, 154). This shows he believed that they all complemented each other, and that the three together could achieve what two – in whichever combination – could not.

Certainly, Gavin Bone devoted himself to helping Farrar with his care and health needs, even down to completing DIY projects around Farrar's home. Bone also negotiated contracts with Farrar's publishers, eventually becoming the couple's business manager. Through Bone's efficiency, experience and responsible attitude (all of which are qualities of *his* Sun sign Capricorn), Stewart Farrar began earning a steady income from the many volumes of books he had written over the years (ibid, 152).

The asteroid Chiron, the Wounded Healer, is angular in the seventh house on the descendant, the area representing partnerships and relationships. In this area in Farrar's chart, Chiron indicates that the 'wound' is in Farrar's relationships – with others or with his self. Chiron's lifelong lesson for Farrar was in learning to know the self through

significant relationships. It was not enough to offer
great personal charm, or to have great popularity –
more was required to sustain them. Relationships,
both personal and professional, required Farrar's
learning and growth.

> **Chiron, the Wounded Healer**
> In our natal charts, Chiron shows our experience of pain, wounding and alienation.

In Farrar's chart, Chiron is making aspects with the angles and a planet comprising of: Chiron opposing ascendant, Chiron square the MC, and Pluto square Chiron. This is further indication that the 'healing' was both significant and substantial in his lifetime. Chiron in Pisces suggests that Farrar attracted 'wounded' people to him who required healing and spiritual support.

It was important for him to recognise his boundaries and not to sacrifice his own energies to the extent that he became drained both physically and spiritually. This is because the compassionate and kind nature of Pisces can be easily depleted if absorbed too much by confused, drowning and vulnerable energies. Perhaps in channelling this energy, he was able to help others by helping them find their own spiritual path and releasing them from any spiritual confusion. It would have been all too easy for Farrar to have been used by others as a prop for their own deficiencies. Then, once he had helped them, they turned their backs on him, something that unfortunately seems to have happened only too often (ibid, 177).

Uranus is in its ruling sign of Aquarius at 19 degrees and is in the fifth house, i.e. the area that corresponds with love affairs and children. This placement suggests that Farrar sought excitement and constant stimulus in his love affairs and was drawn to independent and free-thinking people. He may have felt a need to choose between his need for freedom and space and having children, since the nature of Uranus enjoys freedom and independence. The Pisces descendant indicates that, in his partnerships and relationships, Farrar needed people who understood the mystical, spiritual and religious side of his nature. It is unsurprising therefore that he had an enduring and satisfying relationship with his last wife Janet, herself a Wiccan and author. They enjoyed both a personal and working relationship together and enjoyed the pairing in coven work as High Priest and High Priestess.

Photo of Stewart & Janet Farrar
© The Daily Mirror, 'Mirrorpix'

The Moon trine Uranus suggests Farrar's need for emotional independence as well as space and freedom on a day-to-day basis. He needed the freedom to go wherever he wanted without the restraints of domestic life, feeling free to adventure and explore as he wanted. It suggests that he cultivated an unconventional lifestyle at home, feeling uncomfortable with conventional domesticity and routine.

The Moon in Gemini suggests he liked having friends to visit, and that variety and exchange of ideas, debate, learning and writing were important to him in the home, as was laughter and light-heartedness.

Uranus in Aquarius and in the fifth house suggests coolness and detachment as well as originality and unpredictability. There is a fixed nature with this placement, and also wild enthusiasm; showing that, at times, Farrar could be determined, stubborn and unyielding – especially when his ideals were at stake. This can be seen, for example, through his rejection of his upbringing as a Christian Scientist to become an agnostic at a young age; likewise, having once been a passionate member of the Communist Party, he later denounced his membership and the party, his ideals being reformed by what he had witnessed during the war. In his fifties, he discovered Wicca, which was to become a spiritually satisfying area of his life.

In his book, *What Witches Do*, Farrar describes how he set about his observations and research on Alex and Maxine Sanders and their coven practices, which was originally for an article he was going to write for *Reveille* magazine. Conscientious and diligent in his research for the book, Farrar decided that, if it was to carry any weight, then he should take the steps to be initiated into the coven, which he did when Maxine Sanders initiated him in February, 1970. Farrar freely acknowledged the debt he owed the Sanders', saying that, "it is as much his book (not to mention Maxine's) as mine" (Farrar, 1995, 9).

The fifth house (as previously mentioned) also governs the area of children and indicates that Farrar believed in allowing them freedom and independence. Yet, Uranus can also denote detachment and disconnection, so it is probable that, when Farrar separated from his spouses, a distance opened up between him and his children. It has been said that, later in life, Farrar was ashamed of his behaviour towards two of his children (Andy and Lindsay), as he cared little for their well-being, provided no financial support and rarely visited them (Guerra and Farrar, 2013, 57).

Since Saturn (in the tenth house in the natal chart and representing him as an authorative figure, i.e. parent) also governs maturity, it could be interpreted that, as his children became older, he had more time and understanding and made himself more available to them. This theme is echoed by Saturn being the ruling planet of the of the fifth house cusp, which associates with longevity and wisdom, as well as limitation and obstruction. There is certainly some evidence that the relationships with his children and grandchildren became more cordial over a period of time, as they attended Farrar's legal marriage to his last wife, Janet.

The quincunx aspect created between Saturn and Uranus indicates a difficult combination of frustration, simmering dissatisfaction and stress. This may have manifested itself throughout Farrar's life as the theme of responsibility vs. freedom, since these are correspondences of Saturn and Uranus, respectively. Certainly, with respectable Saturn in the tenth house of career and status, it is likely this was more important to him than his responsibility to his children, as has been previously discussed.

As already mentioned, love affairs are also connected with the fifth house, and it is well-documented that Farrar had numerous love affairs and it is a theme that reoccurs in his natal chart. The nature of Uranus is independent, liberating and freedom-loving, which may have been frustrating to the committed and responsible nature of Saturn in Farrar's love affairs. Because of the tense nature of a quincunx aspect, it could also be said he took his artistic, leisure and recreational pursuits (also governed by the fifth house) very seriously, yet was also aware how his extra-marital affairs might affect his respectable, high-profile status. Such tensions may have helped Farrar to adopt a pragmatic and realistic approach to unusual situations whilst at the same time being able to break with the norm. The author, Margot Adler, remarked upon his common sense and down-to-earth approach, combined with a lack of ego (Guerra and Farrar, 2013, 183).

The planet Neptune in the sign of Leo (*see box over page*) at 1 degree in the eleventh house indicates an artistic, creative and imaginative profile, since Neptune is able to create illusion, fantasy and vision. We see this in the way Farrar was drawn to areas that allowed him to operate in his own individual manner. For example, he wrote poetry and scripts, enjoyed photography, and wrote a screenplay for a film, scripts for radio programmes, together with both fictional and non-fictional books.

Neptune also corresponds with the feet and dancing, and since Neptune is in the eleventh house which governs friends and groups, we see it reflected in Farrar's dancing skyclad (i.e. naked) in his coven rituals. Neptune's other correspondences include divinity, healing, magic, meditation, mysticism and spirituality. The sociable element of Neptune would have instigated Farrar's need for artistic, compassionate, kind and imaginative friends in his life, and in turn he could offer his friends consideration, generosity, kindness and warmth – which are all qualities bestowed by Neptune.

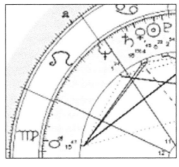

The transcending nature of Neptune suggests that Farrar could 'lose' himself in spiritual groups, in the sense that he could totally immerse himself in a magical and mystical manner, which in turn would have given way to 'loss' (Neptune) of the ego (Leo). This would have helped to blend and transcend, for example, in magical work with others. The kindly nature of Neptune suggests he was altruistic and also that he was accepting of a wide variety of people from different backgrounds, and that he could readily blend and merge easily in group situations. The less helpful side and lower aspect to this placement is that it can denote confusion, deception and gullibility in groups and possibly amongst friends, since Neptune and the eleventh house are, respectively, connected to these areas.

The square aspect created by Jupiter and Neptune indicates that Farrar had strong mystical and spiritual experiences and yearnings. These would have helped him to escape and transcend from mundane daily life, due to his innate understanding that god/goddess is infinite.

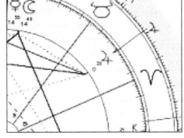

Jupiter is sextile Pluto, which reveals that Farrar was philosophical about death and could explore the themes of Pluto, such as healing, mysteries, the occult, survival and unearthing. As Pluto's nature is able to rejuvenate and transform, it suggests that there was the ability for Farrar to reform in the areas of law, politics and religion, since these are the areas that Jupiter governs. He could be said to have reformed Wicca, in that he made it more accessible to people, allowing them the freedom to practice the Craft without too much emphasis on doctrine and initiation. His books were written in accessible language and, because he had so much experience writing for different audiences, he could connect with a wide range of people.

Jupiter is in the eighth house (*see box above*) and indicates an interest in spiritualism and a philosophical stance where life-after-death matters are concerned, so much so that there may be an optimistic belief that life is better after physical death. Farrar certainly did not fear death, believing the soul's journey did not stop but continued onwards (Guerra and Farrar, 2013, 162).

The eighth house also denotes inheritance, legacies and taxes and, with Jupiter positioned here, it shows the potential for windfalls and luck in these areas. After his

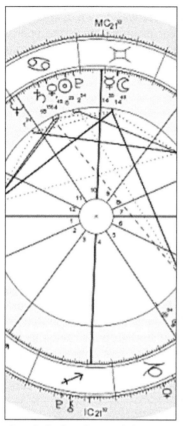

parents passed away, he and his sister inherited his parent's home in Suffolk and he lived there for a short time.

Jupiter in the eighth house also indicates a tremendous drive and passion for areas such as investigation, research and strategy, and also problem-solving. Farrar would have felt driven to unravel mysteries and secrets. Jupiter bestows belief and faith, which would have enhanced Farrar's self-belief. The confidence that Jupiter brings in the eighth house position suggests that Farrar's intuition and perception helped him expose, and uncover, which would have been of great help in his work as a journalist and in his interview technique. The ease created by the sextile aspect between Jupiter and Pluto suggests that whatever Farrar uncovered brought him rewards and success.

Jupiter is at 0 degrees, and in the sign of Taurus. In the book, *World Horoscopes,* by Nicholas Campion (1988, 118), we see this sign governs Ireland, which is where Farrar and Janet went to live. There they totally embraced its customs, culture and people and learned to speak the Irish language. Jupiter is a beneficial planet, so it could be said that Farrar found blessings and transformed his life when he moved to Ireland, where he lived until his death.

Farrar left his physical body on 7th February, 2000, shortly before his 84th birthday at his home in Ireland. At the time of his passing, Farrar was experiencing several major transits with the outer planets; Jupiter, Neptune, Pluto and Uranus. Such involvement at the time of his passing shows he was experiencing a lot of conclusion and tension in his life, since the outer planets call to us to conclude, convert and transform when they are transiting – thus creating an aspect with our natal planets.

At the time of Farrar's passing, transiting Pluto was in Sagittarius at 12 degrees (*see box above left*) and in the third house of communication, opposing the natal Moon in the ninth house.

It could be said that Farrar was already communicating with his new spiritual home as he was preparing to depart from his earthy life. Indeed, in his final journal entry on 10th January, 2000, he wrote, "Home at last and ready for it" (Guerra and Farrar, 2013, 162). This is doubly poignant, since Farrar had been unable to travel anywhere for a long time due to failing health and so, in a way, was already at home in his beloved Ireland.

Due to his experience and knowledge of the spirit world, he must have instinctively known that he was returning to a spiritual home. Astrologically, this was symbolised by the transiting Pluto at the third house of communication, opposing the Moon (a correspondence of home), and in the ninth house of religion, where he was very much at home and which gave him tremendous faith. Pluto at the third house shows how he could communicate his knowledge that he was preparing to pass over, in that final journal entry.

Transiting Pluto was also opposing Farrar's natal planet Mercury in the ninth house at this time, and the opposition suggests he was finding it increasingly difficult to communicate in his speech and his writing. Physically, of course this was true, Farrar having suffered a stroke in 1994 some years before his death. However, perhaps he would like to have expressed more before he finally passed away, and may have become philosophical in knowing that his failing health was inevitably going to prevent him from continuing his great pursuit of teaching and writing.

There was also a quincunx created between transiting Pluto and natal Venus during this time. This suggests an element of love after love, in the metaphorical sense, and that there was a rejuvenation of love after Farrar passed away. Transiting Pluto in the third house and Venus in the tenth house suggests that Farrar's status after his passing gained a greater value and worth. In Pagan society, his authority, influence and power could have taken on even more significance, especially amongst Wiccans. After his death, Janet and Gavin reported experiencing psychic manifestations and other spiritual evidence that Farrar was still very much alive in his new 'home'. This is very much in keeping with the idea that Farrar's transiting Pluto in the house of communication was able to still communicate and express himself albeit using psychic phenomena, and those who were close to him and of a mediumistic nature would easily have been able to continue communication with him in this sense.

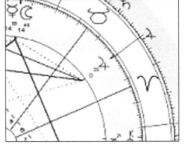

Farrar was experiencing a Jupiter return at this time. Transiting Jupiter in the eighth house (*see box on right*) was conjunct his natal Jupiter, suggesting that Farrar may have found it a blessing to leave the earthly humiliations that old age can bring, and to pass into the spirit realms where he could be rejuvenated and able to explore in his new spiritual home. By this time in his life Farrar had tremendous faith and found peace and solace in his religion of Wicca where he honoured The Goddess and The Horned God.

Jupiter's nature is full of exuberance, growth, optimism and vision and so, by this time in his life, Farrar may have been experiencing a wealth of inspiration, journeying, teaching, travelling and writing, which are all well-known correspondences of Jupiter. In the eighth house, this could have also applied to those areas governing inheritances, mysteries, occult, research and also intimacy.

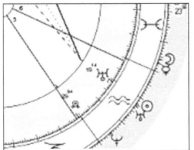

Farrar passed away on his Uranus return, where transiting Uranus in the fifth house (*see box on left*) was creating aspects to the natal Moon, Mercury and Uranus. This transit indicates that Farrar had reached the closure of a cycle in his lifetime and had obtained a certain freedom where he no longer needed to worry about the mundane and routine concerns of everyday life. Reaching the age of 84, Farrar may have been in a position to put his entire life into perspective and relate it to infinity in some way.

Uranus corresponds with technology and so it is interesting he chose to work in the (then) modern media of radio, technology, television and video. Towards the end of his life, he kept his journals on the computer. Less spiritually-minded people may have viewed him as eccentric, shocking and unorthodox – while to those who were more spiritually-minded, he is likely to have been regarded as a genius, humanitarian and unique.

The controversial nature of Uranus should not be ignored here, since Farrar received hate mail (Guerra and Farrar 2013, 158) and when the Farrar's initially moved to Ireland, they were met with a cold and occasionally very hostile reception by some of the local people. They then moved closer to Dublin (ibid, 130).

Stewart Farrar. Photo by kind permission of Janet Farrar.

Farrar passed away after Neptune's half-return; this is a hugely significant time in one's life-cycle and occurs approximately at the age of 82. It demonstrates the end of a cycle and the start of a new beginning. Transiting Neptune was at 4 degrees of Aquarius and creating a quincunx between the natal Sun and Pluto. The planet Neptune symbolises confusion, divinity, healing, loss, sacrifice, spirituality, surrender, transcendence and vulnerability, and it was in Farrar's fifth house for approximately thirteen or fourteen years.

During this transit, at his time of passing, transiting Neptune was creating a quincunx with the natal Sun and Pluto (as previously said). Transiting Neptune quincunx the natal Sun during this period suggests that Farrar may have seemed more elusive to the general public than previously, that he had to make sacrifices and that needed nursing at this time of life. Medication was prominent, and confusion, illusion and solitude may have played a greater part in his life. Meditation, spiritual healing, divine love and mysticism may also have been more significant.

The irritation and stress that a quincunx can bring suggests that Farrar's physical health and energies were depleted at this time leaving him feeling drained and exhausted, as though he was 'spiritually drowning', due to an excess of work. He may even have become unrealistic about what he could achieve and perhaps there was an element of self (Sun) delusion (Neptune), forcing him eventually to surrender to the truth that he could no longer sustain the same level of physical activity as in earlier years.

In the final year of Farrar's life, he was experiencing a transit which comprised of transiting Neptune quincunx natal Pluto, which suggests that Farrar may have experienced religious longings and higher inspiration, becoming obsessed with the divine, since Neptune is akin to these areas and obsession is akin to Pluto.

Stewart Farrar came to Wicca relatively late in his life (when he was 53) and through his work he met Alex and Maxine Sanders. It was to be a major turning point in his life. As a result of this encounter, and through Farrar's curiosity of mind, his life then radically changed and he was embraced into the religion of Wicca, where he became an influential and prominent figure, both as an individual and as a partner of his last wife Janet Farrar (née Owen).

Many established Wiccans and students of Wicca have been inspired and moved by his philosophy, poetry, teaching and writing. During his pre-Wiccan days, Farrar had entertained and informed many listeners, readers and viewers through his work as a journalist, novelist, screenwriter and radio playwright.

His political work would also have contributed both directly and indirectly to humanity and society. Mercury, the winged messenger (and ruler of his natal chart), flew high throughout his long life conveying a variety of messages to wide-ranging audiences, creating a clan of followers who would become friends, family, students and many acquaintances. His influence upon the world of Wicca, witchcraft and the occult was enormous.

ACKNOWLEDGEMENTS, CREDITS AND REFERENCES

The Author and Publisher would like to give special thanks to Janet Farrar and Gavin Bone, for their comments and observations with 'Stewart Farrar' chapter, as well as access to British Pathé films, with which Stewart Farrar was involved. Gratitude is also extended for their very kind permission to use personal photographs of Stewart Farrar.

Archivist & Library Manager at Marx Memorial Library, for *Soviet Weekly* information and direction to SCRSS.

Archive/Honorary Secretary at the Society for Co-operation in Russian & Soviet Studies (SCRSS), for detail on CPGB membership and employment conditions, as well as direction to www.culturematters.org.uk

Public Services and Collection Preservation at the International Institute of Social History, for information on editors and by-lines for editions of *Soviet Weekly* in the 1950s.

Natal chart generated by www.astro.com
Rodden Rating 'A'
Birth data from, *Writer on a Broomstick,* by Farrar, J.

BOOKS

Guerra, E. and Farrar, J. (2013) *Stewart Farrar – Writer on a Broomstick.* Skylight Press.
Farrar, S. (1995) *What Witches Do.* Phoenix Publishing Inc.
Michelson, Neil. F. (1983) *The American Ephemeris for the 20th Century.* Second Edition. ISBN 0917086198. Published by ACS Publications, Inc. (birth data for Janet Farrar).
Campion, N. (1988) *World Horoscopes.* The Aquarian Press.

NEWSPAPERS

Daily Worker articles (all from 1953) by Stewart Farrar:

- 'Minister Delays Rails Pension Scheme.' Tuesday. July 7th, p3
- 'Tories Demand Put Up Rents New Bill is Read.' Saturday, October 3rd
- 'They Packed the Square.' Monday October 19th, front cover and p4
- '7 1/2 Year Wait for Home.' Tuesday October 27th, p4

London Gazette Supplement pdf, 2nd August, 1940: 4735. Accessed on 12/09/2019. Middlesex Regiment, Frank Stewart Farrar (army service number- 140013).

WEBSITES

https://www.britishpathe.com/search/query/stewart+farrar
http://www.callaighe.com/photo_archive/On_the_job.htm – Photographs and tag line of Stewart Farrar on location for Reveille publication. Accessed 04/09/2019.
http://www.witchvox.com/va/dt_va.html?a=usxx&c=passages&id=2655 – Official obituary by Peter J. Doyle.

CHAPTER TEN

Sybil Leek 1917–1982

Astrologer, Witch and Author

SYBIL LEEK (née FAWCETT) was born on 22nd February, 1917, in Hanley, Stoke-on-Trent, Staffordshire, England, and died on 26th October, 1982, in Florida, USA, aged 65. Her parents were Christopher Edwin Fawcett born on 16th January, 1891, in Aberystwyth, Wales (BC); and Louisa Ann Fawcett (née Booth) born on 26th April, 1897 in Hanley, Staffordshire (BC). Leek married four times, firstly to Archibald Tinkler (m.1933), then George R. Key (m.1936), John B. Delves (m.1944), and Reginald B. Leek (m.1952). She had two sons; Julian and Stephen Leek, born 1951 and 1952, respectively.

Sybil Leek was a self-publicising witch and became a prolific writer and lecturer and wrote on various subjects, such as astrology, psychic phenomena and witchcraft. She was also an antiques dealer, psychic, medium, radio and television personality and reporter. Leek emigrated to America in 1964 with her sons and remained in that country until her death in 1982.

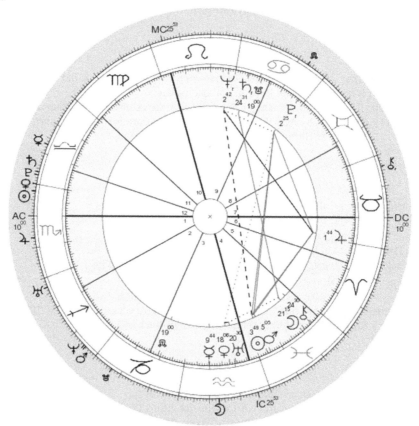

Natal and Transits Chart for Sybil Leek on the day she died, 26th October, 1982.

WHAT SYBIL LEEK'S NATAL CHART SHOWS

Sybil Leek (née Fawcett) was born on 22nd February, 1917, at 11.52pm. At the time of her birth, the Sun was in Pisces at 3 degrees and the Moon was also in Pisces, at 21 degrees; her ascendant sign was Scorpio and her MC (*see glossary*) was in Leo.

The Sun and Moon both in Pisces gives an exceptional Neptunian energy to her nature, revealing that she was artistic and intuitive, as well as imaginative, psychic and mediumistic. It also reveals a need for escapism and retreat as well as romance and understanding.

Confusion and fantasy along with illusion, deception and storytelling are also associated with Pisces and Neptune, and these areas will be discussed more fully later. The Neptunian energy can at times be depleted and strained; overwhelmed by the emotions and situations of other people, such is the compassionate nature of Pisces.

The mutable mode (*see glossary*) of Pisces will have given Leek an ability to adapt and modify. This overall versatility will have given her an ease to deal with change and transformations in her life, and help foster an easy-going approach to life. The mutable presence in Leek's chart is magnified by the presence of planets being in a preponderance of three of the mutable houses; that is the third house of communications and communicating, the sixth house of work and health, and the ninth house of higher education, travel, philosophy and religion.

The four fixed signs on the angles comprise of Scorpio ASC, Aquarius IC, Taurus DC and Leo MC. These positions will have helped provide a determination and stamina in the areas of the self, home, marriage and career (since these areas are symbolised by the angles). There is a preponderance of the female polarities (*see glossary*) in her chart, comprising of Sun, Moon and Mars in Pisces, Jupiter in Taurus, Saturn and Pluto in Cancer. This reveals that Leek was very imaginative and intuitive as well as artistic and receptive.

CREATING AN IMAGE

The Scorpio ascendant shows that the ruling planet of her natal chart is Pluto (Scorpio's ruling planet); this sign is determined and unyielding, as well as being perceptive and enigmatic and its passionate drive can bring about obsession and transformation.

The nature of Neptune, ruler of her Sun and Moon sign coupled with Pluto the ruler of her ascendant, suggests that she was both mysterious and secretive as these qualities are associated with Neptune and Pluto, respectively.

The ascendant is associated with appearance and image; it is no wonder that Leek had an intense air about her in her presentation.

Leek enjoyed wearing dramatic clothes and some of the colours associated with Scorpio/Pluto, such as black and purple. Some Scorpio ascendants have impenetrable, almost hypnotic eyes which feel like they are looking right through you. In photographs and on the television, one can see that Leek certainly had very noticeable and striking eyes. When she

Sybil Leek at a Meeting about Witchcraft at University College in 1964. Photo Licensed by Mirrorpix lived in Burley in the New Forest, Leek was often seen, "... walking through the village wearing a long black cloak with her pet jackdaw (Mr Hotfoot Jackson) resting on her shoulder" (Tucker, Julian's Press). Leek seems to have cultivated an exotic if not eccentric persona. Travelling to America by ocean liner, she was once described as an unforgettable sight. Somewhat overweight, she wore green mascara, snake bracelets and a crystal pendant, all doubtless intended to attract attention (http://spikethenews. blogspot.co.uk).

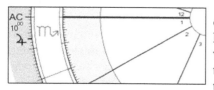

Mercury is square the ascendant. This aspect can produce nervous energy, and so people may have felt overwhelmed both by what they saw and what was being communicated to them. Possibly they felt that she did not listen to them or talked *at* them, which generates a control and forcefulness in relating. The secretive nature of the Scorpio ascendant indicates that Leek concealed much of her private life. For example, she was not entirely truthful towards her readers and the general public about her background, and never even reveals the names of her family or her in-laws in her autobiography, *Diary of a Witch* (apart from her sons Julian and Stephen on the dedication page).

It is curious that on her first marriage certificate, Leek gives her age as 25, when she was in fact only sixteen. This strongly suggests that for some reason she could not provide her father's consent to the marriage (which would have been required under the UK 1929 Ages of Marriage Act for anyone under 21). It seems she married not only without her parents' consent but possibly without their knowledge too. Again, this indicates the secretive nature of the Scorpio ascendant.

Possibly, in later life, Leek felt responsible for her family and believed she needed to safeguard them from any intrusion from the media, a message that is emphasised by both Saturn in Cancer and the Moon trine Saturn. She may also have felt her family deserved privacy, or possibly chose to romanticise about them in her deliberate, self-deceptive Neptunian way.

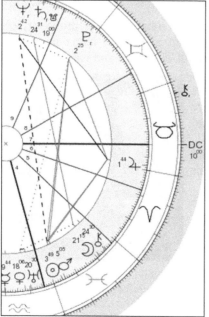

Protecting her family can be seen in Leek's natal chart where Saturn is in the sign of Cancer; this placement is detriment (*see glossary*) and provides an exceptional energy in the chart which would have added force to Leek's intensity and determination in shielding her family. Pluto is also in Cancer and reveals that she felt so intensely emotional and protective about her family that she may have even sought to shield them from any family secrets.

Leek once wrote that, "... positive and negative behaviourism make the perfect Piscean very difficult to distinguish," and that some parts of their personalities make "... the deeds of Judas Iscariot almost a prototype for a Piscean of the least admirable sort" (Leek, 1968, 229).

However, the treacherous and vengeful nature of Judas is more in keeping with Scorpio/Pluto qualities and not, as Leek claimed, an attribute in all Pisceans' natal charts, since astrology is not a one size fits all subject. One wonders if Leek was actually alluding to her own motivations as her own natal chart reveals a strong Plutonian presence, since it is the ruler of her ascending sign and therefore the chart as a whole. Pluto is positioned in its natural (*see glossary*) eighth house, creating aspects with other planets.

For example, Mars trine Pluto (*see box on previous page bottom left*) suggests a compulsive drive for power and a desire to win. Betrayal, spite and vengefulness are all associated with Pluto's darker nature, which Leek alludes to in her analogy of 'Judas'. Leek also writes about Neptune, the ruler of her Sun and Moon sign as being a planet "… of some treachery" in her book, *Astrology and Love* (Leek, 1977, 201).

The MC is Leo (*see glossary*), indicating that Leek would have enjoyed a career where she could lead others as well as working in the field of entertainment and theatre, where creative opportunities and public recognition would have been available to her. She entertained an audience through her interviews on radio and television and featured in television documentaries about witchcraft and psychic phenomena.

Being distinctive and larger than life was important to her and can be seen when she went to America in the mid-1960s, where she sometimes called herself 'Dame' Sybil Leek. Since she was definitely born a commoner, this title would have had to have been awarded by royalty. Yet, there are no formal records of Leek ever receiving 'Damehood'. Clearly this is something she awarded herself, and seems to have revelled in the elevated status it gave her. Even if, initially, it was a genuine mistake by the American media, she never seems to have corrected it. Leek's Sun sign Pisces is attracted to acting, escape and fantasy so, although it is conjecture, perhaps she dreamt of glamour, performing and storytelling to such an extent that she eventually became prey to delusions of grandeur. As we shall see, it was certainly not an isolated event.

When she lived in England, she publicly spoke about herself as a 'witch', yet, when she moved to America, she then described herself as a 'Druid' and claimed, "The Druids are the priests, witches are the working class" (http://www.nytimes.com). This comment reveals something about her attitude towards a sense of having a 'title' and nobility in the Craft as well as her attitude towards class and status within esoteric society.

Leek's *Diary of a Witch* is dedicated to her sons and at the end of the 'dedication' she says of her sons that they "make it easy for me to be their mother and not merely a legend" (Leek, 1968, dedication page). It is a curious turn of phrase for anyone to describe herself as 'merely a legend' and again suggests Leek believed and promulgated her own fantasies, even within her own family. A tendency to self-delusion is associated with the illusionary Piscean nature.

The IC (*see glossary*) is Aquarius, indicating Leek's independent attitude towards family and home; probably her domestic life may have been less conventional than that of many of her contemporaries. For example, in her earlier years, she detached (a characteristic associated with Aquarius) herself from her family and school friends, by playing with the gypsy children of the New Forest. Later, she found a home with the gypsies for a while when she found herself homeless (Leek, 1964, 6 & 29).

Leek wrote that she sent her mother, who at this point was still living in Staffordshire, "some pitiful lying and evasive letters" and arranged for her sons to go and stay with their grandmother on an extended visit (Leek, 1964, 28). By living with the gypsies for a short while, she became one of the 'alienated', in that gypsies were – then and now – considered outsiders.

However, it must be admitted that it is difficult to prove whether or not Leek ever lived with gypsies, although the IC Aquarius in her chart strongly suggests that she

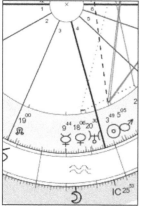

did have an unusual home life and experienced disruptions and unsettlement. Whether these disruptions were physical or emotional is impossible to tell.

The theme of independence and an unconventional domestic life is echoed by Uranus the natural (*see glossary*) ruler of Aquarius, being the house cusp ruler of the fourth house (*see box on left*) in her natal chart. This is the area associated with family, home life and parents.

Aquarius/Uranus is freedom-loving and unconventional and indicates that Leek was individualistic and unpredictable. If her ideals were at stake, she could also be obstinate, since Aquarius belongs to the fixed signs (*see glossary*), which can be inflexible at times. She was likely to have been regarded as eccentric, rebellious and experimental, since these are also areas associated with Aquarius. Leek claimed that in her mid-teens she was "dubbed an eccentric" and that her "… tendency to blurt out some of my psychic perceptions did not help at all" (Leek, 1968, 40). She also stated that, as a child, she "could do telepathic experiments" (ibid, 81).

FAMILY MATTERS

In Leek's natal chart the Sun is in the fourth house, the area that governs domestic-life, family, heritage, legacy and parents. The fourth house is also occupied by the Moon and Mars (as well as the asteroid Chiron), and the Sun is near the IC at a wide conjunction of 8 degrees. This placement reveals that family, heritage and origins were important to Leek and that she needed a family she could be proud of. Being able to share her family roots would have given her a sense of confidence and identity, and she would have found a source of energy in her family and home.

Later in her life, Leek's father, mother and (then) recently widowed maternal aunt moved to the New Forest, where they all lived together in a large Victorian house (Leek, 1964, 33). Leek claimed this had been acquired through a gypsy friend, and that living together for financial reasons helped Sybil and her husband to become more financially secure (ibid). This suggests the family were close enough to pull together in times of need.

Sun in Pisces suggests that, although Leek may have idolised her parents and family, she nevertheless felt the need to fantasise and glamorise them, since these are areas associated with Pisces and its ruler Neptune. Her fanaticising may, however, indicate she was actually not proud of her family. For example, she may have felt ashamed about their occupations, as it did not fit in with her image of her 'glamorised self'.

We see her romanticising nature in her claim to have been born into a family of witches whose ancestry went as far back as 1134 CE (Leek, 1968, 7) a period for which no continuous records exist in Europe, meaning that, like so many of her claims, this also is unverifiable. She also claimed to be related to a Staffordshire witch called Molly Leigh, who lived in the seventeenth century. Molly was an elderly, solitary figure who lived by herself (like so many who were perceived as witches) and, although accused of witchcraft, died before she could be put on trial, later becoming known as The Witch of Burslem. Molly kept a pet blackbird that was accused of turning beer sour, and it is impossible to escape comparisons with Leek's own pet bird, Hotfoot Jackson. However, in making this claim, Leek never actually stated exactly how Leigh was related to her family, and it is almost impossible to prove either way, due to a lack of records for the period.

Leek also claimed that in the tenth century, on her father's side of the family, "… we go back to a staunch family of occultists who were constantly around the royal court of Russia" (Leek, 1968, 9). Civil records for that period were not generally available at the time Leek was writing so, once again, she must have known her claims could neither be proved nor disproved. However, if she did have access to any kind of evidence, she would surely have publicised it.

In Leek's autobiography (published in the USA in 1968) she claimed she was born "… in the classic place for witches, at a crossroads where three rivers also meet, a wild, desolate, witch-ridden part of Staffordshire" (Leek, 1968, 11). Yet her birth certificate shows she was born at home in Hanley, Stoke-on-Trent, Staffordshire, which is an urbanised area, not rural as she had claimed. Her maternal grandparents and parents all lived together in the same home.

However, the Register for Civil Records shows that by 1939, the Leek family were living in a cottage in Cheddleton, Cheshire, where the nearby Endon Brook and the River Churnet meet, running alongside the Caldon Canal in a very rural area (Stoke-on-Trent Archives: email to Author), which is very much how Leek had described her 'birthplace'. Obviously, by this time, Leek would have known she was born in Hanley, so perhaps she chose to think of herself as being spiritually born (or reborn) in Cheddleton, or used some artistic license to describe where she was born in order to evoke a sense of drama.

Another example of her idolising and glamorising, is evidenced when she described her father Christopher, as a "scholarly type" (Leek, 1968, 12), claiming that in his youth he had been a Shakespearean actor and member of the celebrated Frank Benson Theatre Company. Benson's autobiography however fully lists the casts of his touring theatre companies and there is no mention of anyone named Christopher Edwin Fawcett.

In fact, records show that as a young man Fawcett had been employed as an electrician, mechanical engineer and paper-mill worker. When Leek was born, her father was working in the paper-mill industry as a 'back-tenter' (Newspaper article, Pickford). This was someone who minded the machines. If Fawcett *had* been a scholarly type, this certainly was not reflected in his choice of occupation.

In astrology, the Sun can symbolise the father as well as the self and in Leek's natal chart the Sun is in the fourth house, the area of family. The Sun is quincunx Neptune, suggesting she romanticised not only about herself but also her parents, as the nature of the quincunx aspect is to adjust and modify. There are many examples of Leek's 'modifications' in her autobiographical writings.

For example, Leek wrote that, "… on marrying my mother, who was much younger than he, [my father] had given up the stage to go back into the family business of civil engineering" (Leek, 1968, 13). This claim is totally fabricated for her parents' birth certificates show there was a difference of just six years between them; her father being born in 1891 and her mother in 1897. The reference to, "… the family business of civil engineering," is also fabricated since records show that Leek's paternal grandfather Frederick, had been a coal miner, engineer and gas engineer. Official records also show that the Fawcett family moved around many times, perhaps for employment.

Christopher Edwin Fawcett had been born on 16th January, 1891, in Aberystwyth, Wales. Later that same year, he and his parents were registered as living in Norfolk, England, with his mother's parents. By 1901, the family had moved to Stoke and Christopher is listed under his middle name of Edwin. He died in 1964 and his death was registered in Christchurch, Hampshire.

From the movement of this branch of the Fawcett family we can see that maintaining a 'family business' of any description is likely to have been challenging if not impossible. Leek's father was a Sun sign Capricorn which suggests that he would have been a dutiful and responsible person. Securing employment to support himself and his family would have been important to him, such is the Capricorn nature. He would have travelled for employment if that was what it took to secure an income to support his family, as this is in keeping with the Saturnian nature.

Sybil Leek also moved around many times, both in England and then later, when she moved to America and lived in different parts of the States; New York, Los Angeles, Houston and Florida (Guiley, 1999, 198). This shows her restless Piscean nature.

The Moon in the fourth house also indicates frequent change of residence, as the nature of the Moon is inconsistent and the fourth house alludes to the home. The planetary activity in the third house (the area which governs neighbourhoods) supports what we know about her living in many different neighbourhoods and may indicate agitation and restlessness. Leek once said she and her husband had lived in "… derelict cottages, unmanageable barn-like mansions … a flat over a shop" (Leek, 1964, 12). At the age of 47, she stated that she had "never been able to settle down, ever since reaching adolescence and still liked to explore" (Leek, 1964, 9).

Returning to her immediate family, Leek wrote that her mother was a Moon sign Cancer, which is untrue. In her book, *Moon Signs*, she dedicates it to her mother, who, "with her Moon in Cancer, has been the caring, protective bulwark of our family life" (Leek, 1977, dedication page, un-numbered). Yet her mother, Louisa Ann Booth, was born on the 26th April, 1897, and the Ephemeris of 1897 at midnight (www.astro.com) shows that she was actually a Sun sign Taurus and that the Moon is at 0 degrees and 49 minutes in the sign of Pisces. In other words, the Moon was *nowhere near* Cancer on the day Leek's mother was born.

Leek once declared that, "Astrology has been my first love" (Leek, 1968, 137) and for any professional astrologer, accuracy and detail are very important. It is therefore astonishing that Leek should get something so essential so very wrong, whether intentionally or by accident. The Moon takes almost two and half days to move from one sign into another; in astrology, moving from signs Pisces into Cancer is four signs on, which is 120 degrees away. One possible explanation is that Leek cast her mother's horoscope without using an ephemeris and in doing so may have made a mathematical error, which led her to believe her mother's Moon sign was indeed Cancer. Leek's friend and student, Christine Jones, who helped care for Leek in her final years, once said of her that she "… mixed truths with untruths liberally, causing great harm as she went" (https://en.wikipedia.org/wiki/Sybil_Leek).

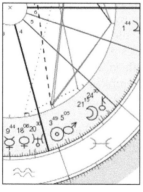

Leek's affection towards her mother is shown again in her book, *Sybil Leek's Book of Herbs* (Leek, 1980, dedication page, un-numbered), where she writes: "To My Mother with love." Even if there was inaccuracy about her mother's Moon sign, Leek's feelings seem genuinely caring and suggest she felt her mother played a significant role in her life. In that same book, Leek describes Moon in Pisces people as being "… artful and *avant garde*" (Leek, 1977, opening page, un-numbered) a description that was particularly apt for herself, as she surely must have known.

As previously mentioned, in Leek's natal chart the Moon is in the fourth house, the area of heritage is at home in this house in the natural zodiac. It can be said that on Leek's mother's side of the family, there was some astrological heritage in them both being born with the Moon in Pisces. The interpretation of this placement in Leek's book, *Moon Signs*, perhaps reveals something about herself and her relationships.

For example, she writes that the Moon in Pisces female "… produces some extremes of deception, and the awakening from the dream that love, sex and marriage are one glorious adventure" (Leek, 1977, 134). Certainly, at times, Pisceans can fanaticise and delude themselves; such is part of the nature of its Neptunian energy, which is helpful for areas such as creating illusion and storytelling.

Leek goes on to say that happiness can be found for lunar Pisceans only if they can find a partner who understands their artistic and sensitive nature. She also observes that Moon in Piscean females are easily taken advantage of by those who "… enjoy playing with your emotions and walk away when they have achieved destruction" (ibid), advising the reader to avoid partners "… who seem to enjoy emotional cruelty" (ibid). It is necessary to look at any natal chart to see if certain themes reoccur and, if they do, then an emphasis can be given to those themes.

In Leek's case however, it is necessary to look also at any aspects created with the Moon which, in her chart, shows that the Moon was trine Saturn, which will be discussed later on. Other famous Moon Pisceans include Aleister Crowley and Doreen Valiente (the latter being the subject of Chapter Eleven in this book). Valiente met Sybil Leek and described her as "an awfully nice person" (Jordan, 1996, 174).

Interestingly, Leek claimed that Crowley was a dear family friend and, when she was a child, he had told her, "This is the one who will take up where I leave off" (Leek, 1968, 19). Yet there is no mention of the 'Fawcett' family name listed in several of Crowley's biographies, or the name Sybil Leek. It has been admitted that Crowley "… was a highly improbable family guest during the 1920s" (Davies, 2013, 210). Leek also claimed (perhaps equally implausibly) that H. G. Wells was a visitor to the family home (Leek, 1968, 14).

The Sun is conjunct Mars which can symbolise that she was at war with herself or was battling and challenging herself, since Mars represents conflict and the Sun represents the self. The Sun Pisces reveals there is symbolism about her self-identity and this is seen regularly with the inconsistencies that keep cropping up whenever she writes about herself. For example, she wrote about an incident where a school mistress called her Sybil Falk and not Fawcett (Leek, 1968, 24), and seemingly Sybil never corrected her.

The Sun quincunx Neptune in her natal chart alludes to a sense of 'self-glamorisation'. It has been said of the quincunx energy that it can manifest as "adjustment, dilemma and re-orientation" (Donath, 1981, 104), which can be seen in the obvious impermanence of Leek's lifestyle. This aspect can also suggest a 'missing/lost father', the Sun representing the father and the 'missing/lost' symbolised by Neptune. In Leek's case, she may have missed her father if he was working long hours in his employment and perhaps felt somewhat lost in not seeing him as much as she would have liked.

Alternatively, the father she would have liked, and perhaps felt she deserved – the academic, artistic father who acted in Shakespeare and worked in the family business – may have been missing from her life, and what she felt was missing was the ideal and not the reality. The idealising and hero-worship of him may have been part of this in her world both as a child and as an adult.

The Sun is trine Pluto and can symbolise self-obsession, since these are areas connected with the Sun and Pluto, respectively. It also reveals that Leek was able to gain an insight into herself through the occult, by accessing subjects such as astrology and numerology, which are both areas associated with Pluto, which associates with the hidden as well as with psychology. In writing about these areas, she could have helped others to better understand themselves, giving a sense of both insight and self-empowerment.

Leek once wrote that both astrology and witchcraft were "… dedicated to the search for ancient wisdom and truth…. Witchcraft is the embodiment of the religion I follow" (Leek, 1968, 138). There is some symbolism of this in her natal chart, where Neptune (witchcraft being an association of Neptune) is in the ninth house, the area that governs religion.

EDUCATION

Mercury and Venus are both in the progressive sign of Aquarius. Mercury in Aquarius suggests that Leek may have been misunderstood as a child, since Aquarius is advanced in its thinking and can be quite futuristic if not clairvoyant. The electric energy of Aquarius also indicates that Leek could have picked up communication and ideas out of the air, as it were, in a telepathic way. It is perhaps unsurprising that Leek wrote books on the subject of ESP and telepathy.

The theme of the 'original mind' is emphasised by the presence of Uranus in the third house, the area connected with communicating (as well as with neighbourhoods and siblings). Uranus in the third house indicates that she had a sharp, inventive mind, often ahead of her time in her ability to think in an unconventional way. At school she may have been considered a bit eccentric by her peers. The disruptive and unruly nature of Uranus in the third house also suggests that Leek's education – perhaps during her schooldays – was somehow disrupted.

We can see this, for example, when she had only been at school for a few weeks and had to stay home because she had diphtheria (Leek, 1968, 14). She also wrote that she had only three years of schooling and that her IQ was 164, which was considered "… unusual for an unorthodox type of upbringing" (Leek, 1968, 13). Typically however, she does not tell us when her IQ was tested or by whom. Leek also wrote that up until the age of eleven years old, she would be visited at home by an Educational Welfare Officer enquiring why she hadn't been attending school (Leek, 1968, 20). Yet she also claims she had a governess at home who taught her, who apparently was a "… former Russian opera star" (Leek, 1968, 20).

Leek also claimed to have been sent to a school in an old English manor house. There the headmistress apparently remarked, "It's very awkward not having an official record of your past education" (Leek, 1968, 24). This could suggest Leek's education had been unsettled and inconsistent, which is in keeping with the unsettled nature of Uranus. However, it might also reveal the extent to which she was determined to conceal the truth about her life which is in keeping with the evasive nature of her solar and lunar sign Pisces, as well as her Scorpio ascendant. She once said, "I think I tried to fit into school life but it was difficult" (Leek, 1968, 27). All in all, it seems that Leek might have felt like an outsider in the orthodox educational system.

Mercury is at home in the third house (as well as the sixth house), as this is the area governed by Mercury and its intellectual air element. This position has been interpreted that a person could be "precocious from an early age … much too slippery to ever get caught" (Hillman, 2007, 117). This may well explain Leek's extravagant claims about herself and her family. She may have regarded herself as outwitting all those she felt were likely to look down on her for her lack of education or unconventional life.

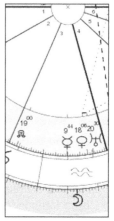

The position also indicates restless energy and an agile mind, revealing that Leek was a natural communicator; observant and witty. For example, she once said to journalists, when she was living in America, that she did not want "to be styled an evangelist for the witch religion" and was not the "Billy Graham of witchcraft" (Davies, 2013, 215).

Another example of her wit is shown when an unwanted telephone caller requested a reading from her and enquired whether she used a crystal ball or tarot cards for her readings. Leek retorted, "I'm not a fortune-teller; I do not have a crystal ball. I collect tarot cards but I prefer to play bridge" (Leek, 1968, 115). However, as the tale comes from Leek herself, we have to regard it with a little caution, although it is certainly something she *might* have said.

The third house also symbolises short journeys where one can expect many trips in one's own country (the opposing ninth house governs overseas journeys). The three planets in Leek's third house reveal that she would have undertaken many journeys in her life, both physically and perhaps also magically.

MESSAGING AND THE ARTS

Mercury is unaspected (also called peregrine – *see glossary*) to any other planets in her natal chart. When a planet creates an aspect with another planet, the energies are blended and forced to work together – but when a planet is unaspected, it has full reign with its own pure energy; no other planets impose limitations on its activities.

If we think of the unaspected planet (in this case Mercury) as an actor in an improvised play, it has the potential to totally dominate the proceedings in communication, or alternatively draws attention to itself by *not* interacting with the other players. This is played out in the natal chart where the person can either dominate with action or govern with passivity. Interestingly, astrologer, Linda Goodman (subject of Chapter Twelve), also had an unaspected Mercury in her natal chart.

The pure energy of an unaspected planet is often overtly expressed in the subject's nature. This is borne out in Leek's life where she spoke and wrote for different audiences. For example, she wrote books and articles on various subjects of the occult (her death certificate gives her occupation as 'journalist' rather than 'author'). Her claim to have once been a 'roving-reporter' on the *Day by Day* magazine programme for Southern TV in England (Leek, 1968, 75) is, like so much else, unverifiable and has since been wildly embellished by her followers.

When unaspected, Mercury – the planet of communication and the mind – can be intellectual and achieve amazing feats both of the spoken and written word. This is borne out by the various articles she wrote, along with books and lectures. Leek worked with a wide variety of people including Hanz Holzer (a parapsychologist, television host and producer) although, an article for the *Journal for the Society of Psychical Research* argued that his use of psychics served to "… cast considerable doubt on the objectivity and reliability of his work as a whole" (Berger & Berger, 1991, 183). She also worked with Bert R. Sugar, who was a sports historian and writer.

Leek said that she found it, "… easy to identify myself with all types of people, good and bad, but never indifferently" (Leek, 1964, 9). She also found no difficulty in talking to people who led different lifestyles to her own. This is perhaps the source of some of Leek's misplaced information and ideas. Mercury in Aquarius adds a sense of absent-mindedness and unpredictability.

Venus is also in the third house and reveals that she had an intellectual appreciation of the arts. Indeed, this is borne out by her argument that when we buy a picture or book of poetry, we give little thought to the artist or poet or even to *the reason* for buying such things, suggesting that people took both art and education for granted (Leek, 1964, 122). She was clearly inspired by poetry, taking the title of her book, *A Fool and a Tree*, from a quotation by the poet, William Blake. Elsewhere she often quoted Shakespeare and also showed her enthusiasm for classical music. Venus in the third house will have been helpful to her when she was lecturing, giving her a natural appeal and charisma.

By acknowledging public indifference to artists and poets, as discussed above, we can see astrology in action by the Mars in Pisces placement in her natal chart. Leek once claimed that she wrote her first poem because of Aleister Crowley, who became her first teacher of the wonders of poetry (Leek, 1968, 17–18). Although it is unlikely that she ever met him in childhood, it is quite possible that once she discovered his work, she then regarded him as a teacher in the sense of the influence of his poetry upon her.

Leek also stated that she had a slim book of poetry published when she was sixteen and that it was read on the BBC Radio by Edith Sitwell (ibid). Curiously however, she does not mention the name of the publisher, the book's title or the date of publication. Despite searching the British Library (which holds copies of most publications), the Author has not managed to identify it. This may, therefore, be a very good example of the excesses of Mercury mentioned earlier.

Poetry, theatre and classical music are all associated with Pisces/Neptune (her lunar and solar signs) and Leek's natal chart indicates that she could be a fluent speaker. This is shown when she was interviewed on the radio and television, where she would try and educate the public about witches, dispelling the common myths and stereotypes.

Mars in Pisces reveals that Leek asserted her energy into the arts and mystical subjects with sensitivity to areas such as colour and mood as well as rhythm and tone. It is a particular useful placement for mediumistic work where her energies have to be open and recipient for receiving the energies of spirits, where transcendence and the ether are of great importance. The position also reveals that she could assert herself also in fighting for the underdog, and this is borne out in the way she looked after homeless or sick animals. Leek once stated that Pisceans could be "… passionately loyal to people or causes" (Leek, 1968, 229). At times, it is true she could be difficult to pin down since her characteristics included escapism and elusiveness, which we have seen in abundance throughout this chapter especially, regarding her personal life.

ASSERTION AND FRIENDSHIPS

The Sun is conjunct Mars in her natal chart as discussed earlier, revealing that Leek could be ambitious, competitive and even daring. In 1951, when she was 34 years old, the Witchcraft Repeal Act was passed, and there was still a certain stigma attached to witches in the UK, despite the change in laws. Yet Leek was courageous enough to step forward and proclaim herself a witch. Yet even she had to admit she was wrong to think it was time to "… emerge into the light to show the world what we knew about witchcraft… . The world even now is not yet ready for witchcraft, as I know all too well" (Leek, 1968, 84).

Taking herself and her two sons to live in America was also a bold move, and would have been quite a radical undertaking in the late 1960s for a single parent to not only emigrate, but also take her children with her (her fourth husband, Reginald Brian Leek, who was the father of Julian and Stephen, did not go with them and remained in Hampshire, until his death in 1974). While in the USA, she fell in love with the country, perhaps feeling it was receptive towards occult subjects and witchcraft.

Whilst still living in Hampshire, England, Leek had claimed that her landlord refused to renew the lease on her antiques shop as she was attracting too much publicity from the media for proclaiming herself a witch. Certainly, her neighbours were not entirely convinced by her claims, with one Dionis MacNair stating that "… people either thought she was a bit of a joke or a fraud" (http://www.bbc.co.uk/insideout/south/series1/sybil-leek.shtml).

Venus in Aquarius indicates that Leek was a loyal friend, as these are areas associated with Venus and Aquarius, respectively. For example, it has been said that she became 'lifelong friends' with the BBC Radio presenter, Annie England, who had once interviewed her; although, again, this is impossible to verify (ibid).

IDEALS AND PRINCIPLES

Leek may have most easily befriended people she regarded as individual, progressive thinkers, as well as those who were original and unconventional. Leek described the paranormal researcher, Hanz Holzer (an Aquarius), and the author and journalist, Jess Stearn (a Taurus), as being "close friends and associates of mine" (Leek, 1974, 6). In Leek's natal chart, the eleventh house cusp ruler is Mercury. This reveals that amongst her friends, she would have had a variety of friendships with authors, businessmen and women, healers, speakers and writers, since these are areas that associate with Mercury.

Venus in Aquarius position also suggests she had high ideals, cared about humanity and may have been involved with good causes where she could help make progressive changes. This is borne out by her frank outspokenness about witchcraft, when others perhaps would have been more cautious.

In an interview in 1969, she claimed it was predictable that there would be a renewed interest in witchcraft, since humanity was about to move into the Age of Aquarius, where people were searching for enlightenment and truth (both qualities associated with Aquarius and its ruler, Uranus), and where religion could accept people as human beings (http://www.nytimes.com). This reveals that she valued the differences in people and understood that we are all unique and individuals. However, she was not the first to recognise this since two years earlier the musical, *Hair*, with its opening song, 'The Age of Aquarius' and (faulty) astrological references, had already paved the way for these sentiments, the musical having been written against the backdrop of the Vietnamese War.

In relationships, Leek valued freedom and appreciated the individualistic nature of people as these are all associated with Aquarius and its ruler, Uranus. Friendship would have been essential to her, as well as partnerships and relationships. In her writing, she collaborated with people such as William I. Kaufman, Bert R. Sugar, together with her sons Julian and Stephen Leek, who provided illustrations for some of her writings.

Leek's understanding that people are individual and unique can be seen in her book, *Astrology and Love,* published in 1977. The information on the back cover describes it as

234 FAMOUS OCCULTISTS AND WITCHES

"… the first really complete guidebook for both gay and straight lovers." Venus conjunct Uranus reveals that she loved to be different and perhaps revelled in being regarded as eccentric and unorthodox. Certainly, her unique Venusian style attracted attention, and not only because she dressed so dramatically in her cloaks and robes.

Aquarius is associated with groups of people and kindred spirits and, at one point; Leek was involved with The Witchcraft Research Association, and so met with fellow witches. She had been involved in its creation, and become its first president, but claimed she was forced to resign from the organisation as many of her colleagues disapproved of her alternative interests to theirs, in particular her "interest in black magic" (Davies, 2013, 212). However, as is so often the case with this subject, despite the Author's own extensive research, shows there is no evidence of such an event. Also, in an interview given on The Amazing Kreskin Show (c.1972), Leek stated unequivocally that if someone followed the Church of Satan, they should change (https://youtu.be/ahBA3uqLwdg).

Leek seems to have gone out of her way to court controversy, for example, writing a book entitled, *Sybil Leek's Book of Curses*, and disagreeing with the ritual nudity that was employed by some other traditions (ibid). These examples show that she did not seem to mind being regarded as unorthodox by her fellow witches, such alienation being associated with Aquarius and its ruler, Uranus. She may even have gone out of her way to court controversy, as highlighted in the Venus conjunct Uranus aspect.

EARNING A LIVING AND USING THE IMAGINATION

As earnings and money are also associated with Venus, whilst Aquarius with the unconventional, it could be said that Leek gained her income in an unusual way and that she was independent in earning an income. Uranus, the ruler of Aquarius, is also associated with radio and television; both at times were sources of income for her. However, as the nature of Aquarius and Uranus can be irregular and unpredictable, it may have been necessary for Leek to also write numerous books in order to provide for her family.

This may have felt precarious, in that she did not know when her next pay cheque would come, or how much it would be. She loved the unusual, so was never going to write about the mundane areas of life, her mystical Piscean nature would have needed to write about esoteric and unusual subjects.

For example, in her books, *A Fool and a Tree* and *The Shop in The High Street*, Leek painted the people in it as real characters, describing their accents and habits as well as their clothes and mannerisms; so much so that the books almost read like a piece of fiction, where the reader could escape into a world of fantasy. Her love of antiques enabled her to dwell upon the past ages connected with items in her shop, such as nineteenth century furniture, jewellery and antiquarian books. She transported herself back in time as she wrote about the origins of her antiques.

BROTHERS, SISTERS AND COUSINS

As previously discussed, the third house also governs siblings, but it has been difficult to discover whether or not Leek had any brothers or sisters. The 1921 Census will be released in 2022 and will probably show if there were any other children living at the family home since, in that year, Sybil would have been three years old. Leek certainly *may* have had siblings; in her book, *A Fool and a Tree*, she described how the local doctor visited the family home when she was sick and "... we children would rush to the front bedroom window, our measly chickenpox-ridden faces beaming at him" (Leek, 1964, 103). Of course, this does not necessarily imply that the other children were her siblings; they may have been neighbour's children or cousins.

The presence of Mercury, Venus and Uranus in the third house suggests that, if Leek did have any siblings, then she may have engaged actively with them, and had a strong bond with a sister as well as the possibility of sibling rivalry. However, this is just supposition until such time as we can establish for certain whether she did have siblings.

As Mars, the planet of anger, is in the fourth house of family and parents, it also suggests that there may have been conflict in the home. The Sun conjunct Mars implies that she may have been involved in those arguments as the Sun represents the self. Leek said of herself once that she had an 'Irish temper' (Leek, 1968, 165).

There is also an indication in the chart that she may have been cut-off from cousins or siblings and also the symbolism that there may even have been 'fostered' siblings in the family home. She wrote that, as a child, "Cousins from other countries would come to visit us during the school holiday" (Leek, 1968, 14). However, she does not elaborate on this, and we do not know which countries they came from. Possibly, since her father and grandfather were Welsh, it may have been her father's family visiting from Wales. The nature of Uranus is to create a detachment and space and this would make sense, as far as there being a 'different' generation around her when she was growing up.

FEATHERED FRIENDS AND OTHERS

Jupiter, the planet of abundance, beliefs, fame and spirituality, is in the sixth house (*see box on right*), which is the area governing work, health and diet, as well as small animals (including birds). The latter is particularly pertinent to Leek as she became famous for appearing with her jackdaw, Mr Hotfoot Jackson. The jackdaw is a relative of the raven and in witchcraft the raven is a magical creature, a winged messenger able to move between the dual worlds of the living and of the dead. Doreen Valiente met Mr Hotfoot Jackson and with affection described how she experienced "his hot little feet on my wrist!" (Jordan, 1996, 174). Corvids are by nature Plutonian, and therefore connected to the underworld, and Pluto is immensely significant in Leek's natal chart, as it is the ruling planet of her natal chart, since Scorpio her ascendant sign is ruled by Pluto as previously discussed.

Such was Leek's affection for her magical companion that she wrote two books dedicated to him after he died, entitled, *Mr Hotfoot Jackson* and *The Jackdaw and The Witch*. As a child, Leek had apparently owned a pet owl, which was a great companion to her (Leek, 1968, 14). Clearly, she loved animals and described how, from her walks in the local neighbourhood in the countryside, "I gradually

Sybil Leek with Mr Hotfoot Jackson on her Head. Licensed by Press Association Images

made our cottage garden into something resembling a miniature zoo" (Leek, 1964, 9). Living in the countryside, she would have also regularly seen foxes, horses, rabbits and ponies.

As a child, her parents may have allowed Leek to keep an assortment of animals but also instilled in her a sense of duty and responsibility, so that she regarded herself as a caretaker of the animals, which is shown in her chart by Moon trine Saturn – symbolised by the Moon as the caretaker and Saturn showing responsibility.

In Leek's natal chart, there is symbolism to show that animals (both domestic and wild) were important to her, and that she loved and valued their unconditional friendship, and also was trustworthy with them. This is shown by planets resident in the third house, which is akin to small wild animals – large wild animals are symbolised in the ninth house, and the sixth house associated with domestic animals.

As an adult, her jackdaw was not her only pet; she also kept a four foot long boa constrictor called Mr Sasha, which she carried around with her on special occasions (Holzer, 1977, 272).

Doreen Valiente commented on Leek's care and compassion for Mr Hotfoot Jackson, saying that "he fell out of the nest and she nursed him up and he grew to be a fine big bird" (Jordan, 1996, 174).

SELF-BELIEF

The aspect of Mars sextile Jupiter can also suggest that Leek did inspire others with her faith, even though so many of her claims are extravagant and unverifiable. For example, she claimed to have been a member of a coven in the New Forest, called the Horsa Coven, which was apparently one of four covens that had been in existence since the time of William Rufus (late eleventh century) (Leek, 1968, 66). Again, this claim about the coven's antiquity is impossible to verify, yet shows her need to claim authority and lineage.

Jupiter in the sixth house also shows that Leek enjoyed her work and gained great satisfaction from it. Jupiter is inspiring by nature (as discussed above) and this can be shown by her work, for example, inspiring and intriguing others such as the solitary Wiccan and author, Scott Cunningham (subject of Chapter Fourteen) (Harrington and Regula, 1996, 11).

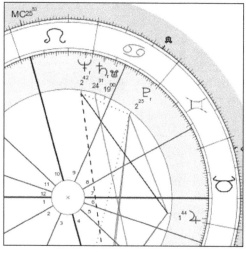

Jupiter is in Taurus (see box on left), indicating that Leek was good at accumulating possessions and spotting bargains, which is an ideal placement to have in a natal chart if you are an antiques dealer. This placement suggests that Leek loved objects that were artistic and stylish, such are the associations of Taurus, for example, paintings and sculptures.

Jupiter also associates with teaching as well as the overseas, both borne out by her emigration to America where she taught and lectured. Actually, America's chart in mundane (see glossary) astrology is ruled by Jupiter, as Sagittarius is its ruling sign.

Perhaps, therefore, it was inevitable that she would move to America. In the natal chart, the symbolism for Leek crossing overseas is found in the ninth house; this will be discussed later.

Faith and spirituality are associated with Jupiter, and these are both subjects about which she spoke and wrote. Jupiter is trine her MC Leo (*see box overpage*), indicating that creativity and originality played an important part in her career and she would have been regarded as a dramatic, colourful and lively character, since these are the associations of Leo. However, this is rather at odds with her comment, "My religion, witchcraft, is not a dramatic thing," while a journalist once described her as "spreading her cape in a pantomime parody of witchcraft" ('Requiem for a Witch', American newspaper).

Sun is sextile Jupiter (*see box on right*), adding a sense of self-aggrandisement along with confidence, pride and strong self-belief. It was once said of her that she was "... full of her own importance" (www.ilovemacc.com) and when describing her teen years she stated, "My good looks and an extroverted happy-go-lucky personality caused me to be invited to all the parties in our community" (Leek, 1968, 40).

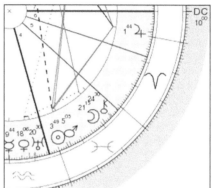

One cannot help wondering whether her success in later life made her re-write the past in order to compensate for a rather lonely, friendless childhood.

HEALER, HEAL THYSELF

When writing about psychic healing, something she had apparently learned from her family, Leek claimed, "... perhaps it would not be immodest to say that I became the most famous person in the Forest for my success in that area" (Leek, 1968, 85). Throughout her life, she seems to have yearned to be not only famous but the *most* famous, and the centre of attention – something we can see through the aspect created by Jupiter trine the MC, Leo.

The aspect Sun sextile Jupiter also provides a generosity, both spiritually and materialistically, and Leek was open-minded toward those regarded as outsiders. For example, the groups of Beatniks who camped near one of her homes (Leek, 1964, 117), and also the Romanies with whom she spent time as a young woman, as well as the bargees (water gypsies), and tramps that she also spent time with as a child, from whom she learnt much about the lore of the countryside and herbs (Leek, 1964, 1). This shows a generosity of spirit towards individuals and groups whom her neighbours may have regarded less kindly.

As mentioned previously the sixth house also represents the area of health. In her autobiography, she reveals that medical astrology is a particular favourite of hers (Leek, 1968, 141–142), claiming that she performed some experiments with members of the medical profession in researching the astrological data in their natal charts; she says that, reluctantly, some of them came to agree with some of her findings. Like so many of her claims, this too is unverifiable.

Likewise, Leek claimed to have received several medals for her work during her nursing career, though she never specified what the names of the medals were and despite this Author's strenuous efforts and extensive correspondence with the appropriate authorities, it has been impossible to substantiate her claims. One cannot help but feel that, had these achievements really happened, Leek would have been eager to share the details. Instead, she dangles snippets of information, knowing her followers will snap at them, rather like fish chasing the bait in a river. This shows the astrology in action with her strong Piscean nature.

Jupiter is excessive by nature, and she may have been referring to her own many health issues when she stated, "It is a family failing.... It has to do with glands and the nervous system" (http://www.nytimes.com). As a child, she had diphtheria and was kept away from school for some time, and was also prone to allergies, asthma and influenza (Leek, 1964, 104, also 1968, 14). She eventually died of cancer.

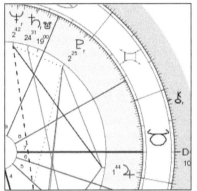

There is something to be said about her emotional and spiritual-well being too, which is an important area for any healer, but particularly for some Pisceans. This is because if the healing sensitive Piscean is around people who are in distress, suffering and need 'rescuing' in some way, then the absorbent energy of Neptune (the ruler of Pisces) can lead the Piscean to feel drained and overwhelmed.

Leek recognised this element within herself and her healing work, as she wrote that in her youth she "... felt intense sorrow for anyone ill and consequently my energy would be drained by my emotions" (Leek, 1968, 86). In time however, she learned how to psychically protect herself. Sun conjunct Mars indicates that she needed to conserve her energy levels, since although Sun and Mars represent energy and vitality, both are in Pisces; a sign which by nature can easily be drained and strained because of its delicate and fragile nature. Psychic self-defence may therefore have been necessary to Leek as "... the process of healing someone through psychic power resulted in a severe strain on my own health" (Leek, 1968, 86). This certainly suggests that, although she was an effective healer, she was nevertheless aware of the risks.

FRIENDS IN HIGH PLACES

Jupiter sextile Pluto in Leek's natal chart (*see box above*) reveals that death, investigation, research and the occult were immensely significant to her and she would have enjoyed mystery and secrecy.

Leek developed an interest in politics, which is also associated with Jupiter; particularly political conspiracy theories. For example, she co-authored with Bert R. Sugar on, *The Assassination Chain*, which looked at subjects such as who assassinated Robert Kennedy and Martin Luther King, offering suggestions implicating the Mafia, the anti-Castro Cubans and the CIA. Conspiracy theories can rarely be substantiated one way or another, rather like many of Leek's other claims.

In 1972, she wrote, *An Astrological Guide to Presidential Candidates*. Leek was also known to mingle with the 'movers and the shakers,' accepting invitations to cocktail parties and other social events; she even met Ronald Regan. Many of these people had an interest in astrology and witchcraft.

At one point, Leek's extensive work schedule in America included organising classes in the occult, broadcasting a nightly radio show and owned a restaurant called, *Sybil Leek's Cauldron* (https://books.google.co.uk/books). Being an entrepreneur was another aspect of Leek's career, as she had previously owned at least three shops in England.

THE OCCULT AND THE UNUSUAL

Pluto is at home in the eighth house of her natal chart, revealing she had tremendous inner power that helped her manage significant changes and crises in her life. The intense nature of Pluto also alludes to betrayal, mania, revenge and sabotage. It is perhaps unsurprising, therefore, with this position of Pluto in the eighth house and her Scorpio ascendant, that part of her work involved literature about cursing and hexing which, as we have seen, was not acceptable in some of her contemporaries' attitudes.

Sun and Mars trine Pluto in her natal chart reveal that Leek had the strength and vitality to work in a mediumistic way. She was a trance medium (*see glossary*) and often worked at helping to clear lost souls and restless spirits. Hans Holzer stated that, after one occasion where Leek had been brought to a haunted house to do some intensive rescue work, she temporarily vacated her own body so the spirit could speak through her (Holzer, 1997, 258).

Leek and Holzer also appeared on American TV to discuss the subjects of ghosts, spirits and witches (Holzer, 2002, 53). Uranus is in opposition to the MC Leo and shows that, although she could communicate about the bizarre and unusual (such as the subjects mentioned above), in doing so she would have drawn attention to herself by speaking about areas which were unconventional; this would then generate a substantial audience fascinated to hear what she had to say. The conflict of the opposition is illustrated when Holzer remarked, "As for her witchcraft, she always considered this her private business, except that she made it a public business by talking about it on air" (http://www.earthsongforums.com).

LIFE OVERSEAS

Neptune, the ruler of Leek's Sun and Moon sign Pisces, can be found in the ninth house of her natal chart. Neptune is the sea-god and the ninth house represents long-distance travel, philosophy and spirituality, as well as beliefs, publishing, law and politics. It is perhaps unsurprising that Leek found spiritual fulfilment overseas, as Neptune associates with dreams and escapism.

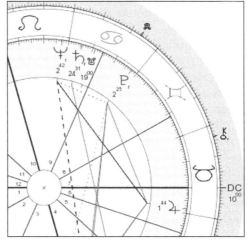

Travel was important to her, perhaps as means of escape from the mundane side of life through magic and make-believe. Jupiter is square Neptune and indicates that perhaps she had big dreams and fantasies, and in order to fulfil these may have had to make sacrifices in her beliefs (*see box on right*).

As mentioned above, the ninth house is associated with publishing, therefore Neptune in this area suggests some confusion, as the energy of Neptune can sometimes be disorderly and mystifying. This can be seen by some of the inaccuracies and vagueness in her autobiographical works, where parts of her life are missed out altogether or seem to have been made up or, at best, exaggerated.

It has been suggested that Leek may have used 'ghost-writers' for her astrology books and that when customers requested their natal charts be interpreted, she sub-contracted out to other astrologers (www.earthsongsforum.com). It has been claimed that these ghost–writers may have included Leek's daughter-in-law, Candice Shoaf-Leek (www.astro.com Shoaf-Leek), as well as Dikki-Jo-Mullen, who was the astrologer for the American magazine, The Witches' Almanac (ibid).

Saturn is also in the ninth house (as discussed previously), indicating that Leek's faith was very important to her and also that she relished the opportunities that travel could bring her. As Saturn is associated with expertise, it is perhaps unsurprising that many regarded her as an authority figure. Wide open spaces are associated with the ninth house and Leek felt spiritually inspired by being at sea (associated with Neptune) and in the countryside (associated with Saturn), both of which are in keeping with vast expanses of space.

As mentioned earlier, the ninth house and Jupiter are associated with beliefs – Leek strongly believed in reincarnation and wrote a book on the subject entitled, *Reincarnation: The Second Chance*. She believed, for example, that she had known her sons in a previous life, dedicating this book to them stating "… my sons in this life, my friends in another" (Leek, 1975, un-numbered).

Leek also believed that she was guided by Madame Helena Blavatsky, the co-founder of the Theosophical Society. Acknowledging that there was a physical resemblance between them, she once declared that "… some of her spirit is forever within me" (Leek, 1975, 6) and felt compelled to complete Blavatsky's work, which had been left unfinished at the time of her death.

REINCARNATION

In the natal chart, there are symbolic points called the Nodes (*see glossary*); the North and South Node, which relate to reincarnation and spiritual advice. However, Leek does not use these areas to illustrate the subject of reincarnation but instead the position of Pluto in aspect, house and sign, as well as the eighth and twelfth house in the natal chart. Possibly, she felt that the Nodes were a little too highbrow for books and articles aimed at ordinary readers without specialist knowledge of astrology.

The eighth house governs death (both physical and metaphysical) and the twelfth house relates to karmic experiences in past lives. Leek effectively describes the twelfth house as "like a memory bank of a computer, in which all past memories are stored and recorded" (Leek, 1975, 61).

She goes on to advise correctly that one's past life memories are not necessarily going to be pleasant but in consulting a spiritual astrologer one can discuss the positive and negative aspects of that area. As discussed earlier, animals were of immense importance to her and she wrote about her belief that animals could be reincarnated either as another animal or a human being.

Leek revealed that one of the most significant turning points in her life was regarding reincarnation after extensive evidential work with Hans Holzer. She stated that previously, when she had lectured on the subject, she had done so with a degree of hesitation. However, after working with Holzer, she felt she experienced differently, and, "… Reincarnation became a fact, not merely a belief" (Leek, 1968, 153).

The Nodes are the karmic points, which are understood to provide spiritual guidance on how to live in order to advance on one's spiritual path. North Node indicates qualities which should be developed, and the South Node qualities which one should inhibit and which have been left over from a previous incarnation.

In Leek's natal chart, we can see that the North Node is in Capricorn and the South Node is in Cancer. This pairing suggests a need for her in this lifetime to have been be more practical and self-sufficient and less emotional and irritable. Capricorn associates with realistic and sensible qualities whilst Cancer associates with emotions and moodiness

Astrologer, Judy Hall, wrote that people with the North Node in Capricorn have a karmic purpose "To develop inner and outer authority" (Hall, 2006, 116). Leek certainly found a platform in her later years when she emigrated to America and became known by some people as an authority on subjects such as astrology and witchcraft. In many ways she did not became truly established and successful *until* she emigrated and this message is echoed again by Saturn (the ruler of Capricorn) in the ninth

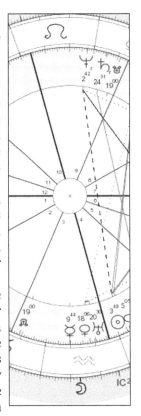

house. Although she achieved relative success in England as a journalist and reporter, it was in America that she found her greatest fame as an author, medium, speaker and witch.

As far as is known, when she had moved to America, there does not appear to be any evidence that she married again or formed a relationship with a lifelong partner. Perhaps age and experience had finally impressed upon her naturally dreamy and poetic Piscean nature that 'all that glitters is not gold' and that she could finally become the independent and self-sufficient person she may have always dreamed of being.

THE END OF THIS LIFETIME

When Leek passed away she was 65 years old and experiencing significant transits to her natal chart. In the twelfth house (the area which governs hospitals, nursing and seclusion), transiting Saturn was sextile the natal Leo midheaven, and square the natal Saturn in the ninth house. When transiting Saturn is in the twelfth house, it can indicate withdrawal and retreat, applied with realism and pragmatism in one's life.

Transiting Saturn sextile the natal Leo midheaven could have helped Leek in deciding to withdraw from public life. Saturn square the natal Saturn in the ninth house may also have helped her decide to limit and retreat from her adventures, exploration, and travel. Decay and the ageing process of Saturn brought inevitability to Leek's final days where limitation and restraint are clearly visible.

Leek died in the Holmes Regional Medical Centre in Melbourne, Florida, and the heading of her obituary in the *New York Times* read, 'Ordinary Witch from New Forest

Dies at 65.' The 'ordinary witch' epithet was apparently how she had once described herself in an interview (http://www.nytimes.com/1982).

Pluto was also transiting in the twelfth house and, in this area of the natal, chart Pluto indicates intensity and privacy. The latter is something that Leek would have certainly needed in the final stages of her life. Pluto is making a significant transit by creating a sextile aspect with the midheaven. This suggests that, at this point in her life, her status was dropping and she was less influential in society. This may have been deliberate, in that she had voluntarily withdrawn, perhaps because of her health. Since the sextile brings an ease in its energy, it indicates that Leek would have accepted the inevitable, perhaps aided by her belief in an afterlife and reincarnation (*see transiting Saturn at twelfth house in box below left*).

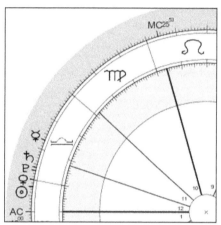

Pluto represents death and rebirths and her MC Leo is ruled by the Sun (*see box to the leftt for this position*) and is associated with the heart in medical astrology. This reveals more symbolism about a transformation of life and a decline in entertaining, performance and show business, in keeping with Leek's natal chart and the strong indication of family, home and roots. Her funeral service and subsequent cremation took place in America. Then, afterwards, her ashes were said to have been flown home to England to be interred (http://www.nytimes.com), showing that, at the end, she wanted to be near her family roots.

Her death certificate gives her name as Sybil Fawcett Leek and her claim to citizenship as being 'Citizen of the U.K. and Colonies under Section 12 (1) (a) – British Nationality Act 1948' (Ref: D/Cert).

Sybil Leek may have created much of her larger-than-life persona but, nevertheless, she cut a powerful, kindly and colourful figure that inspired many to follow in her footsteps and discover more about witchcraft.

ACKNOWLEDGEMENTS, CREDITS AND REFERENCES

The Author and Publisher would like to extend special thanks to the following:

Stoke-on-Trent City Archives Service, for their expertise, dedication, patience and time. Marilyn Stroud, for her tremendous assistance and determination in research.

Birth Certificates: from General Register Office, Southport, Merseyside, PR8 2JD, UK.
Sybil Fawcett – BC: BXCG 946299.
Christopher Edwin Fawcett – BC: WBXZ 514722.
Louisa Ann Booth –BC: BXCH059410.
George Key –BC: BXCH 058114.

Death Certificate: from General Register Office, Southport, Merseyside, PR8 2JD, UK.
CERTIFIED COPY of an ENTRY OF DEATH: Sybil Fawcett Leek – BNDX 000099.

Marriage Certificates: from General Register Office, Southport, Merseyside, PR8 2JD, UK.
MC: MXG 975663 on 19th June, 1933, in the county of Durham for:

Sybil Fawcett (25 yr) Spinster, *to Archibald Tinkler (27 yr)*. Bachelor; Profession: Butcher.
Fawcett's father's profession: Bin man (at time of this marriage).
Tinkler's father's profession: Hay cutter (at time of this marriage).

MC: MXG 977285 on 6th July, 1936, in the district of Fylde in the counties of Lancashire and Blackpool for:
Sybil Fawcett (19 yr) and *George Robert Key (22 yr)*. Profession when married: Musician (Pianist).
Fawcett's father's profession: Mechanical engineer (at time of this marriage).
Key's father's profession: Railway passenger foreman (at time of this marriage).
Courtesy of Stoke-on-Trent Archives Service:
Detail of Louisa Ann Booth's parents and marriage: courtesy of Stoke-on-Trent Archives - Marriage Certificate of Albert E. Booth to Louisa Kent in 1896 (http://www.staffordshirebmd.org.uk).

Details of Sybil Fawcett's husbands/marriages/spouse occupations:

George Robert Key – http://www.lancashirebmd.org.uk/cgi/marrind.cgi
Marriage registered in July, August, September quarter, 1936, Vol. 8, p1983.
George. R. Key born Congelton, Chester, 1914. Occupation: Musician (pianist).

Archibald Tinkler – Courtesy of Stoke-on-Trent Archives.
Occupations: Butcher, Home Guard during Second World War.

John B. Delves (1944) Courtesy of Stoke-on-Trent Archives.
Marriages registered in April, May, June quarter 1944 – Vol. 6b, p784.
Occupation: Butcher.

Reginald B. Leek (1952) Courtesy of Stoke-on-Trent Archives.
Marriage registered in January, February, March quarter, 1952 – Vol. 6b, p412.
Occupation: Antique dealer.

Sybil's Father Christopher Edwin Fawcett – Courtesy of Stoke-on-Trent Archives –
Occupations (incl.) Electrician, and on 1939 Register entered as paper mill worker.

Sybil's Paternal Grandfather – Courtesy of Stoke-on-Trent Archives.
Frederick Robert Fawcett: Courtesy of Stoke-on-Trent Archives.
Occupations (incl.) 1891, 1901 and 1911 Census (incl.): Engineer and gas works engineer.

Sybil's Maternal Grandfather Albert Edward Booth – Courtesy of Stoke-on-Trent Archives.
Occupations (incl.) 1907 and 1912 Census: 'Scavenger'; 1911 Census: Fireman at destructor works – both of these occupations are connected with collection and destruction of waste. When Louisa Ann Booth was born her father's occupation is shown on her BC as 'potter's presser'.

Christopher Fawcett's Family Movement – Courtesy of Stoke-on-Trent Archives.

Taken from Census of 1891, 1901 and 1911:
16th January, 1891, Christopher Edwin Fawcett was born in Aberystwyth, Wales.
Later in 1891, Christopher and his parents were registered as living with his mother's parents in Norfolk.
By 1901, they moved to Stoke and Christopher is listed under his middle name of Edwin, aged ten years.
In 1964, Christopher Fawcett died and his death was registered in Christchurch, Hampshire.

Census of England and Wales, 1911
Head, Albert Edward Booth, Father, aged 42 years. Born in 1869.
Bessie Booth, Daughter, aged nine years, scholar. Born in Hanley, Staffordshire, 1902.
Address: 5 Gilman Street, Hanley, Staffordshire.

Natal chart generated by www.astro.com
Rodden Rating 'A'

Leek, Sybil: Thu, 22nd Feb, 1917, 11.52pm, Stoke-on-Trent, England, UK.
2w10, 53n00.

NEWSPAPERS

Unknown American newspaper, October 1982, Journalist Unknown. Headline: 'Requiem for a Witch – Sybil Leek, Astrologer Dead at 65.'

BOOKS

Benson, F. (1930) *My Memoirs: Sir Frank Benson.* London: Ernest Benn.
Berger, A. & Berger, J. (1991) *The Encyclopaedia of Parapsychology and Psychical Research.* New York: Paragon House.
Davies, O. (2013) *America Bewitched: The Story of Witchcraft after Salem.* Oxford University Press.
Donath, E.B. (1981) *Minor Aspects between Natal Planets.* American Federations of Astrologers Inc.
Guliey, R.E. (1999) *The Encyclopaedia of Witches & Witchcraft.* Checkmark Books.
Hall, J. (2006) *Past Life Astrology.* Godsfield Press.
Harrington, D. and Regula, deTraci. (1996) *Whispers of the Moon – The Life and Work of Scott Cunningham.* Llewellyn Publications.
Hillman, L. (2007) *Planets in Play.* Jeremy P. Tarcher/Penguin.
Holzer, H. (1997) *Ghosts – True Encounters with the World Beyond.* Black Dog & Leventhal Inc.
Holzer, H. (2002) *Witches – True Encounters with Wicca, Wizards, Covens, Cults and Magick.* Black Dog & Leventhal Publishers.
Jordan, M. (1996) *Witches – An Encyclopaedia of Paganism and Magic.* Published by Kyle Cathie Limited.
Leek, S. (1962) *A Shop in the High Street.* London: Jarrolds Publishers Ltd.
Leek, S. (1964) *A Fool and a Tree.* Published by Lambarde Press.
Leek, S. (1968) *Diary of a Witch.* Prentice-Hall.
Leek, S. (1977) *Astrology & Love.* Berkeley Publishing Corporation.
Leek, S. (1977) *Moon Signs.* Berkley Medallion Books.
Leek, S. (1980) *Book of Herbs.* Cornerstone Library.
Leek, S. (1974) *Reincarnation: The Second Chance.* Bantam Books.
Tucker, J. (undated) *Burley: A Brief History.* Printed by Julians Press.

WEBSITES

https://alltacailleach.wordpress.com/pagan-articles-2/ – Written by George Knowles. Accessed on 29/12/2016.
www.astro.com – Ephemeris for 26th April, 1897. Detail of Moon in Capricorn when Louisa Ann Booth was born. Accessed on 30/11/2016.
http://www.astro.com/astro-databank/Shoaf_Candice_biographical_information – Accessed on 08/01/2017.

http://www.bbc.co.uk/insideout/south/series1/sybil-leek.shtml – BBC One Homepage: Inside Out – South: Monday 28th October, 2002.

http://www.ilovemacc.com/2016/06/23/star-wars-worlds-evil-man-witch-wincle/ – Article by Doug Pickford in 2016. Accessed on 25/02/2017.

http://www.nytimes.com/1982/10/29/obituaries/sybil-leek-ordinary-witch-from-new-forest-dies-at-65.html – Journalist, Walter H. Waggoner on October 29th, 1982. Accessed on 29/12/2016.

https://www.youtube.com/watch?v=kCxFchh7PSM – US Game Show, To Tell the Truth, April 13th, 1964. Accessed on 27/12/2016.

http://spikethenews.blogspot.co.uk/2015/02/sybil-leek-ronald-reagan-mk-often-and.html – Virginia Lehman – Passenger.

https://books.google.co.uk/books?id=dGa6F14IXHUC&pg=PT297&lpg=PT297&dq=Sybil+Leek%27s+Cauldron+Restaurant&source=bl&ots=v5BL8jv_4S&sig=qzhR_gL4mjTzAQ06fI6n – Accessed on 28/12/2016.

http://www.earthsongforums.com/forums/archive/index.php/t-12866.html – Nacken and Fetcher. Acessed on 07/01/2017.

http://spikethenews.blogspot.co.uk/2015/02/sybil-leek-ronald-reagan-mk-often-and.html – Accessed on 28/12/2016.

https://uk.pinterest.com/pin/424393964862176189/ – Sybil Leek's Cauldron Restaurant. Accessed on 28/12/2016.

https://pitsnpots.co.uk/2010/04/praise-eccentric – Accessed on 28/12/2016.

https://youtu.be/ahBA3uqLwdg– The Amazing Kreskin Show, YouTube.

CHAPTER ELEVEN

Doreen Valiente 1922–1999

Country Witch, Wiccan Priestess, Author and Poet

DOREEN VALIENTE was born Doreen Edith Dominy on 4th January 1922 in Mitcham, Surrey, England, daughter of Harry and Edith Dominy (née Richardson). Edith had previously given birth to a son, Harold, but sadly he lived less than a year, dying from "… a gastric ulcer and haematemesis" (Heselton, 2016, 15).

Both Valiente's parents were religious; her father's family were Methodists and her mother's were Congregationalist. Valiente attended a convent school but walked out when she was fifteen, as she disliked it so much. Valiente was just eighteen when her father died, and nineteen when her first husband was declared missing, believed drowned. She was 40 when her mother died.

Valiente became one of the founders of modern Wicca in Great Britain, and became affectionately known as the Mother of Modern of Witchcraft. She passionately researched and studied the occult for over 30 years, making appearances on the radio and television, where she discussed her knowledge on areas such as folklore, the occult and witchcraft. She was one of the first to speak openly about witchcraft, when it ceased to be illegal in Britain in 1951.

Valiente's books, including, *An ABC of Witchcraft: Past and Present; Natural Magic; Witchcraft for Tomorrow; Witchcraft: A Tradition* and *The Rebirth of Witchcraft,* were (and still are) extremely popular amongst the Pagan community. She was an exceptional poet and wrote a very significant and beautiful piece of work called, *Charge of the Goddess.*

After her death, her book of poetry was published; *Charge of the Goddess,* and more recently, *Charge of the Goddess – Expanded Edition,* as well as her book of fictional short stories, *The Witches Ball and Other Short Stories.* She was perhaps one of the most influential practitioners and authors of modern witchcraft.

Doreen Valiente died from pancreatic cancer (the same illness that her father died from) in 1999, aged 77.

WHAT DOREEN VALIENTE'S NATAL CHART SHOWS

Valiente was born on 4th January, 1922 (Heselton, 2016, 14), when the Sun was in the earth cardinal sign of Capricorn at 13 degrees, and when the crescent Moon was in the water mutable sign of Pisces at 27 degrees. The combinations of these signs indicate that Valiente was caring and dedicated, as well as intuitive and prone towards significant dreams (the latter will be discussed later). The signs of Capricorn and Pisces both belong to the feminine polarity (*see glossary*) and this reveals talents of artistry, imagination and receptivity. The ruling planet of her natal chart is Mercury, as it rules Virgo, the ascendant sign.

Valiente may have been humble and modest about her abilities and talents as Virgo can be reserved and even self-effacing at times, although, with Saturn present in the first house (the area of the ascendant), it would have helped bring a command and sense of authority which others could have felt in her presence.

Virgo is also associated with diet and health, so she may have been very aware of any ill health pertaining to her and her loved-ones. Allergies, diet, eczema, nervous energy and stress are all areas associated with Virgo and its ruler Mercury, and it is possible that she may have suffered with some of these ailments and conditions.

In Valiente's natal chart, there is a preponderance of the feminine polarities, emphasising her intuitive and sensitive nature. There is also a preponderance of the cardinal mode (*see glossary*). The cardinal energy reveals that she was assertive and pioneering with an action-led nature and a strong work ethic. The cardinal energy in her chart is shown by:

- Sun, Mercury and Venus in Capricorn
- Jupiter and Saturn in Libra
- Pluto in Cancer

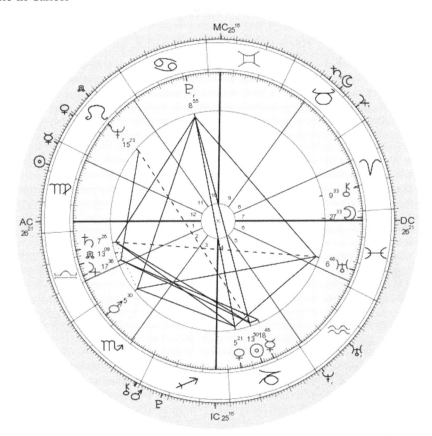

Natal and Transits Chart for Doreen Valiente on the day she died, 1st September, 1999.

FOUNDATIONS

The glyph (*see glossary*) of Capricorn is symbolised by the goat with a fish tail which indicates that all life began in the sea. The image for Capricorn is that of a mountain goat which slowly and determinedly climbs the rough and stony mountain, representing the sign's ambitious and goal-orientated nature.

The earth element rules Valiente's Sun sign, Capricorn, and its qualities include organisation, persistence, reliability, practicality and steadiness. These earthy qualities would have helped whenever discipline and responsibility were required. Capricorn's ruler, Saturn, is known as the taskmaster because of its enduring, persevering and testing nature.

We see this, for example, in her work as an author, where deadlines needed to be met; and also in her research, where she needed to be systematic and thorough. Collecting evidence to illustrate her research would have appealed to the practical and realistic side of her nature.

Valiente's practical approach to her Craft can be seen by the following example, when she was interviewed by author, Michael Jordan, and asked why she was drawn towards Gerald Gardner and a fertility religion. She replied that other groups, such as the Theosophists, were happy to discuss and preach about magic endlessly, but reluctant to see if it worked in practice (Jordan, 1998, 168), which was frustrating and unsatisfying for her.

Working with Gerald Gardner, she found he was open to experimentation and actually worked magic (ibid). We can also see her strength and discipline, when Gerald Gardner asked her to provide a liturgy for the winter solstice rites (probably in 1953), just a few hours before it was to be celebrated. Valiente adapted an existing piece of work called Carmena Gadellica and Gardner was so pleased with it that he included it in his book, Witchcraft Today (1954), as evidence of a seasonal liturgy (Hutton, 2008, 258). Years later, she recalled the occasion of craftily being duped by Gardner to write the ritual, "... the old devil did it on purpose, to see what I could do.... He would land you in something to see what you could do" (Jordan, 1996, 69).

One example of her painstaking collecting of evidence is where she set out to prove the existence of a High Priestess called Dorothy St Quinton Fordham (née Clutterbuck),

Doreen Valiente Photo, with permission of PA Photos Ltd.

who was claimed to have initiated Gerald Gardner in 1939. Writer, Jeffrey B. Russell, Professor of History at the University of California, was unconvinced that Gardner had been initiated by Fordham or that she even existed.

Gardner had spoken to Valiente many times about 'Old Dorothy', as she was affectionately known, and Valiente set out to prove that Russell was incorrect and that her friend Gardner had indeed been telling the truth. That mission took Valiente two determined and focused years to collect evidence that Dorothy St Quintin Fordham had existed, although she never managed to publish proof of Gardner's initiation, as she never found any evidence of his ritual. However, she did find "the house where Old Dorothy was living at the time Gerald was initiated" (Heselton, 2016, 244). In 1982, she wrote in a letter to her friend, Stewart Farrar (subject of Chapter Nine), that she had, "probably stood in the very room where it took place" (ibid). She had asked the (then) occupier of the house to let her take photographs of the house outside, and the owner, a Mrs Ferguson, then invited her in to her home where they chatted some more (ibid). Valiente's work therefore put an end to Russell's claims that Fordham was imaginary, thus restoring Gardner's reputation.

Valiente also adapted Gardner's *Book of Shadows,* which he claimed to have been using since the 1940s. At his invitation, she revised parts of it and in doing so, recognised various passages as being from Aleister Crowley's texts. When she brought this to Gardner's attention, he explained that when he inherited those Wiccan rites, they were disjointed and he had to join them the best that he could. Valiente agreed at his suggestion to amend the *Book of Shadows,* and this she did by replacing much of the material with her own verse, restructuring "… the document into a logical, practical and workable system" (Valiente, 2000, 94).

The end result shows her dedication and thoroughness and also that Gardner respected her and trusted his student to do the job required. They had mutual respect for each other and Valiente described Gardner's uniqueness when she said, "… when they made him they broke the mould" (Jordan, 1998, 168), and referred to his book, *Witchcraft Today,* as an "epoch-making book" (ibid).

Another example that demonstrates Valiente's Capricorn qualities is her position as high priestess in her coven, where accountability and conscientiousness would have been integral to its effective and dynamic energy, and also to any partnership workings. She was trustworthy, recognising the need for discretion and privacy when necessary, "I think you should keep people's secrets and people's confidentiality" (Jordan, 1998, 173). It is possible that here she was also reflecting upon her own experiences, where perhaps her trust was betrayed by people both inside and outside of the Craft. Her natural authority was further recognised when she became Patron of the Centre for Pagan Studies and also in her title 'The Mother of Modern Witchcraft,' which was bestowed on her by the wider Pagan community.

Valiente's life appears to contain several confined and secretive areas, which may or may not be related to what exactly she was doing during World War II. She said upon the topic of secrecy that she thought it instinctive (Jordan, 1998, 174). She observed that there is vital secrecy required of the magician and that "the four powers of the magus [*are*] to know, to dare, to will, to be silent" (ibid).

Mars in Scorpio is in the second house of her natal chart, confirming that she valued confidentiality and could keep another's privacy. Some of her extended family were aware of her secretive nature; for example a cousin commented, "There's a lot about Doreen that's secret … maybe she did something and had to keep it quiet… . She used to disappear and they didn't know where she was, not even her mother" (Heselton, 2016, 39). Mars in Scorpio will be discussed further on in more detail.

It has been speculated that she worked as a translator at Bletchley Park during the war as a Foreign Office Civilian Temporary Senior Assistant Officer (Heselton, 2016, 40). However, investigations by the Author with the archivists and Oral History Department at the Bletchley Park Trust, reveal that they have no records whatsoever of Valiente having ever worked there. Therefore, the speculations are seemingly without foundation, and the subject of employment at this time of her life remains a grey area (correspondence to Author, 06/11/2019).

The angles (*see glossary*) in Valiente's natal chart are in mutable signs (*see glossary under 'mode'*) comprising of Virgo ascendant, Gemini MC, Pisces descendant and Sagittarius IC. The prevalence of mutable signs on the angles suggests that Valiente was practical and curious, compassionate and questing, with a restless yet flexible nature. The mutable energy in the natal chart would have enhanced her ability to adapt and adjust whenever necessary. Interestingly, her friend, Stewart Farrar, also had the same mutable signs on each of the four angles in his natal chart.

Valiente's chart suggests she disliked constraints and needed to be 'on the move' both inwardly and outwardly. This in turn would have created an agitated energy and tension, resulting in a need to journey in life together with a thirst for knowledge and information. Valiente's air sign of Gemini on the MC indicates that she aspired to find an outlet for her ideas as well as for her wit and humour. Flexibility and multi-tasking in her work, together with opportunities to learn and travel would have been important to her.

Gemini is associated with diversity and variety so it is unsurprising that she was known by a mixture of names in her lifetime: 'Ameth' was just one of her magical names, although previously she had a different magical name (as told by Patricia Crowther to the Author). When she married her first husband, a 32 year-old Greek seaman named Joanis Vlachopoulos in 1941, Doreen Edith Dominy was registered on the marriage certificate as 'Doreen Edith (otherwise known as Rachel) Dominy' (email correspondence to Author from Registration Officer at Vale of Glamorgan). Her father was recorded as deceased, while her mother signed as a witness and must have seen the full details already entered, that her daughter was also known as 'Rachel' (ibid). Doreen Dominy would then have become 'Mrs Vlachopoulou' which is the female version of 'Vlachopoulos'. Interestingly, the name 'Joanis' (on the marriage certificate) is not the way it should have been written in English; normally it would be written 'Ioannis' and then pronounced as 'Yannis' (or Giannis); possibly his name was recorded incorrectly, although the Merchant Navy also listed this spelling on the *Pandias*, where he served as an Able Seaman until his death (along with many of the crew) on 13th June, 1941 (https://uboat.net/allies/merchants/crews/person/86876.html). The marriage certificate indicates that Joanis was illiterate as he was unable to sign his name (Tapsell, 2013, 15).

We do not know whether Rachel was a childhood nickname that she kept, but it is certainly interesting. It is of Hebrew origin meaning 'ewe' and can be found in the Old Testament where Rachel was the second and favourite wife of Jacob (https://www.behindthename.com). It seems apt, as Vlachopoulos had been previously married, so Valiente was his second wife. Perhaps he asked her to use the name 'Rachel' or perhaps she had her own personal reasons for using a different name.

Investigations by the Author to various archives and libraries in South Wales reveal no other documents or records of a 'Rachel' Edith Dominy. Some sources give the spelling as Rachael but the entry in the Registrar of Marriages is clear that it was Rachel (see box below). This was not the only time she used a different name in her life, for later, when she was 32 (in 1954), she went to meet Austin Osman Spare, a magical artist and occultist, and she told him that her name was Diane Walden and that her magical name was Ameth (Heselton, 2016, 89).

Domingo, Thomas	Sykes	Nuneaton	6 d	1599
Dominy, Doreen E.	Vlachopoulos E.Glamorgan	11 a	1799
— Doris	Lee	Camberwell	1 d	1443
— Rachel	Vlachopoulos E.Glamorgan	11 a	1799
Domenico, Arturo	Ballard	Edmonton	3 a	2262

Copy of the Entry in the Register for Marriages for East Glamorgan

The Moon is unaspected in Valiente's natal chart. This suggests that she was susceptible to her environment, and that her artistry and highly tuned intuition may have led her to reflect upon dwelling in her inner world, where she could escape from the stimuli of the outer world. This we can see in the way she found expression and retreat in meditation and writing. When she was younger, she had wanted to go to art school but her parents were either unable or unwilling to support her (https://wrldrels.org/2018/08/03/doreen-valiente/).

Because her natal Moon does not create any major aspects with other planets, it tends to magnify the needs represented by the Moon sign, which in Valiente's case is Pisces. This position shows great empathy for her loved ones and others who may have been suffering. It also suggests that Valiente needed to express herself in a caring and nurturing way, but equally needed to create healthy emotional boundaries to avoid burn-outs and exhaustion from others' dependence on her.

The unaspected Moon also suggests that she may have felt emotionally disconnected from her parents as well as other people later in her life (perhaps this is why some areas of her life remain a mystery?). Her strong pragmatic and realistic Capricorn nature would have helped bring balance to the unaspected Moon's energy and make cautious and wise decisions. Valiente wrote extensively about the Moon in her books, poetry and rituals. It has been observed that people with an unaspected Moon in their natal chart can see a great strength in the area of the themes of the Moon (Hamaker-Zondag 2000:72) such as care, intuition, nurturing and healing.

The Sagittarius IC is ruled by the planet Jupiter, suggesting that her upbringing was shaped by a moral, political and religious upbringing since these are areas associated with Jupiter. Valiente's parents were both religious although they held different religious views, her father being a Methodist and her mother a Congregationalist (Heselton, 2016, 18), as already noted.

FLYING HIGH

In Valiente's natal chart, there is an aspect pattern made by the planets called a Kite, which denotes the mark of a distinctive and exceptional person. There is a Grand Trine *(see glossary)* in the water signs comprising of Uranus in Pisces, Mars in Scorpio, and Pluto in Cancer, which reveals her powerful, imaginative intuition and sensitive nature. The opposition *(see glossary)* in the aspect pattern is created between Pluto and Venus.

Interestingly, W. B. Yeats, one of the leading figures in the Irish literary renaissance, also had the Kite in his natal chart. Like Valiente, his lunar sign was in the mystical sign of Pisces. He was a member of the Esoteric Section of the Theosophical Society and the Hermetic Order of The Golden Dawn.

In the Kite, the position of Venus is situated at the base of Valiente's natal chart and shows those areas of her life that would have helped to keep her grounded. Venus in the fourth house suggests that she valued family and home, as they helped her remain grounded and secure.

Kite

Kite is an aspect pattern and is an extension of the Grand Trine whereby a fourth planet forms an opposition to one corner of the triangle, in doing so it creates a sextile to the other two corners.

The position of Pluto situated at the top of her chart suggests the areas of her life in which she excelled. The position of Pluto in Cancer indicates Valiente's ability not only to excel, both in her work and in society, but also to attract and earn respect in her profession. This she certainly did as an author, poet and witch; and her achievements were acknowledged when the City of Brighton and Hove, awarded Valiente a blue plaque (http://www.doreenvaliente.com/). The scheme commemorates prominent figures of the past and the buildings in which they lived and/or worked.

The blue plaque that was awarded in 2013 to Valiente is believed to be the first in the world awarded to a witch and also the building where she lived (a council owned block of flats) was the first local authority property to have a blue plaque (ibid). Not only that, but in December, 2016, a Brighton and Hove bus company named one of its buses after Valiente, in honour of her life (http://history.buses.co.uk/). Valiente may well have felt honoured by the latter, but would also have seen a funny side to it especially as she used buses a lot. Even more pertinent is that buses are associated with Mercury – the ruling planet of her chart! This is just one example which illustrates the excellence and outstanding nature signature, which is in keeping with the 'Kite' aspect pattern found in Valiente's natal chart.

The opposition aspect created between Venus and Pluto in Valiente's chart is interesting, since the aspect could be interpreted as having grounding in the occult, combined with a burning desire to rise, with Venus as goddess. It is interesting that this was the deity that Valiente worshipped and who was so significant in her life.

With such a powerful aspect, it was almost inevitable she became a powerful witch, since Venus is associated with the goddess, while mysteries and the occult (as well as power) are associated with Pluto. This aspect is pertinent to Valiente, since it could be said that one of her greatest achievements was her beautiful text, *Charge of the Goddess*, which has been used and adapted by so many members of the Pagan community.

The aspect also describes major relationship patterns and areas where discord of opposites can generate change. The Venus-Pluto opposition in Valiente's chart indicates a 'relationship crisis', since these are areas associated with Venus and Pluto. This theme was significant in Valiente's life, as she outlived all three of her partners. Her first husband, Joanis, was presumed drowned, lost at sea just five months after their marriage; she married her second husband Casimiro in 1944, and they remained together until his death in 1972. Her third and final relationship was with Ron Cooke, until he died in 1997.

Through her lifetime, Valiente must have had to process the experience of intense emotional suffering and grief several times; all these are associated with the transforming nature of Pluto. In particular, losing her father when she was eighteen and her husband at nineteen was a heavy burden for a teenager. Learning the hard way and endurance are typical traits associated with Capricorn but, as they learn wisdom in harsh circumstances, this can make some Capricorns seem older and more mature than their contemporaries.

In Valiente's natal chart, the Moon is in Pisces (as previously noted) and suggests she was emotional, sensitive and an incurable romantic; this would have helped to keep a sense of optimism along with a yearning for a fulfilling and lasting relationship. Her tenacity comes through via the sustaining nature of Saturn (Capricorn's ruler). The aspect Venus square Saturn reveals hard lessons in love and that there were challenges in her domestic and personal life. Her 'traditional' Capricorn nature would look to marriage as a foundation in her life, through the contract of commitment and loyalty.

Venus is in the fourth house of Valiente's chart as previously discussed. This is the area governing ancestry, home and parents. There is evidence that Valiente was interested in her family's background, in particular about the origin of her father's surname, Dominy, and its meaning (Heselton, 2016, 4).

When she was older, she remembered with fondness her great-grandfather whom she affectionately called 'Great–Gran'fer', who lived in the New Forest. In particular, she remembered his bond with nature, that he was illiterate, made horse liniment and used to sell pea and bean sticks (Jordan, 1998, 171). He apparently erected a prominent notice in the New Forest that read, "Pay & Bane Stiks. Good Oss Ile fer Sale" (sic. ibid). Apparently, her paternal great-grandparents were both psychic and could see ghosts and elemental spirits (known as pixies in the New Forest) and could cast spells (Heselton, 2016, 6).

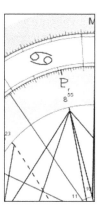

Valiente described her parents as, "very conventional people" (ibid, 17) and in particular said that her mother was, "a prude and a snob." Her comments suggest they may have been a little pretentious living in "genteel poverty" (ibid, 19), although at one point her father "outwitted the bailiff" (ibid). Doreen described her father as a "failed architect" (Heselton, 2016, 11), and he worked only sporadically at draughtsmanship and quantity surveying. However, there is no record of him being a member of the Royal Institute of British Architects (ibid). Perhaps this is why she described him as a failed architect, and his irregular bouts of employment would not have helped fulfil her mother's ambition to live somewhere impressive.

Valiente's biographer, Philip Heselton, suggested that her parents were trying to live beyond their means (ibid). Astrologically speaking, the cluster of planets in the fourth house indicates that there would also be a focus on her home and family-life; this is borne out by the number of times that she moved homes, both as a child and adult.

The peace-loving nature of Venus in the fourth house shows that Valiente valued a harmonious home, and that beautiful objects would have helped create this. There are many photographs of Valiente in the public domain, showing her surrounded by beautiful books and antiquarian objects.

Pluto is in the tenth house where it reveals her ambitious side, and also shows that in her career she would have enjoyed applying investigative and research skills in her work – both are qualities associated with Pluto, along with power, strength and the taboo (one example in her early life being witchcraft).

This would have enabled Valiente to use her strengths for the benefit of society as a whole, rather than to promote her own personal agenda. She preferred to influence society so it could understand witchcraft and make it more accessible, believing that individuals could realise their own power without necessarily being initiated into a coven but by working with nature.

She also applied investigation and research when exploring a wealth of esoteric and occult subjects; the dogged determination in her studies is indicative of the intense and probing nature of Pluto. One small illustration of her using her authority and knowledge to help better understand witchcraft can be seen in some of her contributions to the letters section of the *Psychic News* spiritualist newspaper. She wrote to the newspaper often correcting what other contributors had written about witchcraft. In 1963, she wrote a very educative and informative letter to the editor, explaining what witchcraft was, the origin of the word witch, as well as explaining the definition of magic, and also of white witchcraft and the 'black' cult of evil (*Psychic News* –Valiente, 1963, 6).

Venus in Capricorn suggests that Valiente was attracted to older people, since relationships are associated with Venus and 'being older' is associated with Capricorn and its ruler, Saturn. Her final partner, Ron Cooke, who shared her magical workings, was nearly ten years older; while her first husband, Joanis Vlachopoulos, had been almost thirteen years her senior. Her second husband, Casimiro, however had been just four years older than her and was a Sun sign Aquarius born on 24th January, 1918 (death certificate). Her magical relationship with Gerald Gardner (Chapter Four) is another example of relationships where there was an age gap; Gardner was born in 1884, and was therefore 38 years older.

Valiente's relationship with Gerald Gardner was particularly significant, since she needed to prove to him her commitment and knowledge in studying and devoting herself to the Craft. Much later, she was initiated to the level of third degree, which gave her status as a High Priestess and she visited various covens in this capacity, for example, Bricket Wood in St Albans, Hertfordshire. Her dedication and patience are qualities associated with the persistent nature of Capricorn.

Interestingly, both Cooke and Gardner were Sun sign Gemini with a difference of three days between them; Gardner was born on the 13th June, and Cooke on the 16th June (www.ancestry.com), but in different years. This week in June must have become very significant to Valiente for not only did Gardner's and Cooke's birthdays fall here, but her first husband Joanis Vlachopoulos was lost at sea when his merchant ship the *Pandias* was struck by a torpedo, off the West African coast on the 13th June (Heselton, 2016, 47).

Astrologically, the number thirteen is also significant to Valiente, since in her natal chart the Sun was in 13 degrees of Capricorn and the North Node was in 13 degrees of Libra, the latter being the area associated with reincarnation and past lives. This was a subject about which Valiente held very strong beliefs, once writing, "The witches' number *par excellence* is thirteen" (Valiente, 1994, 255) and this was certainly true of her magical self. In 1951, she wrote a letter to the spiritualist newspaper, *Psychic News*, about the topic of spiritualism and reincarnation (*Psychic News* –Valiente, 1951, 9).

She praised the religion for not requiring its followers to accept anything upon faith, and its willingness to demonstrate the principles it teaches by practical testing. However, when it comes to "teaching from its platforms, doctrines which do not rest upon the rock of truth, it at once loses that unique position and becomes merely another religion founded on blind faith" (ibid). She continued that reincarnation is one of those doctrines and she hoped that spiritualist officials and teachers would consider that point (ibid). This shows her investigative and no-nonsense Capricorn attitude towards reincarnation and her belief that spiritualism sometimes contradicted itself.

Venus in Capricorn also reveals that Valiente valued relationships and took them seriously. Qualities such as reliability and responsibility were important to her and, equally, she will have appreciated being respected. Some of these qualities can be seen for example through her contribution to the work of Janet and Stewart Farrar, her work with E. J. Jones, and also with John and Julie Belham-Payne.

Capricorn is a sign associated with status and tradition; with Venus in Capricorn, this suggests (as discussed previously) that Valiente would have understood that marriage required commitment for one another, all of which are associated with Capricorn and its ruler, Saturn.

We see some of this assurance in her second marriage to Casimiro, who had clearly been emotionally and physically wounded through his experiences in the Spanish Republican Army during the Spanish Civil War and, after that, fighting alongside the Free French during World War II. It is feasible that 'Casimiro Valiente' was not his given name, since many Spaniards who joined the Free French Army enlisted with false names, for fear of being caught by the Spanish Republican Army, from whom the veterans had originally fled (https://www.nbcnews.com/news/latino/).

Possibly, he (Valiente) suffered with what is now known as PTSD (post-traumatic stress disorder), although this would not have been recognised as such at that time. Patricia Crowther, who was a close friend to the Valiente's, once described him as "... such a straight, no-nonsense type – a really good egg!" (Crowther, 1998, 89). However, after Casimiro's death, Valiente apparently revealed to a confidante that her marriage had been very unhappy and that upon reflection she "… should have left him" (Heselton, 2016, 273). His death certificate shows 'Cor Pulmonale' and 'Chronic Bronchitis' as the cause of death (death certificate).

By remaining in an unsatisfactory marriage, we see how the Saturnian themes of duty – fear and security – were powerful influences in Valiente's life. Also at work was the compassionate, romantic and sacrificial nature of Neptune, which was the ruling planet of Valiente's Moon sign, Pisces. She must have sometimes felt that caring for him hindered her esoteric work, research and writing, since these obstructions associate with the aforementioned challenging hard aspects.

The square aspect (see glossary) between Venus and Saturn suggests not only Valiente's disappointment in romance, but also that a secure and loving relationship was only likely in later life. Her first husband was lost at sea, presumed drowned, just five months after their marriage; while her second marriage was apparently unhappy. Feeling isolated and melancholy are both associations of Saturn, while Venus associates with marriage and partnerships. It has been said that during her relationship with Cooke, she was not only at her happiest but also her most creative (ibid, 293).

Venus is sextile Uranus, indicating how Valiente appreciated freedom in relationships, needing independence and space, particularly where her work was concerned. Predictability and routine would not have satisfied her and although she would have appreciated loyalty, a sense of excitement and surprise would have appealed to her independent side. Valiente needed her relationships to be stimulating, requiring strong friendships and kindred spirits, since Venus is also associated with relating and Uranus with truthful and loyal companionship.

There is a sense with this aspect that Valiente valued people's differences and their right to be individual and true to themselves. This is because Venus is associated with value and Uranus with individualism, freedom and truth. We see this in the ways she made it clear to Gerald Gardner that she did not agree with his prejudice against gay people, and would not accept such narrow-mindedness, either outside or within the Craft (Heselton, 2016, 303).

Valiente was independent and unique. In the 1980s, when she was in her sixties, we see an example of her appreciation of liberation and originality by her positive reception to feminist witches, such as Starhawk and Zsusanna Budapest, who were pivotal in environmental activism (https://wrldrels.org).

Valiente was also inspired by feminists who thought positively about women's bodies and their bodily functions. For example, Penelope Shuttle and Peter Redgrove's book, The Wise Wound: Menstruation and Everywoman (ibid), a title which examines the idea that a menstruating woman is a powerful woman (ibid). Valiente was convinced that menstrual blood was sacred to the goddess of the witches and that it helped facilitate witches to work magic (https://wrldrels.org).

Interestingly, Uranus is also associated with being alienated or an outsider. Valiente's relationships with foreign men – her unnamed Polish boyfriend and her Greek and Spanish husbands – may have been seen as shocking and unconventional (both characteristics of Uranus) at that time. In 1943, Valiente was working in South Wales and because she was married to Joanis, a Greek, it has been suggested that she was required by law to register with the police, providing her address and place of employment in accordance with The Aliens Order of 1920. If this obliged her to carry a certificate of registration at all times, it would show that society was already treating her as an outsider (Heselton, 2016, 48).

However, the British Nationality and Status of Aliens Act, 1933 (7.1), specifically provided that a British woman should not cease to be a British subject when she married an alien, unless she acquired her husband's nationality (https:www.gov.uk *see Bibliography*). Unlike, for example, the famous singer, Gracie Fields, who had married an Italian (who was therefore considered an enemy alien) and *wished* to retain her British Passport, Valiente might not, under the 1933 Act, have been *forced* to become an alien. This strongly suggests that when she married, and perhaps for some time afterwards, while waiting to find out whether or not her husband had somehow survived, Valiente self-identified as Greek rather than English.

In Valiente's chart, the Moon is on the descendant (*see glossary*), suggesting she brought a strong caring and parenting role to her relationships. This can be seen in the way she cared for Casimiro, who had been badly wounded in the military. Born under the sign of Capricorn, she could have brought qualities such as maturity, perseverance and respect to her relationship as these are areas associated with this sign. Nursing and caring for him would have come naturally to her, as the Moon in Pisces in the seventh house (the area of marriage and significant partnerships) can also indicate a need to be needed.

The Pisces descendant also suggests that Valiente could have been attracted and committed to a partner who was compassionate and highly spiritual. Although we know that Casimiro was not especially interested in her occult work, we know nothing about his own spirituality. The Pisces descendant (amongst other things) can also indicate having a partner who is at times deeply troubled, vulnerable and seeks help; all these areas are associated with Pisces and its ruler, Neptune. Certainly, her partner, Ron Cooke, shared her spiritual and esoteric interests, unlike Casimiro.

The Moon in sensitive Pisces suggests that Valiente needed love and understanding for herself; she was very gentle, sensitive and easily hurt. It reveals her ability to tune in psychically to others' feelings and emotions, which would have made her a natural healer. However, this placement also suggests she was almost too receptive to the vibrations of others (as discussed previously, in the unaspected Moon).

Her friends, Lois and Wilfred Bourne noted how she could, "… discern quite quickly the difference between truth and fiction, but no one in genuine trouble or misfortune was turned away" (Valiente, 2000, 25). This shows that, although kind, she was no pushover, her Saturnian nature helping to ground her and maintain a realistic approach to life.

In love, Valiente's compassion could have been aroused instinctively with the Moon in Pisces. We have seen that Casimiro needed Valiente's care and nurturing after his traumatic wartime experiences. The Moon in the seventh house can also indicate that Valiente needed such maternal qualities in her partnerships to feel emotionally secure. An emotionally fulfilling partnership would have been important to her, since the seventh house associates with marriage and significant relationships (as noted earlier), and the Moon with nurture.

However, whether Casimiro could satisfy her spiritually, especially since he seems to have had no interest or knowledge in esoteric subjects, is open to question. It must surely have created some emptiness and even tensions in their relationship, perhaps even control issues as demonstrated by the aspect of Venus square Saturn. Marian Green (author, conference organiser and editor), who was a close friend of Valiente, remembers that when she used to visit Valiente's flat, to her, Casimiro was, "a rather dark, silent individual always in the background" (letter to Author, 2016).

Valiente was very fortunate that her later partner, Ron Cooke, did share her interests (she once described him as her 'soul mate') and eventually she initiated him to become her working magical partner, using the witch name 'Dusio' (Heselton, 2016, 241 & 293).

In Valiente's natal chart, Saturn, the ruling planet of Capricorn, is in the first house, the area which represents image, physicality, and the way we appear to others. Saturn is the planetary ruler of her Sun, Mercury and Venus signs, all of which are personal planets (*see glossary*). Saturn's sober nature reveals that Valiente may have initially appeared to others as shy or self-contained, reluctant to reveal her inner self. As a child, she possibly felt isolated, both physically and spiritually, and also experienced loneliness, since these are all areas are associated with Saturn.

The aforementioned aspect of Venus square Saturn also suggests not only fear of rejection but also restricted affection. The strong Capricorn/Saturn energy in the fourth house suggests that in her domestic and family-life she may well have experienced the challenging Saturnian themes, such as discipline, fear, guilt, frustration and sombreness.

The tenth house is also associated with the father and authority figures (including society as a whole). Given that Pluto is resident in this area of her natal chart, it suggests her father may have been domineering, obsessive and intense, driven by  an overwhelming desire for control and power – both qualities associated with Pluto.

Valiente revealed that her father had hit her, and she retaliated by hitting him back; apparently it was this event that led her to leaving home (Heselton, 2016, 36). One wonders if being subjected to a 'clip around the ear' was a frequent occurrence from her father and exactly how severe his discipline had been. She once said that she did not experience any love as a child and the convent school she attended was wretched, as she was bullied emotionally and physically there, especially about her appearance (ibid, 16 & 34). She attended for two years but by the time she was fifteen she could tolerate it no longer and left (which in those days was legal.)

Valiente also remarked how her "… lack of academic distinctions had long been a subject of reproof" (Valiente, 2007, 41). Her childhood and youth were clearly a challenging time for her.

Saturn in the first house (the area which also denotes appearance and impression) indicates that Valiente may have been tall. The occultist, Bill Gray, claimed she was just over six feet (ibid, *272*) and slim, and photographs of Valiente seem to bear this out.

Jupiter is also in the first house and suggests that eventually Valiente embraced the world with confidence, exuberance and optimism. Such qualities would have helped her overcome challenges and tests that Saturn brought in its wake, helping her even from a relatively young age to see the broader picture of life. Certainly, in the Pagan community later on in her life, she appeared an approachable and confident woman, and this can be seen, for example, by her appearances in broadcasts and public speaking.

Valiente's natal chart reveals three planets in the sign of Capricorn: Sun, Mercury, and Venus as mentioned above. Capricornus is one of the constellations in the zodiac and in Latin the name means 'horned goat', which is befitting for some of the magical and ritual work that Valiente practiced. In her book, *Where Witchcraft Lives* (Valiente, 2010, 7), there is a chapter about 'The Horned God in Sussex,' which is very pertinent to the meaning of Capricornus and Valiente's own magical interests.

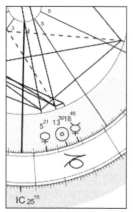

Capricorn is, as we have already seen, an earth sign concerned with the material world, realism and security, and is ruled by Saturn. Areas influenced by Saturn include endurance, longevity, structure and stability, along with maturity and wisdom. Jonathan Tapsell, her first biographer, once said of her, "... perseverance was her chief characteristic" (YouTube, Tapsell). It may have been her innate perseverance that made her stay with Casimiro, even once she realised she was unhappy. Capricorn's less helpful associations are delay, guilt and frustration, as discussed above.

This theme is further emphasised by the energy created by the aspect Sun quincunx Neptune. Amongst other things, it can suggest that Valiente was susceptible to addiction, perhaps her dependence being her need to act as saviour an area associated with Neptune with her first two husbands and eventually as a carer to her last partner, Ron Cooke.

It was therefore very important that Valiente surrounded herself with healthy and positive energy, so as not to be distracted by her immense compassion and devotion to others. This she may have found by her involvement with magical and spiritual groups. We see Neptune positioned in the eleventh house – the area that governs kindred spirits, friends and various groups. Escapism is also associated with Neptune, and as the Sun is in the area of home, perhaps she needed magical outlets to escape from any tensions of her domestic life, which may have seemed like a balancing act at times. Other qualities associated with Neptune in the eleventh house will be discussed further on.

Mercury in Capricorn reveals that Valiente had an organised and practical mindset. The sign's nature is to conserve and retain, suggesting she had a good memory, a faculty associated with Mercury. Valiente studied the occult for over 30 years, which certainly reveals her concentration, and persistence in her studies.

The Sun conjunct Mercury suggests Valiente gained satisfaction from sharing knowledge with others and was keen to learn new things; this aspect is favourable for all forms of communication and education. Mercury corresponds with learning, reading, speaking and writing; the aspect can also indicate an aptitude for languages. Clearly, her appalling experience at her convent school did not deter her enjoyment and natural aptitude for learning and reading as an adult.

Mercury in the fourth house can also denote a sense of the academic in the family home and it is interesting that Valiente's father was nicknamed The Professor; indeed, her cousin Hazel Hall once said of him "... he was so clever, he was weird" (Heselton, 2016, 29). Her father may have had a strong presence in the family home when she was a child, and as Capricorn is sometimes associated with fathers, Valiente's family home may have been a very patriarchal household (especially with the energy of the three planets in Capricorn in the area of the home).

We also know from archives and photographs that, in Valiente's homes (when she was an adult), there were vast number of books, journals and magazines, which illustrates her love of learning and reading and of course she wrote extensively when she was at home which is all keeping with Mercury in the fourth house. During her late twenties she started to regularly contribute letters to the Spiritualist newspaper *Psychic News*, which were published on the Letters' page (*Psychic News* archives, various dates). Her letters continued certainly through the mid nineteen sixties and probably even later than that (*Psychic News* have not, at the time of writing this chapter, digitised their archives for the 1970s and beyond, so it is presently impossible to research beyond 1966).

Valiente may have expanded her knowledge of languages as she researched not only the old religion but also other overseas cultures, religions, and philosophies. Her fascination with these can be seen in pages she transcribed in Italian and Latin in her own, private magical books (private correspondence from Ashley Mortimer). She may also have gained some knowledge of the Greek, Polish and Spanish language through relationships with her boyfriend and husbands who were from the aforementioned countries.

In writing rituals, poetry and becoming an author, the aspect of Sun conjunct Mercury would have helped her in assimilating, processing, and communicating (i.e. sharing information). The conjunct aspect can also provide an ability to educate and inspire other people. This she clearly did, through her books, poetry and also her appearances on radio and television where she spoke on folklore and witchcraft. During her television appearances she often displayed items from her personal collection of witchcraft-related articles. These would have helped illustrate her talk more vividly, which in turn helped her viewers learn and understand more about witchcraft.

Since Valiente lived in a pre-internet era, she had to use libraries (associated with Saturn) in order to do her research. It was once claimed she must have spent over ten years in Bournemouth Library and during her lifetime amassed enough books to rightly describe them as a library (these are now owned by The Doreen Valiente Foundation). Author, Marian Green, who first became acquainted with Valiente in the 1960s, described Valiente's home as "… stuffed with wonderful old books and objects, carvings and ornaments made of antlers and horns" (Tapsell, 2013, 77).

Valiente was inspired by the nature of Mercury  and his rule over medicine, communication, wisdom and magic. She once wrote a poem, *Hymn to Hermes* (the Greek counterpart of Mercury), and it is included in her book of poetry and verse, *Charge of the Goddess* (Valiente, 2000, 16). Mercury is significant astrologically, as it is the ruler of Valiente's natal chart – being the ruling planet of the Virgo ascendant as well as the Gemini midheaven (MC).

In ruling the Virgo ascendant Mercury reveals that Valiente was intelligent, methodical and skilful. Mercury also rules the Gemini MC, revealing that in her career Valiente would have been drawn to areas where she could excel at speaking and writing and where she could learn and communicate her ideas to others – all true Mercurial qualities. Also associated with Mercury and Gemini are correspondence, interpretation, languages and travel along with adaptability and dexterity. The importance of Mercury is further punctuated, as it is the ruling planet of the day on which she was born, Wednesday.

In Valiente's natal chart, Mercury is square Jupiter, indicating she was a broad-minded and a philosophical thinker with an imaginative and rich mind. The energy of this aspect also shows she could be enthusiastic and inspiring, able to look optimistically at life from a religious, spiritual, philosophical and political point of view. She probably always felt the need to broaden her knowledge, since Jupiter governs expansion and Mercury knowledge. Jupiter also associates with seeking and questing, which manifested in her insatiable drive for knowledge. Her interests in philosophy, religion, politics and publishing are all very much in keeping with the Jupiter associations.

She was asked in the late 1990s if she thought there was a future for Paganism in politics. She replied that she thought there was, especially in the areas of ecology and feminism (Jordan, 1998, 171). Since then, people have become further aware of issues such as air and water pollution, energy efficiency and climate change. She pointed out that if we were not more responsible, there would be no more woodlands for the Green Man to be green in (ibid).

Nowadays, over two decades after Valiente made these comments; many developments and much progress have been made in these areas. For example, at the time of writing, there is a Green Party with one MP and, notably, that one MP represents Brighton, where Valiente lived in her later years. There are now also many activist groups and individuals who campaign on climate change and environmental issues. The Pagan Federation organisation (founded in 1971) campaigns and liaises with local authorities on issues that may affect Pagans, such as education. Also, there are more female MPs and since Doreen Valiente's time, there have been two female Prime Ministers, as well as many female chief executives and directors, and there has been *some* improvement in equal pay.

At the time of writing this, the United Kingdom has made the monumental decision to leave the European Union, so clearly a lot has changed as one would expect, since Valiente spoke about how Paganism could be relevant to politics in the 1990s. In 1978, the *Daily Express* reported that Valiente (and other witches) were lobbying their MPs to protect them from discrimination at work (*Daily Express*, 1978, 24). This shows her awareness that being a witch could subject one to intolerance and prejudice, and how she was actively seeking to give Pagans and witches the equality they were entitled to.

In 1973, however, Valiente made the surprising decision to join the far-right political party, the National Front. This organisation was certainly growing in popularity during the early 1970s but given its homophobic views (which we know Valiente strongly disagreed with) and its anti-white immigration stance, it is hard to see why she was drawn to it. Possibly it was because its literature presented it as patriotic and British, and there is certainly some evidence that the National Front deliberately targeted the south coast where Valiente lived (Fielding, 1981, 41)

Valiente remained a member of the National Front for some eighteen months but seems to have become quickly disillusioned. This could have been in part due to the violence at its marches and protests, which was considered serious enough for the National Front to set up 'Honour Guards' by 1974. This was therefore taking place during Valiente's membership. Members of these Honour Guards often carried iron bars and bicycle chains (Walker, 1977, 171).

However, the National Front was not the only political party that Valiente became involved with, for she also joined the fascist organisation, the Northern League (Heselton, 2016, 158). She noted that, "Most, if not all, of the Fascist and Neo-Nazi groups in England have some association with the League" (ibid).

Her letter to Edward Budden (whom she addressed as Ted) of the National Front party in 1974 stated that she would not be renewing her membership because, "I cannot conscientiously support a policy or an attitude which I believe to be profoundly wrong" (Heselton, 2016, 160). It seems she must have been very misled initially, for she must surely have had some firsthand experience of racism when she was married to her two husbands; a Greek and a Spaniard.

However, Valiente also wrote that she hoped that the friendships she had made with its members, including Mr Budden, would not lapse (ibid, 161), showing how she principally disagreed with the party's politics but nonetheless enjoyed the company of some of its members – mixing friends and politics are not always productive! (Budden was a known Neo-Nazi who wrote regularly for *Searchlight* and campaigned as an MP for Hove in 1974).

Apparently, Valiente was influenced by the writing of *Earth Mysteries* author, John Michell, and in particular his book, *The View over Atlantis*, in the early 1970s. Michell was of the opinion that there were ley-lines across the British landscape which channelled earth energies and Valiente set about searching for ley-lines in Brighton (https://en.wikipedia.org/wiki/Doreen_Valiente).

Paul Screeton was a friend of John Michell and described him as having "a charismatic personality and imposing presence," observing that, "he was impatient with those who did not share his Traditionalist beliefs and values" (https://en.wikipedia.org/wiki/John_Michell_(writer)). Michell certainly had affinities with the far right and self-published papers called, *Radical Traditionalist Papers*, in the 1970s and 1980s. It is therefore entirely possible, given his personality and politics, that he exercised some influence over Valiente, perhaps subconsciously.

Many of the National Front's causes (e.g. their opposition to sex education, women's liberation, and the repeal of the laws against homosexuals) were very much against Valiente's beliefs. It has been suggested that she remained with the party for as long as she did because she wanted to investigate and research further before fully making her mind up (Heselton, 2016, 158), and even that she had, "wanted the National Front to be the political wing of the Old Religion" (ibid, 162). However, without further evidence to back this up, it seems a very weak claim, as does Heselton's belief that she was spying on these groups and reporting back to British Intelligence. Other things must have been happening in her life at this time, as we see in her astrology.

At different points during 1973 and 1974, Valiente was experiencing some significant Pluto transits, which were as follows:

- Transiting Pluto square natal Venus
- Transiting Pluto square natal Pluto
- Transiting Pluto conjunct natal Saturn

Transiting Pluto was positioned at the first house (the area governing the *persona* and self). Another important transit during this time was transiting Neptune sextile the natal Saturn. The transiting Neptune was positioned at the third house – the area which is associated with communication, mentality, as well as local community and travel. This shows how areas of the self and communications were prevalent during this period between 1973–74.

What is exceptionally pertinent to Valiente's astrology was that transiting Neptune sextile the natal Saturn was happening exactly (on 20th October, 1974) when transiting Pluto was conjunct natal Saturn. This is very symbolic, as both Pluto and Saturn are associated with endings and beginnings. On or near this date, Edward Budden (the local organiser in Brighton) would have received her letter of resignation from the National Front, dated 12th October, 1974.

The contact between Neptune and Saturn in that transit shows a balancing act between idealism and reality, the former associated with Neptune and the latter with Saturn. Clearly Valiente had by then understood that the National Front Party was not the group she had thought they were, and had decided to terminate her association with them. It was one thing to be a patriot, quite another to be a fascist.

The intense energy of transiting Pluto positioned at the first house shows that Valiente was undertaking a period of transformation, needing to purge anything and anyone that was unnecessary in her life – showing both self-empowerment and perhaps increased perception. Pluto is also associated with compulsion and intensity, and so she would not be interested in areas of life on a superficial level – she needed meaning and truth.

Pluto's energy would have given Valiente increased focus and strength and it is interesting that during the 1970s, her output of writing, especially books and magazine articles, increased. These had been thoroughly investigated and researched over a long period of time (an association with Saturn). Transiting Pluto square Venus would have forced her to let go of the past and move on to a deeper, more profound connection.

This she eventually did, finding her soul-mate; Ron Cooke. His given name was William George but he was known commonly as 'Ron' and had previously been married to Elsie Louise Cooke, who had died in 1975. The 1939 Register of England & Wales shows that at the outbreak of World War II, 'Ron' was a 'heavy-labourer', aged 27, and then lived at 5 Baxter Street, in Brighton, Sussex.

The square aspect generates challenges and even 'big ideas', so that with her wealth of knowledge and information, Valiente would have enthusiastically used books, etc, in her investigative and research work. She was also enthusiastic in sharing her knowledge with others. One example of this can be seen where she apparently provided the ultra-right wing Northern League with information about the allegedly ancient text, the *Oera Linda Book*, which is about the revival of Paganism in Iceland and the Viking ceremony in Scotland, on one of the Shetland Islands (Heselton, 2016, 158). The book is widely accepted as a nineteenth century forgery. However, this again raises questions about her political affiliations.

Moving away from her political life and returning to the subject of Mercury, we see how jesting, pranks and wit are also associated with this planet and, combined with excessive Jupiter, she almost certainly possessed a great sense of humour. However, the Mercury in Capricorn placement would have made her serious-minded about those matters that inspired her.

The contact between Mercury and Jupiter is a hard aspect (*see glossary*), which has potential to create difficulties and tensions. Her humour, for example, may have been too subtle for some people to appreciate. Mercury in Capricorn suggests that her humour was probably dry, since 'dryness' is associated with both Capricorn and Saturn, and also with Mercury's sense of humour. John Belham-Payne, who knew Valiente very well in her later years, once described her as having "… a very wicked and dry sense of humour, she was great company and funny to be around" (Heselton, 2016, 316).

Another association of Mercury is short distance travel, while Jupiter is associated with adventure and exploration. This complex planetary contact almost certainly generated restlessness in her life. Both as a child and as an adult, Valiente moved home numerous times, living in Bournemouth, Brighton, London, the West Country, Hampshire, Buckinghamshire and Surrey, as well as South Wales. Valiente's nomadic spirit was influenced by the restless nature of Mercury in the fourth house, the area which rules the home and family.

TRAINS, BOATS AND PLANES

Valiente travelled in order to practice and teach witchcraft and also to take part in rituals. These are areas connected with Jupiter (as is teaching). Since she did not drive, as a younger woman she had to use public transport, and interestingly, buses, coaches and trains are all associated with Mercury. However, later, when she was in a relationship with Cooke, he had a car and they were able to drive together to places such as Glastonbury in Somerset (Heselton, 2016, 288).

Jupiter is in the sign of Libra and associates with overseas and travel, but Valiente never seems to have left the UK mainland, apart from a possible visit to see Gerald Gardner on the Isle of Man (Heselton, 2016, 290). Such resistance to travelling overseas can loosely be seen in the symbolism of the hard aspect of the square angle created between Mercury and Jupiter, since Mercury associates with flying and travelling and Jupiter with abroad and overseas.

Open spaces (another association of Jupiter) would have appealed to Valiente, along with being at one with the elements. She would have appreciated the natural magic found in the earth, sun, hills, mountains, lakes, moon and even pebbles, wind and trees. In particular, Capricorn and Saturn are associated with land, rocks and stones, which would explain her natural affinity and appreciation for the land. No wonder she self-identified as a 'country witch'.

Valiente visited places such as Glastonbury, Stonehenge, the Chanctonbury Ring in Sussex and the Rollright Stones in the Cotswolds, all of which would have inspired her sense of adventure, exploration, learning and magic. Her lyrical poem, *Night in the New Forest*, is ample proof of how intimately she responded to Nature's majesty (Valiente, 1989, 219).

MUTUAL RECEPTION

Venus in Capricorn reveals that Valiente offered loyalty, trustworthiness and lifetime commitment in her relationships. She took them seriously and it was important to her to be respected in return (as discussed previously). People would have warmed to her pragmatic, business-like, no-nonsense approach to life. Her established relationship with her publisher, Robert Hale, for example, lasted approximately seventeen years.

Venus corresponds with both money and relationships and she not only was prudent with money but also always earned her own income. For example, when she realised that she could not go to art school because her parents would not support her, she secured employment in a factory in order to pay for typing classes at night school (which she eventually did). She worked most of her adult life in a variety of jobs.

Venus and Saturn are in mutual reception to each other (*see glossary*) – Capricorn's ruler Saturn is in Libra and Venus (the ruler of Libra) is in the sign of Capricorn. Saturn is in exaltation (*see glossary*) in the sign of Libra, which corresponds with marriage, partnerships and relationships. This placement suggests that Valiente was charming, well mannered, believed in fair treatment for all and – when in a position of authority – was conscientious and responsible. This is because the earlier qualities mentioned here are associated with Libra and its ruling planet, Venus, while the latter qualities are associated with Capricorn and its ruler, Saturn. This would have been helpful to Valiente, for example, in her position of High Priestess in a coven and as Patron for the Centre for Pagan Studies.

Libra also associates with co-operation, co-workers and collaborations. As we already know, Valiente worked in partnership with a number of occultists and Wiccans, including Robert Cochrane, Gerald Gardner, Ned Grove, Evan John Jones, and John Belham-Payne.

Valiente at times may have felt an inner loneliness during her life, since this is a common feeling amongst Capricorns and with three planets in Capricorn, these feelings were probably heightened. Possibly, she would have kept this to herself because of her underlying feelings of self-containment and self-sufficiency. She outlived all her partners and after Casimiro's death began to "... withdraw into a form of seclusion" (Tapsell, 2013, 72).

Capricorn's ruler, Saturn, often demands that we learn the hard way (as discussed previously), and can be seen with the contact between Mercury and Saturn, since Mercury associates with knowledge and Saturn with challenges. Experience of bereavement came fairly early in Valiente's life, which would have influenced her philosophy about the fragility of life. For example, the nineteen year-old Valiente must have desperately clung to the hope that her first husband had survived the wartime sinking of his ship (http://www.uboat.net/allies/merchants/993.html).

The square aspect created between Venus and Saturn (as discussed earlier) also reveals that action, effort and motivation were present in situations that generated character-building in Valiente's life. Venus and Saturn created themes such as duty before pleasure, loneliness and love later in life. They also suggest relationships with mature, older and experienced partners. As previously mentioned, Valiente had significant partnerships with several people older than herself. Capricorns are often said to be born middle-aged since they appear to have experience and maturity at an early age – this may be partly why she was drawn to those older than herself. Venus opposing Pluto indicates not only profound relationships but also emotional pain in committed relationships, as Venus associates with relating and Pluto brings intensity to a relationship.

The chart suggests Valiente needed a certain amount of freedom in her significant relationships, as indicated by the aspect created by Venus sextile Uranus, and it also suggests she liked an element of the 'unexpected' in her relationships and did not enjoy predictability or routine, preferring there should be room for autonomy, freedom and independence.

The square and opposition aspects in her natal chart generate a T-Square (*see glossary*), which is released through Chiron. The T-Square (*see glossary*) is formed by the Venus and Pluto opposition square Saturn, as well as the Sun and Pluto opposition, which is also square Saturn. Opposing Saturn is Chiron, and this is the focal point in the T-Square. This is particularly significant as, at the end of her life, Valiente would have become the 'wounded healer' of Chiron, since transiting Chiron is in the natal sign of Scorpio. This denotes healing not only through rebirth and transformation but also a physical and metaphorical death, as all are areas connected with Scorpio and its ruling planet, Pluto.

The T-Square in a chart has been described by astrologer and writer, Frank Clifford, as "... like pressure cookers. Underneath, there's a huge amount of tension needing to be released... . T-Squares are usually the source of much energy and edginess and they demand resolution, action and discharge" (Clifford, 2012, 80).

Saturn creates a square aspect with Pluto in her natal chart, suggesting that Valiente experienced lessons of survival and perhaps feared being controlled by those in positions of authority. This may be a product of her childhood, of feeling restricted by environmental and social constraints. For example, she once said, "I thoroughly hated school," when talking about her primary school (Harrington, 1995, 18–22). Her willingness to fight back against injustice and authority, even from quite an early age, is indicative of the Saturn in Libra and Saturn square Pluto aspect.

Valiente was not completely opposed to authority, however, only to its abuse. Yet she seemed to shy away from her own authority and status and apparently disliked the title, *Mother of Modern Witchcraft*, partly because she never wanted children (ibid, 315). She was never someone who 'followed the crowd,' and was a vegetarian long before it really became fashionable (ibid). Nonetheless, she was a natural when it came to effectively carrying authority and responsibility.

She also recoiled at once being described by the witchcraft community as Queen of the Witches, retorting, "The only Queen I know is Her Majesty in Buckingham Palace" (Tapsell, 2014, 100). This suggests she felt uncomfortable with praise and compliments, which is in keeping with some of her natal astrological data – the humble and modest Virgo ascendant, as well as Mercury in Capricorn, which is associated with a cynical and dry sense of humour.

Jean Williams, Wiccan and High Priestess in Gardner's coven in the mid 1970s, recalls an occasion when she was part of a coven participating in a seasonal celebration and where Valiente was leading the ritual in her position as the High Priestess. Williams remarked that, "… nothing had prepared me for the impact of her presence…. . I have never before, or since, witnessed such natural authority" (Valiente, 2000, 77) showing how, despite her modesty and humility, Valiente was much respected by her colleagues.

Saturn is quincunx (*see glossary*) with Uranus in Valiente's natal chart. This suggests that while she could bring discipline and responsibility to her own work, she may have found her co-workers' lack thereof frustrating and irritating. We see this in her partnership with Gerald Gardner, when she wanted to adapt his *Book of Shadows* and make it a serious and useful piece of work for the Craft and Wicca. Valiente intended to ensure that it was no longer fragmented and that it became truly original, so that Gardner couldn't be accused of plagiarising Crowley's work.

Valiente was very practical and level-headed about the claimed antiquity of the Craft, stating "… All sorts of things are being called traditional today that are no older than the works of Gerald Gardner and Margaret Murray" (Valiente, 2007, 81). Nevertheless, she could still invoke the "Ancient Ones of Night" (Valiente, 2000, 12), since that reflected only her own personal gnosis of deity and power.

The Saturn and Uranus quincunx also indicates that her duties and responsibilities could have restricted her personal freedom, causing frustration, which may have affected her nervous system, resulting in ill health and tension. She suffered from both diabetes (which may either have caused or been symptomatic of the pancreatic cancer that finally killed her) and arthritis, which became very debilitating during her later years.

The quincunx in Valiente's chart could generate feelings of distress and tension, which can manifest in one's health. Towards the end of her life, this would have been aggravated by her grief at the death of her partner, Ron Cooke. She withdrew from public life when his health deteriorated and then devoted her time to care for him until he died (https://wrldrels.org/2018/08/03/doreen-valiente/). Only afterwards did she return to the public eye.

The quincunx created between Saturn and Uranus suggests friction between the polarised energies of restriction and freedom, which relate to these planets respectively. This aspect also indicates a situation where adjustment is required, relating to an area in one's life which has been buried, concealed or disregarded. This is illustrated by the presence of Uranus in the sixth house, which is the area of work and health, while Saturn is in the first house of image.

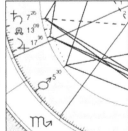

This aspect shows Valiente's need to be conscientious and structured whilst at work, but the nature of her work could sometimes make her appear aloof, idealistic, independent and unsettled, since these are all associations of Uranus. The Virgo ascendant indicates that Valiente applied skills of analysis, detail and efficiency in her work, since these are all areas associated with Virgo and its ruler, Mercury.

Mars is in Scorpio in the second house (*see box on previous page*), the area governing earnings, income, possessions and values; it is also the ruler of the eighth house in Valiente's chart. Traditionally (*see glossary*), Mars rules the eighth house, the area which governs death, inheritance, mysteries, the occult, shared resources and sex. Mars in Scorpio reveals that Valiente had an intense emotional life with a passionate nature, which can be seen through some of her relationships.

It could also be said she possessed a burning desire and passion for both the occult and sex, since these are both areas associated with Mars and Pluto. She once said that, "Sex is an enormously magical thing," showing her understanding of sex as a significant magical force (YouTube: Carlyon). The sextile aspect created between Venus and Mars, which is also partile (*see glossary*), echoes the message about Valiente's passionate nature, showing her desire for a passionate and loving relationship and that she had a lively expression of feeling.

Mars is trine Pluto and addresses themes such as fighting for survival and personal transformations. As the trine is a soft aspect (*see glossary*), this indicates Valiente had a tremendous inner strength that enabled her to overcome any challenges (an association of Mars) or unpleasantly intense situations (an association of Pluto).

For example, Valiente underwent a near death experience when she was 36; her doctor had diagnosed that she had peritonitis and informed her then husband that she had a 50/50 chance of survival (Jordan, 1998, 175). Despite being gravely ill, she could recall how she experienced walking in the Summerlands (*see glossary*) (Heselton, 2016, 306), as well as talking about being in a winter wood and seeing starlight and a beautiful blue light (Jordan, 1998, 175).

Valiente also had highly developed intuition and foresight, which perhaps helped her to survive the Blitz, by listening to her hunches and acting on her sixth sense. This is another example of the perceptive energy of the Mars and Pluto contact in extremely challenging circumstances, such as survival.

The position of Mars in Scorpio also indicates Valiente's clairvoyant and psychic abilities, which she applied in her work and writing. In her book, *The Rebirth of Witchcraft*, she describes receiving spirit communication between 1964 and 1966 from a traditional witch and farmer who identified himself as John Brakespeare (interestingly, farms and farming are also associated with Capricorn and Saturn). In one of his final communications, he gave Valiente his opinions about the Old Religion of his time, comparing it to the way it was in the 1960s. He said, "The Craft today is too full of book-learning. You will learn more from the book of Nature than any other" (Valiente, 2007, 111).

We see the cautious and practical Capricornian nature of Valiente when she writes, "Just how to evaluate these communications I do not know.... . Readers must decide for themselves whether the messages are indeed what they purport to be or whether they are simply the product of my subconscious mind" (ibid, 99). This statement shows her realistic and uncomplicated nature.

We see an example of Valiente's clairvoyant abilities when she had a significant precognitive dream during the war, in early June, 1944 (conflict and war are also associated with Mars). At the time, she was still living in London. She dreamt that an aunt who lived on the south coast frantically warned her to get out of London as the

Germans were "… going to start to shell us from the coast on the thirteenth." (Heselton, 2016, 56).

A few days later, when Valiente went into work, her colleagues were all excitedly talking about a small German plane that had crashed in London; this would have been the first V1 rocket, popularly nicknamed doodlebugs or buzz-bombs. Perhaps unsurprisingly (at least to Valiente), the date was 13th June, the date which was magically significant to her and which she felt proved that her dream *had* been clairvoyant. After that, she accepted that her dreams were a guiding force in her life, holding both literal and metaphorical symbolism. The Valiente's later moved out of London to live in Bournemouth on the south coast of England.

Scorpio's ruler Pluto indicates that Valiente did indeed possess the gift of second sight, and was intuitive and perceptive. It also shows that, with Mars in Scorpio, she was able to keep the confidence and secrets of others. The oath-bound nature of Wicca is a good example of this, and probably appealed to her. It has been suggested that, at one point in her life, Valiente had an interest in the practice of being a private detective and considered becoming a member of the Association of British Detectives, but it never came to fruition (Heselton, 2016, 159).

Drive and initiation are associated with Mars and so, in the sign of Scorpio, it shows that her ambitions and passions were focussed on esoteric subjects, mysteries, the occult, investigation and research; themes of confidentiality, privacy and secrecy are also associated with Scorpio and its ruler, Pluto. For example, she concealed her membership of Gardner's coven from her family by pretending instead that she had become a Druid (which for some reason was deemed a little more respectable!) (Hutton, 2008, 258).

Mars in Scorpio shows that Valiente was not afraid to uncover matters that might be considered 'taboo', such as witchcraft. When she first started researching and collecting articles on this and other esoteric subjects, the Witchcraft Act of 1735 was only just being repealed. In fact, the last person to be charged and imprisoned under that Act was Helen Duncan (the subject of Chapter Six), which happened as late as 1944.

In relation to possessions in the second house, Valiente owned items connected with arcane knowledge and the occult, which all relate to Pluto. Other areas associated with Mars include iron, knives and steel, which are pertinent to her collection of athames, for example. Mars in the second house

Doreen Valiente. Photo by permission of PA Photos Ltd.

is a good position for those who are self-employed, since the Martian energy brings assertiveness, competitiveness and energy in the area that governs earnings and income. These influences would have been of immense help to Valiente's practical and resourceful nature and would have helped her success in business, such as with her writing.

In the natural zodiac (*see glossary*), the sixth house relates to diet, health and work. In Valiente's natal chart, we find Uranus in this house, suggesting she could happily work independently, since she needed freedom and space (which are associated with Uranus, as previously discussed) in her working environment. The unconventional and unorthodox would have appealed to her where work was concerned and, coupled with the Mars in the second house placement; this strongly suggests she found freelance work or self-employment particularly congenial.

Valiente had, like many of her generation, worked in uncongenial jobs such as in a cafe, shop, factory and office, the latter she disliked intensely. Unexpected changes are also denoted in her working life, as the nature of Uranus can also be inconsistent and erratic.

 In relation to the association of health and the sixth house, this suggests that she had an unusual or unconventional attitude towards health, perhaps due to her knowledge of herbs, which she may have used to promote her own health and treat ailments and illnesses. This shows Uranus' qualities of determination and individualism. As an adult, she was vegetarian, which at that time was still considered relatively unusual.

Uranus' nature is free-thinking, innovative and radical – indicating a progressive and reforming attitude towards Paganism and witchcraft in Valiente's work. This theme is echoed by the mutual reception (*see glossary*) of house and sign by Neptune in the eleventh house and Uranus in Pisces – so it is clearly a significant energy in her chart. Pisces and its ruler, Neptune, bestow the gifts of art, poetry and witchcraft; whilst Uranus and the eleventh house are associated with clubs, groups, kindred spirits and societies.

On a personal level, Uranus in Pisces suggests that Valiente was imaginative and enjoyed using her creative, artistic and imaginative talents, which is a helpful placement for her inspirational writing. Uranus areas include groups, organisations and societies (as mentioned above); whilst Pisces corresponds (among other things) with magic and poetry. Valiente was involved significantly in The Pagan Federation, The Pagan Front and The Centre for Pagan Studies. She was in her seventies when she became the Patron for The Centre for Pagan Studies, which was founded in 1995 and, as discussed earlier, she was involved with some political groups for a short period.

Along with Eleanor Bone and Patricia Crowther, Valiente campaigned and led the lobby against what they feared *might* have become a proposed ban on witchcraft in the United Kingdom. This had arisen in part from the activities of Alex Sanders (subject of Chapter thirteen), who courted the media and enjoyed the publicity stunts and showmanship of his form of 'witchcraft'. This caused controversy and unease, especially among the tabloid press.

In April, 1970, for example, the MP Gwilym Roberts asked two brief questions in the House of Commons, stating that he felt witchcraft (which he described as 'medieval nonsense') should be banned because of the attendant risks of drugs and blackmail (HC Debate, 16 April, 1970, Vol. 799, c1555).

Valiente was incensed by Sanders' lack of discretion and what she viewed as his attention-seeking behaviour, foreseeing the difficulties it might cause. She asked to see the MP, and met him and his wife at the House of Commons, just thirteen days later. They spoke at length about the Old Religion and "… as a result of it, Mr Roberts did not proceed with any further requests for legislation against witches" (Valiente, 2007, 79–80).

However, it is unclear just how serious Gwilym Roberts had been about introducing legislation. He seems to have had no particular interest in the subject throughout his career and asked no further questions about witchcraft. Also, Merlyn Rees, the Home Secretary at the time, made it clear that there was existing legislation to deal with any problems arising from bad practices amongst witches.

Valiente had apparently been impressed by the work of the (then) National Council for Civil Liberties (NCCL) (Heselton, 2016, 146), which is now known as 'Liberty'. In 1968, and under the leadership of Tony Smythe, the organisation launched a major campaign on the rights of privacy, producing a pamphlet, *Privacy Under Attack*, written by Donald Madgwick, which was a study of privacy and produced as a contribution to 'Human Rights Year' (Madgwick, 1968, 2).

In Stockholm, in 1967, a conference was held on the right to privacy, which was organised by the International Commission of Jurists. Fundamentally, they urged "that the right to privacy should be recognised as a fundamental right of mankind, but subject to certain limitations in the public interest" (ibid).

Their definition of 'rights to privacy' included practical steps, such as prohibiting "recording, photography or filming," "importuning by the press or by agents of other mass media" and "public disclosure of private facts" (ibid, 3).

The United Nations declared 1968 as being Human Rights Year, which may have prompted the increase in the NCCL's membership. Also, in the same year, the NCCL invited people to report cases of privacy invasion to them (ibid, 40). The organisation "inevitably dealt with minorities and their (not always popular) interests" (Dyson, 1994, 44).

The NCCL embraced these recommendations, and as part of their campaign 'Right to Privacy,' provided evidence to the Home Office's Select Committee on Privacy, which was set-up in 1970 and was finally reported in 1972 (ibid). The verification is now archived at the National Archives in Kew, Surrey (HO264: Committee on Privacy: Evidence & Papers).

Apparently, Valiente "urged witches who had been exposed in press articles to give evidence to the Committee" (Heselton, 2016, 148). Whether any of them followed her advice and wrote to them is unknown since, at the time of writing, due to restrictions caused by the global COVID-19 pandemic, archives services have been forced to close.

Mars is trine Uranus in Valiente's natal chart, indicating that, once she perceived a threat, she acted decisively, letting nothing stand in her way. At times she could be fiercely determined and forceful, such are the qualities associated with the two planets; it was almost as though she had a latent impulse ready to question and rebel. As previously discussed, Mars is also trine Pluto in Valiente's chart, suggesting she understood the concept that out of power came strength and out of strength came power. Her drive for assertion could therefore be used for the greater good in society where others could benefit from her intense yet hidden power.

Pluto in the tenth house, represents not only power in society but also hidden depths, while Mars is assertive and when placed in the second house empowers confronting taboo subjects. This is shown in the way she personally confronted someone like Gwilym Roberts (and others throughout her life) in order to achieve the result that she wanted. The reality of the threat is not at stake here; what matters is that Valiente *believed* it was real and went into action accordingly. She certainly achieved what she wanted in terms of going ahead and securing a meeting with Mr Roberts so she could voice her concerns.

Valiente spoke occasionally about her poetry for the membership organisation of the Poetry Society. In her book of poetry, *Charge of the Goddess*, we read that, during a lecture given there, Valiente described how her poem, *Presences*, "… was written one summer evening, at sunset, on a lonely beach: a place in which I knew I was not alone" (Valiente, 2000, 65).

In that same book, Patricia Crowther's review states that, "Poetry reveals the beauty of the soul and these pages certainly substantiate the truth of this opinion," revealing the evocative power of Valiente's poetry (ibid, 63). Elsewhere in the book, her poem, *Haunted Lake,* illustrates her affinity with the cycles and rhythms of the Moon and water. Professor Ronald Hutton described her as having "amazing poetic talent" (Heselton, 2016, 219).

Valiente enjoyed Aleister Crowley's poetry and dedicated a poem to him called, *To Aleister Crowley* (Valiente, 2000, 80). Valiente also shared some astrological correspondences with Crowley, although whether she was aware of this we do not know (see below for parallels between house, Moon sign and aspects only):

Doreen Valiente	**Aleister Crowley**

Sun Mercury and Venus in the fourth House
Moon in Pisces
Pluto in the tenth House
Mars trine Pluto
Saturn square Pluto

Valiente wrote rousing poetry as well as progressive work for her *Book of Shadows*. For example, as previously mentioned, she reformed and renovated Gerald Gardner's *Book of Shadows* when she recognised text and work in it that had originated from Crowley. Her patience and perseverance in completing her adaptation illustrates her ambitious, diligent, persistent and successful Capricorn nature and self-expression.

ZEST IN THE AWAKENING

Valiente was born when Uranus was in Pisces (as previously discussed). As it is an outer (*see glossary*) planet, it shows that a generation of people were experiencing this cycle of Uranus in Pisces, which spanned from 1919 to 1927 and which popularly became known as the 'Roaring Twenties'. The nature of Uranus is enlightening and progressive, whilst Pisces can be disenchanted and disillusioned.

One example during this cycle is that of the youth who had lived through the era of The Great War which ended in 1918 and who became known as 'the lost generation.' The 'lost' was connected with the pain and suffering experienced during the war. Progressive and rebellious Uranus removes any illusions about war that the Piscean energy had introduced, and in doing so is able to give way to a new vision. Valiente was part of the post war generation that rejected the previous jingoistic thinking about war.

Valiente's progressive approach is shown in her writing about a future age and a progressed society. For example, her books, *Witchcraft for Tomorrow* and *The Rebirth of Witchcraft,* show that, although she was a very traditional witch, she was also aware that the Craft was evolving and that, in order to ride with the changes, she would need to embrace a new generation of the Craft. She often mentions the Age of Aquarius, for example, and believed that, "... the great teacher or avatar of the Age of Aquarius is going to be a woman" (Valiente, 1989, 184).

Visionary Jupiter is in Libra (as previously discussed), suggesting that Valiente enjoyed her life, had successful business partnerships and was good at sharing with others. This placement can also indicate philosophical and spiritual partnerships, since they are associates of Jupiter, while the partnerships are akin to Libra. Jupiter also connects with 'foreign' and 'overseas' relationships; Valiente's first husband was a Greek merchant seaman and her second husband was Spanish.

By using the Moon's Nodes (*see glossary*), signs and house placement in a natal chart, we can begin to astrologically look at the symbolism of reincarnation in Valiente's life. The Nodes provide spiritual advice to help one to find inner happiness in this incarnation for one's life journey. Reincarnation was particularly important to Valiente (as it is to many other witches). She once wrote a poem called, *Reincarnation*, and the title of her book, *The Rebirth of Witchcraft* (first published in 1989), points to a new age of witchcraft that was built upon the older version. Here the Old Religion and the traditional organically fuse together so that the traditional became the modern (Valiente, 2007, 218).

In her famous poem, *The Charge of the Goddess*, Valiente wrote using the *persona* of the goddess, showing the concept of life after death, "... I give the knowledge of the spirit eternal." In, *An ABC of Witchcraft*, she dedicated a whole chapter to reincarnation and believed she had met her last life partner, Ron Cooke, in a previous life. She regarded Cooke as "her soul mate" and "the Sun to her Moon" (Tapsell, 2014, 104).

The astrologer, Melanie Reinhart, observes that the placement of Chiron in aspect to Venus (which is square in Valiente's natal chart) can indicate that one regularly meets people whom we feel we have known from a previous life (Reinhart, 1989, 207). Therefore, the presence of Chiron, the Wounded Healer *(see glossary)*, in the seventh house of marriage and significant partnerships seems to support Valiente's belief that she and Cooke had indeed met in a previous life.

As an adult, she may have had difficulties in her marriages and partnerships especially when trying to ensure that her assertive, bold and competitive nature was not thwarted or swamped by her partners. The difficulty arises through the hard aspect of Venus square Chiron, as the square creates challenges and tensions. Saturn is opposing Chiron and the elder and authority figures areas associated with Saturn. As it is in opposition to Chiron, it could be said that it was possibly Valiente's father who most likely created the wound in her early childhood and that the scars of this persisted into her adult life.

The Sun is square Saturn in her chart which indicates that Valiente's relationship with her father may have been challenging (as previously discussed). When she was in her very early teens, her mother had left her husband taking Valiente with her. The reason for leaving could have been due to his mental health frightening his family, especially his habit of taking an axe to bed with him (Heselton, 2016, 28–29).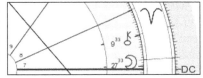

It could be said that the effect that her father had on her as a child may have manifested in her being attracted in adulthood to authority and father-figures in partnerships and relationships, as Saturn carries our shadow, i.e. our fears. It is no wonder that she would later work in partnership with the recognised Father of Witchcraft, Gerald Gardner, from whom she learnt so much. He understood her artistic and sensitive nature as well as respecting her knowledge on the occult and magic, an area which was totally incompatible with her father's religious beliefs. This may show her bravado and fighting spirit, something that often manifests in those for whom Chiron is present in the sign of Aries (Reinhart, 1989, 100) (*see box above*).

The Sun in the fourth house is also creating a square aspect to Chiron and, as previously mentioned, this house is associated with the family and home life. The Sun can also symbolise the father in astrology, another indication that it was her father who created the 'wound' in Valiente's childhood. The Sun square Chiron could be interpreted as Valiente needing a long time to heal from her childhood experience and that, as a child, she may have lacked self-esteem and respect.

The overbearing father is also shown by the aspect of the Sun opposing Pluto in the chart, since power is associated with Pluto and as previously discussed the Sun symbolises the father. It also reveals that Valiente was a magnetic person who had an intense self-awareness and powerful presence, since these are also associates of Pluto.

In Greek mythology, Chiron was the Priest King of Centaurs and his skills included astrology, hunting, medicine, music and warfare. His pupils came to him to learn how to fulfil their highest potential and discover their destiny. It was a sacred teaching that the adept would only learn a divination skill when they were ready to begin their magical quest. Valiente was a skilled tarot reader and owned a collection of rare tarot decks. She was also adept in other forms of divination, such as numerology and scrying.

Before considering the Moon's Nodes in Valiente's natal chart, it is worth considering how these work: The North and South Node represent the traits present in each incarnation. The North Node symbolises our underdeveloped traits, while the South Node symbolises our overdeveloped ones from a previous carnation. The North Node is also known as the Dragon's Head and the South Node the Dragon's Tail. The Moon's North Node in Valiente's chart is in Libra at 13 degrees in the first house, and the South Node is in Aries at 13 degrees in the seventh house.

The placements of her Nodes suggest that Valiente needed to develop a compromising and easy-going approach with other people and learn to be more patient, sensitive and less impulsive. The South Node in Aries holds the residue of a previous life where symbolism suggests Valiente may have felt secure in applying the aforementioned qualities in her hasty and spontaneous nature.

Compromise and co-operation, which are associated with Libra, were significant in Valiente's lifetime. North Node Libra in the first house and South Node Aries in the seventh house, suggests that in Valiente's past incarnation that, pioneering and being first was all-important to Valiente. In being reincarnated and learning from balance, compromise, diplomacy, harmony, mediation, peace and justice were areas where she could find inner happiness and contentment.

The Sun is square the North Node suggesting that Valiente may have sometimes felt thwarted and unable to express herself fully. Certainly, for the first 30 years or so of her life, she would have been unable to have freely expressed her interest in witchcraft and occult matters. During her lifetime she worked with many different people, and shared her exuberance of life with a generosity of spirit and optimism. The Sun square Jupiter suggests that Valiente had tremendous faith about life and herself; she was able to broaden her horizons and had the ability to explore, both mentally and physically.

Being able to see the wider picture and embracing life so fully would have helped her make the most of a bad situation, by adopting an optimistic or philosophical standpoint. This would have stood her in good stead during the dark days when she was waiting for news of her first husband's fate, or when looking after her second husband who had been wounded during the Second World War. Jupiter sextile Neptune shows she would have found freedom in mysticism, which would have enabled her to mentally evade the ordinary and routine of life, enabling her instead to see life in a magical and spiritual way.

The Moon in Pisces placement also reveals her need to withdraw from the world in order to replenish her poetic and sensitive nature. A neighbour of Valiente's, described her in an interview as being, "… very reclusive – she was just there – you knew she was there but you never saw her" (BBC News, Brighton, Sussex), suggesting that seclusion and solitude were sometimes essential to repair her depleted energies and need for privacy. Another neighbour described Valiente as "… very quiet and in the background" (ibid). The background described here is a good example of the Piscean/Neptunian/ twelfth house association of 'behind-the-scenes' activity and secrecy. The seclusion, however, would have been conducive to Valiente's need to channel her magical energies especially in order to write and create poetry and to escape from the mundane in life.

Pisces also alludes to the divine and a higher service, as the Moon symbolises instincts, needs, and feelings. Therefore, it is not surprising that Valiente became absorbed in a world of mysticism, spirituality and worship, all of which were necessary for her comfort and well-being. The Moon in Pisces also dissolves boundaries, which provides escapism for the imagination in areas such as dance, meditation, poetry and music.

Valiente wrote a wealth of exquisite poetry and became known for perhaps the most powerful words in Wicca in, *The Charge of the Goddess*, as well as, *The Witch's Rune*. Dance, gesture, and ritual would have been meaningful to her, for example, in her life as a witch through the celebration of the Esbats and sabbats. One of her poems, *The Gathering for the Esbat*, begins, "Oh Moon, that rid'st the night to wake, Before the dawn is pale" (Valiente, 2000, 12). Moon in Pisces can also add an aura of ambiguity, secrecy and anonymity.

Another example of secrecy at work in Valiente's life and work occurs in her book, *The Rebirth of Witchcraft*, which is described by some as semi-autobiographical. She certainly describes witchcraft, including her studies about the occult and how she met and worked with influential occult figures such as Gerald Gardner. However, there is hardly any autobiographical information about her domestic and personal life in the book and so in this sense it could be said Valiente remained an enigma, which demonstrates the evasiveness of the Moon in Pisces. Her enigmatic self had not gone unnoticed by those who were near to her, "The feeling of not quite knowing Doreen is something her friends all shared" (Heselton, 2016, 318).

Many wiccans and witches assume a Craft name, which creates a separate *persona* for their magical self, and also affords a degree of privacy, something that is particularly important if they feel likely to suffer discrimination. Valiente initially adopted the craft name Ameth, which means 'truth'; she later changed this in the mid-1960s (P. Crowther in conversation with Author).

The Moon in Pisces placement also alludes to the nurturing of magic, something that can be seen at the very beginning of her life, when she describes how, at her birth, she was delivered by, "… a doctor in full evening dress and Masonic regalia" (Heselton, 2016, 14). Apparently, the doctor had been summoned from a Masonic meeting to deliver the Dominy's child. The quotation comes from the draft of Valiente's own planned autobiography (which was never completed for publication) showing that she considered it must have had some influence on her future life and it is interesting that she developed an interest in ceremonial magic too, for example, in The Golden Dawn system of magic, even before she met Gerald Gardner.

Moon in Pisces also denotes the mystic and healer. As a teenager, Doreen had started to practice simple magic. She once made a poppet to prevent a local woman from harassing her mother (ibid, 31). Neptune, the ruler of Pisces, is in exaltation (*see glossary*) in the sign of Leo, which indicates that Valiente was artistic, creative, imaginative and inspired. In fact, as a teenager (as discussed earlier) she had wanted to go to art school but her parents did not support this idea (ibid, 36). One example of her fertile imagination can be seen through her fictional writing of short stories called, *The Witches Ball and Other Short Stories*, which was posthumously published.

Professor Ronald Hutton said of the stories that they "offered real entertainment for readers ... an immensely readable author of fiction, producing occult detective tales on the level of those by Dion Fortune" (Valiente, 2017, outside-back cover). No doubt Valiente would have appreciated the reference to Dion Fortune (the subject of Chapter Five), for whom she had enormous respect. She praised her writing, saying she thought her "... fictional books were more meaningful because there is a lot that is conveyed in fiction that can't be conveyed in non-fiction" (Jordan, 1998, 168).

Valiente's veiled nature is illustrated further by the Sun opposing Pluto. The Sun denotes the self, while Pluto represents the hidden and mysterious, so in this sense one could say there was a hidden self. It is difficult to discover tangible facts and feelings about her early life due to her intense need for privacy.

Pluto is an outer planet so represents generations of people born in this era. Its orbit is very elongated and has a 248 year cycle. Valiente was born when Pluto was in Cancer which was the backdrop of an era which spanned through the First World War to almost the outbreak of the Second World War, i.e. its cycle began in 1913/14 and finished in June, 1939.

Certainly, through this era, survival and transformation (which befits Pluto) were themes that affected many families, especially the collective experience of crisis, bereavement and pain (also befitting of Pluto). This placement also indicates defending one's country as well as the 'death' of family life as it had once been.

Cancer and its ruler, the Moon, symbolise mothers and women, whilst Pluto is associated with power and transformation. It is significant, therefore, that the death of so many men in the wars meant that women gained power and gradually transformed their position, holding more power not only within the home, but outside and politically. For example, women were required to do war work, which gave many of them an independence they could not have previously experienced. This in turn may have increased their awareness of inequality and it is interesting that the rise in violent protest by suffragettes seems to have become more noticeable in 1913, when Pluto was beginning its placement in Cancer. In 1928, women were finally given the right to vote.

On a personal level, Pluto in Cancer denotes Valiente's highly charged emotions and intuitive nature; it also indicates a great deal of pain and worry. Mars is creating a trine aspect with Pluto, which suggests that she could battle and fight when faced with perilous situations. Mars is also creating a trine aspect with Uranus (as previously discussed), which suggests that Valiente was something of a revolutionary; she was certainly original in the way she went about things.

Venus in her natal chart also creates a sextile aspect with Mars (as discussed previously), which denotes personal magnetism and warmth, yet also suggests Valiente could be both assertive while apparently compromising, since Venus is charming and tactful whilst Mars is confident. The harmonious aspect between the two planets creates an affable and conducive energy. It also suggests that Valiente enjoyed putting her energy into doing or creating something which was aesthetically pleasing. Mars likes action and Venus alludes to the earth in a sensuous and tangible way, and so one could say that Valiente was energised by the beauty of the earth and its natural gifts, i.e. the goddess.

Mars and its contact with Venus can symbolise the 'fight for women' and the aspect of Venus opposing Pluto denotes a 'powerful woman'. This indicates Valiente's energy and enthusiasm towards feminism and witchcraft, and indeed she once wrote, "I have always thought of myself as being an upholder of women's rights" (Valiente, 2007, 180). As discussed before, she embraced a new generation of women who were activists, feminists and considered radical by society.

On Midsummer's Day, 2013, almost fourteen years after her passing, Valiente made history when the City of Brighton and Hove acknowledged her accomplishments by awarding her a blue plaque. It is the first blue plaque to be awarded to a witch (Gerald Gardner's was put up the following year) and was placed on the council block where she lived for the rest of her life, until she eventually went into the Sackville Nursing Home in Hove, where she died.

Valiente passed away on 1st September, 1999, at 6.55am, aged 77. By this time, her Sun sign and Venus sign of Capricorn had both progressed (*see glossary*) into the dynamic pioneering sign of Aries. This shows that in her final years, there was a new beginning for Valiente, where she could put herself first without any obligations to others (e.g. such as providing care for her second husband). After her death, two biographies were written about her; *Ameth: The Life and Times of Doreen Valiente*, in 2014 and, *Doreen Valiente: Witch*, in 2016. These books put *her* first rather than her work and in doing so celebrated her life as opposed to her vast knowledge of witchcraft.

At the time of her passing, Valiente was experiencing some major Saturn transits including the transiting Saturn square natal Neptune, transiting Saturn trine natal Mercury, and transiting Saturn quincunx natal Jupiter. When experiencing a Saturn transit, it is quite customary for one to experience depression, sadness, physical and emotional loss in trying to adjust to the new way of life. Also, just two years previously, her long term and magical partner, Ron Cooke, had died, so she was not only suffering a decline in health, but also with loss and grief. By virtue of the hard square and conjunction aspects, this suggests that it was a particularly challenging and daunting period of time for Valiente, especially since her own father had died of pancreatic cancer over 50 years earlier (Heselton, 2016, 37), the same disease that was to take her life.

Hard aspects created between transiting Saturn and natal Neptune suggest that, in matters of health, the planetary contact has the capacity to generate confusion, meaning that potential diseases become difficult to detect and diagnose. We see this in her diabetes which may have been symptomatic of, or the cause of, the pancreatic cancer that eventually proved fatal to her. Transiting Saturn in conjunction with natal Jupiter can suggest that an excess and overburden of responsibilities and work may have finally taken its toll on Valiente's health, since excess associates with Jupiter and responsibilities with Saturn.

It is also possible that, as she became older, so the responsibility of caring for her partner, Ron Cooke, who died just two years before she did, had become very difficult. Transiting Saturn was trine natal Mercury, which suggests that Valiente was applying thought behind earthy and material concerns. Before Valiente had become ill with pancreatic cancer, she may have been involved with long-term projects or plans, such as in her role as Patron for the Centre for Pagan Studies, and in her wish to have her poetry published after she died. She was clearly planning a practical manifestation for her work so that others could be inspired and educated in the future, thus continuing her legacy.

In one of her poems, *A Hymn to Hermes*, she bids the god to "Light me the path into thy hollow hill, when I the dark and mystic way fulfil" (Valiente, 2000, 16). As a humble and modest person, Valiente would probably have been surprised (though honoured) to discover that the author and historian, Professor Ronald Hutton, had her name posthumously entered into the classical dictionary of the *Oxford Dictionary of National Biography* (http://www.oxforddnb.com/view/article/72913). He once described her as "the greatest single female figure in the in the modern British history of witchcraft" (Valiente, 2010, xv).

Her life and work were covered posthumously in various newspapers and books such as, *Obituaries in the Performing Arts (1999)*, (Lentz, 2000, page number unknown) and even abroad in *The New York Times* and *Los Angeles Times* (ibid), as well as in England.

Although it was later that Valiente became known as 'The Mother of Wicca' and 'Mother of Modern Witchcraft', she never called herself a 'Wiccan' or 'High Priestess'. Instead, she preferred to self-identify as a 'country witch' (Author's conversation with Marian Green, June, 2016), although she had been initiated by Gerald Gardner to the third degree and thus indeed was entitled to claim the status of high priestess.

Doreen Valiente was a dignified, experienced and powerful teacher. Her endurance, stamina, longevity and sheer hard work in the Pagan movement illustrate her essential authoritative, disciplined and prudent Capricorn nature. Hutton also said of her that, "Her enduring greatness lay in the very fact that she was so completely and strong-mindedly dedicated to finding and declaring her own truth" (Hutton, 2001, 383). It is little wonder she is known as the Mother of Modern Witchcraft and continues to inspire generations of Pagans.

ACKNOWLEDGEMENTS, CREDITS AND REFERENCES

The Author would like to thank Patricia Crowther, Marian Green and Ashley Mortimer, who were kind enough to read this chapter and advise.

Extended thanks also to Colin Hambrook, for his memories of meeting and participating in workshops with Doreen Valiente in the 1990s.

The Registration Officer at Vale of Glamorgan, for information on registration data for marriage of 'Rachel Dominy'.

Extended thanks also to the Local Studies Assistant at the Local Studies and Maritime Library at Southampton City Council Library, for the address details of the Unemployment Assistance Board Area Office in Southampton.

Natal chart generated by www.astro.com
Valiente, Doreen: Wed, 4th January, 1922, 10.45pm, GMT, Mitcham, England, UK.
0w10, 51n24.
Rodden Rating 'A'
Source: Heselton, 2016, 14.

Doreen Valiente's birth certificate, copy issued by General Register Office, Southport, Merseyside, UK.
No: BXCG 882866. Croydon. Vol. 2a, p683.

William George (Ronald) Cooke's birth certificate (www.ancestry.com –Accessed on 30/01/2016).
Certificate number: 6986018-1. Registered year: 1912. Apr/May/Jun quarter. Registered District: Steyning. Inferred County: Sussex. Vol. 2b, p505.

Casimiro Valiente's birth data: (www.ancestry.com –Accessed on 30/01/2016).
24th January, 1918, Date of Registration: June, 1972. Age: 54.
Registration District: Brighton. Inferred County: Sussex.
Death Certificate: Vol. 5h, p311.

Marriage Certificate Information for Doreen Edith (otherwise known as Rachel) Dominy – from Registration Officer at Vale of Glamorgan, Democratic Services.

Copy from the official Register for Marriages: January, February and March quarter, 1941, for East Glamorgan (Vol. 11a, p1799).

BOOKS

Clifford, F. C. (2012) *Getting to the Heart of your Chart*. Flare Publications.

Crowther, P. (1998) *High Priestess: The Life and Times of Patricia Crowther*. Robert Hale Ltd, London.

Dyson, B. (1994) *Liberty in Britain 34–94: Diamond Jubilee History of the National Council for Civil Liberties*. Civil Liberties Trust.

Fielding, N. (1981) *The National Front*. London Routledge & Kegan Paul.

Hamaker-Zondag, K. (2000) *The Yod Book*. Samuel Weiser Inc.

Harrington, R. (1995) *Pagan Dawn*. Interview with Doreen Valiente No. 117.

Heselton, P. (2016) *Doreen Valiente, Witch*. The Doreen Valiente Foundation in association with the Centre for Pagan Studies.

Hutton, R. (December, 2008) *Modern Pagan Festivals: A Study in the Nature of Tradition: Folklore*. Vol. 119, No. 3.

Hutton, R. (2001) *The Triumph Of The Moon*, Oxford University Press.

Jones, E. J. &Valiente,D. (1990) *Witchcraft A Tradition Renewed*. Robert Hale Ltd.

Jordan, M. (1998) *Witches an Encyclopaedia of Paganism and Magic*. Published by Kyle Cathie Ltd.

Lentz, H. M. (2000) *The 1999 Obituaries of Performing Arts*. McFarland & Co. Inc. Pub.

Michelson, N. F. (1980) *The American Ephemeris for the Twentieth Century*. ACS Publications Inc.

Reinhart, M. (1989) *Chiron and the Healing Journey*. Penguin Books.

Tapsell, J. (2014) *Ameth: The Life and Times of Doreen Valiente*. Avalonia.

Valiente, D. (1978) *Witchcraft for Tomorrow*. Robert Hale Ltd, London.

Valiente, D. (1994) *An ABC of Witchcraft Past and Present*. Robert Hale Ltd, London.

Valiente, D. (2000) *Charge of The Goddess, The Mother of Modern Witchcraft*. Hexagon Hoopix.

Valiente, D. (2007) *The Rebirth of Witchcraft*. Robert Hale Ltd, London.

Valiente, D. (2017) *The Witches Ball and Other Short Stories*. The Doreen Valiente Foundation in association with the Centre for Pagan Studies.

Valiente, D. (2010) *Where Witchcraft Lives*. Whyte Tracks.

Walker M. (1977) The *National Front*. Fontana, London.

NEWSPAPERS

Daily Express – Monday, April 24th, 1978, 24 – Editorial: 'Which Witch is Which?'

Psychic News – Saturday, February 24th, 1951, 9 – Letters: 'Unique Position.'

Psychic News – Saturday, April 6th, 1963, 6 – Letters: 'More about Witchcraft.'

PAMPHLETS

Madgwick, D. (1968) *Privacy under Attack*. NCCL.

WEBSITES

http://www.bbc.co.uk/news/uk-england-sussex-22861672 – Quotes from neighbours (BBC News, Brighton, Sussex). Accessed 12/06/2014.

https://www.behindthename.com/name/rachel – Definition and origins of name 'Rachel'. Accessed on 20/01/2020.

http://www.doreenvaliente.com/Doreen-Valiente-Biography-19.php#sthash.GTRajW6l.dpbs – Accessed on 07/06/2014.

http://www.doreenvaliente.com/Doreen-Valiente-Foundation-3.php – Accessed on 06/02/2016.

http://www.doreenvaliente.com/Doreen-Valiente-Blue_Plaques-7.php – Accessed on 05/02/2016.

http://www.doreenvaliente.com/#sthash.Oqs14cuO.dpbs – Blue plaque award information. Accessed on 02/01/2020.

https://en.wikipedia.org/wiki/Unemployment_Assistance_Board – The Unemployment Assistance Board. Accessed on 30/01/2020.

https://www.gov.uk/government/uploads/system/uploads/attachment_data/file/267907/britnatacts.pdf – Information regarding British Nationality and Status of Aliens Act.

http://history.buses.co.uk/history/fleethist/804dv.htm – 804 Mercedes Streetdeck on route 1: Whitehawk 1A: Doreen Valiente. Accessed on 08/01/2020.

https://www.nationalarchives.gov.uk/cabinetpapers/themes/unemployment-assistance.htm – Information on role of the Unemployment Assistance Board. Accessed on 19/02/2020.

http://www.discovery.nationalarchives.gov.uk/details/r/C9128 – Committee on Privacy: Evidence and Papers. Accessed on 09/02/2021.

https://www.nbcnews.com/news/latino/forgotten-spanish-soldiers-behind-france-s-liberation-nazi-germany-n1045731 – False names. Accessed on 28/01/2020.

http://www.oxforddnb.com/view/article/72913 – Doreen Valiente entry. Accessed on 11/03/2016.

https://wrldrels.org/2018/08/03/doreen-valiente/ – Valiente cared for Ron Cooke until his death. DV wanted to go to art school but instead went to night school. Accessed on 16/01/2020.

https://wrldrels.org/2018/08/03/doreen-valiente/ – Information about menstrual blood used in magic. Accessed on 19/0001/2020.

https://www.youtube.com/watch?v=rXQr2NOQChk – Valiente interviewed by Kevin Carlyon. Accessed on 30/05/2016.

https://www.youtube.com/watch?v=Veg2o02eao0 – Jonathan Tapsell interviewed by Karagan Griffith: Ameth – The Life and Times of Doreen Valiente. Accessed on 30/05/2016.

http://www.uboat.net/allies/merchants/993.html – Information about crew and survivors of the Pandias ship. Accessed on 30/05/2016.

https://www.uboat.net/allies/merchants/crews/person/86876.html – Information about Joanis Vlachopoulos, his age and spelling of his name. Accessed on 18/01/2020.

https://en.wikipedia.org/wiki/John_Michell_(writer)#Embracing_the_Earth_Mysteries – Information about View from Atlantis influencing Valiente. Accessed on 21/01/2021.

http://hansard.millbanksystems.com/commons/1970/apr/16/witchcraft – Question asked in House of Commons by Gwilym Roberts. HC Debate, 16 April, 1970. Vol. 799, c1555. Accessed 20/04/2016.

CHAPTER TWELVE

Linda Goodman 1925–1995

Astrologer, Poet and Writer

LINDA GOODMAN was born Mary Alice Kemery on 9th April, 1925, in Morgantown, West Virginia, USA, and died on 21st October, 1995. She was the only daughter of Robert Stratton Kemery, a newspaper deliverer, and Mazie Kemery (née McBee), a housewife. As an adult, Goodman inspired generations of people through her astrology, numerology and poetry. She began her career writing for newspapers in various parts of USA, and also claimed to have written speeches for Whitney Young, the future President of the National Urban League – a Civil Rights organisation that worked for racial integration and the empowerment of African Americans.

Linda Goodman's Sun Signs was the first astrology book to secure ratings in the bestsellers list in *The New York Times*, and her subsequent book, *Linda Goodman's Love Signs,* was also highly regarded. She wrote other successful books about astrology and poetry and in her later years planned to write a book for children about astrology. She was married twice and had four children. She died at the age of 70 from complications of diabetes.

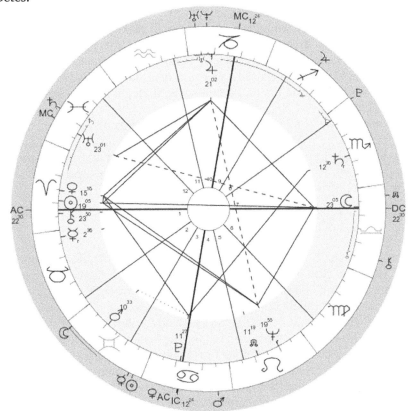

Natal, Progressions and Transit Chart for the day Linda Goodman died, 21st October, 1995.

WHAT LINDA GOODMAN'S NATAL CHART SHOWS

Linda Goodman was born when the Sun was at 19 degrees in the fire sign of Aries, and the opposing Moon was at 23 degrees in the air sign of Libra on 9th April, 1925. Being born on a full-moon and during a thunderstorm was a stirring beginning for a newborn baby. In *Gooberz,* her enchanting, partly autobiographical book of poetry and prose, it states that Goodman was "... born during a spring thunderstorm on an April day" (Goodman, 1959, 2). The spring equinox (in the Northern Hemisphere), the first day of spring, commences with the Sun moving into the first sign of the zodiac, Aries.

Aries
Aries is symbolised by the Ram, and the glyph symbolises the Ram's horns. The glyph can also represent the 'first shoots of spring,' when plants are starting to bud.

Aries begins the zodiacal cycle initiating action, promoting assertiveness, courage and vigour. Mars, which is the ruling planet of Aries, provides a competitive quality, lending itself to drive and rivalry. There is an enterprising, inspirational, and pioneering spirit which requires action and adventure.

Since Mars is governed by the element of fire, Aries has potential to be direct, impulsive and passionate and according to Goodman's son, Michael, she could be 'pushy' (www.nytimes.com). It was also observed that whilst her kindness and generosity drew people to her, they were often driven away by her temper and demands (www.people.com).

The courageous, dynamic, and instinctive nature of Mars provides qualities befitting the hunter and warrior in leadership positions, where 'the Ram' has to approach situations head-on. Being first (symbolised by being the first sign of the zodiac) comes naturally to the impatient, self-assured and warm-hearted Aries. We see an example of her being first when she wrote the first astrology book to get into the best-sellers list in *The New York Times.*

Aries can speak with confidence, enthusiasm and frankness, easily making others aware of their views, as we have seen above in the example of her rage. Mars is unaspected in Goodman's natal chart and this will be discussed in detail further on. Although willing to give interviews, Goodman preferred writing as a way of communicating directly with her audience, i.e. her readers.

ACTION

In Goodman's natal chart, the ascendant (AC), midheaven (MC), descendant (DC) and Imum coeli (IC) (*see glossary*) are in cardinal signs. The cardinal signs comprise of; Aries AC, Capricorn MC, Libra DC and Cancer IC. The cardinal (*see glossary*) mode shows behaviour that is capable of challenge and initiation and this was prominent in Goodman's natal chart. In her book, *Sun Signs,* she describes her own sign of the Aries female thus, "The Mars girl is determined to take the lead, to be the first move to action, and that includes the action of making the first advances in romance" (Goodman, 1972, 22). She describes a typical Aries employee as "... a natural innovator and leader" (ibid, 45). These two quotes and interpretations show how assertive the Aries female can be.

Jupiter is near the MC in the tenth house (*see box overpage*), showing that, in her career, Goodman was destined for fame and success, since these attributes are associated with Jupiter. The Moon is on the descendant and Pluto is on the IC and this astrological data will be discussed later in this chapter.

All the cardinal signs on the axis represent the seasons throughout the year, as when the Sun enters those signs, the seasons change at the equinoxes and solstices. They repeat the theme of initiation, beginnings, fresh-starts and change. The emphasis on the cardinality in the chart shows an ability to begin new projects with a degree of pro-activeness and self-motivation, coupled with a focus to lead, manage and pioneer.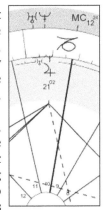

We see this borne out in her life, in that her first astrology book, *Linda Goodman's Sun Signs* (first published by a relatively obscure publishing house named Taplinger in 1968), entered *The New York Times* prestigious best-seller list. This in itself was a pioneering achievement, since it was not only the first astrology book ever to enter the list but did so within a few months of publication. It reveals not only the ground-breaking nature of her work but also how she inspired her readers, which made her first book such a success.

Goodman experienced further success with her follow-up book, *Linda Goodman's Love Signs*, which also entered *The New York Times* best-seller list and is another example of her pioneering achievements. In fact, the paperback rights for her second book set a record in the publishing industry at that time, with the sum of $2.3 million being paid for them (www.timesmachine.nytimes.com). She was also the author of *Venus Trines at Midnight*, which was the first volume of astrological poetry ever published. Three of her books, *Sun Signs* (1968), *Love Signs* (1978) and *Star Signs* (1988), have sold more than 30 million copies in fifteen languages and still continue to sell some 200,000 copies each year (www.timesmachine.nytimes.com).

Of course, those who were not interested in astrology were quick to point out their disdain for astrology in general and Goodman's book in particular, even at the height of her success. For example, one journalist wrote (of *Love Signs*), "There is a category of young woman nowadays who is never happier than when asking what star sign you were born under" (*The Sunday Telegraph*, 1979, 6), he continued in his article, "personally I don't like the sound of any of these star signs" (ibid), although he was quick enough to tell the reader that he was a Pisces!

The Sun on Goodman's ascendant suggests a confident, self-motivated nature with leadership qualities (*see box on left*). When the Sun is in the sign of Aries, it gives self-assurance and an outgoing disposition, coupled with enthusiasm and an ability to encourage and inspire others. Aries on the ascendant indicates a brave, confident and outspoken person; sometimes brusque and sharp. Certainly, having her Sun and ascendant in the same sign would have intensified that Aries energy.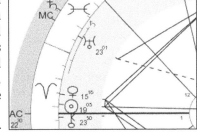

When the Sun is in the twelfth house of 'behind-the-scenes' activity (*see box on right*), there is a degree of self-sacrifice, and the ability to work alone. This placement would have been helpful to Goodman when she was writing, since this is essentially a solitary task. The Sun in the twelfth house also suggests a romantic nature together with a vivid imagination with depths of artistry and intuition. Focus, pride and strength may have been derived in meditation, music, prayer and spirituality, since these are all areas associated with the twelfth house.

This position of the Sun in twelfth house also suggests the aforementioned element of self-sacrifice, where one can be of service to others by providing a selfless love. We see this in the large amount of time that Goodman apparently spent away from her teenage children whilst she went to Los Angeles and New York City in connection with her work, sacrificing family time to pursue her career (www.earthenergyreader.

wordpress.com). It must have been very difficult for her to balance the demands of her career and a busy family life: she had four children, Jill and Michael Goodman (from her first marriage to Sam Goodman), and Bill and Sally Snyder (from her marriage to William Snyder). It has been said that in the 1970s, when the children were teenagers, a couple who were very good friends of Goodman raised them for her while she was away for work (ibid).

The presence of the Moon on the descendant suggests that Goodman needed a partner who was less impulsive and driven than herself, and who could be more agreeable and co-operative. This would have brought a balance into her life that helped to harmonise her partnerships. She would have appreciated qualities

Linda Goodman.
Photo by kind
permission of Hessel
Hoornveld

such as charm, grace and refinement, all of which are associated with Venus, the ruling planet of Libra (and Taurus).

The Moon in Libra suggests that Goodman needed balance, harmony and peace in her life, in that she enjoyed company, and was able to nurture others with charm and kindness. The cordial, gracious and sociable air sign of Libra on the descendant indicates that Goodman was kind and very loving with partners, and valued being part of a partnership. Interestingly, author and witch Doreen Valiente (the subject of Chapter Eleven) also shares this position in her natal chart.

LOVE AND MARRIAGE

One-to-one relationships (both her own and other people's) were of huge significance to Goodman, both personally and professionally. This is perhaps illustrated by the titles of some of her astrological books: *Love Poems, Love Signs* and *Relationships Signs.*

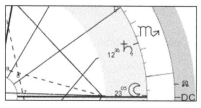

The Moon in the seventh house of marriage and partnerships (*see box on left*) suggests that Goodman may have looked for caring qualities in her relationships (more than most) in order to fulfil her need to feel emotionally secure. Saturn in the seventh house also indicates that she approached partnerships and relationships seriously, fearing making mistakes.

Saturn, the sign of age, maturity and wisdom, indicates that Goodman may have preferred 'older' partners, be they elder in years or in experience, and perhaps sought solid and successful relationships.

For example, Goodman was married to her first husband, William Snyder, for ten years before they divorced. Her second husband, Sam O. Goodman, was a Sun sign Taurus which belongs to the fixed mode. By their nature, the fixed signs are able to bring determination, loyalty and sustenance to a relationship; in turn this may have made Goodman feel secure in her relationship with him. At the very beginning of her second book, *Love Signs* (Goodman, 1978, un-numbered opening page), she pays homage and gives "... a special acknowledgment of gratitude to the patient Bull Sam O. Goodman, without whose steady loyalty and devotion I would not have been able to write this or

any other book." This strongly suggests that he was
mature, realistic and understanding enough to realise
that his wife needed concentration and solitude in
order to help her achieve her aims.

Likewise, in her book, *Gooberz*, she thanks her
husband "... Sam O. Goodman, without whom I
could not have channelled this book, for he spent
many patient hours helping me look within myself
for answers" (Goodman, 1959, un-numbered page).
Her friend and neighbour, Evelyn Stauffer, described
the Goodman's relationship succinctly when she
said of Sam that he, "... was her protector," and that
during their marriage, "... Sam raised the kids and let
her do her thing" (http://consciousevolution.com/

Photo taken in approximately 1968

Astrology/AboutLinda.htm). Apparently, there was little excitement or passion between
Goodman and Sam; something she would later discover with her much younger lover,
Robert Brewer (https://earthenergyreader.wordpress.com/tag/cripple-creek/).

The disciplined and determined nature of Saturn in the seventh house, and in the
sign of intense and powerful Scorpio, suggests achievement in business partnerships.
However, in personal relationships (the seventh house), if there are emotional problems,
there is a capacity to hide that struggle from others, since the nature of Scorpio is to
conceal and veil.

Nonetheless, there is a romantic nature signified in Goodman's chart with; Neptune
in Leo in the fifth house of romance, Sun Aries in the dreamy and romantic twelfth
house, and the Moon in Libra in the seventh house of marriage, and partnerships.

The Sun on the ascendant, opposing the Moon on the descendant, echoes the theme
of a deep longing for emotional security in her relationships. Goodman would have
needed to know that she was loved and cared for, as discussed previously. The afflicting
opposition between the Sun and the Moon indicates that perhaps there was a conflict
in her identity, in that what she sought and what she needed were in opposition. This
created tensions, since her Sun in assertive, forceful, and combative Aries, was opposing
her natal Moon in artistic, gentle, and peaceful Libra, and such oppositions, by their
nature, generate conflict.

The aspect of the Moon sextile Neptune, coupled with her drive and capacity
for partnerships and relationships, helped provide Goodman with sensitivity and
understanding for her astrological readers, who were usually searching for love,
romance and their ideal partner.

The Sun is trine Neptune in her natal chart, bringing gentleness and natural
compassion to her nature. It also adds a sensitive and spiritual dimension, showing she
was attracted to metaphysical subjects, with an innate knowing that there is more to
life than that which meets the physical eye.

However, since the Sun represents the self and Neptune represents dreams and
fantasies, there is the potential for self-deception and self-glamorisation. Goodman may
have dreamed of being special and in turn glamorising her 'self'. Indeed, she may have
recognised this aspect of herself when she gave an interview with the *Los Angeles Times*
and said, "Time is an illusion. But one has to deal with the false reality of it on earth"
(www.nytimes.com). Possibly, Goodman was thinking of herself when she wrote in *Sun
Signs* (1972), about Aries women, "... There's a vain streak in a Mars woman which

makes her sensitive about everything from her age to an innocent remark about how tired she looks" (Goodman, 1972, 29).

This aspect also denotes a naturally gifted soul, with strength and vitality along with altruism and selflessness. There is also imagination and sensitivity, which will have enabled Goodman to easily 'tune-in', bringing to the fore any mediumistic and psychic abilities.

The Capricorn MC suggests Goodman needed a career that offered clear signs of progress and success and writing was certainly a way to achieve this. The confident and visionary Jupiter in the sign of Capricorn, and in the tenth house of career and status in society, boded well for Goodman in having a successful long-term career as well as public fame. Jupiter in Capricorn suggests accomplishment and ambition in business but also a traditional faith and belief in hard work. Her endurance and resourcefulness would have helped her to achieve her goals.

The Sun-Moon opposition (as previously mentioned) is also part of a powerful aspect pattern called a T-Square (*see box on right*), which always produces challenges, akin to a bow and arrow being tensioned. That pressure is then released through the point opposite the planet that is square the opposite planets. In Goodman's chart that release point is 21 degrees of Cancer, which is in the fourth house, the area associated with heritage, domestic life and family.

> **T-Square:**
> A T-Square is a pattern formed when planets in opposition also form a square with another planet. The pattern resembles the letter 'T' when viewed in the chart. The squared planet or point is referred to as the 'focal point'.

Some of the tensions and challenges in Goodman's life can be seen by the following examples. Firstly, her elder daughter, Sally Snyder, who attempted suicide and then in 1973 died from alcohol and narcotics. She had been missing from Goodman's life for several years. At that time, in Linda's chart, transiting Pluto was in the sign of sacrificial natal Pisces which was at Neptune's twelfth house. Pluto symbolises death and rebirth and can bring emotional pain, intensity and fixation.

The obsession is revealed by the way Goodman refused to believe that Sally's body (which was identified by her husband, Sam, who was also Sally's step-father) was really that of her daughter, using astrological evidence to support her theory. It was reported in the media that Goodman developed a mania about her daughter's 'death'. This transit would have triggered the tension at 21 degrees of Cancer and would have created an aspect pattern called a Grand Cross (*see box right*).

The aspect of Moon square Jupiter in Goodman's natal chart gives a warm and embracing spirit that needs to encircle everything and everyone. This could meet with resistance from those in Goodman's life who did not wish her to cultivate or support them. The aspect also suggests that Goodman sometimes reacted in a very emotional, impetuous and even sentimental manner, over-reacting and having temper tantrums. This could have presented challenges in business partnerships and relationships. Jupiter is the sparkling razzle-dazzler of the zodiac and so in this sense could have brought a sense of the diva and drama-queen.

> **Grand Cross**
> A Grand Cross occurs when four planets are all separated from each other by square aspects being 90 degrees apart. It can also be viewed as two oppositions 180 degrees apart, separated from each other by a square. There is a planet in each astrological element but all the planets are in signs of the same modality or quality. It is possible to have a Grand Cross where all the planets are not in the same element (disassociate).

Indeed, she was once described as, "a diva and expected to have people serve her day and night hand and foot" (www.earthenergyreader.wordpress.com). It has also been said that some people enabled Goodman's behaviour by telling her what she wanted to hear (ibid). This not only gives an idea of how fierce Goodman could be, but also that her acquaintances and friends were not always as truthful as they could have been.

It has also been claimed that at times she could be delusional (ibid). For example, after her partner, Robert Brewer, left her (partly because of her demands but also because he found another woman), the break-up affected her so deeply that she was unable to move forward. Afterwards she became "a lonely woman grasping at straws trying to find meaning in something that did not work out and with results that she refused to accept" (ibid). It must have been a tremendous blow to her ego.

It was often said of Goodman that her intensity and generosity attracted false friends, upon whom she would often bestow gifts of cars or expensive jewellery. Mars in the second house suggests that Goodman may have been impulsive with her spending, since Mars is associated with haste and rashness, whilst the second house is associated with earnings and income. Her generosity turned out to be a habit that bankrupted her in the 1980s (www.people.com).

Despite being drawn to her generosity, people were also driven away by her demands and temper. This was a reaction Goodman apparently never seemed to understand, even though perhaps she of all people should have done, since in *Sun Signs* she wrote, "Mars people are often accused of having a terrible temper. They have. But they also have a complete inability to remain angry, and once over with, the grievance is generally buried and forgotten" (Goodman, 1972, 8). Unfortunately, this does not take into account the feelings of those on the receiving end of such outbursts.

The Sun square Jupiter suggests an overreaching of the self, rising to a challenge and trusting to luck and self-belief. The Sun in Aries on the ascendant and square Jupiter in the tenth house indicates a bold, excessive, and optimistic drive for prosperity of work and career. Impulsive and spontaneous decision-making in business are possible with this position. Moderation and restraint would have been helpful at such times.

Venus square the MC suggests that, career-wise, Goodman may sometimes have experienced tense relationships with authority figures, co-workers, managers and supervisors, whenever her arrogance and conceitedness were on display.

INSIGHTS AND SECRETS

Intuitive and perceptive Pluto was opposing the MC in her natal chart, indicating that in her career she might have been working with other people in an investigative, psychological or research capacity. In such fields, confidentiality and trust would have been of paramount importance. Goodman would have found it deeply satisfying to get to the heart of the matter and uncover information in her career.

Pluto on the IC (*see chart in box overpage*) is an ideal placement for psychology which translates into Goodman's astrological work. In her obituary, *The New York Times* journalist, Robert McG. Thomas Jr. suggested that, "… by writing in the first person and drawing on the lives of celebrities, historical figures and personal friends to illustrate her points, Mrs Goodman sometimes seemed more psychologist than astrologer" (www.timesmachinenytimes.com). The placement also denotes the possible presence of mediumistic, occult and psychic abilities in the family.

Another interpretation of Pluto on the IC is that Goodman may have tried to cleanse herself of her past, since Pluto associates with cleansing and purging. This might be

borne out by Goodman's insistence that she was born at her maternal grandparents' home. She seems to have distrusted her family's official account that she was in fact born at her parents' home.

Pluto is in the area of communication (the third house) and of course these attributes would have been at the very heart of her work as an author. Yet conversely, Goodman kept her true age a secret not only from the outside world, but even from members of her own family, secrecy being a correspondence of Pluto. For most of her life, she was able to keep her natal chart a secret. In an interview, Goodman's son, Michael, said (when questioned about his mother's age), "I once asked my grandfather, and he wouldn't tell me either." He also once remarked, "... age was an illusion to her" (www.timesmachine.nytimes.com).

In the third house, Pluto provides a deep and penetrative mind where superficiality has no place. Goodman may have held strong opinions and expressed them forcefully. She would also have been able to keep her thoughts to herself whenever she so wished.

Since the third house also corresponds with networking, her acquaintances and contacts may have confided in her realising that she could keep a secret, maintaining confidences and trust in relationships. Saturn in the seventh house and trine Pluto in the third house indicates that she invested in magnetic, powerful and trustworthy friends. Mutual respect, loyalty and trustworthiness were at the heart of all her relationships, however, as discussed earlier, she could easily drive her friends away if they didn't meet her demands – perhaps this behaviour was an artistic temperament in action! Some of her acquaintances and contacts included the wealthy and political Kennedy family, innovator Howard Hughes, his wife the actress Terry Moore, and astrologer Jacqueline Stallone (www.people.com). Hughes in particular was a famously private person and would not have tolerated Goodman had he not been assured of her total discretion.

Mercury is 2 degrees in the sign of Taurus in the first house and is unaspected by the other planets. Mercury in Taurus suggests caution and practical thinking, employing consideration in making decisions and sticking to routine wherever possible. The Taurean energy will have provided an ease of understanding and straightforwardness in her communicating. Graceful planet Venus, the ruling planet of Taurus, would have helped in adding a certain elegance and style in her communications, which would have been helpful when writing about relationships.

Mercury in the first house indicates a 'first at communicating' approach. It is unsurprising therefore, that as an Aries who likes to be 'first', in her writing she enjoyed writing in 'the first person' (as demonstrated in her books 'Sun Signs' and the semi-autobiographical 'Gooberz'). Also, it is perhaps significant that Goodman liked to be considered first as a writer and second as an astrologer. Her Sun and ascendant Aries conjunct each other, suggests a strong need for attention and recognition, which she certainly got by her books being best-sellers.

Peregrine Planets
A planet which is unaspected is also described as a 'peregrine planet'. The word 'peregrine' derives from the Latin word meaning 'foreign'.

The peregrine Mercury (*see box right*) is apparent to Goodman's talents, in that she was able to communicate as a speaker and writer in various fields. The peregrine Mercury in Goodman's chart has the potential to either dominate with action, or govern with passivity.

Therefore, in this sense, communicating was certainly not 'foreign' to Goodman. Amongst her abundance of achievements, she held positions of employment as newspaper reporter, radio writer, occasional broadcaster, author and poet.

The profusion of the natural energy in Goodman's peregrine Mercury, manifested itself through her work, and the Winged Messenger was able to communicate through the written and spoken word. By directing the pure mental Mercury energy in a positive direction, her communication skills became her strongest asset, helping to offset the potential of an overactive mind that may have been prone to excessive worry and over-thinking.

Returning to Mars, the ruling planet of Aries, and also the ruling planet of Goodman's natal chart; like Mercury, it is also a peregrine planet. The untamed energy of Mars can be potentially lethal, as it is not in contact with any other planets and, given that associations of Mars include anger, impatience, tantrums and rage, it is possible that the scalding nature of Goodman manifested itself through displeasure. Whether she was always ill-tempered or became so as she grew older and became more successful, we do not know. The positive qualities of Mars (which she clearly channelled through her work), include courage, drive, entrepreneurism, motivation and vigour.

Mars is in Gemini – a sign ruled by the planet Mercury (the other sign being Virgo). This placement would have been useful to Goodman, since it would have enabled her to multitask, providing her with dexterity, and making it possible for her to work with a variety of people. In the area of earnings and values in the second house, Mars will have helped drive through an assertive, energetic and resourceful spirit. It brings a competitive and enterprising force, which will have been immensely helpful to Goodman in being self-employed.

Saturn sextile the MC suggests that Goodman tried to be practical and realistic in her work, adopting a pragmatic stance to help her achieve what she wanted in her career. This aspect would have helped balance her artistic, creative and poetic nature. Jupiter in the tenth house and sextile Uranus in the twelfth house suggest she dreamt of a successful future.

Venus, the Goddess of Love placed in the twelfth house suggests Goodman had a very artistic and musical nature, inspired by her imagination and sub-conscious. This will have helped with her poetry and writing. It also indicates that she was drawn to the 'hidden' and the 'unseen' (both areas associated with the twelfth house); at the time she was writing her first book, astrology was sometimes regarded as part of 'the occult'. There may have also been a love of 'letting-go', releasing the self (Sun in twelfth house) through artistic and meditative channels.

This position also suggests she may have found inner peace through retreat and solitude, which could have helped with her writing. There is also the possibility that, through loss and self-sacrifice, Goodman grew more affectionate and devoted, loving and tender. This is borne out by the dedication in the foreword to her book, Love Signs, which reads, "My children ... who have taught me, over the years, many lessons of love." The placement of Venus in the twelfth house also shows a potential for secret love affairs, since the nature of the twelfth house is hidden and secret, and Venus is the planet of love. It is not known whether this was true of Goodman, although Venus is in Aries in her natal chart, suggesting that Goodman needed to keep her relationships fresh and spontaneous. Activity and energy stimulate Venus in Aries, whenever relationships become too comfortable and staid.

The Venus in Aries person is not unlikely to go searching for a new conquest and this was apparently true of Goodman by the following example. After a while, her marriage to Sam Goodman is thought to have become more platonic and, according to a close friend, there was little passion and sexual activity in the marriage (earthenergyreader. wordpress.com). While she was still married to Goodman (although they had separated) she had a brief relationship with Robert Brewer, who was much younger and apparently able to fulfil her sexual appetite (ibid). It has been said that the relationship between Brewer and Goodman eventually broke down, because he was unable to accommodate her 'bossiness and demands'.

Venus is also associated with earnings and wealth, and the twelfth house can also symbolise the deprived and disadvantaged. It is documented that over the course of her lifetime, Goodman relinquished half of all her income to animal rights and ecological organisations. She believed that the more one gave away in life, the bigger reward one received karmically. Unfortunately, this may have ultimately contributed to her bankruptcy in the late 1980s (http://www.linda-goodman.com).

Uranus in the twelfth house has potential for clairvoyance, illumination, truth and vision, since these are areas associated with futuristic and progressive Uranus. Campaigning for charitable causes, for example, working towards a fairer society and generating funds for charities, will have come naturally to Goodman with the energies of Uranus and Venus positioned in the twelfth house. In supporting Civil Rights, animal rights and ecological campaigning, we see that she was well ahead of her time and totally attuned to this characteristic of her chart.

There are also planetary dialogues which indicate that Goodman was an effective healer and medium, drawn to the divine, spiritual and religious. This can be seen through Neptune trine the ascendant, which suggests she could confidently and enthusiastically channel her imagination, mediumship and intuition. She could also carry out spiritual healing through meditation, prayer and visualisation; this is sometimes known as 'absent healing', which would have suited her need to be 'invisible' during the above practices.

At her home in Hayden Street, Colorado, Goodman had spiritually-themed stained glass windows (featuring – amongst others – images of St Francis of Assisi and Mary Magdalene, Isis and Osiris) as well as a chapel area which she designed and furnished (www.earthenergyreader.wordpress.com). The artistic and design element would have been inspiring and satisfying to her Moon sign of Libra. Venus, the ruling planet of her Moon, is trine Neptune; endowing her with creative, spiritual and artistic talents. Goodman loved to listen to Gregorian chants and would light candles to help create peace and tranquillity (www.people.com).

There is a hard aspect of the Moon quincunx Uranus in Goodman's chart. This suggests that at home there may have been an element of eccentricity and unpredictability; it also suggests that Goodman needed domestic independence. The Moon symbolises what nurtures us emotionally while Uranus is associated with individualism and the unconventional.

One example of her perceived unorthodoxy can be seen in a report publicising her book, Love Signs, in the Daily Express newspaper in 1979. The journalist focused on a piece in her book, "...a novel form of birth control has been devised but it only works for starry-eyed lovers" (Daily Express 1979) It goes on to say that only those who believe in astrology would chance the 'astrobiology' method that Goodman claimed to have discovered. The newspaper continued that Goodman believed that, "... there is only one two-hour period when a woman can conceive during a month, which is when the Sun and Moon are at the same angle in the sky as at the time of the woman's birth" (ibid). For the less open-minded, Goodman's method to conceive may have been considered quirky and unconventional, if not a little risky.

Possibly Goodman found it challenging to function harmoniously in group situations with this aspect (Moon quincunx Uranus), as it conflicts with her focus on solitude and withdrawal, and her natal Moon in Libra is more at home with one-to-one situations. Constant extremes of emotion can generate ill health and create strain on the nervous system, which in turn may have resulted in Goodman feeling depleted and diminishing in energy. It has been said of her that, "She almost had a split personality," since she could be extremely difficult, and yet could also show tremendous generosity; she was both inspiring (and inspired) and full of wisdom (www.earthenergyreader.wordpress. com).

SORROW, GRIEF AND SPIRITUALITY

As well as the astrological arts, Goodman had an interest in subjects such as numerology and palmistry. She was also inspired by angels, divine love, karma, miracles, mysticism and reincarnation; which gave her life meaning and understanding.

The area of reincarnation was of deep significance to Goodman. In her semi-autobiographical book, *Gooberz*, she describes in detail how she experienced the end of a past-life before joining this physical plane, being born on the 9th April (Goodman, 1989, 2). The metaphysical death and rebirth provides a degree of symbolism to this, with Pluto on the IC – since Pluto is able to purge and rejuvenate life, while the IC also corresponds with memories and past-lives. Grief, loss and pain through bereavement were familiar to Goodman. She 'lost' children in infancy and an elder daughter died in her twenties. As a young girl, Linda had experienced pain when her animals and beloved grandparents passed away; one's early experiences of bereavement can be particularly bewildering and hurtful.

The theme of loss and disappearance with children is symbolised in the presence of Neptune in the fifth house, the area in a natal chart which denotes children (as well as creativity and love-affairs). Part of Neptune's energy includes demise, pain, sacrifice and surrender, which is borne out by her experience of losing her children through death.

As previously mentioned, Goodman's elder daughter, Sally Snyder, underwent a period of depression, attempted suicide and was hospitalised. She eventually became a casualty of alcohol and narcotics and disappeared in 1970. When Sally's body was found in 1973 in her flat (she had overdosed on pethedine), her step-father, Sam Goodman, identified her body and had it cremated; Linda Goodman refused to accept it was her daughter (http://www.linda-goodman.com) as previously discussed.

However, Sally was not the only individual in Goodman's life who disappeared. Linda's lover, Robert Brewer, a marine biologist, also disappeared (this was sometime after 1972 when he had already left Goodman), but he was never found (www.people. com). Addiction, disappearance and escape are all correspondences of Neptune.

Neptune is in Leo and in the fifth house. This indicates that, as a child, Goodman was artistic, creative, imaginative and spiritually inspired. When she was young, Goodman regularly attended church with her family; she was obsessed as a child to seek answers to the mystery of life, death and rebirth (Pluto on IC and in third house).

From an early age, Goodman seems to have been destined to walk a life where the themes of life and death were prevalent. She was able to self-help, healing her own pain and suffering, yet also helping others by channelling her creativity and spirituality to offer empathy and understanding. The themes of compassion, imagination and creativity repeatedly appear in the astrological data in Goodman's natal chart, so it was inevitable that in her life she applied herself in these areas using these natural gifts.

The asteroid Chiron is in the first house, the area of the self and is in the sign of Aries, where it is conjunct the ascending Sun. In mythology, Chiron is known as the 'Wounded Healer' and in a natal chart it indicates the wounded area that we cannot heal ourselves, but where encouragement, inspiration and motivation can be used to help others to heal themselves in that same area.

The Moon's Nodes

The Moon's Nodes are symbolic points in the sky where the paths of the Moon and Sun cross. The Nodes are karmic points which are believed to be able to provide advice on how to live one's life in order to advance one's spiritual path. This area of astrology may have been of particular interest to Goodman as an astrologer, since she believed in karma and reincarnation.

According to mythology, Chiron was a great astrology teacher who initiated healers, magicians and warriors; he was also skilled at hunting and warfare. Chiron in the first house and in Aries contributes to Goodman's militant and combatant nature, leading with an abundance of courage, drive and enthusiasm to help others realise their potential and strength.

Goodman's North Node in Leo in the fifth house and South Node in Aquarius in the eleventh house, suggest that she needed to find time for her creativity and self-expression, and to foster a less obstinate attitude in her communications with others.

Goodman's Moon in Libra is at 23 degrees conjunct the fixed star of Spica, and the MC in Capricorn is at 12 degrees is conjunct the fixed star of the head of the Archer. Many astrologers believe that Spica is a good influence for those working in science and also the arts, e.g. writers, artists, sculptors and musicians (Ebertin and Hoffmann, 2009, 57), while the head of the Archer possesses a Mars-Saturn nature with some Jupiterian influence. Very few people are considered ready to receive its "spiritual emanations" (ibid, 72). These interpretations for the fixed stars Spica and the head of the Archer are certainly in keeping with the artistic, philosophical and spiritual areas of Goodman's life. It is clear she did indeed benefit from Spica's influence, since she became a world-famous astrologer and author.

The Mars-Saturn and Jupiter influence in the head of the Archer was also significant in Goodman's life and revealed itself in her strong ambition for success. Goodman was always serious about achieving the goals she set herself. The Jupiter nature gave her a belief, faith, optimism and philosophical approach to her aspirations, encouraging her to aim high yet never to let go of her spirituality and vision. She was certainly one of the few who were 'ready to receive the spiritual emanations' of that fixed star, in that she was blessed with both receptive sensitivity and a strong sense of the divine and ephemeral, which in turn infused her sense and understanding of the Infinite.

The aspect of opportunistic Jupiter quincunx dreamy Neptune in the fifth house indicates creativity, spiritual and charitable principles. The less helpful side of this aspect is that it can lead to an excess of work and perhaps even a loss of work where one has been unrealistic in what can be achieved and delivered. Another potential of this aspect is that of tremendous impressionability, susceptibility and vulnerability.

Goodman died in 1995, due to complications from diabetes (www.timesmachine. ny.times.com), which was diagnosed in the 1980s. Since she distrusted orthodox medicine, it is documented that she occasionally refused treatment (ibid) which may eventually have necessitated her having a toe removed as well as a leg amputated. At the time of her death, transiting Neptune was in the tenth house, the area that symbolises career and status in society. Transiting Neptune had created some major aspects to some of her natal planets.

Tenuous Neptune can make it challenging to define a Neptunian transit, since the very nature of Neptune is confusing. It is meaningful, however, when considering the explanation provided about Goodman's death, in that there were 'complications', which arose from diabetes.

Transiting Neptune in the tenth house can bring a change of attitude towards one's career, and areas that had been formalised and structured may dissolve into confusion at this time. Artistic and spiritual endeavours have the potential for accomplishment during this transit. However, practicalities will be less important and investing more in one's intuition will help in building foundations for the future. The major aspects created at this time for Goodman were transiting Neptune; square the natal Sun (on the ascendant), square the natal Moon, conjunct natal Jupiter, and sextile natal Uranus.

WISHING AND HOPING

At its simplest, the blending of these transits suggests that, in her final earthly years, Goodman may have felt her vitality draining away. Lack of sleep and insomnia may have been an issue for her in her later years. She may have felt emotionally vulnerable and the pursuit of fantasies may have been evident, along with some illusion and delusion.

For example, we have already seen that Goodman refused to believe her daughter had died, and subsequently flew to New York in order to search for her 'missing' child. There she spent several days sleeping rough outside St Patrick's Cathedral in Manhattan in order to draw attention to what she believed was an official, high-level cover up (www.people.com). Goodman also dreamed that the other missing person in her life, the marine biologist, her former lover, Robert Brewer, would one day return (ibid). She even continued to set a place for him each day at the dining room table (ibid).

There may have been some delusions of a philosophical nature, and it is possible that some of her personal philosophies may have been weakening. Goodman and her work paved the way for a new group of astrologers, mystics and philosophers, and it has been said that her published work, with its inspiring and uncomplicated style of writing, helped many others to access astrology more easily. In this respect she made a tremendous contribution to the generation of the 'New Age'.

As discussed previously, the ruling planet of Goodman's natal chart is activating Mars, and at the time of her death, transiting Mars was in her eighth house – the area symbolising birth, death, and rebirth. In the eighth house, Mars could also symbolise transformation of the ego, since this is associated with Aries, her Sun sign.

The eighth house is also symbolic of joint resources. Towards the end of Goodman's life, she was befriended by Crystal Bush (thought not to be the actress Crystal Bush) who became a cherished friend and obtained publicity rights to Linda Goodman's name at her death; *Linda Goodman's Relationship Signs* was published posthumously. On the day of Goodman's death, transiting Mars was in the eighth house at the critical 0 degrees in Sagittarius. Associations of the mutable fire sign Sagittarius include the philosophical, spirited and higher-principled. This suggests that Goodman remained enterprising, optimistic and broad-minded right through to the very end of her life.

At the time of Goodman's passing, transiting Pluto was also in the eighth house and in Scorpio. Pluto, the eighth house, and Scorpio are all associates of death and rebirth, which is very significant, particularly as Goodman believed in the 'after-life' and of being 'reborn'. Pluto rules the fixed water sign of Scorpio, and also the eighth house; it is concentrated, intense and passionate by nature. In her book, *Linda Goodman's Love Poems* (1981), Goodman stresses that life can only happen in the presence of love and that, once that happened, there could be no death. This is very typical of her approach to love and life.

Some of Goodman's poetry seems to have had an eerily prophetic quality. As early as 1989, in her semi-autobiographical book, *Gooberz*, she often refers to her 'twin self' and at the time of her passing, Goodman's natal personal planets of the Sun, Moon and Mercury had all progressed into the sign of Gemini (the Twins).

Sun, Moon and Mercury, the progressed planets in the sign of Gemini, coupled with transiting Mars in Sagittarius at the eighth house, indicate that in her last earthly years, Goodman was expending all her energy into her publishing, learning and reading activities. In particular, she planned to write an astrology book for children. That signifies the 'youth' associated with Gemini. Perhaps if it had come to fruition, the book would have been another 'first' for her, since it would have been the first astrology book solely for children at that time. She had already written the manuscript for her next book, *Linda Goodman's Relationship Signs*, which was published posthumously (as previously noted).

Linda Goodman, a pioneer devoted to the elements, stars and Universe, not only nurtured astrology but in doing so created a body of work that inspired a new age of astrologers, making astrology more easily accessible to the public. Her work continues to inspire others and one example of this is that in 2000, Hampton Roads Publishing Company published, *Linda Goodman's Star Cards: A Divination Set Inspired by the Astrological and Numerological Teachings of Linda Goodman*. The deck was illustrated by artist, Frank Riccio, and compiled by Goodman's friend, Crystal Bush. The divination set of cards was described as being "… based on the wisdom of America's favourite astrologer," (https://www.alibris.co.uk/) showing the respectful legacy that Goodman left.

ACKNOWLEDGEMENTS, CREDITS AND REFERENCES

Natal, transits and progression chart generated by http://www.astro.com
Progressed chart date: 18th June, 1925.
Linda Goodman: Thursday, 9th April, 1925, Morgantown, WV, USA.
79w57, 39n38.
Data Collector: Frank C. Clifford.
Source of data: Birth certificate.
Rodden Rating 'AA'

Information detail regarding the parents of Linda Goodman, as seen on her birth certificate, by kind courtesy of Frank C. Clifford.

BOOKS

Goodman, L. (1989) *Gooberz*. Hampton Roads Publishing Co., Inc.
Ebertin, R. and Hoffman, G. (2009) *Fixed Stars and their Interpretation.* American Federation of Astrologers.
Goodman, L. (1981) *Linda Goodman's Love Poems.* Pan Books Ltd.
Goodman, L. (1972) *Sun Signs.* Published by Pan Books Ltd.

NEWSPAPERS

Daily Express. 19th July, 1979. Editorial headline: 'A Star is NOT about to be Born!' Journalist un-named, p3.
The Sunday Telegraph. 22nd July, 1979. Article: 'Tis in our Stars my Love' by Mandrake, p6.

WEBSITES

https://www.alibris.co.uk/Linda-Goodmans-Star-Cards-A-Divination-Set-Inspired-by-the-Astrological-and-Numerological-Teachings-of-Linda-Goodman/book/9175163 – Description of set of cards. Accessed on 22/12/2020.
http://en.wikipedia.org – Accessed on 05/02/2014.
http://www.people.com – 'Linda Goodman Seeks Answers in the Stars' by Sarah Moore Hall and Richard K Rein. Accessed on 05/02/2014.
http://consciousevolution.com – 'Mother of the New Age' by Maria Barron: A Profile of Linda Goodman. Accessed on 05/02/2014.
http://consciousevolution.com/Astrology/AboutLinda.htm – Accessed on 05/02/2014.
https://earthenergyreader.wordpress.com/tag/cripple-creek/ – 'Linda Goodman and a whole lotta shakin' goin' on' by Earth Energy Reader. 4th June, 2012. Accessed on 02/02/2020.
http://www.people.com/people – Article: 'Lost in the Stars' by Cynthia Sanz, 27th November, 1995. Accessed on 05/02/2014.
www.timesmachine.nytimes.com – Obituary: 'Linda Goodman Writer Turned Astrologer Dies' by Robert McG. Thomas Jr., 24th October, 1995, p81. Accessed on 05/02/2014.

CHAPTER THIRTEEN

Alex Sanders 1926–1988

Healer, Magician, High Priest, Occultist, Teacher and Witch

ORRELL ALEXANDER SANDERS (usually known as Alex Sanders) was born to Orrell Alexander Carter (later called Sanders) and Hannah Jane Bibby on 6th June, 1926 in Tranmere, Birkenhead (which then was in the boundary of Cheshire), England. The exact time of his birth is unknown. He grew up, like so many others of his generation, during the Great Depression – a time of high unemployment and great poverty. What made his start in life a little unusual was that when he was born, Sanders' father was married to someone else; a situation much frowned upon in those days. The father moved Hannah and their son to Manchester to start a new life, and apparently the name 'Sanders' was selected from a telephone directory when they moved to Manchester, and thus Orrell and Hannah then became known as 'Mr and Mrs Sanders' (Sanders, 2007, 100). In 1970, Alex Sanders discovered that his real surname was Carter, and then officially changed his name by deed poll from Carter to Sanders (ibid).

Orrell Alexander Carter Snr. was born in 1903, and was apparently a successful and talented musician who entertained in a brass band playing in music-halls and theatres (Johns, 1971, 19). However, his increasing alcoholism eventually led to his dismissal after allegedly appearing drunk on stage. Once his unreliability became known, he never worked in theatres again, which must have had a detrimental effect on the family's income during the hard times of the Great Depression.

In order to help maintain and support his family, he found work as a brick layer's labourer, and he also gave private music lessons on the cornet. Occasionally, he worked at weekends for prize brass or silver bands but, unfortunately, he remained an alcoholic, which caused a great deal of anguish and suffering to his wife and children (ibid, 20). Orrell Carter died of alcoholism in 1968, when his son, Alex was 42. Sanders' mother, Hannah Jane Bibby, was born in North Wales in 1904 (ancestry.com), to a naturally psychic family – a gift that was particularly strong on the female side of the family. Hannah left the family home in Wales and went to Liverpool, where she secured employment in domestic service and eventually met Orrell Alexander Carter.

At first, Hannah travelled with Orrell and accompanied him while he worked at different venues as a musician and, for a while, they were financially comfortable. Once their son was born, she continued for a while to travel with her husband and son, at least until Orrell's alcoholism became a problem. Alex Sanders' birth reunited Hannah with her mother Mary, who by then had been widowed for a long time and who left her home in Wales to be near her daughter and first grandson. Hannah took a variety of jobs, including cleaner and tea-lady, to help supplement Orrell's wages. Even so, times were still extremely hard financially. Hannah died in 1970, two years after her husband.

It was Hannah and her mother who first introduced the young Sanders to occult and esoteric subjects. As a young man, he attended local spiritualist churches, working there as a gifted healer and medium. Yet Sanders' greatest passion would be for the witchcraft tradition that he went on to found with his second wife, Maxine. This became known as Alexandrian Wicca. During his lifetime, Sanders' public *persona* generated a good deal of antagonism and ill-feeling, especially when members of his coven dubbed him 'King of the Witches'. He seems to have been quite happy with this designation, courting the media and paparazzi, and being interviewed on television chat-shows. This courting of publicity did not go down well with everyone, particularly some of the Gardnerian (*see glossary*) witches. Sanders was a pioneer who made a significant global contribution to Wicca and witchcraft and its practitioners, before his death on 30th April, 1988.

WHAT ALEX SANDERS' NATAL CHART SHOWS

On 6th June 1926, the Sun was in the air sign of Gemini, and the Moon was in the fire sign of Aries; since Sanders' exact time of birth is unknown, astrologers use a 'noon' chart to represent an unspecified time of birth. The Moon moves the 'fastest', at approximately 13 degrees a day. This creates a dilemma for the astrologer, since one cannot be absolutely certain of the aspects made to the Moon. One must consider the two possible Moon signs (in this case, Aries or Taurus) – and the aspects and themes in the overall chart – to arrive at a conclusion as to Sanders' Moon sign.

Date:30April
1988UT:0:00:00

Natal and Transits Chart for Alex Sanders on the day he died, 30th April, 1988.

At approximately 7.30pm, the Moon moved into the earth sign of Taurus on 6th June, 1926. The Moon in Taurus suggests a profile of the affectionate and romantic, coupled with sentimentality and warmth. It also brings a natural affinity with the earthy, material and physical world. There is a need for reliability and security, cushioned with creature-comforts. A solid and relaxing home helps to make for feelings of safety and security. Once the 'Moon in Taurus' person has made a commitment, they find it challenging to uproot and change, preferring to keep what they have already built-up. This can manifest as conservatism, inflexibility and rigidity.

Such planetary placement of the Moon in Taurus seems unlikely, since there is a lot of 'adaption and movement' in Sanders' natal chart. The Moon in Taurus provides a reluctance to be ambitious, courageous, daring, impulsive and vigorous. However, all of these qualities can be found when the Moon is in Aries and such themes would have helped make Sanders the adventurous, defiant pioneer that he was. Planetary contacts with the Moon made by Jupiter and Neptune indicate a subject who would have needed themes such as adventure, religion, travel, sacrifice, mysticism, spirituality and the ephemeral in his life. This also would have suppressed the usual need for the material aspects of life.

It seems, therefore, that the Moon in Aries is the more plausible of the two Moon sign options. In the *Book of Law*, Sanders' Aries/Martian personality is well shown in his comment, "I became a pioneer and a very public witch for the sake of my own belief, but before that, for the sake of the craft, I had the courage of my conviction and I stood out" (Sanders, 2012, 6).

In Sanders' natal chart, there are two unaspected planets; Venus and Pluto, and an unaspected pair of planets; the Sun and Mercury. Unaspected planets in natal charts are very rare and extremely significant, undoubtedly playing an important role in the way Sanders became famous, infamous and notorious.

Maxine Sanders wrote that, "No matter what the circumstances, his eyes twinkled with a wicked humour that betokened quiet 'knowing'." She and others have remarked that there were no half-hearted reactions to Sanders, one either loved or hated him. Even the nuns in the local convent near to the (then) Sanders' home sewed his ceremonial robes in exchange for him attending their kitchen on Fridays and holding séances there! (Sanders, 2007, 103).

When the Sun is in Gemini, it suggests a changeable and versatile thinker, a natural and intelligent communicator, someone high-spirited and quick-witted who delights in socialising and meeting new people. Variety is the spice of life for Gemini's, who are sometimes considered colourful, almost chameleon-like characters.

There is a duality to Gemini, the sign being symbolised by 'the Twins' and it is in touch with both its feminine and masculine side, something we see in Sanders' relationships with both men and women and about which he wrote candidly in, *Alex Sanders: Book of Law* (Sanders, 2012, 26). The male and female polarities are equally balanced in the chart – the male polarities representing the elements of fire and air, while the female polarities represent the elements of earth and water. Duality is very important in Wicca, and some branches of witchcraft that emphasise male/female and lord/lady, which is necessary for the symbolism of fertility, and in ceremonial magical practices (such as drawing down the Moon), initiation rites and celebration of the sabbats throughout the magical witches' year.

The theme of duality was prominent in Sanders' life, especially in the student/teacher role. We see it first with his grandmother when he was a young boy, and later with his wife, Maxine, especially in his teaching work with their covens and also his writing and media work.

There is restlessness present whenever the Sun and Mercury are in Gemini and especially if they are conjunct each other, and this shows a presence of adaptability and versatility. Sanders was quick-thinking and versatile, and able to multi-task on a variety of projects at the same time. The duality could also apply to the way he presented himself to others. Stewart Farrar once described him as a loveable old rogue, someone who could be "utterly charming and an old charlatan as well" (Farrar, 1995, 105). Likewise, Sanders' wife, Maxine, commented on the contradictions in his character, meaning he could be both 'saint' and 'showman'; someone who possessed a massive magical ego, yet humility to match, and who could be staggeringly kind, yet ruthlessly frightening (Sanders, 2007, 03).

Stewart Farrar once compared Sanders' flamboyance to that of a gifted court jester (Farrar, 1995, 167) and certainly he was very intelligent, apparently learning to read when he was only three. Often top of his class, when he was eleven, he won a scholarship to the William Hulme's Grammar School (Johns, 1971, 30). Unfortunately, his family's financial difficulties meant he could not take up the scholarship but instead was expected to go out to work as soon as possible and help support them. It is uncertain what employment he took up then to assist his family.

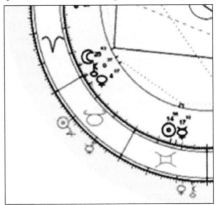

Although it might have been natural for the young Sanders to feel bitter about this, it seems not to have been the case. Perhaps this is due to the lack of hard aspects with the Moon and Pluto and the fact that his Sun and Moon signs are not prone to bitterness or resentfulness. Also, Gemini and Aries are not fixed in nature and these signs would have helped him move on more easily than others and focus on looking to the future.

Despite the setback regarding the scholarship, Sanders never lost his sense of humour, which Stewart Farrar (the subject of Chapter Nine) once described as "puckish" (Farrar, 1995, 167). This is very much in keeping with Mercury's jovial and silver-tongued nature. Youth being an association of Mercury, it gives Gemini a childish streak which can last well into adult life. They can be the original Peter Pan characters, forever reluctant to leave the carefree joys of Never-Never Land. In Sanders' natal chart, Mercury forms part of an unaspected pair of planets (the other being the Sun) which is very unusual in a chart as discussed above This suggests that Sanders was adaptable, intelligent and likeable, coupled with a sense of humour and sociability. He probably enjoyed flitting from one activity to another. Achieving short-term projects, especially ones that required intellectual, verbal or written effort may have come naturally to him. His greatest challenge would be finding perseverance and discipline. His Mercurial mind may have been an asset to him, in that the peregrine Mercury did not prohibit or restrain his intellectual distinction. This message is further emphasised by Mercury being at home in its natural sign of Gemini in Sanders' natal chart, which bestows curiosity and an enquiring mind, along with a certain restlessness.

Sanders' incessant need to move from one activity and person to another was almost certainly influenced by Mercury and Gemini, both of which are flexible and dexterous. One result of this was that working on intellectual, verbal and written projects may have been easy for Sanders, especially where he could apply his knowledge and creative thinking.

When he worked as a book-duster in the John Ryland's Library (a research institution that later merged with the University of Manchester in the 1970s), a friend told him that the library held old manuscripts, including a copy of *The Key of Solomon*. When Sanders applied for the post and was invited for an interview, as soon as he entered the old building, he recognised symbols and hallmarks of a stonemason who had an understanding of witchcraft and carved them into the pillars carved on the walls.

Sanders' mind was further stimulated when he entered into the boardroom to be interviewed. There he saw "magnificent framed papyrus specimens on the walls and the Egyptian bills of sale for servants" (Johns, 197, 67–68). When Sanders told the interviewer that he loved and wanted to care for books, he was immediately offered the position of book-duster, and employed on Tuesday 7th August, 1962 (Lindop, 2018, 117). The role of book-duster was an important one for the library (even though the wages were low). The team of book-dusters was required to wear brown warehouse coats; and gradually work their way around the bookshelves, dusting the books with a soft brush (ibid).

Before the Clean Air Act of 1956, many city libraries faced challenges with dust inside and outside their buildings and the John Rylands Library in Manchester was no exception. Local factory chimneys, domestic coal fires and gasworks, created oily and sooty dust. When the library opened in 1900, it was equipped with an innovative air-filtration system, which was so ineffective, that the exterior and interior stonework became darkened (email communication to Author from Associate Director of Curatorial Practices, John Rylands Library). Sanders soon became familiar with the library and its layout and eventually found the Egyptian section, which particularly captivated him. When he found a copy of *The Key of Solomon*, he was delighted. Gradually, he dismantled the book a few pages at a time, so he could have copies made and then return the originals to the library. Sanders had a friend who worked in an office and had access to a photocopier; through him, Sanders had copies of the originals made. Photocopiers were not generally available to the British public until the 1970s, despite being invented back in the 1950s. This illustrates his improvisational abilities, but also his devious and thrifty Mercurial mindset. However, his behaviour backfired on him, and he was fired for "neglect of his duties" (Lindop, 2018, 115).

As a result, Sanders was investigated by the police at his home for books missing from the library, and two damaged books were found at his home: *The Key of Solomon*, and A.E. Waite's, *Book of Black Magic and Pacts* (Lindop, 2018, 8). He eventually returned the items and narrowly escaped going to prison for theft. The damaged books are still held at the library today, although not available for viewing by the public (ibid, 7).

Interestingly, in 2016, when the John Rylands Library held an exhibition called 'Magic, Witches & Devils in the Early Modern World,' their ex-employee was not included in the exhibition (email communication to Author from Associate Director of Curatorial Practices). More recently, the building has been described as being "like something straight out of Harry Potter" (email communication to Author from a library visitor).

HEALING, PROGRESS AND RECOVERY

The planet Mercury rules the sign of Gemini and also all aspects of communication together with the healing arts. The subject of healing featured significantly in Sander's life, where he successfully applied his talents. For example, he cured a woman who had fibrosis in her back, and a man whose face was disfigured with a twitch. When Joan, his sister, was terminally ill, she stayed with Alex in his home and he administered hands-on-healing to her. She was said to have told him, "You should lay your hands on sick people ... to the one who is suffering they are like angel's hands" (Johns, 1971, 60).

Alexand Maxine Sanders (licensed by PA Photos Ltd)

Sanders performed healing rituals and spells for animals and humans, and Stewart Farrar was particularly impressed by the healing dynamic in the Sanders' coven (Farrar, 1995, 44–45). This shows how the healing arts were of great significance throughout Sanders' life.

He also helped Maxine Sanders' mother who had cancer (Sanders, 2007, 47), and a child who had learning disabilities and epilepsy that caused daily fits (ibid, 42). Gradually the fits stopped and her learning disabilities improved. When Sanders' daughter, Janice, was born with a twisted right foot, doctors at the hospital insisted that nothing could be done for her until she was a teenager, so Sanders set about healing her himself. Praying, he followed the advice given to him clairaudently. This involved applying warmed olive oil to the joint in the foot and manipulating it into its correct position. He did not, however, tell his wife or the doctor about his daughter's recovery, instead allowing them to wonder how Janice's foot had corrected itself (Johns, 1971, 41).

Alex and his wife, Maxine, used music and dance with their coven to help outsiders who were mentally troubled or addicted to mind-altering substances to gain balance and peace. As a child, Sanders had wanted to be a doctor, so he must have felt he had a calling to heal and help others. He may also have been influenced by the way his maternal grandmother nursed him back to health when he was seven years-old and had contracted tuberculosis.

The conjunction between the Sun and Mercury provides a clue about Sander's attitude towards his own health. Possibly, he was unable to be objective about his own contribution to his medical problems, perhaps due to arrogance. For example, in medical astrology, his Sun sign Gemini and its ruler, Mercury, are associated with the respiratory and nervous systems, and so the conjunction in his chart suggests that he functioned with a lot of nervous energy, requiring stimulation so that he was constantly busy. This could have made him very fatigued. This theme is also echoed in the placement of Mars in Pisces, where energy levels may fluctuate and be inconstant. It may have helped Sanders if he could have slowed down and given his faculties a chance to rest.

ALCHEMY, CHEMISTRY AND MAGIC

Other Mercurial attributes include commerce, reading and writing, teaching and speaking; all of which featured significantly in Sander's life. He had many different jobs, including carpenter, salesman, book-duster in a library (as we know) and an assistant in a company of manufacturing chemists, where first he worked in their laboratories and later transferred to their plant, minding a huge calender that made adhesive plaster (Johns, 1969, 36).

He was probably employed by James Woolley, Sons & Co. Ltd; a prominent manufacturing chemist in Manchester, which made plasters for a wide range of health conditions. This would have been around 1946, during World War II, when Sanders was around twenty years-old.

Both the chemist and Mercury are symbolised in alchemy and astrology by the caduceus staff which is entwined by two serpents (the healing caduceus of Apuleius is very similar but has a single serpent and we see a stylised form of it in the logo of the British Medical Association).

In Sanders's natal chart, there is a preponderance of planets in the water signs, comprising: Mars and Uranus in Pisces, Saturn in Scorpio and Pluto in Cancer. The water element in astrology is associated with artistry, imagination, intuition and mediumistic abilities. The planets in the air signs consist of Sun and Mercury in Gemini and Jupiter in Aquarius. The air element is associated with communication, intellectualism and sociability. The planets in the fire signs of Sander's chart comprises of the Moon in Aries and Neptune in Leo. The fire element is associated with confidence, enthusiasm, and instinct. The only planet in an earth sign is Venus in Taurus. The earth element is associated with materialism, practicality and steadiness. The tendencies and qualities of these planetary placements are discussed later on.

CURIOSITY, STUDY AND TEACHING

Sanders excelled at teaching and developed many covens in his capacity as Verbis (his witch name). His friend and student, Stewart Farrar (see Chapter Nine), described him as an excellent teacher, introducing hundreds of people to Wicca, but ultimately leaving responsibility for their spiritual development to the individual (Farrar, 1995, 2). Sanders' infectious enthusiasm for a wide variety of subjects would have rubbed off on his students.

Farrar was impressed with the training offered to members of the Sanders' coven and the way they were nurtured, especially the way everyone was judged as an individual, instead of following a set formula. This assessed them on their own needs, while taking into account the effect they might have on the dynamic of the group. Farrar's lasting impression of an initiation in the Sanders coven was that it was "dignified and moving" (Farrar, 1995, 5). Sanders also recognised the importance of having both young and older witches in the coven in order to maintain balance. This may have been influenced by his own experiences when learning from his grandmother, who had taught him about spirits and magic.

Sanders enjoyed travelling in order to teach his passion for the Craft. His written work included his *Book of Shadows; Alex Sanders: Book of Law* and *The Alex Sanders Lectures.* He enjoyed learning and had an aptitude for languages which would have helped when learning about ancient magical ceremonies and rites from places such as Egypt and India.

As a child, his maternal grandmother had taught him to speak Welsh (Johns, 1971, 24), as well as teaching him witchcraft and runes and told him the old stories and legends. She did not just tell the stories however, but interpreted them, telling the captivated boy how Robin Hood, for example, was really a witch who used his power to help the poor, while Joan of Arc was the Witch Queen of France, who proudly asserted her identity by the way she dressed, at a period in history when the only females who wore men's clothing were witches.

His grandmother had a profound and lasting influence on him, also teaching him about the Craft and cunning-lore on topics such as herbalism. She impressed upon him the importance of witches maintaining their integrity, always first considering the greater good and avoiding using power for selfish purposes, lest it destroy them. When his grandmother passed away, Sanders was in his early teens, and he missed her deeply, especially her stimulating teaching which had helped develop his gifts and talents. Her passing forced him to contact other witches in order to continue his development as a witch and widen his learning about witchcraft.

Sadly, there was a period in his life when Sanders did not heed his grandmother's advice about integrity and avoiding self-interest. There may have been several reasons why he began to abuse his powers as a clairvoyant and witch (Farrar, 1995, 4) and later described it as a period of devotion to black magic. Possibly, after the poverty in his childhood, he had begun to covet a more materialistic lifestyle. This may explain why he started mocking his family for not sharing in his prosperity and refusing his offers of money and help. Partly this refusal was because his mother suspected that his property had not been gained by honest means (Johns, 1971, 55). Also, she probably realised that Sanders was surrounding himself with opportunists and freeloaders. One example of how Sanders acquired property dishonestly was seen earlier in this chapter, when he was employed as a book-duster.

CLEANSING AND PURGING

According to Farrar, Sanders only freed himself from this situation "... with a drastic process of self-purification" (Farrar, 1995, 4). This process would have required the cleansing, intense and transforming energy of Pluto. When Sanders' much-loved sister, Joan, died on 28th June, 1959, it was the third death of a woman he had valued in his life, the other two being his grandmother and a much-loved mistress. Sanders felt he was somehow to blame for their deaths, due to his practice of the Left Hand Path, and that their deaths were some kind of karmic debt. Themes of Pluto include bereavement, grief and transformation, and Sanders may have been able to seek some comfort in the spiritualist belief that there is only physical death, whereas the human soul exists continuously.

When his sister died, Sanders was experiencing some significant astrological transits. For example, transiting Pluto was creating a trine with natal Venus. Because of Sanders' unknown time of birth, it is difficult to see exactly where in his natal chart these transits would have had an effect in his life, since there are no house placements to which we can refer. However, it is possible to address some of the possible influences that Sanders may have experienced during this and other transits.

The trine aspect is a harmonious position which could have been helpful in Sanders' life. Some of the transit's influences may have included death and rebirth cycles, psychological healing, emotionally and sexually rewarding relationships, and delving deeper into the spirit behind sexual acts; since these are all Plutonian themes. Other influences may have included coming to terms with his deepest fears and confronting the dark side of his nature. This may have helped shed light on any previous manipulation and misuse of his power, where he may have been controlling and domineering towards people and situations.

Despite the loss and grief, the year 1959 was probably a new and rewarding time in Sanders' life, helping him once more value those around him. We can see this, for example, with his deepening relationship with Maxine Morris (later to become his wife), to whom he was first introduced in 1960, shortly after Joan's death. In 1964, Maxine was initiated into Sanders' coven and a year later they were handfasted, marrying in a civil ceremony in 1968. By now, transiting Pluto would have stopped creating a trine aspect with Venus.

This all shows the transforming energy of Pluto, and the trine of Venus in Taurus shows a determination and steadiness in his relationships, all of which are associated with the fixed nature of Venus in Taurus in his natal chart. Pluto trine natal Venus aspect helps create permanent relationships. For example, his relationship with Maxine was driven by compulsive and intense energies, for such is the powerful nature of Pluto, helping them both to learn about the inner power which was at work in their relationship.

In 1959, Sanders experienced a harmonious trine aspect between transiting Saturn and his natal Venus, suggesting he could now achieve stability in his relationships, since the nature of Saturn is concrete and disciplined. At such a time he would be less likely to enter into relationships under the influence of romantic illusions. These transits would have helped his growing partnership with Maxine and also promoted the responsibility required in coven relationships.

Saturn is the ruling planet of Maxine Sander's Sun sign Capricorn, as she was born on 30th December, 1946 (Sanders, 20078, 11). In turn, Maxine could also have brought her own Saturnian energy to the relationship, which can include teaching, wisdom and being 'older' in years through experience and wisdom rather than physical years.

Saturn's other associates include conditions, definition and structure, and it also symbolises experience and maturity. Therefore, during this period, Saturn could have helped Sanders to be more serious about his coven work. It could also have helped consolidate relationships with qualities such as growth, patience, realism and responsibility; all of which are associated with Saturn.

BUSINESS AND MONEY

During the transit between these two planets, Sanders may have developed a more responsible attitude towards money and possessions, in marked contrast to his earlier life. He had previously adopted an immature attitude towards money, perhaps because rather than working for it, his benefactors, Maud and Ron (surname unknown), had donated it to him (Johns, 1971, 44–45). His growing responsibility and discipline with financial matters was helped by the harmonious and natural trine aspect.

Unaspected Planet
An unaspected planet is without a major aspect linking it to other planets.

Unaspected Venus in the natal chart suggests a charming, giving and loving nature, which needs to guard against the materialistic side of Venus, so that it does not precede the love element of Taurus. In Sanders' chart, Venus is at home in the earthy and materialistic sign of Taurus which can be prone to laziness, depending on other factors in the chart. The unaspected Venus is uncontrolled as there is no aspect created with other planets; this suggests that Sanders may have experienced strong emotional outbursts. Such inconsistencies may have caused him to distrust his own feelings and ultimately the feelings of others.

The Moon in the fire sign of Aries suggests that Sanders needed action and excitement in his life, and may have been driven by audacity, courage, danger and self-assurance. The Moon in the cardinal sign of Aries) indicates that Sanders was a natural pioneer who could initiate and lead. Working alone will have appealed to him also, especially in his work as a magician when necessary. Mars is the ruling planet of Aries, providing him with courage, energy and a strong entrepreneurial spirit, as previously discussed.

In Sanders' natal chart, there are planets in each of the water signs comprising: Mars in Pisces, Saturn in Scorpio, Uranus in Pisces and Pluto in Cancer. This suggests powerful artistry, imagination, emotion, intuition and sensitivity. Professor Ronald Hutton once observed that Sanders showed great affection and kindness to those who behaved well towards him but responded 'savagely' towards those who did not.

We see a good example of his duality here, in the way his wit could be turned against those he disliked, and how he could exploit these people without compunction, whereas he was "outstandingly generous" towards those he liked and respected (Hutton, 1999, 330). This echoes Maxine Sanders' remark about the "saint and showman" aspects in her husband's character (Sanders, 2007, 103).

ENERGY, FANTASIES AND VISION

In Sanders' natal chart, Mars is in the artistic, imaginative, intuitive, mediumistic and sacrificial water sign of Pisces at 24 degrees. This shows he enjoyed working behind the scenes and being instrumental in artistic and imaginative pursuits. For example, he and Maxine were asked for technical advice during the production of a film called, *The Eye of the Devil* (Sanders, 2007, 107), by Metro-Goldwyn-Meyer and starring David Hemmings, David Niven and Sharon Tate. The director, J. Lee Thompson, wanted to experience first-hand the ambience and mood of ritual magic, before trying to communicate it on screen, and Sanders was hired as a consultant on the film.

Mars symbolises action and Pisces/Neptune fantasy, illusion and imagination. Mars makes a quincunx aspect to Pisces' ruler, Neptune, suggesting an elusive and restless side to his nature, especially where his work was concerned. His best work required an easy-going environment, where he could 'go with the flow' and not have to apply routine and regulation. We see this in Stewart Farrar's remark that Sanders did not "follow any set formula" in his coven work (Farrar, 1995, 44). This may also explain why Sanders found it difficult to remain in the same employment for a long time, especially if method, organisation and systems had to be applied (for example, in his work in the library).

Cardinal Energies

There are three modes in astrology: cardinal, fixed and mutable energies; representing the way in which a sign operates. The cardinal signs are Aries, Cancer, Libra and Capricorn. These are initiators of action, natural leaders with ambition and strong feelings, like champions who break barriers and set out new territory.

There is a sense of fantasy, imagination, theatricality and unreality created between the aspect of Mars quincunx Neptune and the positions of Mars in Pisces and Neptune in Leo. This is because the sign of Pisces and its ruler, Neptune, are akin to distortion, escapism and illusion. Additionally, Mars and the sign of Leo are not only correspondences of I, ego and self but also the actor, who must be dramatic, entertaining and theatrical. As a young child, Sanders was introduced to the world of entertainment and theatre when he toured the music halls and theatres with his father (Johns, 1971, 19). This shows that Sanders was acquainted with theatricality from an early age and understood the importance of an audience. Many feel there was a strong element of fantasy in some of Sanders' stories about growing up. Stewart Farrar felt it reached a point where Sanders might not have been able to distinguish between reality and his own creation of self (Farrar, 1995, page 2 of preface). In particular, Sanders' claim to have copied his grandmother's *Book of Shadows* is unlikely to be true, since his *Book of Shadows* was actually the Gardnerian one, created by Gerald Gardner and Doreen Valiente in the 1950s. Farrar also claimed that Sanders appropriated other people's work but failed to give them credit for it. Apparently, when questioned about this, he said simply, "These teachers meant their work to be used by other teachers" (ibid: page 3 of preface), which is quite blasé and dismissive.

Jupiter in hard aspect to Neptune in Sanders' natal chart suggests that his imagination could ignite endless dreams and fantasies. Author, Dennis Bardens, wrote that, "British witches rejoice in fanciful titles. Alex Sanders had been described as 'King of the Witches'" (Bardens, 1971, 181), and clearly Sanders did not resent the title.

Another example of his fantasising (or boasting) can be seen in one of his letters, published in 1974 in the *Daily Express* newspaper, in which he claimed, "Throughout the country there are now thousands of members of the Alexandrians" (*Daily Express* 1974). NOMIS (the Official Labour Market Statistics for the Office of National Statistics) showed in their research from the 2011 Census for England & Wales that the number of people who followed Wicca as a religion was 11,766, while 1,276 followed witchcraft.

When he appeared on television during the 1960s and 70s, Sanders wore dark glasses, and when asked why, he replied, "These are to protect you from me" (https://www.youtube.com – Maxine Sanders interview, 2018). Maxine Sanders also said that Sanders "… was a natural showman … he wanted to shock and rebel" (Jordan, 1996, 140). This is pertinent to Sanders astrologically, as in his natal chart, Jupiter is in Aquarius and shows that he would have enjoyed shocking people and going to extremes.

Another interpretation and variation (of which there are many) of the hard aspect between Jupiter and Neptune also suggests that Sanders could also be compassionate and kind-hearted, sometimes to his detriment (qualities associated with Neptune), and indeed Maxine Sanders described him as being "generous to a fault" (https://www.youtube.com – Maxine Sanders interview, 2018). This shows his contrasting behaviour, in keeping with the duality of his Sun sign, Gemini.

FREEDOM, INDEPENDENCE AND LIBERTY

Mars is conjunct Uranus suggesting that Sanders may either have had to fight for his freedom, or that he was a revolutionary and struggling for reform, since the nature of Mars is to battle and the nature of Uranus is driven towards independence and progress. It could be said he had to strive for the freedom to live his life in the way he chose at a time when society still enforced its morality on others in terms of sexual freedom and religion. He was even arrested and assaulted for his religious beliefs during the period 1958–73, claiming that the police smashed his teeth and pulled out some of his hair (Sanders, 2012, 6).

Sanders and his wife Maxine were even interviewed during the police investigation into the Moors Murders in the 1960s because they had been at Saddleworth Moor (ibid, 108). Their reason for this was that, during their investigations, the police had searched Ian Brady's flat and found occult books there, so when they saw the Sanders' ritual working on the moor, they jumped to conclusions and incorrectly assumed that Alex and Maxine were somehow implicated.

In both of these examples, we see Sanders' liberty under threat, and his need to fight for it. He told a reporter in 1966, that he looked "… forward to the day when our religion will be seen for the beautiful thing it is and we shall be allowed to worship freely in our temples" (*The Weekender* 1966). The reporter wrote that he felt Sanders' optimism was premature (ibid).

A conjunction between Mars and Uranus can also indicate sudden outbursts of temper, since Mars is direct, frank and impatient; and Uranus is only interested in truths. Sanders was easy going normally, except when confronting dishonesty, something his biographer June Johns noted when interviewing him (Johns, 1971, 124).

The energy with this aspect suggests that Sanders' own physical energy may have been sporadic, since Mars represents action and energy, while Uranus represents unpredictability and the erratic. This is further seen with Mars in Pisces where energy levels fluctuate, presenting as spurts of activity followed by inertia. However, in Sanders' natal chart there is a strong dynamic mental energy, as previously discussed, where the Sun is conjunct Mercury (and Mercury is in its ruling sign of Gemini). Mars creates a quincunx aspect with Pisces' ruler, Neptune, which suggests that although sometimes Sanders may have felt emotionally and physically drained, this may have been due to his inability to set himself realistic boundaries and limits in working with other people.

Returning to the aspect of Mars conjunct Uranus, this is an excellent planetary contact for coaching, encouraging and inspiring others, and would have been beneficial to Sanders in his coven teaching work with Maxine, where their most remarkable gift was "… their ability to inspire people" (Guerra and Farrar, 2008, 106). So many people were inspired either directly by meeting the Sanders', or indirectly, through his Alexandrian work on their spiritual path, that it literally fills a book (*All the King's Children; The Human Legacy of Alex Sanders* by Jimahl di Fiosa. Published by LOGIOS, 2010).

THE UNEXPECTED AND THE UNCONVENTIONAL

Mars and Uranus contact can also indicate a tendency to be accident-prone especially where fires, sharp tools and metal are involved. This is because Uranus associates with accidents and fires, while knives, sharp tools and blood are all associates of Mars. Electricity is also an associate of Uranus so again accidents involving electricity could be more likely for someone with this aspect. Experimentation is also associated with Uranus and so it could be said that Sanders was experimental when working with the Martian athames and swords and creating cones of power, in magic and ritual.

His reputation for being accident-prone may have been due to a combination of impatience, unnecessary risk-taking and a failure to take precaution. In her book, *Firechild*, Maxine Sanders gave a first-hand account of a theatrical production called, *Alex Sanders, King of the Witches, Presents WITCHCRAFT*, in which she and Alex were performing. Since the props included candles and incense, these were considered a health & safety fire risk, so the London Fire Brigade had to be in attendance backstage. Even so, there was a dangerous incident when Sanders threw a censer of burning charcoals at Maxine who was playing the demon Ashtoreth. It must have seemed very effective to the audience, with flames dancing around her sparkling body, but in fact what was happening was that the charcoals had set fire to the glue that was used on the sparkles (Sanders, 2007, 157).

The conjunction created between Mars and Uranus also suggests an unconventional attitude towards sex, since Mars connects with lust and sexuality and Uranus with the unorthodox. It has been claimed that a Mars-Uranus individual is known to be "quick to take his clothes off" (Tompkins, 1990, 208), and certainly Sanders' sexual lifestyle would have fitted this. That said, by the time he was twenty, Sanders had lived through a World War, after which, conventional morality and values would be forever changed for many people. Therefore, when we read about his promiscuity, gay sex and 'sex parties' (Johns, 1971, 50–51), it is important to remember that millions of young people had died in the previous few years. People had learned, due to war, that it was necessary to seize the day.

Sanders' apparent eagerness to remove his clothes was not just about sex; he had also needed to *change* clothes in his modelling work (at one point he worked as a photographic model under the professional name of Paul Dallas, a name he had also used when working in spiritualist churches) and worked sky-clad (naked) in his rituals.

In Sanders' chart, Jupiter is in the sign of Aquarius at 27 degrees. This placement would have been helpful in Sanders in being able to offer novel, original, and unusual ideas in a group setting. It will also have made him enthusiastic in working to support various causes. For example, he undertook charitable works to help blind children such as the 'Sunshine Babies' charity (his first son had been born partially sighted), the old-aged, poor and mentally ill (Sanders, 2007, 103). He often used festivals as an opportunity to raise this money.

Jupiter in Aquarius echoes the message that Sanders enjoyed associating with a wide social network, irrespective of class and race, since expansion is associated with Jupiter and friendships are associated with Aquarius. This placement also indicates a belief in humanity and mankind as Jupiter associates with belief and faith, and Aquarius with humanity and mankind.

Sanders believed that people should be openly able to develop, practice and study their beliefs. Jupiter in Aquarius and Sun in Gemini both contributed to this, bringing him an enlightened, varied and wide network of friends. In this environment, he could have been the life and soul of the party, providing group encouragement and inspiration. Friends and acquaintances came from all walks of life and every social status, something he was careful to maintain in his coven. This illustrates that he felt it was more important to mix with like-minded souls and kindred spirits rather than sticking to a particular social class. For his time, he was very forward-thinking.

FUTURISTIC AND PSYCHIC

The planet Uranus is in the sign of Pisces at 29 degrees, which can bring a zest for rebellion, independence and the unorthodox. Sanders was gifted and talented with an imagination that allowed him to escape into a fantasy world, such is the nature of Pisces, so meditation and trance-work would have come naturally to him. As a child, he frequently demonstrated to his mother that he had the gift of clairvoyance and sensitivity; he regularly used to play with 'spirit children' and engage in a ball game, where he would throw the ball and an invisible being would throw the ball back (Sanders, 2007, 100). As his mother was also 'sighted', she understood that Sanders was playing with spirit children, so was able to accept the gift of her son's sensitivity, whereas other less spiritually aware people may have seen him as odd or eccentric (both associations of Uranus), which would have created a sense of alienation.

At school, Sanders often had premonitions about events he saw happening to his school friends (Johns, 1971, 25), and this prescient energy is another example of Uranus' associations. As Sanders was still a child then, he would just blurt out what he had seen in his visions. On at least one occasion, this resulted in him being beaten, since the recipient did not take kindly to Sanders' revelation. He soon realised he needed to be cautious when telling others about his predictions.

Uranus in Pisces shows an attraction to all things mystical and spiritual, along with the occult and the supernatural. Sanders had the knack of being able to shock, while at the same time was deadly earnest about challenging preconceived ideas (Sanders, 2007, 103). The shock element is also an association of Uranus, whose energy can be surprising and unpredictable; and in bringing an 'awakening', it reveals its enlightening and progressive nature.

Even though Sanders was controversial, he brought witchcraft to the media's attention although, as with Farrar, some people in the Craft questioned his motivation and criticised him for attracting publicity. Behind the showmanship, however, was a strong belief that the more people heard about witchcraft, the less they would fear it (Sanders, 2007, 109). This idea may have taken root in the Sanders' disturbing experiences when questioned by the police in connection with the Moors Murders.

Sanders regularly applied his gift of clairvoyance for self-knowledge by scrying his crystal and reading his tarot pack. In the tarot, Sanders' Sun sign of Gemini and its ruling planet, Mercury, are symbolised by the Magician card, which usually depicts the figure standing ready with his tools, and Farrar once described his friend as "a very powerful magician" (Farrar, 1995, 8). He had his own experience of Sanders' skills.

On one occasion in the early days of their friendship, having discussed clairvoyance and premonition, Sanders told Farrar that within the next month or two he would 'make' about £500–600 from a freelance assignment that was in some way connected with either law or the police. The prediction was uncannily accurate, since Farrar was approached by Thames Television and asked to write an episode of the police series, Special Branch, for the sum of £550! (ibid, 4).

Sanders' Moon sign, Aries, is symbolised in the tarot by the Emperor card, where the Emperor's throne is often depicted with the Aries glyph, Rams head or Ram's horns; Aries is initiating and pioneering. Sanders generated psychic phenomenon, conducted séances, and experimented with magical rituals. The Moon in Aries indicates that he would have enjoyed the freedom that illusion and transcendence can bring, and the lack of invasive boundaries and restrictions enabled him to work with maximum effect.

Saturn in the water sign of Scorpio suggests that Sanders not only controlled his own emotional problems but also hid them from others. Restrictive Saturn brings an intense fear of opening-up emotionally and intimately. Potentially, this could have led to sexual power struggles, since Scorpio and its ruler, Pluto, govern control, power and sex.

The unaspected Venus is uncontrolled as there is no aspect created with other planets; this suggests that Sanders, despite his efforts at self-control (shown by Saturn in Scorpio above), may have had outbreaks of emotional and sentimental instability. These would have caused him to distrust his own feelings and ultimately also the feelings of others. Venus is in Taurus in Sanders' natal chart (as previously discussed), suggesting he enjoyed life's pleasures, such as good food and good living, fine wines, art and music. We see this in his early adult life when he lived in a large house called Riversdale and could access money from his benefactors.

Sanders claimed to have seen the house in one of his premonitions before he had met his benefactors. He regularly visited auctions, collecting antiques and period furniture for his home, spending thousands of pounds refurbishing and restoring it. Perhaps, as a reaction against the poverty of his childhood, he wore hand-tailored suits and employed two cleaners just to polish his Georgian silver and antique furniture! He enjoyed a tipple, and acquired a taste for brandy at that time (Johns, 1971, 45–47). Conversely the natural and simple life can appeal to the Venus in Taurus position, for example, animals, gardening, nature and the countryside. Being at one with the elements would have been hugely satisfying to Sanders and perhaps he found this when he left his various homes in the cities. As a young teenager, he had been evacuated to the countryside in Great Harwood, near Pendle Hill in Lancashire, and he enjoyed holding rituals in the open air at Alderley Edge in Cheshire.

Alex Sanders (photograph by kind permission of Maxine Sanders)

Being out of doors would have appealed to him as Venus enjoys and appreciates the natural world and Mother Nature. Bombarding his senses of smell, taste, hearing sight and touch would have doubtless appealed to his sensuous nature. In return, Sanders showed his devotion and love of the Earth Mother by performing ritual magic in the open air.

When Alex and Maxine lived in Selmeston in Sussex, they very much lived close to nature, housing cats and dogs that the local animal sanctuary were unable to place, along with a horse and two donkeys and also grew their own vegetables (Sanders, 2007, 165). Yet despite living in rather straightened circumstances, he remained generous and always gave what he could, whether that was "food, material objects or information of a magical nature" (ibid, 103). This is very typical of people who have Venus in Taurus.

Sanders' actions also point to Chiron, the Wounded Healer, in Taurus in his natal chart. The wound or healing may be found in Sanders' reluctance in his later life to be imprisoned by items and possessions. It also symbolises the experience of poverty, which is something that was certainly true of his childhood; during his early adult life he may have been drawn to material wealth because of the experience of poverty. However, he gradually learned that wealth did not bring him the happiness he had anticipated.

Sanders was born during the recession of the 1920s, marked by the General Strike of 1926, several years before the UK's Great Depression really took hold. Raising a family during this period must have been exceptionally difficult. The economic consequences were dire for many years afterwards, particularly affecting industrial and mining areas.

Venus in Taurus is very physical and sensuous, seeking security through partnerships, which can be seen through Sanders' long relationship with Maxine Sanders. What Venus in Taurus needs in love is determined by the pleasing of the senses, and so there is an appreciation of form, texture and touch. Taurus is an earth sign, which denotes practicality, and Sanders was very practical, making cloths and vegetable pies for his Craft festivals, decorating them with pastry fertility symbols for his coven-members (ibid, 131). He could also sew garments and Maxine remembers being dressed in "shimmering pale green violet-blue robes" that her husband had made on their old Singer treadle machine (ibid, 125). This shows his skill, since the types of fabric that shimmer are notoriously difficult to sew. Of course, necessity may have been the mother of invention, especially since he would have had no money to buy the sort of robes he wished to own (even had they been available then).

Manual treadle machines were considered old-fashioned, even in the 1970s, but perhaps when he was a boy, Sanders had seen his mother and grandmother using one. It was certainly not common for men to sew 'at home' rather than professionally at that time. He also decorated, painted and wallpapered at home (ibid, 49), showing that he was very capable with his hands, including his healing abilities. In medical astrology, the hands are associations of Mercury, the ruling planet of Sanders' Sun sign.

Saturn is at 21 degrees of the fixed sign of Scorpio and falls in the constellation of Unuk. When Unuk is in Scorpio, it is often interpreted as a 'Martian force' that brings danger and destruction (Ebertin-Hoffman, 2009, 63) and Sanders, as we have seen, could be quite destructive in some areas of his life. Another feature of this placement is the presence of chronic diseases and, as a child, he contracted tuberculosis, which would have certainly caused long-lasting chronic health problems.

CONTROL AND ENDURANCE

In Sanders' chart, Mars is trine Saturn. This is helpful, since it provides a strong measure of perseverance and persistence in fighting to be 'first', in a pioneering sense. The authoritative nature of Saturn is given a forceful domineering energy when trine Mars, resulting in the ability to constantly achieve, to seek and obtain prominent positions and be held in high esteem. This is borne out by being assigned the title of 'King of the Witches' by his coven members, and perhaps also by being the co-founder of the Alexandrian tradition (a term originally coined by Stewart Farrar for his friend) with his wife, Maxine.

By pursuing an interest that motivated him (i.e. witchcraft), Sanders endured opposition and mockery, yet ensured that his legacy was long-lasting. This comes from Mars' ability to motivate and Saturn's to stabilise. Sanders' name and achievements stimulated and inspired many Wiccans and non-Wiccans alike, and continue to do so, even today.

Alex Sanders (photograph by kind permission of Maxine Sanders)

Mars trine Saturn also indicates working with authority figures, elders and the traditional; all of which is demonstrated in his Saturnian and Martian passion for the Craft. This placement would have helped Sanders lay foundations for his passion, for example, in the tradition that he formed with his wife, Maxine. This became known as the Alexandrian tradition (after his first name and perhaps even an indirect reference to their shared love of Egyptology). He also helped to develop other groups, such as the *Ordine Della Luna* and the *Order of Deucalion*.

Challenges and tensions with Jupiter square Saturn on a broad level suggest 'tests of faith,' since Jupiter is associated with religion and beliefs, while Saturn is obstructing and taxing. This is borne out by Sanders being faced with opposition by the authorities and media concerning his beliefs in witchcraft. The nature of fiery and inspiring Jupiter is to expand, while the nature of earthy and realistic Saturn is to restrict, which brings stresses and tensions.

The earth element is less significant in Sanders' chart, suggesting he lacked interest in materialistic and practical matters. Instead, his philosophy was that material things made people sluggish and bound them to the earth, "... all the magical grimoires in the world will not make a man or a magician, without intelligence" (Sanders, 2007, 103). Possibly, this attitude evolved after that period of early wealth in his life, when he took advantage of a kindly benefactor. Only with the passing years did he better understand that money was not what really made a man.

Jupiter is in opposition to Neptune in Sanders' natal chart. This aspect can relate to areas such as excessive dreams, mystical experiences and great sacrifice. It also suggests adventures and opportunities in the areas of mysticism and spirituality. Jupiter represents organised religion, while Neptune indicates vision and spirituality. As both of these planets are in opposition to each other, it is no surprise that Sanders came into conflict with the Church. Sanders' devotion to the mystical and spiritual permeated almost every area of his life, and he must have longed to escape the more mundane and routine areas of daily life, since Neptune has the capacity to escape. Exploring and finding the spiritual side of life in a material world would have been hugely satisfying to him.

Unaspected Pluto brings a magnetic and forceful energy to the chart; powerful people are born with peregrine (*see glossary*) Pluto in their chart. Such is the intensity of the energy in their lives that they can be remembered for centuries after they have died; unaspected Pluto holds power over fame and notoriety. We see this as the Museum of Witchcraft and Magic in Cornwall permanently exhibits artefacts and regalia belonging to Sanders and is educational to those who wish to learn more about him and witchcraft.

Pluto has tremendous capacity to prompt either solitude, or powerful actions that require intense energy, and this we can see through Sanders' need for retreat (particularly when he was very ill), as well as through his magical work. One example of his compulsion in the area of his magical work can be seen by his interest in the Aztecs an area he was quite obsessed with, according to Maxine Sanders (www.youtube.com).

Pluto in the water sign of Cancer suggests an intense, intuitive, emotional and highly charged profile, together with the capacity for emotional transformations in domestic life. Regeneration and unearthing of one's heritage, roots and secret past is also possible. Sanders came from a very psychic family, especially on his mother's side (Sanders, 2007, 101). His maternal grandmother was especially fond of him and they grew even closer when he contracted tuberculosis in childhood, and she helped nurse him back to health. Sanders had an intense instinct and nurturing for the ancient arcane knowledge, as shown by his deep interest and passion in the Egyptian Mysteries.

Sanders also had great empathy for the witches who were persecuted in bygone ages. When he was evacuated to the countryside during the war, he stayed with a man called Uncle Louie who lived near Pendle Hill in Lancashire, a county renowned for its witch-hunts and persecutions in the seventeenth century. On one occasion, whilst on top of Pendle Hill, Sanders received a psychic communication from them, as though they were flickering across his consciousness. He saw their witch-hoods, broomsticks and athames – all items that would later feature in his own magical work (Johns, 1971, 32).

The sign of Cancer pertains to belonging – to one's home, hearth, people, family, country, history and roots. It associates with the archetypal mother, as well as security issues and the domestic arena. It is interesting that the Temple of the Mother was established by Maxine Sanders after Alex went to live in Bexhill, yet he often attended, because there he was able to experience the ritual without the responsibility of leadership of the covenstead. The ritual discipline and boundaries practised within the circle of the Temple of the Mother were quite different to those in his own coven in Bexhill, and there were times he clearly needed and appreciated this freedom.

The Temple of the Mother and its attraction for Sanders is interesting, since Cancer has strong connections to emotions, nurturing and safety; associations of Pluto include brute force, power and even torture. Sander's placement of Pluto in Cancer indicates that he had strong feelings connected to past eras and, in the example of the Pendle Witches, this shows Sanders' empathy for their suffering, and his sensitivity to the atmosphere when he visited Pendle Hill.

Unaspected Pluto is where Pluto in Cancer brings a magnetic and powerful energy to the chart; many influential people are born with peregrine Pluto in their chart as discussed previously. So intense is the energy in their lives that they can be remembered long after their deaths, something that is already happening with Sanders' legacy. Unaspected Pluto holds an incredible capacity for fame and notoriety. It also prompts either solitude or powerful actions which require an intense energy. The solitude can be illustrated by Sanders' solitary work as a practitioner, and the powerful actions by way of his influence and teaching in his coven work, which spread information and made witchcraft more accessible for others.

Neptune is in the fire sign of Leo at 22 degrees and since Leo symbolises the individual and the self, this could be interpreted as either an addiction to the self, a need to escape from the self, or the demise and subsequent loss of the self. Other Neptunian correspondences include: delusion, deception and distortion, which sometimes manifests in Leo as *self*-delusion. Confusion and disappointments will have been familiar to Sanders, for example, as a teenager experiencing the loss of his much-loved maternal grandmother.

Even though he had known since childhood that his birth surname was Carter, he did not change it formally to Sanders by deed poll until 1968, when he was 42. Until then, he had, consciously or not, lived with the shadow of a dual identity, until he decided to legally change it.

Sanders also had to deal with the disappointing nature of those who abused his kindness and took advantage of his hospitality and generosity when he was in his twenties. Yet he too, took advantage of his own benefactors during his early adult life, suggesting that he deluded himself and lived in a fantasy world, presuming there would be an endless provision of money available for his every whim. Dreams, fantasy and illusion are all associated with the romantic and misty nature of Neptune, illustrating Sanders' self-romanticising nature.

Neptune in Leo would have helped him attune to his bewitching, enchanting and spellbinding self, which manifested itself in his creativity, imagination, showmanship and vision – all of which he pursued and enjoyed throughout his life. Neptune also corresponds with dance, film, lenses and photography and it is interesting that Sanders was born into the 'Neptune in Leo' generation, where the age of the silent screen films was in its heyday as part of the 'Roaring 20s'. With this placement, Neptune reflects the artistic, imaginative and enchantment of its time. Perhaps, like many others, he was discovering and enjoying the newness of the age by way of the Neptunian fantasy and illusion, which could so easily be created, displayed and experienced through the lens of film and photography.

Sanders and his coven were, unlike many others, prepared to appear publicly. For example, they featured in the film documentary, *Legend of the Witches*. Through the lens of media attention, he generously shared information about initiations into a coven, dance and rituals. As previously discussed, he and Maxine used dance as a form of escape and healing to aid those who had turned to them for help with drug addictions. A combination of this, together with sound, colour, "… love, kindness and Alex's endless patience," was often remarkably successful (Sanders, 2007, 135).

Neptune in Leo in this instance illustrates the creative and compassionate side to Sander's nature, showing that he was a creative problem-solver able to act on impulse using the medium of dance. Alcohol, dance, escape, drugs, compassion and sensitivity are all associations of Neptune. Leo enjoys an audience, performance, showmanship, taking centre-stage, directing, leading and sharing with a generosity of heart and spirit. However, as we have seen, Sanders was sometimes accused of being too much the showman and too intent on seeking fame.

FULL CIRCLE

Sanders developed lung cancer and passed away at the age of 61 on the witches' sabbat of Beltane, on May Eve, 30th April, 1988. He was experiencing the following transits when he passed away: transiting Pluto trine the natal Pluto, transiting Saturn trine natal Venus, transiting Uranus square the natal Uranus, and transiting Mercury opposing natal Saturn in Scorpio.

The latter transit has particular significance to Sanders' lung cancer since, in medical astrology, Mercury rules the lungs and breathing, and was also the ruler of Sanders' Sun sign, Gemini; the Sun symbolising the self. Saturn symbolises death and finality and is often depicted as 'The Grim-Reaper' and 'Old Father Time'.

Since the planet Mercury opposes Saturn in Scorpio, it adds to Pluto's (the ruler of Scorpio) theme of transformation, death and rebirth. Sanders was cremated on the 11th May, 1988, and had a Pagan service; Saturn's symbolism can be seen in cremation whereby the ashes of the body correspond with the energy of Saturn's finality of bones and matter. Transiting Pluto was trine the natal Pluto at the time of Sanders' death, suggesting a time of insight, intensity and crisis. The trine aspect gives an ease and helps to provide strength in realising the inevitable.

The transit of Saturn trine natal Venus suggests that, at this time, Sanders may have been obliged to foster a pragmatic and realistic approach, especially when dealing with matters related to earnings and possessions. Relationships, both personal and professional, were likely to have meant more to Sanders at this time in his life. He no longer had room for disloyalty, illusion and romanticism; this pragmatic attitude would have provided much-needed stability for him. He would probably have valued his time more, and tried to spend it with his family during this transit.

Transiting Uranus square natal Uranus indicates that a crisis was inevitable, since the square aspect indicates challenges and trials. It would have been these troubling times in his lifetime that Sanders experienced this transit. The first was in his early twenties, when it would have presented as a major and unanticipated change in his life. One significant change at the age of 21 was that he married his first wife, Doreen. The marriage lasted barely four years; perhaps they were both too young and had little in common. They met at his work (when he worked for the chemist), became lovers and she became pregnant. At that time, marriage was inevitable in such a situation.

Doreen did not know that Sanders was a witch, had no interest in spiritualism or witchcraft, and he resented the situation, becoming desperate to find another witch he *could* work with. It was hardly surprising, therefore, that he described himself as feeling trapped almost from the start (Johns, 1971, 40). Perhaps Doreen did too.

Uranus by nature is independent, radical and unconventional, so the energy of Uranus does not easily compliment the traditional domesticity of married life. Uranus rebels against established standards, so possibly an open marriage would have been more appealing to Sanders and may explain why he once told his wife, Maxine, that he loved another man and wished for the three of them to live together (Sanders, 2007, 168–169).

This was not an arrangement Maxine wanted or agreed with, and eventually Sanders left her to go and live with his new partner in Sussex. His parting words to her, "The work is done," reveal just how cold and detached the nature of Uranus can be when it is pushing to assert its determination and independence. The repeated transit of Uranus square the natal Uranus suggests that, during this final phase of his life, there was a hurried change. Through the duration of this transit, he would have had to face the reality that he was approaching old age. He may have felt strained – looking inwardly and questioning what individual contribution he had made to the greater world. This lesson may have given way to feelings of anxiety, nervousness, stress and tension, since the square aspect between transiting Uranus and the natal Uranus is challenging and demanding.

Sun	14Gem	58'20"	145'
Moon	5Ari	42'34"	042'
Mercury	17Gem	9'56"	1428'
Venus	4Tau	7'10"	1653'
Mars	24Pis	3'3"	314'

The planet Uranus symbolises progress, so it seems appropriate at this stage to look at the astrological progressions in Sander's chart on the day of his passing (*see box to the left*).

Three of the personal planets had progressed into the creative, noble and regal sign of Leo. The natal Sun in Gemini had progressed into 14 degrees of Leo. The natal Moon in Aries had progressed into 0 degrees of Leo, and the natal Mercury in Gemini had progressed into 14 degrees of Leo.

Progressions signify the maturity and change of the inner self, whereas transits represent planetary events. It is interesting therefore that Maxine Sanders observed these inner changes in her husband towards the end of his lifetime, noting he had gone from being deeply spiritual to a "showman and egoist" (Sanders, 2007, 280). These are very much the qualities of his Leo progressions.

In the last year or so of Sander's life, others that knew him may well also have seen a change in his behaviour. The progressed planet in Sanders' Sun, Moon and Mercury into the sign of Leo will have generated a more egocentric and self-centred approach in his life. Although justifiably proud of his achievements, he may have developed a greater love for himself (Sun). Emotionally (Moon), he may have become even more comforted and satisfied by a sense of the dramatic and theatrical in his life, where being in the spotlight and flamboyantly expressing himself would have appealed to him.

His communication (Mercury) style may have changed over time too, in that what he wanted to talk about and focus on was himself. In later life, he wrote books and held more one-to-one interviews, which were largely about himself and his life. He may also have taken criticism and judgement more to heart than previously. It might have been helpful to him at this time if he could have adopted a more balanced and co-operative approach in his communications with others, since Leo has the potential to be domineering and inflexible.

The natal Venus in Taurus had progressed 16 degrees into the caring and emotional sign of Cancer, and the natal Mars in Pisces had progressed 3 degrees into the loyal and steadfast sign of Taurus. The personal planets had progressed into signs that would have given Sanders a platform to experience more care, endurance, loyalty and sincerity in his later years. The need for loyalty reliability, security and trust can be shown, for example, where, towards the end of his lifetime, he appointed Maxine Sanders as his next of kin, and charged her to make preparations for his funeral (Sanders, 2007, 208). This shows that, despite his more recent relationships, she was still the one person he trusted to do the right thing by him with dignity and responsibility at such a critical time. This reflects her 'rock-like' practical and responsible Capricorn nature, as did the way she cared for and nursed him towards the end of his life before he had to transfer to a nursing home. Her steadfastness was the mirror that enabled Sanders to truly be himself.

Alex Sanders; Mercury trickster, flighty and playful, juggler of duality, controversial and intellectual, educator, healer and speaker, left this world on May's Eve, 30th April, 1988.

ACKNOWLEDGEMENTS, CREDITS AND REFERENCES

The Author and Publisher would like to thank Maxine Sanders, for her gracious help, encouragement and assistance with this chapter.

Many thanks also to Grevel Lindop, for his enthusiasm and time.

The Associate Director (Curatorial Practices) of the John Rylands Library.

The University of Manchester, for information on the condition of the John Rylands Library in 1900.

The Reference & Discovery Archivist at the University of Manitoba, Canada, for assistance with access to article from *The Weekender*.

Many thanks also to Kevin Rowan-Drewitt, for his assistance and information about the number of Alexandrian witches and Wiccans in England & Wales.

Date of birth: 06/06/1926.

Certified copy of an Entry of Birth for Orrell, Alexander Carter. Birth Certificate No. BXCH994687. From General Records Office, Southport, Merseyside, UK, PR8 2JD.

Rodden Rating– 'X'
Alex Sanders born Sunday 6th June, 1926, time of birth unknown, GMT, Birkenhead, England.
3w02, 53n24.
Flat/noon natal chart generated by www.astro.com
Natal transits and progressions for 30th April, 1988.
Progr. Date: 7th August, 1926, 8:36:12, UT.

ARTICLES

Lindop, G. 'How the King of the Witches Dusted the Books: Alex Sanders at the John Rylands Library'. *Bulletin of the John Rylands Library*. Vol. 94, No. 2 (Autumn, 2018), pp115–125. http://dx.doi.org/10.7227/BJRL.94.2.5

BOOKS

Bardens, D. (1971) *Mysterious Worlds*. W.H. Allen & Co., Ltd.
Di Fiosa, J. (2010) *All the King's Men: The Human Legacy of Alex Sanders*. LOGIOS.
Ebertin-Hoffman. (2009) *Fixed Stars and their Interpretation*. American Federation of Astrologers Inc.
Farrar, S. (1995) *What Witches Do*. Phoenix Publishing Inc.
Guerra, E. and Farrar, J. (2008) *Stewart Farrar: Writer on a Broomstick*. Skylight Press.
Guiley, R.E. (1999) *The Encyclopaedia of Witches & Witchcraft*. Second Edition. Checkmark Books.
Hutton, R. (1999) *The Triumph of the Moon*. Oxford University Press.
Johns, J. (1971) *King of the Witches*. Pan Books Ltd.
Jordan, M. (1999) *Witches: An Encyclopaedia of Paganism and Magic*. Kyle Cathie Ltd.
Michelson, N.F. (1983) *The American Ephemeris for the 20th Century*. ACS Publications, Inc.
Sanders, A. (2012) *Alex Sanders: The Book of Law*. Hob Hill Books.
Sanders, M. (2007) *Firechild: The Life and Magic of Maxine Sanders*. Mandrake of Oxford.
Tompkins, S. (1990) *Aspects in Astrology*. Element Books Ltd.

NEWSPAPERS

Daily Express. Friday, 28th June, 1974.
Letters page, p3 headlines 'These witches aren't exactly spellbound' by Alex Sanders.
The Weekender. Saturday, 6th August, 1966 (the weekend edition of the Canadian newspaper the *Winnipeg Tribune* in Winnipeg). Article heading 'A Night with Today's Witches' by Robert Eddison. No. 37, p7.

FILMS

The Eye of the Devil (1966). Metro-Goldwyn-Meyer.
Legend of the Witches – Their Secret Rituals Revealed. Directed by Malcolm Leigh (first made in 1969).

WEBSITES

https://www.nomisweb.co.uk/census/2011/QS210EW/view/2092957703?rows=cell&cols=rural-urbanfigure – NOMIS Official Labour Market Statistics for Office of National Statistics: Religion QS210EW, by Urban Rural 2011 England & Wales. Accessed on 08/04/2020.
www.noeltyl.com/techniques 31August2007/ – Noel Tyl – Peregrine Island. Accessed on 21/05/2015.
https://www.youtube.com/watch?v=3hWiBSjcvFM – The Museum of Witchcraft & Magic's Simon Costin interviews Maxine Sanders (uploaded to YouTube on 31st January, 2018). Accessed on 07/04/2020.

CHAPTER FOURTEEN

Scott Cunningham 1956–1993

Author and Wiccan

SCOTT DOUGLAS CUNNINGHAM was born on the 27th June, 1956, in Royal Oak, Michigan, USA. He was the second and middle child born to Chester Grant Cunningham and Rose Marie Wilhoit Cunningham who were both Methodists. His older brother was called Gregory and his younger sister Christine. His father was a hugely successful professional writer (Chet Cunningham) and encouraged Scott with his creative projects and written work.

Cunningham spent most of his life in San Diego, California, and also in Hawaii for research, leisure and respite purposes. He enrolled into San Diego State University in

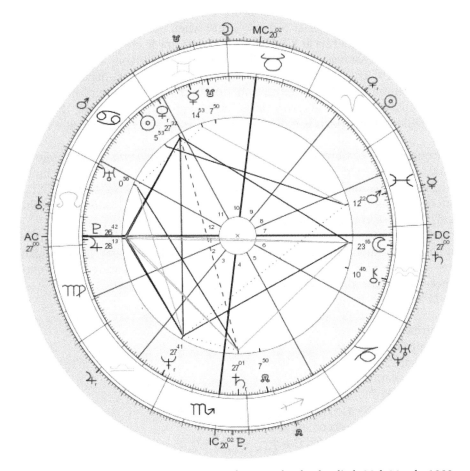

Natal and Transits Chart for Scott Cunningham on the day he died, 28th March, 1993.

1978 to study creative writing but did not complete the course. He was determined to become a full-time writer, frustrated as he had already had more literature published than some of his professors.

During his lifetime, Cunningham helped many people fulfil their potential, which was achieved through his books and public speaking. He was, and still is, hugely influential and helped to transform modern Paganism, making it more accessible. This he did through his books on Wicca, which at that time were still relatively few and far between. He authored many books in different genres in his short lifetime and was a popular educator.

Cunningham died on 28th March, 1993, aged 36. He became ill in 1983 and was initially diagnosed with lymphoma, from which he successfully recovered. However, in March 1990, whilst on a speaking tour in Massachusetts, he suddenly fell ill and was later diagnosed with AIDS-related cryptococcal meningitis; he suffered with several infections because of this illness.

WHAT CUNNINGHAM'S NATAL CHART SHOWS

Cunningham was born on 27th June, 1956, when the Sun was in the cardinal (*see glossary*) water sign of Cancer at 5 degrees and when the Moon was in the fixed (*see glossary*) air sign of Aquarius at 23 degrees. Sun in Cancer indicates that Cunningham had a caring and sensitive nature; Cancer is ruled by the Moon, and Cancer's symbol is that of the crab. The glyph for Cancer represents the breasts; hence the sign being associated with the mother, as well as symbolising the fluid nature of life and feeling. Other symbolism includes the crab's claws, which can cling and retain; the claws also suggest cradling arms, which is indicative of the caring and nurturing side of Cancer's nature.

An acquaintance of Cunningham's once described how Cunningham comforted her following an unexpected relationship breakdown. Crying, she confided in Cunningham who, she said, "took me in his arms and held me in a very soothing way.... He radiated warmth and caring for me" (Harrington and Regula, 1996, 210), showing his ability to respond to distress in an affectionate and caring way.

The sign of Cancer is associated with domestic-life, family and heritage; areas that would have been important to Cunningham. In his natal chart, the Moon (which rules Cancer) has both soft and hard aspects to it, the latter indicating the potential for challenges and issues in Cunningham's life.

The Moon's aspects comprise of:

- Moon trine Venus
- Moon opposing Jupiter
- Moon square Saturn
- Moon trine Neptune
- Moon opposing Pluto
- Moon opposing the ascendant (AC)
- Moon conjunct the descendant (DC)
- Moon square the midheaven (MC)

Such strong aspects to the Moon show that Cunningham was caring, responsive and sensitive and had strong intuitive feelings. Other areas associated with the Moon include family and home, as well as the general public. It also reveals that he was ambitious and pioneering and led the way in his chosen field of writing about magic and Wicca in a way that readers could easily understand.

Health, service and work were also notable areas of importance to Cunningham. This is because they are associated with the sixth house, the place where the Moon is positioned in the natal chart. The Moon is conjunct the DC; and the asteroid Chiron (the Wounded Healer), which is retrograde (*see glossary*), is also positioned in the sixth house – this area will be discussed further on.

The Moon is particularly important in Cunningham's life regarding his work, as it symbolises the female principle; the Moon Goddess and Mother of Witchcraft which were of immense significance to Cunningham through his literature, spirituality and work. The position of the Moon on the descendant (*see glossary*) signifies that Cunningham was instinctively in touch with what the public wanted, which would have been helpful when choosing subjects to write and talk about.

The descendant signifies qualities that we look for in partnerships, as well as qualities we project and seek through close personal relationships. The Moon positioned here suggests that Cunningham needed somebody as caring and sensitive as he was and, potentially, any partners may have needed 'mothering.' This might have caused him to be over-responsive to another person's needs, which would have been challenging for Cunningham. This is because the Moon is in freedom-loving Aquarius which can be cold and detached at times in its energies, other aspects created with the Moon (as highlighted above) show that he had the capacity to restrain his emotions, something that will be discussed further on.

Because the Moon is positioned in the sixth house (*see box on right*), it also indicates that Cunningham was probably a perfectionist in his work, as this area is associated with Virgo, whose very nature is hard working, critical and discriminating. During the time he was 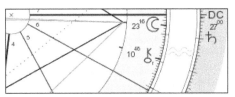 working on his book, *Spell Craft*, he was so thorough in his work that every project in the book was carefully tested and the instructions revised repeatedly (Harrington and Regula, 1996, 167). The purist nature of Cunningham's magical work was due to self-imposed conditions, i.e. that he only used formulas and spells if they either came from an historical source and/or he had tested it out for himself (Kraig, 2012, 78). This shows his professional attitude towards his work, and a combined sense of duty to his publisher as well as towards his readers.

His passion for herbs and flowers started when he was a young boy. When he grew older, he increased his knowledge and learnt how to prepare and use them for magical purposes, which in turn enabled him to write extensively about herbalism. In conjunction with, *Cunningham's Encyclopaedia of Magical Herbs*, and with the assistance of his publishers (Llewellyn Publishing), he made a video in 1987 about collecting and preparing herbs for magical purposes. That was an original and innovative approach at that time, and showed as willingness to reach an audience through a different medium. Through technological advances and progress since 1987, viewers can now see this film on the YouTube website (https://youtu.be/4Y5y9iGspeY).

The Moon is also significant to Cunningham's work, in that it is associated with food and nourishment and Cunningham wrote articles and books on the subject, for example: *Magical Herbs* and *The Magic in Food*, as well as, *Cunningham's Encyclopaedia of Wicca in the Kitchen*. In keeping with correspondences of the sixth house with diet and health, Cunningham also wrote about the then alternative diets such as veganism and vegetarianism and other health alternatives. In *The Magic of Food*, he reveals how he experimented trying a strict vegetarian diet under the guidance of a 'long-time vegetarian and ceremonial magician" (Harrington and Regula, 1996, 31). He was shown how to avoid all animal proteins and fats but, although he persisted, the diet was inappropriate for him as it made him ill and put a strain on his psychic and spiritual energies, so he withdrew from the diet (ibid, 31). This shows how his lunar position in Aquarius was open to experimentation in the area of his diet, health and work (the sixth house).

Researcher and science writer, Michel Gauquelin, observed through extensive research that men born with the Moon on an angle (*see glossary*) often became successful writers. Two examples he found were the songwriter, Gustave Nadaud; and poet, novelist and playwright, Guillaume Apollinaire (Gauquelin, 1976, 133). Certainly, we can add Cunningham as another illustration of this, for writing was his passion and he lived to write.

His book, *Wicca: A Guide for the Solitary Practitioner*, was one of the most successful books ever written on the subject, and Llewellyn Publications declared in the 33rd edition in 2003 that there had been "over 40,000 copies sold." His first book published with Llewellyn was, *Magical Herbalism*, which proved popular and subsequently he wrote many more books for the publishing house including, *Earth, Air, Fire and Water* and *Cunningham's Encyclopaedia of Magical Herbs*.

ARTICLES, NOVELS AND SCRIPTS

Cunningham wrote in other genres too. He moved from writing for magazines and short fiction in 1980, to having his first novel, *The Cliffside Horrors*, published by American Art Enterprises. In the following years, he wrote novels of adventure, horror and even romance (under the pen name of Cathy Cunningham). His books, *The Curse of Valkyrie House* and *Ruling Passions*, were published by Norden Publications and Pioneer Communications Network, respectively. He also wrote a series of Westerns under the pen name Dirk Fletcher, thanks, in large part to his father, who helped him land the job. In the mid-1980s, Cunningham authored a script for the popular American television show *Knots Landing* called 'Misguided Hearts'. He also wrote many articles, some of which included topics about car maintenance; this shows his diversity and talent as a writer.

The changing energy of the Moon suggests that he changed his place of work frequently; this is certainly borne out in his younger years when he was employed by a variety of jobs, which will be highlighted later, and where he worked with an assortment of co-workers in his various roles. Not only is the Moon changeable in energy but also the nature of Aquarius can be unpredictable; this position in the area of work indicates that Cunningham may have faced periods of time when his work offered little or no income. The various aspects made to the Moon also suggest that, at times, Cunningham was both moody and sensitive, as the Moon's energy fluctuates; each of these aspects will be discussed later.

ADAPTION, HUMOUR AND TRADE

The theme of a variety of employment is also shown by the second house the area of income, where the house cusp is ruled by Mercury – a planet that is, by nature, irregular and variable. Mercury is positioned in the tenth house, the area of career and ambition, indicating he could achieve success through his effective communication skills and the ability to work with an assortment of people. Cunningham probably wished to be appreciated as an educated and knowledgeable person, as well as needing to be engaged and stimulated by the people around him, as these are all correspondences associated with Mercury.

Other associations of Mercury include commerce, sales and trade, as well as humour and wit. It is unsurprising, therefore, that Cunningham found himself working in areas of retail where he had to be of service to the public. It has been said of him that he was a joker and prankster with a quick mind; his friend David Harrington said "his wit was sharp and with a well-aimed word could cut through the air with a crackling energy" (Harrington and Regula, 1996, 50). His sister recalls how her brother would make quips and jokes as well as double entendres (Cunningham, 2009, 276). These examples illustrate the Mercury square Mars aspect, which involves communication and directness, which we can see was borne out in Cunningham's jovial and witty nature. The Mercury square Mars aspect in his chart and other interpretations of it will be discussed later.

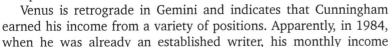
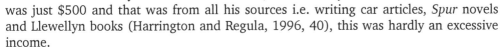

Venus is retrograde in Gemini and indicates that Cunningham earned his income from a variety of positions. Apparently, in 1984, when he was already an established writer, his monthly income was just $500 and that was from all his sources i.e. writing car articles, *Spur* novels and Llewellyn books (Harrington and Regula, 1996, 40), this was hardly an excessive income.

Before he became a full-time writer, Cunningham worked in a variety of jobs that he apparently disliked intensely (ibid, 28). These positions included: data entry clerk, 'on-call' emergency typist, assistant at a marine park, as well as working at various metaphysical and occult bookshops – which he did find stimulating and where he could apply his knowledge and mingle with the customers. Here he became aware of a lack of books available on the subjects he was researching and writing and must have realised that he could write on topics that would fill the gap for customers.

HEALTH, SERVICE AND WORK

Cunningham had also joined the naval service in 1976 for a very short period and was stationed locally. However, the limited and regimented life of the navy was unsuitable for his artistic and sensitive nature and, fortunately, he was allowed to opt out.

As discussed earlier, service is a correspondence of the sixth house, which contains the Moon with the asteroid Chiron, the Wounded Healer, which is retrograde and positioned in the sign Aquarius. In mythology, Chiron was a great teacher who initiated healers, magicians and warriors; this seems particularly pertinent to Cunningham especially in his work, which involved healing and magic. In the natal chart, Chiron represents the area where there is a primal wound which creates an urge to heal, in Cunningham's case it was the area of health, service and work.

Chiron in the sixth house indicates that Cunningham was very much a healer and 'server', who was meticulous in his work. Indeed, medicine and healing became prominent in Cunningham's life. This was borne out by his passion for his work, perhaps even finding that work was healing in its own right. Medicine was also important in his life when he was treated for his various ailments and illnesses, which eventually led to his death. In 1990, he came close to dying through a life-threatening illness, but his devoted Pagan friends collected money to help pay his medical bill (Harrington and Regula, 1996, introduction, xii); he survived for another three years.

Mercury is trine Chiron and indicates that Cunningham had an authorial voice about healing and remedies which was easy and accessible to understand, this is borne out in the success of his magical books.

The themes of originality and objectivity are associated with Aquarius; and Chiron in Aquarius indicates that his wound was about finding a sense of belonging in the community. This may have generated in the following ways:

- Feeling like an outsider and alone when he was in a crowd
- Seeking solitude and feeling relief when he was alone
- Craving contact with a higher being/consciousness

Mercury is in Gemini, which is its natural home, as Gemini (and Virgo) is ruled by this planet. It indicates that Cunningham was a natural communicator, intelligent, observant and witty, as these are all qualities associated with Gemini and Mercury. As this sign and planet are variable in nature, it reveals that Cunningham had tremendous dexterity and could work on a variety of projects at any one time, which he would have found satisfactory and stimulating.

Scott Cunningham. Photo by kind permission of Christine Ashworth, Sister of Scott Cunningham.

Interestingly, Stewart Farrar (the subject of Chapter Nine), who was an inspiration to Cunningham, not only shared the same position of Mercury in Gemini in his natal chart (although in a different house), but also shared the same degree as Cunningham where Mercury was 14 degrees in Gemini. Both were great writers who needed to communicate their ideas through books as well as public speaking.

Throughout the 1970s, Cunningham passionately studied nature and was also educated in a variety of covens of different traditions; eventually, however, he became a solitary practitioner and wrote for people following a solitary path. As well as writing novels, he also increased his knowledge about herbs and began to write textbooks for Wiccans; this was at a time when the subject was still relatively closed. This shows that Cunningham was adept at learning, researching and understanding, while remaining focused to complete his professional obligations for his publishers.

ACCESSIBILITY AND CANDOUR

Returning to the Mercury square Mars aspect of his natal chart; it also indicates that he had a competitive and restless mind and probably found it helpful to channel his agile and nervous energy into writing, where he could apply his quick thinking and put thought into action.

As discussed earlier, Mercury is associated with communication and the mind, whilst Mars is associated with candour and frankness, and so the contact between the two planets indicates that Cunningham could communicate in a concise yet simple way. This may explain his success as an author and public speaker, as his style was accessible and uncomplicated, as well as being witty. Indeed, the author, Raymond Buckland, said of Cunningham that he had "a biting, satirical sense of humour" (Harrington and Regula, 1996, 211).

Cunningham once remarked that "it shouldn't be a difficult task" for those wanting to learn about a different and natural way of worshipping (Cunningham, 2009, 278). This suggests he may have been speaking from experience and felt that perhaps some of the available books about magic and Wicca were not written for beginners. Having worked in metaphysical and occult bookshops, he would have had insight as to what was available, as well as identifying where there was a gap in the market.

THE FEMININE PRINCIPLE

Looking again at the subject of Moon on the descendant, this position also suggests that Cunningham had strong bonds with women and recognised (as previously said) the importance of the feminine polarity in his work, as well as appreciating those women who worked in the Craft.

There was a very close maternal bond between Cunningham and his mother, Rosie, and his sister described how his thoughtfulness and protectiveness towards their mother was very sweet (Cunningham, 2009, 276). This bond is actually unsurprising, as his natal chart has many aspects created with the Moon, which is associated with mother/care-giver and suggests that his relationship with her was particularly significant in his life. Cunningham was devoted to his mother and idealised her, an area which is indicated by the Moon trine Neptune aspect in his chart.

Others have described the dynamic between Cunningham and his mother as "very sweet, and their relationship very close" (Penczak, 2013, 244), which shows the concerned and nurturing temperament of his Sun sign, Cancer. He also sang in the church choir with his mother when he was a teenager (Cunningham, 2009, 275), while his sister, to whom he was very close, described him as "an amazing soul ... an amazing brother" (http://christine-ashworth.com).

Cunningham greatly admired the author and witch, Sybil Leek (the subject of Chapter Ten), and was very affected by her death in 1982, describing her as one of his heroines in the magical community. He even wrote a eulogy for her which was published in *The Shadow's Edge* magazine (Harrington and Regula, 1996, 97).

Another influential female in Cunningham's life was a fellow drama student – teenager, Dorothy Jones. She was also a practitioner of the Craft and they formed a bond where she became his Wiccan teacher (ibid, 12). The Wiccan artist, Robin Wood, also contributed her artwork to some of Cunningham's books, which shows how he admired and respected her artwork.

Two other close female friends from the magical community included de Traci Regula, one of the co-authors of his biography and founder of Isis House publishing, and the Reverend Marilee Bigelow of the Church of The Eternal Source and proprietor of the Star Fire Herb Company, who both had close friendships with Cunningham.

The aspect Moon trine Venus further shows that he not only valued the women in his life, but also qualities of fairness, peace and harmony – the latter qualities being associated with Venus. He was acutely sensitive to other people's suffering, which is indicated by the Moon trine Neptune aspect in his natal chart.

His mother, to whom he was very close, had already been living with multiple sclerosis at the time when Cunningham was admitted into hospital in 1990 (Harrington and Regula, 1996, 158). She was unable to visit him in hospital because of her illness and, being unable to travel, they surely must have missed each other, especially when they were both in such vulnerable situations. His father, however, spent many days by Cunningham's side at Massachusetts General Hospital in Boston, until he was well enough to travel back to San Diego.

LOVE, LIGHT AND PEACE

Neptune is an outer planet (*see glossary*), so represents a specific generation of people. The planet moved from Virgo into Libra between 1942–3 and remained there until October, 1956 – this generation represented the baby boomers who became adults in the 1960s. They became known as the hippy 'flower power' generation who had a beautiful dream of love and world peace, whilst rejecting war. Cunningham was part of this generation, Neptune was 27 degrees in Libra when he was born.

Another example of Cunningham's awareness of suffering can be seen where he sympathised with the soldiers who had to fight in the Vietnam War, which had started in 1955, a year before Cunningham was born. Through his childhood, the war was a backdrop to his life. He wrote about being "terrified of going to Vietnam, constantly seeking escape from the real world, even at that young age" (Harrington and Regula, 1996, 9). Unsurprisingly, reading became his refuge and means of "removing myself from the horrific things that were happening on the other side of the world" (ibid, 10). This shows that he was not only aware of the terrible war that was taking place but also that young men were losing their lives far from home, and this shows his awareness and compassion for those who were killed, injured and bereaved. The war ended in 1975 when Cunningham was almost nineteen years old.

However, when Cunningham was 34, there was yet another conflict – the Gulf war of 1990–91, which also troubled him, since he believed that all war, irrespective of who was right, "... was a foolish waste of human energy and lives" (Harrington and Regula, 1996, 159). This again shows his humanitarian and peace-loving nature.

THE EBB AND FLOW OF THE TIDES

The Moon and Neptune contact is particularly pertinent to Cunningham. Both the Moon and Neptune are associated with the sea, since in astrology they are associated with the water element. This is because they rule the water signs of Cancer (the crab) and Pisces (the fish), respectively, and Cunningham loved being close to water, whether it was for ritual, spell working, research, inspiration or retreat. It has been said that, "Water soothed him both spiritually and physically, especially the sea" (ibid, 57). The ocean also featured in Cunningham's employment when he worked at Scripps's Oceanography at the Ocean Systems Laboratory, as well as at Sea World marine park on the edge of San Diego's Mission Bay (ibid, 28).

Cunningham's father observed that, "He had an abiding love affair with Hawaii" (ibid, 216), and Cunningham's final book, *Cunningham's Guide to Hawaiian Magic and Spirituality* (originally published in 1994 as, *Hawaiian Religion and Magic*), was about its spirituality and religion. No doubt spending so much time on the island surrounded by the Pacific Ocean would have been relaxing for him, where he could escape from the mundane, break the routine of his daily life and recuperate. His father observed that, as a child, Cunningham, unlike his brother, was "more of a loner" (Harrington and Regula, 1996, 6).

Jupiter is sextile Neptune in his natal chart and holds symbolism of how much the sea meant to Cunningham. It shows that by exploring (Jupiter) and escaping to the sea (Neptune) that he could find inspiration and be at one with the goddess, finding it a magical and spellbinding experience. In his extensively researched book about Hawaii, he covered topics such as water (both fresh and salt, and also rain), along with Hawaiian 'birth omens'.

The Moon was significant to the Hawaiians (and to Cunningham!). It was used as a visible calendar as well as a mark of personality traits for people born under each of the lunar months. Being born in late June, Cunningham's birthday fell under the Hawaiian month of Hinaiaeleele, so he may have been amused to discover that qualities associated with this time of year included ignorance, laziness and avoidance of learning! (Cunningham, 2009, 190)

Cancerians enjoy history as they have an appreciation of the past. So, inevitably, being born under this sign, Cunningham would have enjoyed learning about the culture and spirituality of the Hawaiian people in pre-Christian times. For example, he was fascinated with its Fire Goddess Pele; he regularly visited the aromatic and colourful island in order to invocate the goddess, showing that he was gripped by her power, myth and magic.

MAKING WAVES

The Moon in Aquarius suggests that Cunningham needed to retain his individuality and independence, and was instinctively drawn to alternative and progressive ideas. Aquarius is a humanitarian and revolutionary sign, and some of his radical nature can be seen through his politics.

Even as a child, Cunningham was politically aware, painting flowers and writing "bold political statements about the Vietnam War" (Harrington and Regula, 1996, 9). For example, he regularly wrote to local elected representatives on specific bills and issues, believed that voting was essential; even during his last illness, he determinedly ensured that he got to the polling station so that he could vote for Bill Clinton (ibid, 136–137).

1600 PENNSYLVANIA AVENUE

Sadly, Cunningham died in March, 1993, and therefore never saw Clinton complete his term of office as the US President. Interestingly, that same year, President Clinton established the White House Office of National AIDS Policy, the ONAP (www.hiv.gov), to co-ordinate an integrated approach to the care, prevention and treatment of HIV/AIDS. The department helped support people who lived with illnesses related to the Human Immunodeficiency Virus and Acquired Immune Deficiency Syndrome.

Unfortunately, Cunningham did not live long enough to be a recipient of the ONAP's help. In America in the early 1980s, terms such as 'gay cancer' and 'gay plague' were not uncommon and GRID (Gay Related Immune Deficiency) was the original (and cruel) term for the disease known today as AIDS. The 1980s was a period of great confusion about HIV and all the various infections that occur with damaged immune systems.

Cryptococcal meningitis, related to AIDS, was given as the official cause of Cunningham's death (Harrington and Regula, 1996, 182). Meningitis is described as a fungus which is very "common in the soil and can enter the body when breathing in dust or dried bird droppings" (http://www.aidsinfonet.org). This is surely ironic considering Cunningham's deep love and devotion for Mother Nature.

To add further irony, in America, June 27th (Cunningham's birthday) is National HIV Testing-day (https://aidsinfo.nih.gov). Thankfully, medical progress and research since the early 1980s has helped many people to live better with HIV and AIDS and it is no longer the automatic death sentence that it once was. De Traci Regula suggested that some may have criticised Cunningham for screening the true nature of his illness (Harrington and Regula, 1996, 185), but the concealment and privacy of his disease is totally in keeping with his reserved and private nature. Apart from not wanting to be defined as a victim of his illness, he also wanted to guard his family (particularly his mother, who was ill herself) and friends from worry (ibid).

EQUALITY AND GREEN ISSUES

Returning to Cunningham's political side, he believed there needed to be a stronger female presence in politics and, when possible, usually voted for a female politician; apparently he could "be a bit sexist in voting for virtually any female candidate" (ibid), showing that he viewed women as being a source of power that was being inhibited by the then largely patriarchal office in America, and was trying to redress discrimination and inequality.

Environmental and recycling issues were also important to Cunningham, which is hardly surprising for a Wiccan, since the belief system endorses reverence for the earth. However, Cunningham was practicing what he preached long before recycling became trendy. This is one example of his progressive nature as well as being aware that rejuvenation and transformation through recycling was an act of magic in its own right.

THE IMPORTANCE OF FRIENDSHIP

The Sun is positioned in the eleventh house, indicating Cunningham's energy and originality. It also indicates that he was a loyal and independent friend, as well as being interested in helping others; not just his friends, but also other communities and

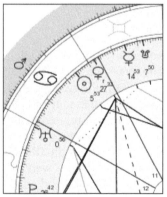

society as a whole. The importance of friendship to him can also be seen by the position of Venus in the eleventh house, which shows he valued companionship and that it could be just as fulfilling and sustaining as a relationship for him without any romantic aspects attached to it. It also suggests that friendship, independence and mutual respect was important in both personal and professional relationships. Cunningham had several close friends (and a large network of contacts), but when it came to his work as an author for Wiccan subjects, he entrusted only his reliable friends to offer their insights and observations about his work. For example, in 1981, when he was writing *Earth Power*, he wrote a draft and then prepared a readers' response sheet for his friends. He asked very specific questions on various areas and relied on honest feedback before then going on to write the second draft of his book (Harrington and Regula, 1996, 100–101).

It has been observed that when Venus is retrograde in the eleventh house, "Friends from past lifetimes will be the friends in this lifetime" (Yott, 1978, 24). Cunningham believed in reincarnation, but his progressive nature shown through his lunar Aquarius suggests he would have placed more importance on learning lessons from one's current life (*see box on previous page*).

The Moon is opposite the Leo ascendant and suggests that, although Cunningham required emotional space in relationships, he also needed a partnership which provided a measure of nurture. One example of cultivation could be seen in the area of work (the sixth house), for example, through co-working with his publishers Llewellyn. They depended on him for his creative material and also coaxed him to write material which he ordinarily may not have considered, such as writing about aromatherapy. Cunningham was not only an author for Llewellyn Publications, but became great friends with the then president, Carl Weschcke, and his wife Sandra in the 1980s, right up until his death in 1993.

The Moon is square the MC and suggests that it may have taken him a while to find the career that brought him fulfilment and happiness; at times, he may have felt tense and unsatisfied. As an author for Llewellyn, he also wrote magazine articles for other publishers on different genres and subjects as discussed earlier and ensured that he met deadlines, showing that he was a dependable contributor and writer. His sensitive nature surely was hurt when he received rejection letters from editors and publishers, when he first approached them looking for a contract to publish his magical books. For example, Avon Books and the New American Library (Harrington and Regula, 1996, 36) both rejected him. Nonetheless his steely determination helped spur him on until he finally secured a contract with Llewellyn Publications.

Cunningham also worked in bookshops to support himself whist he was writing; possibly this would have implemented time restraints on him, which may have made him feel anxious. He was known to have a temper (something that was observed by his sister and roommate), although his frustration was shown particularly when he had issues concerning his writing, such as a typewriter malfunction. A roommate said Cunningham's eyes then flashed and he cursed out loud (Kraig, 2012, 75).

It has been said that Cunningham could "conjure up righteous anger" (Harrington and Regula, 1996, 140), such as shortly before his death, when he was unable to finish his work (Cunningham, 2009, 277). This may have been understandable considering that his life was cruelly cut short; he must have felt there was so much more he wanted to do. He always had a determination to complete his work, which clearly never wavered even when close to death – his passion was evident to those closest to him.

Although at times Cunningham may have been intellectually stimulating, at other times some may have found him rather detached and impersonal, as these qualities are all associated with Aquarius and its ruler, Uranus. The combination of these two luminaries is a challenging one, since Cancer is ruled by the water element, which rules the emotions and can be quite attached; whilst Aquarius is governed by the air element, which can be detached and unemotional. The combination can be successful, however, when working with the general public and where connections with friends, organisations and societies are involved, since these areas are connected with the sign of Aquarius. Interestingly, Gerald Gardner (the subject of Chapter Four) was an inspiration to Cunningham, and also shared the Moon in Aquarius position, which was ideal for his coven work.

Cunningham's natal chart reveals that he was destined to be successful and unique; this is borne out by the data in his chart listed below.

- Kite aspect pattern
- Air Grand Trine
- Two T-Squares
- Fixed signs on the angles

The aspect pattern made by the planets of a kite indicates a distinctive and exceptional person. Doreen Valiente (the subject of Chapter Eleven) was much respected by Cunningham; he referred his readers to some of her work; she also had this aspect pattern in her natal chart. Jupiter and Pluto are on the ascendant in Cunningham's natal chart, and this represents the top of the Kite aspect pattern. The tail end of the Kite is the Moon, whilst Venus and Neptune link the Kite shape altogether (*see box on right*).

The air Grand Trine is created between the Moon in Aquarius, Neptune retrograde in Libra and Venus retrograde in Gemini – this configuration denotes a wealth of ideas and an ability to socialise and network on a large scale. It shows that, whilst Cunningham was at ease in the areas of learning, speaking and writing, when it came to emotional commitments his natural inclination was to remain detached and free to explore whatever attracted his mind. This is because the nature of the air element is abstract and cool and therefore longer-term emotional relationships may have been challenging for him. He would probably have found having a variety of relationships which did not place heavy emotional demands on him more satisfying.

> **Kite**
>
> Kite is an aspect pattern which is an extension of the Grand Trine, whereby a fourth planet forms an opposition to one corner of the triangle. In doing so, it creates a sextile to the other two corners.
>
>

Two of the T-Square configurations (*see glossary*) in the chart, comprise of Jupiter, Moon and Saturn, with the release point being Taurus at the MC, the area which denotes public persona and influences the approach taken in one's career.

The second T-Square comprises of Pluto, Moon and Saturn, with the release point also being in Taurus at the MC. The release points in this position show that Cunningham's career and reputation were significant driving points in his life.

The angles in Cunningham's chart belong to the fixed (*see glossary*) mode, comprising: Leo AC, Taurus MC, Aquarius DC and Scorpio IC. The angles in the natal chart represent the self, home, partnerships, ambition and career. It is in these areas that Cunningham was particularly optimistic, original and reliable. The fixed signs of the mode also indicate that Cunningham was determined and persistent; qualities that would have stood him in good stead in helping him meet deadlines for his editors and publishers. One example of his endurance can be seen where he manually created an index for his non-fiction books, something he believed was essential. This was before computer programmes could write them automatically, and his task was painstakingly time-consuming (Kraig, 2012, 117). It reveals his thoroughness and his awareness of what would be helpful to the reader.

DETERMINATION AND EXPERIMENTATION

Cunningham spent seventeen years preparing and researching for his book, *The Magic of Food* (Cunningham, 1991, un-numbered acknowledgment page); he also studied pre-Christian Hawaiian beliefs for over twenty years, before writing, *Cunningham's Guide to Hawaiian Magic and Spirituality*. This shows not only his stamina but also his passion for his subjects which he explored in depth, underpinning his research with practical experimentation.

The practical side of his research can be seen in the late 1980s when Llewellyn Publications asked him to write a book about aromatherapy and essential oils. This became, *Magical Aromatherapy*, and during the process he not only spent a lot of money buying genuine essential oils but also consulted aromatherapy experts as part of his research (Harrington and Regula, 1996, 142). Indeed, Robert Tisserand, an essential oil educator and founder of the famous Tisserand Institute, offered valuable comments on the manuscript of Cunningham's book.

A less helpful side to the fixed signs on the angles is that it suggests an inflexibility, rigidity and obstinacy, as these are also qualities associated with the fixed signs of Taurus, Leo, Scorpio and Aquarius. Whilst this inner reserve of strength can be helpful in a crisis, at other times it can also create an obstruction, as there is little room for flexibility or manoeuvre. It also shows that Cunningham had tremendous drive and concentration, something which a roommate observed, commenting that when he was working on a book, "nothing could get in his way ... except the need for money" (Kraig, 2012, 67).

The angles also indicate that Cunningham was a creative, determined, unique and powerful person. Leo AC indicates that Cunningham was attracted to artistic, glamorous and successful people, and that he could be a faithful and supportive partner. The Sun is the ruler of Leo and is the ruling planet in the natal chart, as Leo is the ascendant, it also shows that Cunningham was able to live life to the full and accepted himself for what he was.

The Aquarius DC indicates that he would have enjoyed freedom and friendships in partnerships and was drawn to independent people who equally valued liberty and space. Cunningham would also have appreciated truthfulness in partnerships, since Aquarius is associated with openness.

Taurus MC reveals that he needed a career which could bring him security and where, through determination and hard work, he could produce something tangible. He had loyal and successful relationships with his publishers Llewellyn Publications and Mass Market Publications. This brought him financial security and in turn, no doubt the publishing houses benefited from the sales of his books too.

The ruling planet of his MC is Venus and can be associated with working with gems of the earth and nature. For example, crystals, flowers, herbs and trees would have been satisfying to work with and helped in his practice of Wicca and goddess worship. Writing his books and getting them published made his work tangible, which is important to Taureans, since the practical nature of the sign needs to see quantifiable gains. The MC ruler, Venus, is associated with nature, so it is unsurprising that Cunningham found both satisfaction and success in writing about the earth's natural gifts, as earlier discussed.

Scorpio IC suggests that he needed privacy in his home and, at times, that home life may have become intense; an example of this is borne out by the necessity to have seclusion in order to have time without interruptions to meet deadlines. Cunningham needed solitude to express his deepest passions, i.e. through his writing and magical preparations. At home, he may have enjoyed investigating and researching, since these are qualities also associated with Scorpio and its ruler, Pluto.

FAMILY VALUES AND SIBLINGS

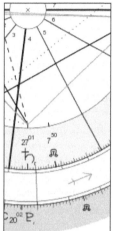

Saturn positioned in the fourth house (*see box on left*) suggests that Cunningham came from a secure and traditional family that valued qualities such as diligence and responsibility, both of which are characteristics associated with Saturn. He once remarked that he was the only person he knew who had a normal childhood (Harrington and Regula, 1999, 8), whilst his sister echoed this sentiment, describing their upbringing as "... a safe, normal, boring childhood" (Penczak, 2013, 239). Normality (as discussed above) comes in different guises and of course what they may have meant was that there were no challenges or issues for them during childhood.

The qualities of Cunningham's siblings can be seen in the third house of his natal chart (*see box below*), where Neptune indicates their nature. Qualities associated with Neptune include compassion and kindness, as well as artistry, dance, music and poetry. His brother Greg, for example, played both guitar and piano; Cunningham himself also played the piano at an advanced level, whilst his sister was a professional ballet dancer and is now a writer. Like Cunningham, his siblings are artistic, creative and musical.

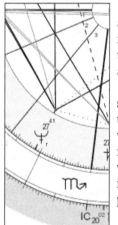

His sister Christine was particularly close to him and they shared a home for a short while when they first left the Cunningham family home (ibid, 241). In his last days, when his sight was fading through illness, she remained caring and offered him practical assistance when necessary (ibid, 243).

Christine remarked that through the normalcy and sense of safety in the family home, it allowed Scott to be who he wanted to be, giving him the freedom to follow his interest in magic and witchcraft when he was in his mid-teens (ibid, 239). Free will was important to Cunningham and he acknowledged that his parents were 'liberal'; something that is suggested by the position of Moon in Aquarius, as the Moon nurtures, while Aquarius is open and progressive.

Returning to the position of Saturn in the fourth house, its characteristics can often be revealed through discipline in the home. For example, as a child, Cunningham was expected to respect his father's need for privacy whilst he worked, and this he did. Cunningham senior was a successful professional writer who worked at home in his office, and so could not always be available to his children whilst working. Cunningham realised early on that confinement and time (characteristics of Saturn) helped bring success in business, especially when working at home, which worked well for both him and his father.

Cunningham senior was mindful of his duties to his children and in reflecting upon fatherhood after his middle child died said, "It's an awesome responsibility raising a brand-new human being into childhood" (Harrington and Regula, 1996, 214). He believed that, when it came to his writing and the creative process, there was no such thing as 'writers block' (http://www.chetcunningham.com). Clearly his son must also have believed this, as evidenced by his prolific output.

DEVELOPMENT, PROGRESS AND DISCIPLINE

Saturn is trine Uranus in Cunningham's natal chart and shows that he could break with tradition and possessed the ability to look at an established (Saturn) subject in a new way (Uranus). This is borne out, for example, when as an adult Cunningham did not follow his parents' Methodist religion, instead choosing to be a solitary Wiccan. He also found new ground in his writing and became an established author, recognised for his progressive thinking, which would help generations on their spiritual path of magic and Wicca.

Uranus is square Neptune in the natal chart and shows that Cunningham was not only innovative and original but also compassionate and sensitive. He needed freedom and independence when practicing his spirituality and writing about the subject.

Jupiter, the planet of abundance, is square Saturn in the natal chart and indicates that the Saturnian principles such as caution, discipline and responsibility were of tremendous importance to Cunningham. He was enthusiastic about needing to apply himself to his work and concentrate, and had surprising stamina – both characteristics associated with Saturn.

ALL WORK AND NO PLAY

Interestingly, this way of working was probably in part due to having watched how his father worked. Saturn is in opposition to the MC and indicates that, at times, Cunningham may have felt lonely and it may have been difficult for people to communicate with him, as he was inaccessible due to the amount of time he had to give to his writing.

This idea is also seen by the quincunx aspect created between Venus and Saturn. It has been observed that ill health as well as professional responsibilities may interfere with social and romantic opportunities and generally the aspect creates "an imbalance between work and pleasure" (Sakoian and Acker, 1972, 32–33). Even at the end of his life, Cunningham was constantly worried about his obligations to his publisher and completing his work, which shows that he was very committed and hard-working.

After Cunningham's death, Carl Weschcke, President of Llewellyn Publications, said that, "He was professional and dedicated to his craft" (Harrington and Regula, 1996, 190), further adding that before he had a computer, Cunningham would completely retype his final draft for the publishing house and that he only included information he had personally checked for accuracy, safety and value (ibid). This shows not only how diligent Cunningham was but also how he held the wellbeing of his readers at heart. The aspect Venus sextile Jupiter shows that, for Cunningham, pleasure (Venus) could be found in his life's work through the belief and philosophy of the goddess (Jupiter).

CONFINEMENT AND DEFENCES

The themes of control and discipline are echoed further by Saturn retrograde being positioned in Scorpio at the fourth house. This is because Saturn is ambitious and realistic, and Scorpio is associated with compulsion and strength, so it is a beneficial position in terms of trying to achieve success in business. However, Saturn in Scorpio can be less helpful in emotional areas, so that in situations where Cunningham may have felt he was losing control or that he was at an emotional crossroads, he may have hidden or repressed his feelings.

Saturn is associated with fear and defensiveness, whilst Scorpio is fixated with emotional control and power. In Cunningham's chart, as we have already seen, Saturn is in the fourth house (associated with parents and home) and is retrograde in the emotionally intense sign of Scorpio. This suggests that, at times, he may have felt he was unable to be truly frank and open with his parents about specific issues. One example of this can be seen where, as an adult, he withheld precise information about the nature of his terminal illness (Harrington and Regula, 1996, 185).

In Cunningham's family life (as discussed earlier), his father worked at home as a professional writer from an office in the family home. The room was kept 'child-free' whilst he worked, and Cunningham described it as 'mysterious' and 'secret', which shows his understanding of privacy (Harrington and Regula, 1996, 6). Perhaps Cunningham was inspired by his father who had come from a newspaper background that required him to write on a daily basis. He therefore approached writing books (he authored literally hundreds) with a very pragmatic attitude, in that he never waited for the muse to 'move' him (www.chetcunningham.com).

This family information indicates some of the qualities and energies of Cunningham's Scorpio IC, which is associated with control, privacy and mystery. The Scorpio IC is also significant to Cunningham, in that investigation is a correspondence of Scorpio, which was hugely important in Cunningham's work, for example, in his research of herbs.

Saturn's nature is barrier building, and Scorpio is an intuitive and perceptive sign; the position therefore indicates a 'psychic defence' where control and power are mastered. An illustration of this can be seen by Cunningham's attitude towards astrology, in particular his belief that one could gain power by seeing someone's birth chart and was therefore reluctant to make details of his own astrological data available to the public (Harrington and Regula, 1996, 243). Only after his death were the details of his birth shared with the general public, through his biography.

Saturn is square Pluto (the ruler of Scorpio) and suggests that Cunningham was persistent and utterly determined to succeed. Themes of survival are also possible with this aspect and will be discussed later when addressing the position of Pluto in the twelfth house.

Jupiter and Saturn are both square the MC (*see glossary*), revealing that Cunningham was confident and optimistic about what he wanted to accomplish in his life and could work steadily and thoroughly to achieve his ambition.

Other aspects in Cunningham's chart emphasise his controlled and hidden feelings, such as Sun in Cancer, Moon square Saturn and Moon opposing Pluto. These show the depth of Cunningham's feelings and sensitive nature, all of which will be discussed later.

FAMILY ROOTS AND SECOND-SIGHT

The IC in a natal chart indicates qualities about one's heritage, family roots and legacy. Cunningham's Scorpio IC is ruled by Pluto and, as discussed previously, associates with areas such as the occult and divinatory arts, and this was also true of some members of Cunningham's family. Two of his female relations had second-sight; Emmy, his paternal great-grandmother, read tea-leaves; while Abby, his great-great-grandmother, believed in and observed the phases of the Moon and, together with her husband, practiced lunar gardening (ibid, 4).

His great-great-grandmother, Abby, believed there were favourable phases of the Moon for carrying out gardening activities such as moving and planting. One of her superstitions was never to move a broom from one house to another; this superstition he included in his book, *The Magical Household*, showing how he valued her insights. Cunningham had the gift of being able to divine (he particularly enjoyed using divination by wax in water) and took it seriously and would not apply it in a frivolous way (ibid, 17).

The Cunningham clan were a mixture of English and German ancestry coupled with touches of French, Irish and Welsh. Cunningham's direct ancestors arrived in the New World in 1635, in Connecticut (ibid, 3). His family ancestry would have been meaningful to Cunningham as people with Sun sign Cancer place much importance on their families and heritage. Scott's paternal grandmother compiled the family history, naming her research *Tapestry* (ibid, 4).

Looking at the astrological data in Cunningham's chart provides insight into his challenges as well as what motivated him in his short, though very successful life, which was sadly cut short at the age of 36.

A PIONEER IN A CROWD

As discussed earlier, the Sun is in Cancer in the eleventh house of Cunningham's chart – the area associated with friends, groups and societies. Examples of this include him being initiated into a coven while he was in high school, as well as being part of a magical group.

As an adult, Cunningham participated in various covens but eventually found more satisfaction as a solitary practitioner. He apparently did not like crowds and although he did attend several Pagan gatherings, he nevertheless needed to be alone; he said he was "… not a tribal person, drums give me stomach aches" (ibid, 85). This ailment is revealing, as it is in keeping with the sign of Cancer and its sensitivities of the stomach as well as the breasts. Cancer is a cardinal sign (*see glossary*), which means he had characteristics that could lead him to be initiating and pioneering, and indeed, he was to become a catalyst in a New Age where his writing inspired a new generation.

The Sun in the eleventh house also suggests that he was a humanitarian at heart and that diversity, freedom and politics were important to him. The Sun in the eleventh house also shows that he was a loyal and independent friend. For example, he was close friends with the (now deceased) Wiccan author, Raymond Buckland, and his wife. Two other friends, David Harrington and de Traci Regula, extended his unfinished autobiography (which became the biography, *Whispers of the Moon*) and worked closely with the Cunningham family, ensuring that what was written after his death was accurate and fair.

Sun trine Mars in the natal chart indicates Cunningham's courage and gusto and his ability to assert himself; his ambition and drive helped make him become a pioneer – particularly in his field of earth magic and Wicca.

ARTISTRY, CREATIVITY AND HEARTBREAK

Mars is in Pisces and when positioned here it suggests an aptitude for being artistic and imaginative, particularly in areas which require 'behind-the-scenes' work, something we can see in Cunningham's writing, as well as his directing work and artistic projects. Occasionally he worked as an assistant director for theatrical productions (ibid, 25).

Mars is positioned in the seventh house, the area which governs partnerships and marriage and suggests that Cunningham, at times, found relationships mystifying. This theme is echoed by the position of Neptune, ruler of Pisces (retrograde), in Libra (associated with relationships), as it shows that he may have found romantic relationships bewildering at times.

It has been said that, by nature, Cunningham was a true romantic but regarded himself as "unlucky in love" and after having experienced early heartbreaks "he avoided romance while idealizing it as a goal he would never achieve" (ibid, 141).

The aspect Venus trine Neptune can be an indicator of relationships which are clandestine, fairy-tale and romantic. Given that Cunningham had seemingly given-up on relationships, it could be said that his most fulfilling relationship was with art, nature and writing (all areas governed by Venus and Neptune). In other words, he chose to sacrifice personal love for his art.

The easy contact between Venus and Neptune indicates that Cunningham valued spiritual relationships, so that celibacy and platonic relationships were also satisfying to him. Indeed, he may even have avoided romance after several unsuccessful relationships, although he probably still idealised it as an unattainable goal (ibid). It may have been a form of self-protection, while allowing the spiritual to remain prominent in his life.

Cunningham's sister, Christine, revealed that during a conversation with him towards the end of his life, she mentioned her regret that he had never "... found a lasting love, a steady partner to share his life with," but her brother only smiled and changed the subject (Penczak, 2013, 245). Again, this may have been a form of self-protection.

GENEROSITY AND PHILOSOPHY

As discussed earlier, the Sun is the ruling planet of the natal chart, as it is the ruler of the ascending sign, Leo. This position shows that Cunningham was destined for greatness, while the position of Jupiter conjunct the ascendant suggests that he presented a carefree and optimistic persona to the world, able to adopt a philosophical stance on any of the challenges life presented to him, as these are qualities associated with Jupiter.

It may have been important both mentally and physically for Cunningham to teach and travel, as these areas are associated with Jupiter. Certainly, he taught classes but claimed that he never had the true need to teach and felt he was not very good at it (Harrington and Regula, 1996, 43). He enjoyed giving small, individual classes more than the gruelling tours that he undertook. Quite apart from the exhausting nature of touring, it may have been that being away from home for any great length of time went against the grain of his home-loving Cancerian nature.

The themes of belief systems and self-exploration are also connected with Jupiter, and these were the areas where Cunningham found fame. In particular, through his belief in Wicca and his magical work, which included meditation and visualisation.

Jupiter in Leo shows that Cunningham had a big personality and could be entertaining, as he enjoyed playing jester to an audience. It also shows that he could be generous and share his happiness with others. He was described by his sister as a giver. To those who never had the pleasure of meeting him, his greatest gift was undoubtedly his books (Penczak, 2013, 247). He had the ability to enthuse others with his optimism and love of life and shared his excitement and vision with all those he met. Author, Laural Jones, described his faith in her when she was a budding writer, "His confidence in me was one of those splendid gifts life sometimes gives us" (Harrington and Regula, 1996, 203).

TAKING THE STAGE

In high school, Cunningham was hugely creative and was attracted to the performing arts, such as dance and drama; he was also an accomplished pianist. He played the part of Benvolio in a production of Romeo and Juliet, his character an unsuccessful peacemaker; these examples show the creative and performing side of Leo, his ascendant sign.

Had he lived, Cunningham would have been proud to know that, *Wicca: A Guide for the Solitary Practitioner* (his most successful book), appeared in a film in 2007. It was a comedy called *Never Say Macbeth* and was about a theatre company who staged the play; a cast member unwittingly jinxes the production by saying the title word. Macbeth's notoriety is because it is Shakespeare's only play based on black magic and witchcraft, and there is a tradition that it is unlucky to say the title before a performance (it is instead referred to as 'the Scottish Play'). The characters consult Cunningham's book in the film to try and find some material to help them understand the curse and lift its hex.

CONTROL, INTRUSION AND POWER

Interestingly, Cunningham's work, *Wicca: A Guide for the Solitary Practitioner*, and some of his other magical books have been criticised for not acknowledging the dark side of human nature, being only an "extremely toned-down, Disneyland version of the Craft" (http://www.wildideas.net). Some felt Cunningham failed to address Wicca as a religion, particularly the themes of polarity, which are integral to it. However, Cunningham may actually have intended to avoid focusing on the dark side of the human nature aspect; another possibility is that his publishers may have required this approach. Another criticism was that "… the version of the Craft that he presented had very little to offer those whose life had not been a bed of roses," as well as his version of the Craft being, "… best suited to an idealised world" (ibid).

Although Cunningham may not have covered these areas in his books, he did not shy away from them completely. He wrote an article for a magical journal called, *The Rose & Quill*, which covered subjects such as chain letters and psychic attack – regarding them as a form of black magic (Harrington and Regula, 1996, 140). In life, he certainly experienced a harrowing situation, when he learnt that his landlord of twelve years had been shot and murdered in a robbery in the building next door to Cunningham's home (ibid, 160). Such an incident would have been upsetting to anyone, and shortly afterwards Cunningham left his flat and relocated (ibid).

Not everyone thought that his work only covered the lighter side of the Craft, however, and some recognised that he wanted to appeal to beginners of Wicca, using accessible language, to explain complex information (https://www.thoughtco.com). This allowed his readers to easily access and make sense of the information in his books, just as the characters in the film *Never Say Macbeth* had done; perhaps this was the underlying appeal of Cunningham's Pagan literature.

INDIVIDUALITY, PRIVACY AND SURVIVAL

Uranus is positioned in Leo at the critical (*see glossary*) point of 0 degrees (*see box below*). Uranus in this sign shows that Cunningham valued individuality, self-expression and believed in living life creatively. Through his writing, he helped lead the way for people to understand their personal journey through the practice of earth magic and Wicca. People no longer needed to find a coven or group; he taught them how to practise as solitaries.

The position of Pluto in Leo in the twelfth house, suggests that Cunningham was driven to work for the good of others; not only did he become an influential and powerful writer, but also transformed his own life and other people's. He once remarked that magic "… should be available to all who wish to use it as a tool of personal transformation" (Harrington and Regula, 1996, outside back cover), revealing that he wanted other people to be aware that magic comes from within and was readily available to all who wished to use it on their individual path in life.

Although Cunningham could appear light-hearted at times, his chart reveals that the persona masked a deeply private and disciplined nature. The Moon is in opposition to Pluto, suggesting that he had intense feelings, while the detached nature of Uranus (the ruler of his Moon sign, Aquarius) would have masked the depth of his feelings, as its associations include detachment and logic. The Moon and Pluto contact indicates that Cunningham was instinctively secretive, preferring to keep both his feelings and his private life concealed. His sister once said of him that he had "always been a private person" (Penczak, 2013, 244–245). The aspect also shows that he had considerable emotional strength and perceptive insights and was well aware of his highly developed intuition and sensitivity.

Buried and hidden feelings are common with the Moon opposing Pluto and shows that Cunningham controlled and repressed his feelings at times; perhaps this was a way of healing and surviving from painful situations where he may have felt emotionally exposed, such as in intimate relationships as discussed briefly above.

In Cunningham's natal chart, Pluto is in the twelfth house, the area associated with:

- Behind-the-scenes/hidden
- Institutions
- Subconscious
- Seclusion
- Secrets

Pluto in the twelfth house suggests that Cunningham had resources of great inner strength and through his extensive knowledge could grow through pain (both inner and outer) and transform himself.

One example of this can be seen through his time in hospital at the age of 27 when he nearly died with lymphoma – a particularly virulent form of cancer. He underwent treatment, which included chemotherapy, radiation and surgery. Cunningham summoned all the inner reserves he could muster, using healing rituals and visualisation, along with conventional medicine to help himself survive (Harrington and Regula,

1996, 95). This shows his ability to use his inner strength to help heal and transform his health. He once said, "You need no initiations to begin experiencing the powers of nature and the energy contained within your own body" (Cunningham, 1988, 158).

The theme of seclusion is hugely significant to Cunningham who found his strength both practicing as a solitary and by writing books for people who were starting to explore Wicca as solitary practitioners. As a writer, he needed privacy so he could concentrate and collect his thoughts, which allowed him to apply his creative energy.

Cunningham's poem, *The Witch Alone*, stresses that solitary witches do not need magical paraphernalia, but can find appropriate correspondences through elements of nature; he also addresses the theme of rebirth in the poem.

Even when he was not writing, he valued his privacy, believing that one's faith needn't be paraded to the general public. He was unwilling to "sacrifice his solitude to further the public acceptance of any part of his life" (Harrington and Regula, 1996, 138).

DEJA VU AND LIFE AFTER LIFE

As mentioned earlier, the twelfth house is also associated with the subconscious and therefore dreams – the psychological realms which we are forced to face through our dream state. This was an area that Cunningham was interested in, and he explored the ability to connect with the higher realms through dreaming. He wrote, *Dreaming the Divine: Techniques for Sacred Sleep*, and addressed areas such as dream interpretation and symbolism, as well as preparation for sacred sleep. Seemingly, Cunningham was well versed in such areas and had vivid recall of his dreams and of at least one previous life.

For a long time, he firmly believed he would die at age of 26, based on a memory of a recent past-life when he had died in World War II (Harrington and Regula, 1993, 106). Pluto is associated with birth and rebirth as well as physical and spiritual transformation. He almost fulfilled this prophecy, nearly dying when he was 27. Nevertheless, he still passed away at the very young age of 36.

This nine-year period (which he must have regarded as something of an unexpected gift) in Cunningham's progressed (*see glossary: Progressions*) chart reveals that, leading up to his death, he was proud of his achievements and originality, albeit in a modest way. His declining health was a major concern in much of his life, although he remained hard-working and industrious, believing he had to provide a service to his employers and audiences.

Through this he eventually achieved his vocation and became known as an important and influential writer, commentator and observer. The Sun had progressed into Leo, the ascendant into Virgo, and the MC into Gemini, by the time that Cunningham had died and indicates not only how he had matured, but also how his life had panned out up until that point of death.

Saturn is square Pluto in Cunningham's natal chart and astrologer, Sue Tompkins, observed that this aspect may be associated with the "... lessons of survival. Sometimes the threat might be of a disease (polio, tuberculosis and AIDS)" (Tompkins, 1990, 236). In Cunningham's case, the 'threat' was in contracting AIDS.

Pluto is conjunct the ascendant and indicates that Cunningham's intense energy will have helped him to concentrate and focus on any crisis and dilemma, helping him to rise from the ashes like a phoenix or a snake shedding its skin. Jupiter is conjunct Pluto on the ascendant, suggesting he had a magnetic and compelling presence and was intensely aware of himself and the impact that he had on other people.

In the natal chart, there are symbolic points called the Moon's Nodes (*see glossary*). These points enable us to deduce information about karmic lessons we have chosen to work with in this lifetime, as well as realising past incarnations. The lunar modes comprise of the North and South Node, the former represents the current lifetime, and the South Node past-lives.

In Cunningham's chart, the North Node is in Sagittarius and South Node in Gemini. The North Node in Sagittarius reveals that his soul's karmic purpose in this incarnation was to search for a philosophy by which he could live, to align with meaning and purpose and to seek the deeper meaning of life, as these themes are associated with Sagittarius.

The South Node in Gemini suggests that, in previous lives, there may have been an element of superficiality. This is because Gemini can collect facts and information arbitrarily but does not necessarily know or understand areas deeply.

The challenge for Cunningham's twentieth century incarnation was to find a deeper meaning to life, something that was achieved by marrying Gemini's mind to Sagittarius' spirit. In past incarnations, Cunningham's life may have been significantly involved with the mind and intellect, as well as communication; and yet had not achieved its full potential.

The North Node is positioned in the fourth house and the South Node in the tenth. This suggests that despite his successful career, he also found huge satisfaction through family and tradition and also by searching inwardly for a sense of belonging and foundation. This combination helped him get in touch with his true inner self, finding his roots, and eventually branching out.

He proposed that there were thirteen goals of a witch, and the first two are: 'Know Yourself' and 'Know Your Craft,' which shows his priorities. 'Know Yourself' in particular is a famous inscription from the Oracle at Delphi, which shows how he looked backwards towards magical traditions from the ancient classical world, feeling they still had much to teach.

AMBIGUITY, MIRRAGE AND SECRECY

As previously discussed, the area of Pluto and the twelfth house is associated with the hidden, privacy and secrets. For example, Cunningham appreciated the power of a well-cast natal chart, believing that having knowledge of somebody else's chart could be used to work against them if in the wrong hands (Harrington and Regula, 1996, 243). When he was alive, therefore, he mostly kept his natal chart details private (ibid).

Other areas associated with Pluto include:

- Investigation
- Lust
- Mysteries
- Occult
- Power
- Sexual taboos
- Survival

Pluto in the twelfth house is a helpful position in terms of Cunningham being able to bury himself in his writing, as well as undertaking investigation and research into areas such as the occult.

The area of sexual taboo largely depends on the culture and time into which a person was born. Pluto's supremacy includes sexual practices, which enlightened people may find acceptable, whilst less open-minded people may find intolerable; these may include issues such as prostitution and same-sex relationships. Essentially, the taboos are practices that lay outside of what many societies endorse. Cunningham was sensitive and deeply private about his intimate relationships, even to his closest friends.

Uranus is also resident in the twelfth house and indicates that he was intuitive and had gifts of clairvoyance and foresight. This would have been helpful because it would have shown him what subjects his readers would be interested in. He once confided in a friend that he knew that he would die at a young age (Kraig, 2012, 133) and, regrettably, Cunningham's premonition came true. Sensitivity to energies, the unknown and the unusual, was part of Cunningham's nature; he astral-projected as a young child and saw a ghost and a UFO (Harrington and Regula, 1996, 8).

His intuition and sensitivity are further emphasised by the position of Neptune in the third house, which shows he could sense underlying currents and recognise subtle meanings. This position also suggests that Cunningham had artistic ability and a fertile imagination, which no doubt will have been helpful to him when writing his romantic novels and Westerns, as well as magical prose and poetry.

BENEVOLENCE AND UNDERSTANDING

Moon opposite Jupiter indicates that Cunningham was a caring, good natured and sympathetic individual who could react and respond to others with great generosity. This is because the Moon is emotional and instinctive whilst Jupiter's nature is excessive, and reveal in ghis innate and abundant kindness. His friend, Raymond Buckland (who died in 2017), once described him as being "… a deeply loving, caring and loyal person who would do anything for a friend in need. He could be generous to a fault" (Harrington and Regula, 1996, 211).

Another indication of the Moon/Jupiter (*see box below*) aspect is Cunningham's innate faith in life; he was inherently driven to areas such as belief, philosophy and politics which are all correspondences of Jupiter. It is apparent through his life that these areas were significant to him through his writing and inspirational public speaking, while his literature brought him fame.

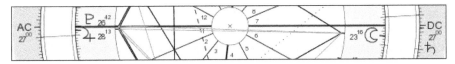

THE CIRCLE CLOSES

Before his death, Cunningham remained focussed on his work and wanted to ensure that he met necessary deadlines for his publisher, which shows his extraordinary determination and strength in a time of crisis. On the day he died, he was experiencing several transits which included challenging relationships with the planets. Pluto and Saturn symbolise beginnings and ends of a cycle in both metaphysical and physical terms. Areas associated with them include restriction and transformation as well as decay and death.

Both these planets were transiting and creating aspects with planets and other points in Cunningham's chart on the day he died. There were several, but the most difficult ones included Saturn positioned in the sixth house and Pluto in the fourth. It is notable that the transits involving the ascendant were significant, as the ascendant represents the physical self and the sixth house the area of health/ill health, as well as work.

Significant transits included:

Transiting Saturn
- Opposing natal Jupiter on the AC
- Opposing natal Pluto on the AC

Transiting Saturn in the sixth house brings extra work and responsibility and Cunningham may have started to find his work testing. Health conditions would have brought restrictions, barriers and confinement in a way not previously experienced. Older people and influential figures in authority may have been of help to him during this Saturn transit, as these (together with earlier areas) are all associated with the taskmaster, Saturn.

His elders were certainly significant at this time; his Llewellyn publisher was in his sixties and remained helpful and loyal to him, whilst Cunningham's parents brought him home from hospice care for him in his last few months. His mother was at his bedside, holding his hand when he passed from this world into the next.

Transiting Saturn opposing natal Jupiter on the ascendant indicates that it was a time of restricted growth for Cunningham and that his enthusiasm and zest for life had slowed down, making his heavy workload no longer feasible. At the end, he would have realised that he needed to restrict himself to deal with the absolute essentials in his life, which he knew was coming to an end.

The other opposition on the ascendant is created with transiting Saturn and natal Pluto and, as discussed earlier, contact between these two planets can indicate that themes of death and survival are possible. One obvious example of this is how Cunningham lived with complications of the AIDS virus and, as a result, in three short years his health underwent a dramatic transformation, as he underwent chemotherapy, radiation and surgery; and eventually, totally lost his sight.

Another possibility of this Pluto and Saturn transit is that Cunningham remained determined to control his circumstances and fulfil his potential as best as he could. For example, he organised sharing out some of his magical possessions, including his many artefacts and books, before he died, so that these would be passed on to his friends, whom he knew would treasure and enjoy the items just as he had.

Transiting Pluto
- Square natal Moon
- Conjunct natal Saturn
- Square Pluto on the AC

Transiting Pluto in the fourth house suggests that Cunningham experienced changes to his home and family life; this was true in that when he became too ill to look after himself he moved back into the family home to be cared for by his parents. He lost one home and gained another during this emotional and physically painful time in his life, and the devastating and transforming nature of Pluto is evident in this life-altering event.

Transiting Pluto square the natal Moon indicates that Cunningham may have been experiencing emotional turmoil and had to deal with issues associated with his mother and/or other women. This may have manifested itself in having to face issues of dependency and feelings of inferiority, catharsis, healing and survival. These themes were clearly evident at this point of Cunningham's life.

Transiting Pluto conjunct natal Saturn suggests that Cunningham was able to shed any self-imposed chains created by the energy of Saturn whilst transiting Pluto, and this would have enabled him to open up in a way he was previously unable to do. Natal Saturn is in the fourth house and so he may have finally opened up to his family about any despair and fears more than in previous years.

Transiting Pluto square Pluto on the AC shows that Cunningham had to confront and break down any barriers in his life and issues around that may have included control, isolation, power and trust; since these are all areas associated with Pluto.

Cunningham was born into the Pluto in Leo generation. As Pluto's orbit is irregular, this suggests that Cunningham's generation may have been called upon, sooner than other age groups, to address Pluto's themes. Such areas include annihilation and healing, for example, and people born into this generation may have found themselves in the spotlight for their uniqueness and ability to shine, which was certainly the case for Scott Cunningham.

He was a catalyst for the New Age generation, educating them through his books and public speaking; he had to make tremendous personal sacrifices in order to produce accessible literature, for people. Through his books, he not only aided them in increasing their knowledge, but also helped them realise that they could pursue their own spiritual paths, without having to be initiated into a coven. Most importantly, they could find within themselves their own power and inner magic.

Scott Cunningham was a diverse author who wrote many forms of literature and is remembered with great affection by those who were close to him. His magical and spiritual legacy lives on through his work.

ACKNOWLEDGEMENTS, CREDITS AND REFERENCES

Natal chart generated by www.astro.com
Rodden Rating 'A'
Cunningham, Scott: Wednesday, 27th June, 1956, 09.25am, Michigan Center, MI, USA.
84w20, 42n14.
Source of birth data and time of birth provided by Scott Cunningham's family in Cunningham's *Whispers of the Moon* biography,

THANKS TO

Christine Ashworth (Scott Cunningham's sister), for granting permission to use a
    publicity photograph of her brother.
Ben Collins, International HIV Partnerships.
The Terence Higgins Trust.

BOOKS

Cunningham, S. (2009) *Cunningham's Book of Shadows: The Path of an American Traditionalist.*
    Llewellyn Publications.
Cunningham, S. (2009) *Cunningham's Guide to Hawaiian Magic and Spirituality.* (Third Edition,
    First Printing) Llewellyn Publications.

Cunningham, S. (1991) *The Magic of Food.* Llewellyn Publications.

Cunningham, S. (1988) *The Truth about Witchcraft Today.* Llewellyn Publications.

Gauquelin, M. (1976) *Cosmic Influences on Human Behaviour.* Futura Publications.

Harrington, D. and Regula, de Traci. (1996) *Whispers of the Moon: The Life and Work of Scott Cunningham.* Llewellyn Publications.

Penczak, C. (2013) *Ancestors of the Craft: The Lives and Lessons of our Magikal Elders.* Copper Cauldron.

Sakoian, F. And Acker, L. (1972) *That Inconjunct Quincunx: The not so Minor Aspect.* Copple House Books, Inc.

Tompkins, S. (1990) *Aspects in Astrology: A Comprehensive Guide to Interpretation.* Element Books

Yott, D.H. (1978) *Retrograde Planets and Reincarnation*: *Astrology and Reincarnation Vol. 1.* Samuel Weiser, Inc., New York.

E-BOOKS

Kraig, M. D. (2012) *The Magical Life of Scott Cunningham.* Llewellyn Publications.

DVDS

Never Say Macbeth. Released in 2007, Vanguard Cinema (genre: comedy).

WEBSITES

https://aidsinfo.nih.gov/understanding-hiv-aids/hiv-aids-awareness-days/163/national-hiv-testing-day – Accessed on 25/03/2018.

http://www.aidsinfonet.org/fact_sheets/view/503 – Accessed on 24/03/2018.

http://www.chetcunningham.com/bio.htm – Accessed on 25/03/2018.

http://christine-ashworth.com/?page_id=2392 – Accessed on 11/02/2018.

https://www.hiv.gov/hiv-basics/overview/history/hiv-and-aids-timeline – Accessed on 05/01/2018.

https://www.thoughtco.com/about-scott-cunningham-2562615 – Patti Widington. Accessed on 05/02/2018.

http://www.wildideas.net/temple/library/letters/cunningham1.html – Liath Cadhoit. Accessed on 02/03/2018.

Glossary of Terms

Alpha et Omega: an occult order, initially named the 'Hermetic Order of the Golden Dawn.'

Angle: the angles in an astrological chart are the four cardinal points which comprise of: the ascendant, the midheaven, the descendant and the Imum Coeli.

Ascendant: the sign of the zodiac ascending at the time of one's birth on the eastern horizon. It is also known as the rising sign.

Aspect: is an angle the planets make to each other in the horoscope, as well as with the ascendant, midheaven, descendant and Imum Coeli (IC).

Aspect patterns: involve three or more planets making a configuration in different ways. There are several of them and examples include: the T-Square, Grand Trine, Yod, Grand Cross and Kite.

Asteroids: are small rocky bodies which vary greatly in size and which orbit the Sun, they are too small to be considered planets. A feature of the solar system is the asteroid belt between Mars and Jupiter that is thought to be a planet that broke up or never formed, and the dwarf planet Ceres is in it.

Astrology: is the study of the influence that planets have on human lives.

Axis: the areas on a natal chart where the ascendant, MC, descendant and IC are situated, they are also known as the 'angles'.

Benefic: a benefic planet is one which bestows positive energies which can, for example, provide construction and supportiveness.

Book of Shadows: sacred text belonging to a witch.

Bundle shape: in planetary shaping, the bundle pattern is where the planets are concentrated within 120 degrees (a trine) and suggests the person has a clear focus, confidence and personal strength.

Cardinal Cross: see definition of Grand Cross.

Chart shapings: indicate the shape the planets make in the chart they comprise of: bowl, bucket, bundle, locomotive, see-saw, sling, splash and splay.

Chiron: is an asteroid and in astrology symbolises the 'Wounded Healer' - it represents our deepest wounds and endeavours to heal it. Chiron orbits the Sun between Saturn and Uranus.

Clairvoyance: means 'clear-seeing' and is a type of psychic gift which allows the psychic to see the hidden.

Conjunction: can be a hard or soft aspect, depending on the energies of the planets involved.

Co-ordinates: (for place birth of birth) show the degrees and minutes for the *place* of birth (longitude and latitude).

Constellation: a group of bright stars which appear close to each other in the sky but in space are actually far apart.

Correspondences: associations, links.

Coven: is a gathering of witches bound into one group and taught and initiated by the same high priest and high priestess. The coven usually has a name, which makes members part of that group and no other.

Critical degrees: the degrees of 0 and 29 in a sign, they are critical because they are the first and final degree.

Decan: each sign of the zodiac is divided into three divisions of 10 degrees. Each sign has three decans, one for each division of 10 degrees. Each decan has a ruler which becomes the sub-ruler or co-ruler of that sign.

Descendant: the descendant is the cusp of the seventh house.

Detriment: a planet which is positioned in the zodiac sign opposite the sign it rules.

Development circle: a group of likeminded people that sit in a circle and do meditation to enhance their spirituality/mediumistic gifts.

Dispositorship: is about rulership, which means that each sign has a planet that rules it. For further explanation please see also 'rulership' in glossary.

Ectoplasm: a substance which is exteriorised by physical mediums associated with the formation of spirits.

Element: the four elements are fire, earth, air and water. Elemental balance is needed to sustain life.

Exaltation: each of the seven traditional planets has its exaltation in one zodiac sign; Sun in Aries, Moon in Taurus, Mercury in Virgo, Venus in Pisces, Mars in Capricorn, Jupiter in Cancer, Saturn in Libra.

Fall: a planet is said to be in fall when it is in the sign opposite the one it is exalted in. When a planet is in fall, it is thought to be debilitated in that sign. For example, the Sun is exalted in Aries and so is in fall in Libra.

Fixed star: appears to not move but in fact does move 1 degree backwards in 72 years.

Flat chart: is a chart which only shows the aspects and planets with no houses.

Focal point: the squared planet or point in a T-Square (see below for 'T-Square' definition).

Gardnerian: is a tradition in the Neopagan religion of Wicca, whose members descend from Gerald Gardner.

Grand Cross: occurs when four planets are all separated from each other by square aspects being 90 degrees apart. It can also be viewed as two oppositions 180 degrees apart, separated from each other by a square. There is a planet in each astrological element but all the planets are in signs of the same modality (cardinal, fixed, mutable) or quality. It is possible to have a Grand Cross where all the planets are not in the same modality (disassociate).

Grand Trine: a Grand Trine consists of three planets that occupy different signs of the same element at 120 degree angles.

Gregorian calendar: A modification of the Julian calendar, introduced in 1582 by Pope Gregory XIII and adopted by most countries at various times over the next 400 years.

Glyphs: are symbols that astrologers use for the planets, signs, asteroids and other points in an astrological chart.

Hard aspect: refers to major angles created between planets, which comprise of the conjunction, opposition and square angles (n.b. the conjunction is variable depending on the energies of the two planets involved).

Horary astrology: is a system of astrology whereby the astrologer tries to answer a question by constructing a horoscope for the exact time and place at which the question was received and understood by the astrologer. It is also called traditional astrology, and doesn't use Uranus, Neptune and Pluto.

Horoscope: an astrological chart that is calculated based upon the date, time and place of birth. A chart can also be calculated for an event, a country and a question.

Houses: a house in the natal chart reveals 'where' planetary energies express themselves. Each of the twelve houses in a chart rule certain areas of life, types of people and relationships, ideas and circumstances of life.

Indirect: the planet appears to be going backwards in the sky.

Imum Coeli (IC): Coeli is Latin for 'bottom of the sky.' The Imum Coeli is the 'nadir' or low point in the Sun's path and, if you could see the Sun, where it would be seen at midnight. It is also the cusp of the fourth house.

Inconjunction: is a minor aspect which creates an angle of 150 degrees with another planet.

Julian calendar: a calendar introduced by the authority of Julius Caesar in 46BC, in which the year had 365 days and every fourth year consisted of 366 days. Outmoded by the Gregorian calendar.

Kite: is an aspect pattern is an extension of the Grand Trine whereby a fourth planet forms an opposition to one corner of the triangle; and in doing so, it creates a sextile to the other two corners.

Locomotive: the planets span an arc of approximately 240 degrees, leaving the other area of the chart void of any planets.

Luminaries: in traditional astrology the Sun and the Moon were described as luminaries since they are the two brightest planets.

Major aspects: comprise of conjunction, opposition, sextile, square and trine angles.

Malefic: a malefic planet tends towards destructive and unsupportive energies in a person's life.

Manifestation: is an object that clearly shows or embodies something abstract or theoretical. It's also how an event or characteristic actually materialises.

Materialisation mediums: are able to allow the spirits with whom they are communicating to make themselves visible to the sitter, either completely or partially.

Medium: the person doing the mediumship, the channel through which spirits communicate and the medium delivers the communication.

Midheaven/MC Coeli: is Latin for heaven, Medium Coeil is the midheaven and is the where the Sun would be at noon at the top of the chart. It is also the tenth house cusp.

Minor aspects: comprise of inconjunction, semi-sextile, semi-square and sesquiquadrate angles.

Modes: there are three modes in astrology which are represented by cardinal, fixed and mutable energies. They all represent the way in which a sign operates. **Cardinal** signs are initiators of action and are the signs of Aries, Cancer, Libra and Capricorn. **Fixed** signs have staying power and are the signs Taurus; Leo, Scorpio and Aquarius. **Mutable** signs have a versatile attitude and are the signs Gemini, Virgo, Sagittarius and Pisces.

Moon's Nodes: North and South lunar Nodes. The Moon's Nodes theorise that one is born with overdeveloped and underdeveloped traits of our character. The North Node indicates traits which we need to develop in order to find inner happiness, and the South Node indicates the overdeveloped traits which we are comfortable with and retain for security purposes. The North Node is also known as the 'Dragon's Head', and the South Node the 'Dragon's Tail'.

Mundane astrology: the study of planetary cycles upon nations.

Mutual reception: is when two planets are in each other's sign of rulership.

Natal chart: a natal chart is a picture of the positions of the signs, planets and angles at the time of one's birth. It contains data such as date, time and place of birth, to generate an accurate astrological chart.

Natural zodiac: is a system where the twelve signs of the zodiac are assimilated to the twelve houses in the birth chart, given that they have similar characteristics. For example, the first sign, Aries, is associated with the first house - both being about the self; the second sign, Taurus, is associated with the second house - Taurus is about possessions, and the second house is about resources, and so on.

Noon chart: a chart erected for the native at noon on the day they were born, when no exact time of birth is known. The credibility for the chart is that it is the time of day on their birthday when the Sun was at its strongest point.

North Node: see the Moon's Nodes for description.

Orbs: An orb refers to a variation of influence in which the aspect between two planets is believed to come into effect. The orb affects the influence and strength of the aspect. The smaller the orb (i.e. the closer the planets are to the exact degree of the aspect), the more powerful the aspect is considered to be.

Opposition: is a hard aspect is which creates an angle of 180 degrees with another planet.

Outer planets: Jupiter, Saturn, Uranus, Neptune and Pluto.

Partile: an aspect is said to be partile when the objects making the aspect are within 1 degree of each other.

Peregrine: an unaspected planet in a chart. Peregrine derives from Latin and means 'foreign' (see unaspected planets description).

Peregrine island: two planets which conjunct each other but do not aspect any other planets.

Personal planets: (the inner planets) Sun, Moon, Mercury, Venus and Mars.

Placidus: A house division system used in Western astrology, where time division is used.

Pluto demotion: Pluto was demoted to a dwarf planet in 2006 by astronomers. However, many astrologers continue to recognise Pluto as a major planet and reflect so in their astrological interpretations, as is the case in this book.

Polarity: there are six polarities in astrology which are natural oppositions. They comprise of: Aries/Libra, Taurus/Scorpio, Gemini/Sagittarius, Cancer/Capricorn, Leo/Aquarius and Virgo/Pisces. The signs are also male and female - the air and fire are masculine, and the earth and water feminine.

Progressions: a system where astrologers equate one day after birth to one year of life, known as 'the year for the day method.'

Psychic phenomena: a type of phenomena that appears to contradict physical laws.

Quincunx: is a minor aspect and is also termed 'inconjunction'. It creates a 150 degree angle with another planet.

Release point: is the square planet or point in a T-Square (see below for definition of a T-Square).

Repeal of the Witchcraft and Vagrancy Act: The act was repealed in 1951 by The Fraudulent Mediums Act, which in turn was repealed in 2008. In 1824 Parliament passed the Vagrancy Act under which astrology, fortune-telling and spiritualism became punishable.

Retrograde: when a planet appears to be moving backwards against the backdrop of stars.

Rodden Rating system: a system developed by astrologer, Lois Rodden, which classifies astrological data by grade to reflect its accuracy, for research purposes for astrologers. Classification starts at 'AA' then 'A' and finishes at 'XX' - for further details see https://www.astro.com/astro-databank/Help:RR

Rulership/dispositorship: the term 'rulership' means that each sign has a planet that rules it, for example Aries is ruled by Mars, Taurus is ruled by Venus and Gemini is ruled by Mercury. In dispositorship, the area of rulership is further developed when what is termed as the dispositing planet is the planet that rules the sign that the other planet is in. For example, when Venus is in Aries, the ruling planet of Aries is Mars, so we would say that Mars is dispositing Venus. If Jupiter is in Taurus, for example, we would say that Venus is dispositing Jupiter, which means that it has rulership over Venus and therefore is stronger.

Sabian symbols: a system of 360 unique images pertaining to each degree of the zodiac, developed in 1925 by Marc Edmund Jones and Elsie Wheeler. The degree in the natal chart needs to be rounded up to the next whole degree in order to obtain the correct number for the Sabian symbol of that sign, e.g. if the Sun is at 26 degrees in Pisces, this is rounded up to 27 degrees - then the Sabian symbol for 27 degrees Pisces has to be read for the interpretation.

Séance: from the French word meaning 'sitting', used to describe a meeting of people who have gathered to receive messages from spirits.

See-saw: a configuration which consists of two groups of opposing planets, separated by a couple of empty houses on each side.

Seax-Wica: is a tradition founded in the 1970s by Raymond Buckland and is inspired by Anglo-Saxon Paganism.

Sextile: is a soft aspect which creates an angle at 60 degrees with another planet.

Skyclad: is ritual nudity in Wicca, Paganism and Neopaganism.

Sling shape: (planetary shaping) is where there is one solitary planet in the chart and the other planets act as a 'bundle-shape', it is through the planets in the bundle that the solitary planet channels its energy.

Soft aspect: refers to major angles created between planets, which comprise of the conjunction; sextile and trine (n.b. the conjunction is variable depending on the energies of the two planets involved).

Summerlands: a term used by Wiccans and witches to describe the place they go to after they have died.

South Node: see the Moon's Nodes for description.

Square aspect: is a planet which creates a 90 degree angle with another planet.

Stellium: multiple conjunctions of planets - a close cluster of three or more planets in one sign and/or house.

Tarot: a tarot deck consists of 78 cards; divided into the major arcana of 22 cards and the minor arcana of 56 cards which are divided into 4 suits of: wands, coins (or Pentacles) swords and cups. The minor arcana cards correspond to the 4 elements: wands-fire, coins/pentacles-earth, swords-air and cups-water. A tarot deck can be used for divination, spiritual advice and self-development.

The Company of Avalon: a group of excarnate monks who had previously lived at Glastonbury Abbey and who communicated psychically through Dion Fortune.

The Guild of Master Jesus: an order set up by Dion Fortune which embodied esoteric Christianity, which was partly influenced from her early involvement with theosophical teachings.

The Hermetic Order of the Golden Dawn: was an organisation devoted to the study and practice of metaphysics, the occult and spiritual development.

The Society of Inner Light: a magical society of charitable status which was founded by Dion Fortune in 1924, which is a mystical school within the Western esoteric tradition, previously named the Fraternity of Inner Light.

The Theosophical Society: an organisation formed in 1875 to advance theosophy.

Traditional astrology: was the type of astrology which was practiced up until the seventeenth century before the arrival of the Age of Reason (aka the Scientific Age). Traditional astrology focused on answering a specific question at a specific time using the traditional planets; Sun, Moon, Mercury, Venus, Mars, Jupiter and Saturn (see above for horary astrology also).

Trance mediumship: deep trance is usually used in physical mediumship and is a sharing of mental and physical energies between the medium and spirit communicator.

Transits: as the planets continue their movement and complete their cycles, they form special relationships to the planets and points in our individual natal charts.

Trine: is a soft aspect which creates a 120 degree angle with another planet.

T-Square: is a pattern formed when planets in opposition also form a square with another planet. The pattern resembles the letter 'T' when viewed in the chart. The squared planet or point is referred to as the release point. T-Squares are made up of each of the modes: cardinal, fixed and mutable.

Unaspected planet: an unaspected planet is without a major aspect linking it to other planets.

Western esoteric tradition: comprises of magical and mystical ideas which direct spiritual insights into cosmology and metaphysics.

Wicca: draws from the old tradition of witchcraft and is a modern Pagan/witchcraft religion.

World horoscopes: is a term given in mundane astrology. This system of astrology is the study of planetary cycles upon nations. A nation's zodiac sign is determined by its day of independence, i.e. its birthday.

Yod: also known as the 'finger of God or 'the finger of fate, it is a rare astrological aspect formed between three planets or points in the horoscope that form a triangle. This rarity occurs when two planets are sextile (60 degree aspect) to each other, and both are quincunx (150 degree aspect) to a third.

Zodiac: the zodiac belt is the circle around which the Sun moves month by month. It moves through the 12 constellation signs which are divided equally by 30 degree divisions.

Lightning Source UK Ltd.
Milton Keynes UK
UKHW031343020222
398093UK00005B/199